Neurocomputing

Algorithms, Architectures and Applications

NATO ASI Series

Advanced Science Institutes Series

A series presenting the results of activities sponsored by the NATO Science Committee, which aims at the dissemination of advanced scientific and technological knowledge, with a view to strengthening links between scientific communities.

The Series is published by an international board of publishers in conjunction with the NATO Scientific Affairs Division

A Life Sciences B Physics	Plenum Publishing Corporation London and New York
C Mathematical and Physical Sciences D Behavioural and Social Sciences E Applied Sciences	Kluwer Academic Publishers Dordrecht, Boston and London
F Computer and Systems Sciences G Ecological Sciences H Cell Biology	Springer-Verlag Berlin Heidelberg New York London Paris Tokyo Hong Kong Barcelona

Series F: Computer and Systems Sciences Vol. 68

Neurocomputing

Algorithms, Architectures and Applications

Edited by

Françoise Fogelman Soulié

Laboratoire de Recherche en Informatique
Bâtiment 490, Université de Paris Sud
F-91405 Orsay Cedex, France

Jeanny Hérault

Institut National Polytechnique de Grenoble, LTIRF
46, avenue Félix Viallet
F-38031 Grenoble Cedex, France

Springer-Verlag Berlin Heidelberg New York
London Paris Tokyo Hong Kong Barcelona
Published in cooperation with NATO Scientific Affairs Division

Proceedings of the NATO Advanced Research Workshop on Neurocomputing – Algorithms, Architectures and Applications, held in Les Arcs, France, February 27 – March 3, 1989.

ISBN 3-540-53278-1 Springer-Verlag Berlin Heidelberg New York
ISBN 0-387-53278-1 Springer-Verlag New York Berlin Heidelberg

Printed in Germany

Printing: Druckhaus Beltz, Hemsbach; Binding: J. Schäffer GmbH & Co. KG, Grünstadt
2145/3140-543210 – Printed on acid-free-paper

Preface

This volume contains the collected papers of the NATO Conference on Neurocomputing, held in Les Arcs in February 1989. For many of us, this conference was reminiscent of another NATO Conference, in 1985, on Disordered Systems [1], which was the first conference on neural nets to be held in France. To some of the participants that conference opened, in a way, the field of neurocomputing (somewhat exotic at that time!) and also allowed for many future fruitful contacts.

Since then, the field of neurocomputing has very much evolved and its audience has increased so widely that meetings in the US have often gathered more than 2000 participants. However, the NATO workshops have a distinct atmosphere of free discussions and time for exchange, and so, in 1988, we decided to go for another session. This was an occasion for me and some of the early birds of the 1985 conference to realize how much, and how little too, the field had matured.

Just looking at the table of contents of both books will show the evolution of the neural networks field: in 1985, it was just the very start of the tide soon to come. The book [1] had sections on mathematics (automata theory), physics (spin glasses), formal neural nets (Hopfield models and the first paper by Y. Le Cun on what was to become the most famous of the present learning algorithms: the gradient back propagation for multilayer networks), optimization and models of biological organization. Many of these topics have now matured or have elapsed from the core of the neural nets field. Today, in the book of the 1989 conference, we have papers more focused towards applications, with sections on neural nets applied to dedicated hardware (Part 2), speech (Part 3) or images (Part 4). Many algorithms are proposed (Part 1) which, in a way, extend our former section on "formal neural nets": these algorithms rely on ideas which were sometimes already present then, but now they are more deeply rooted in the general streamline of computer science, they are compared to other more conventional techniques and their performances are carefully benchmarked. We still have a section on biology (Part 5), but strictly focused now on neuro-biology, where some of the scientists try to look and find new ideas for more powerful algorithms.

This book demonstrates the maturation of the neurocomputing field: it still shows that our domain is not yet really stabilized. The conference was a place for large - and sometimes hot - discussions on many questions linked to the interaction of biology and computer science. We think these interdisciplinary discussions certainly account for a lot of the excitement in the field.

This conference was made possible through the help of the organizing committee: Jeanny Hérault, Bernard Angéniol, John Bridle, Yves Burnod and Jean-Sylvain Liénard. The support of NATO was indeed most appreciated, and we tried to keep their high standards to make the really highest quality program. For that all the participants did a superb job: their talks were always very stimulating (if not their speed in sending back their typed papers!).

Special thanks also go to Sylvia Pelc, who edited a large part of the book and Springer-Verlag who produced the volume in very short time.

Orsay, April 1990 F. Fogelman Soulié

Reference

Bienenstock, E., Fogelman Soulié, F., Weisbuch, G. (eds.): Disordered Systems and Biological Organization. NATO-ARW, Les Houches 1985. NATO ASI Series F: Computer and Systems Sciences, Vol.20, Springer-Verlag, 1986.

Table of Contents

Part 1 Algorithms

Part 4 Image

Part 5 Neuro-biology

1 ALGORITHMS

Incorporating knowledge in multi-layer networks: the example of protein secondary structure prediction

C. Mejia, F. Fogelman Soulié

Laboratoire de Recherche en Informatique
Bâtiment 490
Université de Paris Sud
91 405 ORSAY cedex, France.

Abstract

We present on the example of protein secondary structure prediction various ways by which domain specific knowledge can be incorporated into a multi-layer network so as to increase speed of learning and accuracy in prediction. In particular, we show how to set weight patterns so as to reproduce knowledge of the domain. We illustrate the use of linear learning and Discriminant Analysis to specify the appropriate number of hidden units. Finally, we show that "guided" pruning can improve accuracy while reducing the number of weights. These various techniques can be used for other applications as well.

1. INTRODUCTION [1]

Neural networks have recently been used for many different tasks, essentially of the classification type. In particular, multi-layer perceptrons, or MLPs, have been developed to learn to process data in perceptual problems, such as speech [Bottou, 1989], [Bourlard, 1987], [Waibel, 1987], image [Cottrell, to appear], [Le Cun, 1989], or signal [Gorman, 1988].

MLPs are said to be very efficient, but hard and slow to train. This drawback of the Gradient Back Propagation (GBP) learning algorithm can be overcome in essentially two ways. First, one can try various accelerating techniques instead of the basic gradient-following GBP: this includes conjugated gradients, second order rules [Becker, 1988], [Fahlman, 1988], [Watrous, 1987], ... Or, one can try to reduce the number of weights, i.e. of parameters, in the network. This has also one interesting consequence, linked to the generalization ability of MLPs. The number of cells in the network must always be kept at a minimum: performances on the learning set might increase with an increasing number of cells, but will finally deteriorate on the

---

[1] The work presented at the meeting was realized in the fall of 1988. Since then, the work reported in [Holley, 1989] was published; their results seem rather similar to ours (on the same data base, but split differently between training and test sets). Their architectures were obtained experimentally, when we derived ours from detailed implementation of available knowledge. The comparison with this work thus perfectly illustrates our approach, i.e. to incorporate knowledge beforehand into the network architecture, instead of running many simulations with nets of varying architectures. This is why we decided to add references to Holley's work in the written version of our conference.

NATO ASI Series, Vol. F 68
Neurocomputing
Edited by F. Fogelman Soulié and J. Hérault

test set, because of overfitting effects. With fully connected nets, there exists an "optimal" range for the number of hidden units, large enough to allow for good learning, while small enough for good generalization [Baum, 1989]. The problem, in practice, is to determine that range: trial and error might do, starting with an initial reasonable guess, such as e.g. w = mp, where w is the number of weights, m the number of examples and p the dimension of the outputs. Or, more efficiently, one can set the number of hidden units equal to the dimension of the Discriminant Analysis hyperplane [Gallinari, 1988]. Pruning has also been reported to produce good results by various authors.

However, the best way is certainly to set the connections according to knowledge of the domain. This has been achieved, for example, in the TDNN networks for speech [Bottou, 1989], [Waibel, 1987] or the shared weights networks for image processing [Le Cun, 1989]: the idea there is to impose a constraint on some of the cells of the network so as to make them behave as masks -or feature extractors- passed over the input. The initial structure of the masks can even be set up by looking into image or speech processing manuals and reproducing the classical feature extractors into the masks structures [Loncelle, 1989]. In these architectures, although the number of cells might still be large, the number of free parameters is largely reduced. The networks then learn rapidly and are easy to train, since they have few parameters to learn and these parameters are initialized at "reasonable" values.

In this paper, we will use a problem in Biotechnology as an example for testing these ideas. MLPs have been applied to various problems in Biotechnology: to predict secondary and/or tertiary structures of molecules from their sequence [Holley, 1989; Quian, 1988], to find homologies between sequences or regularities within a structure. Although toy problems are indeed quite illuminating, it is also important to test neural network techniques on hard real-sized problems. All the above problems are hard, of large economic potential, and, at present, do not have complete solutions; gaining a few percents on prediction accuracy is considered of real significance. The area is thus particularly worth investigating with neural net techniques.We will focus here on the problem of protein secondary structure prediction.

The paper is organized as follows: in section 2, we briefly introduce the problem of proteins secondary structure prediction. In section 3, we present various solutions by neural networks, and discuss their performances.

2. PROTEINS SECONDARY STRUCTURE PREDICTION

Proteins represent more than half the weight of cells. By adopting different spatial configurations, they realize many different functionalities: elaborate structures, receive or send messages, protect the organism, serve as enzymes in biochemical reactions... Finding the spatial configuration of a protein is still a very long and painful task, and few proteins have their spatial structure fully elucidated.

Proteins can be viewed as "words" on an alphabet of 20 aminoacids: this word is their **primary structure**. Their 3-D conformation or **tertiary structure** is characteristic of their capacity of entering into specific interactions with molecules, i.e. of their chemical activity. Although the tertiary structure is very often unknown, intermediate local structures have been identified, which are common to all proteins: the **secondary structure** of a protein is then the arrangement of these sub-structures. At present, biochemists have identified two main sub-structures: α-helices, ß-sheets, and more recently more complex sub-structures called domains.

Since systematically identifying the tertiary structure of proteins remains out of reach, many researchers have investigated the somewhat easier problem of predicting their secondary structure. The different methods developed sofar achieve around 60% accuracy; they include statistical methods: [Chou, 1978], [Garnier, 1978], [Gascuel, 1988], [Levin, 1986], knowledge-based methods: [Lim, 1974], or Neural Networks techniques: [Holley, 1989], [Qian, 1988]. It is not always easy to compare those techniques, since they do not use the same data bases. Table 1 shows the results reported by the authors.

Technique	accuracy (%)
Lim	59.3
Chou	49.9
Garnier	55.9
Levin	57.5
Gascuel	58.7
Quian	62.7
Holley	63.2

Table 1. Accuracy on protein secondary structure prediction.

All these techniques are local, in the sense that they predict the sub-structure associated to a residue on the basis of local information only. The fact that no technique can significantly do better than 60% accuracy is not clearly understood: it may be due to the limited size of the available data bases, or much more probably to the need of using long range information for predicting sub-structures. Neural net methods, as we will see in details, share this feature of using local-information-only, and thus have the same limitations. However, they seem to optimally exploit the statistical information included in the data bases, and allow to incorporate biochemical knowledge, thus producing the best existing results. We now describe the methodology used in Neural nets.

3. NETWORK SOLUTIONS

3-1 The data base

We will use Multi-layer networks or MLPs, trained by the Gradient Back Propagation algorithm [Le Cun, 1987], [Rumelhart, 1986]. Our work is intended to show how expert knowledge can be usefully incorporated into an MLP so as to gain increased performances and speed. Our "expert" source has been [Gascuel, 1988].

The data base is taken from [Kabsch and Sanders, 1983] who provided a labelling of the Brookhaven Protein Data bank in three sub-structures: α-helix, ß-sheet and coil (those residues which are neither helix nor sheet). Among the proteins in the data base, some are homologous and their structures are then very close. The data base must be organized so as to take into account homologous proteins: the test set should not contain proteins homologous to those in the training set, since this would artificially **overestimate** the accuracy of the method. In [Holley, 1989], the training set contains the 48 first proteins in the Kabsch and Sanders data base, and the test set the last 14: hence no special care seems to have been taken to avoid homologies. In [Quian, 1988], to study this effect, the authors have investigated various test sets, with and without homologies with the training set, in a data base with 106 proteins from the Brookhaven Data base.

We have used the Kabsch and Sanders data base as described in [Gascuel, 1988]: proteins are considered homologous, if their homology is larger than 30% or if they contain segments of 60 amino acids at least with an homology larger than 30%. 19 homologous proteins have been found in the data base. We have thus used a training set of 41 proteins with no homology and a test set of 19 proteins with homologies (table 2).

1ABP, 1AZU, 1BP2, 1CAC, 1CPV, 1CRN, 1FDX, 1GCN, 1GPD, 1HIP, 1INS, 1LH1, 1LZM, 1MLT, 1OVO, 1PCY, 1PPT, 1REI, 1RHD, 1RNS, 1SBT, 1TIM, 2ADK, 2B5C, 2GRS, 2PAB, 2SNS, 2SOD, 2SSI, 3CNA, 3DFR, 3FXC, 3FXN, 3PGM, 3TLN, 4ADH, 4LDH, 4PTI, 4RXN, 5CPA, 7LYZ

155C, 351C, 3C2C, 3CYT
1APR , 2APP
1CTX, 1NXB
1ECD, 1LHB, 1MBN, 2MHB
1EST, 2ALP, 2GCH, 2PTN, 2SGA,
2ACT, 8PAP

Table 2. data base with Brookhaven identifiers.
The learning set has 41 proteins with no homology (shown in the first 3 lines) and the test set 19 proteins which have homologies among themselves, but not with the learning set: we show the 6 subsets of homologous proteins.

3-2 The network

The network used is of the "NetTalk" type [Sejnowski, 1987], [Quian, 1988]: a window of fixed size is passed over the protein "word" and the network is trained by GBP to produce at the output the sub-structure of the central residue (fig.1). Each position in the window is coded in a group of 21 cells: one for each of the 20 amino-acids and one for the empty position. To determine the size of the window, we have used knowledge [Gascuel, 1988] about the importance of neighbors to determine the structure of a residue. Figure 2 shows these dependences for the three sub-structures: from this figure, we can infer that a window of size 17 would cover most of the important residues. In [Holley, 1989], windows of sizes 3 to 21 have been tried, size 17 happened to produce the best results. We saved these testings by directly using the knowledge available to us.

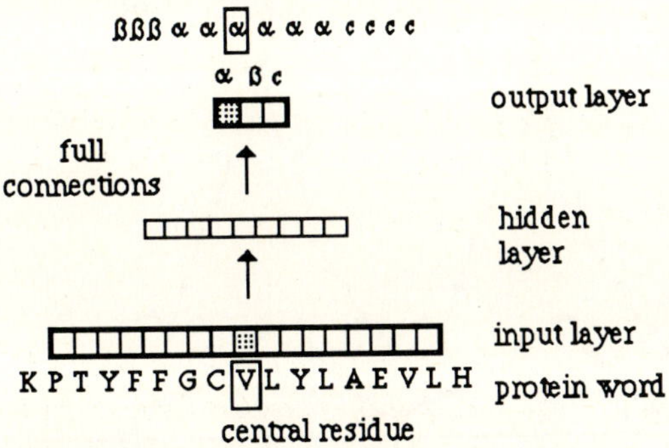

Figure 1. Multi-layer network for prediction of secondary structure of central residue

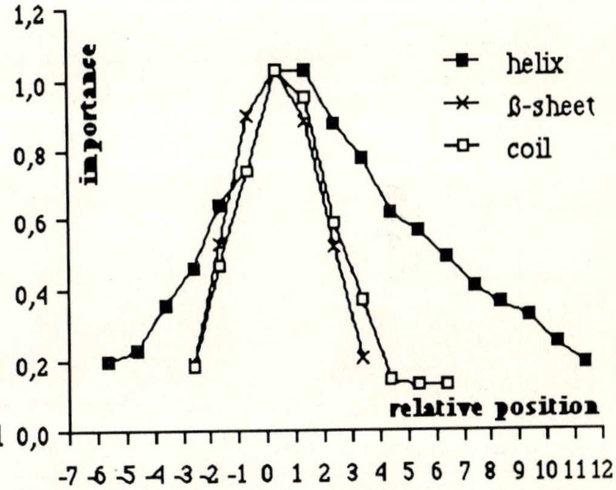

Figure 2. importance of neighbors, at relative position -7 to 12, for the determination of the structure of residue 0, for the three structures.

The output layer has three cells to code, by position, the three sub-structures. The residue is classified in the output category which has the highest activity. The prediction accuracy is measured by $n_\alpha + n_\beta + n_{coil} / N$, where n_i is the number of residues of type i correctly classified and N is the total number of residues. Correlation coefficients can also be used and provide better indications about the quality of the method [Gascuel, 1988]. In addition, it seems reasonable to require that the prediction method be "well balanced", i.e. that the predicted proportions of structures are approximately equal to their observed proportions. Since coil structure is more probable than α-helix or ß-sheet (50% to 30 and 20%), overpredicting coil will overestimate the accuracy. This can be observed in [Holley, 1989] where the prediction accuracy on the test set is 66.9% for coils and only 59.2 and 53.3 for α-helix or ß-sheet.

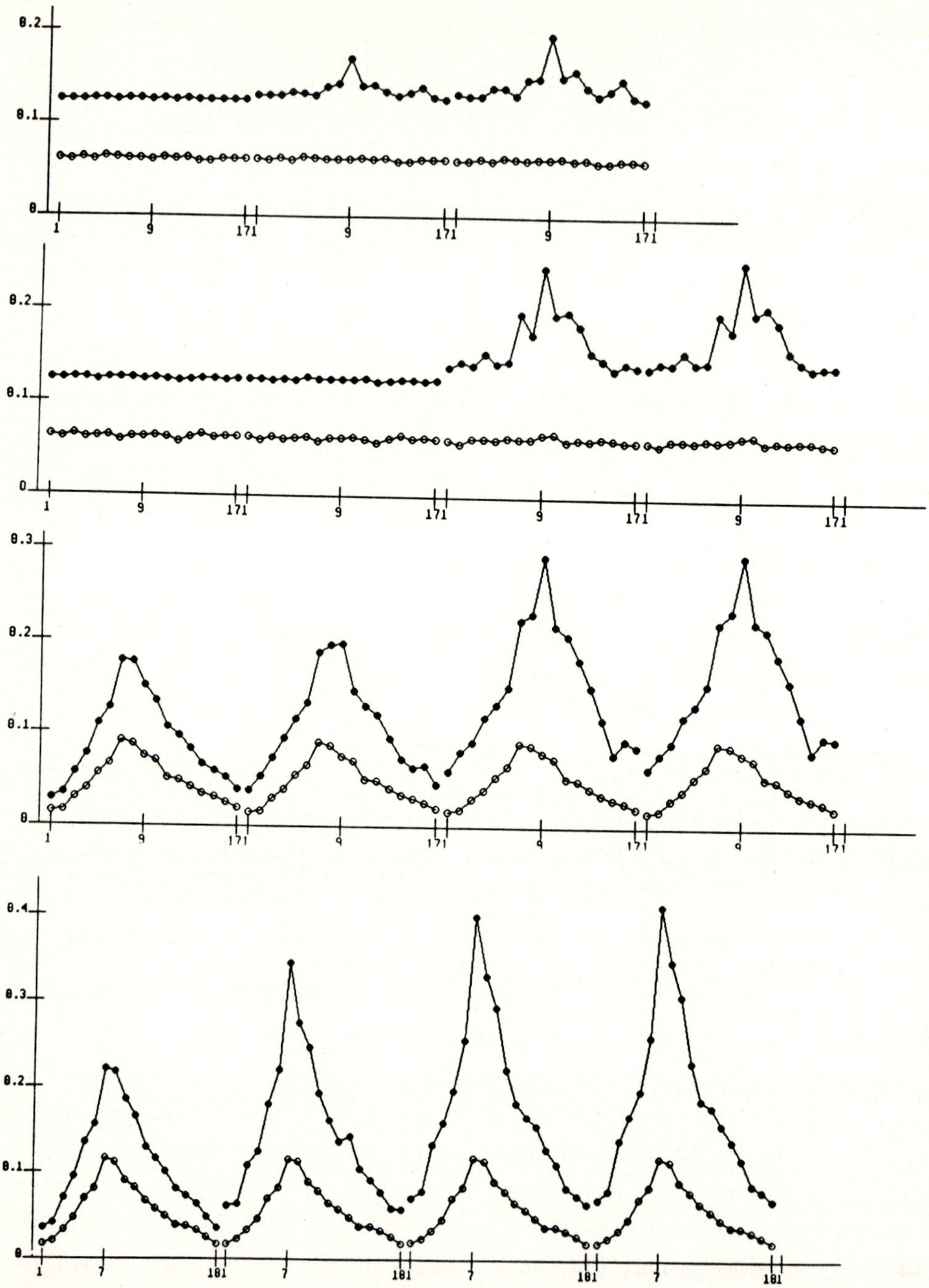

Figure 3. Evolution during learning of weights from one amino-acid, for each of the 17 (nets 1 to 3) or 18 (net 4) cells in the input window, to the hidden layer: the upper curve shows the weights for the amino-acid with maximum weight, the bottom curve the average on all amino-acids. Three periods (for net 1) or four (nets 2 to 4) are shown: period 1 shows initial weights, period 2 shows weights after 20 iterations (sigmoid for net 1, linear otherwise), period 3 after 20 more sigmoidal, period 4 after 100 more sigmoidal.

The hidden layer has a varying number of cells, from 0 to 20: experiments showed that 2 to 3 hidden cells were sufficient. The layers have been fully connected, with random initial weights in the range ± 2.38 / √ fan-in (which is provided by our simulator SN [Bottou, 1988]).

3-3 The trivial solution

The network structure just described involves very little knowledge, except the size of the window: it is the first trivial architecture that one can try. All our results are summarized in table 3: the first results in this trivial case (net 1) are slightly inferior to other classical techniques.

In [Gallinari, 1988], we have shown that MLPs with linear units performed Discriminant Analysis. It is thus reasonable to view MLPs as devices which start by performing DA, especially when the weights are initialized so that the activity of the cells remain in the central, i.e. the linear, part of the sigmoïd. Afterwards, the MLP eventually improves, through non linearity, upon this solution, optimal in the linear case. We have thus used the same network as before, but, during training, we first started with 20 "linear" sweeps, by disabling the sigmoïd, and then followed with the usual sigmoïd sweeps. Table 3 shows that with this trick (net 2), we gained about 5% on test set. Notice that, since the dimension of the DA hyperplane is 2 here, we have a good theoretical reason to use 2 hidden units (which is the optimal number found experimentally in [Holley, 1989]).

Net	Window symmetric	Size of window	Coding of amino-ac.	weights triang.	linear learning	training 41 prot.	test 19 prot.
1	yes	17	21	no	no	55.3	51.5
2	yes	17	21	no	yes	61.2	55.6
3	yes	17	21	yes	yes	63.5	57.9
4	no	18	13	yes	yes	64.5	58.4

Table 3. accuracy (in %) for the different solutions

We have visualized the evolution of weights along learning. Figure 3 shows that, during learning, weights tend to develop triangular patterns similar to those shown in figure 2. We could have initialized those weights directly along triangular patterns and thus save the network the time required to learn this shape. This is what we now show.

3-4 Weights initialization

We have first tested a network identical to net 2, but where the weights are initialized with a triangular shape (fig4). Results are again improved (table 3: net 3). However, if we want to make full use of the information contained in figure 2, we can notice that the windows are not symmetric: for α-helix, the structure of a residue depends upon neighhbors -6 to 11, -3 to 3 for ß-sheet, and -3 to 6 for coils. To use this knowledge, we should thus use windows of different sizes and shapes for the three structures, which is not implementable with our model. We thus use a unique asymmetric window shape, corresponding to the largest case, α-helix, which makes about 26% of the residues in the data base. The window is now of size - 18, and is asymmetric: the network has to predict the structure of residue 0, taking into account residues at relative positions -6 to 11.

We have also used biochemical knowledge [Gascuel, 1988] which links together some amino-acids having similar physico-chemical properties and similar "preferences" for one of the secondary structures. This allows to group those amino-acids and obtain a more compact coding along 13 cells, instead of 21 (fig.5).With this coding, and asymmetric windows, we gain a little more on accuracy (see net 4 in table 3) and weights are almost perfect after 40 sweeps only (fig.3). Notice that our best performances are still less than those reported in [Holley, 1989]: this is due to the fact that, in their test set, some proteins have homologies with proteins in the learning set, which is not the case in ours. Results in [Quian, 1988] are better than ours, but with a much larger data base: 89 proteins for the training set (and 15 for test set with no homology with training set).

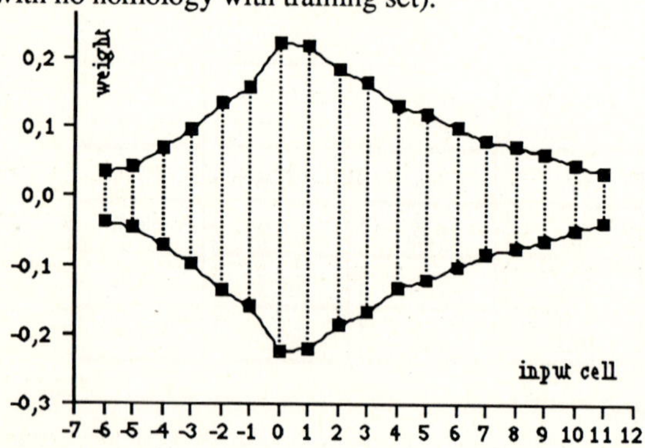

Figure 4. Triangular initialization of weights: for each cell of the window and each amino-acid, the weight is set at random between the two bounds shown.

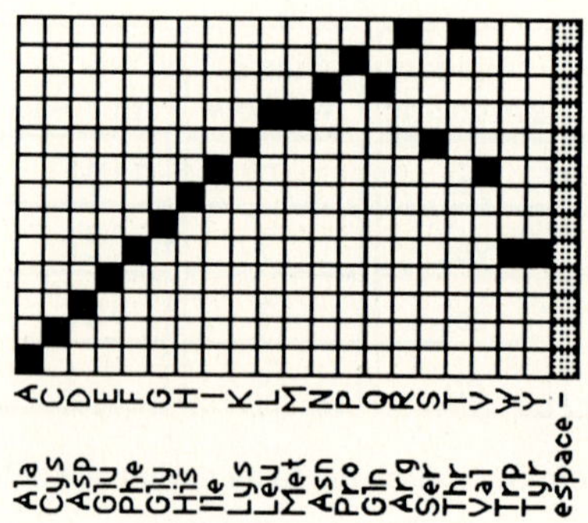

Figure 5. Grouping of "similar" amino-acids, and coding on 13 cells.

3-5 Pruning

Now, suppose we did not know about the DA dimension and we had used a network with too many hidden units, say for example with 20 hidden units. We train the network, and we want to see whether pruning would deteriorate the accuracy. With a network similar to case 4 before, but with 20 hidden units instead of 2, there are 4700 weights in layer 1 and 63 in layer 2. There are different methods for pruning.

We can first try random pruning. We can also use the information in figure 2, that we have partly ignored. Some cells should have a ß-sheet window [-3,3], others should have a coil window [-3,6]. Assume we keep 10 hidden units and out of the remaining 10, prune 6 of them the "coil" way (i.e. kill weights -6 to -4, 7 to 11) and 4 the "ß-sheet" way (kill weights -6 to -4 and 4 to 11). We will thus destroy (11*4+8*6)*13=1196 weights. To do so, we can choose 1196 weights at random or the smallest weights or the smallest cells (those with the smallest average weight) and prune 6 the coil way, 4 the ß-sheet way. The results are given in table 4 and show that, indeed, pruning is not destructive and is definitely more efficient when used with knowledge.

Pruning	learning	test
1. before pruning	64.5	58.3
2. random		
right after pruning	60.9	55.3
after 20 sweeps	61.9	57.7
3. smallest weights		
right after pruning	64.4	58.1
after 20 sweeps	64.1	57.5
4. smallest cells		
right after pruning	64.4	58.8
after 20 sweeps	64.6	58.6

Table 4. Effects of pruning on net 4, with 20 hidden units

4. CONCLUSION

We have shown in this paper various ways by which a-priori domain knowledge could be used to set the architecture of MLPs: patterns of weights can be initialized so as to take into account the importance of particular factors in the input; the dimension of the Discriminant Analysis hyperplane provides a first guess for the number of hidden units; a-posteriori pruning can efficiently reduce the number of weights in the network.

All these techniques can be implemented in many different applications and guide the network designer: MLPs can then be trained faster and lead to better performances in generalization.

We wish to thank Olivier Gascuel, who provided us with his results and data base and very helpful indications at the beginning of our work.

5. REFERENCES

1. Baum, E., Haussler, D.: What Size Net Gives Valid Generalization ?, Neural Computation, Vol. 1. n° 1. 151-160. (1989).

2. Becker, S., Le Cun, Y.: Improving the convergence of bavk-propagation learning with second order methods. In "Proceedings, 1988 Connectionist models Summer School",Morgan Kaufman, 29-37, (1988).

3. Bottou, L.Y., Le Cun, Y.: SN: Un simulateur pour réseaux connexionnistes. "Neuro-Nîmes 88", EC2 Ed., 371-382, (1988).

4. Bottou, L., Fogelman Soulié, F., Liénard, J.S., Blanchet, P.: Speaker independent isolated digit recognition: multi layer perceptrons vs dynamic time warping. Neural Networks, to appear.

5. Bourlard, H., Wellekens, C.J.: Multilayer perceptrons and automatic speech recognition. In IEEE 1st ICNN, San Diego, M. Caudill, C. Butler eds, IEEE catalog n° 87TH0191-7, vol. IV, 407-416, (1987).

6. Chou, P.Y., Fasman, G.D.: Empirical prediction of protein conformation. ANN. Rev. Biochem., 47, 251-276, (1978).

7. Cottrell, G., Munro, P.W., Zipser, D.: Image compression by back propagation: a demonstration of extensional programming. In " Advances in Cognitive Science", N.E. Sharkey Ed., vol2, Norwood NJ Ablex. to appear.

8. Fahlman, S.E.: Faster learning variations on back-propagation: an empirical study. In "Proceedings, 1988 Connectionist models Summer School",Morgan Kaufman,38-51, (1988).

9. Fogelman Soulié, F., Gallinari, P., Le Cun, Y., Thiria, S.: Evaluation of network architectures on test learning tasks. In IEEE 1st ICNN, San Diego, M. Caudill, C. Butler eds, IEEE catalog n° 87TH0191-7, vol. II, 653-660, (1987).

10. Gallinari, P., Thiria, S., Fogelman Soulié, F.: Multilayer Perceptrons and Data Analysis. IEEE 2nd ICNN, San Diego, vol. I, 391-401, (1988).

11. Garnier, J., Osguthorpe, D.J., Robson, B.: Analysis of thje accuracy and implications of simple methods for predicting the secondary structure of globular proteins. J. Mol. Biol., 120, 97-120, (1978).

12. Gascuel, O., Golmard, J.L.: A simple method for predicting the secondary structure of globular proteins: implications and accuracy. Centre de Recherche en Informatique de Montpellier, Technical report, (1988).

13. Gorman, R.P., Sejnowski, T.J.: Analysis of hidden units in a Layered network trained to classify sonar targets. Neural Networks, vol.1, n°1, 75-89, (1988).

14. Holley, L.H., Karplus, M.: Protein structure prediction with a neural network. PNAS, USA, 86, 152-156, (1989).

15. Kabsch, W., Sander, C.: Dictionnary of protein secondary structure: pattern recognition of hydrogen-bonded and geometrical features. Biopolymers, 22, 2577-2637, (1983a).

16. Kabsch, W., Sander, C.: How good are predictions of protein secondary structure? FEBS Letters, 155, 179-182, (1983b).

17. Le Cun, Y.: Modèles connexionnistes de l'apprentissage, Thèse, Paris, (1987).

18. Le Cun, Y.: Generalization and network design strategies. In "Connectionism in perspective", R. Pfeifer, Z. Schreter, F. Fogelman Soulié, L. Steels eds, North Holland, 143-156, (1989).

19. Levin, J., Robson, B., Garnier, J.: An algorithm for secondary structure determination in proteins based on sequence similarity. FEBS Letters, 205, 303-308, (1986).

20. Lim, V.I.: Algorithms for prediction of alpha-helical and beta-structural regions in globular proteins. J. Mol. Biol., 88, 873-894, (1974).

21. Loncelle, J.: Détection de contours par rétro-propagation du gradient. "Neuro-Nîmes 88", EC2 Ed., 373-394, (1988).

22. Quian, N., Sejnowski, T.J.: Predicting the secondary structure of globular proteins using neural network models. J. Mol. Biol., 202, 865-884, (1988).

23. Rumelhart, D., Hinton, G., Williams, R.: Learning Internal Representations by Error Propagation, in Parallel Distributed Processing: Explorations in the MicroStructure of cognition, Rumelhart & McClelland eds, vol 1, chapter 8, MIT Press, (1986).

24. Sejnowski, T.J., Rosenberg, C.M.: Parallel networks that learn to pronounce english text. Complex Systems, vol.1, n°1, 145-168, (1987).

25. Waibel, A., Hanazawa, T., Hinton, G., Shikano, K., Lang, K.: Phoneme recognition using Time-delay neural networks. Preprint ATR Interpreting Telephony Research Laboratories, (oct. 1987).

26. Watrous, R.L.: Learning algorithms for connectionist networks: applied gradient methods of non linear optimization. In IEEE 1st ICNN, San Diego, M. Caudill, C. Butler eds, IEEE catalog n° 87TH0191-7, vol. II, 619-627, (1987).

Product Units with Trainable Exponents and Multi-Layer Networks

Richard Durbin and David E. Rumelhart

Department of Psychology, Stanford University,

Stanford, CA 94305, U.S.A.

Abstract

This chapter reviews and examines a variant type of computational unit which we have recently proposed for use in multi-layer neural networks [3]. Instead of the output of this unit depending on a weighted sum of the inputs, it depends on a weighted product. In justifying the introduction of a new type of unit we explore at some length the rationale behind the use of multi-layer neural networks, and the properties of the computational units within them. At the end of the chapter we discuss a biological model for a single complex neve cell with active dendritic membrane that uses the product units.

1 Introduction

In this chapter we will discuss the trainable product units that we have recently proposed [3], particularly with respect to how such units should be used in multi-layer networks. The output of the proposed unit, y, is given by

$$y = \prod_{i=1}^{N} x_i^{p_i}. \tag{1}$$

Each input, x_i, is raised to some power, determined by a trainable weight, p_i, and then these values are multiplied together. The basic idea is that a single unit can evaluate any polynomial term, depending on the values of the weights p_i. For example, a unit with $p_1 = p_3 = 1$, $p_2 = p_4 = 0$ would calculate the term x_1x_3 on four inputs. As this example shows, each unit can only represent one term: to express a complete polynomial requires a number of units, whose results must then be combined as a weighted sum, using a standard output unit. At first sight this approach is more complex than standard

NATO ASI Series, Vol. F 68
Neurocomputing
Edited by F. Fogelman Soulié and J. Hérault

techniques to learn a function by fitting polynomial coefficients [7]. However it allows much greater control of the number of free parameters, and hence of the generalisation properties of the system. If all the polynomial terms up to some order are to be considered, then in the direct approach an exponentially increasing number of parameters must be estimated, requiring enormous amounts of data. This is what is required by sigma-pi units, as proposed by Rumelhart et al. [10], and Maxwell et al. [5]. In contrast, using the units defined above, we can determine in advance how many terms to allow, without predetermining which terms to use.

This brief discussion has already introduced us to a couple of fundamental issues: generalisation based on the fitting of parameters, and the combination of simple units to perform a more complex task. An important point is that the properties of the "product" units are complementary to, and combine well with, those of standard weighted sum units, which we will call "summing" units in this chapter. Note that we will apply the term summing units broadly, including also units like those in a standard back-propagation network that calculate a nonlinear function of the weighted sum. Later in the chapter we shall discuss the mathematical properties of product units, and show how they operate alongside summing units in networks. First, however, we would like to discuss our views on some of the properties of multi-layer neural networks, and how computational units, such as the product units under discussion in this chapter, are best used in them.

2 Computational Units in Multi-layer Networks

There are two different fields in which neural networks have been justified as being interesting: in modelling of real nervous systems, and as parallel computational systems. We believe that product units of the type proposed above are potentially helpful in both fields. With respect to neural modelling, although a standard thresholded summing unit provides a basic "first order" model of the computational properties of a neuron, there are many cases where it appears that non-linear dendritic processes are very important. In these cases we have proposed that a simple network model, combining summing and product units, provides a better, perhaps "second order" approximation to a single cell. Since this model depends on some of the mathematical analysis of product units we will return to it at the end of the chapter, after reviewing the technical aspects of product units.

As computational systems, let us consider two different arguments for the use of multi-layer neural networks. Both follow from the fact that they tackle hard problems in stages, using successive layers of units. The first argument is that they make use of indirect information, which is often the main form of information available in systems with many interacting components. They do this because they force the formation (in the hidden layers) of intermediate representations. In many cases it is a few higher order combinations of the inputs to the model that are important. Finding such combinations is particularly important when there are several outputs, which are related to each other in the way that they depend on the input data. These relationships are exploited by multi-layer networks.

Since a multi-layer network requires that the hidden layers code information for all of the output units, and each output unit sees all of the hidden layer, the system can and will benefit from generating representations that capture general features useful for the all the tasks under consideration. In other words, the learnt implementations of the output functions will cross-constrain each other, so that the way each one works influences how the others work. As a consequence, for example, Yann LeCun has suggested (pers. comm.) that a network system that is designed to recognise hand-written digits might plausibly be improved by also requiring it to recognise letters, assuming that there is shared structure in the way that people write letters and digits. This type of behavior is hard to achieve with standard interpolation systems, even though it seems to be exactly what is needed for many artificial intelligence applications. A hallmark of intelligent behaviour is that knowledge from a wide variety of related situations has a significant, albeit tangential, effect on a particular task.

The second argument for using a neural network approach takes a more general view of what is happening when training a multi-layer network. We can view a two layer network as comprising two distinct models connected in series. When training the network, the second model is being fit directly, in a traditional fashion, by minimising the prediction errors. In contrast the first model is fit indirectly, on the basis of how well the second model can be made to fit. This process of indirectly fitting a model is potentially very powerful, allowing deep components of a modular system to adapt to data.

Modular systems with sequential components are clearly a good way to approach complex problems. However, in most current modular systems the lower level components are prespecified on *a priori* grounds. We do not claim that data-based training of hidden models is a new discovery of the neural network field — previous examples are the Kalman filter [12] and hidden Markov models [8] — but the neural network approaches open up new opportunities, which had not been previously considered. The power of such techniques is clear from the previous examples (Kalman filters and hidden Markov models), which are both extremely successful, even though they both use linear hidden models (of different types). Neural network techniques, such as back-propagation, use non-linear hiddden stages.

What constraints do these two arguments outlined above make on the type of computational unit to be used in networks? Neither of them requires that the outputs of the network units should depend on weighted sums of inputs. The first suggests that units should have a high interconnectivity and should be sufficiently numerous to allow distributed representation of information. The second suggests that the computation carried out in any one stage should be fairly simple, and that there should be some way to "propagate back" error through units (in a general sense) so as to be able to train lower layers of the whole system. In fact it seems clear that different applications should ideally use different configurations and different types of computation. The traditional approach of fixing the preprocessing components is an extreme version of this. We would argue that fixing a component *a priori* is almost always too rigid, even where there are strong ideas about how processing should be carried out. It is preferable to also have adaptability, so that performance can be optimised for the actual data to be handled. However there are also cases where there are no strong preconceptions about computational organization, especially at intermediary levels. In these cases it is desirable to have general purpose network units that give good learning and generalization behavior.

This is where the product units come in. They are a very natural general form, with a different computational "flavour" to summing units. As such, they are potentially more appropriate in certain circumstances. An example would be where combinatorial or

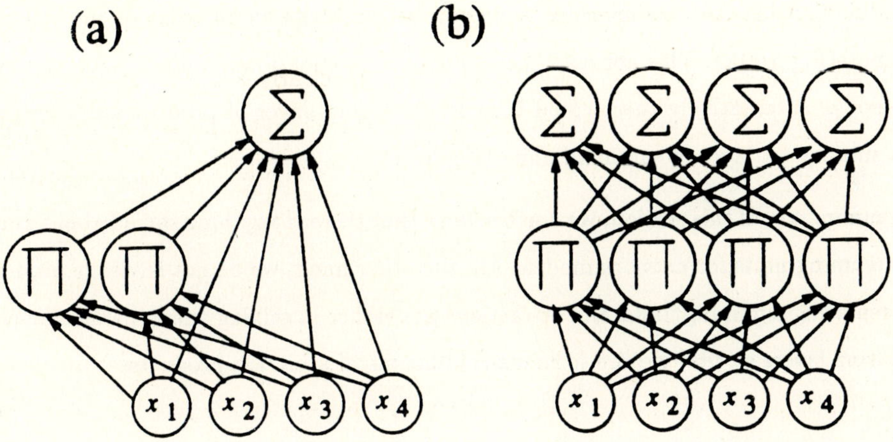

Figure 1. Two suggested forms of possible network incorporating product units. Product units are shown with a Π and summing units with a Σ. (a) Each summing unit gets direct connections from the input units, and also from a group of dedicated product units. (b) Alternating layers of product and summing units, finishing with a summing unit.

switching performance seems to be required, since these are multiplicative-type operations. In a more general sense, product units also appear to be more computationally powerful than summing units (in terms of their information storage capacity per weight, see below).

In cases where there is more than one layer of general type units it seems there is a case for combining product and summing units. There is a natural complementarity between additive and multiplicative type operations. For example this gives rise to the polynomial capabilities that were mentioned above, and are discussed at greater length by Poggio and Reichardt [7]. It is interesting to consider an analogy to boolean networks, where the basic unit operations are conjunction (and) and disjunction (or). These are frequently arranged in alternating layers, as in Figure 1b (called "normal forms" for boolean networks). Although both conjunctive and disjunctive operations can be simulated with either product or summing units, it is natural to consider the product operation as a generalised conjunction, and the summing operation as a generalised disjunction.

There are several ways to arrange the units to achieve these capabilities. One is for a few product units to be made available as inputs to a standard thresholded summing unit, so that the output can now consider some polynomial terms in addition to the original raw inputs(Figure 1a). This approach has a direct neurobiological interpretation (see the discussion). Alternatively there could be a whole hidden layer of product units feeding into a subsequent layer of summing units (Figure 1b).

In summmary of this section, we don't believe that there is anything sacred about standard summing units for network models. On the other hand, we do not envisage product units replacing summing units; the attractions are rather in mixing them, particularly in alternating layers so that we can form weighted sums of arbitrary products.

3 Product Units: Theory and Results

Let us now briefly describe how the proposed product units work. In order to discuss how to train their weights it is convenient to rewrite Equation 1 in terms of exponentials and logarithms.

$$y = e^{\Sigma p_i \ln x_i} \tag{2}$$

In this form we can see that a product unit acts like a summing unit whose inputs are preprocessed by taking logarithms, and whose output is passed through an exponential, rather than a squashing function. In mathematical terms the weighted product operation is said to be *conjugate* to a weighted sum operation, since exponentiation is the inverse of taking logarithms. As a general principle it may be worth while to consider other conjugating functions. Hanson and Burr [4] described several such unit types, mentioning briefly the exponential units that we focus on here.

In order to be able to handle negative inputs x_i, which we would like to be able to do in order to use the non-linearities of the product function around the origin, we must extend Equation 2 to the complex plane. This leads to the introduction of the harmonic functions sine and cosine in addition to the exponential. Exact implementation of Equation 2 would then give rise to an imaginary component of the output of the unit. However it turns out that this can be ignored [3]. The resulting expression,

$$y = e^{\Sigma p_i \ln |x_i|} \cos \Sigma p_i I_i \qquad \text{where } I_i = \begin{cases} 0 & i > 0 \\ \pi & i < 0 \end{cases}$$

is only truly equal to Equation 2 when the p_i are integers. However these correspond to all polynomial terms. One way to view ignoring the imaginary component is that the simplified unit is smoothly interpolating a real-valued function between the polynomial terms. Note that the case $x_i = 0$ was not considered above. This is because Equation 2 is clearly unstable at 0, and so we must ensure that $x_i > \varepsilon$ for some small number ε.

In order to use product (or any other) units in a network being trained by gradient descent we need to be able to calculate two derivatives The first of these is $(\partial y/\partial p_i)$, which is used to update the weights p_i once the error at the output of a unit is known. The second is $(\partial y/\partial x_i)$, which is used to propagate the error back through the unit to the preceeding layer. In this case these two derivatives are

$$\frac{\partial y}{\partial p_i} = e^{\Sigma p_i \ln |x_i|}(\ln |x_i| \cos \Sigma p_i I_i - I_i \sin \Sigma p_i I_i) = y(\ln |x_i| - I_i \tan \Sigma p_i I_i)$$

$$\frac{\partial y}{\partial x_i} = |x_i|^{-1} p_i e^{\Sigma p_i \ln |x_i|} \cos \Sigma p_i I_i = \frac{p_i y}{|x_i|} \tag{3}$$

It might appear that these forms are less well behaved than the equivalent expressions for summing units. This may be so, but it has not prevented adequate convergence in our simulations, given care in a couple of areas. First, it seems empirically that it is necessary to use a smaller value of the learning rate than with summing units (usually 10 to 100 times smaller). Second, it seems often to be important to add a bias term to avoid getting stuck in a local minimum, even when the bias weight eventually decays to 0 (an example is the symmetry task, see [3]). What do we mean by a bias in this case? For summing units the bias can be thought of as a constant input with value 1. For product units the same idea is used, but the appropriate constant is -1, since a positive value would simply multiply the output by a scalar. This would be irrelevant when there was a variable multiplicative weight from the output to a higher level summing unit. As a final note to the potential user: since zero is unavailable as an input value, boolean inputs to product units can not be coded as 0 and 1. It seems best to use boolean values -1 and 1, in which case the exponential terms in Equations 3 disappear, and the units behave like cosine summing units with 1 and 0 inputs.

An important question to ask about any learning system is: how computationally powerful are the basic units? One measure of this is the informational capacity of a unit,

Structure	M	Product unit percentage	Summing unit percentage
6 1	12	92	18
	18	49	3
	20	28	1
12 1	24	100	29
	36	66	0
	40	20	0
6 2 1	24	100	2
	36	82	0
	40	58	0
6 2 1	24	100	0
fixed	36	45	0
output	40	14	0

Table 1. Results on storage of random boolean data. The number of successful storage attempts in 100 trials is shown in the last two columns for various net structures and numbers of vectors, M. Storage is termed successful if all input vectors produce an output closer to the desired output than the undesired one. The "6 1" and "12 1" nets had a single learning unit with 6 or 12 inputs. The "6 2 1" nets had 2 hidden units (either product or summing) and one summing output unit, which was trainable for the first set of results, and fixed with all weights equal for the second set. These results indicate that storage capacity for product units is at least 3 bits per weight, as opposed to no more than 2 bits per weight for summing units, and that fixed output units do not drastically reduce computational power in multi-layer networks.

which is determined by the number of random patterns that it can learn (more precisely the number at which the probability of storing them all perfectly drops to a half [6]). For a single summing unit with N inputs the capacity can be shown theoretically to be 2N [2]. The empirical capacity of a single product unit is significantly higher than this at around 3N (Table 1). The relative improvement is maintained in a comparison of multi-layer networks containing product hidden units compared with ones consisting purely of summing units (Table 1), indicating that product units cooperate well with summing units.

We can also consider the performance of product units when the inputs x_i are real valued. An example is the ability of a network with two product hidden units to learn

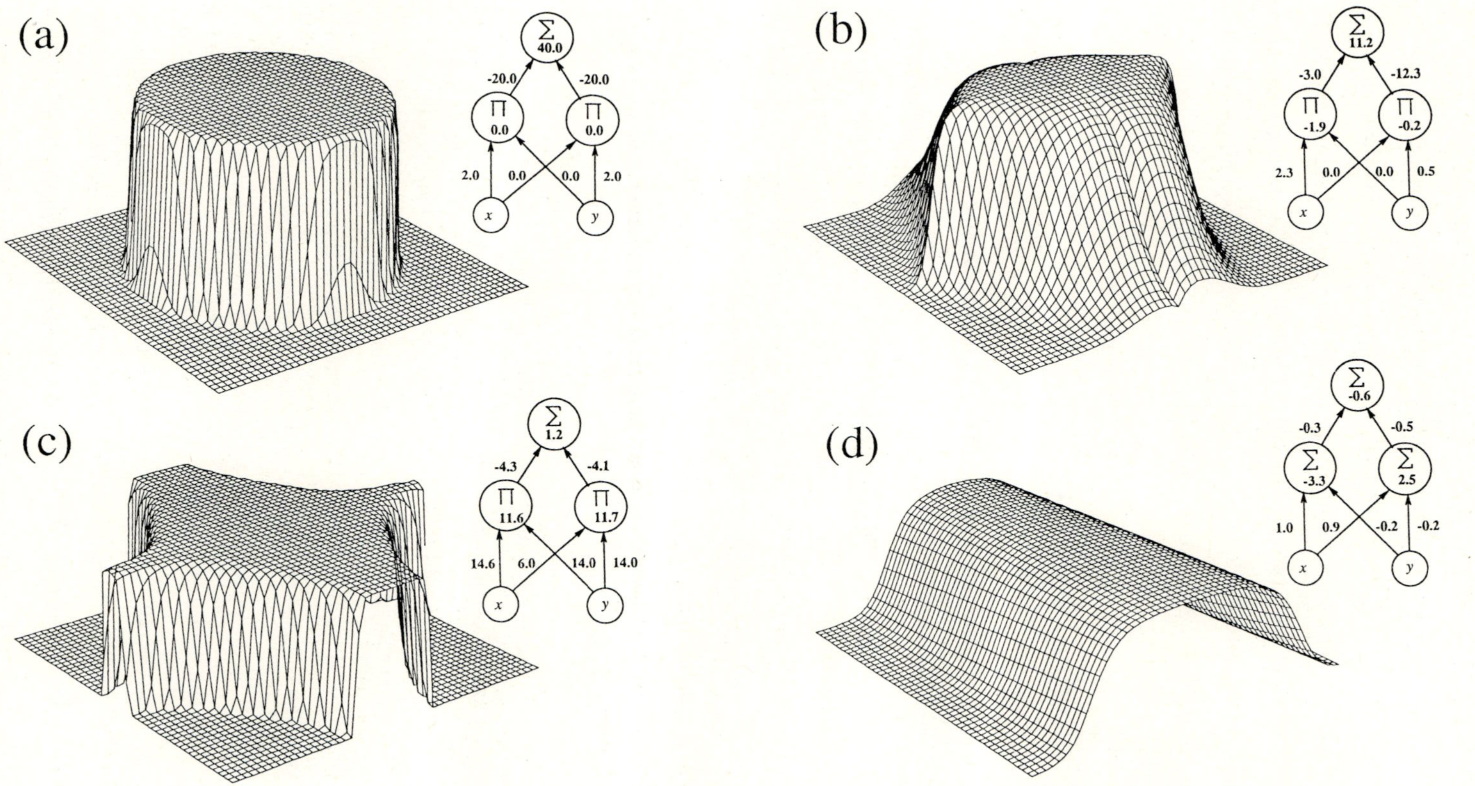

Figure 2. Performance on a task with real-valued input: learning a circular domain. In each case the network and a plot of its response function over the range -2.0 to 2.0 are shown. A variety of local minima were found using two product units (which in theory could solve the problem exactly), whereas there was only one solution found using two summing units. Although non-optimal, the product unit solutions were always better than the summing units solutions. (a) The ideal product unit network, used to generate the data. (b) An example of a good empirical solution with product units (2% missclassified, MSE 0.03). (c) An example of a poor product unit local minimum (13% misclassified, MSE 0.10). (d) The solution essentially always obtained with two summing hidden units (38% misclassified, MSE 0.24).

to respond to a circular region around the origin. In fact it appears that there are many local minima for this problem, and although the network occasionally finds the "correct" solution (Figure 2a), it more often finds other solutions such as those shown in Figure 2b,c). However these solutions are not bad: the average mean square error (MSE) for product unit networks is 0.09 (average of 10) with 88% correct data classification (whether the output is the correct side of 0.5). whereas the best corresponding summing unit network gives an MSE of 0.24, and only 62% correct classification.

4 Neurobiological Model

There is a natural neurobiological interpretation for a particular configuration of product and summing units. The idea is that some types of neuron respond in a non-linear fashion that is better modeled by a number of product units, summing at a central summing unit. The non-linear properties of these cell types arise from active channels in the dendritic membrane, whose properties change with trans-membrane voltage. Examples are cortical pyramidal cells (NMDA receptor channels), and cerebellar Purkinje cells (active calcium channels). It is interesting to observe that these two examples are the major integrating and output neuron types of their brain regions. The local interneurons appear to have more straightforward, linear properties.

The link to the model is best explained via Equation 2, which shows that a product unit acts like a summing unit whose inputs are preprocessed by passing them through a log function, then combined in a weighted sum, then passed through an exponential output function. Each of these stages has a biological analog in the model. Presynaptically, there are saturation effects giving an approximately logarithmic form to the voltage dependency of transmitter release. The released transmitter induces a current across the post-synaptic membrane whose magnitude is dependent on synapse strength. All the currents within a dendritic "region" are then summed. Finally, the voltage sensitive channels cause the post-synaptic voltage response to the summed current to be qualitatively exponential around a critical voltage level [1]. The notion of "dendritic region" depends on passive length constants and arbor geometry. We model the dendritic arbor by a number of discrete product units, but this is clearly a simplification. Standard summing inputs could still be made onto the soma, or onto dendritic regions lacking active channels, or, when the channels are transmitter dependent (as with NMDA receptor channnels), using other neurotransmitters.

As far as learning in the biological model is concerned, it is acceptable that the second layer summing weights, corresponding to the degree of influence of dendritic regions at the soma, are not very variable. Systems with fixed summing output layers are nearly as computationally powerful as fully variable ones, both in theory [6], and simulations (Table 1). Learning at the input synapses is still essentially Hebbian (Equation 3), with an additional term when the input x_i is negative (and so I_i is non-zero). Although the periodic form of this term appears unbiological, some type of additional term is not unreasonable for inhibitory input, which may well have different learning characteristics. Alternatively, it might be that the learning model only applies to excitatory input.

Clearly this model is still an abstraction. The critical issue is whether it describes the next level of qualitative behavior beyond simple summation and threshold models. To the extent that this can be done we would argue that there is an advantage to using a simple mathematical form, for example, keeping the exponential and logarithm functions, which can not be strictly accurate. Further consideration of this neurobiological model is required, but it seems likely that some such approach will lead to a new computional model for some major neuron types that is potentially both more accurate, and, interestingly, more powerful than the standard McCulloch-Pitts model.

Acknowledgements

RMD is a Lucille P. Markey Visiting Fellow and this work was supported by a grant from the Lucille P. Markey Charitable Trust. It was also supported in part by a grant to DER from the Office of Naval Research (Contract N00014-87-K-0671).

References

[1] Collingridge, G.L. and Bliss, T.V.P.: NMDA receptors - their role in long-term potentiation. *Trends Neurosci.* **10**, 288-293 (1987)

[2] Cover, T.: Geometrical and statistical properties of systems of linear inequalities with applications in pattern recognition. *IEEE Trans. Elect. Comp.* **14**, 326-334 (1965)

[3] Durbin, R. and Rumelhart, D.E.: Product units: a computationally powerful and biologically plausible extension to back propagation networks, *Neural Computation* **1**, 133-42 (1989)

[4] Hanson, S.J. and Burr, D.J.: Knowledge representation in connectionist networks. *Technical Report*, Bell Communication Research, Morristown, New Jersey (1987)

[5] Maxwell, T., Giles, C.G, and Lee, Y.C.: Generalization in neural networks, the contiguity problem. in *Proceedings IEEE First International Conference on Neural Networks*, Vol 2, 41-45 (1987)

[6] Mitchison, G.J. and Durbin, R.M.: Bounds on the learning capacity of some multi-layer networks. *Biological Cybernetics* **60**, 345-356 (1989)

[7] Poggio, T. and Reichardt, W.: On the representation of multi-input systems: computational properties of polynomial algorithms. *Biological Cybernetics* **37**, 167-186 (1980)

[8] Rabiner, L.R. and Juang, B.H.: An introduction to hidden markov models. *IEEE ASSP Magazine* **3:1**, 4-16 (1986)

[9] Rosenblatt, F.: *Principles of Neurodynamics*, Spartan, New York (1962)

[10] Rumelhart, D.E., Hinton, G.E. and McClelland, J.L.: A general framework for parallel distributed processing. in *Parallel Distributed Processing*, Vol 1, pp 45-76, MIT Press, Cambridge, Mass and London (1986)

[11] Rumelhart, D.E., Hinton, G.E. and Williams R.J.: Learning internal representations by error propagation. in *Parallel Distributed Processing*, Vol 1, pp 318-362, MIT Press, Cambridge, Mass and London (1986)

[12] Sorenson, H.W. (ed): *Kalman filtering: theory and application*, IEEE Press, New York (1985)

Recurrent Backpropagation and Hopfield Networks

Luis B. Almeida and João P. Neto
INESC
Apartado 10105
P-1017 Lisboa Codex
Portugal

This paper has two parts. In the first one, an intuitively simple proof of the extension of backpropagation to recurrent networks is given. In the second part, preliminary results on the application of recurrent backpropagation to the training of Hopfield networks are presented.

1 - Introduction

Backpropagation is a well known learning technique for multilayer perceptrons. As originally introduced, it was applicable only to feedforward networks, i.e. networks with no recurrent connections [1]. The extension of this rule to recurrent networks was first developed by this author [2]. Pineda [3] independently derived the same result. In this paper, a new form of the derivation is first presented, which is easier to grasp from an intuitive viewpoint. Then, some preliminary results on the training of Hopfield networks through recurrent backpropagation are described. These results suggest that backpropagation is a viable alternative for the training of such networks, possibly yielding some advantages, like the use of hidden units, and the training of analog-valued stable patterns. The paper is organized as follows: Section 2 presents the new derivation of recurrent backpropagation, and section 3 gives the results on training of Hopfield networks. Section 4 concludes.

2 - Recurrent backpropagation

Backpropagation is a gradient optimization technique for minimizing the total quadratic error of the outputs of multilayer perceptrons. As originally developed for feedforward networks [1], it involves a backward propagation of errors which can be viewed as a propagation through an *error propagation network*. As shown in [2], this network can be obtained from the multilayer perceptron by the application of two successive operations: linearization and transposition [4]. In [2], it was mathematically shown that this rule generalizes to recurrent perceptrons, i.e. that gradient optimization can be performed in the same way in these networks, the error propagation network being still obtained through linearization and transposition of the perceptron. Next, we shall give a more intuitive version of this proof.

NATO ASI Series, Vol. F 68
Neurocomputing
Edited by F. Fogelman Soulié and J. Hérault

As a step towards the derivation of the gradient learning procedure, we shall first find a way to compute the partial derivative of an output relative to a weight. Consider a general nonlinear network **P** with an output o and a linear branch of gain a, as depicted in figure 1-a. The external inputs of the network are to be kept fixed during the partial differentiation, and therefore they can be considered to be contained within the network itself, without loss of generality. This is why they are not shown in the figure. The network is assumed to be at a fixed point.

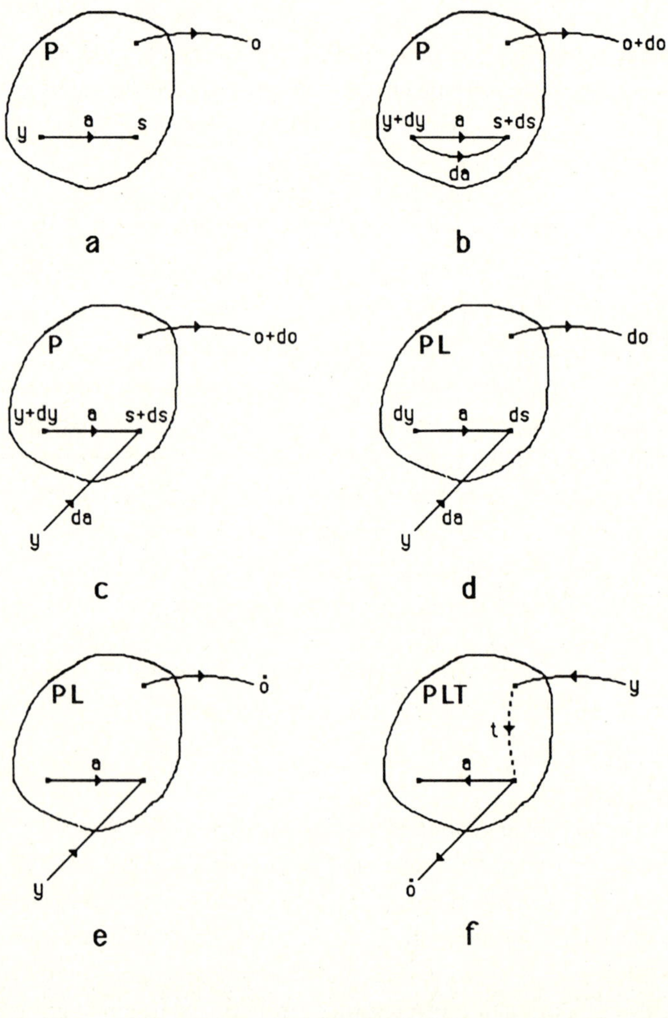

Figure 1 - Computation of the partial derivative of the output of a nonlinear network, relative to a branch weight. See text for explanation.

To compute the partial derivative, we shall give an infinitesimal increment to the branch gain. This is equivalent to adding an extra branch with gain *da* (figure 1-b). Since the network can have feedback connections, there will be increments in all node variables, including the node at the input to the branch under consideration. The net output of the new branch will be $(y+dy).da$, or simply $y.da$, if we discard the higher order term. The same result can be obtained by using and external input with value y, through a branch with gain *da* (figure 1-c). If we now linearize around the original fixed point, considering only increments, we will obtain the network of figure 1-d, which we have designated by **PL**.

Network **PL** is linear, and therefore if we divide its net input by *da*, the output will be divided by the same amount. Dividing the net input by *da* can be accomplished by changing the gain of the input branch to unity, as shown in figure 1-e. The output will now be $\partial o/\partial a$, which we shall designate by o, for compactness.

The network of figure 1-e is linear, and has a single input and a single output. Therefore, the transposition theorem [4] can be applied to it, yielding the transposed network (**PLT**) which, when its input is y, still produces the output o (figure 1-f). If we call t the gain of this network from input to output, we can write

$$o = y\,t$$

We shall now use this expression of the partial derivative to obtain the gradient learning rule. Consider a perceptron (figure 2-a) with a fixed input pattern. We can write for each output o_p (figure 2-b)

$$o_p = \frac{\partial o_p}{\partial a_{ij}} = y_i\, t_{pj} \qquad (1)$$

If the perceptron has several outputs, and O is the set of indexes of the units that produce external outputs, the squared error for the given input pattern is

$$E = \sum_{p\in O} e_p^2$$

where

$$e_p = d_p - o_p$$

is the error of output p, o_p and d_p being the output and the desired value, respectively, for the given input pattern. Now,

$$E = \frac{\partial E}{\partial a_{ij}} = -2 \sum_{p\in O} e_p\, o_p$$

But, using eq. (1)

$$\dot{E} = -2 \sum_{p \in O} e_p \; y_i \; t_{pj}$$

or

$$\dot{E} = -2 \; y_i \sum_{p \in O} e_p \; t_{pj}$$

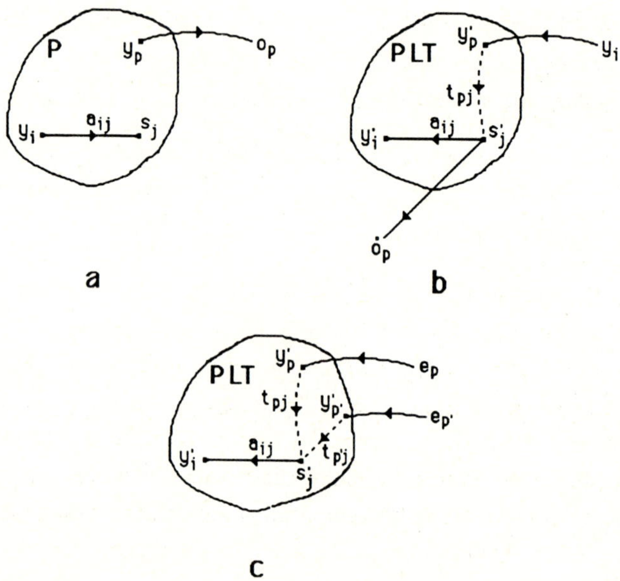

Figure 2 - Computation of the partial derivative in the case of a recurrent perceptron. See text for explanation.

Refering to figure 2-c, and taking into account that network **PLT** is linear, we can finally conclude that:

$$\dot{E} = -2 \; y_i \; s_j'$$

where s_j' is the value obtained at the corresponding node when the output errors are all simultaneously applied to the respective inputs of the transposed network, as shown in that figure. This is a direct extension of the backpropagation rule of feedforward networks: the derivatives are still obtained by applying the output errors to an error propagation network, which is obtained by linearizing and transposing the original perceptron.

3 - Training of Hopfield networks

Hopfield networks [5,6] have been the centre of much interest from researchers. Training methods include Hopfield's original storage prescription [5], pseudo-inverse methods [7] and extensions of the perceptron learning procedure [8]. In this section, we present preliminary results on an investigation of the possibility of training Hopfield networks through recurrent backpropagation.

A fully connected perceptron with no inputs, and with symmetrical weights, i.e., in which $a_{ij}=a_{ji}$ for all i,j is equivalent to a graded Hopfield network [6] if the same dynamical behavior is assumed for the units as was done by Hopfield. The dynamical evolution of such a network can be characterized by an *energy function*. The network evolves in such a way that the energy function always decreases. The points where the network stabilizes are points of stationarity (usually local minima) of this function. In Hopfield networks, the locations of these fixed points are of special interest, since they are used to store patterns. As we have seen, backpropagation can be used to train a network with feedback, moving its fixed points towards desired positions. Therefore, we can conjecture that backpropagation can be used to store a desired set of patterns in a Hopfield network. In the next sections, results obtained with this kind of training, are described. Before presenting these results, however, a point about network initialization should be discussed. The backpropagation procedure can only train fixed points, it cannot train the dynamical behavior of the network. Consider two patterns to be stored, and assume that with its initial weights, the network would evolve from both patterns to the same fixed point. Backpropagation training cannot be expected to split this fixed point into the two that we would desire the network to have. Therefore, steps should be taken to ensure that, initially, each input pattern evolves to a different fixed point.

2.1- Training of fixed points

A 10-unit network was used for this test. The network was fully connected, including connections from each unit to itself (this is slightly different from Hopfield's original topology, but is similar to what has been used by other authors [7]). The patterns to be trained were randomly generated vectors of 10 components each. Each vector component could take the values - 0.8 and + 0.8, with equal probability. The sigmoids used in the network's units had an output ranging from -1 to +1.

Training was performed as follows. As an initialization procedure, the network was first trained with recurrent connections opened, i.e., in a feedforward configuration (see figure 3 for an example). In this mode, it was trained to perform an identity mapping on the training patterns. This training was performed for a number of iterations sufficient to ensure that each training pattern would evolve to a different fixed point, when recurrent connections were closed.

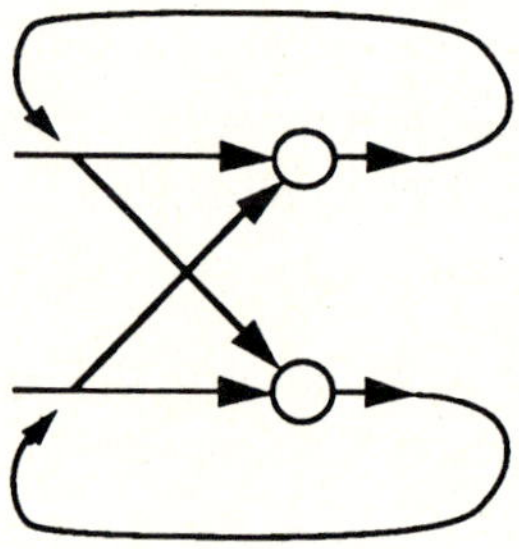

Figure 3 - Illustration of the weight initialization procedure in a 2-unit network.

After this initialization, recurrent connections were closed. Each pattern **p** to be trained was clamped on the network, which was then released, evolving to some fixed point **f**. This fixed point was trained towards the originally clamped pattern, i.e. the output error vector was computed as $\mathbf{e} = \mathbf{p} - \mathbf{f}$, and this error vector was input to the error propagation network in the usual way, for gradient computation. Weight updates were performed after each sweep through the whole set of training patterns.

Table I shows the results obtained for various training set sizes. The statistics were collected after training, by systematically testing the 1024 possible input patterns. Each one was clamped onto the net, which was then released, evolving to some fixed point. The pattern was considered to be stable (and therefore stored) if the signs of the unit outputs at the fixed point were the same as those of the corresponding components of the initially clamped pattern. Spurious stored patterns were those stable ones that did not belong to the training set. The table shows a performance close to what could be expected [9]: the number of spurious patterns is very low initially, and increases steeply when the training set size is of the order of the network size (note, however, that we exert no direct control over spurious states, and that some form of *unlearning* [10] might reduce their number, improving the network's performance).

trained	spurious	trained	spurious
6	0	15	53
8	1	20	145
9	9	30	324
10	14	40	745
12	18	50	917

Table I - Results of training of random patterns; **trained** - training set size; **spurious** - number of spurious stable patterns.

3.2 - Training of regions of attraction

For a better control of the network's performance, one may want to train not only the fixed points, but also each fixed point's region of attraction (in [8], another procedure for training basins of attraction is given). For this purpose, we used the following procedure: We randomly selected a pattern **p**. Assume that this pattern was desired to belong to the region of attraction of some stable pattern **q**. After clamping **p** and releasing the network, the resulting fixed point **f** was trained to move towards the state **q**. Then, a new pattern **p** was randomly selected, and the procedure repeated. Weight update was performed after each pattern presentation. As network initialization we used a very simple deterministic method: we initialized each "self" weight a_{ii} to a relatively large value (typically 3), and each a_{ij} (with $i \neq j$) to zero. In this way, each unit would initially be bistable, and independent of other units, i.e., all possible binary patterns would be stable (note that this initialization could not be used in the case of section 3.1, since there we were training starting only from the desired fixed points, and therefore training would never modify the network's behavior if these patterns were already stable).

Small 2- and 3-unit networks were used in these tests. Figures 4 and 5 depict some of the behaviors that we were able to train, showing that a good control over the regions of attraction can be obtained by this procedure, at least for these small networks.

Figure 4 - Basins of attraction trained on a 2-unit network.

Figure 6 shows an interesting case. This behavior, which was trained on a network of four units (three visible and one hidden), corresponds to the exclusive-or case. It cannot be obtained without hidden units, and therefore it cannot be obtained with any of the other available training methods. The network was operated in the following way. Each pattern was kept clamped onto the visible units long enough for the hidden unit to stabilize. After that, the visible units were unclamped, and the network was allowed to relax to some fixed point. Weight initialization was performed as outlined above, for the visible units. Weights between visible units and the hidden unit were randomly initialized, and that unit's feedback weight was initially set to zero. The remainder of the training procedure was as described above in this section.

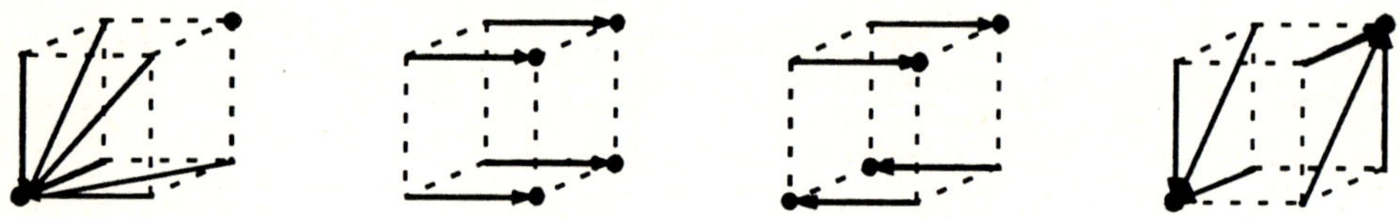

Figure 5 - Basins of attraction trained on a 3-unit network

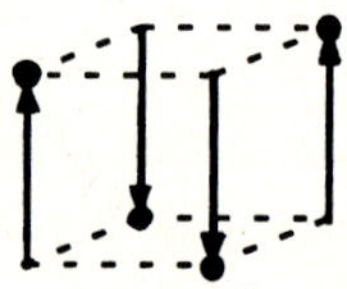

Figure 6 - Exclusive-or behavior trained on a net with 4 units (3 visible and 1 hidden)

3.3 - Discussion

These preliminary results suggest that recurrent backpropagation is a viable technique for training graded Hopfield networks. We have shown that it is possible to train both stable patterns and regions of attraction, and we have given an example of the training of a network with one hidden unit. However, these results also suggest that a better control over the intialization and learning is needed. As an example, a behavior which was hard to train, requiring very precise adjustment of the training of parameteres, and whose success depended on the random ordering of patterns during training, is shown in figure 7-a. Most often, after some training time, the fixed points corresponding to both right-hand patterns would merge, and then the single resulting fixed point would be trained to the left 50% of the time, and to the right another 50%, finally stopping midway, as shown in figure 7-b.

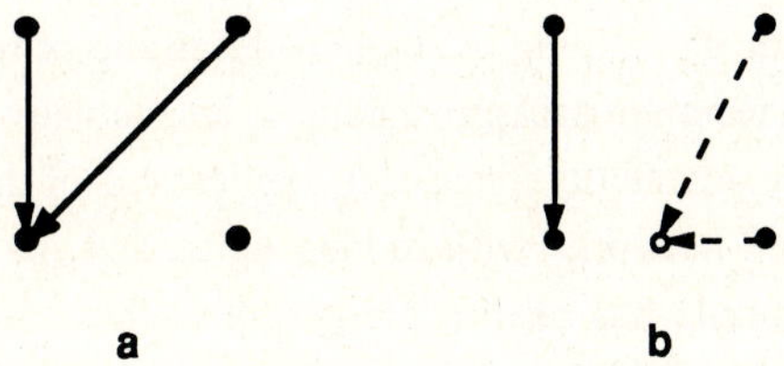

Figure 7 - Example of a problem in the training of basins of attraction; **a** - desired behavior; **b** - behavior that was most frequently obtained.

An interesting application of backpropagation would be to train a graded Hopfield network to have given analog-valued stable patterns. An example of two patterns that were successfully stored in a 10-unit network, using the procedures described in section 3.2, is given in figure 8. However, there is still very little experience on this kind of application.

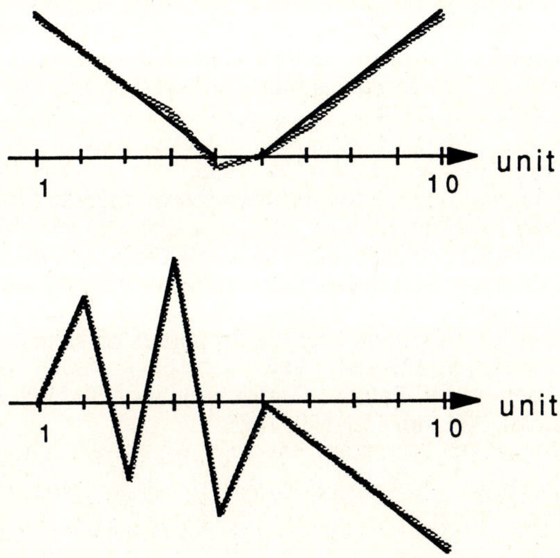

Figure 8 - Two analog patterns that were trained on a 10-unit network. Horizontal axis - unit number. Vertical axis - unit output. The unit outputs have been joined by straight lines for better visibility. Thin black lines - trained pattern. Thick gray lines - recalled pattern.

4 - Conclusions

We have given an intuitively simple proof of the extension of the backpropagation learning rule to recurrent networks. We have also presented results on the application of this rule to graded Hopfield networks, both for the training of stable patterns and of regions of attraction. These results lead us to think that recurrent backpropagation is an alternative method for the training of these networks. Two of the potentially interesting applications of this form of learning, would be the training of Hopfield networks with hidden units, and the storage of analog-valued patterns. Though one example has been presented of each of these cases, further work is needed to assess their general feasibility.

References

1. D. Rumelhart, J. McClelland and the PDP Research Group, eds., *Parallel Distributed Processing: Explorations in the Microstructure of Cognition*, Cambridge, MA: MIT Press, 1986.
2. L. Almeida, "A Learning Rule for Asynchronous Perceptrons with Feedback in a Combinatorial Environment", *Proceedings of the 1987 IEEE First Annual International Conference on Neural Networks*, S. Diego, CA, June 1987.
3. F. Pineda, "Generalization of Backpropagation to Recurrent and Higher Order Networks", *Neural Information Processing Systems*, D. Anderson (ed.), American Institute of Physics, 1988.
4. A. Oppenheim and R. Schafer, *Digital Signal Processing*, Englewood Cliffs, NJ: Prentice Hall, 1975.
5. J. Hopfield, "Neurons with graded response have collective computational properties like those of two-state neurons", *Proceedings of the National Academy of Sciences of the USA*, Vol. 81, pp. 3088-3092, May 1984.
6. J. Hopfield and D. Tank, "Neural Computation of Decisions in Optimization Problems", *Biological Cybernetics*, Vol. 52, pp. 141-152, 1985.
7. L. Personnaz, I. Guyon and G. Dreyfus, ́Information Storage and Retrieval in Spin-Glass Like Neural Networks", *J. Physique Lett.*, **46**, pp. L-359 - L-365, 1985.
8. E. Gardner, N. Stroud and D. Wallace, "Training with Noise, and the Storage of Correlated Patterns in a Neural Network Model", Edinburgh Preprint 87/394, University of Edinburgh, 1987.
9. E. Gardner and B. Derrida, "Optimal Storage Properties of Neural Network Models", *J. Phys. A: Math. Gen.*, **21**, pp. 271-284, 1988.
10. J. Hopfield, D. Feinstein and R. Palmer, "Unlearning has a Stabilizing Effect in Collective Memories", *Nature*, vol. 304, pp. 158-159, 1983.

Optimization of the number of hidden cells in a multilayer perceptron. Validation in the linear case

François VALLET
Laboratoire Central de Recherches
Thomson-CSF
91404 ORSAY (cedex) France

1 Introduction

A general problem for the use of multilayer-perceptrons is the evaluation of the optimal number of hidden units to introduce in the architecture, for a given task. An incremental algorithm has been proposed [1] which is proven to converge. It essentially works for binary outputs and does not necessarily provide the minimal size solution. We propose another approach, in the general case of continuous neurons.

2 The Model

The principal idea is to introduce in each hidden layer an infinite number of neurons, that is to say a continuous density of units, (and to apply the common learning procedure, back-propagation for example...). Then the weight vectors become weight functions. For example, in the discrete representation (when there is only one hidden layer, composed by a finite number N_h of hidden units) the output vector $<O|$ is given as a function of the input vector $<I|$ by:

$$<I| \longrightarrow <O| = \sum_{i=1}^{N_h} f(<I|W_1^i>) <W_2^i|, \tag{1}$$

where $|W_1^i>$ is the transposed vector of the weight vector between the input layer and the ith hidden unit (so that $<I|W>$ denotes the inner product), $<W_2^i|$ the weight vector between this unit and the output layer,

NATO ASI Series, Vol. F 68
Neurocomputing
Edited by F. Fogelman Soulié and J. Hérault

f the neuronal transfer function (sigmoid for example). In the continuous version, the mapping is given by a similar expression, where the discrete summation is transformed in a continuous version:

$$<I| \longrightarrow <O| = \int_0^1 f(<I|W_1(x)>) <W_2(x)|dx, \tag{2}$$

where $|W_1(x)>$ and $<W_2(x)|$ are the weight functions (multidimensional function of a real variable $x \in [0,1]$), and x represents the continuous index of the neuron density. By doing so, we allow the system to solve exactly the problem addressed (there is a infinite number of free parameters). If we add no constraint, it will be very difficult to analyze the solution that has been reached, in order to deduce the minimum number of hidden cells necessary to perform the desired task. Indeed there is an infinite number of solutions, some of them are obtained for example by permuting arbitrary segments in the integration interval $[0,1]$, these permutations giving rise to dramatically complex solutions (non-continuity of the $|W(x)>$'s ...). For analyzing the weights, what we want is the weight functions $|W(x)>$'s to be the smoothest possible. We will fulfill this requirement by adding an elastic energy term, the minimization of which yelds a simple shape for the weight functions:

$$\text{Energy} = \int_0^1 (<W_1'(x)|W_1'(x)> + <W_2'(x)|W_2'(x)>)\, dx, \tag{3}$$

($|W'(x)>$ is the derivative of $|W(x)>$ versus x). We have then introduced geometrical relations between the neurons of the same layer (neighbor hidden neurons have similar behavior). The geometry can be one-dimensionnal (like here) or multidimensionnal (x then becomes a vector).

We think that the relevant information about the complexity of the problem (and in particular the optimal number of hidden cells), is completely embedded in the $|W(x)>$'s, that we can analyze (Fourier transform, wavelets, zero-crossing analysis...). In the case of Fourier analysis for example, as x varies between 0 and 1, the functions can be decomposed on a discrete set of sinusoid functions. The procedure could be to keep in the spectrum only the signifiant components, the number of which could be of the same order than the number of necessary hidden units. Another way is to scan the x segment from 0 to 1, and to create a new neuron i every time a weight vector $|W_1(x)>$ or $<W_2(x)|$ is distant by than more a given threshold ϵ from the weight vector of the preceedingly created neuron $(i-1)$.

3 Validation in the linear case

This approach is mathematically validated in the linear case: the mapping to be learned is a linear operator M (then $f(x) = x$ in the hidden layer as we deal with a linear transformation). The procedure adopted here consists of solving a minimization problem under a constraint. The constraint is that the effective output of the network is equal to the desired one (we impose a functionnal equality):

$$\int_0^1 |W_1(x)\rangle\langle W_2(x)|dx = M. \tag{4}$$

The energy to be minimized is given by (3). To solve the problem, we introduce Lagrange parameters corresponding to the constraint (4), and apply the well known procedure. The solution found is written versus the singular decomposition of M:

$$M = \sum_{i=1}^{R(M)} |E_i\rangle\langle S_i|\lambda_i, \tag{5}$$

where $R(M)$ is the rank of M, $\{|S_i\rangle\}_{i=1\ldots R(M)}$ is a set of orthonormalized vectors of the output space, $\{|E_i\rangle\}_{i=1\ldots R(M)}$ is a set of orthonormalized vectors of the input space and λ_i are positive reals (singular values). We then obtain (Cf appendix):

$$\langle W_1(x)| = \sqrt{2}\sum_{j=1}^{R(M)} \sqrt{\lambda_j} cos(\pi(j-1)x) \langle E_j|, \tag{6}$$

$$|W_2(x)\rangle = \sqrt{2}\sum_{j=1}^{R(M)} \sqrt{\lambda_j} cos(\pi(j-1)x)|S_j\rangle . \tag{7}$$

It is clear in this case, that the optimal number of hidden cells (the rank of the matrix) is given by a Fourier analysis, as it is the number of discrete frequences present in the system.

We remark that this solution gives rise to a delocalization of the hidden cells: as each singular value λ_j can be represented by a localized neuron j in (5) (simple discrete version), a delocalized wave in (6)(7) is provided here. Concerning the energy, we have

$$\text{Energy} = \pi^2 \sum_{n=1}^{R(M)} n^2 \lambda_n, \tag{8}$$

and each numbering $j \longrightarrow \{\lambda_j, |S_j>, |E_j>\}$ provides a different energy (8), each one being a local minimum of (3) under the constraint (4). Then we see that the solution found contains in a straightforward way, all the information about the complexity of the problem.

4 Appendix: derivation of the solution in the linear case

We denote by Z the linear operator effectively implemented by the system:

$$Z \equiv \int_0^1 |W_1(x)><W_2(x)|dx = M. \tag{9}$$

We introduce a Lagrange matrix Λ to take constraint (4) into account. The minimization problem is then equivalent to cancelling the derivative form of (Energy + $Trace(\Lambda Z)$), which leads, after integrating by parts, to:

$$-2\int_0^1 (<dW_1(x)|W_1''(x)> + <dW_2(x)|W_2''(x)>)\,dx + [<dW_1(x)|W_1'(x)>]_0^1$$
$$+[<dW_2(x)|W_2'(x)>]_0^1 + \int_0^1 (<W_2(x)|\Lambda|dW_1(x)> + <dW_2(x)|\Lambda|W_1(x)>)\,dx = 0,$$

(we have used here the fact that Trace$|X><Y| =<X|Y>$ for any vectors $|X>$ and $|Y>$), where $|dW>$ is the differential form of $|W>$. This leads to the following equations:

$$|W_1'(0)>= |W_1'(1)>= 0; \qquad <W_2'(0)| =<W_2'(1)| = 0; \tag{10}$$

$$2|W_1''(x)>= \Lambda^t|W_2(x)>; \qquad 2|W_2''(x)>= \Lambda|W_1(x)>\,. \tag{11}$$

These equations (expressed in the vector base given by the singular decomposition of Λ), combined with the constraint $Z = M$ lead to the solution (6) and (7).

Bibliographie

[1] M. Mézard and J. Nadal. 1989. preprint submitted to *J. Phys. A*.

Single-layer learning revisited: a stepwise procedure for building and training a neural network

S. Knerr, L. Personnaz, G. Dreyfus

Ecole Supérieure de Physique et de Chimie Industrielles de la Ville de Paris
Laboratoire d'Electronique
10, rue Vauquelin
F - 75005 Paris- France

Abstract

A stepwise procedure for building and training a neural network intended to perform classification tasks, based on single layer learning rules, is presented. This procedure breaks up the classification task into subtasks of increasing complexity in order to make learning easier. The network structure is not fixed in advance: it is subject to a growth process during learning. Therefore, after training, the architecture of the network is guaranteed to be well adapted for the classification problem.

1. Introduction

We present a procedure for simultaneously building and training a neural network designed to perform classification tasks. The general motivation behind these investigations is the need for a constructive method which is flexible enough to allow an adaptation of the classifier to the distribution of the classes. Several attempts in the same spirit have been published [1,2,3,4]. Specifically, the most recent studies aim at overcoming the well-known deficiencies of the backpropagation method, namely, that the architecture (number of layers, number of neurons per layer) is fixed a priori by educated guesses. The general guideline for choosing the number of hidden units is the fact that the size of the intermediate layer(s) must be large enough to allow a proper separation of the elements of the training set, and restricted enough for the network to have a good chance to generalize properly. Moreover, the training procedure tends to be time-consuming, and the algorithm is not guaranteed to converge to a good solution, if such solutions exist. Designers usually endeavour to alleviate the task of the network by imposing constraints on the architecture and on the synaptic weights. These constraints are specific to each problem [5,6].

The stepwise construction procedure which is described in the present paper is intended to find a neural network that solves multi-class problems. It consists of several steps of increasing

NATO ASI Series, Vol. F 68
Neurocomputing
Edited by F. Fogelman Soulié and J. Hérault

complexity, starting with attempts at separating linearly each class from all other classes, and subsequently separating classes pairwise with subnetworks. In the latter case, however, training involves the first layer of adaptive connections only.

In the first part, we shall present the building and training procedure; we shall subsequently describe the relevant learning rules and describe the construction of the subnetworks. Experimental results on the contiguity problem will be presented.

2. The building procedure

We assume that the problem involves c classes in R^n. The network will be made of binary state neurons. Figure 1 is a two-dimensional illustration, featuring one class (#3) which is linearly separable from all others, two classes (#1 and 4) which are pairwise linearly separable from all others, and two classes (#2 and 5) which are not linearly separable.

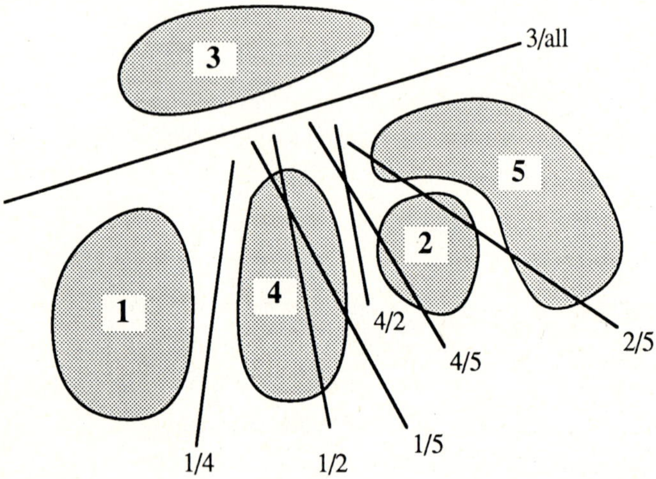

Figure 1

The **first step** of the procedure attempts to separate each class linearly from all others, using c "grandmother" neurons. After training, c_s neurons will perform 100 % correct classification of the examples, and $c_u = c-c_s$ neurons will turn out to be unsuccessful. The latter c_u neurons are discarded. In the case illustrated on Figure 1, there will be one single successful grandmother neuron.

The **second step** consists in attempting a pairwise separation of the c_u remaining classes, using $c_u(c_u-1)/2$ neurons, followed by a layer of AND functions with c_u-1 inputs, which can possibly be implemented in the form of c_u neurons. Training is performed on the first layer of connections only. As a result of this step, the examples corresponding to some classes will be fully correctly classified, whereas examples of other classes will still be misclassified, if the latter are not linearly separable. The AND-neurons corresponding to classes having misclassified examples are discarded, whereas all the neurons of the first layer are retained.

The **third step** has to deal with nonlinearly separable classes. Thus, mutilayer subnetworks must be built. At this point, two possibilities exist : either use of a multilayer Perceptron, trained by backpropagation [7], or use of a pairwise separation procedure, which will be described in a subsequent paragraph. It should be noticed that we now have to deal with the examples of the nonlinearly separable classes only. Thus, the training subset will be much smaller than the initial training set, and each subnetwork will have one output neuron only, so that training will be much easier and faster.

At this point, the structure of the network corresponding to Figure 1 is shown on Figure 2.

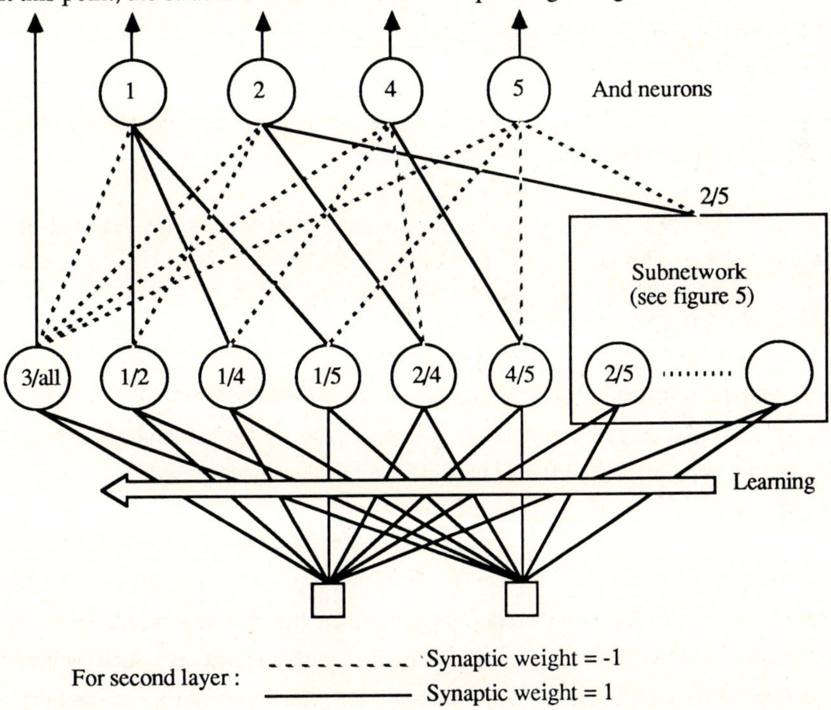

Figure 2

Before going on to discuss the procedure used to build the subnetworks, we shall briefly recall the training algorithms which can be used.

3. Single-layer training algorithms

Single-layer training algorithms have been known for a long time [8,9]. In this section, we shall recall their principles and describe their main properties. Since we consider neurons with binary states, each neuron defines a hyperplane in input space. The synaptic weights $\{C_j\}$ are computed separately for each neuron by a gradient method. In all cases, we deal with supervised learning: the training set is made of pairs $\{\underline{x}^k, d^k\}$ of example vectors $\underline{x}^k$ and their associated desired scalar outputs d^k.

Perceptron learning rule :

Neurons with binary state $s = \{+1,-1\}$ are used for learning and for classification. The criterion to be minimized is

$$J(\{C_j\}) = \Sigma_M(-v^k) \ , \qquad \text{with } v^k = \Sigma_j C_j x_j^k,$$

where M is the set of misclassified examples. The bias weights are connected to a constant input unit $x_0 = +1$, and they are not shown on Figures throughout this paper.

For each example $\{\underline{x}^k, d^k\}$ presented to the network the coefficients are changed in the following way :

$$\Delta C_j = \mu \ (d^k - s^k) \ x_j^k \ .$$

with $0<\mu<1/2$. The convergence of the learning procedure is guaranteed only if the classes are linearly separable. In this case, training stops as soon as the whole training set is properly classified, so that the hyperplanes tend to lie very close to the marginal examples.

A useful variation of the perceptron learning rule is the "pocket algorithm" [10] : after presenting an example and changing the coefficients, the whole training set is tested. If the present classification results are considered to be better than any previous result, the synaptic weights are stored. At the end of the learning phase, the set of coefficients which yielded the best result is kept. This technique can accommodate a variety of criteria for the decision whether a result is better than the previous ones.

Delta rule (Widrow-Hoff):

Neurons with binary state $\{+1,-1\}$ are used. The criterion to be minimized is:

$$J(\{C_j\}) = \Sigma_k(d^k - v^k)^2 \ .$$

The learning rule is expressed as :

$$\Delta C_j = \mu\, (d^k - v^k)\, x_j^k / \|\underline{x}^k\|^2, \quad \text{with } 0 < \mu < 1.$$

The procedure is guaranteed to converge to the least squares solution, which does not necessarily separate the classes, even if they are linearly separable. This will happen when the numbers of examples differ widely from class to class, or if the classes have very different volumes in input space. This is especially true when grandmother cells are used, i.e. when one tries to separate one class from all other classes.

Generalized delta rule :

Neurons with sigmoidal transfer functions $s = f(v) = (\exp(v)-1)/(\exp(v)+1)$ are used for training, but binary state neurons can be used once training has been completed. The criterion to be minimized is

$$J(\{C_j\}) = \Sigma_k (d^k - s^k)^2 .$$

The learning rule is expressed as :

$$\Delta C_j = \mu\, (d^k - s^k)\, x_j^k\, f'(v^k)$$

In the framework of single layer training, the learning rule is guaranteed to converge to the least squares solution. If the classes are linearly separable, the criterion can be made to vanish and the hyperplane will effectively separate the examples, as opposed to the Widrow-Hoff rule. The criterion takes into account the distance of the marginal examples to the separating hyperplane, so that the position of the latter is usually more satisfactory than the position obtained by the Perceptron rule. Therefore, the generalized delta rule takes the best of both worlds, as illustrated on Figure 1, at the expense of using a sigmoidal transfer function for the neurons during learning.

Independently of the learning rule used, there are some situations in which the criterion is minimum if all the examples of the training set lie on the same side of the hyperplane. In such a case, the procedure is trapped. In order to continue, one of the misclassified examples is chosen and the synaptic weights are changed in the following fashion :

$$\Delta C_j = -\,(1+\varepsilon)\, v^k\, x_j^k / \|\underline{x}^k\|^2, \quad \varepsilon > 0 \text{ and small.}$$

This guarantees that example k will be properly classified, and the procedure can be resumed.

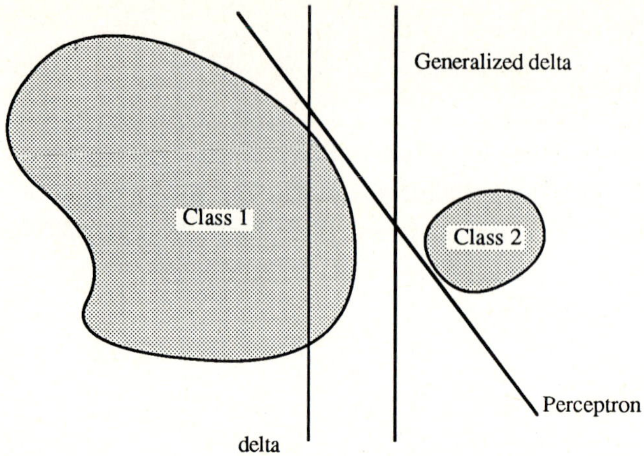

Figure 3

4. Subnetwork construction

We are now dealing with classes which are not pairwise linearly separable. For each such pair of classes, we shall build a subnetwork which is intended to separate them. The procedure is as follows :

- as stated above, pairwise separation was attempted at step two of the construction procedure, resulting in a neuron which failed to separate the classes (e.g. classes #2 and 5 of Figure 1); misclassified examples exist in at least one of the two regions defined by the neuron; this neuron is kept, and each region thus defined is considered separately;
- in each of these regions, we attempt to separate the misclassified examples from the correctly classified examples, thereby generating an extra neuron;
- the procedure is iterated until a satisfaction criterion is met;
- once the criterion is met, the first layer is complete; the subsequent layers perform boolean functions only, thus require no training.

The procedure is illustrated on Figure 4: starting with the neuron separating (unsuccessfully) classes 2 and 5, a neuron A is generated which tries to separate the misclassified examples of class 2 from the examples of class 5; this defines area R1, in which all examples are correctly classified, and the region which is going to be separated into areas R3 (examples correctly classified by neuron A) and R2 (examples misclassified by neuron A); therefore, a neuron B is generated, which separates the examples of area R2 from those of area R3; note that the training set for neuron B includes examples belonging to areas R2 and R3 only. A similar procedure is carried out for areas R4, R5, R6, resulting in the generation of neurons C and D.

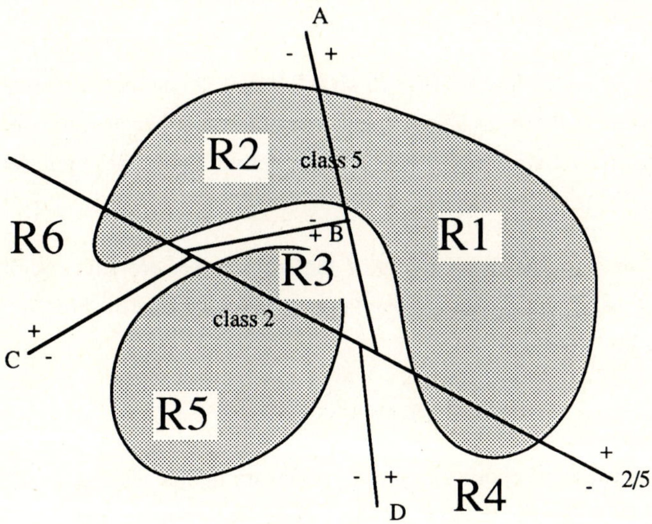

Figure 4

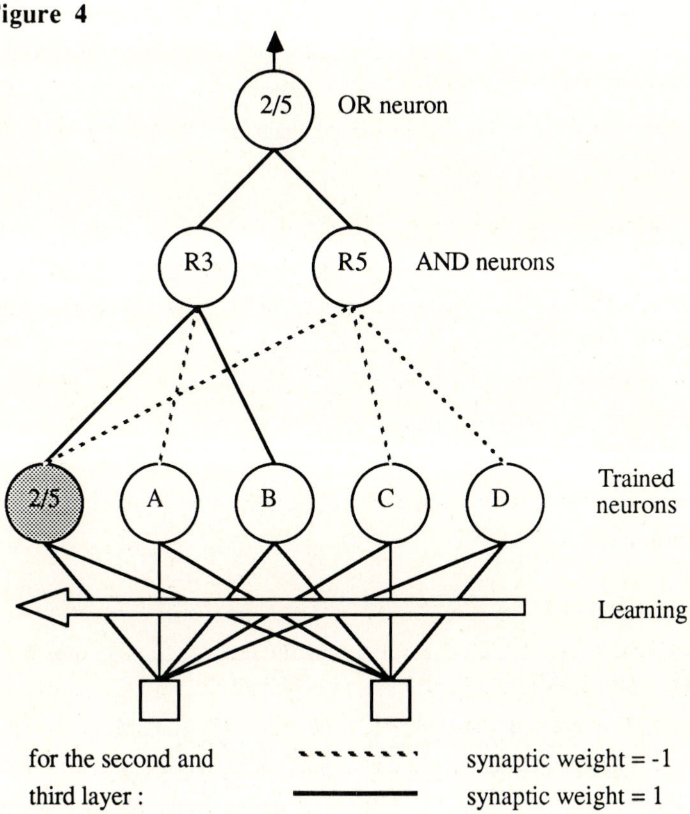

Figure 5

The resulting subnetwork is illustrated on Figure 5.

Neuron labelled R3 is active if the example belongs to area R3, and is inactive otherwise; neuron R5 is active if the example belongs to area R5, inactive otherwise; hence, the output neuron of the subnetwork will be active if either R3 or R5 is active, i.e. if the input data belongs to class 2.

In this example, the procedure stops when all items of the training set are successfully classified. This may not be optimal if two classes are overlapping, in which case the procedure should be stopped before overfitting occurs.

5. Illustrative results

As a first application of our algorithm we chose a problem with binary inputs, which is known as the "two or more clumps problem". A multilayer network trained by backpropagation finds a solution only if one gives it a hint on how the solution looks like.The inputs to the network are one dimensional chains of binary states. This chain is in the form of a closed loop, so that the first and last pixels are neighbours. A set of contiguous black pixels is called a clump. The task is to decide whether there is only one clump in the closed chain, or if there are more. In the first case the desired output is -1; it is 1 otherwise.

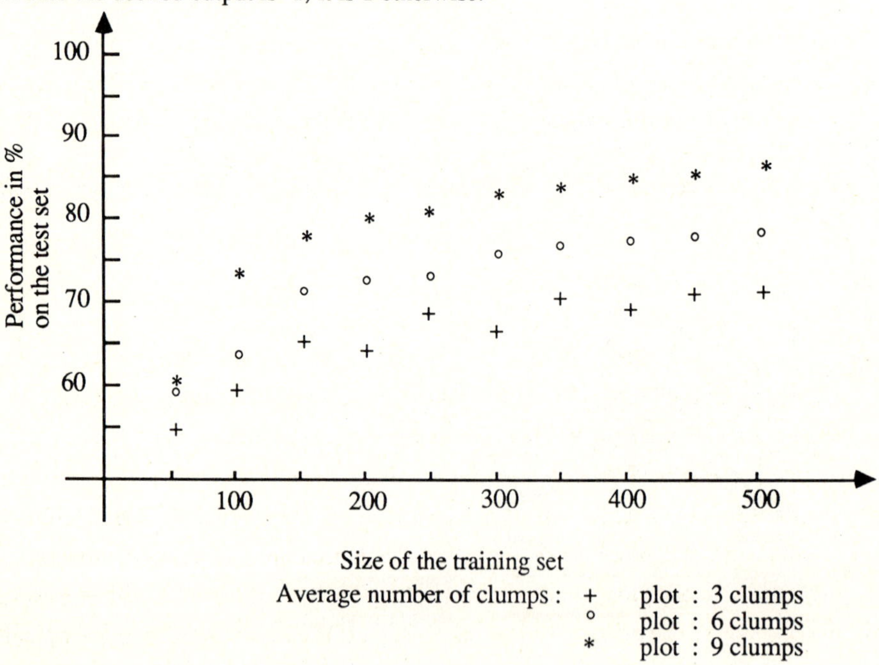

Figure 6

Binary chains of length N=25, with a varying number of clumps, were generated. The training set and the test set had the same size, ranging from 50 to 500 examples with a given average number of clumps and the same number of examples in each class. The stopping criterion for the construction procedure was that all examples of the training set should be correctly classified. Figure 6 shows the results obtained for a given size of the training set, averaged over 10 different instances of the set.

It is not surprising that results are improved when the average number of clumps becomes larger, because it is easier to discriminate a chain with 9 clumps from a chain with one clump than to discriminate a chain with 3 clumps from a chain with one clump. Obviously, the performance also improves with the size of the training set.

Our results are in good agreement with those obtained by the tiling-algorithm [3]. However, the size of the networks, and therefore the training time, compare favourably. Our networks have only one layer of adaptive connections, and two layers of explicit boolean functions, which can even be implemented by standard logic gates. For the case of 500 training examples and an average number of 3 clumps, our network has 16 neurons in the first layer only, plus 15 neurons performing a logic AND in the second layer and one neuron performing a logic OR in the third layer.

As a matter of course, the network was not expected to - and indeed did not - discover the "human" solution (the first layer of which is an edge detector). Note that the above results were obtained without any a priori knowledge of the desirable structure of the network [11].

Results concerning more typical classification problems will be published in a more detailed paper.

6. Conclusions

In the present paper it was shown that a stepwise building procedure with single-layer training offers a potentially powerful alternative to multilayer networks trained by backpropagation. Successive steps of the building procedure are of increasing complexity, thus simple tasks are solved by small networks. Since the network structure is not fixed a priori, the resulting architecture will be well adapted for the classification problem after training. Moreover, convergence of the training procedure in a relatively short time as compared to backpropagation can be guaranteed. In addition, binary state neurons can be used, which makes hardware implementations easier. The performances of the method for automatic classification of pictures and phonemes are under investigation.

References

1. Weaver, C.S.: Some Properties of Threshold Logic Unit Pattern Recognition Networks. In IEEE Transactions on Computers, Vol. c-24, N°. 3, 290, (March 1975).
2. Rujan P., Marchand, M.: Learning by activating neurons: a new approach to learning in neural networks. KFA Jülich preprint, (1988).
3. Mézard M., Nadal, J.P.: Learning in Feedforward Networks: the Tiling Algorithm, L.P.S.E.N.S. preprint, (January 1989).
4. Koutsougeras, C., Papachristou, C.A.:: Training of a neural Network for Pattern Classification Based on an Entropy Measure. In IEEE International Conference on Neural Networks, vol I, 247, San Diego, (July 1988).
5. Waibel, A., Hanazawa, T., Hinton, G.E., Shikano, K., Lang, K.: Phoneme Recognition Using Time-Delay Neural Networks. In IEEE Transactions on Acoustics, Speech and Signal Processing, Vol. 37, N° 3, 328, (March 1989).
6. Le Cun ,Y.: Constrained Networks For Handwritten Numeral Recognition. Snowbird Conference on "Neural Networks for Computing", Snowbird, (April 1989).
7. Rumelhart, D.E., McClelland, J.L.: Parallel Distributed Processing. Bradford Books, Cambridge MA, (1986).
8. Duda R., Hart, P.: Pattern Recognition and Scene Analysis. John Wiley & Sons, (1973).
9. Minsky, M. , Papert, S.: Perceptrons. MIT Press, Cambridge MA,(1969).
10. Gallant, S.I.: Optimal Linear Discriminants. Eighth International Conference On Pattern Recognition, Vol. 2, 849, Paris, France, (1986).
11. Denker, J., Schwartz, D., Wittner, B., Solla, S., Hopfield, J.J.Howard, R., Jackel, L.: Automatic Learning, Rule Extraction and Generalization. In Complex Systems vol 1, 877-922, (1987).

SYNCHRONOUS BOLTZMANN MACHINES AND GIBBS FIELDS : LEARNING ALGORITHMS

Robert AZENCOTT (*)
École Normale Supérieure and Université Paris-Sud

INTRODUCTION

The Boltzmann machines are stochastic networks of formal neurons linked by a quadratic energy function. Hinton, Sejnowski and Ackley who introduced them as pattern classifiers that learn, have proposed a learning algorithm for the asynchronous machine. Here we study the synchronous machine where all neurons are simultaneously updated, we compute its equilibrium energy, and propose a synchronous learning algorithm based on *delayed* average coactivity of pairs of connected neurons. We generalize the Boltzmann machine paradigm to much wider types of interactions and energies allowing multiple interactions of arbitrary order. We propose a learning algorithm for these generalized machines using the theory of Gibbs fields and parameter estimation for such fields. We give quasi-convergence results for all these algorithms, within the framework of stochastic algorithms theory. The links between generalized Boltzmann machines and Markov field models sketched here provide the groundwork for designing generalized Boltzmann machines capable of performing efficient low level vision tasks. These Boltzmann vision modules are described in a forthcoming paper.

The asynchronous Boltzmann machines are widely considered as slow learners. However we emphasize here *their use at suitably selected fixed temperatures*, to avoid long stabilization times due to vanishing temperatures. Moreover *the synchronous versions studied here are structurally much faster*, if implemented on parallel hardware. In collaboration with P. Garda (I.E.F., Université Paris-Sud) and other researchers at DIAM (École Normale Supérieure, Paris), we are currently studying the technological feasibility of such specialized hardware implementations. We feel that Boltzmann machines, in suitable synchronous versions, and with general energies offer a world of learning networks with exciting technological capabilities as well as interesting tentative models for low level human vision.

(*) Chercheur associé aux lab. CNRS : [LMENS] et [Stat. Appliquées Univ. Paris-Sud].
Address : ENS, 45 rue d'Ulm - F-75230 PARIS CEDEX 05 (France)

NATO ASI Series, Vol. F 68
Neurocomputing
Edited by F. Fogelman Soulié and J. Hérault

1. THE ASYNCHRONOUS AND QUADRATIC VERSION (Hinton-Scjnovski-Ackley) :

Let S be the (finite) set of formal neurons or units in such a machine. Each neuron s in S has only two possible states $x_s = 0$ and $x_s = 1$. The interaction between neurons s and t is governed by a synaptic weight w_{st}, and the global configuration $x = (x_s)_{s \in S}$ has an energy

(1.1) $$G(x) = -\sum_{s,t} w_{st}\, x_s\, x_t .$$

The weights are assumed to be *symmetric* : $w_{st} = w_{ts}$.

The dynamics of the machine is stochastic, and controlled by a positive parameter T called the temperature. We first describe *the standard asynchronous version of the machine*, as originally introduced by [H.S.A.]. At each instant $n \in \mathbf{N}$, only one of the neurons may attempt to modify its state. Call s_n its index, which is generally preassigned by a deterministic sequence $(s_1 \dots s_n \dots)$ visiting periodically all neurons s in S, but which can also be drawn at random in the set S. In either case, whenever the current configuration is x, and the neuron s attempts to modify its state x_s, the new value $\hat{x}_s$ of x_s is selected at random with the probability

(1.2) $$\begin{cases} P\left(\hat{x}_s = 1 \mid \text{current state } x\right) = \dfrac{e^{\frac{1}{T} U_s(x)}}{1 + e^{\frac{1}{T} U_s(x)}} \\[2ex] P\left(\hat{x}_s = 0 \mid \text{current state } x\right) = \dfrac{1}{1 + e^{\frac{1}{T} U_s(x)}} \end{cases}$$

where $U_s(x) = \sum_t w_{st}\, x_t$ is the *action potential* of x at site s.

This stochastic dynamics reaches (in the long run) a probabilistic equilibrium which gives to each configuration x the Gibbs probability

(1.3) $$P(x) = \frac{1}{Z_T} \exp - \frac{G(x)}{T} ,$$

where

(1.4) $$Z_T = \sum_{y \in \Omega} \exp - \frac{G(y)}{T}$$

and Ω is the space of all configurations on S.

The use of the Boltzmann machine as a pattern classifier involves selecting two disjoint subsets D and R of S (*data units* and *response units*) which together constitute the set V of *visible units* in S, while the other units constitute the set of *hidden units* $H = S - (D \cup R)$

The environment provides on the data set D a family of "stimuli" which are random configurations $\alpha \in A = \{0,1\}^D$. To each configuration $\alpha \in A$, we want to associate a preassigned response configuration $\beta = F(\alpha) \in B = \{0,1\}^R$, which will achieve the desired classification of pattern α . The map $F : \alpha \rightarrow F(\alpha)$ is assumed known to the superviser of the learning process, at least on a set $A_{ex} \subset A$ of "examples".

The goal of learning algorithms for the Boltzmann machine is to adjust sequentially the weights $(w_{st})_{s,t \in S}$ in the course of alternate periods of "clamped" and unclamped" example presentation. In the "clamped" sequence, one or several examples are presented successively. When α is presented, all the visible units D and R are clamped on α and $F(\alpha)$ respectively, while all the hidden units follow the Glauber dynamics described above. In the "unclamped" sequence, when example α is presented, the data units are tied to the input configuration α , but all hidden and response units evolve freely, according to the stochastic dynamics above.

For each pair of neurons (s,t), the empirical frequencies p_{st} and $\hat{p}_{st}$ of their simultaneous activity are respectively computed during the clamped and unclamped phases by direct observation of x_s and x_t . The current value of the weight w_{st} is then incremented by the rule

(1.5)
$$\Delta w_{st} = \frac{\varepsilon}{T} \left(\hat{p}_{st} - p_{st}\right)$$

where ε is "small".

This interesting algorithm derived by [H.S.A.] has the obvious advantage of using only local computations. However, it is highly stochastic in nature, so that *its convergence is not obvious from a mathematical point of view*. Roughly, it approximates gradient descent for a Kullback distance between marginal distribution on the set of visible units. Even after proving convergence, the optimal qualities of the limit are not obvious either. We will come back on both of these problems below.

2. THE SYNCHRONOUS AND QUADRATIC VERSIONS

Boltzmann machines are reputed to be fairly slow as compared to deterministic versions. These statements deserve to be qualified, but we shall not do it in this paper. In any case, the idea of *simultaneously* updating all neurons $s \in S$ is fairly tempting in view of the "availability " of highly parallel computing machines such as the connection machine, since the speed increase could presumably be of the order of Cardinal(S) .

In this synchronous dynamics, at time n , if the current configuration $X(n) = x$, every neuron s selects at random its next state $\hat{x}_s$, according to the probability distribution (1.1). All these simultaneous choices are *independent* of each other. The new state is then the configuration $\hat{x} = (\hat{x}_s)_{s \in S}$.

Contrary to naive expectations, *the long run limit of this stochastic synchronous dynamics* ***is not*** *the Gibbs measure* (1.2) *associated to* $G(x)$. In fact, *if we define the synchronous energy by*

$$K_T(x) = -\sum_s T \log\left[1 + e^{\frac{1}{T} U_s(x)}\right], \tag{2.1}$$

where $U_s(x) = \sum_t w_{st} x_t$ is the action potential at site s , then we can state the following proposition.

2.2. PROPOSITION.- *Assume the synaptic weights* w_{st} *to be symmetric. The limit probability distribution for the synchronous dynamics is given by the new Gibbs measure*

$$Q(x) = \frac{1}{\Gamma_T} \exp\left[-\frac{1}{T} K_T(x)\right] \tag{2.3}$$

where

$$\Gamma_T = \sum_{y \in \Omega} e^{-K_T(y)/T}$$

and K_T *is given by* (2.1). *Note that* $K_T(x)$ *is temperature dependent in this formulation.*

The details of the computation will be given elsewhere ; they are similar to previous computations of that type (*cf.* Little [L], Peretto [P], Trouvé [T]). Let us point out a few consequences of formula (2.3).

Call N_s *the set of asynchronous neighbours* of neuron s , namely the set of $t \in S$ such that the local conditional laws verify

$$P(x_s = \lambda \mid x_t, t \in S - s) \equiv P(x_s = \lambda \mid x_t, t \in N_s) \tag{2.4}$$

for $\lambda = 1,0$. Intuitively, the neighbours of s are those which "directly" interact with neuron s .

Then for the asynchronous standard limit distribution P , associated to the energy G , one has obviously

$$N_s = \{t \in S \mid w_{st} \neq 0\}. \tag{2.5}$$

However, for the synchronous limit distribution Q an easy computation shows that the set of synchronous neighbours $\tilde{N}_s$ of neuron s is the union of all the $(N_u - s)$ such that N_u contains s . More precisely

$$\tilde{N}_s = \{t \in S \text{ such that there is a } u \in S \text{ for which } w_{us} \neq 0 \text{ and } w_{tu} \neq 0\}.$$

Thus the cardinal of $\tilde{N}_s$ is generally *larger* than N_s in standard setups.

An easy computation shows that *at very low temperature* T , the synchronous energy is equivalent to

$$(2.6)\quad \begin{cases} K_T(x) \sim - \sum\limits_{\{s \mid U_s(x)>0\}} U_s(x) & \text{if } \{s \mid U_s(x) > 0\} \neq \emptyset \\ K_T(x) \sim 0 & \text{if } \{s \mid U_s(x) > 0\} = \emptyset . \end{cases}$$

On the other hand, *at very high temperature* T, the synchronous energy can be replaced by

$$(2.7)\quad \tilde{K}_T(x) \sim -\frac{1}{2} \sum_s U_s(x) .$$

One interesting consequence of (2.7) is that *at very high temperature, the synchronous equilibrium distribution forces the effective stochastic independence of all neurons, with neuron* t *firing at a constant frequency* $p_t = (e^u)/(1 + e^u)$ and $u_t = 1/2 \sum_s w_{st}$. Hence, *at very high temperature, the synchronous machine is in total disorder and no learning can be achieved.*

Also formulas (2.6) (2.7) show clearly that in general the synchronous and asynchronous limit may be extremely different.

This raises the problem of the *feasibility of learning algorithms on the synchronous Boltzmann machines*. Actually, we shall derive a new learning algorithm in this case.

3. A SUITABLE LEARNING ALGORITHM FOR THE SYNCHRONOUS MACHINE

Assume that the environment induces on the set $A = \{0,1\}^D$ *an a priori probability distribution* ν, so that each stimulus $\alpha \in A$ appears with frequency $\nu(\alpha)$.

Call $\Omega_V = A \times B$ the set of all configurations on the visible units $\{D \cup R\}$. When the machine is coupled to the environment through the data units D, a random configuration $Y \in A$ is presented on D, and the machine provides a random response $Z \in B$ when equilibrium is reached. Call $\hat{\theta}$ the probability distribution of the pair (Y,Z) at equilibrium.

Ideally, we would like to select the weights (w_{st}) such that $\hat{\theta}$ becomes as close as possible to θ where

$$(3.1)\quad \begin{cases} \theta(\alpha,\beta) = \upsilon(\alpha) & \text{if } \beta = F(\alpha) \ , \ \alpha \in A \\ \theta(\alpha,\beta) = 0 & \text{if } \beta \neq F(\alpha) \ , \ \alpha \in A , \beta \in B . \end{cases}$$

Recall that F is the desired classification map. More practically, we shall assume that θ has been *replaced* by a probability $\tilde{\theta}$ on Ω_V such that

$$(3.2)\quad \begin{cases} \tilde{\theta}(\alpha,\beta) = (1-\varepsilon)\, \theta(\alpha,\beta) & \text{when } \theta(\alpha,\beta) \neq 0 \\ \tilde{\theta}(\alpha,\beta) = \varepsilon/M & \text{when } \theta(\alpha,\beta) = 0 \end{cases}$$

and $\varepsilon > 0$ is small. The actual value of ε is irrelevant, and $M = \text{card}\{\Omega - \text{support}\ \theta\}$.

One way of evaluating the distance between $\widetilde{\theta}$ and $\hat{\theta}$ is thus to compute the Kullback distance

(3.3) $$d(\widetilde{\theta},\hat{\theta}) = - \sum_{\alpha\beta\in A\times B} \widetilde{\theta}(\alpha\beta) \log \frac{\hat{\theta}(\alpha\beta)}{\widetilde{\theta}(\alpha\beta)} .$$

The vector of optimal weights $w = (w_{st})_{s,t\in S\times S}$ should then minimize $d(\widetilde{\theta},\hat{\theta})$. In particular, we should try to have the zero gradient condition

(3.4) $$\mathrm{grad}_w\, d(\widetilde{\theta},\hat{\theta}) = 0$$

and a natural gradient algorithm is of course to update current values of w by Δw where

(3.5) $$\Delta w \text{ is a (small) multiple of } \left[- \mathrm{grad}_w\, d(\widetilde{\theta},\hat{\theta})\right] .$$

This approach can be carried out in the synchronous case, in view of the explicit formula given above for the synchronous energy, and the computations, which will be given elsewhere, present no serious difficulty ; as a particular case of the general formula (6.6) below, one obtains for the synchronous update Δw_{st}

(3.6) $$\Delta_{\text{synch}}\, w_{st} = \frac{\eta}{T}\left[E^{\text{clamped}}(\gamma_{st}) - E^{\text{unclamped}}(\gamma_{st})\right]$$

where η is a small scalar and

(3.7) $$\gamma_{st} = x_t \frac{e^{U_s(x)/T}}{1+e^{U_s(x)/T}} + x_s \frac{e^{U_t(x)/T}}{1+e^{U_t(x)/T}} .$$

Here $E^{\text{clamped}}(f)$ represents the theoretical expected value of the random variable $f(x)$ when all visible units are clamped on the pairs (stimulus, desired response). Similarly, $E^{\text{unclamped}}(f)$ represents the same quantity when only the input units D are coupled to the environment.

Note that from a practical point of view, these mathematical expectations $E(f)$ can and must be estimated by natural time averages of $f(x)$ at equilibrium.

To understand better the physical nature of γ_{st}, note that

$$\rho_s(x) = \frac{e^{U_s(x)}}{1+e^{U_s(x)/T}}$$

represents the local probability of replacing x_s by 1, when the global actual configuration is x, in the natural synchronous updating of all the $(x_u)_{u\in S}$. Hence, these quantities are locally computed by the machine in a systematic fashion. However, using that remark, we can now give an extremely intuitive interpretation of $E(\gamma_{st})$. Call n an arbitrary instant in the time clock of the synchronous machine. Call $X(n)$ the configuration of the machine at time n, and $X_s(n)$ the state of neuron s at time n. Then in the clamped case, as well as in the unclamped case, we have

$$E(\gamma_{st}) = \lim_{n \to \infty} E\left[X_s(n)\, X_t(n+1) + X_t(n)\, X_s(n+1)\right] \tag{3.8}$$

and thus the interesting formula

$$E(\gamma_{st}) = q_{st} + q_{ts}\,, \tag{3.9}$$

where q_{st} *is the probability of* ***successive firing for neuron*** s ***and neuron*** t . Hence, the meaningful local quantities in synchronous Boltzmann machines turn out to be the (equilibrium) probabilities q_{st} of *delayed co-firing* for ordered pairs (s,t) of neurons. We shall keep *the notation* q_{st} *for the clamped case* and use *the notation* $\hat{q}_{st}$ *for the unclamped case.*

The natural time average estimates for q_{st} , $\hat{q}_{st}$ are of course the empirical frequencies of delayed cofiring (at equilibrium)

$$\frac{1}{1+N}\left[X_s(n)\, X_t(n+1) + X_s(n+1)\, X_t(n+2) + \ldots + X_s(n+N)\, X_t(n+N+1)\right] \tag{3.10}$$

which point out *the relevance of delayed correlations between neighboring neurons in the synchronous activity of the machine.*

We thus propose *the following natural synchronous learning algorithm*

$$\Delta_{\text{synch}}\, w_{st} = \frac{\eta}{T}\left[(q_{st} + q_{ts}) - (\hat{q}_{st} + \hat{q}_{ts})\right] \tag{3.11}$$

where $q_{st}\, q_{ts}\, \hat{q}_{st}\, \hat{q}_{ts}$ are estimated by the empirical frequencies of delayed cofiring (3.10). Note that the computations involved are purely local and extremely simple.

The mathematical results on stochastic gradient algorithms ([B.M.P.] [Y]) strongly recommends the use of *a slowly decreasing coefficient* η (the "gain" of the algorithm) to make convergence possible. A mathematically classical choice is

$$\eta(k) = \frac{c}{b+k} \tag{3.12}$$

where c,b remain constant during learning and the integer $k \in \mathbf{N}$ denotes the *index of the current weights updating.*

4. CONVERGENCE OF THE LEARNING ALGORITHMS

It turns out that the learning problem for Boltzmann machines wether synchronous or asynchronous is quite similar to the problem of maximum likelihood estimation for partially observed Markov fields. Thus most of the sophisticated probabilistic techniques used by Younes in his doctorate thesis (*cf.* [Y]) are relevant in this context.

Here of course the parameter to be discovered is the unknown vector of weights w and hence may be high-dimensional. Consider again the problem of minimizing in w the function $\phi(w) = d(\tilde{\theta},\hat{\theta})$, defined by (3.3).

As is easily checked, the function $w \to \phi(w)$ is often *not convex*, and hence the stochastic gradient algorithms proposed for learning in synchronous or asynchronous Boltzmann machines may very well be trapped in local minima of ϕ. Note here that our statements concern learning at fixed temperature which we consider as quite relevant in artificial vision applications for instance, as will be explained elsewhere.

In generic situations, the theory of stochastic gradient algorithms following the lines of [B.M.P.] and [Y], can thus only prove quasi-convergence of learning algorithms. This means essentially that if the successive learned values $w(k)$, $k = 1,2,\ldots$ of the vector of weights come back infinitely often within any single well of the energy landscape associated to the function ϕ, then the sequence $w(k)$ becomes ultimately trapped at the bottom of that well. Hence for all practical purposes, either the sequence $w(k)$ explodes, or it is bound to achieve *local* optimisation, in generic Boltzmann machines.

Another result of the same kind is that if the starting point $w(0)$ for the vector of weights lies close enough to a non degenerate absolute minimum $\tilde{w}$ of $\phi(w)$, and if the coefficient η regulating the gain is small enough, then the learning algorithm will converge towards the absolute minimizing weight vector $\tilde{w}$. From a practical point of view, this last point means that *small variations of the environment characteristics can be successfully corrected by learning once the machine has initially been properly tuned.*

As for learning using decreasing temperature schedules, it can be studied through similar stochastic techniques, but we shall come back to this question elsewhere.

5. GENERAL BOLTZMANN MACHINES WITH MULTIPLE INTERACTIONS

In the standard quadratic Boltzmann machines, interaction between neurons is limited to *pairs of neurons*. Actually, one can usefully develop a learning theory for much more geenral stochastic machines, within the formalism of Gibbs measures.

As a first and innocuous generalizing step assume that each neuron may now take a finite family of values $\lambda \in \Lambda$ instead of the only values $0,1$. Consider an *arbitrary family* Γ of subsets C of S. Each C in Γ will be called a *clique of neurons*, and its degree of activity will be quantitatively measured by an *interaction potential* $J_C(x) = J_C(x_s \ldots x_s)$ if $C = \{s_1 \ldots s_k\}$. These interaction potentials are *arbitrary numerical functions of the clique configuration* x_C.

For each clique $C \subset \Gamma$ introduce a numerical parameter $w_C \in \mathbf{R}$ which will be called the *clique weight*. The vector $w = \{w_C\}_{C \in \Gamma}$ will be called the *weights vector* and will define completely the generalized Boltzmann machine.

Indeed we introduce the asynchronous energy function

$$G(x) = \sum_{C \in \Gamma} w_C J_C(x) \tag{5.1}$$

which measures the *weighted activity of the cliques* to compute the global activity of the configuration. A classical Glauber type of asynchronous stochastic dynamics can now be defined to ensure that the asynchronous machine has at equilibrium (in the long run) a Gibbs probability distribution on the set Ω of configurations given by

$$P(x) = \frac{1}{Z_T} e^{-G(x)/T}, \tag{5.2}$$

where Z_T is as before the partition function, and T a positive fixed temperature parameter.

Define the set N_s of neighbours of neuron s as the set of all $t \in S$ such that $t \neq s$ and there is some clique $C \in \Gamma$ containing both s and t. Then the *local action potential* at s is defined as $U_s(x) = U_s(x_s, x_N\ )$ by

$$U_s(x_s, x_{N_s}) = -\sum_{\{C \ni s\}} w_C J_C(x). \tag{5.3}$$

And the proper random updating of a single neuron s is here to select the next state $\hat{x}_s \in \Lambda$ with the probability

$$p(\hat{x}_s) = \frac{e^{U_s(\hat{x}_s, x_{N_s})/T}}{\sum_{\lambda \in \Lambda} e^{U_s(\lambda, x_{N_s})/T}}. \tag{5.4}$$

To compare this setup with the standard asynchronous quadratic Boltzmann machine, take the set Γ of active cliques to coincide with the set of arbitrary *pairs* of neurons, and interaction potentials

$$J_C(x) = J_{\{s,t\}}(x) = -2\, x_s\, x_t. \tag{5.5}$$

Then the weight w_C of the clique $C = \{s,t\}$ is simply the synaptic weight w_{st}, and the random updating (5.4) is exactly the one we recalled earlier in (1.2).

The problem is now to define a suitable learning algorithm for the asynchronous generalized Boltzmann machine. To do this, we have to compute the distance $\phi(w) = d(\tilde{\theta}, \hat{\theta})$ between clamped and unclamped distributions on Ω_V and evaluate the gradient $\partial\phi/\partial w$.

A direct computation shows that one has

$$T \frac{\partial \phi}{\partial w_C}(w) = E_{\text{clamped}}\left[J_C\right] - E_{\text{unclamped}}\left[J_C\right] \tag{5.6}$$

and thus the *natural learning algorithm for asynchronous general Boltzmann machines* consists in updating the vector w of clique weights by

(5.7) $$\Delta w_C = \frac{\eta}{T}\left\{E_{\text{unclamped}}(J_C) - E_{\text{clamped}}(J_C)\right\}$$

where the (small) gain η decreases slowly at the rate $\eta(k) = c/(b+k)$ where k is the weight update index.

Of course in the now classical quadratic case, for clique $C = \{s,t\}$, the expected value of $1/2\, J_C = - x_s x_t$ is simply $(- p_{st})$ where p_{st} is the probability of simultaneous firing for neurons s and t, at equilibrium. Practically a good estimate of $E(J_C)$ is provided by *a direct time average of the clique activity* $J_C(x)$. Thus, *computations remain local* and just as feasible as in quadratic machines.

The network should then be viewed as a double network $S \cup \Gamma$ where to each index $C \in \Gamma$ is associated a cell or processor which we call a *clique indicator* and whose states belong to a finite subset of $\mathbf{R}$. Namely, whenever the network S is in configuration x, *the state* y_C *of the clique indicator* C is

(5.8) $$y_C = J_C(x) .$$

The connection between neuron $s \in S$ *and clique indicator* $C \in \Gamma$ *exists if and only if* s *belongs to the clique* C. Moreover, this connection is simply a *message transmission channel.* From s to C, it transmits the state x_s to the processor C, which once it has gotten hold of all the $(x_s)_{s \in C}$ computes deterministically its state $y_C = J_C\,(x_s\,,\, s \in C)$.

Conversely from C to s, the connection transmits the state y_C, that is the corresponding cell activity, with the weight w_C. Then by a simple sum over all cliques C connected to s, the neuron s can compute its action potential

(5.9) $$U_s(x) = -\sum_{C \text{ containing } s} w_C\, y_C$$

and then neuron s uses this number for its own random updating. Several detailed setups corresponding to this random update can easily be proposed and will be described elsewhere.

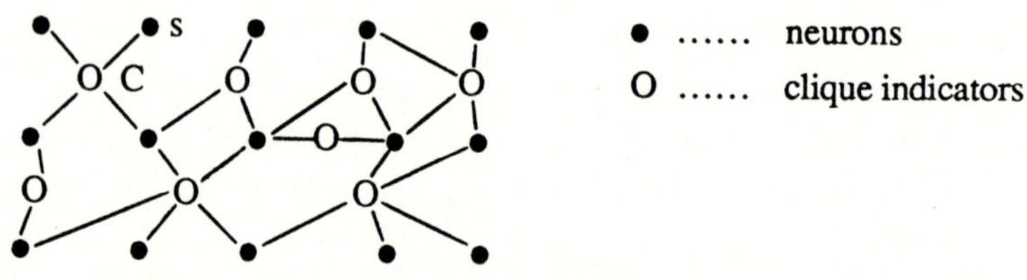

Example of a small network with cliques of various cardinals

The configuration x of S thus provides a direct computation (a deterministic one) of the configuration y of Γ, which in turn permits a proper mechanism for random updating of x.

The updating of the weights requires essentially a time monitoring of the clique indicator activity, a simple computation which can be done by a local processor included in C.

Hence the asynchronous generalized Boltzmann machine looks like an interesting learning tool, in pattern recognition. Indeed in artificial vision, many tasks of low-level vision have been studied through Markov field modelizations following the breakthrough papers of D. and S. Geman (see [A] [C] [G] [GG] among many others). Many of these models can be suitably reinterpreted in the context we have just described, to design asynchronous generalized Boltzmann machines which achieve low-level vision tasks such as contour detection and segmentation. We shall come back to this exciting topic in another paper.

6. THE SYNCHRONOUS GENERAL BOLTZMANN MACHINE

For a general Boltzmann machine, the study of the synchronous equilibrium energy is much more difficult than in the case of standard Boltzmann machines. The difficulty here is not linked to the fact that we abandon quadratic forms, *but to the existence of multiple interaction of order* ≥ 3, which prevents the explicit computation of the synchronous equilibrium distribution. We have recently solved this problem in [A]. In this brief note, *we shall limit ourselves to the much easier case of general Boltzmann machines with pairwise interactions only.*

Call $J_{st}(x_s,x_t)$ the interaction potentials corresponding to pairs $\{s,t\}$ and w_{st} the weight of the clique $\{s,t\}$. The action potential $U_s(x_s,x_{S-s})$ is given by (5.3) as before and the synchronous energy $K_T(x)$ for this Boltzmann machine can be computed using microbalance equations, to show that

$$K_T(x) = -T\sum_s \log\left[\sum_{\lambda\in\Lambda} e^{U_s(\lambda,x_{S-s})/T}\right] \tag{6.1}$$

with synchronous equilibrium distribution

$$Q(x) = \frac{1}{\tilde{Z}_T}\, e^{-K_T(x)/T}\,. \tag{6.2}$$

One can now check that the gradient of the Kullback distance $d(\tilde{\theta},\hat{\theta})$ involves *the average delayed interactions*

$$d_{st} + d_{ts} = \lim_{n\to\infty} E\left\{J_{st}\left[X_s(x),X_t(n+1)\right] + J_{st}\left[X_s(n+1),X_t(n)\right]\right\} \tag{6.3}$$

where $X(n)$ is the global neuron configuration at time n.

These average delayed interactions can be correctly estimated by *empirical delayed interactions*

(6.4) $$\frac{1}{N}\left\{J_{st}\left[X_s(n),X_t(n+1)\right]+\ldots+J_{st}\left[X_s(n+N-1),X_t(n+N)\right]\right\},$$

which we still denote by d_{st} in the clamped case and $\hat{d}_{st}$ in the unclamped case.

Then one can prove that the synchronous learning algorithm by gradient descent must compute the update Δw_{st} of the clique weight w_{st} by

(6.5) $$\Delta w_{st} = \frac{\eta}{T}\left[(\hat{d}_{st}+\hat{d}_{ts})-(d_{st}-d_{ts})\right]$$

with a slowly decreasing gain η, as before in (3.12). Recall that in the standard quadratic case $1/2\, J_{st}(x_s\, x_t)$ is $(-\, x_s\, x_t)$ so that these formulas do generalize those of § 3.

7. FURTHER EXTENSIONS

One may want to evaluate the clique activity from several quantitative points of view and weight these points of view according to their relative importance. This is handled by vector valued interaction potentials J_C and clique weights w_C.

It is also possible to imagine more realistic partially synchronous updates, in which at each tick of the clock, only a fixed proportion of the neurons S are drawn at random and allowed to perform simultaneous random updates. As long as the probability of having 3 or more simultaneous updates within a single active clique is kept small, the theory of learning for partially synchronous updates should strongly resemble the totally synchronous update for pairwise interacting machines. Hence, in such cases, learning by using average delayed interactions as described above should still perform a good gradient descent.

BIBLIOGRAPHY

[A] R. AZENCOTT - *Markov fields and low-level vision tasks*. Proc. Int. Cong. App. Math., ICIAM, Paris (1987).

- *Gibbs fields, simulated annealing, and low-level vision tasks*, Proc. Congress on Pattern Recognition AFCET - INRIA, Antibes (1987).

- *General Boltzmann machines with multiple interactions* (to appear in IEEE PAMI, 1990).

- *Parameter estimation for synchronous Markov fields* (to appear 1990).

[B.M.P.] A. BENVENISTE, M. MÉTIVIER, R. PRIOURET - *Algorithmes stochastiques*, Masson, Paris (1988).

[C] B. CHALMOND - *Image restoration using an estimated Markov model*, IEEE PAMI (1988).

[G] D. and S. GEMAN - *Gibbs fields, simulated annealing, and Bayerian reconstruction of images*, IEEE PAMI (1984).

[G.G.] S. GEMAN and C. GRAFFIGNE - *Gibbs fields and image segmentation*, Proc. Int. Cong. Math. (1987).

[H.S.A.] G. HINTON, T. SEJNOWSKY, D.H. ACKLEY - *Boltzmann machines : constraint satisfaction networks that learn*, Technical report Carnegie Mellon Univ. (1984).

[L] W.A. LITTLE - *The existence of persistent states*, Math. Biosci 19 (1974).

[P] P. PERETTO - *Collective properties of neural networks*, Preprint (1984).

[T] A. TROUVÉ - *Parallelization of simulated annealing*, C.R. Ac. Sci. (1988) and preprint (1988).

[Y] L. YOUNES - *Parameter estimation for Gibbs fields*, Ann. Inst. H. Poincaré (1988) and doctorate thesis Univ. Paris-Sud (1988).

Fast Computation of Kohonen Self-Organization

J. Lampinen and E. Oja
Lappeenranta University of Technology
Dept. of Information Technology
Box 20 SF-53851 Lappeenranta
Finland

Abstract

A new computational algorithm, the Probing Algorithm, is introduced for the subproblem of finding the best matching unit in Kohonen's self-organization procedure. It is compared to exhaustive search and four other algorithms, and shown to be roughly 6 to 10 times faster for the case of high-dimensional vectors.

1. Introduction

The Kohonen Self-Organizing Feature Map [5] is a mapping of a high dimensional space of input vectors onto a low dimensional (usually 1- or 2-dimensional) discrete lattice of units, or formal neurons. The aim of the self-organizing is to generate a topology preserving mapping, where the neighborhood relations in the input space are preserved as well as possible in the neighborhood relations of the units on the map.

If the algorithm is simulated on a conventional computer, a central problem is to locate the best matching unit for each input vector in turn. Since self-organization takes typically a very large number of steps, devising a fast algorithm for this subproblem would be very desirable.

There exist several methods, developed within Computer Science, for the problem of finding nearest neighbors. Some of them are reviewed and the negative conclusion is drawn that in typical situations they are inefficient for locating the best matching unit on the feature map. A new algorithm which takes advantage of the lattice neighborhoods is introduced. We call it the Probing Algorithm. Its feasibility and speed are demonstrated

---

Work on this paper was supported by Tekes Grant 4196/1988 under the Finsoft project.

NATO ASI Series, Vol. F 68
Neurocomputing
Edited by F. Fogelman Soulié and J. Hérault

by an artificial example of a 10×10 map with a 9-dimensional input space.

2. Self-Organization and The Nearest Neighbor Bottleneck

2.1. The Self-Organization procedure

Assume a one, two, or higher dimensional discrete lattice of units indexed with index i of corresponding dimensionality. Thus, i gives the location of the unit in the lattice. Let d be the dimensionality of the input sample space U. Each unit i carries a d-dimensional reference vector w_i. A point $x \in U$ is *mapped to* a unit j for which

$$\| x - w_j \| = \min_i \| x - w_i \| \tag{1}$$

i.e., a point x is mapped to the unit whose reference vector is the nearest neighbor of x among all the reference vectors. This is called the *best matching unit*.

The self-organization procedure can be summarized as:

1) Draw a sample x from the probability distribution of the input samples and find the best matching unit j, for which $\| x - w_j \|$ is minimum.

2) Adjust the reference vectors of all units in the neighborhood of j by

$$w_i^{new} = w_i^{old} + \gamma h_r (x - w_i^{old}) \tag{2}$$

where γ is the learning step size and h_r is a function of the distance $r = \| i - j \|$ of the units measured along the lattice. Usually h_r is monotonically decreasing in r. Both γ and the size of the neighborhood are slowly decreasing in time.

The optimal computing environment for the feature map would be a highly parallel special architecture [6], since all the units are independent and parallel in nature. Unfortunately such computers are yet costly and unfriendly to program. Most of the research is thus done on traditional serial computers simulating the parallelism. The computational costs of the self-organization on a serial computer concentrate at finding the best matching unit at each step. Especially at the end of the iteration, with a neighborhood of 0 to 1 points, it turns out that computing the distances between the reference vectors of all the units and the input vector takes practically all the time.

Exactly the same problem occurs in nearest neighbor classification which is a well-known decision procedure in pattern recognition, as well as in database problems where the best-matching record has to be found for a search key. A lot of methods have been published to tackle the problem. In the following, some fast algorithms for finding the nearest neighbor to a point are reviewed, with special emphasis on the range of parameters characteristic of feature maps.

2.2. Finding The Nearest Neighbor Quickly

Friedman et al. [1] first *ordered* the reference vectors according to their projection values on a given coordinate axis. The problem is to find the closest reference vector to a *test point*, as would be the case on one step of the self-organizing algorithm. The search begins from the reference vector with the smallest projected distance from the test point. This vector becomes the first candidate for the nearest neighbor, with its total distance from the test point becoming the candidate for the minimum distance. The rest of the reference vectors are now examined in order of their projected distance, updating the candidate if possible. When this distance becomes larger than the distance from the current candidate for the nearest neighbor, the search can be terminated.

In the full procedure Friedman orders the reference vectors on all of the coordinates and the one with the smallest local projected density in the neighborhood of the test point is chosen for searching.

Friedman shows that the expected number of distance calculations is $O(N^{1-1/d})$, where N is the number of reference points and d is the dimensionality of the input space. Although the method is quite effective in low dimensional cases, both theoretical results and simulations show that it gives no advantage over the brute force method (linear search over all the points) if N is small (< 1000) and d is large (> 8) which are very typical for feature maps.

Yunck [8] proposed the cube method which is based on an ordered list on each coordinate axis. Yunck places a hypercube around the test point and iteratively changes the size of the cube until it contains exactly 1 reference point (or more if desired). The expected number of distance calculations is dependent on the metrics used, and is shown to be $O(1)$ and $O(constant^{1-1/d})$ for the maximum (Chebychev) and the Euclidean metrics, respectively. In addition, the algorithm requires, for any metrics, a large number of shift operations, namely $O(dN^{1-1/d})$, which makes also this method unreasonable for large d and small N.

Fukunaga and Narendra [2] first partitioned the reference points with k-means clustering and then searched the tree with the branch-and-bound algorithm for the nearest neighbor to the given test point. Kamgar-Parsi and Kanal [3] improved the method by adding rules to eliminate points without distance calculations. However, our simulations show the same behaviour as with the two previous methods as a function of d and N.

Kim and Park [4] proposed an algorithm based on ordered partitions. The reference points are partitioned first along one of the coordinate axes and the partitions are repartitioned along another coordinate axis, and so on. To find the nearest neighbor, the resulting tree is searched with the branch-and-bound algorithm. Searching will require no distance calculations, and the number of nodes to be searched is independent of the number of points. In low dimensions the method is strikingly fast, but as the dimensionality increases, the number of searched nodes increases exponentially. When $d > 8$ ($N < 1000$), the method is no faster than the brute force approach.

In his extensive article Omohundro [7] reviews some classical search algorithms, noting that with special arrangements these algorithms have behavior resembling that of artificial neural networks (i.e. associative memory, matching by partial key, nonlinear mappings and topology-preserving dimension reduction). However, since the algorithms are essentially the same as described above, nothing is gained by trying to simulate neural net behavior by these methods in the present case.

3. The Probing Algorithm

In computer simulations, the self-organizing feature map is often high dimensional (up to 16) and the number of units is rather small (some hundreds). Both of these factors make all the previous algorithms, as efficient as they are in some other problems, unusable for this application as such. We will next present an algorithm that will not suffer any slowing down in high dimensions. It is based on the topology preserving property of the map and we have called it the Probing Algorithm since, having found a candidate for the best matching unit, the algorithm probes around in the lattice trying to find a better candidate. The algorithm is *not* a general purpose nearest neighbor method, since there is no way to assure that the result is the true nearest neighbor. However, the real goal of the self-organizing is not to find the exact nearest neighbors but to develop a topological feature map. The algorithm will make errors in finding the closest reference vector to an input vector, but in such a consistent way, that it will not disturb the self-organization.

The Probing Algorithm can be summarized as:

1) Given the reference vectors, try to find the nearest neighbor to a test point with any algorithm in a predetermined number of steps (e.g. 2 to 6 steps at most, one step consisting of choosing a new reference vector, computing the distance to the test point, and comparing to the current minimum distance. If more steps would be required, go to 2.

2) Examine the *lattice neighbors* of the current candidate for the nearest neighbor, and if they contain better candidates, select the best of them and repeat 2. If none of the neighbors is closer to the test point than the current candidate, terminate the search.

Note how, at step 2, the method takes advantage of the neighborhood relations among the reference vectors, induced by the lattice of the corresponding units. It may be evident why the method would work if the map is already organized, and the reference vectors of the lattice neighbors are close to each other.

The algorithm, as it is described above, stops immediately at the first local minimum. Escaping the local minima would be tedious, first finding out that the point is not the exact nearest neighbor, then determining the next searching point. On the other hand, an organized map tends to be locally smooth, which suggests a low error probability in finding the nearest neighbor in case of an organized map. When the map is still in an unorganized state the search will more often get stuck to a local minimum, but since the updated neighborhood is large, the fold causing the local minimum will be pulled towards the minimum and eventually smoothed out, while the original algorithm gets often folded in early stages of organization and requires a substantial number of iterations to stretch the folds out.

When choosing the method for the initial search in Phase 1 of the Probing Algorithm, one must consider the amount of preprocessing required. Most of the methods reviewed in Section 2.2 are based on restructuring the reference vectors before searching for the nearest neighbor. However, now the reference vectors are changing during the self-organization, and the preprocessed data (partitioned tree or sorted coordinate list) must be updated after every change, which can be very time-consuming. We chose Friedman's algorithm [1] since sorting the coordinate values is faster than rebuilding a balanced tree or reclustering the points. Since the map changes slowly and the initial point is not very critical for our algorithm, we reordered the points after a fixed number of iterations (usually 100) and to keep all the dimensions balanced we chose each dimension in turn.

The maximum number of candidates considered by Friedman's algorithm in Phase 1 of the Probing Algorithm, and the number of probing steps in Phase 2, are weakly dependent. For the 10×10 map, the best choice was 6 Friedman steps, resulting in 10 probing steps on the average. Compare this to 100 steps required by the brute force method.

4. Simulation Results

In our simulations we considered two criteria for the algorithm: first, how well the algorithm is able to generate a topology preserving mapping, second, how the speed of the algorithm is affected when dimensionality increases.

4.1 Does the Probing Algorithm produce self-organization?

For the first criterion we used several tests; a rough measure of the convergence to a self-organized state is the variance of matching rates of the units. The matching rate is measured by taking samples from the input space according to the input probability distribution and measuring how many times a given unit is the best matching unit. The variance of the matching rates of all the units will stabilize to a non-zero value since the units have different matching probabilities, as can be seen from Fig. 1., showing the variances of matching rates as the self-organizing proceeds. The solid curve is the original self-organizing procedure, in which the best mathing unit has been found at each step exactly, while in the case of the dashed curve, the Probing method has been used instead. The map had 10 by 10 units in 9 dimensions and the input samples were drawn from two Gaussian distributions with variances 1.0 centered at $(0,\ldots,0)$ and $(1,\ldots,1)$.

The Probing Algorithm is based on the smooth topology of the map, and the initial state of the map is random. Consequently, the map must be in a somewhat organized state before there is any sense in using the topology for navigation. Therefore, in Fig. 1., the Probing Algorithm is started after organizing the map first for 1000 iterations by the exact method.

Fig. 1. indicates that the map organizes in the same number of iterations to the same variance as by the exact algorithm. This is a typical convergence curve for the Probing Algorithm; some hundreds of exact iterations seem to be sufficient at first, after which it will follow the same convergence.

If the mapping is topology preserving, a small movement of an input sample will cause

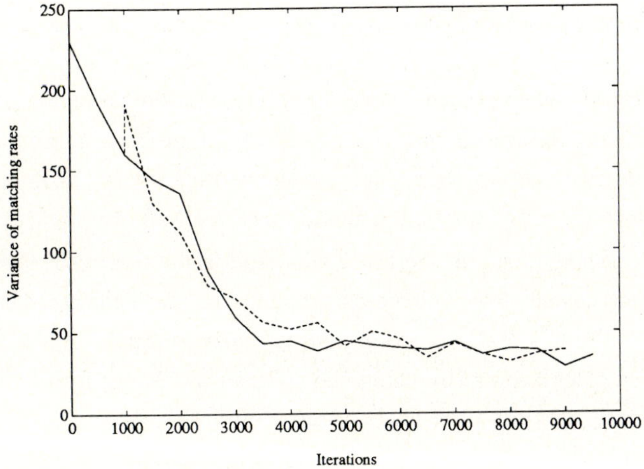

Fig. 1. Variance of matching rates during convergence
Solid line - exact nearest neighbor, dashed line - Probing

a small movement of the response on the map. We examined this by moving a test point by very small steps through the input space and tracking the trajectory of the response. Fig. 2. presents trajectories from the maps after 10000 iterations. Teaching the map with exact nearest neighbors will produce a slightly smoother trajectory, but in both cases the response moves continuously from a unit to a neighboring unit.

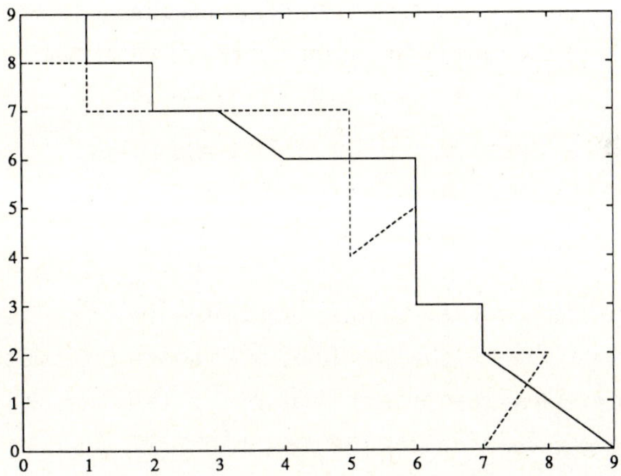

Fig. 2. Trajectories of responses of the 10×10 map
to a line in 9D.
Solid line - exact nearest neighbor, dashed line - Probing

Does the Probing Algorithm speed up the job?

Experiments confirmed, as expected, that the average computational complexity of the Probing Algorithm in finding one (approximative) nearest neighbor is roughly *independent of the dimensionality* . Fig. 3. shows how many times faster the different algorithms are as compared to the brute force method (horizontal line at 1.0). The solid steep decreasing curve is the full Friedman's algorithm with the $O(N^{1-1/d})$ complexity. The dot-dashed lower curve corresponds to the Probing Algorithm with initial search by Friedman's method, examining at most 6 points. If the initial search required no distance calculations (by using the ordered partitions for example), saving the 6 points, the result would be the dashed upper curve.

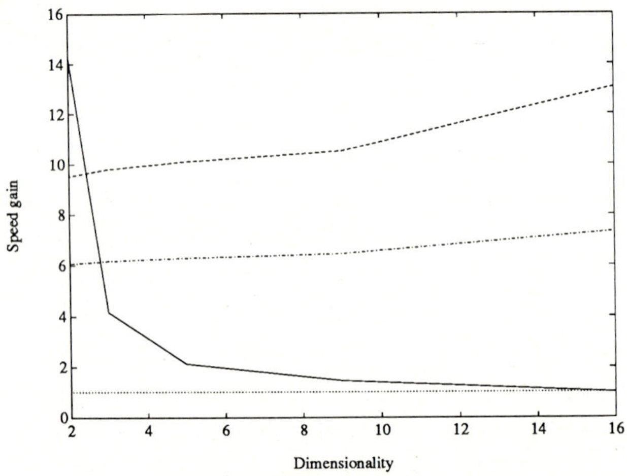

Fig. 3. Speed gain of the Probing Algorithm
See the text for explanations.

In fact, the average complexity of the Probing Algorithm decreases slowly as the dimension increases, because it requires more folding to fit a two-dimensional map in to a higher dimensional space. This creates more local minima to get stuck to, making the search slightly faster on expense of raising the error rate.

To make clear the speed advantage of the Probing Algorithm, Fig. 4. shows the same convergence curves as Fig. 1., but redrawn as functions of *computer time* required. Both cases have the same number of iterations.

With a general purpose nearest neighbor algorithm the error probability would be a major consideration, if any errors would be tolerated at all. In this algorithm, however,

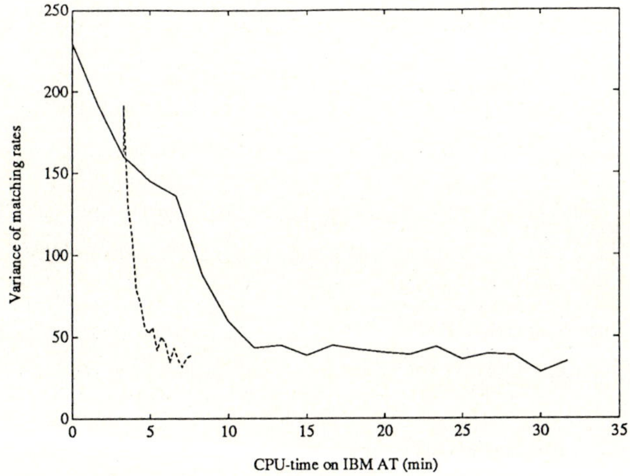

Fig. 4. Variance of matching rates during convergence as functions of required CPU-time.
Solid line - exact nearest neighbor, dashed line - Probing

the error rate does not have such significance, since the errors occur systematically at the same locations; they define another mapping from the input space onto the lattice, which maps a point and its neighborhood on the same unit, thus not destroying the self-organization.

Despite the error rate, the Probing Algorithm can be used for nearest-neighbor type classification, since a point and its local neighborhood map to the same unit on the map (see the trajectories in Fig. 2.). We labeled the units by collecting a large number of samples from the two Gaussian 9-D distributions, and tested the performance with a new set of data, trying to separate the two distributions. The error rates were 8.7% and 9.2% for maps taught by exact nearest neighbors and the Probing Algorithm, respectively. The difference of classification accuracy was rather small, while the error rate in finding the exact nearest neighbor by the Probing Algorithm was in fact 17% .

5. Conclusions

We have presented a version of the self-organization algorithm, the Probing Algorithm, that is from 5 to 10 times faster than conventional algorithms, and will not suffer any slowing down when the dimensionality of the input space gets high. The algorithm is suitable for self-organization and classification, but it is not a general purpose nearest neighbor algorithm. The main usage for the algorithm can be summarized as follows: if computing of the self-organization takes too long due to heavy distance calculations in finding the best mathing unit, one can plug in the Probing Algorithm for this task.

The algorithm will terminate the nearest neighbor search after a few steps and continue along the topology of the map.

6. References

1. Friedman J.H, Baskett F. and Shustek L.J.: An Algorithm for Finding Nearest Neighbors, IEEE Trans. Comput., vol C-24, Oct. 1975, 1000-1006

2. Fukunaga K. and Narendra P.M.: A Branch and Bound Algorithm for Computing k-nearest Neighbors, IEEE Trans. Comput., vol C-24, July 1975, 750-753

3. Kamgar-Parsi B. and Kanal L.N.; An Improved Branch and Bound Algorithm for Computing k-nearest Neighbors, Pattern Recognition Letters 3, 7-12, 1985

4. Kim B. S. and Park S. B.: A Fast k Nearest Neighbor Finding Algorithm Based on the Ordered Partition, IEEE Trans. PAMI, vol. PAMI-8, No. 6, Nov. 1986, 761-766

5. Kohonen T.: Self-Organization and Associative Memory. Springer-Verlag, Berlin, 1988

6. Koikkalainen P. and Oja E.: Specification and Implementation Environment for Neural Networks Using Communicating Sequential Processes, Proc. IEEE ICNN-88, San Diego, CA, July 24.-27., 1988, 533-540

7. Omohundro S. M.: Efficient Algorithms with Neural Network Behavior, Complex Systems 1, Complex Systems Publications, Inc, 1989, 273-347

8. Yunck T.P.: A Technique to Identify Nearest Neighbors, IEEE Trans. Syst. Man. Cybern., vol SMC-6, Oct. 1976, 678-683

Learning algorithms in neural networks: recent results

Marc Mézard

Laboratoire de Physique Théorique de l'Ecole Normale Supérieure
24 rue Lhomond
75231 Paris Cedex 05- FRANCE

Abstract

We review two new algorithms for learning in neural networks of Boolean units. The first applies to the problem of associative memory: Hopfield model or perceptron. The algorithm optimizes the stability of learned patterns, which enlarges the size of the basins of attraction. The second algorithm builds a multilayer feedforward network: it allows one to learn an arbitrary mapping input $\rightarrow$ output. The convergence of the growth process is guaranteed. The generalization properties look very promising.

This paper gives a short review of some work done at ENS on learning in neural networks, basically in collaboration with W. Krauth and J.P. Nadal. I shall not give any details (the reader is referred to the original papers), but I shall rather point out the basic ideas and some results.

Associative memory

The first problem we have considered is that of associative memory. Consider a neural network of N Boolean units $S_i = \pm 1$, coupled through the coupling constants (= synaptic efficacies) J_{ij}, evolving through the dynamics (sequential or parallel) :

$$S_i^{t+1} = \text{Sign} \left(\Sigma_j \; J_{ij} \; S_j^t \right) \tag{1}$$

One wants to memorize in such a network a set of p patterns

$$x^m = \{ x_i^m = \pm 1, i = 1, \ldots N \} ; m = 1, \ldots p.$$

The necessary condition of stability of pattern m on site i is :

$$D_i^m = \Sigma_j \; J_{ij} \, x_i^m \; x_j^m > O \tag{2}$$

NATO ASI Series, Vol. F 68
Neurocomputing
Edited by F. Fogelman Soulié and J. Hérault

These p. N inequalities decouple from each site i to another. Therefore we are left with the following problem on each site i: given p vectors y^m with N components ($y_j^m = x_i^m \cdot x_j^m$), find a N component vector J^i such that, for each m, $J^i \cdot y^m > 0$.

Clearly the same problem appears in a perceptron [1] : in order to map an input pattern I_j^m to an output O_i^m, we need that for each output site i :

$$O_j^m = \mathrm{Sign} \; (\Sigma_j \quad J_{ij} \cdot I_j^m) \tag{3}$$

which is again of the same form $J^i \cdot y^m > 0$, where the dimension of the vectors J^i and y^m is the number of neurons in the input layer, and now : $y_j^m = O_i^m \; I_j^m$

The above conditions just ensure the stability of patterns to be learnt. In order to use these networks as associative memories, one wants the patterns to have large basins of attraction. It has been postulated in [2] that this can be achieved if the stabilities of the patterns are large, where the definition of the stability on site i for pattern m is :

$$T_i^m = (\Sigma_j \quad J_{ij}\, x_i^m\, x_j^m)\; (\Sigma_j \; J_{ij}^2)^{-1/2} = J^i \cdot y^m / \; \| J^i \| \tag{4}$$

From now on we shall drop the index i.

The fact that the sizes of the basins of attraction increase with the stabilities has been checked in several works, numerically for the case of Hopfield's model [3,4], analytically for the case of the perceptron [5].

Within this hypothesis - that the sizes of the basins of attraction essentially depend on the stabilities of the parameters - the learning problem can be phrased as an optimization problem : Find the vector J such that $\| J \| = 1$ and the smallest stability, inf T^m, is maximal. This problem is solved by the MINOVER algorithm [2], which is a variant of the usual perceptron learning algorithm [1]. As for the case of the perceptron, the algorithm is guaranteed to converge if the problem is linearly separable, i.e. if there exists at least one J such that all the stabilities be positive. We have tested the algorithm on the case of learning of random patterns, $y_j^m = \pm 1$ with probability 1/2. Then the optimal value K of inf T^m has been computed by E. Gardner [6], as a function of the storage ratio $\alpha = P/N$, in the limit of a large number of neurons $N \rightarrow \infty$. K is a decreasing function of α which goes to zero when $\alpha = 2$, which is the maximal capacity of these associative memory networks for random patterns.

The MINOVER algorithm reaches the predicted value K, and it can indeed store up to 2N random patterns. Other methods for trying to reach large values of inf T^m have also been proposed [7].

Multilayer feed forward networks: the tiling algorithm, a constructive algorithm.

In order to go beyond associative memory we soon encounter more complicated problems which are not linearly separable [1]. Then the fully connected structure with feedback used in the Hopfield model becomes quite complicated to understand. For practical applications it is simpler, within present knowledge at least, to use feedforward networks with several layers. We consider such networks with Boolean units. Each unit receives inputs from the previous layer only, and reacts according to (1), where t is now a layer index.

The learning problem is then to find all the couplings between the layers, in order to implement the mapping $x_i^m \rightarrow o^m$, where m = 1,..., p are the patterns to be learnt (the elements of the training set), and i = 1,..., N, (N is the size of the input). For simplicity we keep here to the case of just one binary output $o^m = \pm 1$ (yes or no answer). The generalization to several output units is in principle straightforward, although it can be done in a more or less clever way.

Recently we proposed a constructive algorithm which builds a network solving this learning problem [8]. Each hidden unit is generated one after the other, until convergence. Two simple ideas govern this growth algorithm. First of all, in each hidden layer one gets an internal representation of the problem. Suppose we look at a hidden layer with N' neurons: to each input pattern x^m corresponds a set of activities of the N' neurons, say $Z_i^m = \pm 1$, i = 1,..., N' : these activities are obtained by propagating the input x^m through the previous layers, using (1). Some patterns can have the same internal representations ($Z_i^m = Z_i^n$, i = 1,..., N'). We call **class** a set of patterns with the same internal representation. A trivial remark is that, for the internal representation in this hidden layer to be valid, one needs any two patterns m, n in the same class to always have the same outputs $o^m = o^n$. If this is the case the classes are named **faithful**. The growth (adjunction of new units) within each hidden layer corresponds to adding "**ancillary**" units until one gets faithful classes (see [8]). The second idea is to use, in each layer, a special neuron called the **master** unit, which gives the best possible approximation in this layer of the desired output. We measure the error in layer L as the number of patterns in the training set such that the corresponding activity of the master unit in layer L differs from the desired output o^m. A convergence theorem [8] gives a way to generate the master unit such that the error strictly decreases from one layer to the next.

Therefore this algorithm is guaranteed to exactly learn any training set (unless there are inconsistent data, in which case it can learn the largest possible subset). To our knowledge this property is shared only by the algorithm of Rujan and Marchand [9] which generates only one hidden layer, but is unfortunately limited so far to inputs of small size N. We use perceptron learning which allows large inputs ; we can also relax the condition of exact learning and tolerate a certain number of errors in the training set.

After training, the next obvious question is : what are the generalization properties ? The usual belief is that generalization will be better whenever the training set has been learnt with a smaller number of hidden units [10,11]. This is precisely the idea which prompted us to find a constructive algorithm, which will generate only the units it needs, instead of having the size of the network imposed from the beginning. We have tested the algorithm for generalization on the problem of detecting domain walls. In a string of N bits (N = 25 or N = 50 in our simulations), the output should be one if there are at least three domain walls (a domain wall is a set of two consecutive neurons which point in opposite directions). In the most difficult case we presented in the training and in the test sets random patterns with an average number of domain walls precisely equal to three. With 600 patterns in the training set we get a rate of generalization of 68 % [8]. This is much better than back propagation which does not generalize in the same conditions [11]. In fact this rate is remarkable because we have not given to the network any insight on the problem, in particular the system does not know about the one-dimensional nature of the problem.

This means that the problem we are really addressing is the detection of domain walls, but the examples from which we learn could be mixed up by an arbitrary fixed permutation of the neurons. This is clearly a hard problem.

In order to help the network one must provide it with some more information on the problem, for instance on its one-dimensional nature. This could be done with our tiling algorithm in the following way. For the generation of the first hidden layer, we do not use any master unit : the aim is just to get a faithful internal representation in this layer, but we can add one constraint, namely the fact that each unit must receive inputs from at most k neighbouring units of the input layer. This gives a hint of unidimensionality. This is easy to implement within our algorithm for generating ancillary units : given an unfaithful class, and the k neurons which are to be connected to the new unit, one must learn the restrictions of the patterns in the unfaithful class to these k neurons. This strategy has not been tested yet, but it should be very useful for all applications in which the inputs have a spatial structure. Another variant of the algorithm has also been studied recently by J.P. Nadal [12].

References

[1] Minsky, M., Papert, S. : Perceptrons, MIT Press, Cambridge, MA, (1969).

[2] Krauth, W., Mézard, M. : Learning algorithms with optimal stability in neural networks. J. Phys. A, 20, L 745, (1987).

[3] Forrest, B.M. : J. Phys. A21, 245 (1988).

[4] Krauth, W., Nadal, J.P., Mézard, M. : Basins of attraction in a perceptron-like neural network. Complex Systems 2, 387 (1988).

[5] Krauth, W., Nadal, J.P., Mézard, M.: The roles of stability and symmetry in the dynamics of neural networks. J. Phys. A, 21, 2995-3011, (1988).

[6] Gardner, E. : Europhys. Lett. 4, 481 (1987)

Gardner, E. Derrida, B.: Optimal Storage Properties of Neural Network Models. In J. Phys. A, 21, 271-284, (1988).

[7] Gardner, E., Stroud, N., Wallace, D.: Training with Noise, and the Storage of Correlated Patterns in a Neural Network Model, Edinburgh Preprint 87/394, University of Edinburgh, (1987).

Pœppel G. and Krey U. : Europhys.Lett. 4, 481, (1987).

[8] Mézard, M., Nadal, J.P. : Learning in feed-forward layered networks: the tiling algorithm. J. Phys. A, 22, 2191-2203, (1989).

[9] Rujan P., Marchand, M.: Learning by activating neurons: a new approach to learning in neural networks. KFA Jülich preprint, to appear in Complex Systems, (1988).

[10] Carnevali, P., Patarnello, S. : Europhys. Lett. 4, 1199, (1987).

[11] Denker, J., Schwartz, D., Wittner, B., Solla, S., Hopfield, J.J.Howard, R., Jackel, L.: Automatic Learning, Rule Extraction and Generalization. In Complex Systems vol 1, 877-922, (1987).

[12] Nadal, J.P. : Study of a growth algorithm for a feedforward network. In Intl Journal of Neural Networks, 1, 55-59, (1989).

Statistical approach to the Jutten-Hérault algorithm*

Pierre Comon

THOMSON-SINTRA,
BP 53
F-06801 Cagnes sur Mer - France

Abstract

One year ago, the Jutten-Herault (JH) network was the only existing tool for recovering p stochastic "source" processes from an unknown mixture [1]. With guidance provided by neurosciences analogies, the unsupervised learning JH algorithm has been adjusted and implemented on an array of p linear neurons totally interconnected [0] [1]. Because of its numerous applications ranging from image processing to antenna array processing, the JH algorithm received much attention during the last few years [2], but no rigorous derivation has been proposed to date. We attempt in this paper to analyze it from a statistics point of view. For instance, it could be shown that the updating term of the synaptic efficacies matrix, δC, cannot be the gradient of a single C^2 functional contrary to what is sometimes understood. In fact, we show that the JH algorithm is actually searching common zeros of p functionals by a technique of Robbins-Monro type.

1. Properties inherent in the problem

Denote $x_i(t)$ the source processes, $1 \leq i \leq p$. They are assumed zero-mean, stationary up to the fourth order, and mutually independent. Denote $e_i(t)$ the observations, obtained by an unknown memoryless linear transform of the sources. Then we have in compact form the relation between both vector-processes e and x:

$$e(t) = A\, x(t), \tag{1}$$

* This work was supported by DRET, Paris, France

NATO ASI Series, Vol. F 68
Neurocomputing
Edited by F. Fogelman Soulié and J. Hérault

where A is an unknown pxp matrix. The goal is to retrieve the source processes $x_i(t)$ by using solely their statistical independence. It is obvious that the solution, if it is obtainable, is necessarily given by a linear transform:

$$s(t) = F\, e(t). \tag{2}$$

Notice that if a process x(t) has independent components, then so do the process $P\Lambda x(t)$, where P is any permutation matrix, and Λ any regular diagonal matrix; in other words, we may have $FA = P\Lambda$. The consequence is that among the p^2 unknowns (the entries of F), p of them are undetermined. It suffices to impose p entries in F to get a well-posed problem. One way of doing this would be to impose that the variances of the outputs $s_i(t)$ be all equal to 1 [4]. Another is to look for a matrix F under the form:

$$F = (I + C)^{-1}; \tag{3}$$

with Diag{C} = 0.

This constraint is assumed in the JH algorithm. Now, it remains to find matrix C, that is, only p(p-1) unknowns. Ideally, there are *several* equivalent solutions

$$C = AP[\mathrm{Diag}(AP)]^{-1} - I, \tag{4}$$

where P describes the set of permutations in dimension p. If we resort to a second-order description of the stochastic processes, then the problem is undetermined. In fact, there are p(p−1)/2 cross-moments and their cancellation yields independence of the outputs at order 2, and provides us with p(p−1)/2 quadratic equations, which is half less than the number of unknowns. For instance, the solution given by the principal components analysis of the covariance matrix $E\{s(t)s(t)^T\}$ provides uncorrelated outputs $s_i(t)$, that may not be pairwise independent whenever they are non-Gaussian. Since Gaussian processes in the strict sense are never observed in the real world, this solution is not satisfactory. The need of p(p−1)/2 additional equations may be faced by utilizing higher-order moments.

2. A statistical measure of independence

Based on a quantitative criterion of independence of higher order, namely higher-order output cumulants, a more "classical" approach may be derived [4]. These tools are briefly described below. If the variables s_i are mutually independent, then by definition the joint characteristic function $\phi_s(u)$ splits into the product of p marginal characteristic functions $\phi_{s_i}(u_i)$. This yields by taking the logarithm:

$$\ln\phi_s(u) = \sum \ln\phi_{s_i}(u_i). \tag{5}$$

Suppose we compute the Taylor expansion of both sides of (5). Then all the terms in the left hand side where products between different variables u_i enter must be zero since there are no such terms in the right hand side. In other words, all the *cross cumulants* of any order must vanish. For instance, for p=2 and at order 4, this means:

$$\begin{aligned} \Gamma_{13} &= M_{13} - 3\, M_{20}\, M_{11} = 0, \\ \Gamma_{22} &= M_{22} - M_{20}\, M_{02} - 2\, M_{11}{}^2 = 0, \\ \Gamma_{31} &= M_{31} - 3\, M_{02}\, M_{11} = 0, \end{aligned} \tag{6}$$

where $M_{ij} = E\{s_1{}^i s_2{}^j\}$ denote the moments of order i+j, and the Γ_{ij}'s are the corresponding cumulants. Cross-cumulants of order 4 seem better to use than those of order 3 which can be identically zero regardless of C for symmetric probability densities. Let us turn to the JH algorithm which is a means to cancel higher-order moments.

3. JH adaptation rule

3.1. Searching the zeros of a function

Let $\Phi(x)$ be a real deterministic function defined as the expectation of a random function $\varphi[x,s(x)]$, s(x) being a random variable depending on the unknown parameter, x. One of the simplest ways of finding the zeros of $\Phi(x)$ is to run the algorithm:

$$x(k) = x(k-1) + \mu\, \Phi(x(k-1))$$

where μ is a constant, $0<\mu<1$.

It is easy to see that if $\Phi(x)>0$, then x increases, whereas if $\Phi(x)<0$ x decreases. This iteration is thus able to find the zeros of $\Phi(x)$ that have a negative derivative. A similar iteration may be used to find the zeros with positive derivative just by changing the sign of μ. In a stochastic approximation context, $\Phi(x)$ is unknown to the user as well as the probability density of φ. However, one may substitute $\varphi[x,s(x)]$ for $\Phi(x)$ in the above iteration, yielding the Robbins-Monro stochastic iteration [3, p42-43]:

$$x(k) = x(k-1) + \mu\, \varphi[x(k-1),s(x(k-1))]. \tag{7}$$

Convergence in probability of the Markov process x(k) to a root of $\Phi(x)$ needs among other conditions that μ depends on k. More precisely, the sequence $\mu(k)$ must be nonsummable and

$\mu(k)^2$ must be summable. If $\mu(k)$ does not tend to zero, then x(k) will be able only to achieve a neighborhood of the root but there will be a non-zero residual. This is what occurs in the JH algorithm, but it could be easily palliated if required. However, a minimal positive value of $\mu(k)$ is desired in a nonstationary environment.

3.2. Searching common zeros of several functions

Now, let the dimension of x be larger than 1. Assume we observe several functions $\varphi_i[x,s(x)]$, and assume we know in advance that the functions $\Phi_i(x) = E\{\varphi_i[x,s(x)]\}$ have a common zero. The previous iteration may be used along each coordinate in turn. In such a case, the ith component of x is updated only once each p steps, if p is the dimension of x, according to a relaxation scheme.

3.3. JH algorithm as a pipelined search

Omitting the high-pass filter that was originally implemented together with function g, the adaptation rule used in JH algorithm may be written as:

$$C(t) = C(t\text{-}1) + \mu\ \delta C(t), \tag{8}$$

where

$$\delta C_{ij}(t) = f(s_i(t\text{-}1))\ g(s_j(t\text{-}1)) \qquad \text{for } i \neq j,$$

and the functions f(x) and g(x) are suggested to be (**i**) different (**ii**) different from identity (**iii**) odd [1] [2]. Clearly, iteration (8) is attempting to simultaneously cancel the functions $E\{f(s_i(t\text{-}1))\ g(s_j(t\text{-}1))\}$ with respect to the entries of C. The difference with the relaxation scheme described above is that iterations along each coordinate are computed all together at the same time step. If the step is very small, the principle does not change much and the difference may be viewed as a pipeling operation. On the other hand, if the step is large, then algorithm (8) may not converge. In the next section, we shall point out some of the convergence limitations which are definitely due not only to the search algorithm but also to the choice of the functionals themselves.

Let us review the conditions recommended for functions f and g: (**i**) They must be different from each other in order for the matrix C to be able to take unsymmetric values, this is necessary. Conditions (**ii**) and (**iii**) are sufficient to avoid the function $\Phi_{ij}(C)$ to be a third order cumulant. But they are too strong; for instance, taking

$$\{f(x) = x^3 \text{ and } g(y) = y\}$$

is also acceptable, and works almost as well as

$$\{f(x) = x^3 \text{ and } g(y) = \text{atan}(\alpha y)\}.$$

Moreover, $E\{x^3y\}$ is garanteed to vanish when x and y are independent, which is not garanteed with $E\{x^3\text{atan}(\alpha y)\}$ neither for $E\{x^py^q\}$ when p,q>1.

In the moment

$$\Phi_{ij}[C_{ji},C_{ij}] = E\{s_i^3\text{atan}(\alpha s_j)\}$$

higher order moments are implicitely involved (this would be obvious if αs_j were almost surely in the unit disk). The consequence is that the functional $\Phi_{ij}[C_{ji},C_{ij}]$ is not polynomial anymore, and may have a lot of spurious zeros providing statistically dependent outputs. This is verified with simulations (see next sections).

4. Behavior of the JH algorithm

4.1. Restriction to a one-dimensional study

The purpose of this section is to show various conditionings of JH algorithm, and in particular those that cause problems. Our present investigation focuses on the case p=2 for the sake of clarity; nonetheless the results are representative of the behavior at higher dimensions since all outputs are processed pairwise. Now, matrix C has only two free parameters, C_{12} and C_{21}. The first goal of the algorithm is to provide uncorrelated outputs, and the next is concerned with higher-order independence. This first task is less interesting to study for two reasons: (a) there exist many classical methods carrying it out (b) JH algorithm has been shown to converge quite rapidly to uncorrelated outputs whereas the next phase dealing with higher order independence take a fairly larger amount of iterations [1] [2]. In this section, we shall restrict the study to uncorrelated (but statistically dependent) inputs. In such a case, the matrix C to estimate is necessarily skew-symmetric. So denote from now on $C_{12} = \theta = -C_{21}$.

4.2. Explicit computation of the functionals implicitely cancelled by JH

Assume the inputs $e_1(t)$ and $e_2(t)$ are uncorrelated (at order 2). Then algorithm JH is attempting to simultaneously cancel

$$\Phi_{12}[\theta] = E\{s_1^3(t)\text{atan}(\alpha s_2(t))\}$$

and $$\Phi_{21}[\theta] = E\{s_2^3(t)\text{atan}(\alpha s_1(t))\} \tag{9}$$

with: $\alpha=10$

$$s_1(t) = [e_1(t) - \theta e_2(t)]/(1+\theta^2) \text{ and } s_2(t) = [e_2(t) + \theta e_1(t)]/(1+\theta^2). \tag{10}$$

For given inputs, it is possible to estimate accurately both functionals as functions of the unknown transform parameter, θ. For this purpose, it suffices to substitute the values of $s_1(t)$ and $s_2(t)$ in (9) for their values given by (10) and to replace the expectation by a time averaging over a long period $1 \leq t \leq T$. This must be of course repeated for each value θ to be scaned, and therefore involves a rather large computational burden.

4.3. Simulation examples

Figures 1 and 2 show the functionals obtained for T=2000 with two types of inputs. Inputs are obtained from independent sources via the orthogonal transform A = [0.319 0.948; −0.948 0.319]. In the first case, the sources are identically and uniformly distributed white processes, and in the second they are binary and trinary random white processes respectively. Sources are zero-mean and of unit variance. The ideal solutions are, from(4), $\theta = 3$ and $\theta = -0.3$. Be careful that figures (b) plot Φ_{21} as a function of $-C_{21}$ and not $+C_{21}$, in order to make it easier to compare solutions θ obtained on figures (a) and (b). Thus, attractors of JH are the zeros with *positive derivative* on figures (b), and *negative derivative* on figures (a).

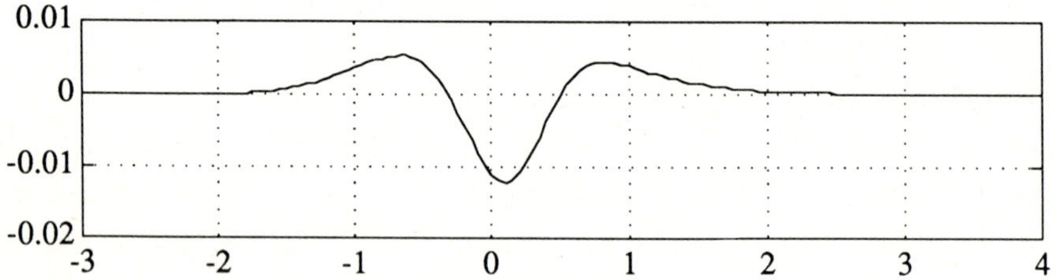

Figure 1 (a). Attractors for C_{12}: -0.3, +3
Associated attraction basins:]-2.1, 0.5[,]0.5, +∞[

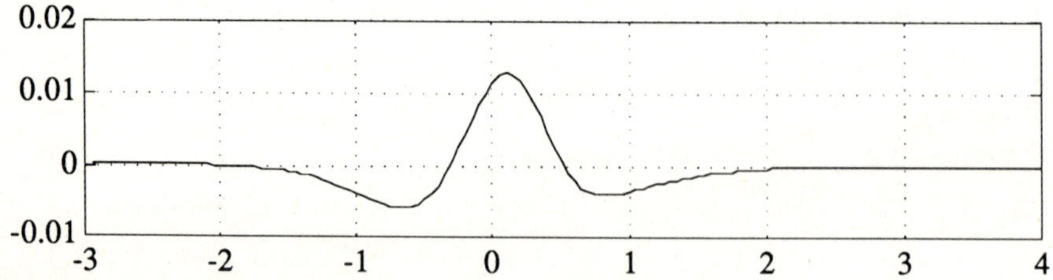

Figure 1 (b). Attractors for $-C_{21}$: -0.3, +2.4
Associated attraction basins:]-1.8, 0.5[,]0.5, +∞[

On figure 1 we can see that the attractors obtained coincide exactly with the solutions expected. However, one can check that if $\{C_{12},-C_{21}\}$ is initialized to $\{-3,-2\}$, then the algorithm diverges to $\{-\infty,-\infty\}$; if it is initialized to $\{3,3\}$ then it converges fairly slowly. On the other hand, the second figure sheds light on more embarrassing results. There are spurious attractors, and some attractors have split into two close attractors. For instance on figure 2a attractor -0.3 does not exist any more, but attractors -0.6 and -0.1 have appeared; as a result there is an unstable basin limit at -0.3. Experiments run with zero starting values all led to $\{C_{12},-C_{21}\}=\{-0.6,-0.3\}$ which is an unaccurate solution anticipated by our analysis. Note that attractor -0.1 has been skipped in that case, because of too little averaging at the beginning of the process.

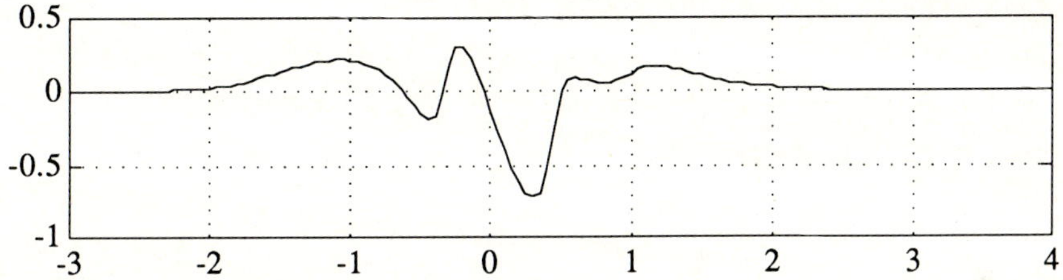

Figure 2 (a). Attractors for C_{12}: -0.6, -0.1, +3
Associated attraction basins:]-2, -0.3[,]-0.3, 0.5[,]0.5, +∞[

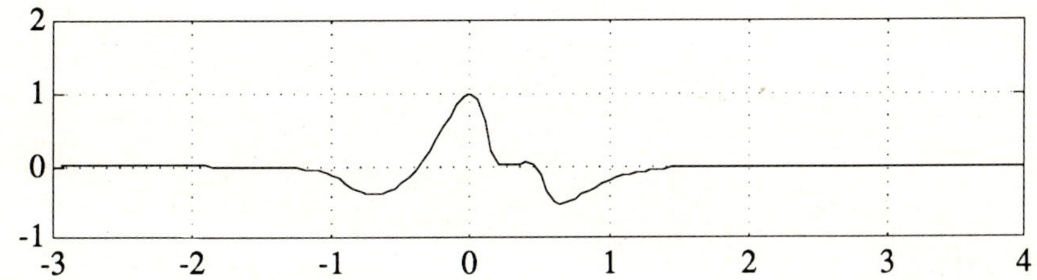

Figure 2 (b). Attractors for $-C_{21}$: -0.3, +0.3, +1.7
Associated attraction basins:]-1.8, 0.2[,]0.2, 0.5[,]0.5, +∞[

5. Improvements to the method

The Robbins-Monro algorithm has specific limitations that are shared with the JH algorithm. For instance, the speed of convergence of a sequence x(k) to a zero x_o of $\Phi(x)$ depends upon the ratio $\mathrm{Min}\{\Phi(x)/(x-x_o)\}$. The possible improvements are two-fold. First, one can change the nature of the functionals, by using cumulants for instance. Second, the iterative search can be speeded up, or even replaced by a direct computation when it is feasible [4] in order to get rid of the initialization sensitivity. As a conclusion, it must be said that this problem is related to overdetermined polynomial systems of *several variables* which are difficult to solve, and all methods that could be invesitgated would have to cope with spurious solutions, and might have the same inconveniences as the JH algorithm.

References

[0] Jutten, C., Hérault, J.: Analog Implementation of a Permanent Unsupervised Learning Algorithm. This volume.

[1] Jutten, C., Hérault, J., Ans, B.: Détection de Grandeurs Primitives dans un Message Composite. Colloqium GRETSI, Nice, France, (may 20-24, 1985).

[2] Jutten, C., Hérault, J.: Independent Component Analysis versus Principal Component Analysis", Conference EUSIPCO, Grenoble, France, (sept 1988).

[3] Ljung, L., Soderstrom, T.: Theory and Practice of Recursive Identification, MIT Press, (1983).

[4] Comon, P.: Separation of Stochastic Processes whose Linear Mixture is Observed, ONRNSF - IEEE Workshop on Higher-Order Spectral Analysis, Vail, Colorado, (june 28-30, 1989).

The N Programming Language

Gaël de La Croix Vaubois, Catherine Moulinoux, Benoît Derot
Thomson-CSF / DSE
BP 150
F-92223 Bagneux Cédex

Abstract

Expecting a wide use of neural network algorithms in the near future, our objective is to get a complete software development environment for programming and testing new applications. We intend to produce a high level language for neural network specification, as a part of such an environment.

The language we propose is characterized by a high degree of modularity, based on parameterizable data structures, with functionalities in the form of update methods attached to them. Composition rules of structures and methods enable to build, step by step, more complex structures from smaller ones previously defined. Objects are viewed as autonomous modules which are linked through plugs for communications. We particularly cared for the parallelization of methods running concurrently on different objects of the network. The syntax is largely related to those of the C and C++ languages.

This research work takes place in the Pygmalion ESPRIT II project 2059.

Neural Network Programming System

In order to promote the use of neural networks algorithms for a wide range of applications, a Neural Network Programming System (NNPS) is designed to provide a standard programming environment for all types of hardware, including dedicated neurocomputers. The programming system executes on a host computer and generates a specific net simulator/emulator to be executed on a target computer. Monitoring of the simulator/ emulator is done from the host through a command language and visualization of the network evolution is allowed by a set of adequate graphical tools. NNPS is organized into five parts.

Neural networks are defined by a *High Level Language (HLL)*. It allows for the description of the network topology and its dynamics in an object-oriented form. New networks are built from parameterized modules of existing networks or sub-networks. A number of such objects, written in HLL and validated, will be available to the user. They constitute a basic *Algorithms Library*.
Compilation of a network from HLL to a particular hardware requires two steps. First, the network is precompiled into an *Intermediate Level Language (ILL)* which is the lowest machine-independent level. Compilation towards various computers is then carried out from this unique format. Direct access to any element of a running network for visualiza-

NATO ASI Series, Vol. F 68
Neurocomputing
Edited by F. Fogelman Soulié and J. Hérault

tion and update is enabled by the *Graphic Monitor*, which interacts with the ILL description of the network.

NNPS is completed with a *Simulation Control Language* allowing the user to set up a simulation context, to follow the evolution of the network parameters, and to keep a textual trace of experiments.

The N language

The N language is the High Level Language we develop for neural networks specification. It is largely inspired by SLOGAN (1), an object-oriented language which runs in a Lisp and Symbolics computer environment. N is an actor language running in a C environment.

In N, a neural network is built from connected and hierarchically structured modular elements. Any object of a network may be designed from previously defined models. A complex object may comprise a number of more elementary ones. These objects include methods to be activated by incoming messages. Methods belonging to an object are part of its definition. A message received by an object may activate one of its own methods, or just be forwarded to the sub-objects it is composed of. An example using N for the definition of a backpropagation network is given in Figures 1 and 2.

An object in N is called a model. The definition of a model may contain :

- *Private* variables as fields for internal use. These variables may be seen only by the own methods of the model. No access is allowed from any other model at any level.
- *Submodels* : the models which the current model is composed of.
- *Plug* variables for input or output. They ensure communication with the other objects in the structure. A plug variable must be either plugin or plugout.
- *Above* read-only variables, whose value must be given by a model at a higher level.
- *Accessed variables* which are available to any submodel where they are declared as *above* variable.
- *Connection* function : Each plug variable of the current model or of submodels may be linked to another one with respect to the direction of data transmission.
- *Methods* which may be activated by a model at the level just above the current one. They can access the own variables of the model they belong to, its own *plug* variables, *plug* variables of its immediate submodels, and the *accessed* and *above* variables. A *method* has no other access to any variable of any models, even submodels of the model it belongs to.

A model is entirely autonomous, except for communications through plugged variables and accessed variables. The true parallelization of a complex model on a suited architecture will be obtained by distributing objects on processors. Each model will run on a single processor, in order to have all internal variables and methods on site. At the opposite, its sub-models may be distributed on distant processors. As communication between sub-models of a given model, and between a model and its sub-models are allowed only through plugs and links, only these links will give rise to communication between processors. The regularity generally obtained for the links structure of a network allows an easy protocole for communications between processors.

```
somatype _soma(int ns, int nu) {
plugin :
 float in[ns], inback[nu];
plugout :
 float out, outback;
private :
 float potential,backpotential,
       state;
method :
 void propagate(int ns) {
   potential = 0;
   for(int i=0;i<ns;i++)
     potential += in[i];
   state = sigmo(potential);
   out = state;}
 void back(int nu) {
   backpotential= 0;
   for(int i=0;i<nu;i++)
     backpotential += inback[i];
   outback = backpotential
             * sigmoprim(state);}};
```

```
synapsetype _synapse() {
plugin :
 float in, inback;
plugout :
 float out, outback;
private :
 float weight = nrand(min,max),
       state,backstate;
method :
 void propagate() {
   state = in;
   out = state * weight;}
 void back() {
   backstate = inback;
   outback =  backstate * weight;
   weight = weight
            + lambda * state
              * backstate;}
 void printweight() {
   cout << " " << weight;}};
```

```
newtype _neuron(int ns, int nu) {
plugin :
 float in[ns],inback[nu];
plugout :
 float out,outback[ns];
private :
 _synapse synapse[ns+1] = new{()};
 _soma soma = new(ns,nu);
 connect(int ns) {
     // threshold value :
   synapse[ns].in = -1.0;
   for(int i=0;i<ns;i++) {
     link(synapse[i].outback,
          outback[i]);
     link(synapse[i].in,in[i]);}
   for(i=0;i<ns+1;i++) {
     link(synapse[i].inback,
          soma.outback);
     link(soma.in[i],
          synapse[i].out);}
   link(soma.out,out);
   link(soma.inback,inback);}
method :
 void propagate(int ns) {
   for (int i=0;i<ns+1;i++)
     synapse[i].propagate();
   soma.propagate(ns+1);}
 void back(int ns,int nu) {
   soma.back(nu);
   par(int i=0;i<ns+1;i++)
     synapse[i].back();}
 void printweight(int ns) {
   par(int i=0;i<ns+1;i++)
       synapse[i].printweight();}};
```

Figure 1 – Description of a backpropagation network in N. This excerpt describes the "neuron" model to be used in the backpropagation algorithm.

Conclusion

The N Neural Network Programming Language we are designing is intended to be used by expert users, thanks to its high flexibility, as well as application developers who will take advantage of its modularity to use predefined models contained in an algorithm library. A complete simulator in C is expected to be running in the begining of 1990, before N is integrated in a wider software development environment, and compiled towards parallel hardware.

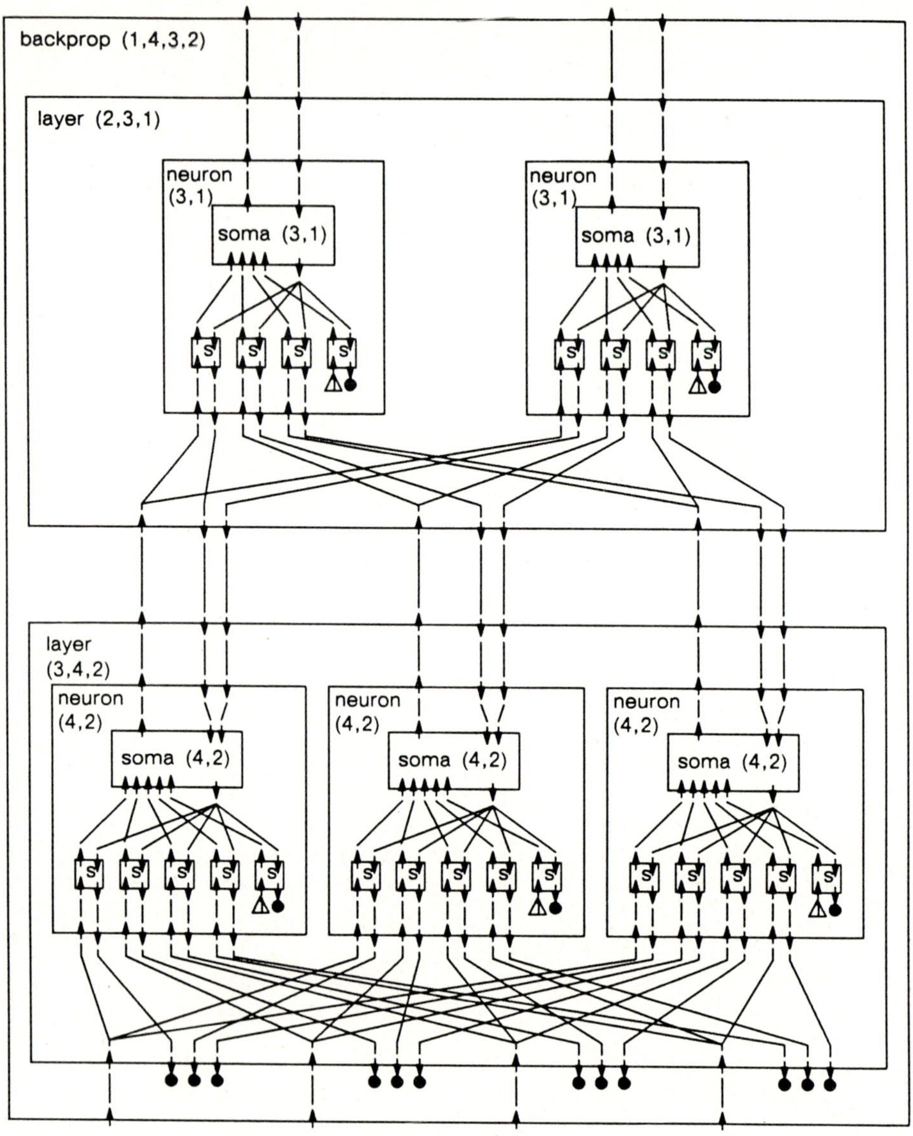

Figure 2 – Schematic representation of a complete backpropagation network based on its description in language N. In this instanciation of the "backprop" model, the network has 1 hidden layer, 4 entries, 3 neurons on the hidden layer, and 2 neurons on the output layer.
NB : "s" stands for "synapse" in the figure.

Reference

1. Angéniol, B., Le Texier, J. Y., Mateu J. B. : SLOGAN : an object-oriented language for neural network specification. To appear in the Acts of the nEuro '88 Conference at ESPCI Paris, June 1988.

Neural Networks Dynamics

Eric Goles *
Departamento de Matematicas
Escuela de Ingenieria, U. de Chile
Casilla 170/3, Correo-3
Santiago, Chile
e-mail: egoles at uchcecvm

Abstract. In this paper we study some dynamical aspects of the synchronous update of Neural Networks. We exhibit Lyapunov Functionals for discrete neural networks (binary states) and also for continuous local rules. By doing so we prove, in the context of binary networks, the convergence to cycles of period one or two for symmetric weights. Also we prove that "almost symmetric" Neural Networks admit large cycles (non-bounded in the size,n, of the array) and that the synchronous update with symmetric weights may have an exponential transient time in order to reach a fixed point. Finally, for continuous local rules we give the explicit expression of Lyapunov operators for synchronous and sequential iterations and we characterize the network dynamics for periodic trajectories.

1. Introduction

In this paper we present some results about the dynamic behaviour of Neural Networks. This class was introduced by Mc. Culloch and Pitts [19] to modelize the nervous system. They proved essentially that such a network may simulate any finite automaton and, if an infinite number of sites is available, a Turing Machine. Also, this model is the origin of the mathematical concept of Regular Language. In this context, Kleene proved the equivalence between these two concepts [18]. Moreover, Mc. Culloch's model was used in the sixties to develop a neural learning algorithm called the "Perceptron" [20]. Furthermore, in the last five years this class has had an enormous development, either theoretical or in applications. Theoretical studies have been possible by using tools coming from computer science and also by interpreting this class, in the particular case of symmetric links, with the spin glass model [16] . From the conception of a more powerful procedure for learning tasks in a neural array, the Back Propagation algorithm [21], interesting applications have been developed for several problems concerning for instance: learning, associative memories, image restoration and discrete optimization. More information about applications may be seen in [2,5,21].

A Neural Network may be formalized as follows; given a nxn matrix W and a n-dimensional vector b we define:

$$y = \mathbf{1} [W x - b] \tag{1.1}$$

where x and y are vectors in the hypercube $\{0,1\}^n$.

The entries of W may be interpreted as the synaptic weights and b as the threshold values of the formal neurons.
Each component, $\mathbf{1}[v]$, of the function $\mathbf{1}[u_1, .. ,u_n] = (\mathbf{1}[u_i])$ is defined as follows:

---

* Partially supported by FNC/89, DTI U. Chile, EHEI U. Paris-V and F. Andes-Chile/89

NATO ASI Series, Vol. F 68
Neurocomputing
Edited by F. Fogelman Soulié and J. Hérault

$$\mathbf{1}[\,v\,] = \begin{cases} 0 & \text{if } v < 0 \\ 1 & \text{otherwise} \end{cases}$$

We may see the previous network as an automata network by taking the local version of (1.1) :

$$y_i = \mathbf{1}[\sum_{j=1}^{n} w_{ij} x_j - b_i] \qquad (1.2)$$

A dynamics may be introduced in several ways: sequential, with memory, synchronous, etc. The most used update modes are the sequential and the synchronous one. The former consists in updating each site one at a time in a prescribed order. The latter consist in updating all the sites in parallel, i.e:

$$x_i(t+1) = \mathbf{1}[\sum_{j=1}^{n} w_{ij} x_j(t) - b_i] \qquad (1.3)$$

As was mencionned above an arbitrary neural net is a very powerful computing machine, hence in order to study the dynamical behaviour some hypothesis on the network regularity are needed. In the context of applications and the classical theory of cellular automata, a relevant assumption is to consider neural networks whose lattice is an undirected graph, i.e. the interconnection weigths verify: $w_{ij} = w_{ji}$ for any couple of sites in the lattice. With this hypothesis and by assuming that the diagonal terms w_{ii} are non-negative, it was proved in [7] that the sequential iteration only admits fixed points. Later, in the context of modelisation of associative memories this result was also obtained by using the analogy between this network and the spin glass problem [16]. In fact the author proved that a random sequential update on Neural Networks with a Hebb connection matrix admits the Ising Hamiltonian:

$$H(x) = - \sum_{i,j=1}^{n} w_{ij} x_i x_j \qquad (1.4)$$

and that it is decreasing. That same formalism was used in [3] to study the transient length of sequential iteration.
For the synchronous update (1.3) with a symmetric interconnection matrix, it was proved that the dynamical behaviour is very simple: convergence to fixed points and/or two cycles from any initial configuration in the hypercube [6]. Furthermore, in [13] we associate to this network a Lyapunov operator driving its dynamics and by doing so, we give bounds for the transient phase; i.e. the time needed to reach the steady state. It is important to point out that for the two update modes the symmetry is a crucial hypothesis to characterize the dynamics. When W is no longer symmetric we may yet obtain Lyapunov operators in some particular cases; e.g. W being an antisymmetric matrix [9], but Hamiltonian or Lyapunov functionals usually do not work for more general interconnection matrices. A more surprising result, that we shall explain in the paper, is the fact that, instead of assuming symmetry, the convergence time to steady states may be exponential in the size, n, of the network [14,15].
Also we study the dynamics when the local transition functions are monotone, i.e. each site of the network changes its state according to a non-decreasing local rule. In this context we have the sigmoid and the multithreshold functions, the BSB model, etc. For this class of networks we usually have an infinite set of states (for instance [-1, +1] for sigmoidal functions and the BSB model) then it is not possible to prove that any synchronous or sequential trajectory always converges to periodic steady states. For continuous symmetric Neural Networks we exhibit Lyapunov operators driving their synchronous or sequential dynamics and by doing so we prove that the periods, if they exist, are one or two [4,5,11]. The fact to have Lyapunov functionals for continuous rules is important for instance to determine local optima in some Combinatorial Optimisation Problems [17].

2. Dynamics of Discrete Neural Networks

Let us consider the synchronous iteration scheme (1.3) where matrix W is symmetric. Under this condition it was proved in [6] that the network only has fixed points or two cycles as steady states. The idea of the proof is the following: since the phase space is finite (only 2^n binary vectors) and the iteration scheme is deterministic, any initial configuration converges, in a finite time, to a cycle of period T given by { x(0), x(1), ..., x(T-1) } where x(t+1) is the configuration at time t+1 obtained by the synchronous update of configuration x(t). We define the quantity:

$$V(x_i, x_j) = w_{ij} \sum_{t=0}^{T-1} x_i(t)\,(x_j(t+1) + x_j(t-1)) \tag{2.1}$$

where the indexes t are taken modulo T and , for any site i, $x_i = (x_i(0), ..., x_i(T-1))$. Since the matrix W is symmetric , we get:

$$\sum_{i,j=1}^{n} V(x_i, x_j) = 0 \tag{2.2}$$

From the definition of the local update rule, if the local vector x_i has a period larger than two, then:

$$\sum_{j=1}^{n} V(x_i, x_j) < 0 \tag{2.3}$$

and this previous quantity vanishes when x_i is one or two periodic [5,6].

The proof of property (2.3) is non trivial. The crucial trick consists to determine a maximal modulo-two partition of the support of vector x_i ; i.e. the sets of indexes as follows:

$$\{ t, t+2, t+4, ..., t+2q \ / \ x_i(t+2k) = 1 \text{ for } 0 \le k \le q, \text{ and } x_i(t-2) = x_i(t+2q+2) = 0 \}$$

and to verify that for each partition set the quantity (2.3) is negative [6,7] .

Clearly, from properties (2.2) and (2.3), it is easy to conclude that the only admissible periods are one (fixed points) or two.

For the sequential update a similar operator is determined :

$$V(x_i, x_j) = \begin{cases} w_{ij} \sum_{t=0}^{T-1} x_i(t)\,(x_j(t) - x_j(t-1)) & \text{if } i<j \\ 0 & \text{if } i=j \\ w_{ij} \sum_{t=0}^{T-1} x_i(t)\,(x_j(t+1) - x_j(t)) & \text{if } i>j \end{cases} \tag{2.4}$$

and, under the non-negative diagonal assumption, we proved, in a similar way, that there exist only fixed points [7].

Previous operators may be seen as the difference of two local potentials such that in the steady state they are invariant. From that it is not difficult to determine local quantities which drive, not only the steady state, but all the dynamics of the network. These new expressions are similar to the Hamiltonian of spin glasses evaluated in two succesive time steps for the synchronous iteration [12,13], and in one step, t, for the sequential one. They are noted E_{syn} and E_{seq} respectively:

$$E_{syn}(x(t)) = -\sum_{i=0}^{n} x_i(t) \sum_{j=0}^{n} w_{ij} x_j(t-1) + \sum_{i=0}^{n} b_i (x_i(t) + x_i(t-1)) \tag{2.5}$$

$$E_{seq}(x(t)) = -\frac{1}{2}\sum_{i=0}^{n} x_i(t) \sum_{j=0}^{n} w_{ij} x_j(t) + \sum_{i=0}^{n} b_i x_i(t) \tag{2.6}$$

From previous assumptions, E_{syn} and E_{seq} are Lyapunov operators for synchronous and sequential trajectories respectively and it is easy to see that they are strictly decreasing in the transient phase [5,12,13]. For instance, for a synchronous trajectory $\{x(t)\}$, since W is a symmetric matrix, we get:

$\Delta_t E = E_{syn}(x(t)) - E_{syn}(x(t-1)) =$

$$\Delta_t E = -\sum_{i=1}^{n} (x_i(t) - x_i(t-2)) \{ \sum_{j=1}^{n} w_{ij} x_j(t-1) - b_i \} \tag{2.7}$$

and the i-th term in (2.7) verifies:

$$(\Delta_t E)_i = -(x_i(t) - x_i(t-2)) \{ \sum_{j=1}^{n} w_{ij} x_j(t-1) - b_i \} \leq 0 \tag{2.8}$$

Furthermore, since it is always possible to assume that $\sum_j w_{ij} u_j \neq 0$ for any site i and any vector u in the hypercube [4,13]: $x_i(t) \neq x_i(t-2)$ implies $\Delta_t E < 0$. Hence, E_{syn} is a Lyapunov functional for the synchronous update and it is strictly decreasing in the transient phase. From that the two-cycle behaviour follows directly.

For the particular application of Associative Memories (i.e.W being a pattern correlation matrix and $b = 0$) the sequential energy was introduced in [16]. In a more general framework it was studied in [3].
When matrix W is no longer symmetric, the synchronous iteration admits non bounded cycles. Let us take the network given by:

$$x_0(t+1) = \mathbf{1}[\ w x_{n-1}(t) + (w - \varepsilon)\, x_1(t) - w\ ]$$

$$x_i(t+1) = \mathbf{1}[\ (w - i\varepsilon)\, x_{i-1}(t) + (w - (i+1)\varepsilon)\, x_{i+1}(t) - (w - i\varepsilon)\ ] \quad \text{for } 1 \leq i \leq n-2 \tag{2.9}$$

$$x_{n-1}(t+1) = \mathbf{1}[\ (w - (n-1)\varepsilon)\, x_{n-2}(t) + (w - n\varepsilon)\, x_0(t) - (w - (n-1)\varepsilon)\ ]$$

where w is a positive integer and $0 < \varepsilon < 1/n$.

It is not difficult to see that the matrix W coding scheme (2.9) is "almost symmetric"; i.e. all the entries are symmetric except the couple $w_{0,n-1}$ and $w_{n-1,0}$ but the difference of these two entries may be set arbitrarily small: $| w_{0,n-1} - w_{n-1,0} | = (n-1)\varepsilon$.

On the other hand the configuration $x(0) = (1,0, \ldots , 0)$ belongs to a cycle of period n. Thus the periodicity is non-bounded in the size of the network. For instance, for n = 6 with weights and thresholds given by:

$w_1 = w-\varepsilon,\ w_2 = w-2\varepsilon,\ w_3 = w-3\varepsilon,\ w_4 = w-4\varepsilon,\ w_5 = w-5\varepsilon,\ w_{05} = w,\ w_{50} = w-6\varepsilon$
$h_0 = w, h_1 = w_1, h_2 = w_2, h_3 = w_3, h_4 = w_4, h_5 = w_5.$

By taking $w = 1$, $\varepsilon = 1/36$ and the initial condition (1, 0, 0, 0, 0, 0) we get a 6-cycle.

In a similar way it is possible to build a one dimensional almost symmetric lattice which has non-bounded periods for the sequential update [5].

Equations (2.5) and (2.6) may be used to bound the transient time. In fact, since the hypercube is a finite set, these quantities are bounded. Let ε be the minimun of $|\Delta E|$, hence one may bound the transient time by $O((\|W\| + \|b\|)/\varepsilon)$, where $\|W\| = \sum_{ij} |w_{ij}|$ and $\|b\| = \sum_i |b_i|$. Clearly the bound depends on the size of the interconnection matrix and vector b. For integral matrices (i.e. $w_{ij} \in Z$) the bound is reached. In this case $\varepsilon = \min|\Delta E| = 1$ and for the synchronous update the bound is given by:

$$T_r \leq \frac{1}{2}(\|W\| + 3e - n) \tag{2.10}$$

where e is the number of even lines in matrix W

A Neural Network that reaches the bound (2.10) is the following:

$x_0(t+1) = \mathbf{1}[\, x_1(t) - 1/2\,]$

$x_i(t+1) = \mathbf{1}[\, x_{i-1}(t) + x_{i+1}(t) - 1/2\,]$ for $1 \leq i \leq n-2$

$x_{n-1}(t+1) = \mathbf{1}[\, x_{n-2}(t) + x_{n-1}(t) - 1/2\,]$

Clearly $\|W\| = 2n-1$ and $e = n-1$, hence the bound is $2(n-1)$. On the other hand, the initial configuration $x(0) = (1,0, \ldots , 0)$ has this same transient time $T_r = 2(n-1)$.
Since expression (2.10) depends on matrix W, even in the symmetric case we may expect that there exist large transients. One may build such networks by recurrence. Let us take the couple (W, b) in R^2 given by: $w_{11} = -1$, $w_{12} = w_{21} = 1$, $w_{22} = 1$ and $b_1 = -1/2$, $b_2 = 1$. It is direct that its synchronous trajectory is: **(0,0)** → **(1,0)** → **(0,1)** → **(1,1)**, where **(1,1)** is a fixed point. It is important to point out that the trajectory travels through all the vectors of the two-hypercube. By adding three sites to the network, one may travel through the 3-hypercube, it suffices to take the couple (W, b) :

$$W = \begin{vmatrix} -1 & 1 & 1 & -2 & 1 \\ 1 & 1 & 1 & -3 & 2 \\ 1 & 1 & 0 & 6 & 0 \\ -2 & -3 & 6 & 0 & 4 \\ 1 & 2 & 0 & 4 & 0 \end{vmatrix} \qquad b = (-1/2, 1, 2, 1, 4)$$

This network may be visualized as follows:

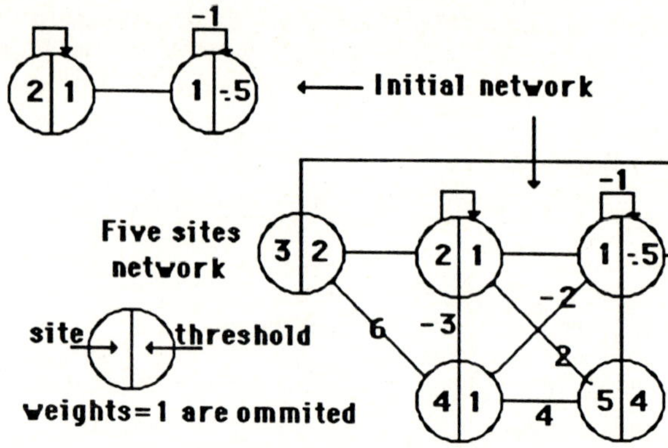

Figure1. Neural Network whose synchronous dynamics travels through the 3-hypercube

The new sites { 3, 4, 5 } are used as control units to repeat twice the dynamics on the 2-hypercube. The dynamics for the initial condition x(0) = (0, ... , 0) is the following:

3	**2**	**1**	**4**	**5**	site number
0	0	0	0	0	
0	0	1	0	0	
0	1	0	0	0	
0	1	1	0	0	
1	1	1	0	0	
1	1	1	1	0	
1	0	0	1	1	
1	0	1	1	1	
1	1	0	1	1	
1	**1**	**1**	**1**	**1**	fixed point

Table1. Synchronous dynamics travel through the 3-hypercube

The sites { 1,2,3 } travel through the 3-hypercube. For that, the 4-th site is on if and only if the first travel of the 2-hypercube is finished. Also, it switches off the sites {1,2}. On the other hand, site-5 rules out all the external weights to sites one and two. By doing so these sites repeat the initial trajectory on the 2-hypercube.
From this it may be proved by recurrence [4,14,15] that it is always possible to double the transient lengths only by adding three cells; i.e. with n cell we may build a symmetric network such that its transient time to reach the fixed point (1,...,1) is $O(2^{n/3})$. On the other hand, since we may always simulate a parallel dynamics by a sequential one by doubling the number of sites without changing the symmetry assumption [15,23], we also exhibit exponential transient trajectories for the sequential update. For the previous construction, the sequential transient time is $O(2^{n/6})$.
As a remark, the fact to add three cells in the inductive process is imposed to maintain the symmetry of matrix W. Otherwise it is easy to build longer transient trajectories.

3. Continuous Neural Networks

In this paragraph we shall study Neural Networks with continuous local functions. More precisely , each automaton has a real continuous function, f, strictly increasing on an interval]a, b[and constant outside. For instance, f may be a truncated sigmoid, a BSB model, etc.
As in previous paragraphs, the local equations are the following:

$$y_i = f\left(\sum_{j=1}^{n} w_{ij} x_j - b_i\right) \tag{3.1}$$

We define the total weighted input as follows:

$$A_i = \Sigma_{j=1,n}\, w_{ij}\, x_j - b_i \tag{3.2}$$

Then the synchronous update is given by: $x_i(t+1) = f(A_i(t))$ (3.3)

Without loss of generality we shall suppose that $a < 0 < b$ and $f(0) = 0$. By assuming that the interconnection matrix W is symmetric we may associate to any synchronous trajectory, $\{x(t)\}$, a Lyapunov functional given by:

$$E_{syn}(x(t)) = \sum_{i,j=1}^{n} w_{ij} x_i(t)\, x_j(t-1) - \sum_{i=1}^{n} \left\{ \int_0^{A_i(t)} f(s)\, ds + \int_0^{A_i(t-1)} f(s)\, ds \right\} \tag{3.4}$$

In fact, since W is symmetric we get:

$$\Delta_t E_{syn} = E_{syn}(x(t)) - E_{syn}(x(t-1)) = \sum_{i,j=1}^{n} w_{ij} x_i(t-1)\,[\,x_j(t) - x_j(t-2)] - \sum_{i=1}^{n} \int_{A_i(t-2)}^{A_i(t)} f(s)\, ds$$

$$= \sum_{i=1}^{n} f(A_i(t-2))\,[\,A_i(t) - A_i(t-2)] - \sum_{i=1}^{n} \int_{A_i(t-2)}^{A_i(t)} f(s)\, ds$$

From the mean value theorem we have:

$$\Delta_t E_{syn} = \sum_{i=1}^{n} \{\, f(A_i(t-2))\,[\,A_i(t) - A_i(t-2)] - f(z_i)\,[\,A_i(t) - A_i(t-2)]\}$$

where $z_i \in\ ]\,A_i(t-2), A_i(t)\,[$. Hence:

$$\Delta_t E_{syn} = \sum_{i=1}^{n} [\,A_i(t) - A_i(t-2)]\,[f(A_i(t-2)) - f(z_i)\,]$$

since f is increasing, it follows that $\Delta_t E \le 0$. That is to say, E_{syn} is a Lyapunov functional.

It is not difficult to see that, since $f(0) = 0$ we may write equation (3.4) as follows:

$$E_{syn}(x(t)) = -\sum_{i,j=1}^{n} w_{ij} x_i(t)\, x_j(t-1) + \sum_{i=1}^{n} b_i\,[\,x_i(t) + x_i(t-1)\,] +$$

$$+ \sum_{i=1}^{n} \left\{ \int_0^{x_i(t)} f^{-1}(s)\, ds + \int_0^{x_i(t-1)} f^{-1}(s)\, ds \right\} \tag{3.5}$$

Similarly, when the matrix W is symmetric and its diagonal is non-negative (i.e. $w_{ii} \geq 0$) we determine a Lyapunov functional for the sequential update:

$$E_{seq}(x(t)) = -\frac{1}{2}\sum_{i,j=1}^{n} w_{ij} x_i(t) x_j(t) + \sum_{i=1}^{n} \{ \int_0^{x_i(t)} f^{-1}(s)\, ds + b_i x_i(t) \} \tag{3.6}$$

Expression (3.6) is similar to the Lyapunov functional given by Hopfield in the particular case of a sigmoid local function [17]. The integral term of (3.5) and (3.6) may be considered as a perturbation for the quadratic Lyapunov functionals obtained in paragraph 2 for the discrete case (binary states).
Clearly, since f is not necessarily a discrete function, the synchronous iteration does not always converge to fixed points or two cycles, but with the same arguments as in the discrete case we conclude, by using expressions (3.4) or (3.5), that if the trajectory converges to a cycle, its period must be one or two [4,11]. On the other hand, for the sequential iteration, under the previous hypothesis there exist only fixed points [4, 11].

Lyapunov functional may also be obtained for non-strictly decreasing functions [4,5,8] such as multithreshold local rules, i.e.:

$$f_i(x) = a_k \quad \text{iff} \quad b_k \leq \Sigma_{j=1,n} w_{ij} < b_{k+1} \quad \text{for } k = 0, \ldots, p-1 \text{ and } i = 1, \ldots, n$$

where the state set is given by the real numbers: $a_0 < a_1 < a_2 < \ldots\ldots < a_{p-1}$ and the threshold values are given by: $b_0 = -\infty < b_1 \leq b_2 \leq \ldots\ldots \leq b_{p-1} \leq b_p = +\infty$

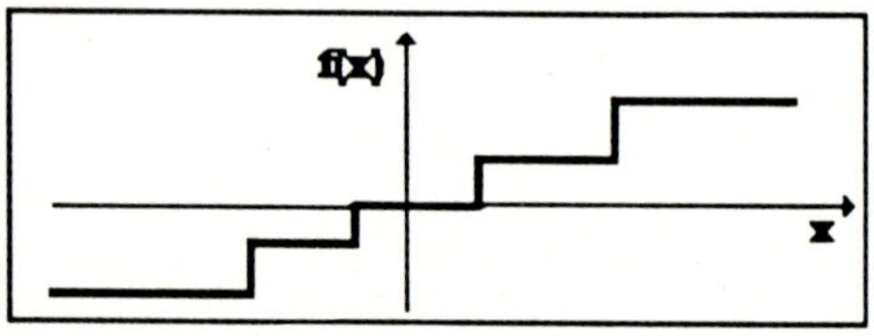

Figure2. Multithreshold local function with five states.

In fact there exist Lyapunov operators for any symmetric Neural Network with monotone local rules. The proof is similar to previous cases but longer [4,5,11].

4. Conclusions

We have presented some exact results on the dynamical behaviour of Neural Networks. These results have been possible because the networks studied here have a regular interconnection structure, i.e. a symmetric matrix. For this class we exhibit Lyapunov operators driving the network dynamic and by doing so we characterize the periodic and the transient behaviour.The general problem to characterize the dynamics for any structure of interconnection weights is not possible because Neural Networks may simulate any finite automaton or a Turing Machine for infinite arrays. Nevertheless, we think that some others regularities on the weights may be studied in a similar way. For instance, we conjecture that if any interconnection link (i, j) belongs to a three circuit then the periodicity of the synchronous network dynamics is three. On the other hand, from the fact that continuous Neural Networks have the same periods under the symmetry assumption, the 2-periodic behaviour for the synchronous update does not depend on the cardinality of the state set but only on the local threshold function and the parallel update.

An other generalization of our approach consists in taking non-linear arguments for the local threshold functions as follows:

$$f_i(x) = \mathbf{1}[\sum_{j_1,\ldots,j_s=1}^{n} w_{j_1 j_2 \ldots j_s} x_{j_1} x_{j_2} \ldots x_{j_s}] \qquad (4.1)$$

In this situation we assume a generalized symmetry of weights:

$$w_{ij_1 \ldots j_s} = w_{p(ij_1 \ldots j_s)} \qquad (4.2)$$

where p is an arbitrary permutation of the indexes. Hypothesis (4.2) generalizes the symmetry. In fact for linear arguments we obtain $w_{ij} = w_{ji}$.
For the sequential update of (4.1) we also assume a non-negative diagonal property; i.e.

$$w_{ij_1 \ldots j_s} = 0 \qquad (4.3)$$

if there exists indexes m, k such that $j_m = j_k$

which corresponds to $w_{ii} = 0$ in the linear case.

Under conditions (4.2) and (4.3) it is easy to see that the sequential update admits the following Lyapunov Operator:

$$E(x) = -\sum_{j_1,\ldots,j_s=1}^{n} a_{j_1 j_2 \ldots j_s} x_i x_{j_1} x_{j_2} \ldots x_{j_s} \qquad (4.4)$$

And, from that, it is direct to infer that any initial condition converges to fixed points.

The study of the synchronous update on this model seems difficult and we do not know energy operators. Furthermore, when the argument is a conbination of terms with different polynomial degrees it is possible to build networks which, under previous assumptions, admit n-cycles for the synchronous iteration [5].

References

[1] Bienenstock E., Fogelman-Soulie F. Weisbuch G., Disordered Systems and Biological Organisation, Procc Les Houches, NATO ASI series, Springer Verlag, 1986

[2] Fogelman-Soulie F., Robert Y., Tchuente M., Automata Networks in Computer Science, Manchester Univ. Press, 1987

[3] Fogelman-Soulie F., Goles E., Weisbuch G., Transient length in sequential iteration of threshold functions, Disc. Appl. Maths., 6, 95-98, 1983

[4] Fogelman-Soulie F., Goles E., Martinez S., Mejia C., Energy functionals in Neural Networks with continuous local functions, Res. Rep. EHEI, Paris-V, 1988, submitted to Complex Systems

[5] Goles E., Martinez S., Dynamics on Generalized Neural Networks, to appear in Kluber Pub. (ex Reidel), 1990

[6] Goles E., Olivos J., Comportement periodique des fonctions a seuil binaires et applications Disc. Appl. Maths., 3, 93-105, 1981

[7] Goles E., Fixed point behaviour of threshold functions, SIAM J. on Disc. and Alg. Meths., 4, 529-531, 1982

[8] Goles E., Dynamics on Positive Automata Networks, Theor. Comp.Sci., 41,19-32, 1985

[9] Goles E., Antisymmetric Neural Networks, Disc. Applied Maths., 13, 97-100, 1986

[10] Goles E., Martinez S., Properties on positive functions and the dynamics of associated automata networks, Disc. Appl. Maths., vol 18, 39-46, 1987

[11] Goles E., Martinez S., Lyapunov functionals for Automata Networks defined by ciclically monotone functions, Res. Rep., Dep. Mat., U. de Chile, 1987, submitted to SIAM J. Disc.Maths.

[12] Goles E., Vichniac G., Lyapunov functions for parallel neural networks, in Neural Networks for Computing, Snowbird 1986, Denker ed., Am. Inst. Phys. , 151, 165-181,1986

[13] Goles E., Fogelman-Soulie F., Pellegrin D., Decreasing energy functions as a tool for studying threshold functions, Disc. Applied Maths., 12, 261-277, 1985

[14] Goles E., Olivos J., The convergence of symmetric threshold automata, Inf. and Control, vol 51, 2, 98-100, 1981

[15] Goles E., Martinez S., Exponential transient classes of symmetric neural networks for synchronous and sequential updating, Res Rep. Dep. Matematicas, U. de Chile, 1989, submitted to Neural Networks.

[16] Hopfield J.J., Neural Networks and physical systems with emergent collective computational abilities, Proc. Nat. Acad. Sci, USA 79, 2554-58, 1982

[17] Hopfield J.J.,Tank D.W., Neural Computation of Decisions in Optimization Problems, Biol. Cybern., 52, 141-152, 1985

[18] Klenne S.C., Representation of events in nerve nets and finite automata, in Automata Studies, Shannon C. E., Mac Carthy J. eds., Princeton Univ. Press, 1956

[19] Mc. Culloch W., Pitts W., A logical calculus of the ideas immanent in nervous activity, Bull. of Math. Biophys., 5, 1943

[20] Rosenblatt F., Principles of Neurodynamics, Spartan, Washington, 1962

[21] Rumelhart D. E., Hinton G., Williams R. J., Learning Integral Representation by Error Propagation, in Parallel Distributed Proccesing, MIT Press, Vol 1, 318-362, 1986

[22] Shingai R., Maximun period of 2-dimensional neural networks, Inf. and Control 41, 324-341,1979

[23] Tchuente M., Sequential simulation of parallel iterations and applications, Theor. Comp. Sci., 48, 135-144, 1986

DYNAMICAL ANALYSIS OF CLASSIFIER SYSTEMS

M. Compiani, D. Montanari, R. Serra, P. Simonini
Enidata, Via Aldo Moro 38 - 40127 Bologna (Italy)

Abstract

Classifier systems use both dynamical and inferential operations in order to perform complex tasks. Their relationship with neural networks is briefly discussed. While dynamical features are crucial for learning, we investigate their role in the solutions which are finally discovered by the system, showing that some truly dynamical solutions exist and that they can perform a specific task with a smaller number of classifiers than purely "inferential" solutions. The stability of the rules under the action of genetic operators is also briefly discussed.

1 Classifier systems, dynamical systems and Artificial Intelligence

Connectionist models are particularly attractive, because of their properties of robustness against various kinds of noise or damages and of their capabilities for adaptive learning. They therefore provide a promising approach to problems which are very hard for classical AI.

Similar features of robustness and adaptivity can be found also in other, non neurally inspired dynamical systems. In this paper we will discuss some features of classifier systems, which have been proposed in order to exploit the usefulness of genetic algorithms in Artificial Intelligence [Holland, 1986,Holland *et al.*, 1986].

Classifier systems are particularly interesting because they take advantage of both classical Artificial Intelligence techniques and the theory of dynamical systems; two mechanisms are in fact at work, one based upon matching and inferencing, the other upon dynamical evolution equations [Serra 1989]. Moreover, they allow a straightforward introduction of *a priori* domain knowledge, which is necessary in several complex tasks. This makes classifier systems much appealing since the introduction of previous knowledge is still a much debated problem in current research on connectionist models [Fogelman *et al.*].

Classifier systems consist of

NATO ASI Series, Vol. F 68
Neurocomputing
Edited by F. Fogelman Soulié and J. Hérault

- a population of rules of the condition/action type (classifiers)
- a set of numerical variables (called strengths) associated to the classifiers, which measure their "fitness"
- a message list (ML)
- a set of input devices (detectors)
- a set of output devices (effectors)

At each cycle, all the classifiers check in parallel whether their conditions are matched by messages present on the ML and, if it is so, they try to post a new message specified by their action part. Also input/output information is coded in the form of special messages.

Classifiers trying to post messages enter a competition process, where winners are selected either in a probabilistic way or according to a deterministic algorithm involving a nonlinear function of their fitness.

Learning takes place in a supervised way, according to two different learning mechanisms which operate on different time scales. The "teacher" directly reinforces or weakens the fitness of the rules leading to correct or incorrect answers respectively. The back–propagation of fitness changes from the last rules of each chain (i.e., the rule which posted an output message) to the preceding ones is achieved by the so-called bucket–brigade algorithm. This gives rise to the fast learning dynamics, the population of classifiers being fixed. Analytical considerations on the asymptotic behaviour of the bucket–brigade can be found in [Compiani *et al.*, 1989b].

A slower dynamics runs in parallel with the bucket–brigade and provides the classifier system with a mechanism for changing the population of rules, by means of suitable genetic operators.

Classifier systems and neural networks are both dynamical systems for AI applications. Their relationship can be elucidated by building an "image network" of a classifier system, on the basis of the correspondence

- formal neurons / messages
- connections / classifiers
- firing / being in the message list

In both cases learning takes place through modifications of the connection strengths. However, classifier systems display a less collective activation mechanism than neural nets. It is worth noticing that, while most neural models do not provide means for modifying their own structure (i.e. creating new connections), classifier systems accomplish this task through genetics. A detailed comparison of classifier systems and neural networks has been carried out elsewhere [Compiani *et al.*, 1989a].

A major reason of interest in classifier systems is that they implement a mixing of dynamics and inferencing. Dynamics is always necessary in the learning phase, where the bucket-brigade algorithms determines the strength distribution which, in turn, is used by genetic algorithms in order to choose the most appropriate partners for mating.

An important question is whether the dynamical properties of classifier systems can be exploited also in the "final solution" which is devised by the system, i.e. if mixing dynamics and inferencing may be an effective way to solve problems.

2 A taxonomy of solutions

We have tested the capabilities of classifier systems in a particular task domain, proposed by [Robertson *et al.*, 1988], using the CFS-C simulation package [Riolo 1986]. Starting with a random set of classifiers, the system is cyclically fed with a finite sequence of letters which are "read" one at a time. The system is expected to learn to predict correctly (after a suitable learning phase) the next coming letter in the sequence on the ground of the currently read letter.

Two cases can be identified: *i)* Markovian (or "unambiguous") sequences, where knowing the current letter determines the following (like, e.g., $A\ B\ C\ D$), and *ii)* non–Markovian (or "ambiguous") sequences of the type $A\ A\ B$

The first class of sequences poses an hetero–associative task, which can be solved associating a different output with each different input.

The second class of sequences forces the system to search for a more sophisticated strategy in order to deal with the ambiguity, due to the fact that the same symbol "A" is followed by two different letters. In fact the system must now develop the capability of memorizing the previous readings in order to successfully discriminate between the two occurrences of the letter "A".

In the following we will concentrate upon the latter case, which is much harder and interesting. Starting from an initially random population of classifiers, the system usually succeeds in solving this task, for short sequences where the knowledge of the current and of the previous letter is sufficient to determine the next one. Occasionally, the system does not succeed in achieving the desired disambiguation, due to population dynamics effects in the learning phase, which have been discussed elsewhere [Compiani *et al.*, 1989b,Compiani *et al.*, 1989c].

We will now describe some different kinds of solutions which are discovered by the system, starting from an initially random population of rules, with reference to the simplest possible ambiguous sequence (i.e., $A\ A\ B$). The solutions will be described here in plain words (for a detailed description, see [Compiani *et al.*, 1989b].

The first kind of solution may be called "anthropomorphic", since appears "natural" to a human observer. The strength dynamics was necessary to reach it but it is no longer essential after learning. This solution is based upon the following classifiers;

- if input is A and if the previous letter was B then guess A
- if input is A then remember A
- if input is B then guess A
- if input is B then remember B
- if input is A and if the previous letter was A then guess B

The system keeps track of the reading made on the previous step , through a process of self–organization, by generating an internal message which represents a "memory of the past".

Another solution may be appropriately called "dynamical", since it makes an essential use of the competition mechanism, and it provides a tight coupling between inferential and dynamical features. The layout is the following:

- if input is A then guess A
- if input is A then remember A

- if input is B then guess A
- if input is A and if the previous letter was A then guess B

The first classifier does not make use of internal messages, and it would make mistakes, if it were allowed to post guesses whenever it matches the input message. But if both the current and the previous letters are A, it must compete with the last classifier. Due to the form of the competition equations, the latter prevails thus leading to the correct prediction.

There exists also another kind of solution ("symbiosis"), which is also dynamical in nature and which is based upon a cyclic oscillation of the strengths, synchronized with the external signal, which resembles well known phenomena in physical oscillators. The relevant rules involved are:

- if input is A then guess A
- if input is B then guess A
- if input is A or if the previous guess was A then guess B

In this case, no explicit internal message is present. The first and the last classifier always match the input message, if it is an A. The first and third classifiers' fitnesses oscillate periodically, with a frequency equal to that of the environment, in such a way that the correct one prevails at the right time.

Different solutions, which rely upon "hidden variables" for disambiguation, are described in [Compiani *et al.*, 1989b].

3 Conclusions

We have shown that truly "dynamical" solutions are actually developed by classifier systems in the task domain considered. These dynamical solutions can perform the disambiguation task with a smaller number of rules than anthropomorphic solutions, which are based upon inferencing only. On the other hand, dynamical solutions are less easy to read, and "explanation" may be more complicated in this case.

A crucial issue for the performance regards the stability of the knowledge, either spontaneously developed or introduced *a priori* by a knowledge engineer. In this connection it is important to elucidate several mechanisms which can destabilize the solution devised by the system. Particularly dangerous situations occur when the population of classifiers is almost completely composed by subpopulations of rules with the same phenotype, their strengths being almost equalized. In this case, the newborn classifiers, which are generated by a random mechanism, enter the system with a strength which is close to that of the old rules. The latter can therefore be beaten in the competition for firing: an error is produced, whose effect can be amplified by the autocatalytic action of error-triggered genetic operators. The system then enters an instability phase, for some ranges of parameters' values.

Detailed analysis of the problems of stability can be found, in the case of predicting letter sequences, in [Compiani *et al.*, 1989c]. This paper also discusses the importance of several parameters upon the system performance and upon its learning capacity.

References

[Compiani *et al.*, 1989a] Compiani, M., Montanari, D., Serra, R. & Valastro, G. (1989a). Classifier systems and neural networks. In E. Caianiello (Ed.) *Parallel architectures and neural networks*, p. 105. Singapore: World Scientific.

[Compiani *et al.*, 1989b] Compiani, M., Montanari, D., Serra, R. Simonini, P. & Valastro, G. (1989b). *Dynamical systems in Artificial Intelligence: the case of classifier systems.* To appear in R. Pfeifer (ed.) *Connectionism in perspective.* Amsterdam: Elsevier

[Compiani *et al.*, 1989c] Compiani, M., Montanari, D., Serra, R. & Simonini, P. (1989c). *Asymptotic behaviour of classifier systems.* To appear in *Proceedings of the third international conference on genetic algorithms and their applications.* Los Altos: Morgan Kaufmann

[Fogelman *et al.*] Fogelman Soulie, F., Gallinari, P., LeCun, Y., Thiria, S. (in press). Network learning. To appear in Y. Kodratoff & R. Michalski (Eds.) *Machine Learning*, Vol.III.

[Holland, 1986] Holland, J.H. (1986). Escaping Brittleness. In R.S. Michalski et al. (Eds.), *Machine learning. An artificial intelligence approach*, Vol.II (pp.592-623). Los Altos (CA): Morgan Kaufmann

[Holland *et al.*, 1986] Holland, J.H., Holyoak, K.J., Nisbett, R.E. & Thagard, P.R. (1986). *Induction.* Cambridge (MA): MIT Press

[Riolo 1986] Riolo, R. (1986) CFS-C: A package of domain independent subroutines for implementing classifier systems in arbitrary, user-defined environments. Internal report, Logic of Computers Group, University of Michigan.

[Robertson *et al.*, 1988] Robertson, G.G. & Riolo, R. (1988). A tale of two classifier systems. *Machine Learning* 3: 139-160

[Serra 1989] Serra, R. Dynamical systems and expert systems. To appear in R. Pfeifer (ed.) *Connectionism in perspective.* Amsterdam: Elsevier

Neuro-Computing Aspects in Motor Planning & Control

Pietro Morasso, Gianni Vercelli and Renato Zaccaria

University of Genoa, DIST - Department of Computer Science
Via Opera Pia 11A, I-16145 Genoa, Italy

Abstract - *Planning robot movements in an unstructured environment is investigated from the point of view of common sense reasoning as the simulation of a complex dynamical system. We first show how motor redundancy can be solved by simulating passive motion (what we call Passive Motion Paradigm). We then extend this concept in terms of Abstract Force Fields, that allow to express a variety of problems in addition to trajectory formation (force/position control, obstacle avoidance, concurrent tasks, etc.). We show the analogy between this approach and Hopfield nets. We define the notion of Hybrid Motor Schema as the composite ensemble of an analogic component (which consists of the "mental" simulation of model dynamics) and a symbolic component (which contains rules and methods for instantiating the analogic component in a given context: goal, environment, expectations, constraints, ...). Simulation results of preliminary implementations are presented.*

Subfield: Robotics
Keyword: Planning, Common Sense, Redundancy, Complex Dynamics, Potential Fields.

1. Introduction

Planning robot movements in an unstructured environment is a typical problem of dealing with the real world. Planning is not only trajectory formation, but also redundancy, complex 3D modelling, pattern recognition, and knowledge-based representation. All these are aspects of the same problem, in the sense that the complexity of planning should be analyzed in a global manner, and then spread out in a distributed manner using different computational models, or knowledge structures, or schemas, that help us in the comprehension of the domain of the problem.

Humans are *complex dynamical systems*, robots should be: *Redundancy* is the characteristic feature of the human motor system, so only redundant robots should be able to perform complex motor tasks (Morasso et al.,1988). Redundancy comes from an imbalance between the set of independently controllable variables and the set of system variables, while Concurrency stresses the importance of multiple-level computational models when the dimensionality of system grows dramatically. Works on complex dynamical systems use "mapping" approaches that start both from equilibrium dynamics (e.g. spin glasses) and from non-equilibrium dynamics (e.g. reaction-diffusion systems, Steels, 1988).

We investigate how planning actions could be exploited through an hybrid approach, formulated in connectionist terms, and based on analogical models and complex dynamics: the unifying concept we found is called **Abstract Force Fields**, shortly **AFF**.

Trajectory formation, for open and closed kinematic configurations, as well as force generation, can be formulated as a flow of signals in the multiple-constraints satisfaction network that

NATO Advanced Research Workshop "*Neuro Computing: Algorithms, Architectures and Applications*",
Les Arcs, France, February 27 - March 3, 1989.

NATO ASI Series, Vol. F 68
Neurocomputing
Edited by F. Fogelman Soulié and J. Hérault

correspond to a collective evolution towards states of minimum potential energy. The analogy between this approach and connectionist models is obvious, particularly with Hopfield nets and Boltzmann machine. The pattern recognition part of the planning process (e.g. the selection of grasping sites) can be formulated in connectionist terms, as the learned association between shape representations and motion parameters (multi-layer perceptron). Reaching, collision-avoidance, fine grasping tasks could be also formulated in terms of sequential networks (Jordan, 1988).

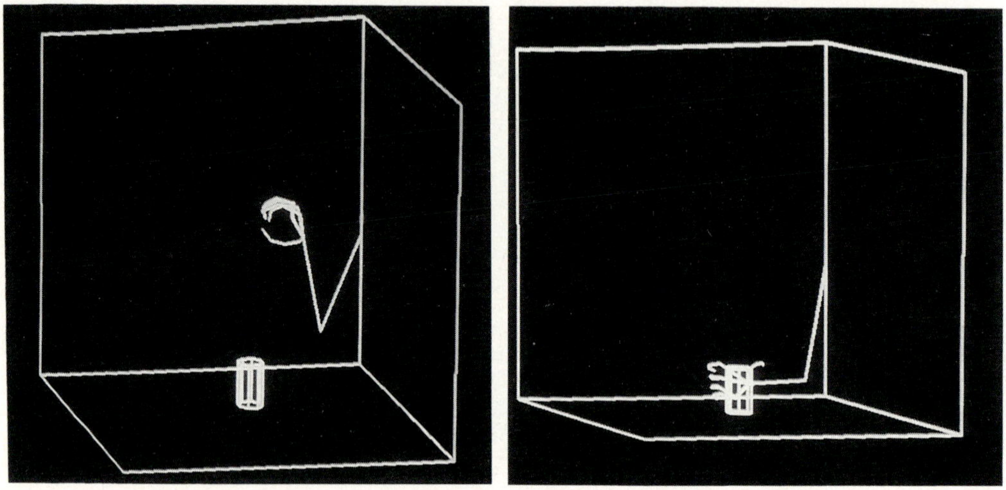

Fig. 1-2 3D-Simulation of a reaching-grasping movement.

2. Complex Dynamics and Abstract Force Fields

Motor Planning and Control (shortly P&C) for complex, human-like, dynamical systems clash with Redundancy and Concurrency. The basic problem is how to coordinate the degrees of freedom and the actuators of a redundant system while carrying out concurrent tasks of highly variable nature. In a previous paper (Mussa Ivaldi et al., 1988), we suggest a general principle for approaching this problem that we call **Passive Motion Paradigm (PMP)**. PMP sounds this way: "*For an action in 3D space incrementally prescribed as a force/displacement vector, displace the attractor posture by the same amount that would result if the vector were applied passively*".

According to this principle, planning a human movement, i.e. generating the synergy of muscle activations, is an internal simulation of passive movement, that is a motor "relaxation" between several different postures. *Postures* are equilibrium configurations that "attract" the different body segments. Postures are coded by the distribution of neuromuscular activity and can store, in this sense, a sort of elastic potential energy.

The starting point to introduce the notion of **AFF** is exactly the elastic nature of human muscles, which are neither pure force generators (like dc motors) nor pure position generators (like stepping motors) but are viscous-elastic actuators with controllable elastic characteristics (rest-length and stiffness). This means that for any distribution of muscle activities we can identify a conservative force field in the configuration space and a corresponding potential function: the point of minimum potential energy is the stable posture encoded by the set of muscle activities. This posture is an *attractor* that can be exploited in order to address the problems listed above. The muscular force field in configuration space is the physical substrate upon which we can build abstract representations (AFF's) necessary to formulate the problems in computational terms.

From the motor planning&control point of view, the *attractor posture* is a representation that can be programmed incrementally (with respect to the *current posture*) to obtain two complementary results in configuration space: generation of prescribed trajectories (if the motion is free) or of prescribed interaction forces (if the intended movement is inhibited by external constraints). The relationship between the two entities is given by the *stiffness matrix*:

$$\tau = K\,\delta q$$

where δq represents a small displacement from an attractor posture, τ is the corresponding restoring force/torque vector and K is the stiffness matrix. The computational device for implementing this concept is an (approximate) internal representation of the muscular force field in terms of a graph of relations among different force/position vectors (Morasso and Mussa Ivaldi 1986, Morasso et al. 1987). The generality of this device is that we can build upon it different representational layers that capture diverse aspects of motor P&C in the same framework. For example, the constraints due to joint limits can be easily accomodated by another AFF where repulsive forces steeply increase the potential function in the neighborhood of forbidden joint configuration regions. The problems that plague force control (e.g. instability) are overcome because interaction forces are not controlled explicitly but arise implicitly from the intrinsic controllable stiffness/compliance of the system.

Other P&C issues are better formulated in 3D space, for example trajectory formation or obstacle avoidance, and this implies a mapping of the AFF between configuration space and 3D space. This mapping must satisfy the principle of invariance of virtual work:

$$\delta q \cdot \tau = \delta x \cdot f$$

where δq and δx are virtual displacements in the two spaces and τ and f are the corresponding force vectors. From this it is possible, in principle, to determine the passive behaviour of the system when a disturbing force f or a passive displacement δx is applied: δq identifies indeed the resulting dislocation from the attractor posture and τ is the corresponding restoring force vector.

The power of the method is threefold: We reduce free movements and interaction movements to the same paradigm, we overcome the redundancy issue (planned trajectories are guided in the direction of minimum potential energy), and we open the window to a variety of generalizations of the $< f \mid \delta x >$ representation. At the basic level, $< f \mid \delta x >$ specifies an attractor that implements the inverse kinematic problem of a (redundant) kinematic chain. More general is the case of a whole humanoid, composed of a set of (possibly closed) kinematic chains: This requires to segment the $< f \mid \delta x >$ representation in order to specify an attractor for each limb of the humanoid. Moreover, obstacle avoidance can be expressed as a repulsive force field emanating from the obstacles, overlapped with the attracting field associated with the target.

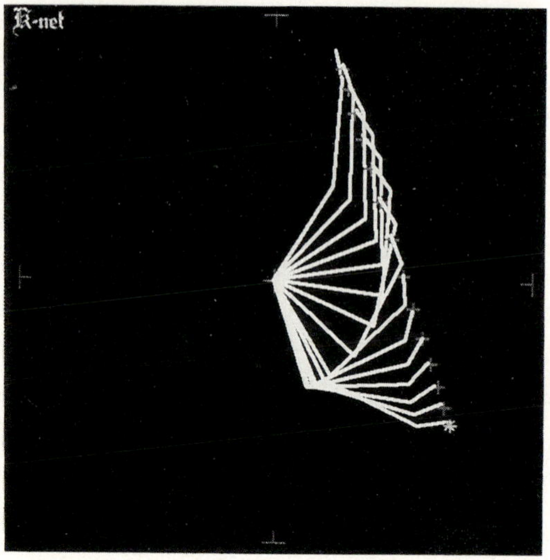

Fig. 3 Redundant arm: open kinematic chain.

The technique of overlapping multiple AFF's (some of them intended to attract and some to repel the motion of the robot) can be extended to the time axis, allowing the smooth composition of complex trajectories driven by discrete instantiation of guiding postures/spatial patterns, in a similar way to the segmentation of continuous speech in overlapped phonemes or of cursive script handwriting in overlapped graphemes. Furthermore, the technique can be used for both off-line planning and on-line correction.

3. Hybrid Motor Schemas

Hybrid motor schemas (HS) are intended to capture the complexity of actions in the real world. Let us consider "grasping", for example. Its structure can be detailed from different points of view:

- There are different grasping modes;
- The shape of objects and their physical nature provide several virtual "handles";
- The layout of the working environment provides constraints on the approach phase and the selection phase.

A grasping schema needs analogic representations for the different grasping modes, parametrized in such a way to adapt them to the specific dimensions of the handles. It also requires rules for selecting grasping modes and parameters according to the context.

While the purpose of activating schemas is usually that of directly producing inferences, the purpose of a hybrid motor schema, such as the grasping schema, is to set up an AFF whose simulation details the plan of movement. The coordination among all the fingers as a function of the specific shape of the grasped object, for example, is not explicitly represented in the schema but is an indirect result of simulating the complex dynamics of the force field. The different phases of the planned actions (e.g. approach and grasp) can be joined together by singling out a limited set of "key postures" (Morasso, Vercelli, Zaccaria, 1988). In summary, an hybrid motor schema is a representation of the whole movement or a particular chunk of it which is conceptually divided into two parts:

- *an analogic part*, i.e. kinematic and/or dynamic and/or eidetic descriptions;
- *a symbolic part*, i.e. micro and/or macro features that specify something of the movement.

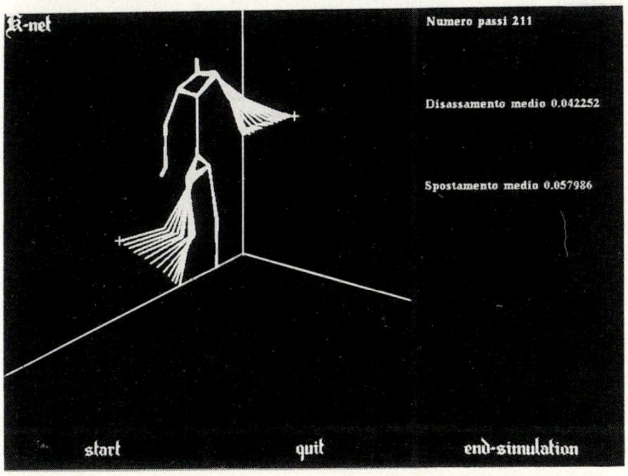

Fig. 4 Redundant structure: open and closed kinematic chain.

4. Results

Translating the AFF and HS concepts into practical computational terms is our long-term goal. We have just begun to set-up a few tiles of the mosaic, developing software tools for various simulation purposes. One such tool is a prototype of a human grasping movements planner, called OCTOPUS. This system is able to solve reaching-grasping problems, starting from a set of icons (3-D kinematic skeletons) of the hand and from a hybrid schema of the action.

Icons are organized as a knowledge base. They represent the *analogic* part of the planner, in the sense that the analogic model of the HS (e.g. the network representing the "virtual" hand) stores iconic information during the learning phase and compute the right sequence of actions during the execution phase. The planner itself performs symbolic computation, or *reasoning*, on icons' properties, also described in the KB.

An icon is usually a virtual target for a part of a movement, as a final or intermediate posture; in some case, an icon can be a *repulsing* posture, having the meaning of a forbidden (e.g. dangerous) configuration. Several icons may be (and usually are) simultaneously targets, so that no one will be exactly part of the actual motion. The aim of the planner is to:

- choose the proper icons (related to the the particular object, and the given grasping type), e.g. a suitable grasping posture ;
- *adapt* the icons to the actual problem (changing parameters so that they correspond to the shapes of objects); e.g. the grasping posture is made fit to the object;
- set the appropriate Force Fields associated to the set of icons (which may include obstacles, constraints etc.).

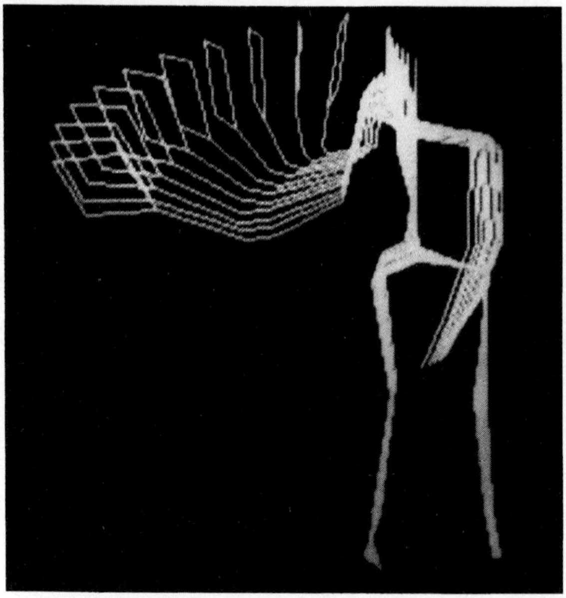

Fig. 5 Example of movements using AFF and HS.

The planner carries out its task on the symbolic "summaries" of the icons, also stored in the KB. After the planner has decided and set up the *analogic model* for the action, a *realizing process* starts, which generates the movement. This may be done using the P&C paradigm described in the previous section. Currently, computation is carried out by procedures written in NEM language. The *NEM language* (Marino et al., 1985,1986) allows building arbitrary structures of geometric frames, to compute geometric relations among them, and to specify relative motions in a concurrent way.

Figures 1-2 are simulation outputs of the planner: the reaching task is performed by an inverse kinematic module that is the HS "arm reaching task", while grasping task is performed by an interpolation module that is the HS "handle grasping task".

For the organization of such HS's we started building a tool for *body models*, that encodes the special geometric constraints of degrees of freedom, a tool for *compliant actuators*, that sets up the graph implementing the attractor posture, and a tool for *obstacle modeling* that implements the repulsive force fields as AFF. The figures show some examples of simulations performed within such a software environment. Figure 3 is an example of inverse kinematics for a redundant arm (open kinematic chain). Figure 4 extends the example to a closed chain, resulting from right arm movement while legs are grounded. Figure 5 shows the generation of a whole body movement from two subsequent attractor postures.

References

- Jordan M., (1988) Supervised learning and systems with excess degrees of freedom, COINS Tech. Rep. 88-27
- Hopfield J.J., (1982) Neural network and physical systems with emergent collective computational abilities, Proc. of the Nat. Acad. of Sciences USA 79:2554-2558.
- Marino G., Morasso P. and Zaccaria R. (1985) Motor Knowledge Representation. Proceed. IJCAI (Los Angeles, California):1110-1112.
- Marino G., Morasso P. and Zaccaria R. (1986) NEM: a Language for the Representation of Motor Knowledge. In Human Movement Understanding (P. Morasso and V. Tagliasco Eds.):125-156. North Holland:Amsterdam.
- Morasso P. and Mussa Ivaldi F.A. (1986) The role of physical constraints in natural and artificial manipulation. Proc. IEEE Conf. Robotics and Automation. San Francisco: 1901-1905.
- Morasso P., Mussa Ivaldi F.A. and Zaccaria R. (1987) Redundant Robotic Manipulators. I: Regularizing by Mechanical Impedance. NATO ARW Kinematic and Dynamic Issues in Sensor Based Control, 25th-31st October.
- Morasso P., Vercelli G., and Zaccaria R. (1988) Rappresentazione del movimento in Robotica: modello, ricostruzione, data base cognitivo in un caso antropomorfo, 4-th SIRI National Conf., Milano.
- Mussa Ivaldi F.A., Morasso P., Zaccaria R., (1988) Kinematic networks - A distributed model for representing and regularizing motor redundancy, Biol. Cybernetics, in press.
- Rumelhart D., McClelland J.L., et al., (1986) Parallel Distributed Processing. Explorations in the Microstructure of Cognition, MIT Press, Cambridge Ma.
- Steels L., (1988) Steps towards Common Sense, Int. Conf. "Connectionism in perspective", Zurich.

This research was partly supported by Esprit projects 419, 595 and Eureka project Prometheus.

NEURAL NETWORKS AND SYMBOLIC A.I.

Matthew K. O. Lee†

Department of Computer Science
University College London
WC1 6BT (email: mlee@uk.ac.ucl.cs)

This paper examines neural networks in the context of conventional symbolic artificial intelligence, with a view to explore ways in which neural networks can potentially benefit conventional A.I. systems. The focus is on the integration of the two paradigms in a complementary manner rather than on the complete replacement of one paradigm by another. Since Knowledge-Based Systems (KBS) are arguably the prime manifestation of A.I. systems in practice, they are used as a focal point for investigation. The paper looks into one particular venue, viz.. the maintenance of the consistency of information in a KBS, for incorporating neural networks into conventional KBS. In particular, the problem of how to use neural networks to perform tedious Truth Maintenance System (TMS) functions of a multiple-context and/or non-monotonic KBS is addressed. A way of mapping a TMS problem onto neural network is illustrated. Some practical implementation issues are discussed.

1. Introduction

Under the broad umbrella of Artificial Intelligence (A.I.), a number of areas have received much attention in the past few decades, the commonest of which include: knowledge based systems, natural language processing, image understanding, planning systems, and robotics. Among these, KBS perhaps represent the most important area for the application of symbolic A.I. techniques. KBS typically exist in the shape of "knowledge based expert systems", employing separate knowledge bases and have non-trivial inferencing abilities. Although neural networks have been successfully used in other A.I. areas like natural language processing and image understanding, most KBS still employ conventional symbolic A.I. techniques almost exclusively. Both neural network (NN) technology and conventional KBS technology have their own strengths and weaknesses. It is natural to ask how the best features of these two technologies can be combined to complement each other. There are at least 4 possible approaches:

1. Use NN to replace some of the structural components of a conventional KBS.
2. Use NN to help increase the efficiency of various mechanisms within a conventional KBS.
3. Use conventional KBS technology to control and organize neural networks.
4. Find a unifying theoretical framework for both technologies.

As a first step towards integration, this work concentrates on how conventional KBS can be improved

† The author wishes to acknowledge the support of British Telecom for this work.

NATO ASI Series, Vol. F 68
Neurocomputing
Edited by F. Fogelman Soulié and J. Hérault

using NN technology, i.e. approaches (1) and (2) above. Modern KBS often require Truth Maintenance Systems (TMS) to work alongside inference engines. As an example, the problem of performing TMS functions using neural networks is addressed in this short paper.

2. Neural Networks as Truth Maintenance Systems

In situations where an inference engine has to reason non-monotonically or under multiple contexts, a *truth maintenance system*[McAl80] is often required to maintain the consistency of beliefs in the knowledge base. Among the varieties of truth maintenance systems a Logic-based Truth Maintenance System (LTMS) can be most naturally represented as a constraint network which could be tackled as a constraint optimization problem using neural network models. To map this problem onto a neural network the following tasks must be tackled:

1. Choose a representation scheme which allows the problem and its solutions to be expressed in terms of network state.
2. Formulate an energy function whose minimum corresponds to a possible problem solution.
3. From the energy function derive the link weights and threshold value for every node in the network.

LTMS represents knowledge as a set of propositions. Each proposition can possibly be represented by a network node in the sense that if a node is on then the corresponding proposition is true and vice versa for a proposition that assumes a false value. Now the consequence of a clause such as E1 => E2 can be written in conjunctive normal form as:

$ (E1 bar or E2 or {(E1 => E2) bar}) and (E1 or {(E1 => E2)}) and (E2 bar or (E1 => E2)) $

Each conjunctive term above (there are three such terms) can be viewed as a constraint equation. If a value of 1 is assigned to a true disjunctive proposition inside a conjunctive term and each 'or' connective is taken as a summation operator then each term must correspond to a value which is at least 1 which signifies the minimum requirement for constraint satisfaction. A neural network representing the above clause will have 3 nodes representing the propositions E1, E2, and E1 => E2 respectively. The three resulting constraint equations will be embodied in the energy function which will reflect the constraints by appropriate link weights in the network. Basically the constraints are that each of the constraint equations must have a resulting numeric value of at least one. If the problem is to find the minimum set of true propositions that are capable of maintaining consistency then the problem can be framed as an optimization which tries to find the minimum of an energy function with a value equal to the total sum of all numeric values represented by the constraint equations.

For example, two implications such as E1 => E2 and E2 => E3 will be represented in the LTMS context as six constraint equations plus a further one denoting a global quantity to be optimized. If these equations are given numeric values in the manner as mentioned before, they can be written down as follows:

$ E1 bar + E2 + {(E1 => E2)} bar >= 1 (1) $
$ E1 + (E1 => E2) >= 1 (2) $
$ E2 bar + (E1 => E2) >= 1 (3) $
$ E2 bar + E3 + {(E2 => E3)} bar >= 1 (4) $
$ E2 + (E2 => E3) >= 1 (5) $
$ E3 bar + (E2 => E3) >= 1 (6) $
$ E1 + E2 + E3 + (E1 => E2) + (E2 => E3) = M (7) $

The quantity M in equation (7) is to be minimized subject to the constraint equations (1) to (6). A neural network for solving the above problem would have 5 nodes each corresponding to a term in equation (7). Supposing an energy function can be formulated which contain 7 terms each representing 1 of the equations above, then from it the link weights of the network can be derived analytically in a way similar to what has been done in Travelling Salesman Problems (TSP) [Bout88]. The initial state of the network corresponds to initial assumptions on the truth values of the 5 propositions in equation (7). For example, if all the consequences of a true E1 and (E1 => E2) are to be explored then the initial network state will have the nodes representing E1 and (E1 => E2) held at the on state but the states of other nodes (called "don't care nodes") will be let free running. A "don't care node" corresponds to a LTM clause with an unknown state. From this initial state the network will iterate and the energy function will steadily decrease. Throughout the process nodes E1 and (E2 => E2) must be held high. After the network has stabilized, the network state will correspond to a minimal set of true propositions that are consistent with the initial assumptions of E1 and (E1 => E2) being true. In this case the network should stabilize to a state where the nodes representing E1, (E1 => E2), and E2 are on while others are off. If a larger set is required than a further constraint equation may be added to increase the lower bound to the value of M in equation (7). When more than one set of propositions are possible as a solution, the network will converge into a state representing one of the sets depending on the actual initial states of the "don't care nodes".

In fact, the equations above constitute a problem resembling that of integer linear programming. Generally speaking, inference over a set of propositional clauses can be construed as an integer linear programming problem. Propositional clauses are transformed into constraint equations which are then regarded as a system of linear integer programming equations. Then neural network is then used to solve this system of linear equations. In this way, theorem proving involving only ground clauses can be performed on a neural network. Indeed, very recently there has been reports of successful applications of neural network in solving the Job-Scheduling problem (which is a class of np-complete problem) via an integer linear programming formulation [Foo88]. Such an approach offers potential advantages in speed and development time that conventional heuristic and deterministic methods cannot match. Furthermore, there are good prospects for direct hardware implementations.

3. Practical Issues

Although a LTMS problem may be mapped onto a neural network in the manner described above, there are several issues still to be resolved before this can become an effective approach in practice.

3.1 Choosing the Right Network

Both the Hopfield and Tank model (and its variants) and the Boltzmann machine are obvious first choices due to their proven ability in optimization and the present state of knowledge existing about these models. However, a more detailed and quantitative characterization and comparison of these models must be made within the context of this particular problem area in order to arrive at the most appropriate model. For instance, a Boltzmann machine, although much slower and more costly than other models, does provide an additional mechanism for controlling the search for energy minima in the network dynamics. The temperature of a Boltzmann machine can be judiciously adjusted during annealing to control the actual minimum that the network eventually settles on. This may be used to affect the size of a possible solution in much that same way as to install an extra constraint equation into the system as would be necessary for a Hopfield and Tank model without annealing.

3.2 Determining Network Parameters

For optimization networks, network parameters are link weights and threshold values which are determined by the form of the designated network energy function. In turn, the energy function encompasses all the constraint equations which specify the problem at hand. For a typical LTMS problem the size of a network is directly proportional to the number of clauses (i.e. both facts and premises) that are to be dealt with. An effective methodology must be developed for the automatic transformation of a problem into integer linear constraint equations, and from there an appropriate energy function is automatically formulated which is followed by the direct derivation of network parameters. Such a methodology is likely to be network dependent. For instance, if a Boltzmann machine model is employed then there are further parameters to be decided regarding the cooling schedule used in the annealing process.

3.3 Imposing Strong Constraints

Neural networks are often thought to be good at solving weak constraint problems. The fact that a single energy function is used to embody all the constraint equations may lead to the network finding a solution which violates some of the constraints while overall the total energy is still low enough for the network to settle. This may not be a serious problem in situations where an approximate solution will suffice already. However, in some other situations (e.g. logic theorem proving) even a small violation of a constraint may render the whole result meaningless. More effort must be made to study ways of formulating energy functions that allow strong constraints to be effectively imposed (e.g. via a large penalty term for each violation etc.).

4. Conclusions

This paper has illustrated one way of using neural networks in typical Knowledge-Based Systems. The particular example used is the so-called truth maintenance system which is employed in many modern KBS. For this problem the central issue is how to map a TMS problem onto a neural network as an optimization problem. It appears that the LTMS variety of truth maintenance systems is suitable for this mapping, and a novel way of achieving this is illustrated. However, a number of practical issues are still to be resolved to reach an efficient implementation.

TMS is used in this paper as an example to illustrate one way of incorporating neural networks into KBS. There are, of course, other more obvious examples such as the use of neural network associative memories as basic memory components of a KBS, and the use of neural network to effect learning in KBS etc. These examples are discussed in [Lee88].

References

[Bout88] Bout, D.E. and Miller, T.K., "A Traveling Salesman Objective Function that Works", Proc. of the Second IEEE International Conference on Neural Networks, Vol.2, pp.299-304, San Diego, July 1988.

[Foo88] Foo, Y.P.S. and Takefuji, Y., "Integer linear programming Neural Networks for Job-Shop Scheduling", Proc. of the Second IEEE International Conference on Neural Networks, Vol.2, pp.341-348, San Diego, July 1988.

[Lee88] Lee, M.K.O., "Neural Networks for Knowledge Based Systems", Research Note RN/89/36, Dept. of Computer Science, University College London, 1989.

[McAl80] McAllester, David A., "An Outlook on Truth Maintenance", Report AIM-551, Artificial Intelligence Laboratory, MIT, Cambridge, MA, 1980.

2 ARCHITECTURES

Integrated artificial neural networks: components for higher level architectures with new properties

Michel Weinfeld

Laboratoire d'Informatique
Ecole Polytechnique
91128 Palaiseau Cedex- France

Introduction

Artificial neural network architectures exhibit properties (associative memory, classification, generalization,...) which roughly approximate some of our elementary brain properties. Classical or parallel computer simulations have been, and still are, invaluable tools for investigating their behavior, but require more and more power, becoming increasingly costly. The regularity of most networks architecture make them good candidates for hardwiring, and even better, integration in silicon. In this case, it is also expected to take advantage of the intrinsic robustness of neural architectures, which could make acceptable some defective circuits which would otherwise be rejected by current standards. One can expect to gain orders of magnitude in overall efficiency when simulations are done on these specialized circuits. We shall quickly review some current developments in silicon, especially the digital 64 neurons feedback network with included learning circuitry that we develop in cooperation with the ESPCI group. We shall also give some information on a long term project of wafer-scale integration.

Beyond these descriptions, we think that these circuits will not be anything more than components to be used for designing more elaborate architectures. In effect, whatever interesting their properties are, these properties are nevertheless to be considered as low level with respect to the mental processes we try to understand and reproduce. This is why the future of integrated networks probably does not lie in a huge increase in unitary size, which could be made possible by several technological improvements expected in semiconductor industry. Biology indicates that information processing in the nervous pathways, from the initial sensors to the deepest areas, is made by numerous series-parallel processes, involving dynamic invocation of specialized units, which could perhaps be modeled by integrated components of reasonable size, capable of self-modification (learning), such as the network described later in this paper. Moreover, we want to insist on the essentially dynamic nature of this information processing, which, in biological systems, never reaches a final state, but follows an endless trajectory in state space. Until now,

NATO ASI Series, Vol. F 68
Neurocomputing
Edited by F. Fogelman Soulié and J. Hérault

the ANN community has tried to build machines (real or simulated), dedicated to certain kinds of tasks having rather well defined initial and final states, as for instance in pattern recognition. We think that it is worth thinking about coupling such machines or circuits into dynamic auto-adaptive architectures, that might open the way for implementing artificial intelligent functions, closer to what life suggests.

Some current developments in silicon

To our knowledge, all of the discrete or integrated neural network circuits so far published implement the fully connected feedback architecture such as the so-called Hopfield [1] or Boltzmann [2] architectures. This is due to their totally regular structure, not related (except for the size of the network) to any particular problem. Multilayered networks, having a less regular architecture depending rather strongly on the problem to solve, and more complicated learning rules, are less interesting and more difficult to build as whole circuits.

Massive parallelism for a whole feedback net and smooth transfer function for the individual neuron is easily implemented using operational amplifiers, the synapses being represented by conductances. This analog circuitry approach has been the easiest way used in early and recent circuits [3-6], with the severe drawback of poor or null synapse programmability. Several designs have been or are underway to overcome this problem, using many ingenious solutions, such as charge-coupled devices [7], charge storage in floating gates [8,9] or in independent capacitors [10] to modulate the transconductance of MOS transistors, scaled geometry transistors connected in parallel [11], switched-capacitors techniques [12], etc... The common features to all these designs is a relatively low precision (generally no more than the equivalent of four bits plus sign), the requirement of auxiliary digital circuitry for control and programming, and, of course, a rather strong dependency of the whole design on process technology issues. Only one of them [11] implements in-circuit learning, all the others requiring an external computer to calculate the synaptic coefficients. Nevertheless, some people advocate analog design as being the only genuinely looking "biological", because of native asynchrony and the natural presence of noise, among other properties [13].

Purely digital designs are relatively few. Digital circuitry is reputed for making massive parallelism implementation much more difficult, if not impossible, thus slowing down the architecture, for being more complex, thus requiring more silicon area for a given net size, and finally for requiring some kind of sequencing and clocking. These points are absolutely true, but not decisive, and one has to take into account the numerous advantages induced by digital design, for instance the almost total immunity to noise, the complete flexibility of circuit implementation and programmability, the naturally good coupling to the external world, which is almost always numerical, the use of virtually technology-independant design tools, etc... In addition, as we shall show later, it may be very interesting to implement learning as well as relaxation in the network: this can represent only a small overhead if one uses digital circuitry. Generally, the designs use varieties of systolic architectures to realize a kind of spatio-temporal massive connectivity [14], use bit-serial arithmetic [15], or, in a simpler way, realize basic building blocks which can be combined to make various architectures, including multi-layered networks [16].

The LIX-ESPCI circuit with included learning

The circuit under design with ESPCI has been described elsewhere [17,18]. It is a fully connected systolic CMOS feedback network with 64 binary neurons. The learning rule uses the Widrow-Hoff algorithm, which can be iterated [19] to make the synaptic coefficients tend towards the non local projection rule coefficients [20]. It uses 9 bit wide synaptic coefficients and a simple fixed-point arithmetic unit. The coefficients are stored locally in each neuron, in a shift register memory minimizing the surface and the power consumption with respect to traditional random access circuitry. The circuit implements an automatic combinatorial convergence detection, which speeds up the serial-parallel output operations. The whole circuit is to be interfaced to a Macintosh II microcomputer through a special MCP™ development card. This computer will serve only as a workbench, and not as the usual host for computing coefficients. The overall size of the complete circuit will be around 4.10^3 transistors, and will be processed using 1.5μm or smaller technology. We have investigated the design of an additional random serial bit generator to be used as a device implementing in a very simple way a finite "temperature" in the network, which is known to improve the convergence (see below). During each updating cycle of the network, this additional circuitry generates a 64 bits vector with a determined number of randomly distributed ones (the greater this number, the higher the pseudo-temperature), which is xor'ed with the network state vector at the end of the cycle, so as to flip some intermediate neuron states. This rather crude mechanism approximates individual independent neuron probabilistic transfer function, and has the great advantage to be rather easily designed and to adapt itself well to the general circuit architecture.

The LIX-ESPCI-CSI wafer-scale integration project

Taking into account our systolic basic design, our colleagues from the Laboratoire des Circuits et Systèmes Intégrés in Grenoble are working on the design of reconfigurable networks, either feedback or multilayered feedforward [21], having Wafer Scale Integration (WSI) as a goal. The design will implement multivalued neurons, that is to say a rather smooth transfer function, and also on-silicon learning. The elementary neuronal cell is based on fixed point arithmetics, the sigmoidal transfer function being calculated by a quadratic approximation. Depending on the chosen configuration and the precision of the coefficients, several kinds of networks can be implemented on a standard wafer. For instance, it is expected to integrate 200 to 800 neurons on a 4 inches wafer using current technologies.

Here also, the robustness of neural architectures is an interesting research issue. This project will probably be a candidate as a demonstrator in the European program JESSI (Joint European Submicron Silicon Initiative), in the Basic Level Research (BLR) subprogram.

Are unitary networks able to deal with interesting problems ?

Some authors expect that forthcoming circuitry and technologies will give rise to networks with many more neurons. Of course, circuits with about one hundred cells can probably not lead to very interesting applications when used alone. Dedicated feedforward multilayers or feedback networks need more probably several thousands cells, especially if we take into account the need for a certain sparsity in representing the data. They will await the availability of real submicronic technologies and cascadable building blocks. But still they will need a lot of external overhead just to take advantage of their properties. Let us take for instance a feedforward network, the generalization of which can be proved to be never equal to 100%: in real use, what would detect that the response lies actually in the bad region ? The same question could be asked for a feedback network, converging into a parasitic attractor. In all cases, the fundamental and certainly unavoidable limited precision of what the networks can do obliges to use them in some kind of dynamic structure, with no rest state, but with localized or more global cost – or energy – function. Single networks, as good as they can be to solve certain kinds of model problems under the supervision of an instructor knowing the good response in advance will remain interesting, but mostly research objects, not very usable for applications.

We strongly believe that the future lies in more complicated structures, using basic networks such as those that are presently being designed, as elementary components: all integrated networks, when they become usable as research tools, will certainly give momentum to investigations on these more complex architectures.

As an example of an interesting "auto-adaptive" feature, we shall describe a simple mechanism of attractor-labelling in a feedback network, allowing it to discriminate by itself whether its final state, after relaxation from any stimulus, is a learnt attractor (prototype) or a parasitic one.

Self discrimination of prototypes and parasitic attractors in a feedback network.

We started from an idea of Personnaz, Dreyfus and Guyon [22], who made a Hopfield network learn the rasterized pictures of handwritten digits. They added to the information field of the learnt vectors a supplementary field of ten bits identifying the attractor, using a "1 in 10" code. This is a rather simple way to qualify the contents of the net state after convergence. Nevertheless, this labelling is information-dependent, which is a severe disadvantage. We imagined (in view of a modification of the integrated 64 neuron circuits mentioned above) to use a labelling inspired by error-correcting codes: a certain amount of bits in the vector contains the result of some calculation on the remaining bits. The constraints are: the coding subfield must be small with respect to the information-carrying field, and the calculation must be simple enough to be easily incorporated in silicon. We first tried a Hamming code [23] with different label width. When a prototype is learnt to the network, it includes the calculated label. Before a stimulus (distant from the nearest prototype by a Hamming distance H_i) is presented to the network, it is submitted to an identical label calculation and initialization. When the network has stabilized, we make a comparison between the label field of the attractor, as it appears, and the label as calculated from the information-carrying part of the attractor, and mark a success in case of equality, which means that the network has recognized that it has relaxed on a prototype. Figure 1 shows the results: for a learning rate of 25% (16 prototypes on a 64 neurons net), five bits of code are enough to get a failure rate smaller than 5% even for an initial distance of 28 bits; with 6 bits this rate is divided by a factor of two, meaning that we have a success rate of approximately 98% in identifying prototypes versus parasitic attractors.

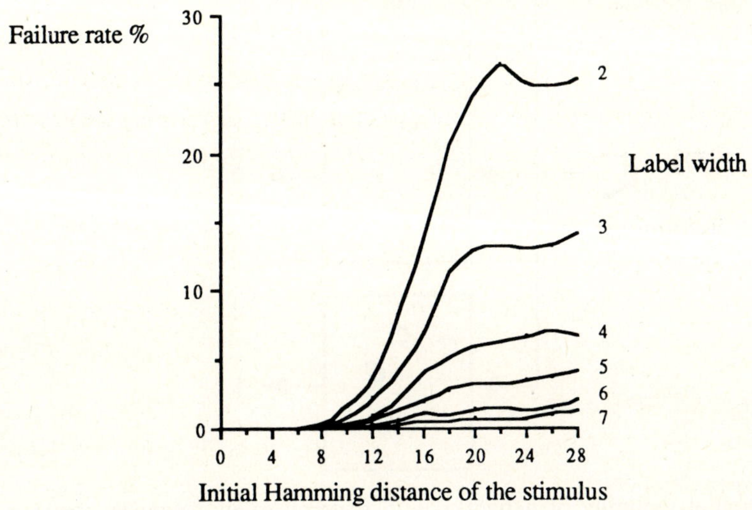

Figure 1. error rate for identifying a prototype, as a function of initial Hamming distance of the stimulus from the prototype. The parameter is the label width in bits. The network has 64 cells, and has learnt 16 prototypes.

As it is known, spurious states in feedback networks are often linear combinations of prototypes. The Hamming code, being linear, is unable to detect them. Moreover, the silicon design of the adequate circuitry is somehow bulky. To overcome these two drawbacks, we implemented a cyclic code (using the 6,1,0 polynomial) which has a simpler silicon footprint, has been shown by simulation to discriminate linear combinations of prototypes as spurious states, and has very similar success rates.

A step towards auto-adaptivity ?

To summarize, we have showed that a simple input-output preprocessing layer implementing a cyclic code, used as a filter in the network I/O, is able to give a very good attractor labelling, allowing to differentiate internally between prototypes and spurious states. This property opens the way to several steps towards auto-adaptivity. First, identifying that the network is stuck in a spurious state allows to automatically start an annealing process, using the special circuitry mentioned earlier. Without getting into details, which will be published later, let us mention that a labelling-annealing strategy has been shown to improve the overall success rate of the network by as much as 25%.

Another possibility, to be thoroughly explored, is the grouping of several networks.

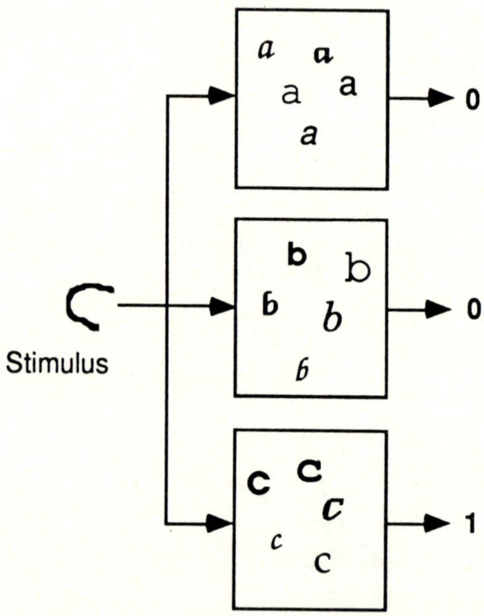

Figure 2. Parallel grouping of networks with flagging of the "winner", implementing a classifier with localized fast learning.

Figure 2 shows a conceptual view of one of many possibilities: each network is in charge of the recognition of variants of a same generic pattern (shape and/or position), for instance several instances of the same letter. The unknown pattern is submitted in parallel to all nets, which all asynchronously converge towards a steady state, but the one raising its label-fitting flag has the good answer. In case of conflicts, some logical combination of the flags may lead to a satisfactory decision.

Other architectures could implement for instance hierarchical symbol processing, with automatic low-level recognition on segments of the symbols if high-level recognition fails, as indicated by the labels. These low-level tasks, dynamically triggered by high-level circuitry may provide in turn partially or totally error-corrected segments, thus facilitating a new attempt of high-level recognition. In case of failure, the learning of the unknown pattern might be chosen. Other kind of hierarchical groupings of networks can be studied, the point being that *self-labelling opens the way to automatic routing and processing of the information in a network of networks.*

Back to biology, it is nowadays currently admitted that information processing in nervous systems proceeds along multiple parallel pathways, involving several modular structures [24] in a way which is yet far from being clear. The use of the word "pathway" involves also of course serial processing, that is a chronology of events. We think that our approach could be helpful to "hard-simulate" structures inspired by these considerations.

Bibliography

1. Hopfield, J. J.: Neural networks and physical systems with emergent collective computational abilities. Proc. Natl. Acad. Sci. USA, vol. 79, pp. 2554-2558, 1982
2. Ackley, D.H., Hinton, G.E. and Sejnowski, T.J.: A learning algorithm for Boltzmann machines. Cognitive Science, vol. 9, pp. 147-169, 1985
3. Sivilotti, M., Emerling, M. R., and Mead,C.: A novel associative memory implemented using collective computation. In: Proc. Chapel Hill Conf. on VLSI, pp. 329-342, Computer Science Press 1985
4. Moopenn, A., Langenbacher, H., Thakoor, A. P. and Khanna, S.K.: A programmable binary synaptic matrix chip for electronic neural networks. IEEE Conf. on Neural Information Processing Systems, Natural and Synthetic, Denver (USA), 1987. In: Neural Information Processing Systems, Natural and Synthetic, D.Z.Anderson, ed., American Institute of Physics, 1988
5. Schwartz, D. B., Howard, R. E., Denker, J. S., Epworth, R. W., Graf, H. P., Hubbard, W., Jackel, L. D., Straughn, B. and Tennant, D. M.: Dynamics of microfabricated electronic neural networks. Appl. Phys. Lett., vol. 50, pp. 1110-1112, 1987
6. Verleysen, M., Sirletti, B., Vandemeulenbroecke, A.M., Jespers, P.G.A.: Neural networks for high-storage content-adressable memory: VLSI circuit and learning algorithm. IEEE Journal of solid-state circuits, vol. 24, no. 3, pp. 562-569, 1989
7. Sage, J.P., Thompson, K. and Withers, R.S.: An artificial network integrated circuit based on MNOS/CCD principles. In: Neural networks for computing, J.S.Denker ed., American Institute of Physics, 1986
8. Rückert, U. and Goser, K.: VLSI design of associative networks. International Workshop on VLSI for artificial intelligence, Oxford (GB), July 1988. In: VLSI for artificial intelligence, J.G. Delgado-Frias and W.Moore eds., Kluwer Academic, 1989

9. Holler, M., Tam, S., Castro, H.and Benson, R.: An electrically trainable artificial neural network with 10240 "floating gate" synapses. Proceedings of International Joint Conference on Neural Networks, Washington D.C., June 1989
10. Schwartz, D. B. and Howard, R. E.: Analog VLSI for adaptive learning, Neural Networks for Computing, Snowbird, 1988 (unpublished).
11. Alspector, J., Allen, R. B., Hu, V. and Satyanarayana, S.: Stochastic learning networks and their electronic implementation. IEEE Conf. on Neural Information Processing Systems, Natural and Synthetic, Denver (USA), 1987. In: Neural Information Processing Systems, Natural and Synthetic, D.Z.Anderson, ed., American Institute of Physics, 1988
12. Tsividis, Y.P. and Anastassiou, D.: Switched capacitor neural network. Electronic Lett. vol. 23, pp. 958-959, 1987
13. Hopfield, J.J.: On the effectiveness of neural network hardware. Proceedings of the workshop "Hardware implementation of neuron nets and synapses", San Diego (USA), P.Mueller ed, pp. 120-124, January 1988
14. Blayo, F. and Hurat, P.: A systolic architecture dedicated to neural networks. nEuro'88 conference, Paris, June 1988. In: Neural networks, from models to applications , L.Personnaz and G.Dreyfus, eds., IDSET, 1989
15. Murray, A. F., Smith, V. W. and Butler, Z. F.: Bit-serial neural networks , IEEE Conf. on Neural Information Processing Systems, Natural and Synthetic, Denver (USA), 1987. In: Neural Information Processing Systems, Natural and Synthetic, D.Z.Anderson, ed., American Institute of Physics, 1988
16. Duranton, M., Gobert, J. and Mauduit, N.: A digital VLSI module for neural networks. nEuro'88 conference, Paris, June 1988. In: Neural networks, from models to applications. L.Personnaz and G.Dreyfus, eds., IDSET, 1989
17. Personnaz, L., Johannet, A., Dreyfus, G., Weinfeld, M.: Towards a neural network chip: a performance assessment and a simple example. nEuro'88 conference, Paris, June 1988. In: Neural networks, from models to applications, L.Personnaz and G.Dreyfus, eds., IDSET, 1989
18. Weinfeld, M.: A fully digital CMOS integrated Hopfield network including the learning algorithm. International Workshop on VLSI for artificial intelligence, Oxford (GB), July 1988. In: VLSI for artificial intelligence, J.G. Delgado-Frias and W.Moore eds., Kluwer Academic, 1989
19. Diederich, S. and Opper, M.: Learning of correlated patterns in spin-glass networks by local learning rules. Phys. Rev. Lett., vol. 58, no. 9, pp. 949-952, 1987
20. Personnaz, L., Guyon, I. and Dreyfus, G.: Collective computational properties of neural networks: new learning mechanisms. Phys. Rev. A, vol. 34, pp. 4217-4228, 1986
21. Ouali, J., Saucier, G. and Trilhe, J.: A flexible wafer scale network.ICCD Conference, Rye Brook, (USA), September 1989
22. Personnaz, L., Guyon, I. and Dreyfus, G.: Designing a neural network satisfying a given set of constraints. In: Neural networks for computing, J.S.Denker ed., American Institute of Physics, 1986
23. Peterson, W.W. and Weldon, E.J.: Error correcting codes, MIT Press, 1972
24. Nature's 11th international conference "How the brain works", Cambridge (USA), September 1988. Nature vol.335, pp.489-491, October 1988

Basic VLSI Circuits for Neural Networks

Karl Goser
Bauelemente der Elektrotechnik
University of Dortmund
Emil-Figge-Str. 68
4600 Dortmund 50
F.R.G.

Abstract

The most important basic circuits of neural networks are the memory cells for the adaptive weights, the complex connections between the neurons, and special circuits to support the learning. We present new circuits which implement these functions, and show concepts of functional integration in silicon. Additional circuits improve learning, e.g. an input layer with fuzzy logic or associative memory cells is preprocessing the information. The evaluation of these concepts reveals a better system performance and a higher integration level than that of pure digital concepts. A short outlook about new technologies based on silicon, as cooled circuits, optoelectronics, and molecular electronics, closes the overview.

1. Introduction

If artificial neural networks should offer a severe alternative to conventional information processing, we have to carry out these systems in hardware. The research on hardware concepts is going on and the development of VLSI systems is just at the beginning /2,11,18/. Due to the fast progress in microelectronics - today we are at the introduction of the "Mega-Logic" - these networks are now becoming feasible with a large enough storing capacity. One of the main design problems is to find out effective learning algorithms for such microelectronic components.

This paper describes new circuits and design principles. They offer the basis for implementing a wide variety of network types in silicon. In future we expect that a broad spectrum of applications in microelectronics will further push forward silicon technologies towards cooled circuitry, optoelectronics and molecular devices. These developments will impact neural networks, too. This context demands an effective interaction between both systems and circuits.

2. The basic problems with regards to integration

Neural science can offer almost all mathematical theory of neural networks /2,5,9,14,18/. This framework is very coarse and leaves open many degrees of freedom. The theory, however,

NATO ASI Series, Vol. F 68
Neurocomputing
Edited by F. Fogelman Soulié and J. Hérault

reflects the highly parallel, regular and modular architecture of neural networks making them attractive for VLSI systems. Such VLSI systems arise the following problems concerning integration:

- The units processing (synapses) must be compact in order to accomodate many of them on a chip.

- The memory cells should store the adaptive weights as analog values which should be variable.

- The technology should offer solutions to the problem of the complex connectivity between the units.

- The learning algorithm must take into account the possibilities and restrictions of the technology.

The design problem leads to the following question: Should we design neural networks only with a top down strategy as neuroscience does? Or, should we chose a bottom up strategy where we are looking around for new suitable devices and circuits which are available for other applications in any case? The first way concentrates more or less upon the main stream of digital MOS technology. The second way tends to functional integration with some analog technology . Both lead to a higher performance of the neural nets. Therefore it may be a good strategy for design to meet in the middle.

3. Silicon Technology

In the following we discuss some basic integrated circuits for solving the above mentioned problems of connectivity, storing adaptive weights and learning functions.

3.1 Analog versus digital circuitry

Digital concepts are very important since they use the mainstream of technology. In addition they surprise by a quite good performance that is enough for many applications /11,17/. One of several concepts is the Palm matrix where only zero's and one's are used for weights /14, 16/. We have designed and integrated the main building blocks for such a concept. Fig. 1 shows the photomicrograph of a matrix with 96 rows and 16 columns. The advantage of the concept is its modular structure so we can achieve a quite large fully interconnected neural network of several hundred neurons by mounting only a few chips on a printed circuit board /15/.

In our opinion, however, the analog version is more attractive because of size, power and speed. The accuracy of analog circuits is not as high as for digital circuits, but more appropriate for highly parallel signal transfer operations. Therefore almost all VLSI systems for neural networks up to now make use of analog computation. Especially for signal processing the implementation in analog technique is appropriate because of the time-dependent signals. Herault and Jutten /5/

Fig. 1. Microphotograph of a VLSI-chip with 7 x 8 mm^2 and 40.000 transistors. The VLSI system bases on the modified Palm concept /14/ and has modular architecture.

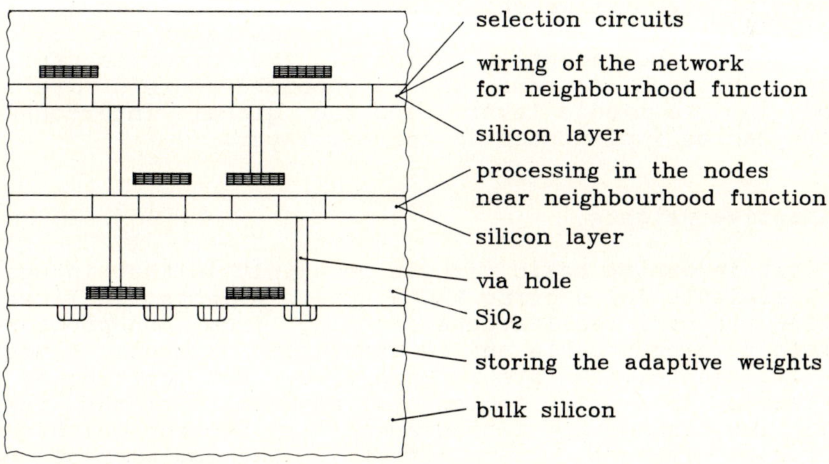

Fig. 2. Three-dimensional integration technique using SOI with laser annealing /7/. Three layers of integrated circuits may be suitable for neural networks.

proposed a very simple network which is able to extract independent unknown sources in signals issued from unknown mixtures of that sources. In this network there are OpAmp's and high-value resistors for the analog operations. Recent developments in analog CMOS techniques lead to high performance circuits where OTA's replace the high-value resistors. In addition our cell concept allows a quick design of a complex network on a small area, since all cells fit together well /6/.

3.2 Connectivity

The usual way to solve the connectivity problem in electronics is the use of the time as an additional grade of freedom. Therefore we find multiplexing, shift registers for input/output buffers, pulse modulation, or systolic arrays. Weinfeld et al., for example, developed sophisticated architectures which use the time axis extensively /20/.

In the following, however, we will concentrate on technology to improve the data exchange in the networks. Besides a multilayer for connections the three-dimensional integration offers interesting aspects for solving the problem of connectivity. One of the most interesting 3D techniques is the silicon on insulator technology (SOI-technique) which will play an important role for intelligent sensors in future.

Such a concept is highly feasible, since the research work on 3D integration is going on intensively. In our laboratory we have developed a method for annealing a polysilicon film by a laser beam /7/. The annealing temperature is high enough for integrating CMOS circuits into the silicon film. Its annealing temperature, however, is low enough so the process does not affect the integrated circuits in the bulk underneath.

For neural networks we should provide three circuit layers for example (Fig. 2): The bulk at the bottom takes the circuitry for storing the adaptive weights. The circuits for data exchange between neurons and neighboured neurons are integrated in the middle layer, and the global interconnection network can be implemented in the top layer.

3.3 Adaptive weights

The most important basic circuit certainly is the integration of the elements for storing the adaptive weights. In literature we find several realizations ranging from non-programmable discrete to programmable analog connection elements. Almost all VLSI implementations are non-adaptive, but learning or self-organization do require incremental adjustment of the weights. In our view, analog and reprogrammable connection weights are a significant feature of an effective VLSI emulator of neural networks. Therefore we propose two concepts in the following: a pure analog and a hybrid digital/analog concept for storing elements.

3.3.1 The storing element with floating gate transistor

As already proposed in earlier publications /4/ the so-called floating-gate transistor or FAMOS transistor (Floating Gate Avalanche MOS) offers a good way for a functional integration of a storing element. Today the electrically erasable and programmable read only memories (EEPROMs) use this type of transistor. Based on it we developed a new storing element with dual drain and dual control gate, as depicted in Fig.3 /4,16/. The device acts as a nonvolatile storage cell at which the electrical charge on the floating gate represents the information, in our case the adaptive weight. Since the charge can vary continously, the storage cell works analog. It holds the stored information independently of the power supply.

The cell matches the requirements for operating within a processing unit quite well. During association an activated input line causes the memory cell to feed a current into the column line. This current depends on the threshold voltage which is proportional to the stored charge in the floating gate. The current source mode seems to be the most adequate operation for the transistor.

Tunneling of electrons into the floating gate shifts the threshold voltage. The charge on the floating gate represents the adaptive weight. Their characteristics resemble to the adaptation function of a neuron. The dynamic range is equivalent to 4 to 8 Bits. Since both positive and negative pulses are necessary for the inhibitory and exhibitory operations, there are two polarities of programming pulses which need high voltage CMOS driver circuits on the same chip /16/.

At the present state of the art some degradation effect due to charge trapping within the thin oxide limits the satisfactory longtime operation of this device. Around a million of modification cycles leaves only a small threshold voltage shift so the cell becomes inoperable in a matrix. The technological results tend toward lower degradation by using better insulation layers. On the other hand the cell characteristics of today are sufficient for learning a network once.

3.3.2 The storing element with CCD loop

A storing element with charge coupled devices (CCD) overcomes the disadvantages of low accuracy and longtime degradation of the floating gate transistor. The build up of such an element is more complex since the element requires a three dimensional integration with at least two layers of silicon (Fig. 4). In the first layer, in the bulk substrate, there is a CCD loop together with a regenerator and an input/output stage as well as the clock lines for the CCD. The number of CCD's in the loop yields the accuracy of the connection weight since the number of charge packets corresponds the weight value, and only the area limits it. The cycle time for the CCD's depends on the leakage currents and can be relatively long in standby operation.

In the second layer three MOS transistors represent the

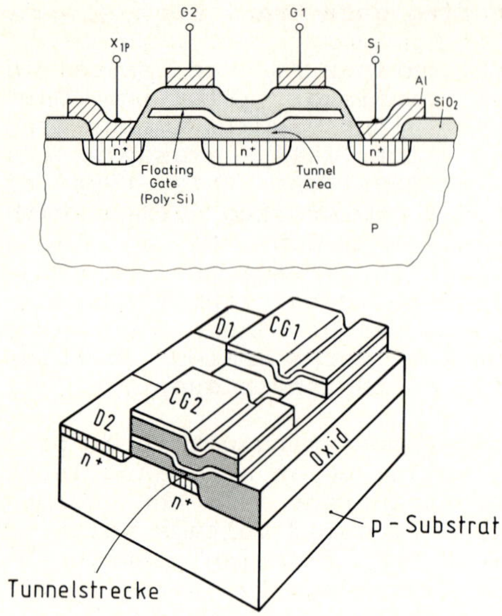

Fig. 3. The floating gate transitor as an adaptive weight. In addition the U-formed transistor takes the selection, the multiplication and the adaptation /4,16/.

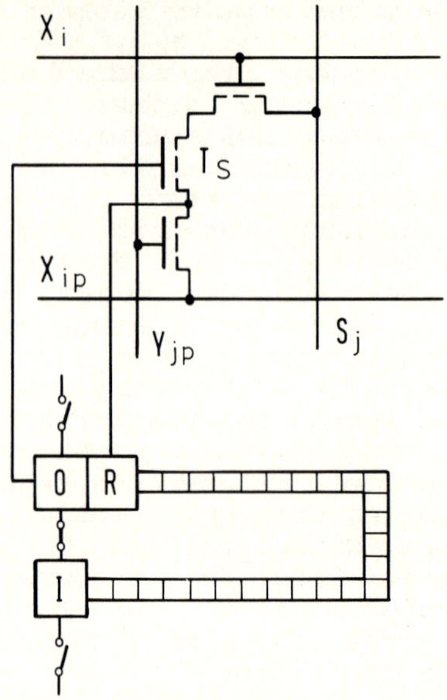

Fig. 4. CCD loop cell as adaptive weight. The circuitry can be built in SOI-techniques /15/.

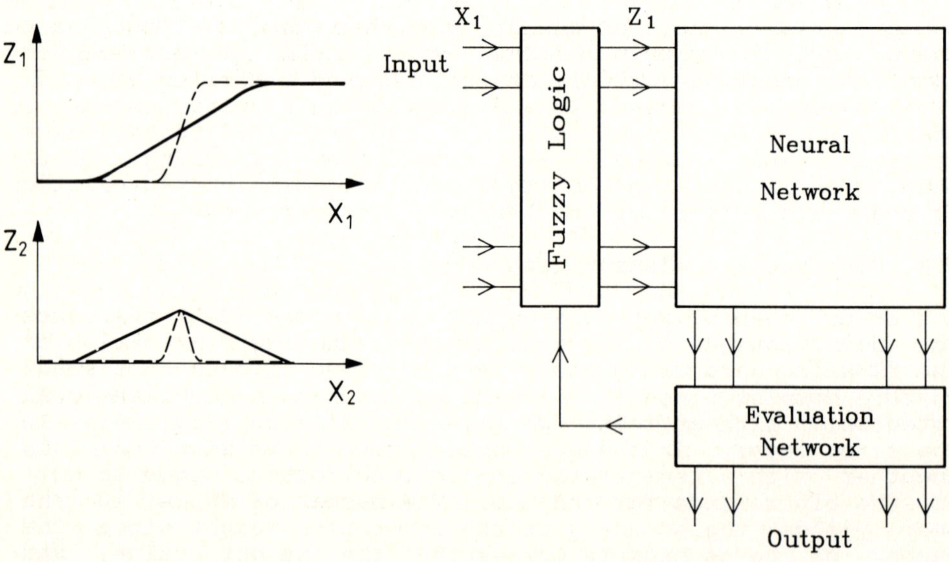

Fig. 5. The learning of a neural network is improved by a one- or two-layer of fuzzy logic for preprocessing the input information.

connection element itself, since one of the gate capacitance collects the charge packets of the CCD loop. The higher the electrical charge the lower the resistance or the higher the current through this transistor. The power supply lines and the input lines also are on top of this layer as suggested in Fig.2.

A further advantage of this element is that the information stored into the loops can be read out by opening the loops and by switching all loops in series. In this way the output of the chip receives the charge packet strings of each storing element. An external memory, e.g. a magnetic disc, can store these data. On the reversed way the adaptive weights can be written into the loops from outside, so the time consuming process of learning can be omitted /15/.

3.4 Learning

The problem put in microelectronics is to find an effective learning algorithm for a VLSI system with a certain integration level and with limitations set by the technology. Such limitations are quantization of signals, parameter spread, delay times, and switching times.

The Boltzmann machine is an example for difficulties which arise from the technological limitations /10/. Since this machine uses statistics for learning, we have the advantage to find the global minima in the network at storing the information. In addition the network is fault tolerant which is a very attractive aspect for VLSI systems /17/. The statistical process makes use of the Fermi function. Since at high and low energy levels the probability is either one or zero, the learning of the network is worse the lower the system temperature is. Present research work tries to solve the problem by introducing additional noise sources or by using other algorithms.

Fuzzy logic aims at modeling the imprecise modes of reasoning that play an essential role to make rational decisions in an environment of uncertainty and imprecision, as in pattern recognition /21/. Although fuzzy logic has similar characteristics as neural networks, it seems that both principles exclude each other. The example of self-organizing maps, however, shows that fuzzy cells in one or two layers can be used for preprocessing the information so the neural network can adapt better (Fig. 5), /6,9,11/. At the beginning of learning the input data range can be wide, at the final state the fuzzy cells can narrow it to the relevant range. In this case the neural network directly controls the slopes of the fuzzy cells. By the fuzzy cell layer at the input the neural network becomes more effective.

A similar way to accelerate the learning is to use an adaptive associative memory layer only at the input /4/.

3.5 The potential of integration technologies

In future the integration technology will probably proceed as quickly as in the past. In Europe the JESSI project will cause a progress from 1 Mega bit memory chips to 64 Mega bit chips, even 256 Mega bit chips are feasible /8/. These pilot products will use sub-micron-technologies down to 0,3 μm. This program ranges to 1997 and should provide Europe with high level integrated systems. It is also a challenge for neural networks vice versa respectively.

Today, research institutes can realize 10 to 100 neurons on a chip. For complex digital concepts as the Boltzmann machine we can only expect one neuron on a chip. Selected companies which own such a sub-μm-technology have the possibilities to design chips up to 1.000 neurons. At the end of the JESSI program we can expect chips with about 10.000 neurons in analog technique if one weight can be stored in a single device; but this goal does not only require an adequate technology but also powerful design tools and test equipments /12/. Even at such high-sophisticated technologies the number of neurons is quite small in comparison with that in biological systems. Therefore it will be a challenge to develop integration technologies beyond the scope of the JESSI program.

4. Aspects of future technologies

In the following we discuss some technologies which all base on silicon and which will be available for other important applications in microelectronics in any case.

4.1 Low temperature circuits on silicon

The simplest way to high performance networks seems to be the cooling of the CMOS circuits. The results are not only a higher performance of digital logic but also a longer time constant for discharging a MOS capacitor. The leakage rate of a MOS capacitor reduces by three orders of magnitude by cooling the circuits to -50°C and by five orders of magnitude by cooling to -100°C. The low temperature may solve the problem of storing the analog weights.

The low temperatures offer the opportunity to introduce superconductor as lossless transmission lines so high data rates are practicable. The wiring with high temperature superconductors will be an important goal for future VLSI chips. In addition, it may be possible that superconductor rings store adaptive weights as a magnetic flux. Since a Josephson junction allows to change the flux step by step, the cell operates in an analog way. The summation of the signals in a neuron is the sum of the currents of all magnetic fluxes, the read operation can be reversible and lossless if special circuits are used.

Low temperatures will offer interesting aspects for neural nets. Since this technology will probably come for large systems, it will support the application of neural nets as accelerators.

4.2 Optoelectronics on silicon

Since silicon is a relatively cheap substrate, the research efforts have the goal to integrate light wave guides, photo diodes and light emitting sources into silicon. The first two components can be realized without difficulties as new results show, the last one is still open. On one side the molecular beam epitaxy may alter the crystal structure of silicon so light emitting devices are just ahead, on the other side there are light emitting effects in silicon devices which we can probably develop further /19/.

4.3 Molecular electronics on silicon

Molecular electronics is a vision which promises to solve all technological problems of neural nets /1/. Self-building and self-organizing in three dimensions offer the outlook to huge neural networks with high performance. In reality, however, the biological molecular electronics will be very slow, and the physical molecular electronics is just starting with the first test structures /13/.

The delta films deposited on silicon by molecular beam epitaxy make possible new devices /3/. Our experiments show that capacitors with such films have a capacitance which is one magnitude higher than that of usual MOS capacitors. The appearance of new devices as vertical switches or tunnel switches impacts neural nets, since these devices open new ways for functional integration. In addition the quantum effects linked to such thin films are quite interesting as regards storing adaptive weights.

5. Conclusion

The main stream of integration technology concentrates on digital memories. This technology is not well suited for the implementation of neural networks but it offers a good opportunity. Since a broad application of microelectronics needs a diversity in any case, it is worthwhile to look if such special technologies offer advantages for the integration of neural networks. Indeed, such advantages exist, as shown above, and we should adapt the architecture and the algorithms of neural networks to the facilities of these technologies. It means for the design strategy that we should meet in the middle.

Acknowledgements

The author thanks the coworkers U. Rueckert, I. Kreuzer, K.M. Marks, U. Hilleringmann, and V. Tryba for the cooperation, and he is grateful to the DFG (Deutsche Forschungsgemeinschaft) and to the EC (project BRAIN and ESPRIT) for the financial support.

References

/1/ Conrad, M.: The Lure of Molecular Computing. IEEE Spectrum, Vol. 23, pp. 55 - 60, 1986

/2/ Eckmiller, R; v. d. Malsburg, C.: Neural Computers. Springer Verlag 1988

/3/ Eisele, I.: Delta-Type Doping Profiles in Silicon, Applied Surface Science, Vol. 36, pp. 39 - 51, 1989

/4/ Goser, K.; Fölster, C.; Rückert, U.: Intelligent memories in VLSI. Information Sciences, Vol. 34, pp. 61 - 62, 1984

/5/ Herault, I.: Brain and Neurocomputing. IEEE EUSIPCO '80, Grenoble

/6/ Heite, C.; Goser, K.; Schumacher, K.: Fuzzy Logic Cells in CMOS. ESSCIRC '89, Vienna, to be published

/7/ Hilleringmann, U.; Goser, K.: CMOS-Schaltungen in laser-kristallisierten Siliziumschichten. GME-Fachtagung Mikroelektronik, Baden-Baden '89

/8/ Klar, H; Ramacher, U.: Microelectronics for Artificial Neural Nets. VDI-Verlag 1989

/9/ Kohonen, T.: Self-Organizing and Assoziative Memory. Springer Verlag 1984

/10/ Kreuzer, I.; Goser, K.: A Modified Model of Boltzmann Machines for WSI-Realization. EUSIPCO '88, Grenoble

/11/ Mannel, F.: Are Artificial Neural Networks Finally Ready for Market? Electronics 61, pp. 85-88, Aug. 1988

/12/ Mead, C.: Analog VLSI and Neural Networks. Addison-Wesley 1988

/13/ Mehring, M.; Sixl, H.: Molecular Electronics: Storage and Transport. WOPPLOT '86, Springer Verlag 1987

/14/ Palm, G.: Neural Assemblies, an Alternative Approach to Artificial Intelligence. Springer Verlag 1982

/15/ Rückert, U.; Kreuzer, I.; Goser, K.: VLSI-Design of Associative Networks. VLSI for Artificial Intelligence, Kluwer Academic Publisher 1989

/16/ Rückert, U.; Goser, K.: VLSI Architectures for Associative Networks. IEEE ISCAS, Helsinki, June 6 - 8, 1988

/17/ Rückert, U.; Kreuzer, I.; Tryba, V, Goser, K.: Fault-Tolerance of Associative Memories based on Neural Networks. IEEE COMPEURO '89, Hamburg, to be published

/18/ Shriver, B.; Editor: Artificial Neural Systems. IEEE Computer, Vol. 21, pp. 8 - 117, 1988

/19/ Torinmi, A.; Yoshimi, M.; Iwase, M.; Akiyama, K.; Tamiguchi, K.: A Study of Photon Emission from m-Channel MOSFET's. IEEE Trans. on Electron Dev., ED-34, pp. 1501-1507, 1987

/20/ Weinfeld, M.: A Fully Digital Integrated CMOS Hopfield Network Including the Learning Algorithms. VLSI for Artificial Intelligence, Kluwer Academic Publisher 1989

/21/ Zadeh, L.A.: Fuzzy Logic. IEEE Computer 21, pp. 83 - 92, 1988

An Analog VLSI Architecture for Large Neural Networks

Michel Verleysen, Paul Jespers

Université Catholique de Louvain
Microelectronics Laboratory
3, pl. du Levant
1348 Louvain-la-Neuve, Belgium

Introduction

Neural networks seem to be very interesting in problems such as optimization, pattern recognition and many tasks where perception is more important than a huge amount of computations. However, the interesting properties (speed, fault-tolerance, convergence,...) do not exist when these networks are simulated on conventional computers; the need for dedicated VLSI chips is thus obvious, but the problem is to realize chips where a great number of neurons and synapses can be connected together and integrated on the same chip.

Since a neural network consists in a set of simple processors (neurons) connected to a great number of synapses, it would be difficult to realize them with digital electronics: a simple 100-neuron fully interconnected network would require a hundred 100-input adders, and the area occupied by these cells would be too large for practical applications. Analog techniques will then be used, in order to reduce the size of some elements, even despite a loss of precision.

Analog VLSI architecture for neural networks with synaptic current sources

In artificial neural networks, the elementary processing elements (called neurons by analogy with biological models) are connected through a programmable coupling network. In the model proposed here, each neuron receives information about the state of all the other neurons, weighed by connection strengths (Hopfield's fully interconnected network [1]). A connection between two neurons (called a synapse) can be either excitatory (positive) or inhibitory (negative). Each synapse can source or sink current to the input line of the connected neuron; the direction of the current is determined by a combination of the output of the neuron to which the synapse is connected and a weight value memorized into each synapse. In our model, the output of each neuron is boolean: the logical function of a neuron is thus only a weighed sum of the other neurons with a sign discrimination. Furthermore, only three different connection values are allowed in each synapse: +1, 0 and -1. The direction of the current results from the product of these two values (the neuron output and the connection strength): a product equal to

NATO ASI Series, Vol. F 68
Neurocomputing
Edited by F. Fogelman Soulié and J. Hérault

1 means a sourced current, to -1 a sunk one and to 0 no connection. The architecture proposed here can be generalized if more than three different states are required.

One simple way to realize this architecture is the solution proposed by De Vegvar and Graf [2]; in this circuit, the synaptic currents are either sourced by a P-type transistor or sunk by an N-type one (Fig. 1). However, this solution presents a major drawback: the matching of currents through the N- and P-type transistors is impaired by the mobility differences between electrons and holes. Since in our model, the logical function of each neuron is to detect the sign of the sum of the sourced and sunk currents, the total mismatching between the P- and N-type transistors on each input line must not exceed one single synaptic current. As the synaptic current itself has to be small enough to allow several single currents to be summed on the same line, mismatching constitutes a strong limitation to the maximum number of neurons that can be put together on the same chip.

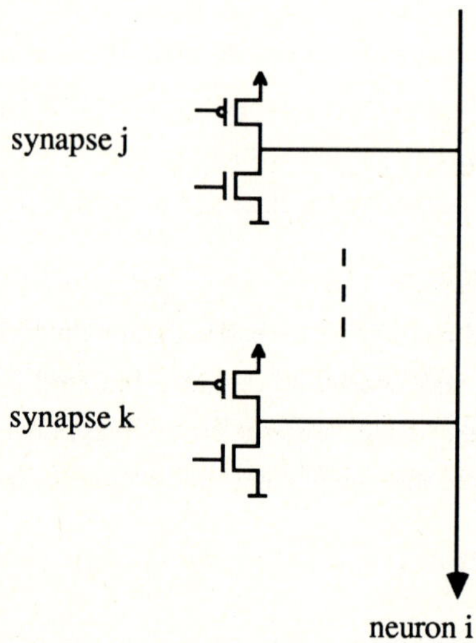

Figure 1. Synapses with P-type and N-type current sources

The problem can be avoided by using the same type of transistors to sink and source current on the input line of the neuron. To realize this, we used two distinct lines to sum the currents: one for excitatory currents, the other for inhibitory currents.

Each synapse is a programmable current source controlling a differential pair (Fig. 2). Three connection values are allowed in each synapse. If "mem1"= 1, current is delivered to one of the two lines with the sign of the connection determined by the product of "mem2" and the output of the neuron to which the synapse is connected. If "mem1"= 0, no connection exists between neurons i and j, and no current flows either to the excitatory line or to the inhibitory line.

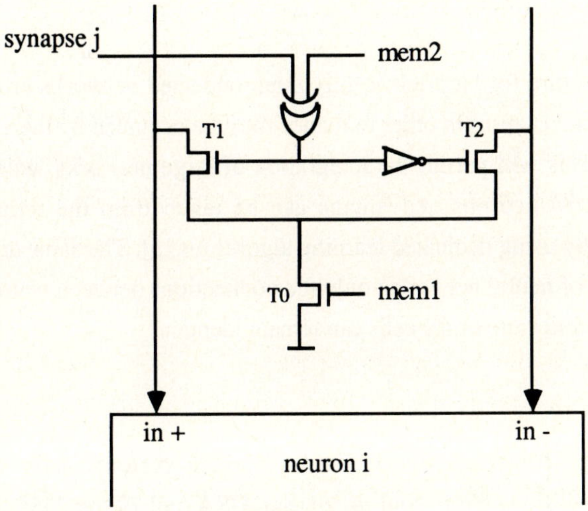

Figure 2. Synapse

Depending on the state of the XOR function, the current may be sourced either on the line i+ or on the line i-. In the neuron, the comparison of the two total currents on the lines i+ and i- must be achieved. This is done by means of the current reflector shown in Fig. 3. The currents on the lines are converted into voltages across transistors *T3* and *T4*; these voltages themselves are compared in the differential input reflector formed by transistors *T5* to *T9*. Because of the two-stage architecture of the neuron, the gain may be very large and the output *(out)* is either 5V if the current in *neuron i-* is greater than the one in *neuron i+*, or OV in the opposite case. The digital output of the neuron can then be fed back into the synapses.

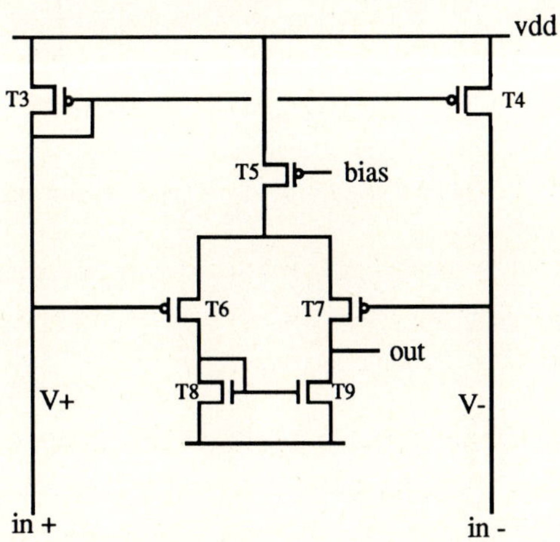

Figure 3. Neuron i

Conclusion

The VLSI architecture for Hopfield's fully interconnected networks proposed here uses very simple neurons and synapses in order to reduce the area occupied by these cells when integrated in a VLSI chip. This will permit the integration of large networks, with several hundreds of fully interconnected neurons. Advantage can be taken from the reduced precision of the synaptic weights by using dedicated learning algorithms [3]. The same architecture can also be used for any type of neural networks: only the connections between neurons and synapses will change, but the architecture of the cells can remain identical.

References

1. Hopfield, J.J.: Neural networks and physical systems with emergent collective computational abilities. Proc. Natl. Acad. Sci. USA, vol.79, pp.2554-2558 (April 1982)
2. Graf, H.P., de Vegvar, P.: A CMOS implementation of a neural network model. Proc. Stanford Conf. on Advanced Research in VLSI, P.Losleben (ed.), MIT Press (1987)
3. Verleysen, M., Sirletti, B., Vandemeulebroecke, A., Jespers, P.: Neural networks for high-storage content-addressable memories: VLSI circuit and learning algorithm. To be published in IEEE Journal of Solid-State Circuits (June 1989)

Analog implementation of a permanent unsupervised learning algorithm

Christian Jutten [1], Jeanny Hérault

INPG/ENSERG/Lab. TIRF
46, avenue Félix Viallet
F-38031 GRENOBLE Cedex- France

1. INTRODUCTION

Today, most applications of neural networks are devoted to pattern recognition in the fields of speech and image processing. The main connectionnist tools used for this purpose are associative memories [9], particularly multi-layer networks associated with the well-known algorithm of the backpropagation of the error gradient [10, 11, 13]. To obtain the best results with these devices, it is necessary to apply some preprocessing which increases the orthogonality degree of the prototypes to be stored. For instance, KOHONEN proposed such a preprocessing, very simple but efficient, with a Laplacian filter [9, pp. 170-71]. First, consider these prototypes, that is the input vectors of these memories. In fact, they come from the outputs of sensors (cameras, microphones or eyes, ears and so on...). These sensors are multi-sensitive : the signal provided by one sensor is a superimposition of signals emitted by all the sources of the neighbourhood. It is clear that decisions and classification of such a set of multi-dimensional data (prototypes) is difficult or even impossible, because of the redundancy of the components of prototype vectors associated to the mixtures. So, separating the independent sources in these mixtures is a very powerful preprocessing.

In the following, this paper is divided in three parts. The first part is devoted to the presentation of the theoretical problem of separation of sources and an adaptive algorithmic solution. In the second one, we propose an analog implementation of that algorithm with discrete electronic components of a simple 2-neuron network. At last, we emphazise in the conclusion the main interesting points emerging from this realization and we discuss of its interest for integrated implementations of others learning algorithms.

---

[1] present address (March to July 1989) : EPFL - Lab. de Microinformatique, avenue de Cour 37, CH-1007 LAUSANNE

NATO ASI Series, Vol. F 68
Neurocomputing
Edited by F. Fogelman Soulié and J. Hérault

2. THE PROBLEM AND A SOLUTION

2.1. The problem.

The problem of separation of sources that we speak about in the introduction is a very classical and difficult problem in Signal Processing. For instance, signals received by antennas are typically mixtures of sources (radio, radar or sonar). We may assume that these sources are providing statistically independent signals. The independence seems to be a very strong property. In fact, if we consider different and pinpoint sources, this hypothesis is consistent. In practice, because both mixtures and sources are unknown, the solution corresponding to a "blind identification procedure" is a complex problem. This problem is also relevant in natural systems : biological signals issued from eyes, ears, temperature sensors of the skin or strecht sensors of the muscles are mixtures of the various sources emitting in their receptor fields. For example, in the case of strecht sensors, it has been shown [6, 12] that the signals transmitted to the Central Nervous System by Ia and II fibers are spike trains which instantaneous frequency codes a mixture of informations about speed and position of the joint. Moreover, it is well-known that fibers Ia (called dynamic fibers) are more sensitive to the speed while fibers II (called static fibers) are more sensitive to the position of the joint. A simple linear (but consistent with physiological knowledge) model of mixtures of these two independent quantities has been proposed [1] ; such a model may easily be extended for mixtures of more than two independent signals.

Consider now a set of p sensors sensitive to the signals $X_i(t)$ emitted by n sources. Let $E_k(t)$ be the signal at the output of the sensor k. If we assume a linear model of the mixtures, we may write the p following equations :

$$E_k(t) = \sum_{i=1}^{n} a_{ki}.X_i(t) \ , \quad 1 \leq k \leq p . \tag{1}$$

In these equations, let us remember that the coefficients of the mixtures a_{ki} and the independent sources $X_i(t)$ are unknown. We may also write the previous equations in matrix notation :

$$E(t) = A.X(t) \ , \tag{2}$$

where E(t) is a p-component vector, X(t) is a n-component vector and A is a rectangular matrix with p rows and n columns.

For the sake of simplicity, we impose n = p. So, the matrix A becomes a square one, that we suppose regular. Solving the problem of separation of sources consists of finding a matrix B such than the product B.A is equal to a product D.P where D is a diagonal matrix and P is a permutation matrix.

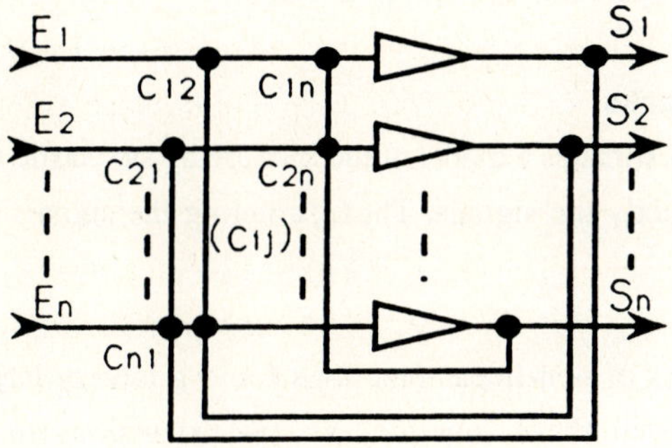

Figure 1. Recursive network architecture.

2.2. An adaptive solution.

We proposed in 1985 [5] a neuromimetic solution to this problem. In this purpose, we use a recursive network of p fully interconnected neurons (figure 1), so that the output $S_i(t)$ of the neuron i of this network is :

$$S_i(t) = E_i(t) - \sum_{k=1}^{n} c_{ik}.S_k(t) \ , \qquad (3)$$

where c_{ik} is the synaptic weight from the neuron k (source) to the neuron i (goal), and $c_{ii} = 0$.

It is easy to compute a set of values of the connections matrix C according to the coefficients of the mixture matrix A, such that the output vector is : $S(t) = D.P.X(t)$. Unfortunately, we don't know the matrix A, and we propose an adaptive rule to estimate the matrix C. This rule is based on the independence hypothesis of the unknown sources $X_i(t)$. The coefficients c_{ik} must be updated until the outputs $S_i(t)$ are also independent. We approximate an independence test by introducing high order crossmoments by means of non-linear odd functions in the adaptive rule, which has the form :

$$dc_{ik}/dt = -\gamma.c_{ik} + a.f(S_i(t)).g(s_k(t)), \qquad (4)$$

where γ is a forgetting rate, a is the learning rate, f and g are two non-linear odd functions, and $s_k(t)$ is a zero mean estimation of the signal $S_k(t)$. This estimation does not need great precision, and a simple first order high-pass filter can be sufficient :

$$s_k(t) = S_k(t) * (\delta(t) - \exp(-t/T)), \qquad (5)$$

where * denotes the convolution operator, $\delta(t)$ is the Dirac function and T is the time constant of the filter.

More precise explanations about this algorithm have already been presented [7, 8], and more theoretical results (based on cumulants) about the convergence and an analytical result have just been developed by P. COMON [2] in this book.

2.3. Some remarks.

First, the network estimates a model of the mixture by stochastic approximation method, but does not process directly the signals. Thus, sampling the signals according to Shannon theorem is not necessary.

Secondly, the class of non-linear functions f and g is very large : they must be odd functions. So, suppose that these functions accept expansions in Taylor Series, these expansions contain only odd powers and it is clear that the high order moments of the product $f(S_i).g(s_k)$ are equal to zero if the signals $S_i(t)$ and $S_k(t)$ are independent. Another explanations of the role of these odd functions are proposed by L. FETY [3].

Last, in the equation (4), the filtering (equation 5) to compute s_k is very important and must be applied even in the case of zero mean signals. This estimation of zero mean signals are approximative, which imply non stationary estimations of variances of signals. Moreover, it can easily be shown [7] that in the plane (c_{ik}, c_{ki}), the locus $< s_i.s_k > = 0$ is a family of hyperboles which depends on the variances of the sources and of the mixture matrix A. If the variances of signals are time dependent, the only common point of these hyperboles is the point characteristic of the mixture, that we are looking for.

3. ANALOG IMPLEMENTATION

We study in this part the analog implementation with discrete electronic components of a 2-neuron network. The recursive network deduced from the figure 1 is shown at figure 2.a. It contains only 2 neuron like elements and 2 synaptic connections, because weights of self-connections between elements are null. According to relaxation and adaptation equations (3, 4) of this network, we may derive the following synoptic representation (figure 2.b). In figure 2.b, bold lines are associated to the relaxation equation, and the blocks in the dotted frame are associated to the adaptation rule.

3.1. Implementation of functional blocks.

The 2-neuron network is done with 2 operational amplifiers used as inverter of gain -1. The products $- c_{ik}.S_k$ are designed by using 2 Field Effect Transistors (FET) as resistors controlled by the gate. The voltage applied to each gate must be an image of the coefficient c_{ik}.

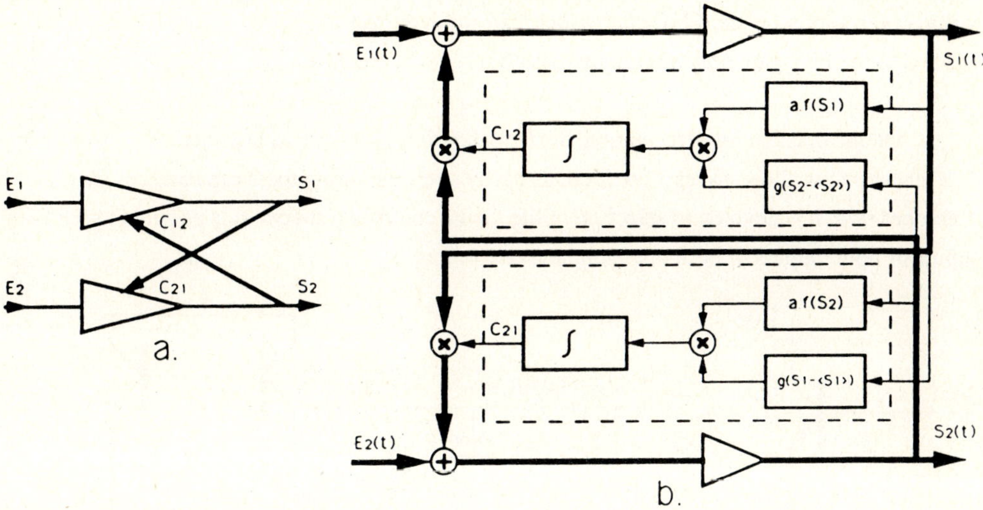

Figure 2. a. 2-neuron network architecture.
b. Functional synoptic of the network of Fig. 2.a.

The adaptation increment Δc_{ik} is the product of 2 non-linear functions. We choose here : $f(S_i) = a.S_i^3$ and $g(s_k) = \tanh(s_k)$. By using non-linear abilities of transistors, such functions are very easy to implement. We propose to model the function f by appropriate linearization of exponential response I(V) of a bipolar transistor (figure 3.a). The bias current I_b of the differential pair of the figure 3.b is then a cubic function of the signal S_i.

The estimation of the zero mean signal s_k is simply done with a C_f-R_f cell, which correspond to a first order high-pass filtering of S_k. For the implementation of function g, we use the well known response of a differential pair whose output is a current proportional to the hyperbolic tangent of the differential input voltage (between the transistors'bases). In fact, the output current of the differential pair is also proportional to the current bias of the pair. Thus, the output current I_s corresponds finally to the adaptation increment (figure 3.b).

To obtain on line the updated value of the coefficient c_{ik}, it is necessary to integrate along the time the adaptation increments. In that purpose, we use a capacitance C_m whose voltage increases or decreases according to the value of the current I_s. To avoid large and fast voltage variations on the FET gate which can induce instability, the voltage capacitance is applied to the FET gate only after a low-pass filtering (figure 3.b).

On the practice implementation, the front board is as simple as possible :
* 2 reset buttons allow to reset coefficients c_{ik} by short-circuiting the 2 capacitances C_m,
* another switch is devoted to selection of the visual control on scope : it is possible to see both inputs or both outputs or both one input and one output.

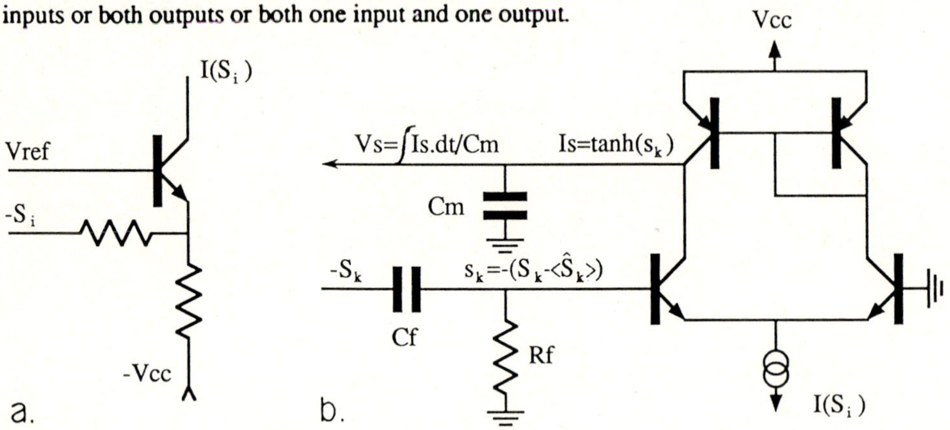

Figure 3. a. Implementation of the function $f(S_i) = a.S_i^3$.
b. Implementations of the estimation of zero mean signals, of the function $g(s_k) = \tanh(s_k)$, and of the integration of adaptation increments.

3.2. Results.

To experiment this device, we use two independent signal sources (for instance, function generators, tape recorders, etc.), we mix them and we apply them to the inputs of the machine. As long as the reset buttons are on, the coefficients c_{ik} are null ($C_m = 0$), outputs and inputs are equal. After the release of these buttons, the time evolution of the outputs is very fast : the separation of the sources is reached in less than a second, with a real time visual control on the scope. The same experiment needs about 500 iterations (network relaxation and weights adaptation) which demands about one minute on a personal computer HP 9816 (200 series).

In figure 4, we present results obtained in the case of mixtures of triangle and sine waves. Figure 4.a. shows the mixed inputs which feed the neural network. Before the learning ($c_{ik} = 0$), outputs are equal to these input signals. Figure 4.b. shows the outputs after about one second of learning. Because the learning is permanent, we can remark some error on these outputs : the triangle wave in Fig. 4.b. contains yet a bit of sine wave and vice-versa.

However, the permanent learning is very interesting for tracking abilities in case of time dependent mixtures.

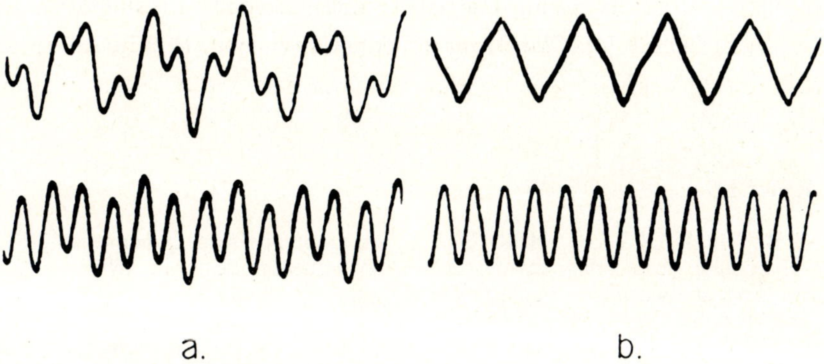

Figure 4. a. Mixed inputs feeding the network.
b. After less than one second outputs have discovered independent signals present in the mixed inputs.

4. CONCLUSION

This implementation is very simple, however it is interesting for many reasons, that we want emphasize now. First, it shows that the precision of analog components is sufficient. Moreover, in a recursive architecture as we use here, the precision must only maintain the stability of the network. This allows a large scale of functions and of values of the parameters and start-up is very easy. Secondly, we can notice the abilities of analog structures to model various non-linear functions : in our implementation, we model a cubic function by using piecewise linearization of exponential response of a bipolar transistor, which implies one transistor and two resistors only, and a tanh function with a differential pair, which needs four transistors. The speed of convergence of the network is very fast, less than one second, about 100 times faster than computer simulations. Moreover, real time actions and controls are possible by using single analog generators (generator of functions, tape or cassette recorder) and a scope. For instance, it is easy to see tracking performances if the mixture is varying, or to verify theoretical results if the two signals (mixtures) presented to the two inputs of the network are proportional. At last, we prove here that the use of a simple capacitance is possible, because the permanent learning and the continuous nature of signals which are fed into the network. So, we think that it can be very interesting to adapt classical algorithms in such a way that learning becomes permanent, or to use this capacitance as short term memory which allows fast learning (but also fast forgetting) associated with long term analog memory (for example, floating gate MOS transistor).

At the moment, a first integrated version in analog CMOS of this algorithm has been already designed in the Swiss Federal Institute of Lausanne (EPFL/LEG) by X. ARREGUIT and E. VITTOZ. The first prototypes have been tested and a 2-neuron network is working now (March 1989). Two other analog integrated implementations are studied in Dortmund University by K. GOSER [4] (CMOS) and in Berlin University by H. BERGER (Bipolar Gate Array).

REFERENCES :

1. ANS B., GILHODES J.-C., HERAULT J., Simulation de réseaux neuronaux (SIRENE). II - Hypothèse de décodage du message de mouvement porté par les afférences fusoriales Ia et II par un mécanisme de plasticité synaptique. C. R. Acad. Sc., Paris, 297, série III, pp 419-22, 1983.
2. COMON P., Statistical approach to the Jutten-Hérault algorithm for separating independent signals.NATO Advanced Research Workshop on Neuro Computing : Algorithms, Architectures and Applications, Les Arcs, 1989, in this book.
3. FETY L., Méthodes de traitement d'antenne adaptées aux radiocommunications. Thèse de l'ENST, Paris, 1988.
4. GOSER K., Basic VLSI Circuits for Neural Networks. NATO Advanced Research Workshop on Neuro Computing : Algorithms, Architectures and Applications, Les Arcs, 1989, in this book.
5. HERAULT J., JUTTEN C., ANS B., Détection de grandeurs primitives dans un message composite par une architecture de calcul neuromimétique en apprentissage non supervisé. Xème GRETSI, pp. 1017-22, Nice, 1985.
6. HOUK J. C., RYMER W. Z., CRAGO P. E., Nature of the dynamic response and its relation to the high sensitivity of muscle spindles to small changes in length. In "Muscle Receptors and Movement" (H. Taylor and A. Prochazka, Eds.), MacMillan (London), pp. 33-43, 1981.
7. JUTTEN C., Calcul Neuromimétique et Traitement du Signal. Analyse en Composantes Indépendantes. Thèse d'état ès Sciences Physiques, INP-USM Grenoble, 1987.
8. JUTTEN C., HERAULT J., Une solution neuromimétique au problème de séparation de sources. To appear in Traitement du Signal, 1989.
9. KOHONEN T., Self-Organization and Associative Memory. Springer-Verlag, 1984.
10. Le CUN Y., A learning scheme for asymetric threshold network. COGNITIVA 85, pp. 599-604, Paris, 1985.
11. PARKER D. B., Learning-Logic. Invention report, S81-64, File 1, Office of Technology Licensing, Standford University, October 1982.
12. ROLL J.-P., Contribution de la proprioception musculaire à la perception et au contrôle du mouvement chez l'homme. Thèse d'état, Univ. d'Aix-Marseille I, 1981.
13. RUMELHART D. E., Mc CLELLANDS J. L. and the PDP Research Group. Parallel Distributed Processing: Explorations in the microstructure of cognition. Vol. 1 : Foundations.

An Analog Cell for VLSI Implementation of Neural Networks

E. Pasero*, L. M. Reyneri**

* II Università di Roma "Tor Vergata", Dip. Ing. Elettronica
Via O. Raimondo, 1 - 00173 Roma - Italy
** Politecnico di Torino - Dipartimento di Elettronica
C.so Duca degli Abruzzi, 24 - 10129 Torino - Italy

This paper presents a silicon implementation of a basic cell for Artificial Neural Systems, which uses analog techniques to implement the computing kernel. The network has a built-in learning facility that implements a discrete delta rule. A prototype chip is actually under development, whose performance has been tailored to typical pattern recognition applications.

Introduction

The interesting perspectives offered by Artificial Neural Systems[1] (ANS) can be efficiently supported by technologies that were not conceivable until a few years ago. The characteristics of these networks require a large number of operations to be executed in parallel, taking remarkable execution time unless several computing units are available. Since the elementary operations required are simple, the easiest way to achieve massive parallel computing is by means of analog circuits.

Studies on Artificial Neural Systems often neglect hardware implementation problems and usually refer to software simulations. The scope of the work described in this paper is to design and implement an ANS on a VLSI silicon chip, flexible enough to fit most user requirements, in terms of interconnection topology, accuracy, response time and learning capabilities.

Analog and digital implementations have been analysed and their performances compared: digital neurons may have as much accuracy as required, virtually unlimited, yet the accuracy influences either the physical size or the computation time. On the other hand the accuracy of analog neurons is limited by noise, drifts and non linearities[2] and it can be related either to the neuron size or to the integration time but it cannot be better than roughly 0.1÷1%.

Some existing models of ANS have been simulated to verify the minimum accuracy required for proper operation, both during learning and in the recognition phase, and it turned out that the accuracy available with analog processors is sufficient for most applications provided that appropriate learning rules are used.

NATO ASI Series, Vol. F 68
Neurocomputing
Edited by F. Fogelman Soulié and J. Hérault

Analog cell for Artificial Neural Systems

The Neural Network presented in this paper is based on the McCulloch and Pitts model and is shown in Figure 1. It is made of a linear array of neurons (vertical columns) with digital inputs and outputs multiplexed on a smaller count of I/O pins to reduce the device package size. Each neuron is made of an array of synapses plus an output signal conditioner, as shown in Figure 2.

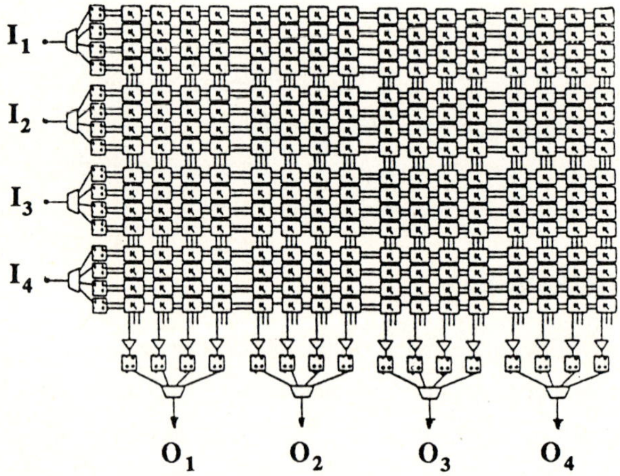

Figure 1 Artificial Neural Network on VLSI chip

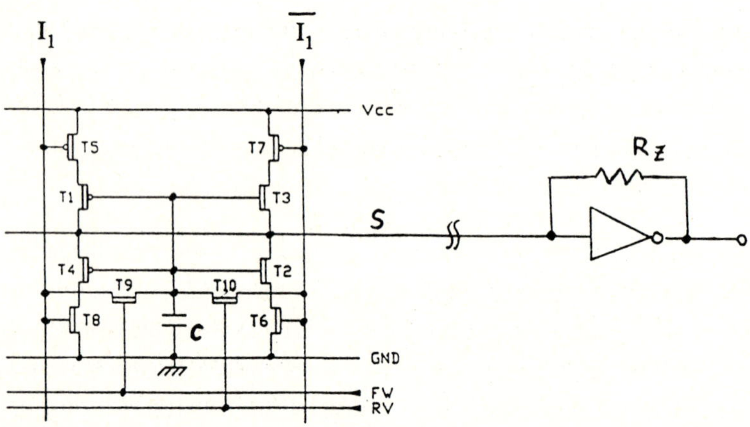

Figure 2 Basic cell for analog ANS

Each neuron computes the weighted sum of the inputs to the network, which are binary signals where the logical *one* and *zero* levels (electrical Vcc and 0 voltages) correspond to +/- 1 values respectively. The weights are stored in each synapse in the form of a charge stored on the capacitor C. Since the absolute value of the input signals is always unity, the multiplier behaves as a sign inverter. The synapse generates (or sinks) a current proportional to the absolute value of the weight with a direction that is a function of the input signal and the weight sign. All the currents are injected on the same summing line S and the sum is converted into a voltage by means of the output transconductance amplifier. The amplifier holds the voltage on the line S at a constant value $V_{CC}/2$ via the resistor feedback R_Z.

From Figure 2 it can be seen that each synapse behaves as a variable resistor controlled by the voltage V_C stored on the capacitor. The synapse receives both the input I_i and its logical complement. When the input I_i is at logical one, transistors T_7 and T_8 are turned on and enable transistors T_3 and T_4 which behave as variable current sources controlled by the voltage V_C. The current will be either positive or negative if V_C is higher or lower than $V_{CC}/2$ respectively. On the other hand when I_i is at logical zero the other four transistors (T_5, T_6, T_1 and T_2) are enabled and the circuit behaves in a similar way but the versus of the current is reversed. Formula (1) gives the theoretical weight of the synapse as a function of the voltage V_C.

$$W_i^j = \left\{ \begin{array}{ll} \frac{K_T}{K_A} \cdot \left(\left(V_C - \frac{V_{CC}}{2} \right) - V_{th} \right)^2 & \text{if } V_C > \frac{V_{CC}}{2} \\ \frac{K_T}{K_A} \cdot \left(\left(\frac{V_{CC}}{2} - V_C \right) - V_{th} \right)^2 & \text{if } V_C < \frac{V_{CC}}{2} \end{array} \right\} \tag{1}$$

The synapse has also a built-in learning capability given by the transistors T_9 and T_{10}, controlled by two lines which are shortly pulsed only when the neuron output does not correspond to the target: FW (*forward*) is pulsed when the target is at logical one, RV (*reverse*) otherwise. It has been proven via simulation that the weights converge and the network learns.

Optimization of the Neuron Size

The goal of the study was to reduce as much as possible the size of each neuron without affecting significantly the overall performance. It has been found that the physical size of the neuron depends on the *target current* which is the maximum current allowed to flow in each transistor (i.e. when the weight is maximum)[3]. For low levels of current each transistor must have a small W/L (width/length) ratio, namely below unity so that the area is inversely proportional to the target current, while for large values of current each transistor must have a W/L ratio above unity so that the area becomes directly proportional to the target current. A similar analysis holds also for the feedback resistor and the output inverting amplifier. Further, the neuron size is affected also by the required accuracy. Figure 3 (taken from [3]) plots the total size (excluding interconnections) of a 30 inputs neuron versus the total current (flowing in the summing line) for a simplified version of the same cell (with no correction transistor) and a required accuracy of ≈2%. It is clear that the area shows a minimum for a given total current $I_{opt} \approx 0.3$ mA (target current ≈ 10 μA). This corresponds to given sizes for all the elements, namely: Ratio W/L for T_2 and T_3: 2/20 μm; Ratio W/L for T_1 and T_4: 2/7 μm; Resistor R_Z: 5 KΩ; Ratio W/L for output inverter: 90/2 μm (pull-up).

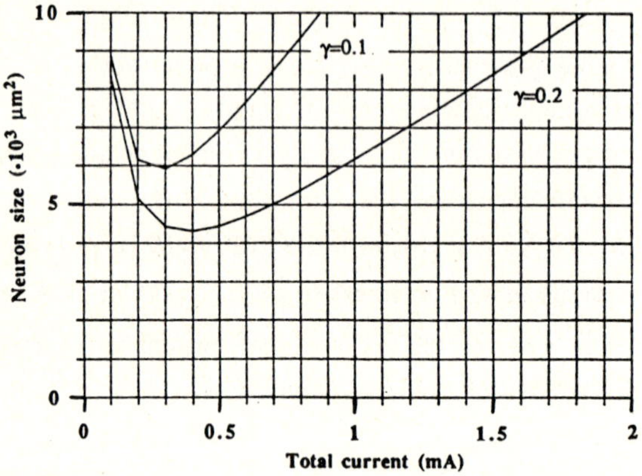

Figure 3 Neuron size versus total current (with 30 inputs)

Conclusion

The feasibility of an analog cell for Artificial Neural Networks has been demonstrated, and a prototype chip is currently under development implementing a fully connected array of 32 neurons with 32 inputs. The neuron size has been optimized for given (typical) performances.

References

[1] Carpenter, G.A., Grossberg, S.: The ART of Adaptive Pattern Recognition by a Self-Organizing Neural Network. Computer, (March 1988).

[2] Mead, C.A. : Analog VLSI and Neural Systems. Addison-Wesley, (1988).

[3] Mourad, K., Portinaro, N.: Progetto e Ottimizzazione di un Sommatore Analogico per Reti Neurali in Tecnologia CMOS. Internal Report, Politecnico di Torino, (April 1989).

Use of Pulse Rate and Width Modulations in a Mixed Analog/digital Cell for Artificial Neural Systems

D. Del Corso, F. Gregoretti, L. M. Reyneri

Politecnico di Torino - Dipartimento di Elettronica
C.so Duca degli Abruzzi, 24
10129 Torino- Italy

Abstract

The paper presents a silicon implementation of a basic cell for Artificial Neural Systems. Information is represented and processed by means of pulse rate and width modulations and the cell uses a mix of analog and digital circuitry. In the prototype currently under development the resolution of the processing elements can be varied to suit the requirements of different network architectures and applications.

1- Introduction

Studies on Artificial Neural Systems (ANS) often refer only to software simulation[1] and do not take care of hardware implementation problems. The goal of the work described in this paper is to design and implement an ANS on a VLSI silicon chip with enough flexibility, in terms of interconnection topology, accuracy, response time and learning capabilities, to enable its use for experiments on various application architectures.

Current VLSI technology allows the mixing of analog and digital circuits on the same silicon chip[2]. Both techniques have relevant advantages and disadvantages, and a good overall performance can be achieved using, in each functional block, the most suitable approach. The circuit described here uses pulse rate modulation to move information among different neurons, and pulse width modulation for input weighting. Since both types of modulation use two-level signals, they can be handled by standard digital circuitry, while the input weighting and summation is better accomplished with the simple analog circuits presented further. Also other processing techniques which operate on pulse streams are currently being studied, with the aim of achieving minimum area occupation for a given accuracy.

2- Representation of information

Physical quantities are easily represented by means of *analog* signals, which can assume any value within a certain range and are time-continuous. Analog signals are affected by various types of

NATO ASI Series, Vol. F 68
Neurocomputing
Edited by F. Fogelman Soulié and J. Hérault

noise which puts inherent limits on the achievable accuracy. Time- and amplitude-discrete signals (respectively called *sampled* and *numeric*) are preferred for processing, because noise can be removed from them. The accuracy of numeric variables depends only on the number of digits (bits) used, and can be preserved during information transmission and processing. The last reason has made digital computers the preferred tool to simulate the behaviour of analog systems but, if lower accuracy can be tolerated, the analog approach may offer higher processing power for the same silicon area[3].

There are techniques which can represent continuous quantities using binary signals, such as *pulse rate* and *pulse width modulations* which are shown in fig. 1. Pulse rate modulation (PRM) associates the information to the interval between two pulses (T_R) while pulse width modulation (PWM) uses the width of each pulse (T_W).

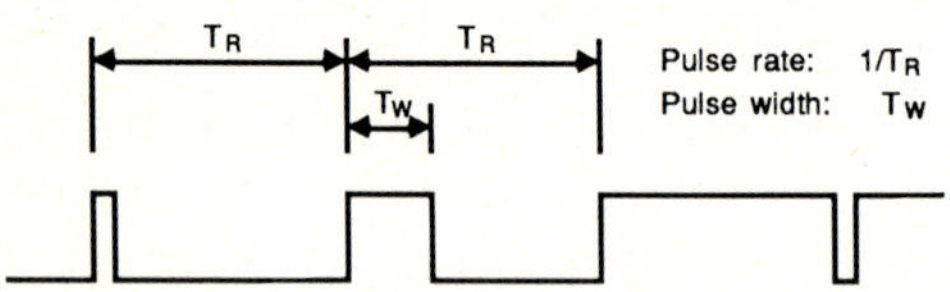

Figure 1. Pulse rate and width modulations

3- Rationale for the use of pulse rate modulation

Pulse rate modulation has also other advantages than those mentioned above. It is known that some natural neuronal structure uses, among other methods, pulse phase modulation which associates information to the time skew between two (or more) pulses carried by the same or even different axons. Although similar to pulse rate modulation, this technique has faster response because information is associated only to a pair of pulses and not to an average pulse rate meaned over several periods. In this way information is transmitted only when required, while keeping the system (i.e. the neurons) in a low-power, no-activity (idle) state otherwise.

The neural network proposed here can be easily adapted to that form of information encoding, by appropriately selecting the time constant of an output filter. It is not yet obvious which choice is more appropriate to electronic circuits, and both pulse stream and pulse-pair encoding will be considered in the further developement of ANS with the PR-PW cells.

4- Analog vs. Digital tradeoff

As a general rule, analog circuits are well suited to those cases where processing is simple (e.g. summations, simple non-linear functions, integrations and filtering) but accuracy is not critical, while the physical size must be minimized. Digital circuits are better suited to the transmission of information with a high noise immunity and to an easy long-term storage of information. Digital circuits allow higher accuracy, at the expense of an increase in the bit count, which corresponds to a larger silicon area. Since state-of-the-art VLSI technology allows integration of both analog and digital circuits on the same silicon chip, it is useful to design circuits by combining both methods in such a way to obtain the best from each of them. The accuracy limits of the analog parts shall be compensated by the choice of a proper network architecture.

In the case of ANS the circuit density and interconnection complexity are critical factors, and this claims for simple information transfer techniques combined with small processing circuits. With PR and PW modulations, the former goal is achieved by using binary signals, and the second by using analog processing circuits.

5- Basic principle of the cell for Neural Networks

The energy of a square wave (in this case, its mean value) is proportional to the product of the pulse width and the pulse rate. If each pulse is stretched by an amount proportional to the weight, it is possible to use that principle to multiply the input value by the stored weight. A block diagram of the circuit which performs this function is shown in figure 2. The pulse stretcher is a down counter, which is loaded, at each pulse, with the value stored in the weight memory. The terminal count signal of the counter is a waveform with the same rate as the input signal and a width proportional to the weight, thus a mean value proportional to the product of the input value and the weight.

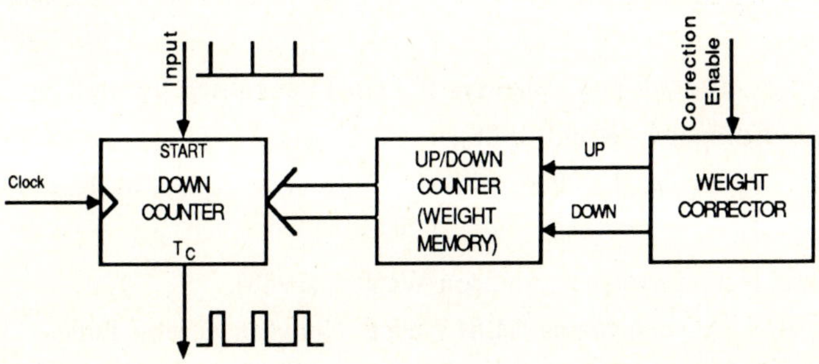

Figure 2. Pulse stretcher: block diagram

The stretched pulse enables, within each synapsis, a current source (or sink, for the logical zero), therefore the currents from each synapsis are directly summed on a virtual ground node that enters a transconductance amplifier, as shown in figure 3, the output of which is filtered and converted back to a pulse stream, rate-modulated. A proper combination of current mirrors reduces the simmetry problems improving the overall linearity of the system.

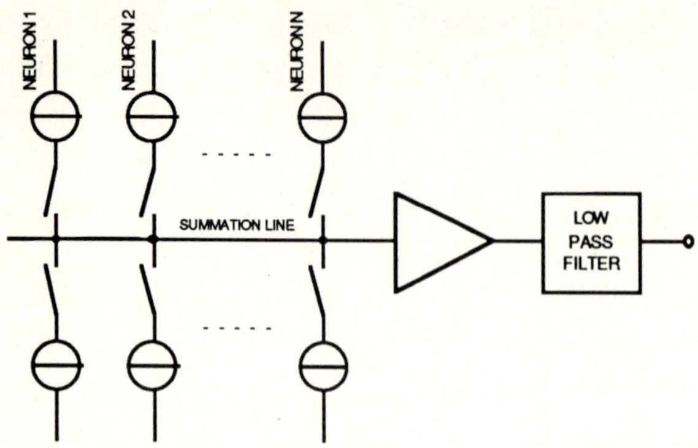

Figure 3. Analog adder with current sources

6- Performance analysis

The performances of the network can be adapted to fit different requirements, in terms of response time, accuracy and resolution. The neuron response time T_R has been evaluated as:

$$T_R \approx K \cdot T_W \cdot D$$

where T_W is the minimum pulse width allowed by the chip technology, D is the weight dynamic (i.e. the inverse of the weight resolution or the system accuracy) and K is a correction factor ranging from 1 to 10 that takes into account the filter type.

7- References

[1] Carpenter, G.A., Grossberg, S.: The ART of Adaptive Pattern Recognition by a Self-Organizing Neural Network. In Computer, (March 1988).

[2] Kubo, M., Masuda, I., Miyata, K., Ogiue, K.: Perspective on BiCMOS VLSI's. In IEEE JSSC, Vol 23, n. 1, (February 1988).

[3] Mead, C.A.: Analog VLSI and Neural System. Addison-Wesley, (1988).

[4] Murray, A.F., Smith, A.V.W.: Asynchronous VLSI Neural Networks Using Pulse-Stream Arithmetic. In IEEE JSSC, Vol 23, n. 3, (June 1988).

Parallel Implementation of a Multi-Layer Perceptron

F. Baiardi, R. Mussardo
Dipartimento di Informatica, Università di Pisa, Corso Italia 40, 56100 Pisa (Italty)

R. Serra, G. Valastro
ENIDATA, viale Aldo Moro 38, 40127 BOLOGNA (Italy)

Abstract

In this paper we describe a parallel implementation of a multi-layer perceptron for a message-passing parallel architecture following the vertical-slicing approach. A theoretical analysis shows that linear scalability may be achieved both in recognition and learning, at the expense of a proper replication of data structures in order to optimize the communication phase.

Scalability is a function of the number of neurons per processor, of the communication bandwidth and of the ratio between processing time and communication time. We show how, given a particular neural network, the number of processing elements that minimizes the execution time can be determined.

The theoretical analysis has been confirmed by an actual implementation in the case of a Transputer-based system with 40 processing nodes.

1. Intrinsic parallelism in back-propagation

The back-propagation algorithm, which is particularly interesting in neural network research [1][2], is intrinsically parallel [3], [4], [5]. It is possible to find out two major types of parallelism.

Neuron parallelism: neurons belonging to the same layer can compute in parallel their outputs in the forward phase, while in the learning phase they can compute in parallel the gradients of the cost function and modify the weights accordingly.

Synapse parallelism: a finer grained parallelism inside each neuron can result from the weighted sum in both phases.

In our implementation we have exploited only the neuron parallelism which is better suited to a coarse grain parallel computer; it would be possible to exploit both types of parallelism on a fine grain parallel machine or on a coarse grain parallel machine with a Vector Processing Unit.

To exploit the neuron parallelism we have chosen the 'vertical slicing' [3] approach. In a multi-layer perceptron only one layer at a time is allowed to update its own state; therefore the

NATO ASI Series, Vol. F 68
Neurocomputing
Edited by F. Fogelman Soulié and J. Hérault

maximum degree of parallelism may be exploited by partitioning the computational load associated with the neurons belonging to the same layer on all processors ('slice' process). The allocation of neurons on processors may be a random one since full connectivity between the layers of the neural network is assumed.

Each processor, after computing its own part of layer (h), communicates its outputs to all the other processors and then it computes its part of layer (h+1). The weights of the connections between layer (h) and layer (h+1) are allocated on layer (h+1); a duplication of the same weights on layer (h) reduces the number of communications required in the learning phase.

2. The recognition phase

Let N(h) be the number of neurons of layer h, d the number of links per processor (8 in our case), c_m the cost of computing one term of the weighted sum (1 multiplication + the time for memory access), c_f the cost of computing the sigmoid function $f(x)=1/(1+e^{-x})$ (exponential + the time for memory access), c_b the cost of the communication of 1 byte on a link (included the time for memory access). Let us also call k_i various overhead constants,*SP* the set of 'slice' processes used in the computation, p the number of processors and $D \approx d\,p\,/\,2$ the total number of link in the communication network.

We can estimate the execution time for the recognition phase in a sequential implementation as:

$$T_R^{seq} \approx \Big(\Sigma_{h=1,..(L-1)} \ (c_m\, N^{(h)} N^{(h+1)} + c_f\, N^{(h+1)} + k_1) \Big) + k_2 \,.$$

In a parallel implementation, the execution time for the recognition phase is the sum of elaboration and communication; in the communication phase we can use only *broadcast messages*. Under the assumptions that : i) all the nodes broadcast their messages simultaneously and ii) the load due to these communications is uniformly ditributed among all the links of the network, we have (6):

$$T_R^{par}(P) \approx \big(\Sigma_{h=1,..(L-1)} \ (CE_h / p + CC_h / D)\big) + k_3 \qquad \text{where}$$

$$CE_h = (c_m\, N^{(h)} N^{(h+1)} + c_f\, N^{(h+1)} + k_4)$$ is the cost of the elaboration of the layer (h+1), so that $\Sigma_{h=1,..(L-1)}\, CE_h = T_R^{seq}$, and

$$CC_h = \Big(\Sigma_{s \in SP}\, \Sigma_{r \in SP - \{s\}} \ (\, c_b\, (w\, N^{(h)}/\, p + z) + k_5)\,\Big)$$ is the global cost of the communication between layer (h) and layer (h+1); w and z are respectively the number of bytes used to code the output of a neuron and the number of bytes used for the message headers (in our implementation w=4, z=8).

In order to simplify the equations, we shall consider the case where the number of neurons per layer (**N**) is constant, therefore:

$$T_R^{par}(p) \approx (L-1)((c_m N^2 + c_f N + k_4)/p + (2(P-1) c_b (w N/p + z)/d) + k_5)) + k_6 \quad (2)$$

From Eq. (2) we can find p_{ott}, i.e. the number of processors for which the time $T_R^{par}(p)$ is minimum:

$$p_{ott} = (d/2 z c_b (c_m N^2 - (w c_b/d - c_f) N + k_4/N^2))^{1/2} \approx (d c_m / 2 z c_b)^{1/2} * N .$$

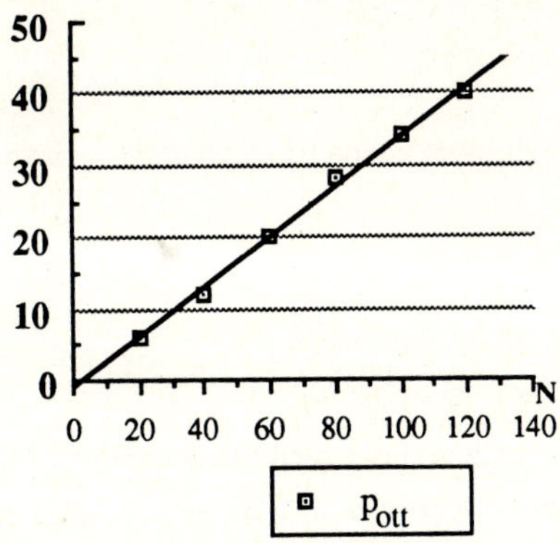

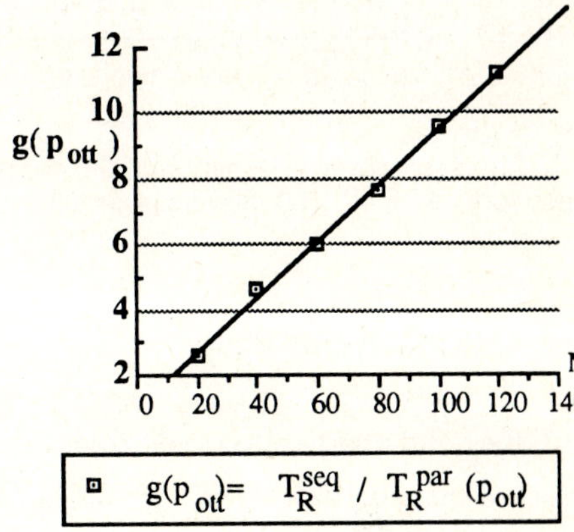

Fig. 1. optimal number of processors and speed-up in the recognition phase with optimal density of neurons per processor (three-layer network).

Therefore the speed-up is maximum when the number of neurons per processor is *constant*; the experimental results shown in Fig. 1, confirm the validity of the teoretical approach; the angular coefficient is approximately 1/3.

The optimal execution time can be obtained from Eq. (2) by replacing p by p_{ott}. From the Eqs. (1) and (2), we obtain the optimal speed-up that is approximately:

$$g(p_{ott}) = T_R^{seq} / T_R^{par}(p_{ott}) \approx 1/(2(z r)^{1/2} + w r) * N + k_9 , \quad \text{where} \quad r = 2 c_b / d c_m$$

Fig. 1 shows that the experimental results are in accordance with the previous equation; the angular coefficient is approximately 1/11.

3. Non optimal mapping

Equations (1) and (2) show that, by increasing the number of neurons per processor, the value of the speed-up becomes near to the number of processors used (Fig 2) but it is always less then the value of the optimal speed-up obtainable with $p = p_{ott}$ if enough processors are available.

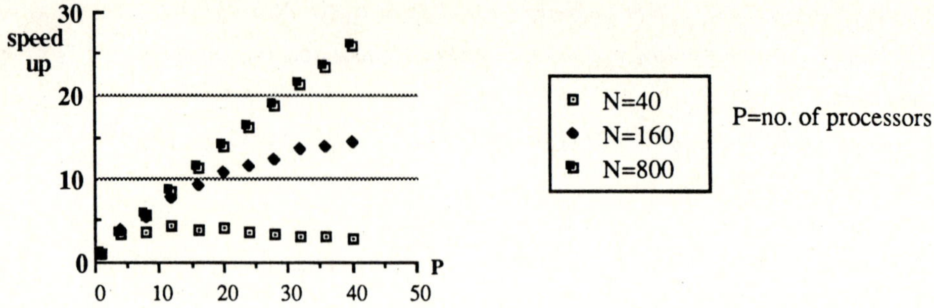

Fig. 2. speed-up as function of the number of processors in the recognition phase (two-layer networks with 40, 160, 800 neurons per layer)

4. The learning phase

If c_p is the cost of the modification of a weight (2 multiplications + memory access), c_s the cost of the modification of a threshold (1 multiplication + memory access), $c_{f'}$ the cost of computing $f'(x)=e^{-x}/(1+e^{-x})^2$ (exponential + memory access), we can estimate the execution time for the recognition phase, with sequential updating, as:

$$T_L^{seq} \approx T_R^{seq} + \{\Sigma_{h=1,..(L-1)} [(c_p+c_m) N^{(h)} N^{(h+1)} + c_s N^{(h+1)} + c_{f'} N^{(h)} + k_{10}]\} + k_{11} .$$

If there are **N** neurons in every layer, then:

$$T_L^{seq} \approx (L-1)(2\, c_m + c_p) * \mathbf{N}^2 + (L-1)(c_f + c_s + c_{f'}) * \mathbf{N} + (L\, k_{12} + k_{13}) .$$

Learning phase, first version.

If the weights of the connections between layer (h) and layer (h+1) are allocated on layer (h+1), each processor computes its own part of the gradients of layer (h+1), and then it sends the pertinent weighted sums to each other processor with *point-to point* messages. If the routing is optimal we have:

$$T_{L1}^{par}(p) \approx T_R^{par}(p) + \Sigma_{h=1,..(L-1)} (CM_h / p) + \Sigma_{h=2,..(L-1)} (CC_h / D)$$ where

$CM_h = ((c_p + c_m) N^{(h)} N^{(h+1)} + c_s N^{(h+1)} + c_{f'} N^{(h)} + k_{14})$ is the global cost of modifying both the weights between layers (h) and (h+1), and the thresholds of the layer (h+1),

$CC_h = (\Sigma_{s \in SP} \Sigma_{r \in SP-\{s\}} [\mathit{dist}(s,r)\, c_b\, (w\, N^{(h)}/p + z)\,] + k_{15})$ is the global cost of the communication from layer (h+1) to layer (h).

In this case, *dist*(s,r), i.e. the distance between processors s and r, plays a critical role: in fact $T_{L1}^{par}(p)$ is of the same order as $T_R^{par}(p)$ only if $\forall r,s \in SP$ *dist*(s,r) is constant, that is if the network is fully connected; if the interconnection topology is a ring $T_{L1}^{par}(N)$ is $O(N^2)$,.if the interconnection topology is a mesh $T_{L1}^{par}(N)$ is $O(N^{3/2})$. The asymptotical behaviour of the speed-up in a ring is constant and in a mesh is $O(N^{1/2})$.

Learning phase, second version

If the weights of the connections between layer (h) and layer (h+1) are allocated on layer (h+1) and they are duplicated on layer (h), processors have to compute the weights modification twice, but they can use *broadcast* messages which are much more efficient than *point-to point* messages. If the routing is optimal we have:

$T_{L2}^{par}(p) \sim T_R^{par}(p) + \Sigma_{h=2,..(L-1)} (CM_h / p) + \Sigma_{h=2,..(L-1)} (CC_h / D) + CM_1 / p$ where

$CM_h = 2 ((c_p + c_m) N^{(h)} N^{(h+1)} + c_s N^{(h+1)} + c_f N^{(h)} + k_{17})$ is the global cost of modifying the (duplicated) weights between layers (h) and (h+1), and the thresholds of the layer (h+1),

CC_h is the same as in the previous calculation, and

$CM_1 = ((c_p + c_m) N^{(1)} N^{(2)} + c_s N^{(2)} + c_f N^{(1)} + k_{18})$ is the cost required to modify both the (not duplicated) weights between layers (1) and (2), and the thresholds of the layer (2).

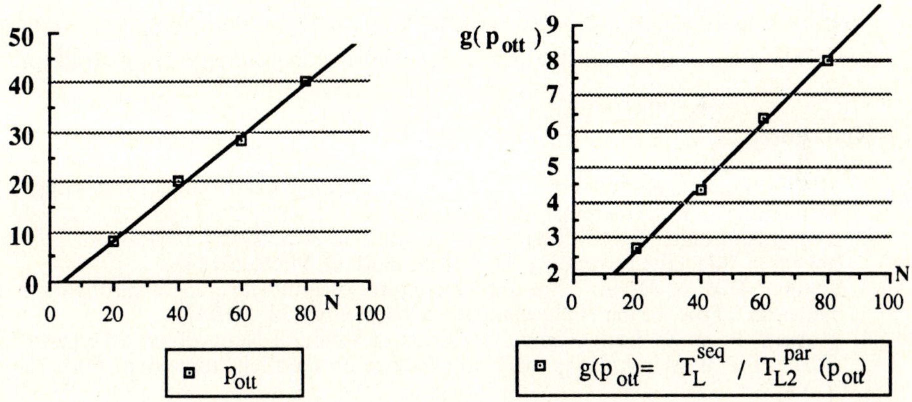

Fig. 3. optimal number of processors and speed-up in the learning phase with optimal density of neurons per processor (three-layer network).

If the number of neurons per layer (N) is constant, we obtain:

$T_{L2}^{par}(N) \approx [(L-1) c_m + (2L-3) (c_p + c_m + 2 (w+z) c_b/d)] * N + (L k_{19} + k_{20})$.

The linear behaviour of T_{L2}^{par} (N) has also been experimentally confirmed.

In the learning phase too we can obtain the number of processors for which the time $T_{L2}^{par}(P)$ is minimum and the speed-up is maximum. Also in this case, the optimal number of neurons per processor is *constant* and it is typically lower than the corresponding one in the recognition phase. In Fig. 3 we show experimental results concerning the optimal number of processors and the corresponding speed-up .

5. Conclusions

In this paper we have described a parallel implementation of a multi-layer perceptron for a message-passing parallel architecture with a small number of links per processor. A proper replication of data has been adopted, in order to optimize the communications in the learning phase.

A theoretical analisys of the performance has been done: in particular we supposed that in a communication intensive parallel computation, in which each processor broadcasts messages to the other processors, the critical aspects are the communication bandwidth of the interconnection network and the way how the routing algorithm uses it. The number of links per processor and the interconnection topology are important essentially for their influence on the communication bandwidth.

We have shown that it is possible to obtain a linear scalability in both the recognition and the learning phases. Given a particular neural network, we have shown how the number of processors which minimizes the execution time can be computed, and we have proven that it corresponds to a constant number of neurons per processing node. The theoretical analysis has been confirmed by experimental results so far involving up to 40 processing nodes.

References

1. Mc Clelland,J., Rumelhart, D.E. et al. : "Parallel Distributed Processing", vol. 1, Cambridge MA, MIT Press, (1986).
2. Fogelman-Soulie, F., Gallinari, P., Le Cun, Y. & S. Thiria : "Network Learning", to appear in "Machine Learning", vol. 3, Kodratoff, R. Michalski Eds.
3. Beynon, T. & N. Dodd: "The implementation of multi-layer perceptrons on transputer networks", Proc. of the 7th Occam User Group, Grenoble, (1987).
4. Robert, F. & S. Wang: "Implementation of a Neural Network on a Hypercube F.P.S. T20", IFIP Working Group 10.3, Conference on Parallel Processing, Pisa, Italy (April 1988).
5. Forrest,B., Roweth, D., Stroud, N., Wallace, D., & G.Wilson: "Neural network models", Edinburgh preprint no. 87 / 419, (1987).
6. Baiardi,F., Mussardo, R., Serra, R. & G. Valastro: "Feedforward Layered Networks on Message Passing Parallel Computers", to appear in "Proceedings of the 1989 Workshop on Parallel Architectures and Neural Networks", E.R. Caianiello editor, World Scientific Publishers, London, in press.

A monolithic processor array for stochastic relaxation using optical random number generation

P. Garda, K. Madani, F. Devos
I.E.F., C.N.R.S. L.A. 22, Bat. 220, Un. de Paris Sud, F-91405 ORSAY

P. Chavel, P. Lalanne, J. Taboury
I.O.T.A., C.N.R.S. L.A. 14, B.P. 43, F-91406 ORSAY

Abstract

The architecture of an electronic retina for image processing by stochastic relaxation is described. It consists of a 2-D array whose PE implementation uses both analog and digital devices, and is specifically designed to take advantage of an optical random number generator. It is well suited to applications where the input data is a grey-level picture, the output data is a binary picture, and the energy model is a generalization of the Ising model with external field.

0. Introduction.

Neural networks are currently used for several low level image processing tasks. Regarding these tasks, some of their features may be underlined, as they make easier the design of the network. Firstly, the parameters of the net may generally be considered as shift invariable. Secondly, the relations between the network vertices may be restricted to neighbors. Finally, some weights adapted to the problem may be suggested by the designer instead of resulting from a learning phase. Whereas taking advantage of these features generally leads to lower quality results, it also greatly simplifies both the network and its implementation.

By the way, several special purpose hardware implementations of neural networks are currently under design. When these hardware are dedicated to low level image processing, it is particularly efficient to map the local dependance and shift invariability of the tasks to the hardware itself. That is to say the architecture consists of a 2-D array of identical processing elements (P.E.), each of them being connected to its nearest neighbors. Moreover when the P.E. are small enough for a complete system to fit in a single chip, then giving each P.E. its sensor results in a so-called electronic retina.

Talking about retinas, we present in this paper such devices dedicated to image processing by simulated annealing. Simulated annealing has been more and more popular since its introduction in [1] as a generic optimization procedure. An increasing number of applications to image processing - called stochastic relaxation - and related developments have been reported

NATO ASI Series, Vol. F 68
Neurocomputing
Edited by F. Fogelman Soulié and J. Hérault

after [2]. The interest of these techniques are their good performances from the image processing viewpoint and their good statistical modeling. Unfortunately they require a high computational power. Some parallel implementations have been described, but real time executions are still out of reach [3]. On the other hand, electronic retina are useful in a number of applications, where compactness and fast processing time are important, but their implementation constraints make them compute bound. Thus one can try to use stochastic relaxation to increase their image processing performances.

In this paper, we describe an electronic parallel mesh array which performs very fast stochastic relaxation thanks to an optical random number generator and specific analog and digital implementations. The paper has three parts : we present at first image processing by stochastic relaxation, then the overall architecture specification and design choices, and finally the implementations functionalities.

1. Stochastic relaxation.

We sketch here the use of stochastic relaxation for image processing. More detailed descriptions can be found in [2] and [4]. In this case we consider discrete pictures only, i.e. pictures which are temporally and spatially sampled with quantized pixels. Now a first step is to state the low level image processing task to be performed as an optimization problem. That is to say some cost function has to be defined, such that the pictures whose value through the cost function is minimal among all possible pictures are considered as the best results for this low level task.

Once the low level image processing task has been modeled as an optimization problem, one still has to find a way to minimize it practically. This procedure is a Monte Carlo algorithm, called simulated annealing, as it consists of the numerical simulation of the thermal annealing of some physical system which is equivalent to the cost function tailored for the low level task. For this purpose some procedure replacing the thermal agitation has been described, as well as some temperature decreasing schedule . One will generate a sequence of pictures such that from one iteration to the next only one site in the picture may change. This sequence is computed in a way such that it converges in some sense to a picture of minimal energy.

Now let us describe the perturbation which leads from the n-th picture to the (n+1)-th in the sequence. In the case of the Metropolis dynamics [5], the site whose pixel value may change is chosen at random among all picture sites under some uniform distribution law. Let s_0 be this site. The pixel value q of the particle at this site may change according to the following rule : choose at random a new pixel value q' under a uniform law on the set of pixel values Q. Let I be the n-th picture and I' the picture I where only pixel value at site s_0 is changed to q'. Compare the energy of I' to that of I : if it is lower, then let I' be the (n+1)-th picture. If it is higher, let ΔE be the quantity (E(I') - E(I)). Now perform some coin tossing with probability $\exp(-\ \Delta E / T)$: if its answer is positive, then let the (n+1)-th picture be I', otherwise let it be I.

This rule gives the procedure to compute the change of a single pixel value from one picture to the next in the sequence of pictures which converges to a minimum energy picture. Clearly the use of this procedure for a parallel processor rises some questions which will not be covered in this paper. Incidentally the temperature parameter, which is controlled by the experimenter, has to decrease slowly in order for that convergence to be insured. Theoretical temperature schedule follow $O(K / \log(n + 1))$, whereas practical ones follow $O(K * T^{n})$. In the next section we describe the architecture of a parallel processor dedicated to this approach.

2. Processor architecture.

2.1. Functionalities.

As we intend a short term monolithic implementation, we cannot afford the hardware for the general case which has been previously described. Both computational and memory requirements can be restricted if one uses only binary pictures as the evolving states. We feel that the following energy gives a common framework to a number of simple low level tasks such as digital halftoning or edge detection :

$$E(B) = \sum_{ij}\left(\alpha_{ij} + \sum_k \beta_k\ e_k(B_{ij+V_k})\right)$$

where α_{ij} is some integer grey level picture ;

$(\beta_k)_k$ is some integer convolution kernel ;

e_k is some local boolean function whose support is included in V_k;

B_{ij} is the computed binary picture ;

$e_k(B_{ij+V_k})$ is a boolean expression whose variables sites are located inside $(ij+V_k)$.

2.2. Architecture.

The architecture consists of a 2-D processor array which works in a SIMD mode. The PE are connected according to a mesh, that is to say each PE is connected to its four nearest neighbors in the North, East, West and South directions. The links between PEs and between the PE units are one bit wide digital lines and all communications between the units are made in a bit-serial way.The PE is organized around three units as needed by the previous computations (figure 2) :

- an Acquisition and Memory Unit, (AMU) whose functionalities are to acquire some grey level picture A and to store it as well as a binary picture B ;

- an Energy Evaluation Unit (EEU), whose purpose is to compute the variation ΔE in the energy from one iteration to the next at the given site ; these computations are made on a local basis ; the accumulation of the different elements appearing in the accumulation of the conditional sum which makes the energy expression are done sequentially, and each of the integer terms is accumulated serially ;
- an Exponential Random Number Generation Unit, (ERNGU) which makes a coin tossing with exponential law out of the parameter ΔE. ΔE is given in a serial way, and the binary result of the coin tossing is output of the unit.

3. Implementation.

We sketch here the implementation lines that we are following. Their main objectives are to result in a processor array which fits in a single chip and which could execute the Metropolis dynamics for the energy described in a time as close as possible to real time.We require a granularity of the parallel machine to be well-suited to the use of optical computing means to achieve compactness and fast processing time.

The network is implemented thanks to a 2-D two-way shift register. It easily allows all neighboring communications at an arbitrary distance and provides at the same time the memorization of a one bit picture.

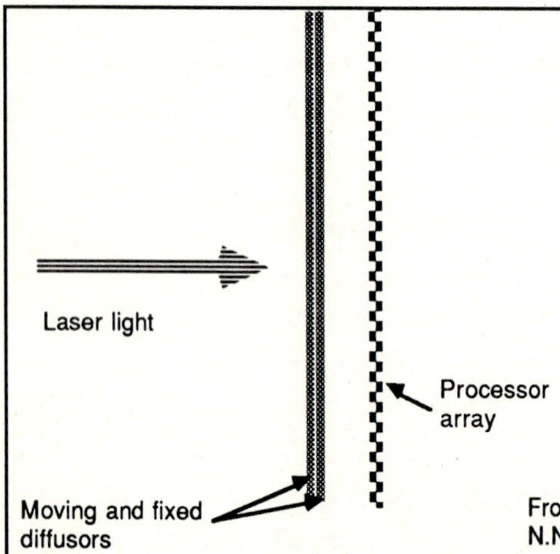

Figure 1 : optical R.N.G.

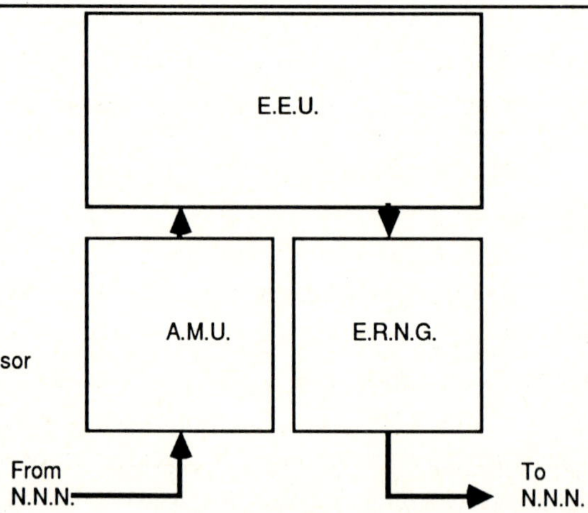

Figure 2 : P.E. organization

As far as the implementation of the PE units is concerned, we suggest to follow an approach which is well suited to low grey scale resolution pictures, small extent and low dynamic kernel coefficients. We try to use, as long as possible, mixed analog and digital cells, and even opto-electrical for the ERNGU.

- The AMU consists of a photodiode and an analog memory, whose interface with the interconnexion network is digital ;
- The EEU may be a serial digital accumulator whereas an analog implementation was suggested in [6] ;
- The ERNGU is implemented as a hybrid optical and electronic device (figure 1). The main point is to rely on some physical process to generate 2-D random pictures. It has been described in [7]. After some investigations, laser speckle as been preferred, and a theoretical evaluation has been done. The optical setup which is built in front of the focal plane array consists of a laser and two diffusers in rotation. It has been shown in [8] that a suitable choice of the setup geometric parameters should lead to the following results:

- the spatial independence of neighboring samples is guaranteed;
- the temporal independence of successive samples at a given site is guaranteed;
- the distribution law of the samples is exponential;

Finally this generator can lead to an ERNGU provided that one samples it with an integration time which is proportional to ΔE.

Clearly the test of the array presents a number of problems. Firstly, the A.M.U. and E.E.U. may be functionally tested as usual. However one should take care of the array structure for the test. Secondly the E.R.N.G.U. may be tested statistically, i.e. its performances may be tested through some statistical test.

4.Conclusion.

In this paper we have sketched a parallel architecture for its implementation for a class of stochastic picture processing algorithms. We have given the main design choices which make it suitable for a mixed analog, digital and optical implementation. In a 2μ 2 metals CMOS process, the PE density would be about 30 x 30 PE per cm^2, and a single halftoning Metropolis iteration for a 3x3 constant kernel with a 20 MHz clock frequency on a 5 bit picture could be expected to take about 400 μs.

Acknowledgements.

This work has been granted by GCIS of CNRS and partly by D.R.E.T. under convention 87/292.

References.

1. Kirkpatrick S. & al.: Optimization by simulated annealing. Science, 8, 67, (1983).
2. Geman S. & al. : Stochastic relaxation, Gibbs distribution and the Bayesian restoration of images. IEEE Trans. PAMI, Vol. 3, 721-741, (1984).
3. Murray D.W. & al. : A parallel approach to the picture restoration algorithm of Geman and Geman. Image Vision Computing, Vol. 4, N° 6, 133-142, (August 1986).
4. Carnevalli P. & al.: Image processing by simulated annealing. IBM J. of res. & Devlpt., Vol. 29, N° 6, 569-579, (Nov. 1985).
5. Metropolis N. & al. : Equations of State calculations by fast computing machines. J. Chem. Phys., 21, 1087, (1953).
6. P.Garda & al. : A massively parallel image processor for stochastic relaxation using optical random number generation. Optical Computing 88, Toulon , 08-30/09-02, (1989).
7. Devos F. & al. : Optical generation of random number arrays for on-chip massively parallel Monte Carlo cellular processors. Optics Letters, Vol. 12, N° 3, (March 1987).
8. Chavel P. & al. : Utilisation du speckle comme générateur rapide de tableaux aléatoires binaires: optimisation des paramètres. Annales des Télécommunications, (March 1988).

Dedicated neural network
A retina for edge detection

D. Collobert, S. Salaün, P. Guyader, J. Guerin, B. Vinouze

Centre National d'Etudes des Télécommunications
BP 40
22 301 Lannion cedex - FRANCE

1- Introduction

Metals, insulators and also semi-conductors are already available from thin film technology by the way of deposition techniques. Glass substrates allow large area (100 cm ^{2}) devices. With a rule pattern of 10 µm, the built up of 100 000 components on a single chip is quite at hand. This technology has been developed in our laboratory especially for neural networks purposes.

2- The retina

The attractor of our work is an active retina which extracts the contours of real images incoming on one of its faces and gives the edged images on its other face (Fig. 1).

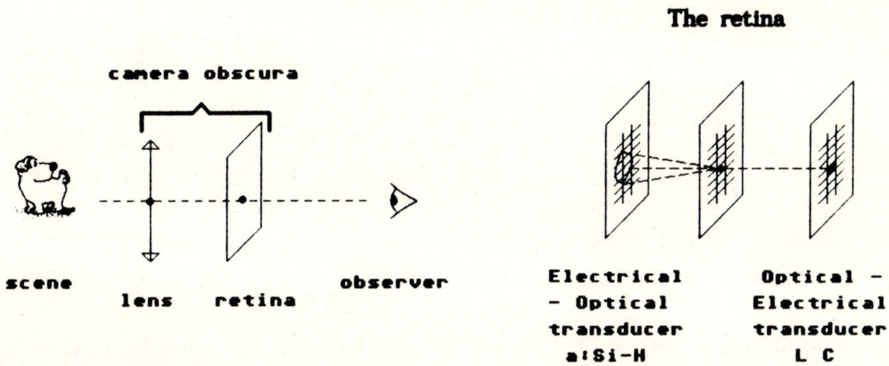

Figure 1. The set up

The retina is split in 3 functional parts:

- the first one is an array of photoreceptors. We choose amorphous hydrogenated silicon (a:Si-H) for its photoelectrical properties and the opportunity to deposit it by the way of the so-called Plasma Enhanced Chemical Vapour Deposition technique (PECVD).
- the second part of the retina is an array of automata, the neurons: each of them processes electrical information provided by some photoreceptors located in its neighbourhood.

NATO ASI Series, Vol. F 68
Neurocomputing
Edited by F. Fogelman Soulié and J. Hérault

- the last part of the retina is an array of electrical-to-optical transducers. We choose liquid crystal because they need low level power supply which is not the case for other materials presently available in thin film technology like electroluminescent materials.

A black matrix is deposited onto the rear of the retina in order to prevent light from passing through it and inducing trouble to the observer.

3- The omega point

The ultimate point of our work is drawn on Figure 2. There, the human eye is replaced by a black and white video camera and some electronics performing standard data compression method in order to transmit images of contours (512x512 pixels, 25 images/sec, 64 Kbits/sec) on a specialized telephone network (NUMERIS which is the French commercial name of ISDN).

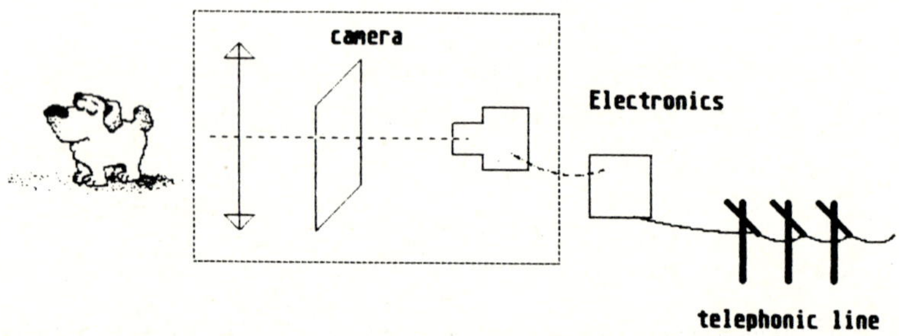

Figure 2. The retina as a mean to transmit edged images.

In this arrangement, the retina makes the parallel computation of edges, and the black and white camera the serial transformation required for transmission.

Before going further, let us discuss contours images and answer the question of how such images are understood by people.

We realized a video tape of half an hour (by computer simulation) with different kinds of sequences and we tested this film with deaf people. The deaf are able to understand the edged film, either the sign and body language sequences or the lip reading sequences. The success score was 65% [1]. The conclusion is that these cartoon-like images should be a good mean of communication among the non-deaf community.

4- Edge detector

Many types of edge detectors are used in digital image processing. Most of them are based on local computation of gradients and most techniques are limited to processing over 3x3 windows [2]. Nonlinear edge detection utilizes nonlinear combination of pixels as a means of edge enhancement before thresholding.

In Figure 3, we have drawn a simple mask with a pixel ponderation of 8 in the middle and -1 in the surrounding. It is easy to see that if the window applies on a uniform grey region, the result of the computation is zero. Otherwise the result is different from zero, and there is an edge at this point.

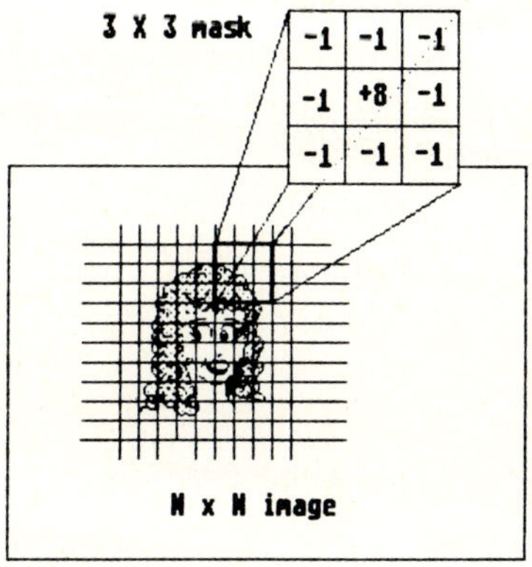

Figure 3. A sliding window is used to obtain the contours in digital image processing.

The most powerful detector is the so-called SOBEL. It consists of the sum of two masks making enhancement at right angle directions. Notice that the result is the sum of the two absolute values given by each mask. (See first part of Figure 5). Of course, there is also a thresholding.

5- Silicon implementation: principles

A single operator could be represented in three different ways as reported on Figure 4.

- The first way is the 3x3 window as used in digital image analysis.
- The second is a neural representation. The "neuron" computes the weighted sum of its inputs and thresholds the result. The "synaptic" coefficients are the different values of the mask.
- The third is the electrical equivalent. Here the inputs are positive or negative but have the same absolute value. The values of the resistances R are such that their conductance (1/R) are proportionnal to the desired value. In the case of the nine values mask, there are nine synaptic

weights per neuron, i.e. nine resistances, (and one neuron per pixel) and the currents passing through each resistance are summed up on a single wire. In our case this summing up develops some voltage on the liquid crystal cell. If this voltage is high enough, the transparency of the display changes.

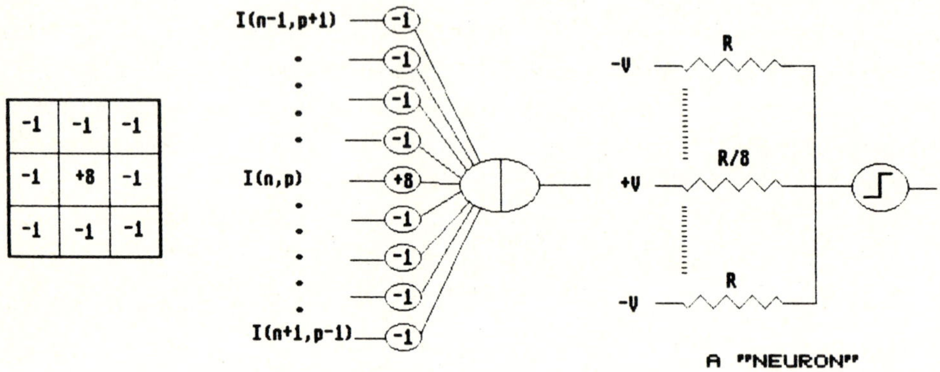

Figure 4. Three ways to represent a mask.

6- Sobel

The Sobel is composed of two operators with a total amount of 12 non null weights. As we have to physically build these weights, a problem of congestion arises for it is difficult to have two resistances at the same place, each of them computing one part of the total Sobel. Moreover, it is difficult to connect all the resistances in the whole image plane.

A solution is to take back some of the resistances, namely those at opposite corner, as shown on Figure 5.

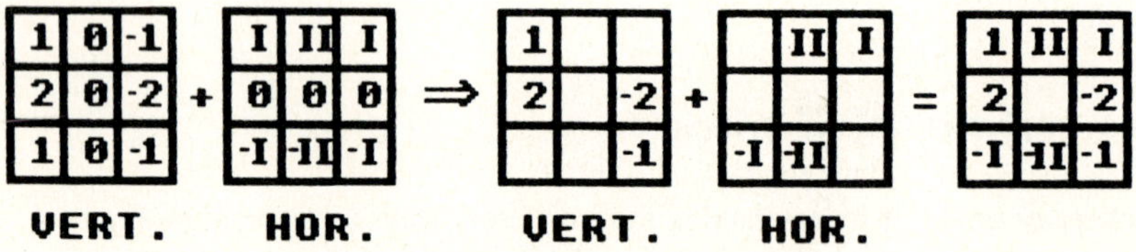

Figure 5. The true Sobel (left) and the modified Sobel (right)

On this figure, numerals are for the horizontal detector, arabics for the vertical one. So we obtain a modified Sobel. Simulations, as proposed in [2] p 495, show that the modified Sobel works nearly as well as the true Sobel. More precisely the performance criteria (as defined by equation 17.5-1 of ref 2) of the modified mask is only 5% less than the unmodified, when the signal to noise ratio is less than 10. Above this SNR, both are equivalent.

7- Feeding and thresholding

How can we cope with the problem of doing the sum of two absolute values and with the problem of thresholding?

The trick is to use two properties of the liquid crystal. The first property is that LC is a thresholding device with a sigmoidal threshold between 3 and 6 Volts, depending on the very mixture in use. The second property is that the LC is only sensitive to rms voltages.

Finally, we use two sets of supplies as those shown on Figure 6. In each set the two supplies are in opposite phase, and the two sets are out of phase of $\pi/2$.

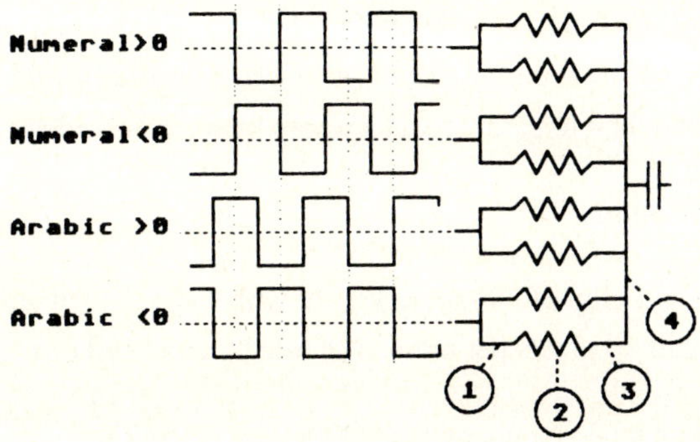

Figure 6. The full set of supplies

It is easy to show that the overall rms voltage one gets on the summing wire is proportional to the desired sum.

8- The sketch of the device

is shown on Figure 7.

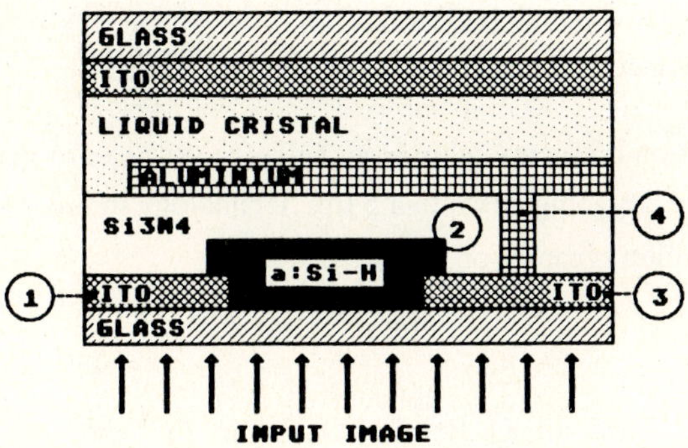

Figure 7. Schematic view of one resistance

The first part of the device is a sheet of glass covered with a layer of ITO (Indium Tin Oxyde), a transparent and conductive material. ITO is patterned in order to make the wires numbered 1 and 3 on Figure 6. Wire 1 supports the incoming current, wire 3 the outgoing current. Between these two wires a tiny plot of amorphous silicon stuffes up the hole.

The layer of silicon nitride ($Si_3 N_4$) insures the collecting wire (4) is not short circuited with feeding wires.

The last layer (Al) has a square shape to delimit the pixel area. It sums up all the elementary currents passing through the corresponding 8 resistances by means of 8 holes patterned in the insulating layer.

There is also a second sheet of glass covered with a uniform layer of ITO to insure closing of the electrical circuit. Not shown on the sketch, is a black matrix, a grid of non transparent material to avoid incoming light to pass through the gap between two adjacent pixels.

9- Results and conclusions

The state of the art now is a chip of 30 mm x 30 mm with 120 x 120 pixels. Each pixel is 250 µm on a side, which means 16 pixels per mm^2. The rule pattern is 10 µm.

The 14 400 neurons with a total amount of 115 200 synapses work in full parallelism.

The operating rate could reach 50 images per second although it is difficult to evaluate this performance.

The needed illumination of the scene is in the order of 500 lux, which is obtained without special floodlighting.

Unfortunately, until now we have not succeeded to make a chip with zero defect. The chip we presented at the meeting has about 20 broken lines. It is the reason why we present on Figure 8 only the result obtained when a single neuron scans a colored image.

The need of zero defect on a 10 cm^2 chip is a challenge we hope to master in a very near future. From now on, we are going down to a 5 µm technology in order to obtain 240 x 240 pixels and near half a million synapses on a chip.

Acknowledgements

We thank P. Anizan, D. Bardouil, O. Bernier, O. Collin, G. Leroy of the neural network group at CNET for helpful comments.

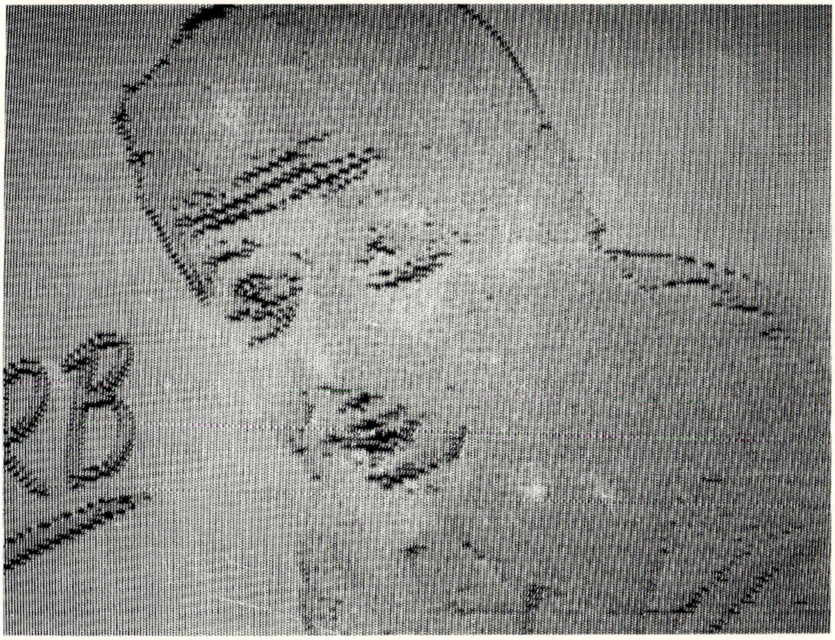

Figure 8. The result obtained with a single neuron scanning an image

References

1- Zambrano, J., Besson, R.: Studies on the use of telephone networks for deaf communications. In X Congress of deaf world federation. Helsinki, (1987).

2- Pratt, W.K.: Digital image processing. John Wiley & Sons, (1978).

Neural Network Applications in the Edinburgh Concurrent Supercomputer Project

M.G. Norman, N.J. Radcliffe, G.D. Richards, F.J. Smieja, D.J. Wallace,
Physics Department, University of Edinburgh, Edinburgh EH9 3JZ.
J.F. Collins, S. J. Hayward,
Biocomputing Research Unit and Molecular Biology, University of Edinburgh.
B.M. Forrest,
Institut fur Festkörperforschung, Kernforschungsanlage Julich.

Abstract

The Edinburgh Concurrent Supercomputer Project is built around a Meiko Computing Surface, with presently some 400 floating point transputers and 1.6 Gbytes of memory. The first part of this paper gives a brief overview of the Project's origins and status. In the second part we review work in neural network models, including analogue neurons for image restoration, studies of texture discrimination and protein structure predictions using a multi-layer perceptron simulator. The problem of optimisation of machine topology is also discussed in the context of irregular graphs and genetic algorithms.

1. Project Origins

Work at Edinburgh on the use of parallel computers for Physics applications began in 1980, on the ICL Distributed Array Processor at Queen Mary College. This initiative was spearheaded by Stuart Pawley, whose main interest was in molecular dynamics, but the work rapidly expanded into lattice field theory as we appreciated the potential of this fine-grain SIMD machine. We were successful in acquiring a dedicated machine at Edinburgh in 1982, through funding from the Science and Engineering Research Council and a collaborative agreement for software development between ICL and the Edinburgh University Computing Service. Within a year we were able to persuade ICL to donate a second DAP. These machines exemplified many of the strengths of parallel architectures. For example, with off-the-shelf mid-70's technology, they provided a sustained 20 Mflops for a range of problems including lattice field theory, neural networks and molecular dynamics, and outperformed all existing vector supercomputers for problems involving boolean variables or short word problems, such as the Ising spin model and molecular

NATO ASI Series, Vol. F 68
Neurocomputing
Edited by F. Fogelman Soulié and J. Hérault

sequence analysis. This was all the more remarkable when one notes that the total capital and maintenance funding required over a period of 5 years was only £300K. The machines had to be decommissioned in 1987, on the replacement of the ICL hosts which acted as the University mainframe resource. At that time some 180 publications had resulted from the work; a summary can be found in [1].

The anticipated replacement of the ICL host machines, and the now large community dependent on high performance computing obliged us to look for alternative machines. We were convinced then that the only way we would have access to the required power with the budgets we might expect was through exploiting parallel machines with novel architectures. We already had a relationship with Inmos, who were supporting a student in parallel computing for particle theory, and were fortunate to obtain one of the earliest Meiko Computing Surfaces in April 1986, with the support of the Department of Trade and Industry and the Computer Board. This demonstrator system consisted of 40 T414 transputers each with 1/4 Mbyte, along with a display system, and was file served and networked through a MicroVAX host. The reliability of this system, the imminent loss of the DAPs and a survey of existing parallel machines formed the cornerstone of the proposal for the Edinburgh Concurrent Supercomputer (ECS). The proposal in collaboration with Meiko sought some £3.4M from the SERC, DTI and Computer Board to fund a machine built around 1024 T800 transputers (with floating point capability) each with 1 Mbyte of memory, to provide an electronically reconfigurable multi-user resource. After some three months the three funding agencies agreed in principle to consider jointly funding the machine. Phase 1 funding for the machine infrastructure and compute resource of 200 T800s each with 4 Mbytes was secured during 1987, multi-user service for code development was established in September 1987, and the first T800 compute resource installed at the end of that year.

2. Present status

2.1 Funding

The present (April 1989) level of commitment to the Project is shown in Table 1. The initial DTI contribution funded the infrastructure for the machine, including cabinets, inter-cabinet link boards, 32 host boards for code development, 4 display systems and some 5 Gbytes of disc. Their contribution has recently been increased by £569K of Phase 2 support, which has enabled us to expand the compute resource with another 195 T800s and 900 Mbytes of memory. The Computer Board and SERC support includes some £600K for hardware, which provided the Phase 1 T800 compute resource and a frame grabber and fast I/O system. Their contributions also contain some funds for software, maintenance, and up to three people for up to five years. Meiko have also contributed very significantly in hardware, maintenance and software; in addition they site two people at Edinburgh and have considerable in-house software activity to meet the Project requirements. The University has committed £60K in cash in this year alone, as well as three computing officers for service management and support.

Department of Trade and Industry	£1144K
Computer Board	£575K
SERC (Science and Nuclear Physics Boards)	£400K
Meiko Limited (excl. personnel)	£779K
Scottish Development Agency	£10K
Industrial Affiliation (cash and kind)	£700K
Edinburgh Univ. 3 Computing Officers, infrastructure	£76K

Table 1. Funding support for the ECS as at April 1989

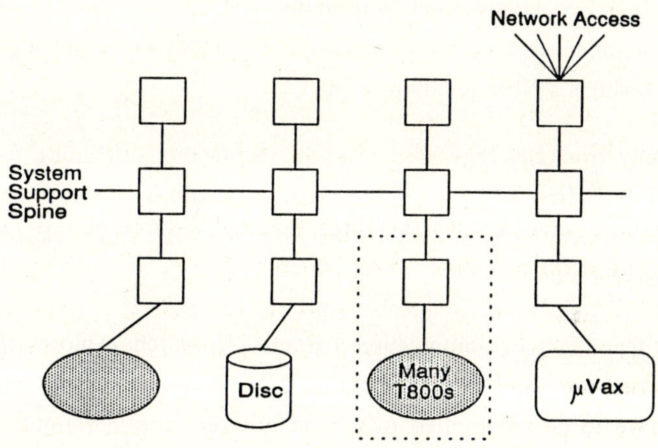

Figure 1. Schematic diagram of Computing Surface organisation

2.2 Hardware configuration

General information about the transputer, the Computing Surface and the occam language can be found in [2]. The machine organisation is shown schematically in figure 1. It is built around a transparent communication spine which is also built from transputers. Various other devices are also attached to the machine through the spine. The MicroVAX host of the original demonstrator system is now retained as one of the file servers, and to provide a VMS environment. The main file service is provided by a number of HP discs running a Berkeley 4.2 BSD file system. Access is provided by direct lines and from JANET via a reversed PAD, soon to be replaced by an ethernet. To provide multi-user capability the compute resource is divided into domains; the size and number of these is controlled by the system manager, and in practice is changed twice daily (exploiting the software reconfiguration) to match day and night time user needs. At present there are typically more than 20 domains on the service machine; a separate machine for system development can support a further 8 users. At login, the user is presented with a menu of domains; she boots an available domain and a file server and has then a personal parallel machine. Back-up is provided by Exabyte cartridges.

2.3 Software and projects

The multi-user system outlined above, MMVCS, provides the user with the occam programming system OPS and UNIX file serving utilities (UNIX is a trademark of AT&T Bell Laboratories). There are also C and Fortran compilers for single transputers and a range of utilities is available or under development at Meiko. At the time of writing, the UNIX system, MEIKOS, is mounted and under test on the development machine. Among the work being performed on the development machine is a porting of the AT&T System V utilities, which is close to completion.

There are currently over 200 registered users of the facility, including some 42 M.Sc. students. The Project Directory [3] gives a snapshot of the 60 projects underway as of September 1988; the number continues to increase. Among those related to topics of interest in this workshop are:

* A topology independent communication harness [4], which explores the transputer configuration at run time and sets up point-to-point communications and broadcasts. Code does not have to be recompiled to run on different configurations. The start-up latency is 17 microseconds and the through-routing CPU overhead time is 19 microseconds per node with a realised bandwidth of around 1.4 Mbytes per second per link. The flexibility of this utility has been used to explore the properties of irregular graphs [5], which have many attractive features, including mean interprocessor distance and diameter which increase only logarithmically with the number of (fixed-valency) nodes, and are very close to the optimal bound. Such graphs provide a framework for shared memory emulation on distributed memory machines, following the work of Valiant [6].

* An improved environment [7] for developing and running programs, providing split-screen facilities supporting the selective presentation of, for example, debug

information through the Meiko system bus, incremental reconfiguration (i.e. step by step modification of the topology of the array), and planned reconfiguration during a run.

* The porting of other packages and utilities such as GKS.

* A parallel 3-d graphics facility [8].

Further information about these and other projects can be found in the Project Directory [3] and also in the Project Newsletters. We turn now to some neural net applications on the machine.

3. Optimisation by analogue neurons

Analogue neurons were introduced by Hopfield and Tank [9] as a general technique for optimisation problems involving boolean variables. The method was applied by them originally to the travelling salesman problem, although it turns out not to be effective at that particular task [10]. It has also been used to perform analogue-to-digital conversion [11] and load balancing in parallel computing [12]. We focus here on image restoration, using the algorithm of Geman and Geman [13] for binary images which have been corrupted by noise; see also the work by Murray et al [14] using the simulated annealing algorithm [15]. The analogue neuron scheme [16] involves representing the array of pixel intensities as a network of neurons, each of which can 'fire' on a continuous scale from non-firing ('black' pixel) to fully-firing ('white' pixel).

The technique of analogue neurons is directed towards finding good minima of a cost function in which the variables are boolean, e.g. $E = -\frac{1}{2}\sum I_i I_j J_{ij} - \sum U_i I_i$, where J_{ij} and U_i are given and the I_i (0 or 1) are the variables. The method proceeds by introducing a real variable $\phi_i(t)$ which evolves according to the coupled differential equations: $d\phi_i/dt = -\phi_i/\tau + \sum J_{ij} I_j + U_i$, where $I_i(\phi_i)$ is the usual logistic function, $(1 + \exp(-g\phi_i))^{-1}$. This evolution is motivated by analogy with currents and resistors in a network. As discussed in [9], the flow is governed by a Lyapunov function, so that the ϕ variables tend to a fixed point which for large gain g is close to 0 or 1.

The Geman and Geman formulation of image restoration starts from the Bayesian relation $P(I|D)P(D) = P(D|I)P(I)$ for the joint probability of the clean image I and the noisy data D. The problem is posed in terms of finding the image I which maximises $P(I|D)$, i.e. in terms of minimising a cost function $E \equiv -\ell nP(I|D) = -\ell nP(I) - \ell nP(D|I)$ + constant. The first term must capture the statistical properties of clean images. In the simplest case, we can enforce scarcity of edges by introducing a nearest neighbour interacton, $J_{ij} = J > 0$ between neighbours i and j on the pixel lattice. Further, if we model the noise generation by the probability p that each pixel is flipped (wrong), the term $\ell nP(D|I)$ can be written in terms of a threshhold term with a given value of U_i.

This problem is intrinsically SIMD-parallel, with short-range communications, so that it can be expected to run efficiently on most parallel machines; at Edinburgh it was studied both on the DAP [16] and a comparative study made of DAP and Computing Surface implementations [17].

The performance of the restoration by this analogue neural network method was compared to that of a simple majority-rule scheme in which each neuron continually adopts the intensity of the majority of its four nearest neighbours, or remains unchanged if exactly two of its neighbours are 'white', until the image stabilises. A third restoration method - performing a gradient descent - was achieved by restricting the neuron firing rates to discrete values ('on'/'off'). The analogue neural network method consistently finds better solutions [16] than these schemes, as illustrated in figure 2.

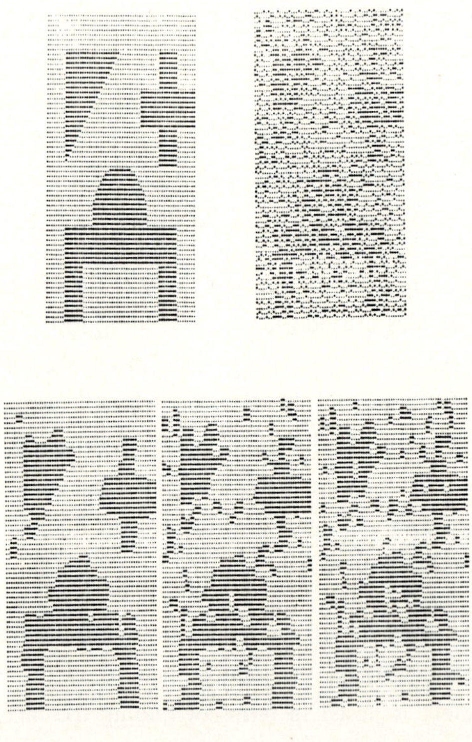

Figure 2. Image restoration by analogue neurons in the framework of Geman and Geman [13]. The top two images are an original, and with 30% noise. The bottom three are from (a) analogue neurons, (b) gradient descent and (c) a majority rule. From [16].

4. Multi-layer perceptron simulator.

A general purpose simulator for layered networks with error correction by back-propagation has been implemented on the Computing Surface. There are many levels of potential parallelism in a multi-layer perceptron (mlp) network; the basic strategy in the simulator is to distribute the weight matrix for each layer over the array which is configured as a torus, so that each processor is responsible for a part of the weight matrix in every layer. The user specifies either interactively or from a file the number of layers, nodes in each layer, the structure of connectivity, and the various net parameters (weight change factor, momentum factor etc) and the net is then mapped transparently on to the array. The software has been sold and used successfully for commercial purposes. Further information about it is given in [18,19].

An early use of the simulator was in the study of structured training, to illustrate how the organisation of a training set (so that easy examples are presented first and then progressively more difficult ones) can be an effective strategy for successful training in hard problems [20]. Three other projects underway are described below.

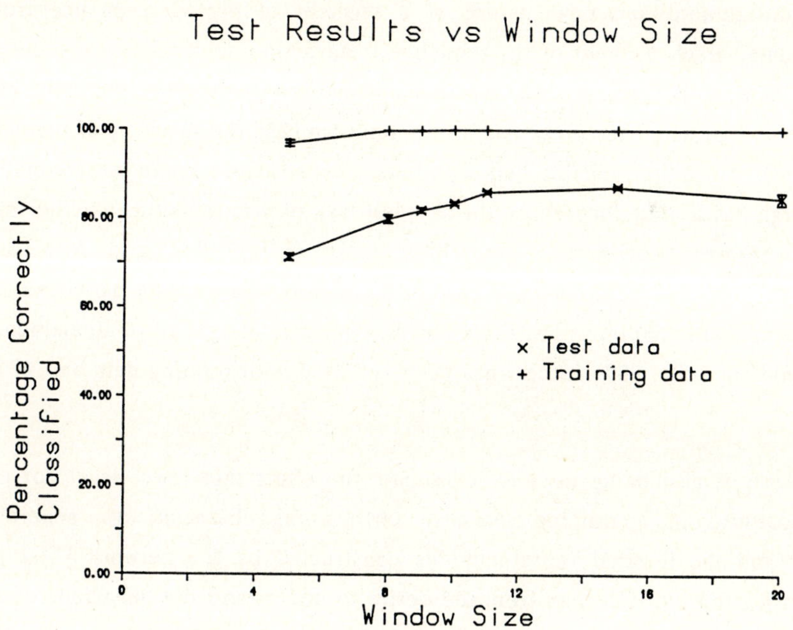

Figure 3. Discrimination of four of the textures of Brodatz [22] using a multi-layer perceptron. The percentage of correct identifications is shown as a function of the size of the window for the training and test data.

The first is the problem of texture recognition. In this application, the inputs are grey-levels in a window of a texture and the target output is a 1 in the node representing that texture and 0 in the others. Following earlier work [21], the aim of the study at Edinburgh (G.D. Richards, unpublished) is to explore how the performance of the net scales with the size of the window, and how the size of window required to achieve discrimination depends on the correlation lengths in the textures. The use of a hierarchically structured net to capture the two-dimensional nature of the texture and to facilitate the exploration of correlations on many length scales is also being investigated. The textures under study include a set from the Brodatz collection [22] and configurations of the two-dimensional Ising model at different values of the coupling, i.e. with different correlation lengths. The latter are particularly challenging because they are statistically the same out to the smallest of the correlation lengths in the examples. Preliminary results are illustrated in figure 3, for the case of four of the Brodatz textures; they show how the performance on the test data continues to improve out to windows as large as 11×11; the levelling off for larger windows may be a limitation of the size of the training set used to date.

The second example is the prediction of protein secondary structure. The goal here is to establish the three-dimensional nature of a segment of protein sequence from the sequence data. Each element of the sequence is an amino acid; there are some twenty different elements. The output is the secondary structure (alpha helix, beta sheet, coil) for the segment of the sequence presented at the input (in [23], the structure of the centre of the segment). Since the available data with beta sheet structure is still rather small, work at Edinburgh has to date focused on the simplest task of discriminating whether or not a particular segment corresponds to alpha helix (J.F. Collins and S. Hayward, unpublished). In preliminary results based on the Brookhaven data bank and using a three layer net, with 200 input units (i.e. corresponding to a segment of 10 elements) and up to 40 hidden units, 98% success has been achieved with training data and 80% with test data.

The simulator is also being used to investigate the effect that lower level correlations between patterns in a training set have on training characteristics, generalisation behaviour and the internal representations constructed by the network [24,25]. The motivation for this work derives from the desire to understand the behaviour of an mlp in learning large 'naturally meaningful' training sets such as the texture and sequence applications cited above. It is hoped that by studying the behaviour in training sets with identifiable correlations of specific order, we may get some insight into how best to deal in the mlp with other problems for which such simple generation rules cannot be so easily defined.

5. Topology optimisation and genetic algorithms.

There are two key tasks in the efficient use of a distributed memory computer with a fixed topology of connections: the application of interest must be broken down into tasks which can be performed in parallel (in most cases with communication of data between them, of course); and these tasks must be mapped onto the processor array in such a way as to load-balance the computation and to minimise the communication involved. It is this problem which has been studied by Fox and collaborators [12] using analogue neurons. In reconfigurable transputer arrays, there is the additional freedom to choose the topology or configuration of the array to optimise performance.

The problem is formulated in terms of a 'virtual machine architecture' with the following characteristics: many processing units capable of independent computation and with direct access only to local memory; interprocessor communication by means of links, with only a limited number of these per processor; through-routing of messages between processors which are not directly connected by one of the links. This can be viewed as a graph matching problem, which could in principle be studied by neural net methods (see the lecture by Bienenstock in this volume), but work at Edinburgh has focused on the use of genetic algorithms for this problem. In this case the quality of a topology is determined either by the speed at which it runs a program, or is alternatively modelled by some cost function.

In genetic algorithms, one maintains a population of solutions (in this case topologies) which is generated randomly or by using other optimisation techniques. Each solution is represented as a bit or character string, and individual solutions change under idealised genetic operations akin to mutation and inversion. In addition, pairs of solutions are selected for crossover i.e. combined according to rules analogous to those governing genetic recombination. Finally the new solutions so obtained are considered for inclusion in the population according to their cost. In general the method is particularly well suited to study on medium-grain parallel computers since one may simply run (relatively) isolated sub-populations on the individual processors; this may have inherent advantages, since it can help to sustain genetic diversity (i.e. keep a 'view' in the ensemble of several different regions of potentially good solutions) [26,27].

In order to demonstrate the principle of the use of genetic algorithms for topology optimisation [28], the class of graphs allowed was restricted to Hamiltonian graphs, i.e. those with a closed cycle which visits each node of the graph precisely once. Since the hardware of interest involves transputers, the nodes are assumed to have four links. The processors are intrinsically ordered along the Hamiltonian path, which is connected (conventionally) by links 0 and 1. This leaves links 2 and 3 to make up the other connections in the topology. Without loss of generality, fully connected topologies can be assumed to have link 3 of each node connected to link 2 of another. The representation of the graph is then in terms of the processor to which link 3 is connected, starting with processor 0, and is thus simply a permutation of the n labels of the nodes for an n node graph. This representation is illustrated in figure 4.

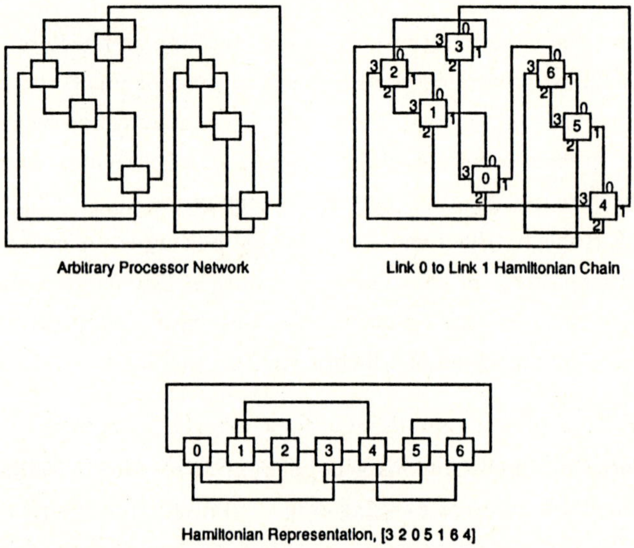

Figure 4. A processor graph, and the representation it may generate.

With this representation, mutation is effected by swapping components, i.e. interchanging two elements of the list. Inversion is effected by reversing a sub-list of the node labels. These two operations involve only individual members of the ensemble. Crossover involves swapping compatible subgraphs from two members; details are given in [28]. One may anticipate that the first two operations might be adequate for finding local minima of the cost function and that the second would be needed to find a good global one. This is indeed the case, as is illustrated in figure 5.

A number of different cost functions have been studied, including test functions with pernicious optima and such measures as average interprocessor distance; see also [5]. The implementation on the Computing Surface itself runs in parallel and provides graphics output showing the best current topology and the quality of solutions on each of the processors. Communications are asynchronous and use the topology independent harness mentioned earlier.

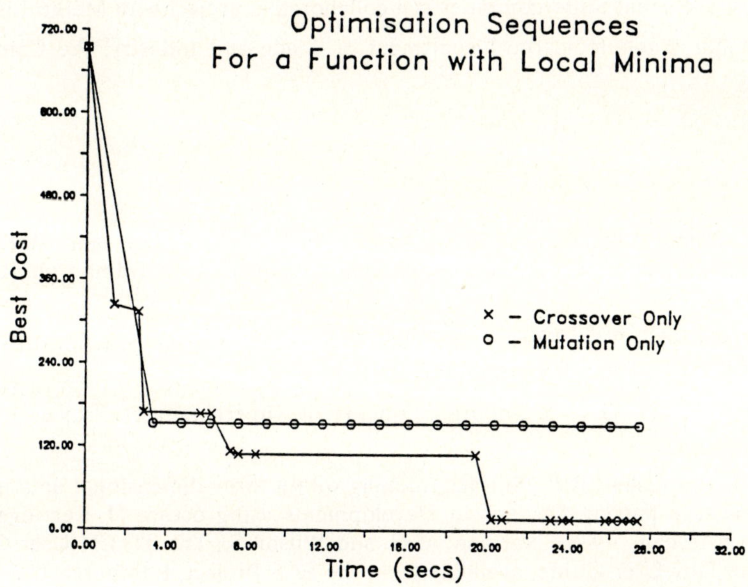

Figure 5. Example of the optimisation sequence for a topology function with local minima, showing the limitation of mutation only, and the importance of crossover. From [28].

6. Concluding remarks

In this paper we have tried to present a snapshot of the development of a large transputer array facility; it is inevitable that the information will be somewhat dated when the article appears in print, and the interested reader should contact the authors for further information.

We have reviewed briefly some of the results obtained to date, using a multi-layer perceptron simulator, in image restoration by analogue neurons, and in processor topology optimisation by genetic algorithms. Other work under way includes automatic theorem proving and Linsker's model for the development of feature detectors by training with random noise.

Finally, we have focused on the parallel computing aspects of our work but no paper on the neural net activity in Physics at Edinburgh would be complete without acknowledging the enormous impact which Elizabeth Gardner made, and the loss to us and the wider community on her tragic death in 1988.

Acknowledgements

The Edinburgh Concurrent Supercomputer is a collaborative project with Meiko Limited, supported by major grants from the Department of Trade and Industry, the Computer Board and SERC.

References.

1. Bowler, K.C., Bruce, A.D., Kenway, R.D., Pawley, G.S., Wallace, D.J. and McKendrick, A., Scientific Computation on the Edinburgh DAPs, University of Edinburgh Report, December 1987.

2. Bowler, K.C., Kenway, R.D., Pawley, G.S. and Roweth, D., An Introduction to Occam 2 Programming, Chartwell-Bratt, Bromley 1987.

3. Wexler, J. and Wilson, G.V., Edinburgh Concurrent Supercomputer Project Directory, 1988.

4. Norman, M.G. and Fisher, R.B., Surface tracking within three dimensional datasets, using a generalised message passing harness, in Developments using occam (J. Kerridge, ed.) pp77-82, IOS Amsterdam, 1988. Norman, M.G. and Wilson S., The TITCH User Guide; Clarke, L.J., The Tiny User Guide, available from the ECS Project, Edinburgh University Computing Service.

5. Prior, D., Radcliffe, N.J., Norman, M.G. and Clarke, L.J., Concurrency: Practice and Experience, to appear.

6. Valiant, L.G., Optimally universal parallel computers, in Scientific Applications of Multiprocessors (R.J. Elliott and C.A.R. Hoare, eds.) pp. 17-20, Prentice Hall International Series in Computer Science 1989.

7. Clarke, L.J., Rian User Guide, available form ECS Project, Edinburgh University Computing Service.

8. Norman, M.G. and Maclachlan, S., submitted to Conf. on Engineering Applications of Transputers, Liverpool, 1989.

9. Hopfield, J.J. and Tank, D., Neural computation on decisions in optimisation problems, Biol. Cyber. 52, 141-152 (1984).

10. Wilson, G.V. and Pawley, G.S., On the stability of the travelling salesman problem of Hopfield and Tank, Biol. Cyber. 58 63-70 (1988).

11. Tank, D.W. and Hopfield, J.J., AT&T Bell Labs preprint (1985).

12. Fox, G.C. and Furmanski, W., The physical structure of concurrent problems and concurrent computers, in Scientific Applications of Multiprocessors (R.J. Elliott and C.A.R. Hoare, eds.) pp. 55-88, Prentice Hall International Series in Computer Science 1989.

13. Geman, S. and Geman, D., Stochastic relaxation, Gibbs distributions and the Bayesian restoration of images, IEEE Trans PAMI 5, 721 -741 (1984).

14. Murray, D.W., Kashko, A. and Buxton, B., A parallel approach to the picture restoration algorithm of Geman and Geman, IVC 3 133-142 (1985).

15. Kirkpatrick, S., Gellat, C.D. and Vecchi, M.P., Optimisation by simulated annealing, Science 220, 671-680 (1983).

16. Forrest, B.M., Restoration of binary images using networks of analogue neurons, in Parallel Architectures and Computer Vision (I. Page, ed.) pp. 19-31, Oxford University Press 1988.

17. Simmen, M. and Wilson G.V., A comparison of two parallel implementations of the Durbin and Willshaw algorithm for solving the travelling salesman problem, submitted to Concurrency: Practice and Experience.

18. Richards, G.D., Implementation of back-propagation on a transputer array, in Proc. 8th Technical Meeting of the Occam User Group (J. Kerridge, ed.) pp. 173-179, IOS Amsterdam 1988.

19. Richards, G.D., Documentation for Rhwydwaith, available from the ECS project, Edinburgh University Computing Service.

20. Smieja, F.J. and Richards, G.D., Hard learning the easy way - backpropagation with deformation, Complex Systems, to appear.

21. Dodd, N., Texture discrimination using multi-layer perceptrons, Pattern Recognition Letters, in press.

22. Brodatz, P., Textures - A Photographic Album for Artists and Designers, Dover, New York (1966).

23. Qian, N. and Sejnowski, T., Predicting the secondary structure of globular proteins using neural network models, J. Mol. Biol. 2020, 865-864 (1988).

24. Smieja, F.J., The significance of underlying correlations in the training of a layered net, presented at the INNS Conf., Boston, 1988. Edinburgh preprint, unpublished.

25. Smieja, F.J., MLP solutions, generalisation, and hidden unit representations, in Proc. DANIP Workshop, Bonn, 1989

26. Muhlenbein, H., Gorges-Schleuter, M. and Kramer, O., Evolution algorithms in combinatorial optimisation, Parallel Computing 7 65-85 (1985).

27. Radcliffe, N.J., Early clustering around optima, Edinburgh preprint in preparation.

28. Norman, M.G., A genetic approach to topology optimisation for multiprocessor architectures, submitted to Parallel Computing.

THE SEMI-PARALLEL ARCHITECTURES OF NEURO-COMPUTERS

Pierre Peretto, Robert Van Zurk, André Mougin and Christian Gamrat
C.E.N.Grenoble DRF/SPh
85X 38041 Grenoble Cedex FRANCE

1- General principles of neurocomputation and machines categorization

1-1 Neuronal dynamics.

A neurocomputer is a machine which is built to work along the principles of the dynamics of neuronal networks. Actually there exists two types of dynamical variables, the neuronal states and the network parameters (the synaptic efficacies and the thresholds). The second dynamics corresponds to learning whereas the first dynamics corresponds to solving tasks.

In this text the main concern is relaxation dynamics. Indeed the principles of neuronal states dynamics seem to be fairly well established and they are worth implementing in hardware architectures. On the contrary the general principles driving the learning dynamics are still not so well founded and it is wise to build machines wherein the learning algorithms are not frozen. This approach implies that the computation of the parameters of the network has to be carried out by a powerful host computer or by inboard micro-processors.

Let us recall the basic steps of the neuronal states dynamics :

▪ A neural network is made of a number of neurons i; i= 1, 2,... , N which interact through connexions J_{ij} .

- Choose a neuron i at random, i ranging from 1 to N
- Compute the local fields

$$h_i^o = \sum_j J_{ij} \cdot \sigma_j$$

- Substract the thresholds θ_i .
- Add a noise η, a random number with a given probability distribution, the wider the distribution the larger the noise.
- Compare the resulting field to zero

  If $h_i = h_i^o - \theta_i + \eta > 0$ then $\sigma_i = +1$

  If $h_i < 0$ then $\sigma_i = -1$
- Iterate the process.

▪

A classical program implementing this neuronal dynamics involves two nested loops :

- the inner one of length N computes the local field h_i of neuron i

NATO ASI Series, Vol. F 68
Neurocomputing
Edited by F. Fogelman Soulié and J. Hérault

- the outer one, also of length N, updates the neuronal states σ_i.
As a whole the computation time scales as N^2.

1-2)- Scaling behaviours of computational times

A neurocomputer is a machine which essentially aims at shortening the computational times t_{comp} and the various types of neurocomputers can be characterized by φ an index which determines how t_{comp} scales with N the size of the network :

$$t_{comp} \propto N^{\varphi}$$

- In biological systems the computation of membrane potentials (the local fields) and the updating of neurons are all carried out in parallel and therefore the computation does not depend on the size of the network. Machines working in this fashion are *parallel neurocomputers* with index φ=0. These are the most powerful but also the most material demanding machines.
- *Serial neurocomputers* are characterized by φ= 2 as in ordinary computers. This is the way the components are arranged inside the machine which allows the time gain.
- φ= 1 characterizes the *semi-parallel machines*. Here the computation time increases linearly with the size of the network. Semi-parallel machines represent a good compromise since the time gain factor is N with respect to serial machines and the gain factor in material and connections is N with respect to fully parallel machines. This last statement must be taken with a grain of salt since whatever the machine the N^2 synaptic efficacies must be stored somewhere. Actually this is the number of chips, be them memories or logical devices, which scales as $N^{2-\varphi}$.

1-3 A classification of semi-parallel neurocomputers

Semi-parallel neurocomputers are machines which carry out one or the other of the two loops of the dynamics in parallel. There are two sorts of semi-parallel types of neurocomputers accordingly, those which process the updating of neuronal states in parallel and those which process the updating in series. For each sort there are in turn two ways of computing the local fields and therefore the semi-parallel designs are classified along 4 types of architectures :

- Parallel states updating : Type I - Systolic field computation
  : Type II - Serial field computation

- Serial states updating : Type III - Systolic field computation
  : Type IV - Parallel field computation

The dynamics of the computation of local fields is depicted in Fig. 1 for each type of neurocomputer.

$$h_1 = J_{11}.\sigma_1 + J_{12}.\sigma_2 + J_{13}.\sigma_3$$
$$h_2 = J_{21}.\sigma_1 + J_{22}.\sigma_2 + J_{23}.\sigma_3$$
$$h_3 = J_{31}.\sigma_1 + J_{32}.\sigma_2 + J_{33}.\sigma_3$$

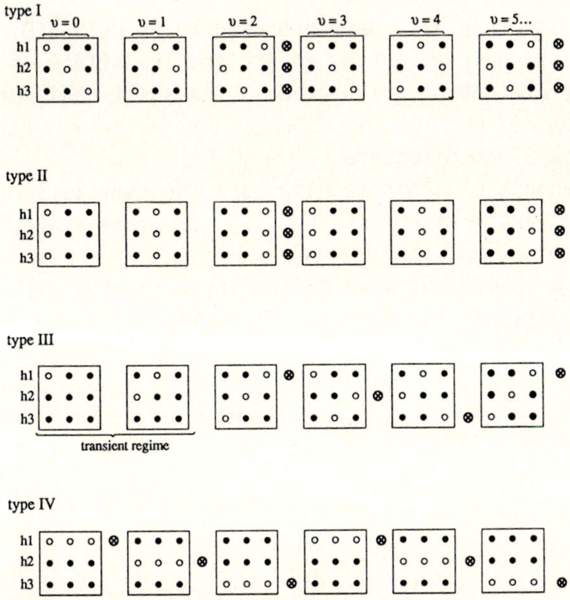

Fig. 1. The four types of semi-parallel neurocomputers architecture.

2- Semi-parallel neurocomputers

2-1 The serial states updating semi-parallel architectures

These machines are built around a shift register which stores the states of the system. They are made of N cells which perform the elementary operations of the neuronal dynamics in parallel and store the result of calculations. The cells i are made of a memory which stores the connections J_{ij} ; j= 1, 2,..., N , of a register to store the field h_i, of an other one for the threshold, eventually of a memory to store a noise distribution, an adder, a multiplier and of a comparator which is made active by a gate δ.

a) The type I (systolic) architecture

In this design the cells have access to the states of the shift register they are facing (see Fig. 2). At time ν the field h_i of cell i transforms according to:

$$h_i \rightarrow h_i + J_{ij} \cdot \sigma_j$$
$$j = (\nu + i) \text{ Mod}(N)$$

After a complete turn the threshold and the noise contributions are added and the fields are compared to zero. The comparator gates are then open and the new states are fed in parallel in the shift register. Afterwards the contents of the field registers are reset to zero and the system is ready for a new cycle.

This architecture has been proposed by M. WEINFELD. In this approach the operations are carried out by an ALU and the effect of noise is simulated by directly disturbing the states in the shift register.

b) The type II architecture

The components of this machine are the same as in the previous one. The difference lies in the fact that the very same state, that stored in a

position of the shift register defined by a pointer, is fed through a bus line to all units of the computer (see Fig. 3). The increase in the field at time is given by :

$$h_i \rightarrow h_i + J_{ij} \cdot \sigma_j$$
$$j = \nu \text{ Mod}(N)$$

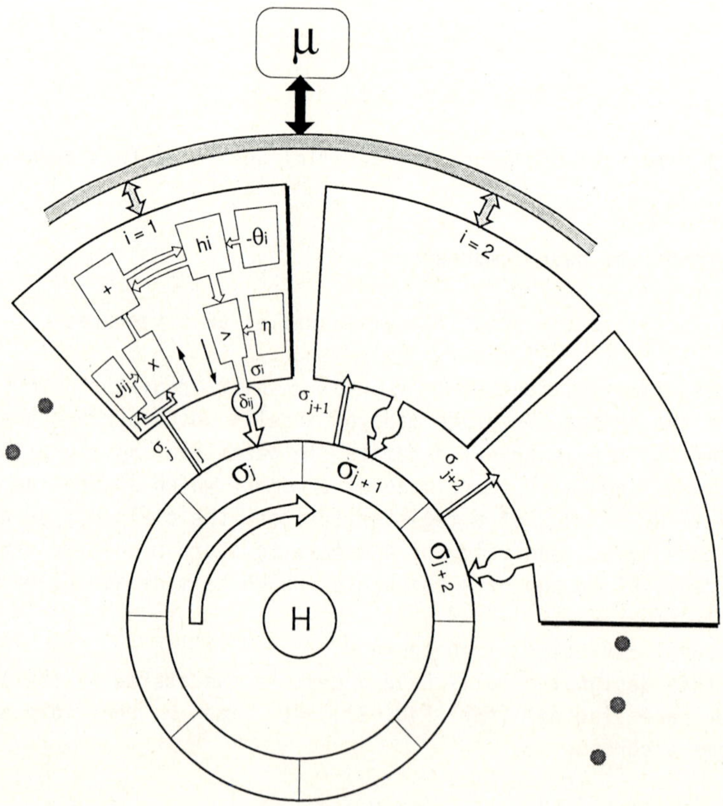

Fig. 2 . Type I semiparallel systolic architecture (WEINFELD).

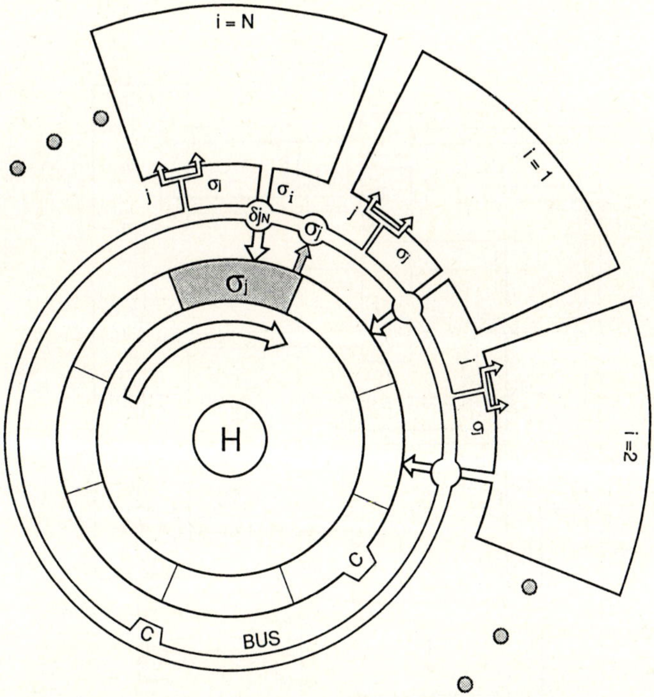

Fig. 3 . A type II design which combines a parallel states updating and a serial field computation.

2-2 The parallel states updating semi-parallel architectures

These systems are made of cells j which contain a storage memory for connections J_{ij} ; i= 1, 2,..., N (note the swapping of the role of indices i and j with respect to the serial semi-parallel architectures), a register for state j, a multiplier and a gate δ for updating. The whole set of thresholds and the noise distribution are stored in two independent memories.

a) The type III (systolic) design

The systolic chain is a string of adders and registers which store the partial fields (see Fig. 4). At time ν the field stored in register j (that facing cell j) is increased according to :

$$h_i \rightarrow h_i + J_{ij} \cdot \sigma_j$$
$$i = (\nu - j) \text{ Mod}(N).$$

The thresholds and the noise are added in the first stage of the line and one neuronal state, that of index i= Mod(N), is updated at every step.

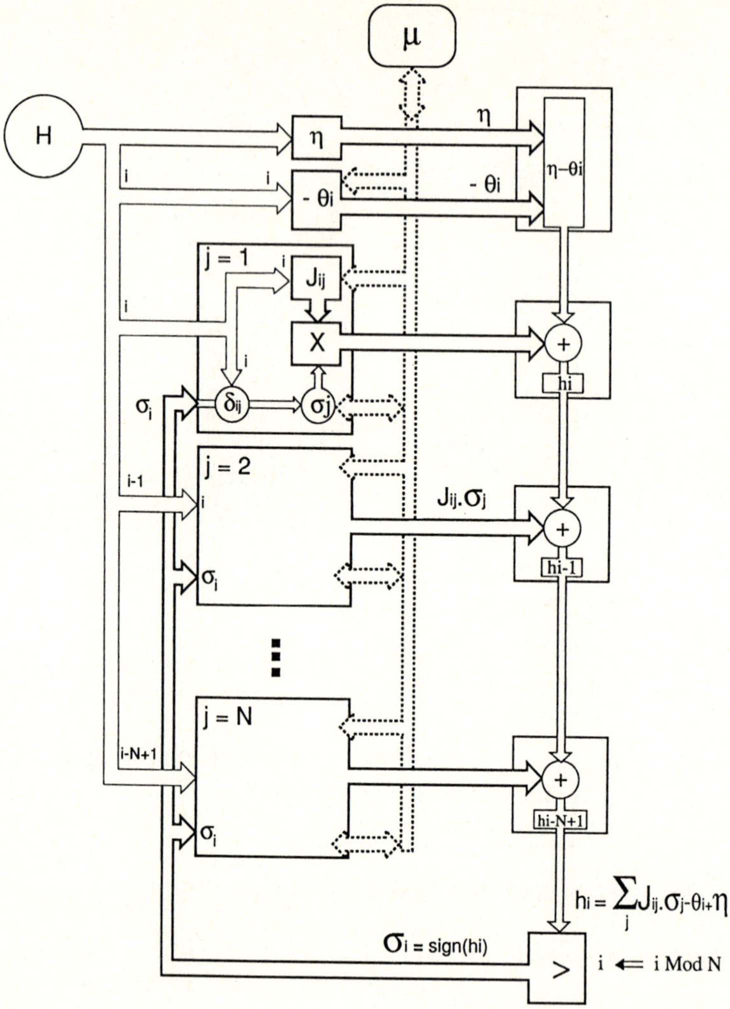

Fig. 4 . Type III semiparallel architecture. The field computation is systolic and the neuronal states are updated in series.

b) The type IV (parallel) design

This is the most simple architecture one can concieve : all contributions $J_{ij} \cdot \sigma_j$ of the field of a given neuron i are computed in parallel and the state of i is updated accordingly (see Fig. 5). The problem is to carry out the parallel addition. There are two solutions ; either one appeals to an analog adder or to parallel digital adders. The first approach has been put at work in several machines in particular in MIND-128 a neurocomputer built at CEA in 1986. This machine is more carefully described in the next section. Digital designs must appeal to WALLACE adders.

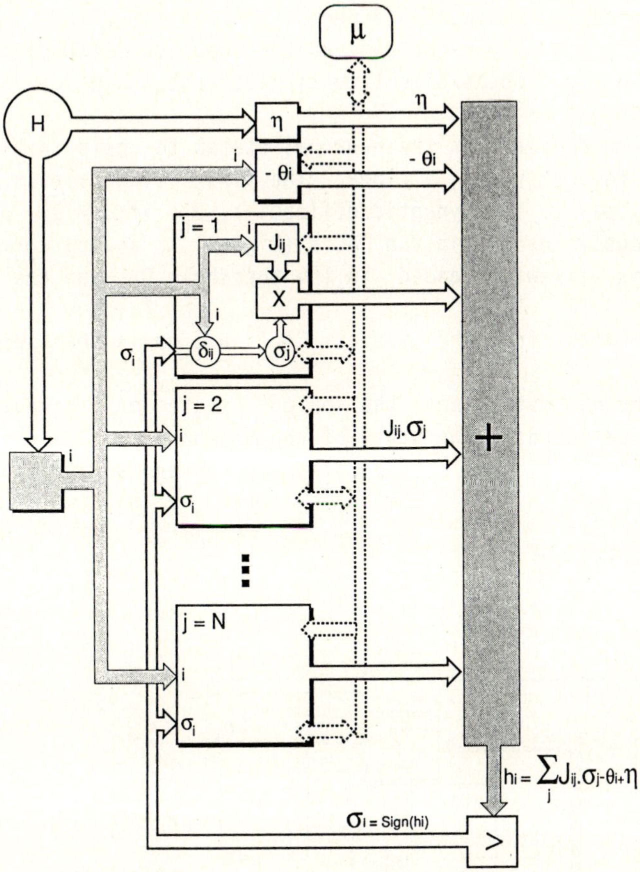

Fig.5 . Type IV semiparallel neurocomputers. Parallelism is used to compute the local fields but the neuronal states are updated in series.

2-3 MIND-128 : A semi-parallel asynchronous neurocomputer

MIND is an acronym for "a Machine Implementing Neural Devices". In this machine the neuronal states are binary, the synaptic efficacies and the thresholds are stored in RAM memories (see Fig. 6). The parallel computation of all local fields is carried out analogically by the summation of currents and the state of the active neuron is determined by an analog comparator. The noise signals are stored in a E^2PROM memory which is filled according to the noise distribution which has been chosen. Likewise the string of labels of neurons to be updated is memorized into an other E^2PROM. The dynamics of this neuro-computer proceeds along the following steps :

■

• The host computer calculates the N=128 thresholds and the N^2= 16,384 synaptic efficacies associated with a given problem.

These values are loaded into the corresponding memories through the ports of the host computer. A synaptic memory of 256×4 bits is associated with every neuron j. It contains 2 pages. The left page say, is devoted to the efficacies J_{ij} and the right page to the opposite efficacies $-J_{ij}$. This trick avoids carying out explicit multiplications $J_{ij} \cdot \sigma_j$ by associating a page with a neuronal state.

- The host computer sets the neuronal states to their initial values.
- The system comprises a clock. The first tick selects the first neuronal label, say i. The synaptic efficacies, J_{ij} if $\sigma_j = 1$, $-J_{ij}$ if $\sigma_j = -1$ are simultaneously loaded in the DAC's (Digital to analog converter). The threshold θ_i is likewise loaded in the threshold DAC and the first noise contribution η
- All currents from the various DAC's add up in the bipolar charge line.
- The current determines the output state of a comparator. This output is used to reupdate the state of the neuron i.
- The following tick selects an other neuron and so on ...

■

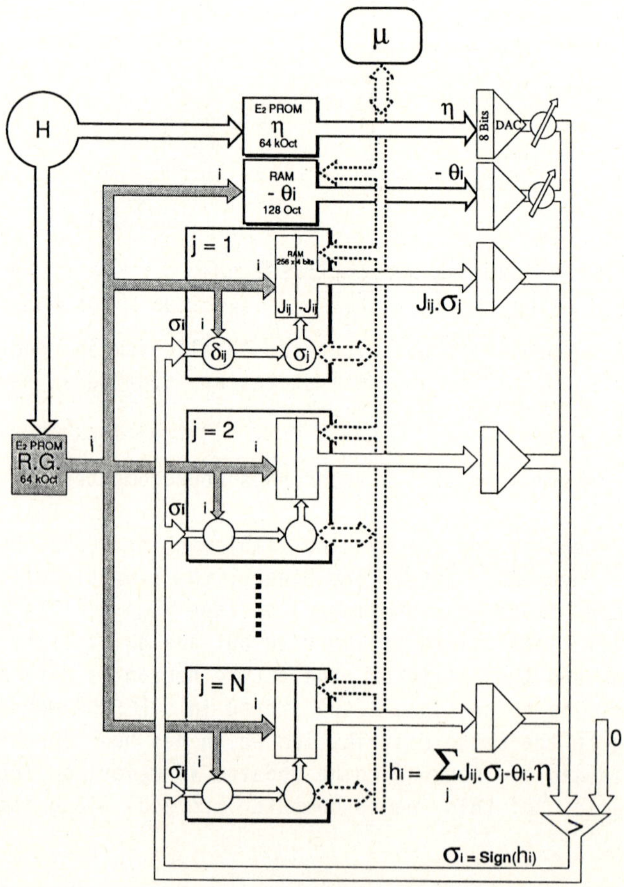

Fig.6 . MIND-128 ; an analog type IV neurocomputer comprised of 128 units. The computation of the field is carried out by using currents summations.

The synaptic efficacies range is 4 bits, that of thresholds is 8 bits. To make the electronic design as simple as possible, we chose RAM memories with separated input and output lines. We also used 8 bits DAC's. The synaptic efficacies feed the 4 most significant bits of the DAC's. In that way the accuracy of the total current on the line is better than half of the change due to the modification of one single less significant bit of efficacies. The system is built on a series of boards. There are 16 boards housing 8 neurons each, one board for the comparator, one board for the noise, one for the thresholds and one for the interface with the host computer, that is 20 boards plugged into a VME bus line. To minimize the fluctuations due to the current sources every board is given its own current source. A nice feature of this architecture is that the source associated with the noise DAC can be made adjustable, thus giving a very practical mean of controlling the noise amplitude (the temperature of the network). The thermal annealing process can be carried out "by hand". The states of neurons are directly made visible on an array of 8×16 diodes.

This neurocomputer works quite satisfactorily. It solves all the problems of associative memory, of combinatorial optimization and of solid state physics (2-dimensional magnetism), it is programmed for.

We did not intend to make the machine as fast as possible. The fastest speed we use is a clock frequency of 150 kHz which is really slow when it is compared with the 15 or 20 MHz clocks of modern microcomputers. The speed is actually limited by the memories we use. However, even so the machine prove to be three times faster than the fastest serial machine one can find on the market, the Cray-XPM. The convergence times measured on a benchmark associative memory problem is 3 mSec for the system and 8 mSec for the Cray-XMP using the same fully vectorized algorithm (and look-up tables to generate the random numbers when necessary).
The consumption of the machine is 20 watts.

A 32 neurons machine made at JPL by THAKOOR, MOOPENN, LAMBE and KHANNA in 1987 and IRENE a neurocomputer comprising 1024 units made by the THOMSON firm in 1988 have also been built using this architecture.

3- The limits of analog architectures

The reliability of semiparallel analog machines are limited by the accuracy of analog components they are made of, that of the DAC's in particular. The accuracy of a DAC is of the order of its less significant bit and the current fluctuations due to the DAC's in the current summation line is therefore of the order of $N^{1/2}$. This must be smaller than the change brought about by the smallest variation of one synaptic efficacy. Let b_D be the number of bits of a DAC, the number of irrelevant bits (which means that the synaptic efficacies are coded on the $(b_D - b_J)$ most significant bits of the DAC's) and $N= 2^n$ the number of neurons. Then one must have

$$b_J > n/2$$

and

$$b_D - b_J > b_E$$

where $b_E = k \cdot n$ is the number of bits which are necessary for the neurocomputer to tackle the problems it has to solve. The maximum size of a network is then given by :

$$n = b_D/(k+1/2) = \mathrm{Log}_2(N)$$

There exists 14-bits DAC's and even DAC's with higher number of bits. But more accurate devices reach their equilibrium so slowly that the time gain due to parallelization is lost. With $k = 1/2$ and $b_D = 14$, 4096-units analog neurocomputers would be feasible and with $k = 1$ the size would be limited to 1024 neurons. $k = 1$ is the value which is necessary to program combinatorial optimization problems in neuro-computer. Actually there are many other sources of noise in those machines which limit the size to even lower values. 512 neurons seems to be the limit size of general purpose analog neurocomputers.
For associative memory only one-bit J_{ij}'s are needed since clipping the synaptic efficacies only reduces the memory storage capacity by a factor of 2 or so. Then $k = 0$ and $N \lesssim 16 \times 10^6$ neurons : There is no practical limitation to the size of the network in that case.

4- Conclusions

Semi-parallel architectures seem to be the best way of conciling two antagonistic constraints one is faced in neurocomputers designs. The first is the necessity of making as fast machines as possible and the other is that of keeping the involved material within sensible limits. Semi-parallelism is a compromise which secures large gains on both sides. Among the four possible families of semi-parallel neurocomputers we strongly favour type IV , a design which carries out the local field computation in parallel and the updating of neuronal states in series. It is a very flexible approach which allows digital or analog realizations, cascadability, synchronous or asynchronous dynamics and versatility in the handling of stochastic dynamics , a feature which is vital in thermal annealing protocols for example.

3 SPEECH

Speech coding with multilayer networks

Yoshua BENGIO*, Regis CARDIN*,
Piero COSI **, Renato DE MORI* and Ettore MERLO*

*School of Computer Science
Mc Gill University/CRIM
3480 University Street
MONTREAL,QUEBEC
CANADA, H3A2A7

**Centro di Studio per le
Ricerche di Fonetica CNR
via G. Oberdan, 10
35122 PADOVA, ITALY

Abstract

A set of Multi-Layered Networks (MLN) for Automatic Speech Recognition (ASR) is proposed. Such a set allows to integrate information extracted with variable resolution in the time and in the frequency domain and to keep the number of links between nodes of the networks small in order to allow significant generalization during learning with a reasonable training set size.

1. Introduction

Important efforts have been devoted in the last years to the coding of portions of the speech signal into **representations**. An example of such coding is vector quantization that describes a speech interval with a label belonging to a given vocabulary. Such method for obtaining descriptions of speech intervals has been applied to speech transmission and to Automatic Speech Recognition (ASR). Extensive and successful experiments [1] have been performed on the automatic recognition of large vocabularies with speaker-dependent coding. This chapter introduces a new partially implemented coding scheme for speaker-independent ASR based on the conjecture that coding speech for recognition does not have the same objectives than coding speech for transmission.

In order to capture speech **properties** useful for ASR and characteristic of a large population of speakers, decision functions, which have to describe the existence of **phonetic properties** in speech intervals, have to be learned by examples rather than being defined by algorithms conceived by the coder designer. The main motivation for such a new approach to coder design is that perceptually significant features have to exhibit small distortions in a **perceptual** space whose dimensions and metrics are not a-priori known.

Different descriptions from acoustic data can be extracted by **Property Extractors (PE)**. PEs can associate spectral samples collected in a short time interval with heterogeneous descriptions relative to larger intervals and extracted by knowledge-based algorithms.

NATO ASI Series, Vol. F 68
Neurocomputing
Edited by F. Fogelman Soulié and J. Hérault

Recently, a large number of scientists are investigating and applying learning systems based on **Multi-Layer Networks (MLN).** Definitions of MLNs, motivations and algorithms for their use can be found in [2]-[4]. Theoretical results have shown that MLNs can perform a variety of complex functions[3]. Applications have also shown that MLNs have interesting generalization performances capable of capturing information related to pattern structures as well as characterization of parameter variation ([5]-[7]). Algorithms exist for MLNs with proven mathematical properties that allow learning to be **discriminant** and to focus on the properties that make different two patterns belonging to different classes. Another reason for the interest in MLNs is the possibility of conceiving efficient architectures for them.

We will investigate in this chapter how **phonetic features** can be generated by MLNs performing a sort of **intuitive inference** on the data based on rules that are represented by links and are difficult to hypothesize just based on speech knowledge. Each MLN is trained separately. The reason for using phonetic features is that they can be grouped into sets each of which is characterized by a **complete** collection of features (e.g. places of articulation).

The coding function that an MLN should perform is unknown. In principle an MLN can implement every function a digital computer can implement provided that a suitable number of nodes, a suitable topology and a suitable choice of weights for internode links are chosen. In fact, a digital computer can be implemented using threshold logic. The problem here is that of **learning** internode weights that characterize an acceptable model of an ideal coder that will detect phonetic properties whenever they are present in a pattern even if not all the instantiations of a property have been used for training the coder.

The available learning procedures have interesting mathematical properties but it is difficult to predict the value of what the networks based on them can produce. For the case of speech coding, only an a-posteriori evaluation can be established with new experiments on new speakers. Knowing very little about acceptable schematizations of input patterns it is not possible to build a theory for predicting the effectiveness and the complexities of these networks. Nevertheless, phonetic features can be chosen in such a way that the corresponding patterns in the domain of acoustic data differ by small distortions that can be well generalized by MLN learning techniques.

There have been discussions on the risk of using weak methods in training MLNs. These methods may lead to local minima of a function and the learning procedure may stop on one of these minima without reaching the absolute minimum. It appears from our experience that **learning strategies** have a large influence on the performance of the networks.

Some of the MLNs we use are **Feed-Forward Networks (FFN)**. They have an input layer, one or two intermediate layers and an output layer that collects information from groups of second-layer nodes. All the nodes of a layer are connected with all the nodes of the next layer only. Each link is associated a weight that has to be learned. Some networks have a feed-back on the hidden layer. These networks will be referred to as **Networks with Feed-Back (NFB).** A new algorithm, suitable for use in ASR has been recently introduced [8].

The topology of some networks has been simplified by clustering nodes at a given level and connecting them only to the relevant nodes at the lower level. The possibility of using networks with links between every pair of nodes following the paradigm of Boltzmann machines has also been investigated [9]. As this paradigm is more computationally expensive than the one described in this paper and it does not introduce remarkable improvements for the problems we try to solve, it was decided not to continue using it.

Each network output corresponds to a **phonetic feature** and may assume values between zero and one corresponding to a **degree of evidence** with which that feature has been observed in the data. Word models can be built using MLNs or other coders in conjunctions with Hidden Markov Models (HMM). The phonetic features obtained by the networks of MLNs can be used alone for recognition or they can be used for driving search with knowledge based on descriptive symbols, for word spotting, for a preliminary generation of word hypotheses, for estimating probabilities in multiple models in conjunction with more classical approaches. The proposed coder can also be used for predicting endpoints of word hypotheses in continuous speech. These hypotheses can be evaluated on the basis of the evidence of phoneme features. Definitions of high and low evidence can be obtained without comparing evidences of different words.

2. Structure of the coder

The structure of the coder is shown in Figure 1. A general description of the coder will be provided in this Section. Signal is processed by an Acoustic Property Extractor (APE) whose output feeds two networks, namely **PLART**, for the computation of the **place of articulation** and **MANNER** for the computation of the **manner of articulation**.

The output set O_1 of PLART is defined as follows:

O_1 : { labial, labio-dental, dental, PL1, PL2, PL3, PL4, PL5, alveolar, non-speech} (1)

where PLk ($1 \leq PLk \leq 5$) is a value of the place of articulation of a sonorant oral sound (PL1 is for "back", PL5 is for "front"), while other places are for nonsonorant and nasal sounds. A rejection class "non-speech" is introduced for other sounds. Notice that O_1 is **complete** in the sense that every sound must have a place of articulation.

The output set O_2 of MANNER is defined as follows:

O_2 : {MN1,MN2,MN3,MN4,MN5, nas, v-fr, v-pl, u-fr, u-pl, sil} (2)

where MNk (1≤PLk≤5) is a value of the place of articulation of a sonorant oral sound (MN1 is for "low", MN5 is for "high"), while other places are for the manner of articulation of other sounds, v- is for "voiced", u- is for "unvoiced", pl is for "plosive", fr is for "fricative", nas is for "nasal" and sil is for "silence".

If T is the sampling interval for the calculation of feature hypotheses, nT corresponds to the n-th sample and $\mu_j(n)$ is the degree of evidence of the feature associated to the j-th coder output, distributions of feature evidences for all places and manners can be represented by a vector

$$M(n) : M(n) = (\mu_1(n),\ \mu_2(n),\dots\dots,\ \mu_j(n),\dots\dots\dots,\ \mu_J(n)) \tag{3}$$

The values of M(n) can be used directly for recognition or can be "vector-quantized" in two independent code-books, one for the place and one for the manner of articulation. In fact, based on phonetic considerations, it can be assumed that place and manner of articulation are independent features. Following this approach the two code-books can be added to other code-books and used in multi-codebook Hidden Markov Models. (HMM).

Another attractive approach can be considered based on a recent paper by Bourlard and Wellekens [5]. This paper shows that under certain conditions, MLNs can estimate a-posteriori probabilities of classes given the data. In our case, place and manner of articulation can be considered as independent and probabilities about them can be used for computing the a-priori probability of a phoneme.

Let d(n) be the speech data in the n-th interval of analysis, ph(j) be a phoneme hypotheses, pl(j) and mn(j) be respectively its place and manner of articulation, then the a-priori probability of ph(j) at time nT can be computed as follows:

$$\Pr\,(\,d(n)/ph(j)) = \frac{\Pr\,(pl(j)/d(n))}{\Pr(pl(j))}\ \frac{\Pr(mn(j)/d(n))}{\Pr(mn(j))}\ \Pr(d(n)) \tag{4}$$

The probabilities Pr(pl(j)) and Pr(mn(j)) can be obtained from the training data while the computation of Pr(d(n)) is not required if the (4) has to be used for comparing competing candidates. If some hidden units of the MLNs are with feed-back, the probabilities in (4) are conditioned, among other things, by the history of the MLN states. This aspect makes the use of networks with feed-back interesting because often the interpretation of an acoustic segment has to take into account its **acoustic context**.

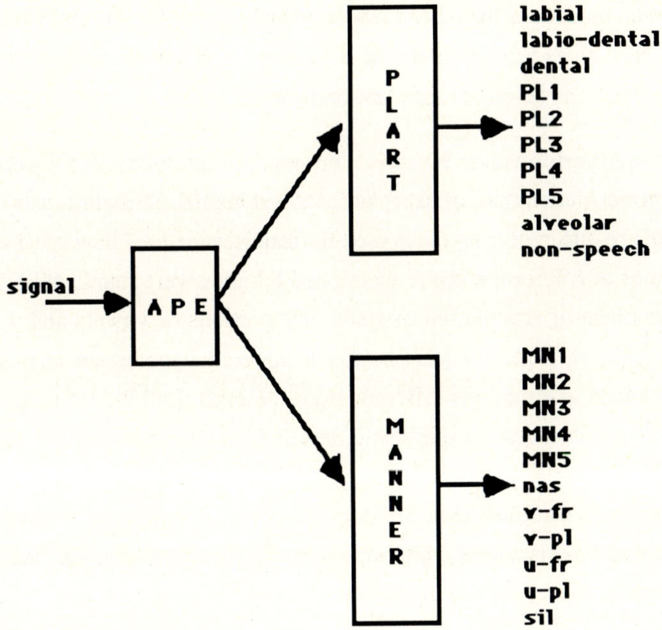

Figure 1. The proposed coder

Unfortunately the conditions under which MLNs estimate probabilities are not always verified, so the latter approach can be followed as a first attempt in which probability estimation may not be the best one. The great advantage of this approach is that with it the only required training is for the MLNs.

3. Description of the network PLART.

Figure 2 shows a scheme of the network PLART as well as the details of APE that is also used by MANNER. In order to characterize sonorant segments that are produced by most of the phonemes, cover the largest portion of a speech signal and are characterized by narrow-band resonances, an ear model with a synchrony detector has been introduced. Such a model produces a spectral analysis every 10 msecs. Each spectrum is represented by 40 energy samples spaced in frequency between .1 and 8 kHz according to a bark scale. The synchrony detector acts as a Property Extractor (PE) that spans the signal and produces 120 parameters every 10 msecs. These parameters are normalized and sent to the inputs of MLN11 and MLN12.

MLN11 is a Feed-Forward Networks (FFD) with 120 input nodes and a hidden layer of 20 nodes. MLN11 has been initially trained with 5 outputs corresponding to the places of articulation PLk ($1 \leq PLk \leq 5$). These outputs are connected to the general output layer of

PLART. The weights of these connections have been learned when all the other MLN1i were connected. In this way, MLN11 gives at its outputs the evidences of places of articulations under the conditions that the input data belong to sonorant-oral sounds.

Training of network MLN11 was performed on 10 vowels pronounced in monosyllabic words by 12 different speakers (5 pronunciations per speaker) as described in [10]. The words as well the speakers used for training are different from those used for test. Results on 7 new speakers are reported in [10]. Error rates of 8% for the above mentioned features were found. MLN11 was trained to recognize the place of articulation of stationary portions of vowels and was expected to have generalized its knowledge in order to be able to correctly hypothesize the place of articulation of sonorant sounds in situations different from the ones used for training. A good generalization capability was observed in experiments described in [10] due to the fact that places of articulation are related to relative positions of spectral peaks well extracted by the synchrony detector. Such relations establish that, although places of articulations can vary continuously as well as their spectral correlates, variations of spectral peaks corresponding to the same place (sound) are represented by limited translations of spectral peaks.

Network MLN12 has been implemented as a Feedback Networks (FN) as described in [8]. The use of FNs seems particularly attractive when the acoustic patterns of a place of articulation are affected by context as in the case of nasal sounds. A new model of FN has been developed for this purpose that allows to control the network stability and the time interval for which the context is taken into account. Details of this model are discussed in [8]. MLN12 has 120 input nodes and 10 hidden nodes with feedback that is local to each hidden node.

Training of MLN12 was performed using nasal and vocalic sounds from 70 speakers pronouncing monosyllabic words. Test was performed using 10 new speakers with an error rate of 6% for the test set. MLN12 has 5 outputs; it was trained to recognize the place of articulation when nasal sounds were pronounced and to reject other sounds. The outputs of MLN12 are connected to the output layer of PLART.

MLN13 and MLN14 receive input from Property Extractors (PE) that extract energies in certain frequency bands. These PEs are mostly rectangular windows subdivided into cells and are characterized by a vector of time resolutions (VT) and a vector of frequency resolutions (VF) describing the size of the cells (time values are in msecs., frequency values are in kHz).

PE13 of MLN13 is characterized by the following vectors:

$$\text{PE13:} \quad VT = \{30,30\} \quad VF = \{1.0,2.0,3.0,4.0,5.0,6.0,7.0\} \tag{5}$$

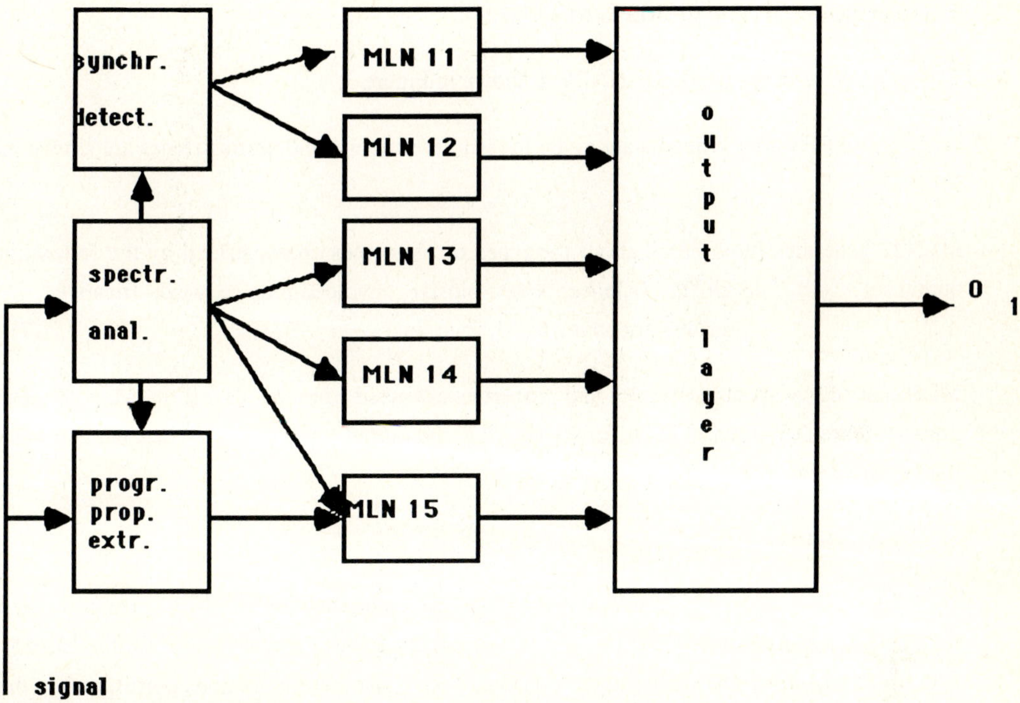

Figure 2. The network PLART

MLN13 is a FFN with 16 nodes in the first layer and 10 nodes in the hidden layer. Il has been trained for extracting the place of articulation of fricative sounds by analyzing the spectra every 10 msecs. with two successive windows of 30 msecs. The network has been trained separately with letters pronounced four times by 70 speakers, it has at the output four places of articulation and two rejection outputs. Experiments on 10 new speakers pronouncing four times all the plosive sounds gave a 6% error rate.

MLN14 is supposed to extract burst properties and is fed by the data coming from the following property extractor PE14:

$$\text{P14:} \quad VT = \{5,5,5,5\}$$
$$VF = \{2.0,3.0,4.0,5.0,6.0,7.0\} \tag{6}$$

MLN15 receives at the input normalized properties of the time evolution of energies in various bands as well as properties extracted from the speech waveform. This is a subset of the properties defined in [11] and has the objective of providing additional properties for the place of articulation of plosive sounds as well as providing additional information for weighting the outputs of the other networks in order to produce correct evidences at the output O_1 of PLART. The integration of the network outputs has not been implemented yet.

4. Description of the network MANNER

The structure of the network MANNER is shown in Figure 3.

MLN21 is a FFN whose details are given in [10]. Its structure and performances are similar to MLN11.

MLN22 generates hypotheses about the types of phonemes characterized by the following output set : O(31) : {silence, voiced-plosive, unvoiced-plosive, weak- fricative, strong- fricative, nasal, sonorant} (7)

MLN22 is fed by spectral samples and properties extracted from the waveform. Most of these properties are described in [11]. As for PLART, the output layer of MANNER has not been implemented yet.

5. Word models

Word models are represented by finite-state diagrams, each transition of which corresponds to a phoneme or a transition between two phonemes. Figure 4 shows a word model for the letter K. The first transition corresponds to the consonant /k/, other state transitions correspond to the speech transition /kae/, the vocalic segment /ae/ the speech transition /aei/ and the vowel /i/. More sophisticated diagram could be conceived for the same word involving more speech transition segments. For example, the transition /aei/ could be represented by several units, namely /aei1/, /aei2/ etc. ; the segment /aei1/ represents the beginning of the transition of the diphthong /aei/ just after the vocalic segment, /aei2/ represents the continuation of the transition and so on. Each transition can be represented by a value of place and a value of manner of articulation. Word models can be compared with real data using dynamic programming as the coder generates evidences of feature hypotheses every 5 msecs. Distances can be computed as the euclidean distance between features computed at the output of the MLNs in a time interval and the features associated to a transition.

The above mentioned comparison method can be used just for alignment. Once the alignment has been performed, probability densities of features for state transitions can be learned together with probabilities of state transitions in word or SU models. In such a way Continuous Densities Hidden Markov Models can be obtained for each SU and for a large speaker population. Preliminary experiments have been performed with spoken digits using only MLN11 and MLN21 with no training on words. An error rate of 6% has been found.

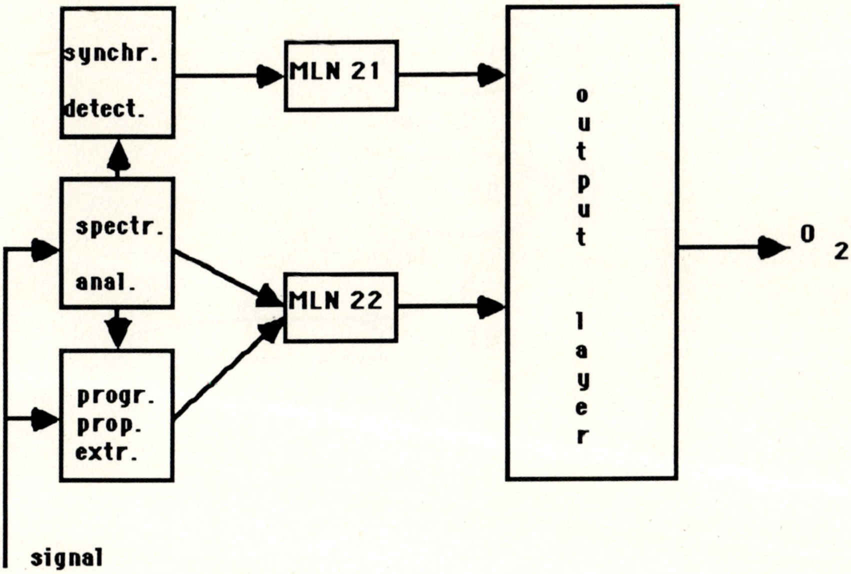

Figure 3. The network MANNER

6. Conclusions

The major contributions of this chapter are the following.

New evidence is provided that speech sounds can be coded by features related to the place and manner of articulation. The presence of these features can be represented by degrees of evidence based on which stochastic performance models can be derived.

New evidence is provided that information about frames of short duration combined with information about intervals of longer duration allows to obtain a better characterization of important speech sounds in view of automatic recognition.

Under the conditions described in this paper, MLNs can be trained effectively with a reasonable number of data allowing to conceive a single model for several sounds.

Acknowledgements

This work was supported by the Natural Science and Engineering Council of Canada (NSERC). The Centre de Recherche en Informatique de Montreal (CRIM) kindly provided computing time on its facilities. Discussions with L. Stringa (IRST) have been very useful.

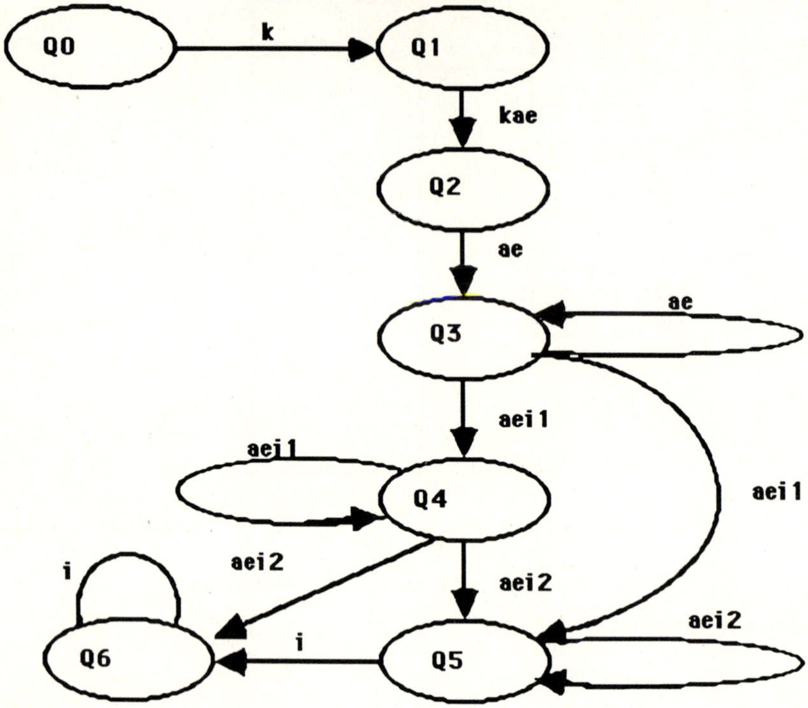

Figure 4. A word model

References

[1] Jelinek, F.: The development of an experimental discrete dictation recognizer. IEEE Proceedings, pp.1616-1624, (November 1984).

[2] Rumelhart, D.E., Hinton, G.E., Williams, R.J.: Learning internal representation by error propagation. In Parallel Distributed Processing: Exploration in the Microstructure of Cognition, vol. 1, MIT Press, 318-362, (1986).

[3] Plout, D.C., Hinton, G.E.: Learning sets of filters using back propagation. Computer Speech and Language, vol. 2, 35-61, (1987).

[4] Hinton, G.E., Sejnowski, T.J.: Learning and relearning in Boltzmann machines. In Parallel Distributed Processing : Exploration in the Microstructure of Cognition, vol. 1, MIT Press, 282-317, (1986).

[5] Bourlard, H., Wellekens, C.J.: Links between Markov models and multilayer perceptron. IEEE Conference on Neural Networks, Denver Co. , (1988).

[6] Watrous, R.L., Shastri, L.: Learning phonetic features using connectionist networks. Proceedings of the 10th International Joint Conference on Artificial Intelligence, 851-854, (1987).

[7] Waibel, A., Hanazawa, T., Hinton, G.E., Shikano, K., Lang, K.: Phoneme recognition : neural networks vs hidden Markov models. IEEE Transactions on on Acoustics, Speech and Signal Processing, (1989).

[8] Gori, M., Bengio Y., De Mori, R.: BPS : A learning algorithm for capturing the dynamic nature of speech. In Proceedings ICNN-89, Washington, D. C, (1989).

[9] Bengio Y., De Mori, R.: Speaker normalization and automatic speech recognition using spectral lines and neural networks. In Proceedings of the Canadian Conference on Artificial Intelligence (CSCSI-88), Edmonton, Al., (May 1988).

[10] Cosi, P. , Bengio Y., De Mori, R.: On the generalization capabilities of multilayer networks in the extraction of speech properties. In Proceedings of the 11th International Joint Conference on Artificial Intelligence, Detroit Mi., (Aug. 1989).

[11] De Mori, R., Lam, L., Gilloux, M.: Learning and plan refinement in a knowledge-based system for automatic speech recognition. In IEEE Transactions on Pattern Analysis and Machine Intelligence, vol. PAMI-9, No.2,289-305, (1987).

Statistical Inference in Multilayer Perceptrons and Hidden Markov Models with Applications in Continuous Speech Recognition

H. Bourlard [†,‡], N. Morgan [‡] & C.J. Wellekens [†]

([†])Philips Research Laboratory Brussels
Av. Van Becelaere 2, Box 8,
B-1170 Brussels, Belgium.

([‡])International Computer Science Institute
1947 Center Street, Suite 600
Berkeley, CA 94704 USA.

Abstract: Speech recognition must contend with the statistical and sequential nature of the human speech production system. Hidden Markov Models *(HMM)* provide a powerful method to cope with both of these, and their use made a breakthrough in speech recognition. However, the a priori choice of a model topology and weak discriminative power limit *HMM* capabilities. Recently, connectionist models have been recognized as an alternative tool. Their main useful properties lie in their discriminative power while capturing input-output relations. They have also proved useful in dealing with statistical data. However, the sequential aspect remains difficult to handle in connectionist models. The statistical use of a particular classic form of a connectionist system, the Multilayer Perceptron *(MLP)*, is described in the context of the recognition of continuous speech. Relations with Hidden Markov Models are explained and preliminary results are reported.

1. Introduction

Hidden Markov Models (HMM) are widely used for automatic speech recognition and inherently incorporate the sequential and statistical character of the speech signal. However, their discriminant properties are weak if they are trained along the *Maximum Likelihood Estimate (MLE)* [Brown, 1987]. An algorithm based on another criterion, *Maximum Mutual Information (MMI)* [Brown, 1987] provides more discrimination but the mathematics become trickier, and many constraining assumptions must be made. Finally, the incorporation of acoustic or phonetic contextual information requires a complex *HMM* and a large (possibly prohibitive) storage capacity.

On the other hand, connectionist architectures, and more particularly *Multilayer Perceptrons (MLP)*, have recently been recognized as an alternative tool for pattern recognition problems such as speech recognition. Their main useful properties are their discriminative power and their capability to deal with non-explicit knowledge. Also, contextual information can easily be taken into account. Good results for phonetic decoding have already been reported [Bourlard & Wellekens, 1989a], but are so far restricted to local decisions, as *MLPs* are feedforward machines generally used for classification of static inputs where no sequential processing is involved. If the connections are supplied with delays, feedback loops can be added providing dynamic and implicit memory. Several authors [Jordan, 1986; Watrous, 1987; Elman, 1988] have proposed original architectures along this line.

In this paper, the link between stochastic models used in speech recognition and connectionist devices used as classifiers [Bourlard & Wellekens, 1989b] is discussed. The hypotheses made when using Markov models are compared with the potential solution offered by *MLPs*. Preliminary results and new questions are reported.

NATO ASI Series, Vol. F 68
Neurocomputing
Edited by F. Fogelman Soulié and J. Hérault

2. Hidden Markov Models

In the generic discrete *HMM*, the acoustic vectors (e.g., corresponding to 10 ms speech frames) are quantized in a front-end processor where each one is replaced by the closest (e.g. according to an Euclidean norm) prototype vector y_i selected in a predetermined finite set $\mathcal{Y}$ of cardinality I. Let $\mathcal{Q}$ be a set of K different states $q(k)$, with $k = 1, \ldots, K$. Markov models [Bahl & Jelinek, 1975] are then constituted by the association (according to a predefined topology) of some of these states. If *HMM* are trained along the *MLE* criterion, the parameters of the models (defined below) are optimized for maximizing $P(X|W)$ where X is a training sequence of quantized acoustic vectors $x_n \in \mathcal{Y}$, with $n = 1, \ldots, N$ and W is its associated Markov model made up of L states $q_\ell \in \mathcal{Q}$ with $\ell = 1, \ldots, L$. Of course, $L \neq K \neq N$ since the same state may occur several times with different indices ℓ, since all states do not appear in the model and since loops on states are allowed. Let us denote by q_ℓ^n the presence on state q_ℓ at a given time $n \in [1, N]$. Events q_ℓ^n are mutually exclusive so that probability $P(X|W)$ can be written for any arbitrary n:

$$P(X|W) = \sum_{\ell=1}^{L} P(q_\ell^n, X|W) \; , \tag{3}$$

where $P(q_\ell^n, X|W)$ denotes thus the probability that X is produced by W while associating x_n with state q_ℓ. Maximization of (3) can be worked out by the classical forward-backward recurrences of the *Baum-Welch* algorithm [Brown, 1987].

Maximization of $P(X|W)$ is also usually approximated by the *Viterbi* criterion. It can be viewed as a simplified version of the *MLE* criterion where, instead of taking account of all possible state sequences in W capable of producing X, one merely considers the most probable one. To make all possible paths apparent, (3) can also be rewritten as

$$P(X|W) \;=\; \sum_{\ell_1=1}^{L} \cdots \sum_{\ell_N=1}^{L} P(q_{\ell_1}^1, \ldots, q_{\ell_N}^N, X|W) \; ,$$

and the explicit formulation of the *Viterbi* criterion is obtained by replacing all summations by a "*max* " operator. Probability (3) is then approximated by:

$$\overline{P}(X|W) \;=\; \max_{\ell_1, \ldots, \ell_N} P(q_{\ell_1}^1, \ldots, q_{\ell_N}^N, X|W) \; , \tag{4}$$

and can be calculated by the classical *dynamic time warping (DTW)* algorithm. In that case, each training vector is then uniquely associated with only one particular transition $\{q(k) \rightarrow q(\ell)\}$ between two states $\in Q$.

In both cases (*MLE* and *Viterbi*), it can be shown that probabilities $P(X|W)$ and $\overline{P}(X|W)$ can be recursively computed from "local" contributions $p[q_\ell^n, x_n | Q_1^{n-1}, X, W]$, where Q_1^{n-1} stands for the state sequence associated with the previously observed vector sequence $x_1, \ldots, x_{n-1}$. As it is generally assumed, for simplicity reasons, that the model is a first order Markov model (i.e. conditional state sequence restricted to the previous state only) and that the acoustic vectors are not correlated (i.e. overlooking X in the conditional), these "local" contributions are then estimated from the set of local parameters $p[q(\ell), y_i | q^-(k), W]$, for $i = 1, \ldots, I$ and $k, \ell = 1, \ldots, K$. Notations $q^-(k)$ and $q(\ell)$ denote states $\in \mathcal{Q}$ observed at two consecutive instants. In the particular case of the Viterbi criterion, these parameters are estimated by:

$$\hat{p}[q(\ell), y_i | q^-(k)] \;=\; \frac{n_{ik\ell}}{\sum_{j=1}^{I} \sum_{m=1}^{K} n_{jkm}}, \quad \forall i \in [1, I], \quad \forall k, \ell \in [1, K] \; , \tag{5}$$

where $n_{ik\ell}$ denotes the number of times each prototype vector y_i has been associated with a particular transition from $q(k)$ to $q(\ell)$ during the training. In order to reduce the number of parameters it is sometimes assumed that (5) may be split into an *emission probability* $p(y_i|q(\ell))$ and a *transition probability* $p(q(\ell)|q^-(k))$. However, it is clear that criterion (3) and estimates (5) do not minimize the error rate, either at the word level or at the acoustic vector level. Indeed, no discrimination is taken into account when the models are trained to give a *MLE*. For instance, the local probability (5) is not the suitable measure for the labeling of a prototype vector y_i, i.e. to find the most probable state given a current input vector and a specified previous state. Indeed, the decision should ideally be based on the "optimal" *maximum a posteriori probability (MAP)*, also referred to here as the Bayes probability. In that case, the most probable state $q(\ell_{opt})$ is defined by

$$\ell_{opt} = \underset{\ell}{\operatorname{argmax}} \; p[q(\ell)|y_i, q^-(k)] \,, \tag{6}$$

and not on the basis of (5).
It is easy to prove that the estimates of the Bayes probabilities in (6) are:

$$\hat{p}[q(\ell)|y_i, q^-(k)] = \frac{n_{ik\ell}}{\sum_{m=1}^{K} n_{ikm}} \,. \tag{7}$$

It is thus worth noting that the optimal criterion, minimizing the decoding error rate at the word or at the frame level, should be based on the *MAP*. That fact was also explained in [Nadas et al., 1988] where the role of the different probabilities used in stochastic speech recognition were clearly explained. More particularly, it was also shown that the *MAP* estimate appears safer for the training of speech recognizers when the language model is poor i.e. when the a priori probabilities are poorly estimated. However, the conclusions of this paper were only valid for isolated word recognition and did not apply to local probability definition, i.e. the lower level decoding process.

In the next sections, it is shown that, whatever the inputs to an *MLP* are, the output values will be estimates of *MAP*-like probabilities, i.e. (7) or something more general depending on fed back information which may be supplied to the input field. It is also shown that, by extending the input field to the contextual surroundings of the considered acoustic vector and by a particular output feedback, it is possible to generate output probabilities depending on a fixed window back into the recent past on both states and observations. These essential requirements were recalled in [Poritz, 1988].

3. Statistical Inference in Multilayer Perceptrons

Let $q(k)$, with $k = 1, \ldots, K$, be the output units of an *MLP* associated with different classes (each of them corresponding to a particular state of $\mathcal{Q}$). Let us assume that the training is performed on a sequence of N vector quantized inputs $\{y_{i_1}, \ldots, y_{i_N}\}$ where $y_{i_n} \in \mathcal{Y}$. The training of the *MLP* parameters is usually based on the minimization of the following *mean square criterion (LMSE)*:

$$E = \frac{1}{2} \sum_{n=1}^{N} \sum_{k=1}^{K} [g(i_n, k) - d(i_n, k)]^2 \,, \tag{8}$$

where $g(i_n, k)$ represents the output value of unit k given y_{i_n} at the input and $d(i_n, k)$ is the associated target value and is equal to $\delta_{k\ell}$ (Kronecker delta) if the input is known to belong to class $q(\ell)$. Multiple presentations of the same current prototype are not necessarily associated with the same class (inconsistent training). Expanding summations to collect all terms depending on the same y_i, (8) can be rewritten as:

$$E = \frac{1}{2}\sum_{i=1}^{I}\sum_{k=1}^{K}\sum_{\ell=1}^{K} n_{ik} \cdot [g(i,\ell) - d(i,\ell)]^2 \ , \tag{9}$$

where n_{ik} represents the number of times y_i has been classified in $q(k)$. Thus, whatever the *MLP* topology is, i.e. the number of its hidden layers and of units per layer, the optimal output values $g_{opt}(i,k)$ are obtained by canceling the partial derivative of E versus $g(i,k)$. It can easily be proved that, doing so, the optimal values for the outputs are then

$$g_{opt}(i,k) = \frac{n_{ik}}{\sum_{\ell=1}^{K} n_{i\ell}} \ , \tag{10}$$

which are the estimates of the Bayes probabilities (7) where the transition probabilities are not taken into account. However, these optimal values can be reached only provided the *MLP* contains enough parameters and does not get stuck into a local minimum during the training. In the next Section, it will be shown how probabilities (7) or also something more general can be generated at the output by feeding back some output information as the previous classification to the input field.

These results follow directly from the minimized criterion and not from the topology of the model. It is also interesting to notice [Bourlard & Wellekens, 1989b] that the same optimal values (10) may also result from other criteria as, for instance, the entropy or relative entropy of the targets with respect to the output. This optimal solution, obtained by cancelling the partial derivative of the error criterion (*LMSE* or entropy) versus the output vector g, could, in theory, be reached by the algorithm actually used for the training of the *MLP*, i.e. the *error back-propagation algorithm (EBP)*, which cancels , by a gradient procedure, the partial derivatives of the error versus the weight parameters W.
Indeed:

$$\frac{\partial E}{\partial w_{ij}} = \nabla_g^t E \,.\frac{\partial g}{\partial w_{ij}} \quad , \forall i,j \ ,$$

where t signifies the transpose operation. Thus, a minimum in the output space ($\nabla_g E = 0$) is also a minimum in the parameter space ($\partial E/\partial w_{ij} = 0$, $\forall i,j$). However, it is also clear that $\partial E/\partial w_{ij} = 0$, $\forall i,j$, does not necessarily lead to $\nabla_g E = 0$ which corresponds then to a *local minimum* of the training procedure. In that case, it is no longer guaranteed that the output values look like probabilities, i.e. that they sum up to unity. An elegant way to circumvent that problem is to replace the classical sigmoidal function applied at the output units by a "softmax" function [Bridle, 1989] defined, for any i, as:

$$g(i,k) = \frac{e^{x(i,k)}}{\sum_{\ell=1}^{K} e^{x(i,\ell)}} \ , \tag{11}$$

where $x(i,k)$ is the output value of unit k before the nonlinearity for an input y_i. This function generalizes the sigmoid and exhibits nice relationships with the Gibbs distribution [Bridle, 1989].

Thus, for discrete inputs, in classification mode (using "one-from-K coding", i.e. one output for each class, all targets are zero except for the correct class where it is unity), if there are enough parameters in the system and if the training does not get stuck in a local minimum, the output values of the *MLP* will approximate the a posteriori probabilities (Bayes probabilities). Section 4 will describe some empirical evidence for this conclusion.

This conclusion can also be generalized to continuous inputs. Indeed, it is known by regression theory that a *LMSE* criterion (as a lot of other criteria , including the entropy) converges, if there is enough training data, to the conditional expectation of the output given the input, i.e. to $E[d(t)|v(t)]$, where $v(t)$ stands for the input vector at time t and $d(t)$ the associated desired output. In classification mode, as $d(t)$ is a "one-from-K coding", we have then $E[d(t)|v(t)] = P[d(t)|v(t)]$, i.e. the probability distribution over classes conditioned on the input.

Of course, since these results are independent of the topology of the models, they remain also valid for linear discriminant functions. But, as we are then limited by the number of parameters, it is not guaranteed that the optimal values (10) can be reached (even if we can escape from local minima). However, it can be shown [Devijver & Kittler, 1982, see pages 171-172] that the discriminant functions obtained by minimizing a *LMSE* criterion retains the essential property of being the best approximation, in the sense of mean-square-error, to the Bayes probabilities.

4. Experiments

As shown in Section 3, the *MLP* can at best approximate Bayes *(MAP)* probabilities. The only potential advantage of using *MLP* instead of counting as (7) is their interpolating capabilities in the case of insufficient training data for the input space. This fact is clearly illustrated in the following experiments.

In the experiment reported in Table I, a German data base consisting of 100 training and 100 test sentences (both from the same speaker) were used for training of a *MLP* for recognition of phonemes at the frame level, as well as to estimate emission probabilities for use in a dynamic programming algorithm for a discrete *HMM*. Vector-quantized (132 prototypes) mel cepstra were used as acoustic vectors. To simplify the representation of the input data, each vector was replaced by its index coded by a simple binary vector with only one bit "on". Multiple frames were used as input to provide context (9 frames) to the network. Thus, the input field contained $9 \times 132 = 1188$ units, and the total of possible inputs was thus equal to 132^9, which makes the simple counting in (7) impossible. While the hidden layer was varied from 20 to 200 units, the size of the output layer was kept fixed at 50 units, corresponding to the 50 phonemes to be recognized.

There were 26767 training patterns and 26702 independent test patterns. Of course, this represented only a small fraction of the possible inputs, and generalization was thus potentially difficult. For comparison with classical approaches, results obtained with maximum likelihood *(MLE)* and maximum a posteriori probability *(MAP)* are also given. In those cases, it is not possible to use contextual information, because the number of parameters to be learned would be 50×132^9 for 9 frames of context. Therefore, the input field was restricted to a single frame. This restriction explains why the Bayes classifier, which is inherently optimal for a given pattern classification problem, is shown here yielding a lower performance than the potentially suboptimal *MLP*. Large values for the parameterization ratio (# parameters / # training measurements) correspond to a slight degradation of generalization performance (3.3% over a factor of 10 in number of parameters). The iterative estimation process was stopped when generalization degraded for an independent data set (cross-validation) [Morgan & Bourlard, 1989], which explains the insensitivity of test set classification scores to the net size.

# hidden units	# parameters/ # training patterns	training	test
5	.23	62.8 (1.010)	54.2 (1.012)
20	.93	75.7 (1.030)	62.7 (1.035)
50	2.31	86.4 (1.018)	61.4 (1.000)
200	9.3	86.9 (1.053)	59.4 (0.995)
MLE	.25	45.9	44.8
MAP	.25	53.8	53.0
50 NCI	.34	53.5 (1.011)	52.7 (1.012)

Table I. Classification rates at the frame level on German data base

Therefore, an *MLP* can be useful in estimating Bayes probabilities associated with acoustic vectors in a temporal context which is too large for the training of a classical *HMM*. The numbers in parentheses give the average sum, over all the training or test patterns, of the *MLP* output values. Since these outputs approximate *MAP*, their sum is approximately unity. The line denoted "50 NCI" stands for the results obtained from the training of a *MLP* with 50 hidden units and *no contextual input* (only the current acoustic vector coded by 132 input units). It can be observed that the *MLP* solution converges to the *MAP* one (53.5 instead of 53.8 for the training set and 52.7 instead of 53.0 for the test set), which is, of course, the optimal one in that particular case. Again, the average sums of the output values are very close to unity. Another result worth considering is the mean and the standard deviation of the error between the " 50 NCI" output values and the actual *MAPs* (which can be obtained by counting); for the training and the test sets, the mean errors were respectively equal to $2.78\ 10^{-4}$ and $2.93\ 10^{-4}$ and the standard deviation was $1.15\ 10^{-2}$ in both cases, which leads to the confidence interval:

$$P(|g(i,k) - p(q_k|y_i)| > 0.04) < 0.001 \ .$$

All these results clearly suggest that the training did not get stuck in a very suboptimal local minimum.

Another problem considered was speaker-independent continuous speech recognition using the SRI discrete features extracted from the TIMIT data base [Murveit & Weintraub, 1988]. In that case, each acoustic vector is described by 4 features, the mel-cepstrum (f_1), the delta mel-cepstrum (f_2), the energy (f_3) and the delta energy (f_4). These features are respectively and independently described by 256, 256, 25 and 25 prototypes. Even for no contextual information from the input field, it is impossible to directly estimate the probability of observing a set of 4 features given a class (or a state) q_k without any independence assumption (as there are $256 \times 256 \times 25 \times 25$ or 4×10^7 possible inputs):

$$p(f_1, f_2, f_3, f_4|q_k) = \prod_{i=1}^{4} p(f_i|q_k) \ . \tag{12}$$

If we now consider an *MLP* with four input groups, each of them coding a particular feature ($256 + 256 + 25 + 25 = 562$ input units), the $k - th$ output will approximate, in theory, the *MAP* probability $p(q_k|f_1, f_2, f_3, f_4)$ without any independence assumption. Of course, the *MAP* estimate associated with the independence assumption can be calculated by:

$$\hat{p}((q_k|f_1, f_2, f_3, f_4) = \frac{\prod_{i=1}^{4} p(f_i|q_k).p(q_k)}{p(f_1, f_2, f_3, f_4)} \ . \tag{13}$$

Preliminary results are reported in Table II where classification rates obtained from *MLE* (equation 12), *MAP* estimates (equation 13, i.e. under the hypothesis of independence of the 4 features) and *MLPs* (no independence assumption) are compared. The TIMIT data base was described on the basis of 60 phonemes and "1 x 562 - 60" and "7 x 562 - 60" stand for *MLPs* with respectively one input frame (no contextual information) and seven input frames.

	training	test	validation
1 x 562 - 60	41.4 (1.176)	36.1 (1.116)	37.3 (1.129)
7 x 562 - 60	69.8 (1.043)	40.3 (0.998)	40.9 (0.960)
MLE	36.0	29.2	30.2
MAP	42.2	36.4	38.2

Table II. Classification rates at the frame level on TIMIT data base

The classification rates obtained from the *MAP* estimated by (13) are similar to those obtained with the *MLP* without contextual input (1 x 562 - 60). This suggests that the correlation of the input features is not sufficiently class-dependent to make a difference in the recognition scores. However, it is also true that the training procedure is not guaranteed to reach the optimal solution. If some contextual information (7 x 562 - 60) is added , the network performance is somewhat better. As in Table I, the numbers in brackets give the average sum, over the training set, test set or validation set, of the output values. Again, it can be observe that these values are very close to unity.

All of these results were obtained by maximizing the probability of a correct frame classification. Unfortunately, this does not guarantee the best performance for the recognition of words in continuous unsegmented speech, which is the actual practical problem we are trying to solve. In fact, preliminary experiments have shown us that the use of *MLP* outputs as probabilities for a discriminant *HMM* leads to worse performance at the word level than we can obtain using classical methods. However, it appears that these effects are significantly recuced if the output values of the *MLP* are divided by the prior class probabilities observed over the training set. Further work will be required before we can conclude that there is any real advantage to using an *MLP* for continuous word recognition. These considerations should be kept in mind when one sees comparisons between *MLP* systems, which are optimized for frame or steady-state phoneme classification, and *HMM* systems which are optimized for word recognition in continuous speech.

5. Integrating an MLP into an HMM

In Sections 3 and 4, each acoustic vector is classified independently of the preceding classifications and the sequential character of the speech signal is not modeled, except in the sense of the time-space mapping which is done to use the context of multiple time frames in the classification of each frame. The system has no short-term memory from one classification to the next one, and successive classifications may be contradictory. As shown by both the theoretical and experimental results above, *MLP* output values may be considered to be *MAP* probabilities for pattern classification. Either these, or some other related quantity (such as the output normalized by the prior probability of the corresponding class) may be used in the Viterbi search *(DTW)* to determine the best time-warped succession of states (speech sounds) to explain the observed speech measurements. This hybrid approach (*MLP* to estimate probabilities, *HMM* to incorporate them to segment continuous speech into a succession of words) has the potential of exploiting the interpolating capabilities of *MLPs* while using the *DTW* procedure to capture the dynamics of speech. While we know of no one who has been successful at using this or any other method to recognize continuous speech with an *MLP* (at an accuracy as good as that of conventional statistical systems), it is likely that any successful effort of this sort must make use of some method (such as the *DTW*) to recognize the succession of states which comprises an entire continuous utterance.

Thus, a feedforward *MLP* can be used to estimate the emission probabilities of an *HMM*. When recurrent connections are added to the *MLP*, state transition probabilities as well may be incorporated. Several recurrent networks have already been proposed for speech recognition. In [Prager et al., 1986], a particular Boltzmann machine dealing with sequential inputs was defined where some of the hidden units, called "carry units", were supplied as extra inputs with the purpose of generating time dynamic. In [Watrous & Shastri, 1987], sequential processing is obtained with the "temporal flow model". Delayed self-loops are added to the hidden and output units of the *MLP*. The system described in [Elman, 1988] is also an alternative implementation of this network where the output self-loops are eliminated and where the delayed hidden unit values are fed back as supplementary input units. Feedback is easily implemented by extending the input field with an additional vector containing the hidden unit values generated by the preceding input frame. All these machines can be referred as "hidden-to-input feedback models". Approximation of these recurrent networks over a finite time period has been presented in [Waibel et al., 1988]. In that case, the loops at each layer are replaced by the explicit use of several preceding activations values. The activations in a particular layer are computed from the current and multiple delayed values of the preceding layer.

In the *HMM* formalism, the speech signal is supposed to be produced by a (first order) Markov source for which the probability of reaching a particular state depends entirely on the previous state and on the observed acoustic vectors associated with the speech time slots. In this framework, it can be shown [Bourlard & Wellekens, 1989b] that local contributions as (7) can be generated by an *MLP* feeding back, to the input field, the output values associated with the previous input frame. Canceling the partial derivative of the associated *LMSE* criterion versus the outputs leads to the estimates given in (7) which take the transition probabilities into account. The basic architecture of the corresponding *MLP* (using contextual information for the input acoustic vectors) is similar in design to the net developed in [Jordan, 1986] to produce output pattern sequences. It can be referred as "output-to-input-feedback model". Again, the generated local contributions can be used in a *DTW* process to achieve a global discriminant recognition. A straightforward generalization can me made to more general or high order Markov models by replicating outputs corresponding to several previous frames in the input field. Another way to take account of previous decisions is to represent, in the same extra input vector, a weighted sum (e.g. exponentially decreasing with time) of the preceding outputs [Jordan, 1986]. That can be achieved by adding a self-loop on the fed-back units with a scalar weight μ, with $0 < \mu < 1$. In that case, the $k-th$ output unit will estimate the a *posteriori probability* of state $q(k)$ given the current input vector and given the probabilities that previous vectors where classified into $q(\ell)$, $\ell = 1, \ldots, K$.

The main advantage of the "output-to-input-feedback" topology, when compared with other recurrent models proposed for sequential processing [Elman, 1988; Watrous, 1987], over and above the possible interpretation in terms of *HMM*, is the control of the information fed back during the training. Indeed, since the training data consists of consecutive labeled speech frames, the correct sequence of output states is known and the training is supervised by providing the correct information. However, all these recurrent nets can be interpreted in terms of state space equations of "nonlinear" control theory [Robinson & Fallside, 1987].

6. Conclusion

It is now clear, both from a theoretical perspective and from empirical measurements, that the outputs of an *MLP* (when trained for pattern classification using the mean square criterion) approximate the Maximum a Posteriori *(MAP)* probabilities, or the class probabilities conditioned on the input. It has also been shown that these estimates, given the use of contextual inputs to the *MLP*, lead to frame classification performance which is significantly improved over the corresponding performance for simple Maximum Likelihood probabilities, or even *MAP* probabilties without the benefit of context.

The recognition of words in continuous speech is not so simply improved by the use of an *MLP*. When dynamic time warping *DTW* is used for decoding *HMM* it not only tackles the variability of speech pronunciation, but is also an efficient tool for connected speech segmentation. This property is difficult to achieve using a "neural" architecture. Indeed, even assuming a perfect dynamical system taking the complete history into account, the output of these machines is just the "instantaneous" activation value of each output class (e.g. associated with words or phonemes) and does not give any idea about the underlying segmentation. For example, with the *HMM* approach, even if we were able to build a very high order Markov model, the time warping would still be useful. Avoiding explicit *DTW* for a real task continuous speech recognition remains thus a challenging problem. On the other hand, it is also questionable whether it is even desirable to replace the *DTW* algorithm, as it is well known that this process is very effective, and also has efficient hardware implementations [Murveit & Brodersen, 1986]. Lippmann & Gold (1987) have defined a neural net architecture, called the "Viterbi Net", that can implement a *DTW* decoder, but there is no obvious advantage to its use. In short, we have yet to learn how to incorporate "neural" networks to any advantage in the recognition of words in continuous speech. However, the progress that has been made for the levels which we appear to understand (e.g., frame classification) seems to justify our further investigation.

References

1. Bahl, L.R. & Jelinek, F. (1975). Decoding for Channels with Insertions, Deletions, and Substitutions with Applications to Speech Recognition, *IEEE Trans. on IT*, vol. 21, no. 4, pp. 404-411.

2. Bourlard, H. & Wellekens, C.J. (1989a). Speech Pattern Discrimination and Multilayer Perceptrons, *Computer, Speech and Language*, vol. 3, pp. 1-19.

3. Bourlard, H. & Wellekens, C.J. (1989b). Links between Markov Models and Multilayer Perceptrons, *Advances in Neural Information Processing Systems 1*, Morgan Kaufmann, pp. 502-510,

4. Bridle, J.S. (1989). Probabilistic Scoring for Back-Propagation Networks, with Relationships to Statistical Pattern Recognition, *Neural Network for Computing*, Snowbird, UT.

5. Brown, P. (1987). The Acoustic-Modeling Problem in Automatic Speech Recognition, *Ph.D. thesis*, Comp. Sc. Dep., Carnegie-Mellon University.

6. Devijver, P.A. & Kittler, J. (1982). *Pattern Recognition: A Statistical Approach*, Prentice Hall International.

7. Elman, J.L. (1988). Finding Structure in Time, *CRL Tech, Report 8801*, University of California, San Diego.

8. Jordan M.L. (1986). Serial Order: A Parallel Distributed Processing Approach, UCSD, Tech. Report 8604.

9. Lippmann, R.P. & Gold, B. (1987). Neural Classifiers Useful for Speech Recognition, *1st Int. Conf. on Neural Networks*, pp. IV-417, San Diego, CA.

10. Morgan, N. & Bourlard, H. (1989). Generalization and Parameter Estimation in Feedforward Nets: Some Experiments, *Neural Networks for Computing*, Snowbird, UT, also in *ICSI Technical Report TR-089-017.*

11. Murveit, H. & Brodersen, R.W. (1986). An Integrated-Circuit-Based Speech Recognition System, *IEEE Trans. ASSP*, vol. 34, no. 6, pp. 1465-1472.

12. Murveit, H. & Weintraub M. (1988). 1000-Word Speaker-Independent Continuous -Speech Recognition Using Hidden Markov Models, *Proc. Int. Conf. on ASSP-88*, pp. 115-118, New York.

13. Nadas, A., Nahamoo, D. & Picheny M.A. (1988). On a Model-Robust Training Method for Speech Recognition, *IEEE Trans. on ASSP*, vol. 35, no.9, pp. 1432-1436.

14. Poritz, A.B. (1988). Hidden Markov Models: A Guided Tour, *Proc. Int. Conf. on ASSP-88*, pp. 7-13, New York.

15. Prager R.W., Harrison T.D. & Fallside F. (1986). Boltzmann Machines for Speech Recognition, *Computer, Speech and Language*, vol. 1, pp. 3-27.

16. Robinson, A.J. & Fallside, F. (1987). The Utility Driven Dynamic Error Propagation Network, *Tech. Report* CUED/F-INFENG/TR.1, Cambridge Univ., UK.

17. Waibel, A., Hanazawa, T., Hinton, G., Shikano, K., Lang, K. (1988). Phoneme Recognition: Neural Networks vs. Hidden Markov Models, *Proc. Int. Conf. on ASSP-88*, pp. 107- 110, New York.

18. Watrous, R.L. & Shastri, L. (1987). Learning Phonetic Features Using Connectionist Networks: an Experiment in Speech Recognition, *1st Int. Conf. on Neural Networks*, pp. IV-381-388, San Diego, CA.

Probabilistic Interpretation of Feedforward Classification Network Outputs, with Relationships to Statistical Pattern Recognition

JOHN S. BRIDLE
Speech Research Unit
Royal Signals and Radar Establishment
St. Andrews Road Great Malvern
UK WR14 3PS

Abstract

We are concerned with feed-forward non-linear networks (multi-layer perceptrons, or MLPs) with multiple outputs. We wish to treat the outputs of the network as probabilities of alternatives (*e.g.* pattern classes), conditioned on the inputs. We look for appropriate output non-linearities and for appropriate criteria for adaptation of the parameters of the network (*e.g.* weights). We explain two modifications: probability scoring, which is an alternative to squared error minimisation, and a normalised exponential (**softmax**) multi-input generalisation of the logistic non-linearity. The two modifications together result in quite simple arithmetic, and hardware implementation is not difficult either. The use of **radial units** (squared distance instead of dot product) immediately before the **softmax** output stage produces a network which computes posterior distributions over class labels based on an assumption of Gaussian within-class distributions. However the training, which uses cross-class information, can result in better performance at class discrimination than the usual within-class training method, unless the within-class distribution assumptions are actually correct.

1 Networks and Probabilistic Models

1.1 The stochastic model paradigm

Currently the most successful approach to automatic speech recognition is based on *Stochastic Models.* The approach generalises parametric statistical pattern recognition, and is also important in other application domains, such as computational vision.

NATO ASI Series, Vol. F 68
Neurocomputing
Edited by F. Fogelman Soulié and J. Hérault

The method consists in treating the data as if it were the output of a stochastic system (one governed by probabilistic laws) [1]. The structure of the model is a pattern of direct dependencies between internal (hidden) and external (visible) random variables, and it is usually informed by insight into the structure of the data or of the real generator (*e.g.* vocal tracts in the case of speech). There is also a (possibly large) set of parameters of the model, which need to be estimated (such as conditional probabilities, means and variances). There are usually separate algorithms for recognition (interpreting the data in terms of the model) and for learning (estimating parameters.)

The basis of the recognition process is often to compute the likelihood of the data conditioned on some unseen random variable of interest, such as the class of the pattern: $P(\text{Data} \mid \text{Class})$. Using Bayes rule, the class conditional probabilities are then

$$P(\text{Class} \mid \text{Data}) = P(\text{Data} \mid \text{Class})P(\text{Class}) \Big/ P(\text{Data}),$$

where $P(\text{Class})$ are the prior probabilities (often assumed equal) and

$$P(\text{Data}) = \sum_{\text{classes}} P(\text{Data} \mid \text{Class})P(\text{Class}).$$

If we only require the most likely class then this denominator can be ignored.

One of the simplest stochastic models (and one we shall return to below) is a set of Gaussian distributions, one for each class. In this case the parameters are the priors, the means, and the covariance matrices. We may choose to restrict the covariance matrices in various ways, such as zero except on the diagonals (independence assumption), or still more by assuming the covariance matrix is unit diagonal times a constant. We might also assume that the covariance matrices for the different classes are related (*e.g.* equal). We would usually estimate the means etc. from the sample means, etc. (*i.e.* maximum likelihood estimation for each class separately).

1.2 Feed-forward nonlinear "neural" networks

In contrast to the stochastic model approach, a neural network approach typically starts with assumptions about the form of a suitable recognition process, such as a non-linear feedforward network, and we adjust its parameters (*e.g.* weights) to optimise some measure of performance.

The standard "multi-layer perceptron" (MLP) can be taken as a semi-linear logistic feed-forward network with squared error minimisation, trained using some optimisation technique exploiting the error back-propagation method for computing partial derivatives with respect to the weights. Such MLPs are often used for pattern classification, using one-from-N coding at the output. (*i.e.* One output for each class, targets are zero except for unity at the true class line.) However, this structure is really only suitable for cases where the outputs correspond to (approximately) independent properties of the input, such presence/absence of objects which may appear together, or in the use of componential representations, *e.g.* [2]. Later we consider a more appropriate structure for 1-from-N classification problems.

The usual criterion for adjusting the parameters (θ) of a network is minimum squared error between outputs and targets (y).

$$\min_{\theta} \mathrm{E}\left[(Y - F(x,\theta))^2\right]$$

The structure of the network may not allow this optimum to be reached, and if it does the search method may not find it. What we *should* try to optimise is the expected performance on *unseen* samples (but from the same distribution as the training data). In practice we minimise not the expected value of the squared error, but the average over the training set. Optimisation of a squared error criterion can tend towards networks producing estimates of the posterior distribution of classes. Later we consider an alternative score which is concerned with probabilities of correct classification decisions.

2 Stochastic models with neural network solutions

A natural way to think of the function of a neural-style network when used for pattern classification is in terms of conditional relative class density estimation, which is equivalent to the probability distribution over class labels conditioned on the input (i.e. the posterior distribution over class labels, $P(\text{Class} \mid \text{Data})$). The relative densities may need less parameters than the set of individual class densities, and the relative densities are precisely what matter in discrimination tasks.

To illustrate the connections between networks and stochastic models, we consider two simple stochastic models for which the relative densities are a semi-linear logistic funtion of the inputs.

2.1 Boolean random variables separately dependent on another BRV

As a simple example of a stochastic model, consider a set of Boolean random variables (BRVs) $\{X_i\}$ which are independent apart from their dependence on another BRV Y. The $(2n+1)$ parameters are $p_y \triangleq P(Y=1)$, $p_i \triangleq P(X_i=1 \mid Y=1)$ and $\tilde{p}_i \triangleq P(X_i=1 \mid Y=0)$. Suppose we are given observed values of the Xs, $x_1, \ldots, x_n$. and we wish to estimate the value of Y.

It can be shown that

$$P(Y=1 \mid x_1, \ldots, x_n) = 1/(1 + \exp -(w_0 + \sum_i w_i x_i)),$$

where

$$w_i = \log \frac{p_i}{(1-p_i)} - \log \frac{\tilde{p}_i}{(1-\tilde{p}_i)}, \quad \text{and} \quad \mathrm{w}_0 = \log \frac{\mathrm{p}_y}{(1-\mathrm{p}_y)} + \sum_i \log \frac{(1-\mathrm{p}_i)}{(1-\tilde{\mathrm{p}}_i)}.$$

Thus the semi-linear logistic is just what is needed in this case, to compute the probability of the unseen BRV, Y, being 1, as a function of the observed values of the Xs.

2.2 Equal covariance Gaussians

Consider next the case of discrimination between two classes, each univariate Gaussian distributed, differing only in the values of their means (m_a, m_b) and priors($p_a \triangleq P(\text{Class}=a), p_b \triangleq P(\text{Class}=b)$) (*i.e.* equal variances, σ^2). The two probability density functions have the form

$$P(x \mid a) \triangleq P(X=x \mid \text{Class}=a) = \frac{1}{\sqrt{2\pi\sigma^2}} e^{-\frac{(x-m_a)^2}{2\sigma^2}}.$$

The posterior probability of class a, given an observation x, is

$$P(\text{Class}=a \mid X=x) = 1 \Big/ \left(1 + \exp -(w_0 + w_1 x)\right),$$

where

$$w_0 = \log(p_a/p_b) - \frac{(m_a^2 - m_b^2)}{2\sigma^2}, \qquad w_1 = \frac{(m_a - m_b)}{\sigma^2}.$$

Thus a single semi-linear logistic unit can compute the posterior distribution of class labels. This result extends to multi-variate distributions with equal covariance matrices.

Multi-layer networks are useful when the relationships between input and output are more complicated. In the following sections we are concerned only with the form of the output non-linearity and the criterion which is optimised by adjusting the weights. We treat first the case of independent outputs, which is relatively well established, then the case of present interest, which is a one-from-N classifier.

3 Networks with multi-component, independent outputs

If each output value, O_j, from a network is to be treated as a probability that an associated random variable, Y_j, is true, then we require that all N outputs lie between 0 and 1.

Given a set of unconstrained scalar input values, I_j, which may be weighted sums of outputs from other units ($I_j = \sum_i w_{ij} O_i$) we wish to produce outputs of the network, $O_j = F(I_j)$ which satisfy the $0 > O_j > 1$ constraint. The term sigmoid is used for any non-decreasing function which maps the real line to the unit interval. The most commonly used sigmoid function is the logistic or (offset) hyperbolic tangent:

$$O_j = F(I_j) = \frac{1}{1+e^{-I_j}} = \frac{1}{2}\left(1 + \tanh\frac{x}{2}\right).$$

One way to score such a system against the true values, $\{T_j\}$, is to say we shall use the Os to guess the true values. We shall guess that $Y_j=1$ with probability O_j. If $T_j=1$ we shall be correct O_j of the time, and if $T_j=0$ we shall be correct $(1-O_j)$ of the time. The probability of all the (independent) guesses being correct is

$$\prod_{j=1}^{N} O_j^{T_j}(1-O_j)^{(1-T_j)}.$$

This is also appropriate if the Ts are between 0 and 1, signifying the *probability* that the random variable is true.

In fact we minimise minus the log of this product:

$$J = -\sum_j (T_j \log(O_j) + (1 - T_j) \log(1 - O_j)).$$

To compute the gradient of J wrt parameters of the network (*e.g.* weights) we need

$$\frac{\partial J}{\partial I_j} = \frac{\partial J}{\partial O_j} \frac{\partial O_j}{\partial I_j} = \frac{O_j - T_j}{O_j(1 - O_j)} O_j(1 - O_j) = (O_j - T_j).$$

The difference between this partial derivative and the usual squared-error derivative is simply the removal of the $O(1-O)$ factor.

This type of probability or entropy score for backpropagation networks has been suggested several times in different forms [3, 4, 5, 6]. It is essentially the same as the G measure used in the Boltzmann machine [7] and the recent Boltzmann Perceptron Network [8], which is a deterministic feedforward network closely related to the system presented in the next section. To our knowledge it has not yet been shown convincingly that such a score provides better performance than squared error in practice, but it certainly seems more appropriate for some purposes from a theoretical point of view. The closely related Maximum Mutual Information estimation method has been shown to improve results of hidden Markov model based speech recognition [9].

4 1-from-N Classifier Networks

For 1-from-N classifiers the *set* of outputs should have the form of a probability distribution over class labels, conditioned on the input:

$$O_j = P(c{=}j \mid \text{input}),$$

so we require

$$O_j > 0 \quad \forall j \quad \text{and} \quad \sum_{j=1}^{N} O_j = 1.$$

To enforce this stochastic constraint, we suggest a *normalised exponential* output non-linearity,

$$O_j = \mathrm{e}^{I_j} \Big/ \sum_k \mathrm{e}^{I_k}.$$

This "**softmax**" function is a generalisation of the logistic to multiple inputs. It also generalises maximum picking, or "Winner-Take-All", in the sense that that the outputs change smoothly, and equal inputs produce equal outputs. Although it looks rather cumbersome, and perhaps not really in the spirit of neural networks, those familiar with

Markov random fields or statistical mechanics will know that it has convenient mathematical properties. Circuit designers will enjoy the simple transistor circuit which implements it.

Softmax can approach arbitrarily close to a WTA effect by increasing an optional gain factor, $1/T$ (now use $e^{I_j/T}$. As $T \to 0$ the outputs approach a Kronecker delta function indicating the position of the maximum in the inputs. We have found it useful to consider replacing WTA with **softmax** in various algorithms. The result is often insight or an improved algorithm. It is easy to add an extra output with a constant input, to deal with rejects (inputs not in any of the main classes).

For scoring we assume that we shall pick one of the labels $(1, \ldots, N)$ based on the outputs treated as a distribution. (Pick j with probability O_j.)

First let us assume that for each input training pattern we have the true probability distribution over labels, $T_j = P(c = j \mid x)$. We wish our set of outputs, $\{O_j\}$ to be as close as possible to the true probabilities. An appropriate measure of similarity of the two probability distributions is the relative entropy of the Ts with respect to the outputs [10] (*i.e.* the extra information given by the T when we already know the Os)

$$G \triangleq -\sum_j T_j \log \frac{T_j}{O_j} = -\sum_j T_j \log T_j + \sum_j T_j \log O_j = H(T) - J,$$

where $J = -\sum_j T_j \log O_j$.

The first term is the entropy of the T distribution, and is independent of the outputs. The second term is the log of the probability of a long run of correct guesses, if we choose from the O distribution. If the true class, c, is known, the probability of choosing the correct class is O_c, and the expression for relative entropy simplifies because $H(T) = 0$ and $J = -\log O_c$.

In back-propagating the partial derivatives we note that each output depends on *all* the inputs to **softmax**, so:

$$\frac{\partial J}{\partial I_j} = \sum_k \frac{\partial J}{\partial O_k} \frac{\partial O_k}{\partial I_j}.$$

$$\frac{\partial J}{\partial O_k} = -\frac{T_k}{O_k}.$$

For the **softmax** output nonlinearity,

$$\frac{\partial O_k}{\partial I_j} = O_k(\delta_{kj} - O_j),$$

so

$$\frac{\partial J}{\partial I_j} = (O_j - T_j).$$

We conclude that **softmax** and the entropy score suit one another well.

5 Transistor circuits

It is well known that a long-tailed pair (differential pair) of transistors, each with an exponential transconductance characteristic (*e.g.* bipolar transistors or sub-threshold CMOS) has a logistic relationship between (differential) input voltage and output current. (In an amplifier we use the central, linear, portion of this transfer characteristic, and in a logic gate (*e.g.* ECL) we use the endpoints.) The **softmax** function can be implemented in a generalisation of the longtail pair, with one transistor per input value.

6 A Practical Example

To illustrate the use of the softmax nonlinearity, probability scoring and relationships between networks and conventional classifiers, we constructed a ("one layer") network which computes the posterior distribution over class labels under the following assumptions: the within-class distributions are all Gaussian, with equal covariance matrices (all the unit matrix times a known constant) and equal priors.

The outputs of the network were:

$$O_j = \mathrm{e}^{I_j} / \sum_k \mathrm{e}^{I_k},$$

where the inputs to the **softmax** were

$$I_j = -\sum_i (x_i - m_{ij})^2.$$

The components, m_{ij}, of the means of the distributions were the only free parameters, and they were adjusted using a back-propagation-based method, starting from the values of the within-class data means:

$$\frac{\partial J}{\partial m_{ij}} = \frac{\partial J}{\partial I_j}\frac{\partial I_j}{\partial m_{ij}} = 2(0_j - T_j)(x_i - m_{ij}).$$

The data was a set of first and second formant frequency values for spoken vowel sounds, in 11 vowel classes, spoken by many male and female American speakers [11][1].

The standard parameter estimation technique is maximum likelihood for each class separately. With the above assumptions about the form of the distributions, the parameters are the class means, and the ML estimates are the data means. The Bayes decision regions are shown in figure 1 (the steps in the lines are an artifact). Each point on the plane is labelled with the class of the nearest mean. Figure 1 also shows correctly classified training points as dots, and wrongly classified training points as letters corresponding to true classes.

[1] We are grateful to Richard Lippmann of Lincoln Laboratories for his version of this data [12]

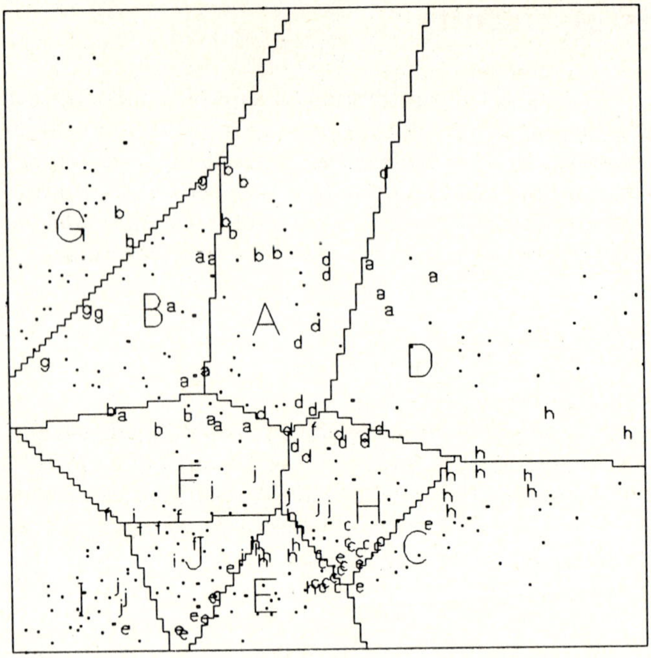

Figure 1. Decision boundaries etc using data means

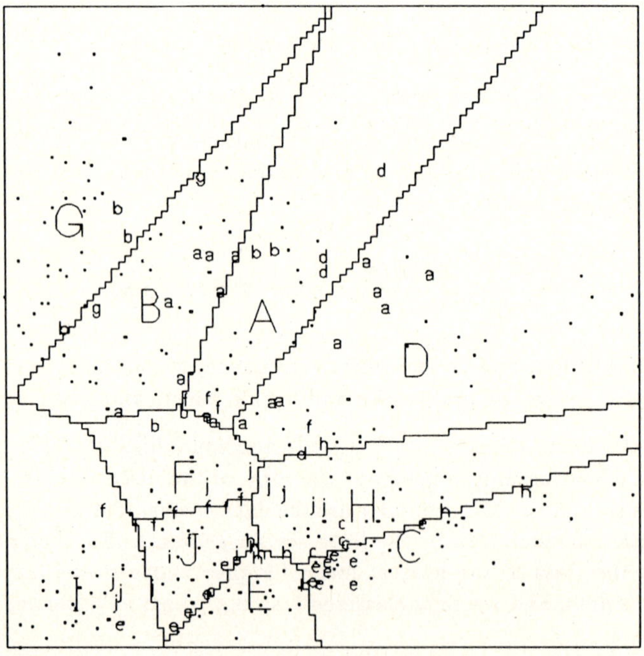

Figure 2. Decision boundaries etc after network training

68% of a separate test set was correctly classified by this "Euclidean distance to class mean" rule. When the reference points were adjusted further using the network method, the performance on the test set improved to 78% correct. The new decision boundaries and wrongly labelled training points are shown in figure 2. This improvement may seem surprising, until we remember that the assumptions about the distributions are not very good. In this case we have enough data to estimate a separate covariance matrix for each class, and performance with a Mahalanobis distance is close to that of the discrimination-optimised isotropic distributions.

7 Conclusions

We have shown how some "neural networks" can be understood in terms of parametric statistical pattern recognition, and that modifications of the usual network structures and scoring methods can make them more appropriate for delivering posterior probabilities. Training the network can improve on the equivalent standard model-based parameter estimation methods if the assumptions of the model are incorrect. It remains to be seen whether these modifications make a significant difference in practice, and whether more interesting types of parametric pattern recognition method (such as those based on hidden Markov models, as used in speech recognition) can be cast as adaptive networks.

References

[1] D R Cox and H D Millar. *The Theory of stochastic processes.* Methuen, 1965.

[2] T J Seinowski and C R Rosenberg. *NETtalk: A parallel network that learns to read aloud.* Technical Report JHU/EECS-86/01, Johns Hopkins U. EE&CS, 1986.

[3] L Gillick. Probability scores for backpropagation networks. July 1987. Personal communication.

[4] G E Hinton. *Connectionist Learning Procedures.* Technical Report CMU-CS-87-115, Carnegie Mellon University Computer Science Department, June 1987.

[5] E B Baum and F Wilczek. Supervised learning of probability distributions by neural networks. In D Anderson, editor, *Neural Information Processing Systems*, pages 52–61, Am. Inst. of Physics, 1988.

[6] S Solla, E Levin, and M Fleisher. Accelerated learning in layered neural networks. *Complex Systems*, January 1989.

[7] G.E. Hinton, T.J. Sejnowski, and D.H. Ackley. *Boltzmann machines: constraint satisfaction networks that learn.* Technical report CMU–CS–84–119, Carnegie–Mellon University, May 1984.

[8] E Yair and A Gersho. *The Boltzmann Perceptron Network: a soft classifier.* Technical Report CIPR TR 88-11, Center for Information Processing Research, Dept. of E&CE, UCSB, November 1988.

[9] L R Bahl, P F Brown, P V de Souza, and R L Mercer. Maximum mutual information estimation of hidden Markov model parameters. In *Proc. IEEE ICASSP86*, pages 49–52, 1986.

[10] A J Viterbi. *Principles of Digital Communication and Coding.* McGraw-Hill, 1979.

[11] G E Peterson and H L Barney. Control methods used in a study of vowels. *J. Acoust. Soc. Amer.*, 24(2):175–184, March 1952.

[12] W M Huang and R P Lippmann. Neural net and traditional classifiers. In D Anderson, editor, *Neural Information Processing Systems*, pages 387–396, Am. Inst. of Physics, 1988.

Data Compression Using Multilayer Perceptrons

Pascal Blanchet

LIMSI/CNRS
BP 30
91 406 Orsay cedex
France

Abstract

This paper describes the use of Multilayer Perceptrons to perform data compression tasks. It has been shown that an MLP with two fully connected layers of linear units, performs a principal component analysis when used for auto-association [2]. Further work has been carried out in the field of MLP and data analysis which has proven that such networks can also perform discriminant analysis when used for classification [3]. The main property of MLPs is that the compressed representation of an input is the activity vector of the cells contained in the hidden layer, therefore the rank of dimensionality reduction is the size of this layer. We applied this idea to other network architectures and trained them with the backpropagation algorithm [4,5] for French phoneme classification and auto-association.

The Data

The experiments were carried out on speech data. The signal was FFT-analysed then passed through a sixteen-channel filter bank. This analysis transforms the signal into a sequence of sixteen-dimensional vectors called "frames". We then averaged each frame and preserved the mean value as a seventeenth coefficient.

We gave the networks the frames corresponding to stable phonemes pronounced in different contexts by a single speaker [1]. This way, only one frame should be sufficient to identify one phoneme, and the set of frames corresponding to the same phoneme should constitute an almost convex cluster in a specific region of the data space. The training set contained twenty-three phonemes and phonetic features, including thirteen vowels, six fricatives, M and N, and the voiced and unvoiced silences of plosives.

Classification Training

A network used to perform a kind of discriminant analysis needs to be trained for classification: in our experiment we chose to code the desired output with twenty-three values so that each cell was at plus one for a given phoneme and minus one for all the others.

NATO ASI Series, Vol. F 68
Neurocomputing
Edited by F. Fogelman Soulié and J. Hérault

In the case of a two-layer perceptron, the data is projected in the hidden layer, and then separated by the output layer. Therefore the decision regions found by the output layer to separate the projected clusters are single hyperplans. But we know that a single hyperplan may not be sufficient to separate one cluster from all the others. For this reason, our networks were augmented by a second hidden layer containing twenty cells to help cluster separation. The type of architecture we have just described was previously used in [5] for a simple classification problem.

Three different networks with this kind of architecture were trained. With three or four cells in the first hidden layer, the recognition rate at the output was 91% and 94% and no phonemes were under 75%. These results show that each phoneme was located in a specific region of the projection space, which means that the networks found subspaces which separated the phonetic clusters rather well.

But with only two cells, the recognition rate fell to 70% and some phonemes were completely ignored by the network (they were completely overlapped by other phonemes). Those poor results were probably obtained because the solution to the problem, which consists of projecting our data set on a plane preserving the phoneme separation, does not exist. Therefore, if we want such a planar representation of that speech data, we need to introduce non linearities, which, for example, can be done by simply adding to the network a twenty-cell layer above the reduced one (Fig. 1). This way, the compressed representation provided by the reduced layer is not a projection. In fact, the first hidden layer positions the phoneme clusters so that they can be projected into separated regions of the plane.

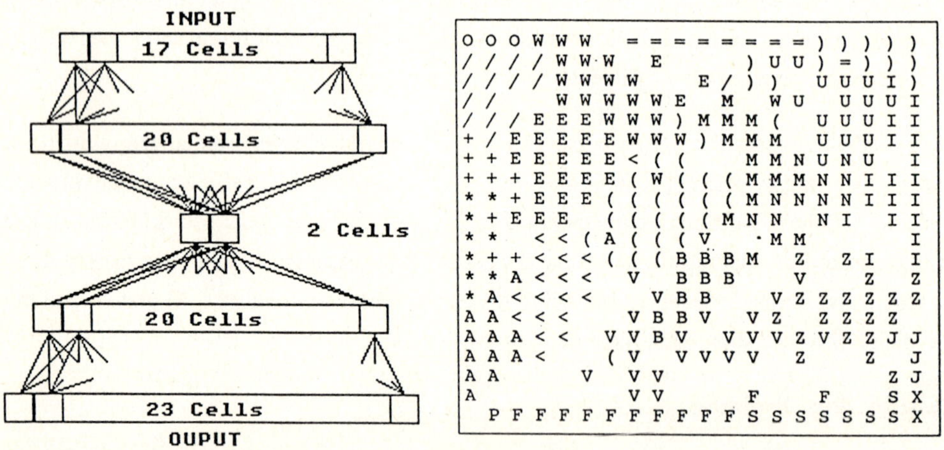

Figure 1 Network architecture for non linear compression and compressed representation obtained after training (see Table 1 for the phonetic codes)

The results show a recognition rate of 88% and no phoneme was ignored by the network. Besides, with a two-dimensional space, we can see that the phonemes are located in a specific region of the plane. The map of Figure 1 shows the activity space of the two-cell layer. The coordinates of each label are the couple of cell activities obtained after propagation of a frame (the plane was divided into a 20x20 grid and the squares were labeled with a majority-voting criterion).

Auto-association Training

The next step of our work was to try the same kind of architecture for auto-association. The twenty-three cells of the output layer were replaced by seventeen to match the input dimension. It is noticeable that the best results were obtained with a network containing two internal layers between the reduced one and the output one. So our network was a five-layer perceptron.

The non linearities above the reduced layer enable the network to provide a compressed representation which is not a projection of the input space. Because of the two hidden layers below the reduced one, the image of the plane in the output space is a curved surface which matches the shape of the training frame cluster better than a plane.

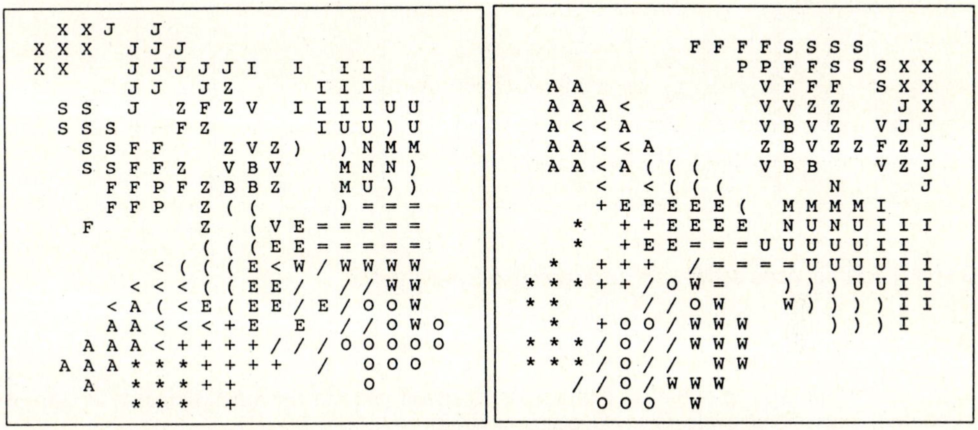

Figure 2 The two planar representations obtained by auto-association training

We compared the results with those obtained by a two-layer perceptron, which performs principal component analysis. Figure 2 shows the two planes provided by these networks. The first plane is the PCA and the second is the non linear compression.

We can see two things in the second plane that are not in the first one. There is a gap between vowels and consonants, and the phonemes 'U' and ')' are well separated from each other and from the nasals 'M' and 'N'. On the other hand, 'O' and '/' completely overlap in the second plane.

To decide whether or not non linear compression is better, we have computed two different criteria. The mean overlapping rate (the percentage of frames falling into a wrongly labeled square) was 29% on 2855 frames for the first plane and 20% for the second one. Also, the output square error of the non linear compression was less than half that of the PCA.

Conclusion

The results obtained by these different experiments show that using MLPs is another way to reduce the dimensionality of a space. The main problem of this approach is the possibility of getting stuck in a local minimum during the training phase. However, non linearity and gradient descent seem to be useful in building a continuous compressed representation of a high dimension space. This non linearity enables the networks to improve some properties of the classical dimensionality reduction algorithms.

API	LIMSI
ɔ	+
a	A
ã	*
i	I
y	U
e	)

API	LIMSI
ɛ	(
œ	E
ø	=
o	O
õ	/
u	W

API	LIMSI
ɛ̃	<
p	P
b	B
f	F
s	S
ʃ	X

API	LIMSI
v	V
z	Z
ʒ	J
m	M
n	N

Table 1 API phonetic codes and corresponding LIMSI codes

References

1. Adda-Decker M.: "Evaluation d'unités de décision pour la reconnaissance de la parole continue", Thèse 3ème cycle, Orsay (December 1988)
2. Bourlard H., Kamp Y.: "Auto-Association by multilayer perceptron and singular value decomposition", Manuscript M217, Philips Research Laboratory, Brussels, Belgium (November 1987)
3. Gallinari P., Thiria S., Fogelman-Soulie F.: "Multilayer perceptrons and data analysis". Second Annual International Conference on Neural Networks, San Diego, I-391-401 (1988)
4. Le Cun Y., Fogelman F.: "Modèles connexionnistes de l'apprentissage", Intellectica vol. 1, n°2/3, 114-143 (1987)
5. Rumelhart D.E., Hinton G.E., Williams R.J.: "Learning internal representation by error propagation". In D.E.Rumelhart and J.L.McClelland (eds) Parallel Distributed Processing, MIT Press, vol. 1, 318-362 (1986)

Guided Propagation: current state of theory and applications

Dominique G. Béroule

LIMSI - CNRS
BP 133
91403 ORSAY cedex - FRANCE

Abstract

This paper presents a parallel processing principle: its origin, current state of development and future trends. Implemented in a modular network of processing units, this so-called Guided Propagation principle is presently applied to pattern recognition tasks and psychological modelling.

I. Introduction

The question of Representations, their physical support, the way they are built and used, is a principal one in Cognitive Sciences. Inside a memory space, the lowest level of representation has three main dimensions: a coded one (what is stored for an item), a topographic one (where an item is put), a temporal one (when an item is accessed). This means that any representation is based on a combination of these three components. For instance, a computer-oriented memory is filled in with codes, the position of which are usually not significant: representations are of the coded type, possibly completed by the topographic organization of registers. An alternative machine could instead consider as significant the relative locations of a set of world items. In such a machine, the activation of some memory units (or Feature-Detectors) by incoming stimulations would mean that their associated items are accessed. But the problem is then: how could Feature-Detectors be activated under the influence of highly variable incoming stimulations ?

Connectionism is a possible solution to this problem. As a matter of fact, some connectionist systems implement Feature-Detectors. In Perceptrons, weights of links between the memory units can be regulated so as to induce the propagation of input stimulations towards possibly a single output cell. This kind of system must be told the memory output position to be assigned to each item, in accordance with a supervised learning algorithm (Rosenblatt 59) (LeCun 85). In the memory model presented in this paper, the temporal dimension is combined with the topographic one, in such a way that the position to be assigned to an unexpected item can be determined by the system itself. Internal representations supported by this model are accessed through Guided Propagation, a processing principle which is presented now, together with its current applications.

NATO ASI Series, Vol. F 68
Neurocomputing
Edited by F. Fogelman Soulié and J. Hérault

II. Foundations of Guided Propagation

Motivated by the inadequacy of the functional architecture of computers in dealing with real-world A.I. problems, this work is aimed at designing alternative processing strategies (Béroule 85, 89a). Two sources of data have principally inspired or reinforced the memory model which supports these strategies: Pattern Recognition and Psychophysiology.

II.1. Pattern Recognition features

Initially developed within the framework of Automatic Speech Recognition, this system had to take into account the strong constraints brought in by the characteristics of real-world patterns. First of all, patterns are very variable: their occurrences can be incomplete, distorted and noisy. There now exists some relatively efficient methods for processing pattern distortions; for instance, temporal variations are managed by the Dynamic Time Warping (DTW) algorithm (Gauvain 83). Even if we should not try to simulate the same signal processing and pattern matching algorithms as classical tools, these systems have to be looked at, since they provide us with a set of limitations and open problems.

Inside the broader field of Human-Computer Communication, there is no real-time architecture for managing the many parallel processes involved in a human-like communication. The different knowledge levels of a continuous speech understanding system are accessed sequentially, according to a bottom-up or top-down strategy (Mariani 82), whereas any piece of knowledge should participate in the interpretation process at any time. Speech synthesizers, however close to real voices they may be, do not approach the on-line control performed by a human producing phrases. No speech understanding system can identify speech when mixed with other speech signals.

Thus, the aim of an alternative approach should be twofold:
- providing alternative solutions to problems currently "solved" by classical methods,
- proposing solutions to open problems.

Current speech recognition systems produce some results in dealing with variability by using an average signal analysis. Since our aim is to design a learning machine capable of extracting features of any given precision, another strong constraint arises from the uncertainty principle, which states that a high resolution cannot be obtained over both spatial and temporal dimensions. In a parallel system, each module could be tuned to one of the pattern dimensions, thus providing simultaneous high resolution analyses.

II.2 Psychophysiology

Research in the field of Psychophysiology has produced data and models that may inspire some alternative processing strategies. At a peripheral level, the physiological properties already discovered can be interpreted from a functional point of view (Schwartz 83) (Béroule & Schwartz 86). At a central level, which is much less known, general theories of learning and memory have been propounded. Hypotheses concerning the functional architecture of the nervous system have already become integrated in biological models (Burnod 88).

In the peripheral auditory system, speech is represented by at least two means, place coding and time coding. Place coding involves feature-detectors having their own characteristic spectral frequency (a type of representation previously referred to as topographic). Independently of their frequency channel, the first nervous fibers also reproduce in their discharge rate the main spectral frequencies (coded representation). the synchronization of the spikes with spectral components may also participate in the representation (temporal representation), compatible with a more general fact. The summation of Post Synaptic Potentials arising at neurons dendrites exhibit the following property: whereas a single input induces temporal summations which may not be sufficient to trigger a response, spatial summations from many inputs are more efficient. Indeed, the more synchronized the spikes coming from different locations to a nervous cell, the faster it is activated. From a simplified functional point of view, a neuron can thus be considered a detector of coincidence between internal signals, a property that might be extended to populations of cells.

At a more macroscopic level, synchronization seems also to be significant, as shown by experiments where the spontaneous propagation of nervous signals along some pathways were enhanced and synchronized by incoming stimulations (Verzeano 77). Concerning the formation of the physical support of the nervous activity, current hypotheses are referred to as: reinforcement (Hebb 49), sprouting and selective stabilization (Changeux & al 73). Contrary to a classical distinction in Computer Science, information storage and information retrieval might be based on the same physiological events (Bloch & Laroche 84), and thus would occur in close temporal relationship.

Returning to the periphery of the nervous system, a striking fact is the similarity of the visual and the auditory systems architectures. Both of these systems have two sets of receptors; the largest one is connected to a few nervous fibers (<10%), whereas the smallest set of receptors contacts most of the fibers. The role of this double-channel organization might be related to the uncertainty principle previously mentioned: This dual organization could correspond to complementary analyses performed in parallel on the same input signals (Béroule 85). The dynamic behaviour of the inner ear, possibly controled on-line by a bundle of efferent fibers

Figure 1. The memory pathways, along which a flow of internal signals propagate spontaneously. Signals come from the origin of the pathways (left side of the picture a/), and may reach some characteristic memory locations situated at the ends of this so called cross bundle of pathways.

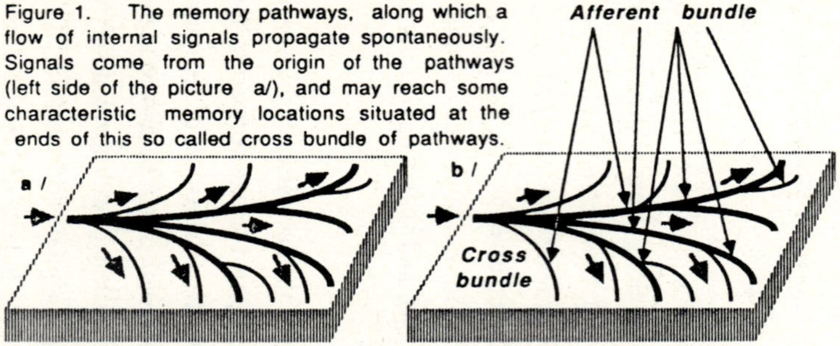

b / The spontaneous propagation of internal signals is rendered more selective under the influence of a second bundle of pathways (afferent bundle), issued from a set of feature detectors. Each internal pathway can be selectively stimulated by a particular sequence of discrete signals conveyed by the afferent bundle.

Thus, propagation can be guided along one of the pathways, which then inhibits the spontaneous propagation which occurs along the other elements of the cross bundle, thanks to transveral and bi-directional inhibitory paths (not represented).

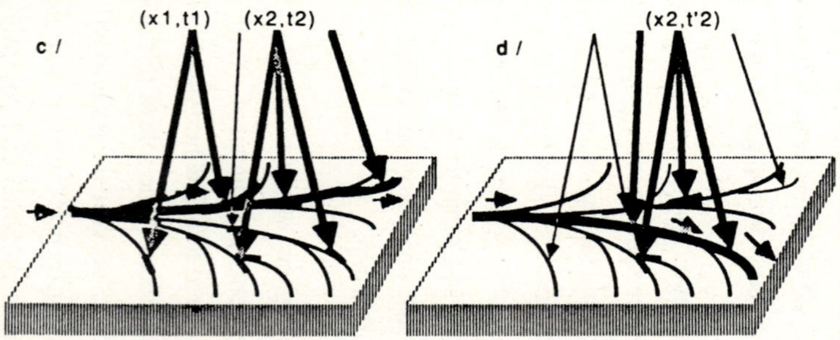

c/ For instance, a signal coming at time t2 from the feature detector x2 spreads over many memory pathways. On the pathway represented by a heavy line, the contribution of x2 enhances the previous action of x1; on the other stimulated pathways , x2 does not occur in a favourable context, and thus remains inneficient.

d/ When the contribution of x2 follows the action of another feature detector, the signals propagating along the cross bundle are then guided along another pathway.

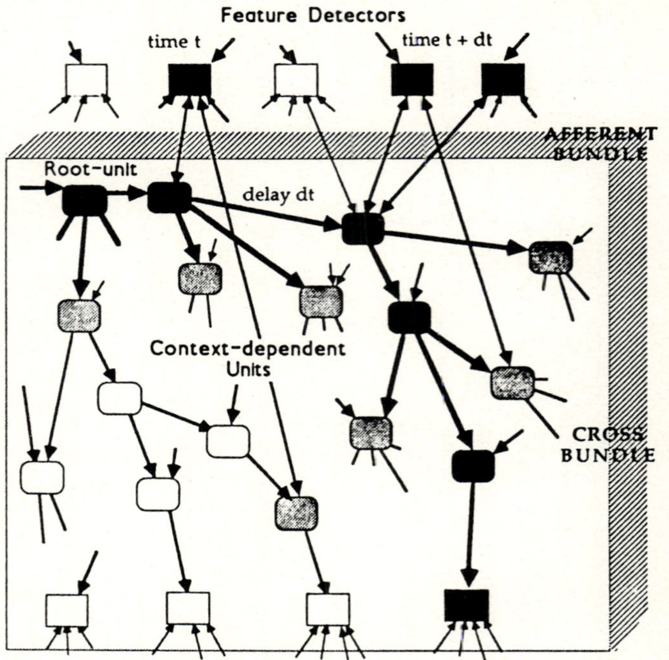

Figure 2. The afferent bundle of pathways is issued from a bank of feature detectors. The cross bundle is issued from a root-unit which provides it with internal signals. Context-Dependent units intersect the two bundles. In the figure,the units represented in white do not receive any signals; the grey units are partly activated, but not enough to generate a signal. The dark units are activated by an internal signal and incoming signals, and thus produce an internal signal.

(Davis 83), is another example of the differences between the signal processing strategies involved in the nervous system and current automatic devices. Among the physiological phenomena already observed, lateral inhibition (Kohonen 84) and short-term adaptation (Delgutte 84) can be viewed as operators aimed at extracting features from the input receptors.

II.3. Description of the processing principle

In the system that we propose, patterns are represented in memory by pathways leading to feature-detectors. The recognition process consists in guiding the spontaneous propagation of internal signals along the pathway which corresponds the best to the stimulations extracted from the current pattern. The similarity criterion is the spatial and temporal coincidence between an internal flow of signals (system's knowledge) and an incoming flow of stimulations (input data).

Consider a memory module inside which a bundle of pathways leads to characteristic memory locations or feature-detectors (fig.1). Assume the spontaneous propagation of a flow of internal signals in parallel along these pathways, and suppose that each pathway stands for a pattern's internal representation. The recognition process will then consist in selectively activating the pathway which corresponds to the current module input. For this purpose, a new bundle of pathways is brought into play, which conveys incoming stimulations from the input pattern: as the internal flow of signals proceeds along the memory pathways, it is selectively fed by a sequence of incoming stimulations.

At a given instant, this mechanism can be viewed as a search for the intersection between different memory subsets: - the part of memory currently activated by the internal flow; - the subsets activated by the stimulations. If activations are summed, the intersection will be the more activated. Processing units distributed in memory would detect coincident signals from different origins. Accordingly, the learning process consists in forcing -the spatial coincidence by directing a group of stimulations and a context signal to the same processing unit, -the temporal coincidence by associating a certain time-delay to each input to this unit.

III. Formalization of Guided Propagation

III.1. A modular network of processing units

Although internal pathways are the main components of this memory model, their activation is significant only when synchronized with a feed-forward flow of stimulations. This function can be performed by processing units set at the points of intersection between the internal flow and the input flow. In this way, each module of the system appears as a connectionist network, inside which three kinds of processing units can be distinguished (fig. 2) :

- The root-unit initiates the spontaneous propagation along memory pathways,
- The Context-Dependent (CD) units form the pathways and detect coincidence between a short-term context signal and stimulations from more peripheral modules.
- The Feature-Detectors stand at the end of the pathways and form the module's interface. They accept input to the system, they feed the pathways of the deeper modules, and can also be preactivated by them (background context).

Before having been shown patterns, the network consists of a set of pre-wired modules, the content of which is limited to a single processing unit (the root of the future pathways). When the system is given a first pattern, its associated pathway grows inside each module from the root-unit and is connected with the activated input feature-detectors. The spontaneous activity of the root-unit then flows along this pathway. If the same pattern occurs again, the internal flow if fed by a similar sequence of stimulations, as it proceeds towards the end of the pathway where stands the pattern-detector. If the set of stimulations does not roughly coincide with the spatio-temporal configuration represented by the pathway, then a new branch may be created, thus enlarging the set of memory references. The complete system appears as a modular network (fig. 3).

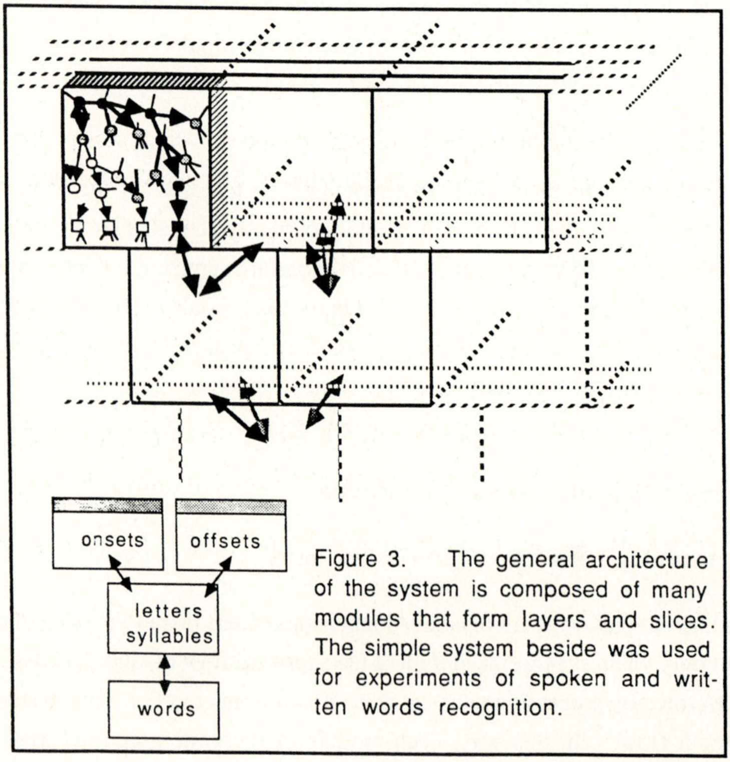

Figure 3. The general architecture of the system is composed of many modules that form layers and slices. The simple system beside was used for experiments of spoken and written words recognition.

III.2. Parameters of the units

Mathematical optimality is not guaranteed for the total network structure that results from the current learning process. However, the local behaviour of a processing unit has been related to its adaptive parameters.Two kinds of parameters may be distinguished: those which determine the local transformations of each input to a unit, and those which define the unit Transfer Function.

- input parameters: Each discrete signal getting to a unit is transformed so as to be synchronized with other input signals, weighted according to the frequency of its occurrences; it also causes an activation of a certain duration.

Synchronization is obtained by delaying with tij the signals issued from unit i and feeding the unit j; if tn is the time at which the unit n is activated, tij is set to tj - ti when the connection between Ui and Uj is created. Time-delays are then adapted to new occurrences. It is shown (see (Béroule 85) pp. 120) that if time-delays of a unit input are averaged, the resulting value converge if the duration Tij of the internal signal tends to decrease from its initial value. Tij is the time interval during which the internal signal may overlap with other incoming signals in order to reach the unit's threshold. There are two initial values for this parameter: the duration of the context signal and the duration of the stimulations (see IV.1).

The weights are used to code the frequency of the Context-Stimuli associations, following a simple Hebbian rule completed by a forgetting process which acts in the opposite way. Weights are mainly aimed at regulating the balance between Context and Stimuli signals (parameter R of the transfer function): the information retrieval process does not depend on the weights of the links between units, but on the system's architecture.

- transfer function: Local decisions are taken by each unit Ui, in order to evaluate the coincidence of its input signals (fig.4). For this purpose, transformed signals are summed and passed through a threshold function. The threshold qi has been defined as a certain ratio Ei of the maximum input to Ui : qi = S + C / Ei (Stimulations + Context signals). Another parameter Ri defines the relative contribution of C and S to the activation of the unit: Ri = C/S.

Parameters Ei and Ri determine three processing modes which correspond more or less to a classical distinction concerning recognition strategies. In the usual "restricted propagation" mode, both context and stimulation signals are required for the decision threshold to be reached; the unit is knowledge-driven in the "extended propagation" mode, and data-driven in the "forced propagation" mode (fig.5).

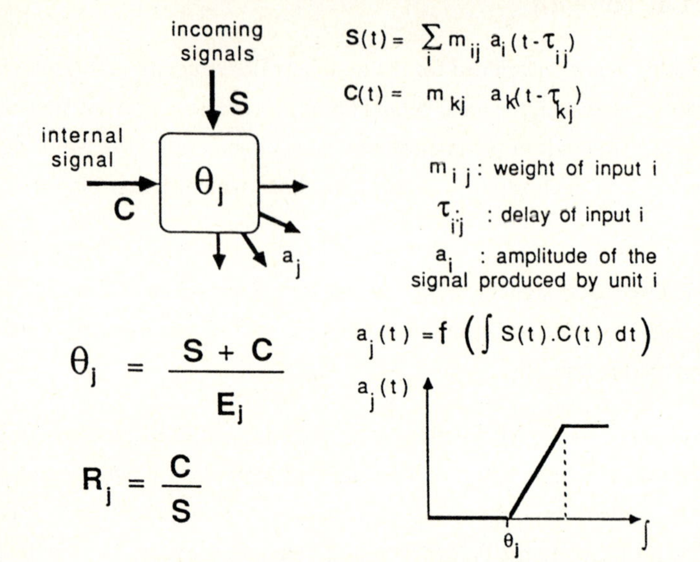

Figure 4. A processing unit forms the delayed and weighted sum of its inputs, calculates the correlation between incoming and internal signals, and passes the result through a threshold logic function.
The behaviour of the unit depends on the two adaptive parameters E_j (Excitability) and R_j (Ratio internal / incoming signals).

Figure 5. The self-regulation of the two parameters Ej and Rj can follow the trajectory represented by a dotted line on the graph below. The left-hand point corresponds to initial values, which increase each time unit j is submitted to reinforcement. Consequently,the transfer function is modified as shown on the graph beside. When Ej is low, the threshold is close to the maximum input (function in grey); as Ej and Rj increase,the threshold decreases and the max. input increases (dotted line).

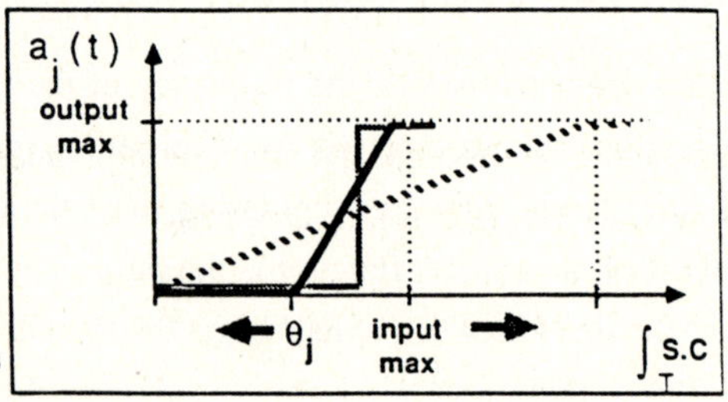

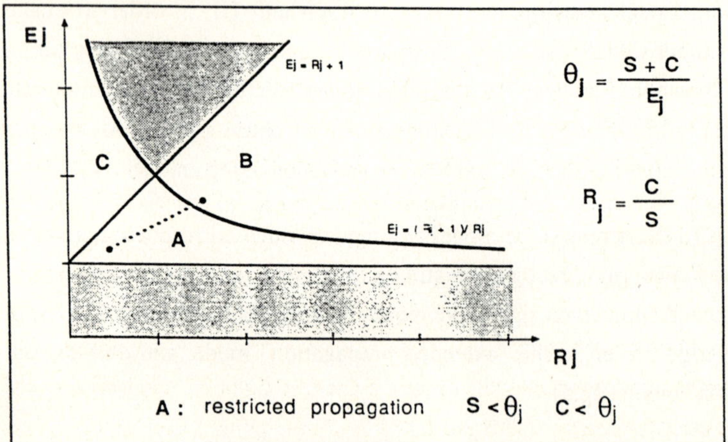

A : restricted propagation $S < \theta_j$ $C < \theta_j$

B : extended propagation $S < \theta_j$ $C > \theta_j$

C : forced propagation $S > \theta_j$ $C < \theta_j$

The steeper the slope of the transfer function, the more the unit reacts in an all-or-none fashion. The greater the number of events for a unit, the more global its decision, since it concerns a larger amount of stimulations (large receptive fields). The longer the duration of the internal signals, the broader the temporal distortions supported by a unit. According to this, a global analysis module would involve units working in the forced propagation mode, with linear transfer functions, long-duration internal signals and receptive fields as large as the whole pattern. A network architecture has been proposed (Leboeuf 88) which is equivalent to such a module, the pathways of which are limited to a single processing unit. This network module has a trend to generalize, finding similarities between input patterns. It always provide an output, due to the lax decision criterion.

III.3. Feature extraction and clustering

Pattern classification is usually expressed in terms of the partition of feature space into mutually exclusive regions. An input pattern is assigned a single vector in a N-dimensional feature space, and the decision area surrounding a given vector is the class to which its associated pattern belongs. A different view is proposed here.

In order to guide propagation in the peripheral modules, real-world signals have to be transformed into patterns of a specific format. Any input must be assigned a set of discrete events distributed in time and space (fig.6).

Assume a pattern be decomposed into a set of n independent discrete events (or vectors) inside a 2D space ((x1, t1), (x2, t2), ... (xn, tn)).

1/ Each constituent vector is allowed to belong to different pathways, since it is the spatio-temporal relationship it shares with other vectors which determines the cluster it is owned by. This means that clusters can overlap.

2/ The variability of the whole pattern is distributed over a set of vectors along only 2 dimensions. Each vector is allowed to vary in position inside a certain area (Dxi,Dti) relatively to other constituent vectors. The union of these elementary areas defines the complex area (or receptive field) inside which vectors can occur for the pattern to be recognized with the best matching score. Since vectors are independent, the high variability of a certain amount of them do not impede the contribution of the other ones to the activation of a threshold unit.

Complex receptive fields can be formed in a single unsupervised trial, using a priori values for Dx and Dt. An event (xi, ti) encountered in a new context is automatically linked to a specific memory unit, the coordinates of which are taken in the neighbourhood of the subnetwork currently fed by the internal flow (current system's expectations). The exact position assigned to an event depends on the learning strategy (Béroule 88a). The strategy currently implemented consists in linking the corresponding input feature detectors with a CD unit the activation of which coincides with stimulations; the set of possible feeding stimulations for this unit is thus enlarged (learning by Generalization). This may happen in case of extended propagation (strong expectation), or if the event occurs simultaneously with an expected event. If the activation of the input feature detectors does not coincide with any CD unit, a new CD unit is created, starting a new branch which will lead to a new detector (Learning by Differentiation). A supervised strategy consists in using corrections from the user. The initial value of the parameters, such as the internal signal durations, are chosen so as to favour generalization. In case of wrong activation of a unit, the durations of the input signals are automatically regulated so as to decrease their coincidence next time; the procedure now investigated tends to remove the overlapping parts of the signals that are summed by a defective memory unit.

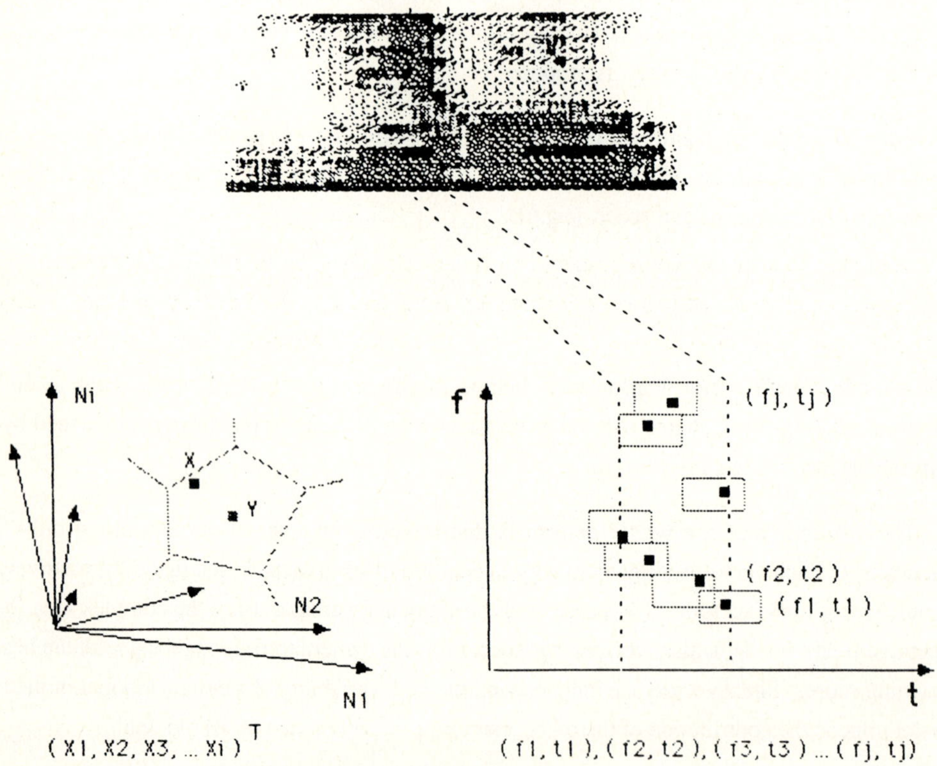

Figure 6. Two representations of a speech sample.
A single N-dimensional vector inside its decision area, or many 2-dimensional (time and frequency) vectors with their respective decision areas.

III.4. Software simulation

Software simulations of this memory model have been applied to pattern processing tasks, and developed in close interaction with its theoretical aspects (Béroule 85) (Leboeuf 87) (Béroule 88b). This provides an efficient way to face new theoretical developments with applied tasks, and conversely to discover new problems that were not specified in the theory.

Due to the dynamic nature of the network, the usual matrix calculus could not be used. Simulations make use of symbolic programming techniques instead. The main components of the network (signals, links, processing units, modules) are considered as objects that are manipulated by a set of list processing procedures. An object owns a set of properties and a list of pointers to other objects. For instance, the C-language structure that represents a processing unit is composed of slots giving the instantaneous values of the unit parameters, together with a list of pointers to input and output links. Whereas the lists of pointers can be modified only through sprouting and dissolution, the parameters values may change every processing steps. This is the case for counters that are decremented in order to simulate time-delays; this is also the case for the sum of the input signals to each unit, which is compared with the unit's threshold.

The management of feature-detectors for the possible extension of the network is an example of list processing: when they are activated, feature-detectors are concatenated to a special list of their module; when a context-dependent unit is activated above its threshold, feature-detectors that participated to its activation are removed from the list. In this way, the list finally comprises the unit which did not participate in the guided propagation process, which is a criterion for enlarging the network.

IV. Applications of Guided Propagation

IV.1. Speech

If speech recognizers are now capable of reasonably good performance in laboratories, they do not yet deal properly with real-world constraints. Whereas efficient pattern-matching algorithms such as DTW are responsible in a large part for successful experiments, we argue that the distinction between pre-processing and actual processing is a cause of performance drop in noisy environment and everyday free pronunciation. Moreover, the usual restriction of learning to a preliminary phase of pattern samples acquisition hinders the system's adaptation to new surroundings.

Concerning Automatic Speech Recognition, the aim of Guided Propagation is twofold:
- providing an alternative to the DTW algorithm.

- replacing the pre-processing concept by a distributed and parallel extraction of features.
- management of distortions in time and space

If a chunk of speech is viewed as a sequence of vectors (coded representation), temporal variations in the input pattern are expressed by the changeable values of some parameters. If, as we propose, a speech event is represented by a discrete memory position reached at a certain instant (topographic and temporal representation), variations may occur along these two dimensions.

Until now, spatial distortions have been envisaged in two ways:

- by immersing the spatial coordinates of every feature detector into a receptive field assigned to a CD unit, which only allows local variations.
- by transforming spatial variations into temporal ones (see section IV.2).

Time distortions are managed in a more straightforward way. When new links are created, the time-delays of signals to a processing unit are regulated so as to force coincidence. The duration of the internal signals that are summed by a processing unit Ui is much involved in the management of time variations (Béroule 89c). Assume that unit Ui integrate a subset of spectral events. The duration of the Contextual signal to Ui defines the size of the time interval during which can occur the group of events associated with Ui. This duration corresponds to the group variations of the event set. The duration of each S-signal to Ui defines the time-interval during which it can overlap with other signals, allowing thus local variations: According to the condition of convergence of time-delays, these durations are chosen wide at initialization and are then possibly decreased in case of wrong generalization.

A related problem is the segmentation of the speech stream into groups of events to be associated with the CD units of a pathway. For robustness to time variations, each CD unit must be fed by events that tend to vary together over time. Presently, a variability function (Liénard 72) is used in the following way: when the spectral variability remains below a given threshold for a certain amount of time, a boundary is detected. The segmentation process is then inhibited until a significant negative variation is encountered. The resulting boundaries can be found in stable sounds such as vowels and fricatives; groups of events then correspond to the transient parts of speech, whereas no events are detected in the stable sounds, the duration of which is very changeable.

- Spectral transformations

As stated above, Guided Propagation requires specific input pattern representations. The preferred direction taken by the internal flow depends on the localized input stimulations from a few channel at any given time. The problem is thus to transform the continuous speech waveform into discrete standard signals. This could be performed while these signals are propagated towards a specific memory location: Pre-processing and actual processing would thus be united. Such a strategy is aimed at extracting features in dynamic manner, depending on current task and possibly on current context. As a matter of fact, it is known that the same set of parameters does not fit equally well for a speaker identification task, an experiment in noisy environment, or speaker independent recognition. But if the transformation operators were integrated into the network, their parameters could be regulated on line. The non-linear operators presently studied (lateral inhibition and short-term adaptation) could be implemented in the connectivity of the network. These transformations have been used in a preliminary experiment of speech recognition (Leboeuf & Béroule 87), showing the robustness of the approach to superimposed speech signals (Fig.7).

pre-processing	8 cepstral coefficients every 12.8 ms	64 elementary signals possibly every 2 ms
algorithm of recognition	Dynamic Time Warping	Guided Propagation
processing time (VAX 11/750)	1 cpu h	4 cpu h
corpus	10 * 10 digits + noise ("dix")	
recognition rate noise - free	100 %	98 %
with added speech (S/ N = 0 db)	53 %	86 %

Figure 7. Compared performance of two speech recognition systems working on the same corpus: the digits and a single speech noise carefully pronounced by the same person (from: Leboeuf & Béroule 87). The grey column corresponds to an implementation of Guided Propagation in the "forced" mode (see fig.5), with a noise-free supervised learning phase, and performing recognition on the training set (self-consistency). The DTW algorithm is used in the word-spotting mode. Comparable results are presently obtained with another implementation involving much fewer processing units, real-time unsupervised learning carried out on a single series of noise-free digits, and recognition of a different set of the same digits, some of which may be superimposed. It is shown that two superimposed signals can be recognized in parallel by the network.

1/ The distribution of events along a temporal and a spatial dimension of memory is obtained through Fourier Transform.A bank of feature detectors is mapped onto the frequency dimension, so that each input detector react to a frequency channel. The number of detectors required mainly depends on the size of the analysis window.

2/ Lateral inhibition enhances the spectrum, the maxima of which are thus better located (topographic representation). It can be implemented by moving a Mexican Hat Function along the frequency dimension, so that each channel be activated by its closer neighbours and inhibited by its more distant neighbours. The content of the resulting representation depends on the range of the excitatory and inhibitory areas, and also on the weighting coefficients.

3/ Short-term adaptation detects local variations along the time dimension inside each channel (spectral onsets and offsets) and inhibits the channel during a certain period following a detection. It can be implemented with a variability function and a detection threshold.

IV.2. Modelization of reading

Contrary to what one might intuitively expect, the eyes do not perform a smooth scanning during reading, but proceed discretely by a series of jumps. But what controls the decision as to when and where to move the eye is not well understood. According to the "current fixation" model, this control is dynamically carried out, depending on the information extracted from the text processed on the current fixation (Rayner & Pollatsek, 81). This model is compatible with Guided Propagation, when applied to simple spatial patterns. Since this mechanism requires a few instantaneous stimulations distributed along the temporal dimension, pattern features are extracted from a narrow window which is moved discretely.

The current implementation works as follows. The network, organized in three layers (letters, words, sentences) reacts to items viewed from a narrow window. The set of feature-detectors that forms the network input is distributed over this window.Another larger window surrounding the narrow one allows the extraction of information concerning the position of neighbouring letters and words.

Whenever a feature, letter or word detector is activated by its deeper layer, a saccadic movement of both windows is triggered. The length of the saccade depends on the position on the page of the next item the type of which is the same as the detector's (feature, letter, word detectors). For instance, if a letter detector is activated, the large window is brought into play for finding the position of the next letter where the scanner is to be moved.

The triggering activation of a detector is either provoked by incoming stimulations or by the internal flow. In the first case, the detector feeds its associated CD units in the deeper layer; if at least one of them becomes activated, this one sends in return a signal to the detector and a saccade is triggered (otherwise, a backward saccade or learning occurs). In the second case, the direct activation of a CD unit by a heavy context (extended propagation) flows towards its associated detectors at the more peripheral layer. This causes a saccade before the actual recognition of the corresponding items (fig.8).

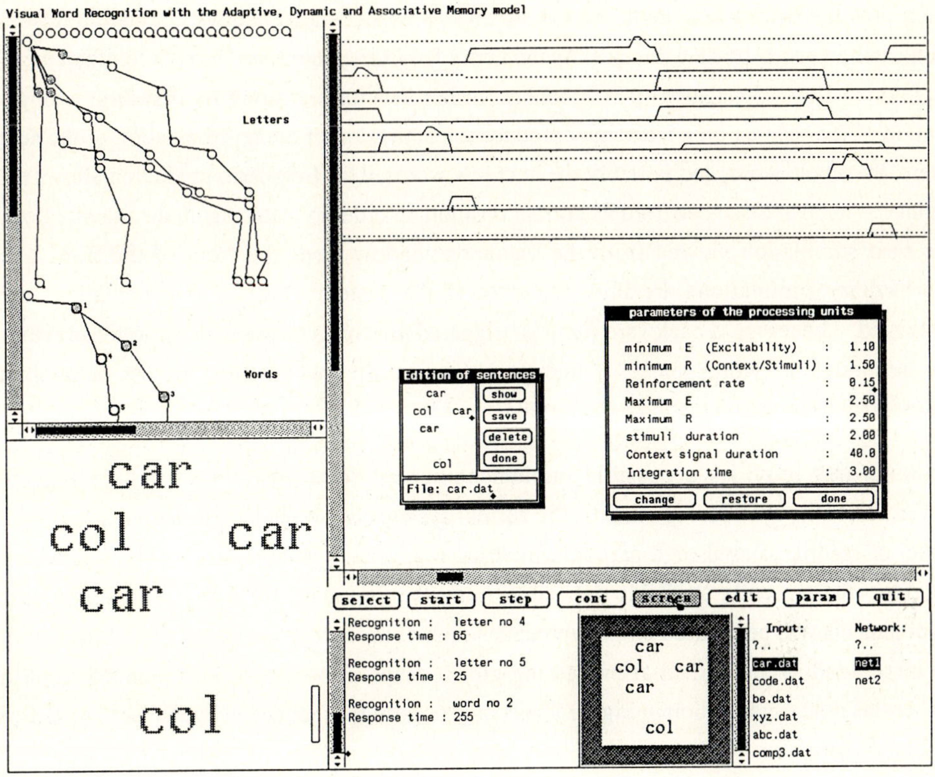

Figure 8. Influence of word familiarity on the duration of their recognition.

In this experiment, the system was shown two neighbouring words on a page (bottom-left graphic window). At the top of the page, the word "car" is encountered three times, the less frequent word "col" only once. Thus, the pathway representing "car" is more reinforced than the other one. when the scanner jumps at the last word of the page, the recognition of the first letter "c" also induces the activation of the representation of letter "a" and the pre-activation of letter "r". Due to this strong expectation, the second letter is skipped by the scanner. Since the third letter does not match the expected one, a backward saccade is triggered and the left-to-right scanning recommences more slowly. Because the expectation was wrong, the response-time of the less frequent word is increased.In the top left graphic window is displayed the network built during this experiment (for clarity of the display, the bi-directional links between feature-detectors and pathways are only represented when activated; the bi-directional inhibitory links between pathways are not represented). The initial network only comprised the top row of feature detectors, distributed along the scanning window (displayed in the bottom-right square of the page representation), and a root-unit inside every module. The Letters, Words and Sentences modules are built all at once as the scanner proceeds along the page. Reinforcement of a pathway acts on the E and R parameters of the units involved, increasing their value according to the parameters displayed in the central window. The graph at the top-right of the screen displays the activity histograms of the unit which belong to the word pathways. The dotted lines stand for the units thresholds; the long duration signals (40 clock steps) are generated by Contextual signals (C), the shorter ones by the stimulations (S). The topmost histogram corresponds to the first unit of the pathways (letter "c" in first position inside a word) ; when both C and S signals are summed across the threshold, a C signal is sent towards the two next units (2nd and 3rd histograms).One of them being activated directly above its threshold, extended propagation occurs, preactivating the next unit (4th histogram).A saccade puts the scanning window on the third letter. Since the stimulations (which appears on the 5th histogram) is not the expected one, a backward saccade occurs. Then the recognition of letter "o" activates the unit corresponding to the 3rd histogram, and guided propagation goes on towards the end of the right pathway (5th and 7th histograms).

When provided with a new item, the system creates its associated pathway, scanning it from left to right in a step-by-step manner. As the item's familiarity increases through reinforcement, the internal flow propagates spontaneously further and further along its pathway: a single fixation of the scanner on a letter may produce the activation of the representation of the next letters, the whole word, and possibly the next few words. This long-term prediction allows the scanner to jump at distances from its current position, in order to match again the internal flow. The next stimulation viewed from the scanner's window feeds the front of the flow. The intermediary stimulations are thus neglected if the system's long-term expectations are confirmed. Otherwise, a backward jump is triggered towards a position closer to the previous one, scanning the word gently. If unexpected items are encountered, the set of internal representations is completed through learning.

Although this provides a possible implementation of some hypotheses concerning the movement of the eyes during reading, the current system cannot yet be considered as a proper model of reading. Based on a particular internal representation of visual words, it does not integrate the presently available data concerning the first stage of visual perception. Next developments will be focused on the implementation of another peripheral module linked with the large window and aimed at processing global shape information. It is planned to push further this dual organization in higher levels of processing, as proposed by the BLC model of reading (Taylor 88).

IV.3. Other applications

The ultimate goal of this research work is to design a complete man-machine communication system based on the same parallel processing principle. Such a system would comprise many modules working simultaneously and respectively devoted to complementary tasks: pattern perception and interpretation, reasoning, pattern generation. So far, only pattern recognition modules have been investigated. Other modules should treat abstract information, manipulate symbols, and produce patterns of activity.

The application of Guided Propagation to syntactic processing is currently under investigation. In a first implementation, sequences of word clusters were learned from examples, using contextual information (Roques 89)(Blanchet 86). But syntactic rules cannot be implemented with the purely topographic representation presently used. The general problem encountered by the connectionist approach is not only to represent symbolic structures, but also to manipulate symbols. Contrary to an A.I. program, a connectionist system does not dispose of a temporary working memory, created in the course of processing for copying, combining and matching rules.

Trying to fill the gap between rule-based A.I. tools and our approach, we proposed to take the content of the propagated signals into account (Béroule 89b). This new trend of the memory model can be justified is many ways:

First, bringing up the subject of representations again, it appears that A.I. symbolic programming tools such as LISP have brought into play both coded and topographic dimensions (the first element of a LISP cell points out a particular code, the second one giving the position of another cell). Thus, the basic coded representation of computers had to be completed by the topographic one for the purpose of manipulating structures. Accordingly, the basic topographic representation of the memory model should be completed by the coded one for the same purpose.

Second, the components of a network are fixed through learning and can hardly be manipulated. On the other hand, due to their dynamic nature, internal signals can be considered as symbols; they can be propagated towards symbolic processing modules the units of which respond to a particular combination of codes by generating other codes. To keep close to real-world signals, a code could be represented by a specific frequency of the propagated signals.

Third, the nervous system, which inspired this model, also makes use of the content of the nervous signals. Even at the periphery, both topographic and coded representations are available (place coding and time coding). As a matter of fact, when the content-related information will be fully integrated in the memory model, it will not be limited to higher level processing. Symbolic processing will also certainly be performed in the peripheral modules.

Semantic and Syntactic treatment can respectively be viewed as spatial and temporal analyses performed simultaneously on words (Béroule 89c). According to this, the same kind of dual architecture used for signal analysis could be used for more abstract representations, possibly completed by symbolic processing modules (fig. 9). In this way, the robustness of the more peripheral layers would also exist in deeper layers. Internal representations of written language could be developed via the learning procedure. They would then be robust to noise, distortions and missing information and be of use in processing spoken language.

V. Conclusion

Ideas can be separated from the way they are implemented. As a matter of fact, the leading ideas of the approach presented in this paper have inspired some implementations in the framework of physical or mathematical theories. For instance, sequences of items can be implemented as successive states of activity in a thermodynamic network (Guyon & al 88); time-delays are helpful for applying Back-Propagation to Speech recognition (Waibel 88); the

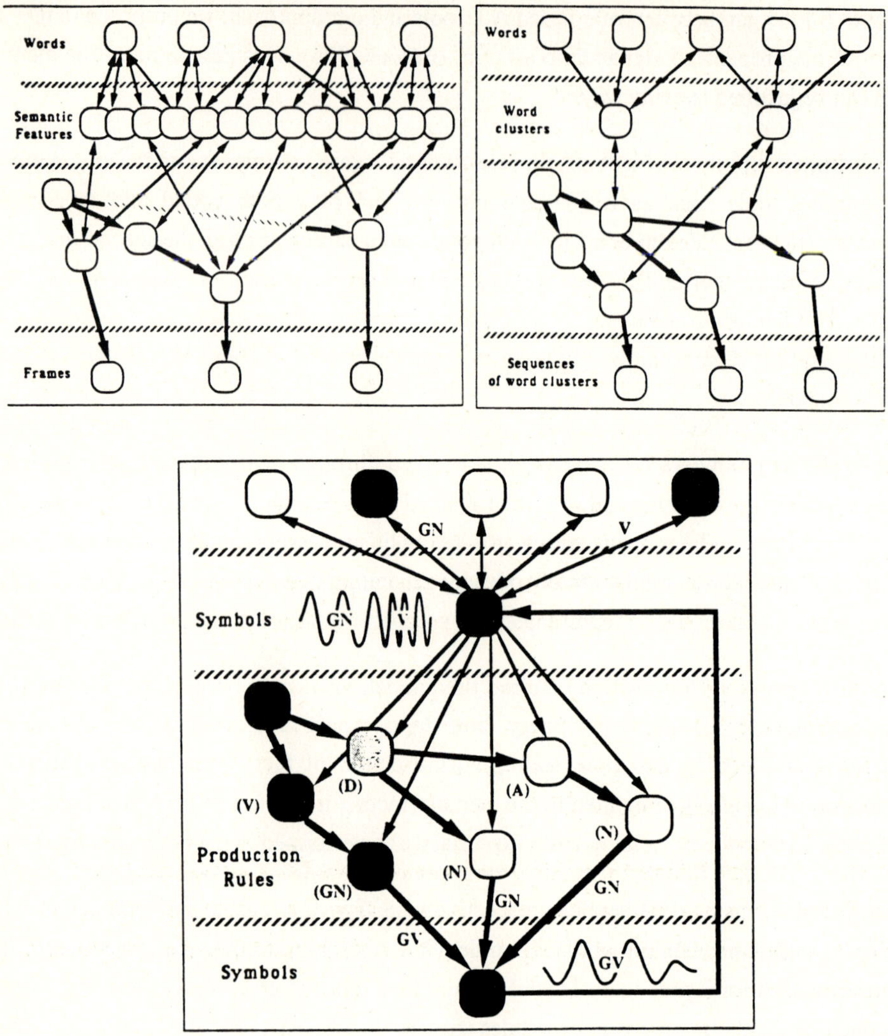

Figure 9. Three complementary architectures.

The "semantic" module performs an accurate spatial analysis; the "syntactic" module is interested in the sequential structure of groups of words (temporal analysis). The "symbolic processing" module owns units which respectively respond to a characteristic input signal frequency, considered as a symbol (in brackets at the left-hand side of the CD units). Sequences of symbols feed in parallel every pathways which produce other symbols, thus implementing production rules (V+GN -> GV, D+N -> GN, D+A+N -> GN).

data-driven creation of perceptron layers can also be considered as a way to deal with expensive fully-connected networks (Nadal 89)(Mezard 89). However, even if not supported by a strong mathematical background, these ideas are integrated in a coherent way within the Guided Propagation framework. Being stimulated by sequences of items is a condition for the system to work; time-delays were not artificially added to an existing theory: they are the main parameters of a system based on the detection of coincidences. The growth of the network is interesting because not performed in a preliminary learning phase, but combined with recognition; in this way, on-line expectations can drive the clustering process.

As a physiological model, this system implements current hypotheses concerning learning and memory (sprouting, selective reinforcement or dissolution) without requiring a preliminary supervised learning phase. Concerning information retrieval, the S-R (Stimulus-Response) behaviorist schema takes the form: C-S-R where C stands for contextual information. The processing strategy involves many parallel modules representing the different dimensions of world signals, and a few input channels. Thus, instead of a convergent feed-forward architecture integrating a lot of simultaneous stimulations into a single "grandmother" cell, a few stimulations participate in the feeding of many parallel modules, leading to the activation of many detectors.

As a psycholinguistic model, this system is compatible with the model of Logogens (Morton 69) and more explicit theories stating a left-to-right lexical access (Marslen-Wilson 80) mediated by syllabic units (Segui 83)

In the field of Pattern Recognition, this system can be viewed as a parallel implementation of a Markov model applied to a particular spectral representation of speech: a parallel flow of 2D vectors, a representation which already exhibited some ability in dealing with the recognition of superimposed signals.

Our long-term goal, to design a complete man-machine communication system based on Guided Propagation, may be attained, provided that symbolic processing methods be developed.

Aknowledgements
I am grateful to Jean-François Jodouin without which this article would have appeared stranger than it is.

References

[1] Béroule, D., Schwartz, J.L.: Essai de formalisation de faits et hypothèses de physiologie concernant le traitement de l'information pour la reconnaissance automatique de la parole, Proceedings of the 15th JEP, Aix-en-Provence. (1986)

[2] Béroule, D.: Un modèle de mémoire adaptative, dynamique et associative pour le traitement automatique de la parole, Thèse 3ème cycle, Orsay. (1985)

[3] Béroule, D.: Guided Propagation inside a Topographic Memory, IEEE First International Conference on Neural Networks, San Diego, June 21-24. (1987)

[4] Béroule, D.G.: The Never-Ending Learning, Neural Computers, R.Eckmiller, C.v.d. Malsburg (Eds), Springer Verlag. (1988a)

[5] Béroule, D.: SunADAM: a software simulation of the Adaptive, Dynamic and Associative Memory Model for the SunWorkstation, IPO report, Eindhoven. (1988b)

[6] Béroule, D.: The adaptive, Dynamic and Associative Memory Model: a possible future tool for vocal Human-Computer Communication, The Structure of Multi-modal Dialogue, M.M.Taylor, F.Néel, D.G.Bouwhuis (Eds.), Amsterdam: North-Holland. (1989a)

[7] Béroule, D.: Traitement Connexionniste du Langage, in: Histoire, Epistémologie et Langage, tome 11 fascicule 1: Sciences du langage et recherches cognitives, F.Rastier Ed. (1989b)

[8] Béroule, D.G.: Management of time distorsions through rough coincidence detection, Proceedings of the 1st European Conference on Speech Communication and Technology, Paris. (1989c).

[9] Blanchet, P., Coupet, P., Dore, L., Lajaunie, T.: Approche d'un apprentissage syntaxique par un modèle connexionniste, DEA report, LIMSI, Orsay. (1986)

[10] Bloch, V., Laroche, S.: Facts and hypotheses related to the search of the engram, Neurobiology of Learning and Memory, Guilford, New-York. (1984)

[11] Burnod, Y.: Cerebral Cortex and Behavioral Adaptation: a possible mechanism, Masson. (1988)

[12] Changeux, J.P., Courrege, P., Danchin, A.: A Theory of the Epigenesis of Neuronal Networks by Selective Stabilization of Synapses, Proc.Nat.Acad.Sci. USA, Vol 70, No 10, 2974-2978. (1973)

[13] Davis, M.: An active process in cochlear mechanisms, Hearing Research, No 91, 79-90. (1983)

[14] Delgutte, C.: Codage de la parole dans le nerf auditif, thèse d'état, Paris VI. (1984)

[15] Gauvain, J.L.: Reconnaissance de mots enchainés et détection de mots dans la parole continue, thèse 3ème cycle, Orsay. (1982)

[16] Guyon, I., Personnaz, L., Dreyfus, G.: Of Points and Loops, Neural Computers, R.Eckmiller, C.v.d. Malsburg (Eds), Springer Verlag. (1988)

[17] Hebb, D.: The organization of Behaviour, Wiley, New-York. (1949)

[19] Kohonen, T.: Self-Organization and and Associative Memory, Springer-Verlag. (1984)

[20] Leboeuf, J.: Présentation d'une simulation du modele ADAM, LIMSI report 86-2, Orsay. (1986)

[21] Leboeuf, J., Béroule, D.: Processing of noisy patterns with a connectionist system using a topographic representation of speech, European Conference on Speech Technology, Edinburg. (1987)

[22] Leboeuf, J.: Un système connectionniste appliqué au Traitement Automatique de la Parole, Thèse Doctorat, Orsay. (1988)

[23] LeCun, Y.: Une procédure d'apprentissage pour réseau à seuil assymetrique (A learning schema for assymetric threshold network), Cognitiva 85, Paris. (1985)

[24] Liénard, J.S.: Analyse, Synthèse et Reconnaissance Automatique de la Parole Continue, Thèse d'état, Paris VI. (1972)

[25] Mariani, J.J.: ESOPE: un système de Compréhension de la parole continue, Thèse d'état, Orsay. (1982)

[26] Marslen-Wilson, W.D. Speech Understanding as a psychological process, Spoken Language Generation and Understanding, D.Reidel. (1980)

[27] Mezard, M.: Learning algorithms in layered networks, this book. (1989)

[28] Morton, J. A functional model of memory, Psychological Review, (1969).

[29] Nadal, J.P.: Study of a Growth Algorithm for a Feedforward Network, International Journal of Neural Systems, vol.1, n°1, 55-60, World Scientific. (1989)

[30] Rayner, K. , Pollatsek, A.: Eye movement control during reading: Evidence for direct control, Quartely Journal of Experimental Psychology, 351-373. (1981)

[31] Roques, M.: Apprentissage et Reconnaissance de séquence de classes lexicales, DEA Report, LIMSI. (1989)

[32] Rosenblatt, F.: The Perceptron: A Probabilistic model for information storage and organization in the Brain, Psychological Review, 65, 386-408. (1959)

[33] Schwartz, J.L. L'organisation de l'information nerveuse à la sortie du système auditif périphérique, LIMSI report 83-1, Orsay. (1983)

[34] Segui, J.: The syllable: A basic perceptual unit ?, Attention and Performance: Control of Language Process, Hillsdale. (1983)

[35] Taylor & Taylor, Psychology of Reading, Academic Press, New-York London.

[36] Verzeano, M.: The Activity of Neuronal Networks in Memory Consolidation, Sleep and Memory, Drucker-Colin J. Mc Gaugh Eds, New-York Academic Press. (1977)

[37] Waibel, A., Hanasawa, T, Hinton, G., Shikano, K., Lang, K.: Phoneme recognition using time-delay neural networks. IEEE, Transactions on Acoustics, Speech and Signal Processing. (1988)

Speaker adaptation using multi-layer feed-forward automata and canonical correlation analysis

K. Choukri*, G. Chollet**, C. Montacié**

* Cap Sesa Innovation, Cap Gemini Sogeti Group,
118 rue de Tocqueville, F-75017 Paris

** CNRS URA 820,
ENST Dept. SIGNAL, 46 rue Barrault, F-75013 Paris

Abstract

Intra and inter-speaker variability is a major source of error in Automatic Speech Recognition (ASR). This paper reports on a series of experiments that allow us to control some aspects of this variability and therefore perform an adaptation of standard recognizers to new speakers. The first experiments concern spectral transformation using linear approaches based on some powerful data analysis techniques. In a second series of experiments spectral transformations using Multi-layer Feed Forward Automata (MLFFA) are introduced. Compared with linear techniques, the MLFFA approach offers some improvement.

Introduction

Inter-speaker variability shows up drastically on acoustic spectral parameters. This variability is primarily due to functional (and anatomical) differences between speakers. A transformation of the spectral space of a reference speaker could be adapted to match the spectral space of a new speaker. Different techniques could be used to perform this transformation, which might be linear or non-linear. Several linear techniques have been introduced and experimented in [2,3]. The best approach we experimented so far, was based on data analysis techniques, namely Canonical Correlation Analysis (CCA), versus Linear Multi-variate Regression (LMR) or Procust Analysis. It will be briefly described in a following section. It is of interest to investigate non-linear transformations. A simple approach, based on MLFFA, will be described. In order to compare these approaches, evaluation was performed on a subset of the TI isolated word data base [4].

Spectral transformations

Spectral parameters corresponding to the same sound Ω_i uttered by two speakers (S and N) differ systematically. Speaker-independent recognizers usually take this variability into account using stochastic models and/or multi-references. A better approach consists in learning **spectral mappings** to perform the best match between reference and new speaker's

NATO ASI Series, Vol. F 68
Neurocomputing
Edited by F. Fogelman Soulié and J. Hérault

corresponding spectra. These mappings are then exploited to obtain a new spectra better adapted to the new user.

General formulation

In the most general form, transformations could be applied to reference speaker and new user spectra as illustrated below:

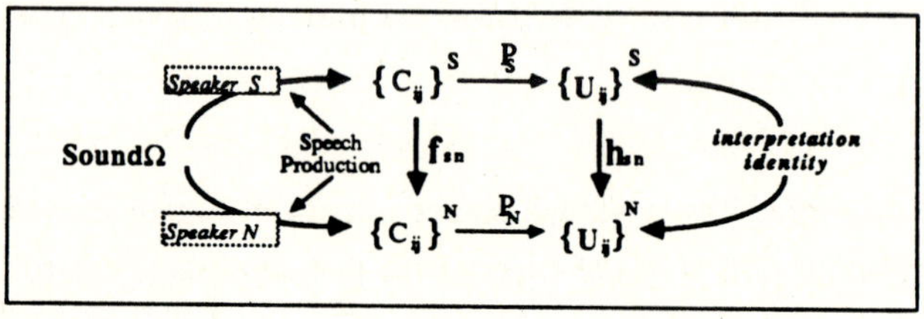

Figure 1. Interpretation space

The transformations Ps and Pn should be found such that the averaged error E_i is minimum over a representative set of sounds Ω_i. Formally: $P_n (C_{ij})^n = P_s (C_{ij})^S + E_i$. It should be noted that the transformation Ps can be used to adapt the reference spectra at once (at the end of the adaptation phase).The transformation Pn must be applied as a normalisation procedure during recognition phase. In the following sections linear and non-linear transformations are considered.

Linear Case

CCA is a data analysis technique which allows to compute linear transformations P_s and P_n [2,3]. This technique is used as a reference in the context of this study. According to figure 1, it seems natural to search for an operator that permits a direct transformation of the standard speaker into the current one. Then Pn is the Identity transformation. If P_s is kept linear then it coincides with a LMR of the standard spectra to match the new spectra. An adaptation procedure based on LMR has been evaluated in [2]. It was shown less efficient than a procedure based on CCA. The limited performances of the linear approches used up to date encourage us to investigate the non-linear case. Different techniques allow for the computation of non-linear functions P_s. They are based on polynomial filtering, decomposition into Volterra series, etc... The use of a MLFFA [5] is a simple alternative with the possibility of a linear initialisation.

Non-linear spectral transformation based on MLFFA

A MLFFA could be trained to perform the (possibly) non-linear spectral transformation. This automaton produces a spectrum in the new speaker space, associated to a spectrum of the standard speaker. A MLFFA using a single-layer (no hidden layer) is equivalent to the linear technique based on LMR for normally distributed data. Adding hidden layers could only upgrade performances, since in the worst case the added layer operates in a linear mode and could be suppressed. In the scope of this work the MLFFA contains only one hidden layer, for statistical reasons, as the training data consists in a set of 200 parameters. Input and output parameters are centered and normalized. The evaluation shows that the reconstruction error (difference between desired outputs and actual ones) with this architecture decreases by 25% compared to the LMR.

Evaluation

The most widely available speech recognition algorithm and data base were chosen to evaluate comparatively the MLFFA and CCA spectral transformation techniques [1]. The TI isolated word data base provides sufficient samples for our purpose. It consists of 20 English words (including the digits) recorded 26 times by 16 different speakers. Three speakers (GNL, REH, and SAS) were selected for the test corpus. The first repetition of the 20 words are reference templates, tests are conducted on the remaining 25 repetitions. The reference system, available on the "SAM" workstation [1], is used as an isolated word recognizer. Speech is parametrized with 8 Mel-Frequency Cepstral Coefficients (MFCC) every 20 ms. Pattern matching is based on Dynamic Time Warping (DTW). Adaptation is always performed with the 5 words: "One, Five, Two, Six, No" of the first repetition by each speaker. These adaptation words are time aligned with the corresponding reference words (using DTW). As a result about 200 spectra are associated and used to train the MLFFA or to perform CCA. The MLFFA contains 8 nodes on each layer and 500 cycles of training are used. All results are given, in the following table, as a confidence interval which insures a 95% chance to contain the correct recognition score.

Confidence intervals for Recognition scores

Experiment	Results
Mono-speaker (before adaptation)	96.4 - 98.0 %
Cross-speakers (before adaptation)	73.9 - 77.0 %
Cross-speakers (adaptation using CCA)	86.3 - 88.6 %
Cross-speakers (adaptation using MLFFA)	88.2 - 90.4 %

Before adaptation, the cross-speaker scores fall as low as 55%. On the average the CCA adaptation provides a 12% improvement and adaptation with this MLFFA provides a 14%

improvement as compared to the non-adapted results. The MLFFA and CCA spectral transformations show different patterns of improvement in recognition performance.

To qualify the adaptation efficiency an adaptability ratio is commonly used. It is defined as:

$$\rho = \frac{\tau^{a}_{sn} - \tau_{sn}}{\tau_{ss} - \tau_{sn}}$$

where τ_{sn} is the recognition score when the references are provided by the speaker S and the user is N, τ^{a}_{ss} is the mono-speaker recognition score, and τ_{sn}s the recognition score after adaptation. The value of rho is in the closed interval [0,1]. The closer to 1, the better is the adaptation. The results of these experiments give:

$\rho_{CCA} = 49\%$
$\rho_{MLFFA} = 57\%$

and an advantage to the MLFFA approach.

Conclusion

This contribution focusses on some techniques that allow the references of a recognizer to be adapted to new speakers or environments. The adaptation procedures consist of transformations of the speech parametric representation, taking the specific acoustical characteristics of new users into account. Several linear and non-linear supervised learning techniques are considered and evaluated in case of an isolated word recognition system with single dictionaries.

These techniques are being applied to another topic concerning speech synthesis. The spectral transformation is used to obtain a new parametric space adapted to the current user. These new parameters can be used for speech synthesis instead of speech recognition. This is commonly refered to as Voice conversion.

References

[1] Chollet G., Choukri K. & Montacié C.: A test workstation for the evaluation of speech recognition algorithms, applications, and data bases , in proc. 7th FASE Symposium (Speech '88), Edinburgh,145-151, (August 1988).
[2] Choukri K.: Several approaches to Speaker Adaptation in Automatic Speech Recognition Systems. PhD Thesis, ENST, Paris, France, (1987).
[3] Choukri K. & Chollet G.: Unsupervised and Dynamic learning of Spectral transformations using canonical correlation analysis for adaptation of ASR to new speakers. in Computer and Speech Language, Vol 1, N° 2. Academic Press Inc. 95-107, (1986).
[4] Doddington G. R. & Schalk T. B.: Speech recognition: turning theory to practice, In IEEE Spectrum, 26-32, (1981).
[5] Lippman R.: Computing with neural nets, in IEEE ASSP, Vol. 4, n° 2, 4-22, (1987).

Analysis of linear predictive data as speech and of ARMA processes by a class of single-layer connectionist models

Frank Fallside

Cambridge University Engineering Department
Trumpington Street, Cambridge CB2 1PZ- UK

1. Introduction

Since the first application of linear predictive or autoregressive analysis to speech by Atal [1] its use has become widespread throughout the analysis of speech - for coding, recognition and synthesis; see for example successive Proceedings of the International Conference on Acoustics, Speech & Signal Processing (ICASSP).

There has recently been an upsurge of interest in the analysis of pattern data by connectionist models/artificial neural networks, see for example Rumelhart & McClelland [2]. This has included the analysis of speech, for example [3,4], using the error-back-propagation algorithm. Most such studies preprocess speech into the frequency domain and employ spectral pattern data as input to the neural net. There are a few examples where the speech waveform itself has been applied as input to the neural net, notably by Elman & Zipser [5].

Because of the importance of linear predictive or autoregressive analysis, which is carried out in the time-domain, it is of interest to study the analysis of time series such as speech by neural nets and to relate this to linear predictive analysis. This is the subject of the present paper. It is concerned mostly with the analysis of a class of single-layer connectionist models, the relationship of the class to conventional linear predictive analysis and to the back propagation algorithm. A few computational results are given, leading to a form of connectionist vector quantisation (CVQ) for preprocessing of speech. Finally the equivalent result is given for the case of an autoregressive moving average (ARMA) process.

A preliminary version of this paper, without the proofs or the ARMA analysis, was read at [6].

NATO ASI Series, Vol. F 68
Neurocomputing
Edited by F. Fogelman Soulié and J. Hérault

2. Single layer connectionist model

2.1 Unconstrained model

The network is as shown in Fig.1. This has $\{y_i\}$ as the L+1 input data sequence and,

$$\sigma_k = \sum_{j=o}^{L} w_j \, y_{k-j} \quad ; \quad w_o = 1 \tag{1a}$$

and an output

$$0_k = f(\sigma_k) \tag{1b}$$

where $f(\sigma_k)$ is for example the sigmoid function commonly used in back propagation nets.

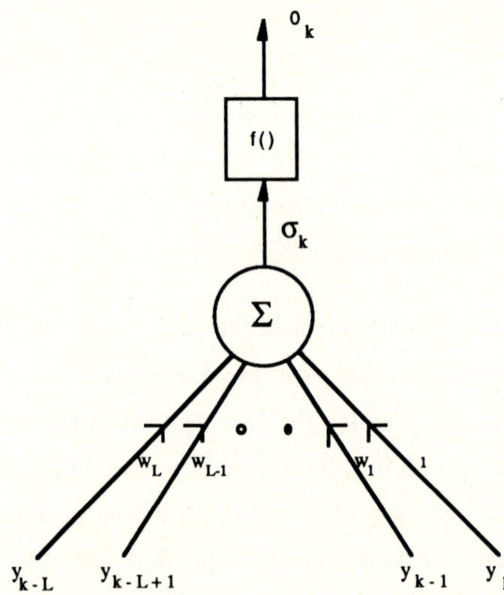

Figure 1 Single layer connectionist model

Such networks can be trained from the minimisation over a training set of N input patterns,

$$J_N = \min_{w_1..w_L} \sum_N (0_k - 0_T)^2 \tag{2a}$$

where 0_T is the target output. For the moment we will concentrate on the linear version and the minimisation

$$J = \min_{w_1..w_L} \sum_N (\sigma_k - \sigma_T)^2 \tag{2b}$$

and we will choose $\sigma_T = 0$, thus

$$J = \min_{w_1..w_L} \sum_N \sigma_k^{\ 2} \qquad (2c)$$

2.2 Constrained model

For input data $\{y_i\}$ which is a linear predictive or autoregressive process, the minimisation of eqn (2) is constrained and hence the w_i are constrained. One way of proceeding is to insert the constraints and then carry out the minimisation.

In linear predictive analysis the current sample y_i is estimated as y,^i, a linear combination of the previous p samples or observations,

$$\hat{y}_i = - \sum_{j=1}^{p} a_j \, y_{i-j} \qquad (3)$$

Introducing the estimation error e_i

$$e_i = y_i - \hat{y}_i \qquad (4)$$

the constraint equations are

$$e_i = \sum_{j=o}^{p} a_j \, y_{i-j} \quad ; \quad a_o = 1 \qquad (5)$$

This structure is as shown in Fig. 2.

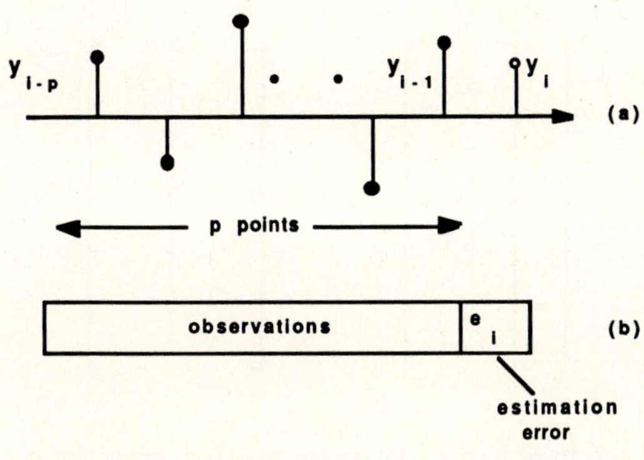

Figure 2 Linear prediction analysis
(a) estimation (after Parsons [7]) (b) estimation error and observations

The network equation is

$$\begin{aligned} \sigma_k &= y_k + [y_{k-1} \; y_{k-2} \cdot\cdot \; y_{k-L}] \;\; [w_1 \; w_2 \, .. \, w_L]^T \qquad (6) \\ &= y_k + \mathbf{z} \, \mathbf{w} \end{aligned}$$

We note that if L=p then the connectionist model is simply solving the conventional linear predictive analysis with $w_j=a_j$, $\sigma_k=e_i$. However in this paper we are concerned with the more general case L>p.

Since the data $\{y_i\}$ is dependent on p variables a_j let us try a generating solution

$$\mathbf{w} = \mathbf{I}_L + \alpha\,\mathbf{a} \tag{7}$$

where $\mathbf{I}_L$ is an L column unit vector, and α is an Lxp coefficient matrix and $\mathbf{a}$ is the p column vector of lp coefficients a_j. Thus

$$\sigma_k = I_{T,L+1}\ [\,y_k, y_{k-1} \cdot\cdot\, y_{k-L}\,]^T + \mathbf{z}\,\alpha\,\mathbf{a} \tag{8}$$

Now since the connectionist filter of Fig.1 is (L+1) wide and the lp filter has p observations, there can be m=L+1-p estimates within the connectionist filter. As a result the lp constraint equations

$$e_i = y_i + [y_{i-1}\ y_{i-2} \cdot\cdot\, y_{i-p}]\ [\,a_1, a_2 \cdot\cdot\, a_p\,]^T \tag{9}$$

can be written for the m estimates as

$$\mathbf{e}_m = \mathbf{y}_m + \mathbf{x}_m\,\mathbf{a} \tag{10}$$

Inserting these in σ_k gives

$$\sigma_k = \mathbf{I}_{L+1}^T \left\{ \begin{bmatrix} \mathbf{e}_m \\ - \\ y_{k-m} \\ \cdot \\ \cdot \\ y_{k-L} \end{bmatrix} - \begin{bmatrix} \mathbf{x}_m \\ - \\ \\ \mathbf{0} \end{bmatrix} \mathbf{a} \right\} + \mathbf{z}\,\alpha\mathbf{a} \tag{11}$$

Now since the second and third terms contain the coefficients $\mathbf{a}$, for σ_k to be a function of $\mathbf{e}_m$ alone, the last p elements of $\mathbf{I}_{L+1}$ must be zero and we will call the result $\mathbf{I}_{L+1,p}$ and correspondingly

$$\mathbf{w} = \mathbf{I}_{L,p} + \alpha\mathbf{a} \tag{12}$$

Thus

$$\sigma_k = I_{T,m}\, e_m - I_{T,m}\, x_m\, a + z\alpha a \tag{13}$$

Finally for σ_k to be a function of e_m only

$$I_{T,m}\, x_m = z\alpha \tag{14a}$$

Now

$$I_m^T x_m = z \underbrace{\begin{bmatrix} 1 & & O \\ 1 & 1 & \\ \cdot & 1 & \\ 1 & \cdot & 1 \\ & 1 & 1 \\ & & \cdot \\ O & & 1 \end{bmatrix}}_{\langle\; p \;\rangle} \begin{matrix} \wedge \\ p-1 \\ \vee \\ \wedge \\ m \\ \vee \end{matrix} \;\; L \tag{14b}$$

$$= z \begin{bmatrix} I_m & & O \\ & I_m & \\ & & \cdot \;\; \cdot \\ & O & & I_m \end{bmatrix} \tag{14c}$$

$$= zS_m \tag{14d}$$

and so the condition is

$$\alpha = S_m \tag{15}$$

So, subject to the lp constraints on the data, for the weights

$$w = I_{L,p} + S_m a \tag{16}$$

there is

$$\sigma_k = I_m^T e_m \tag{17}$$

$$= \sum_{j=k-m+1}^{k} e_j$$

2.3 Solution of linear problem

The solution of the constrained linear problem

$$J = \min_{w_1..w_2} \sum_N \sigma_k^2 \tag{18a}$$

reduces to the solution of the unconstrained problem

$$J = \min_{a_1..a_p} \sum_N (\mathbf{I}_{T,m}\, e_m)^2 \tag{18b}$$

The analysis and the connectionist network problem is simplified by defining some new variables

$$\sigma_k = \mathbf{I}_{T,m}\, [\, e_k\, e_{k-1} \cdots e_{k-m+1}\,]^T \tag{19}$$

$$Y_k = \mathbf{I}_{T,m}\, [\, y_k\, y_{k-1} \cdots y_{k-m+1}\,]^T \tag{20}$$

Using eqns (1a) and (16) for example we find

$$\sigma_k = Y_k + \sum_{j=1}^{p} a_j\, Y_{k-j} \tag{21}$$

Writing

$$\hat{Y}_k = -\sum_{j=1}^{p} a_j\, Y_{k-j} \tag{22}$$

and

$$\sigma_k = Y_k - \hat{Y}_k \tag{23}$$

we see that the connectionist model is behaving as a particular kind of linear predictor with σ_k as its estimation error, analogous to the conventional linear predictor of eqn (5).

Eqn (21) can also be written :

$$\sigma_k = Y_k + \mathbf{X}_k\mathbf{a} \tag{24}$$

Since the connectionist filter is longer in general than the lp filter, the way the data $\{y_i\}$ is incremented through the filter affects the cost function. It is found that if the increment is m then J is a perfect square in σ_k (otherwise it is a quadratic form). Under these conditions we can write the vector of σ_k for all the training data as

$$\sigma = \mathbf{Y} + \mathbf{X}\,\mathbf{a} \tag{25}$$

We can now solve the training problem using the orthogonality principle (eg Parsons (7)). For some other weight vector say $\mathbf{c}$, then σ becomes say Θ and

$$\begin{aligned}\Theta &= \mathbf{Y} + \mathbf{X}\,\mathbf{c} \\ &= \sigma + \mathbf{X}(\mathbf{c}-\mathbf{a})\end{aligned} \tag{26}$$

So the cost function

$$\begin{aligned}\Theta^T\Theta &= (\sigma + \mathbf{X}(\mathbf{c}\text{-}\mathbf{a}))^T(\sigma + \mathbf{X}(\mathbf{c}\text{-}\mathbf{a})) \\ &= \sigma^T\sigma + \sigma^T\mathbf{X}(\mathbf{c}\text{-}\mathbf{a}) + (\mathbf{c}\text{-}\mathbf{a})^T\mathbf{X}^T\sigma \\ &+ (\mathbf{X}(\mathbf{c}\text{-}\mathbf{a}))^T(\mathbf{X}(\mathbf{c}\text{-}\mathbf{a}))\end{aligned} \tag{27}$$

Now under the condition

$$\begin{aligned}\mathbf{X}^T\sigma &= \mathbf{X}^T(\mathbf{Y} + \mathbf{X}\mathbf{a}) = 0 \\ \Theta^T\Theta &= \sigma^T\sigma + |\mathbf{X}(\mathbf{c}\text{-}\mathbf{a})|^2 \\ &\geq \sigma^T\sigma\end{aligned} \tag{28}$$

with equality only for $\mathbf{c} = \mathbf{a}$. Thus the solution, the normal equations for this problem, is

$$\mathbf{X}^T\mathbf{X}\mathbf{a} = -\mathbf{X}^T\mathbf{Y} \tag{29}$$

and

$$\mathbf{J} = \sigma^T\mathbf{Y} \tag{30}$$

The condition $\sigma\mathbf{X}^T = 0$ is that each error σ_i is required to be orthogonal to the observations Y(i-1),..,Y(i-p). In other words the sum of each m lp errors, is to be orthogonal to the sum of their observation data.

Without pursuing it here we notice that if the lp estimation errors are uncorrelated

$$< e_i \, e_j > = 0 \quad ; \quad i \neq j \tag{31}$$

then

$$\mathbf{J} = \min_{a_1..a_p} \sigma^T\sigma \tag{32}$$

$$\rightarrow \min_{a_1..a_p} \mathbf{e}^T\mathbf{e} \tag{33}$$

In other words if the estimation errors are uncorrelated, the minimisation or training of the connectionist model establishes the same coefficients **a** as does conventional lp analysis. It is well known that for speech the estimation errors are not uncorrelated, but that the conventional lp analysis produces a useful parameterisation of speech and we might expect the same for the connectionist analysis.

We also note that if L=p, the connectionist model carries out a conventional lp analysis.

2.4 Solution of the non-linear problem

So far we have looked at the solution to the network of Fig.1 which minimises the cost function of the linear variable σ_k,

$$J = \min_{w_1..w_L} \sigma^T\sigma \tag{34}$$

$$= \min_{w_1..w_L} (\sigma_{N1}^2 + \sigma_{N1+1}^2 + ... + \sigma_{N2}^2) \tag{35}$$

The non-linear problem is

$$J_N = \min_{w_1..w_L} ((0_{N1}-0_T)^2 + (0_{N1+1}-0_T)^2 + ..+ (0_{N2}-0_T)^2) \tag{36}$$

$$= \min_{w_1..w_L} (g^2(\sigma_{N1}) + g^2(\sigma_{N1+1}) +..+ g^2(\sigma_{N2}))$$

However if

$$\sigma g(\sigma) \geq 0 \tag{37}$$

and $g(\sigma)$ is a monotonically increasing function

then

$$| g(\sigma_1 | > | g(\sigma_2 |$$

for

$$| \sigma_1 | > | \sigma_2 |$$

and in particular, using the nomenclature of the previous section,

$$g^2(\theta_i) > g^2(\sigma_i) \tag{38}$$

and the minimisation conditions for the linear problem of eqn (34), which are independent of the range N, are also the minimisation conditions of the non-linear problem of eqn (36).

Most non-linearities used in neural networks can satisfy the requirements of eqn (37). For example the sigmoid function commonly used in back propagation,

$$f(\sigma) = \frac{1}{1 + e^{-\sigma}} \tag{39}$$

satisfies the requirement when

$$0_T = 0.5 \tag{40}$$

2.5 Relation to error back propagation analysis

We see that the cost function eqn (34) or (36) used in the analysis which produces the solution of eqns (16),(29),(37) is the same as that used in error back propagation, which is solving the same problem using the steepest descent algorithm.

3. Properties of the class

Some of these are best seen by example. Take the case L=6 as shown in Fig.3(a) and assume p=2. Therefore the number of estimates in a connectionist frame of data is m=L+l-p=5.

Hence

$$\sigma_k = e_k + e_{k-1} + e_{k-2} + e_{k-3} + e_{k-4} \tag{41}$$

$$\mathbf{I}_{L,p} = \begin{bmatrix} 1 \\ 1 \\ 1 \\ 1 \\ 0 \\ 0 \end{bmatrix} ; \quad \mathbf{S}_m = \begin{bmatrix} 1 & 0 \\ 1 & 1 \\ 1 & 1 \\ 1 & 1 \\ 1 & 1 \\ 0 & 1 \end{bmatrix} \tag{42}$$

$$\mathbf{w} = \mathbf{I}_{L,p} + \mathbf{S}_m \, [\, a_1 \; a_2 \,]^T \tag{43}$$

$$\begin{bmatrix} w_1 \\ w_2 \\ w_3 \\ w_4 \\ w_5 \\ w_6 \end{bmatrix} = \begin{bmatrix} 1 \\ 1 \\ 1 \\ 1 \\ 0 \\ 0 \end{bmatrix} + \begin{bmatrix} a_1 \\ a_1 + a_2 \\ a_1 + a_2 \\ a_1 + a_2 \\ a_1 + a_2 \\ a_2 \end{bmatrix} = \begin{bmatrix} 1 + a_1 \\ 1 + a_1 + a_2 \\ 1 + a_1 + a_2 \\ 1 + a_1 + a_2 \\ a_1 + a_2 \\ a_2 \end{bmatrix} \tag{44}$$

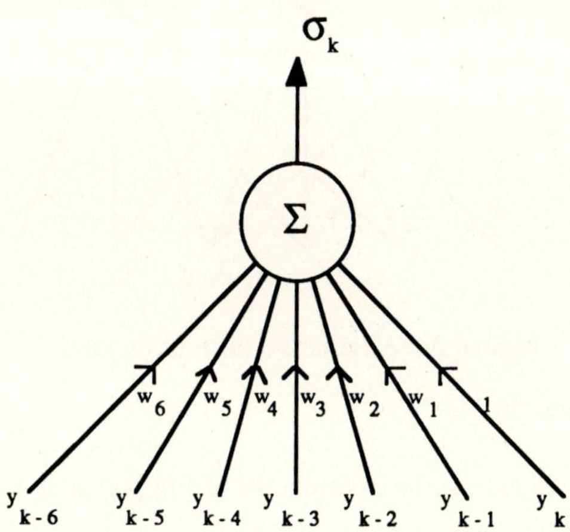

Figure 3(a) Single layer model, L=6

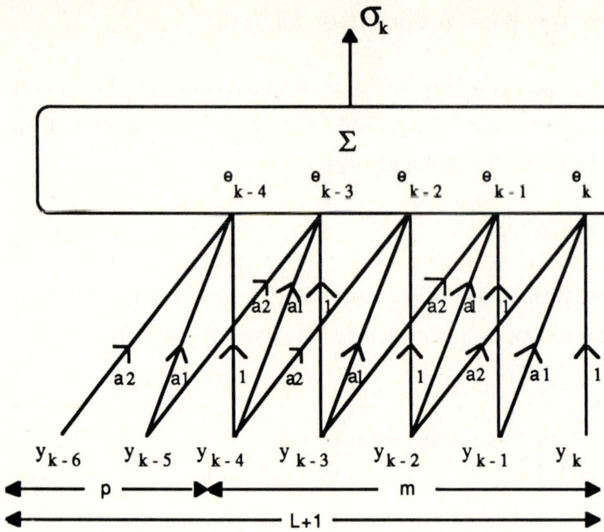

Figure 3b Single layer model with expanded weight values

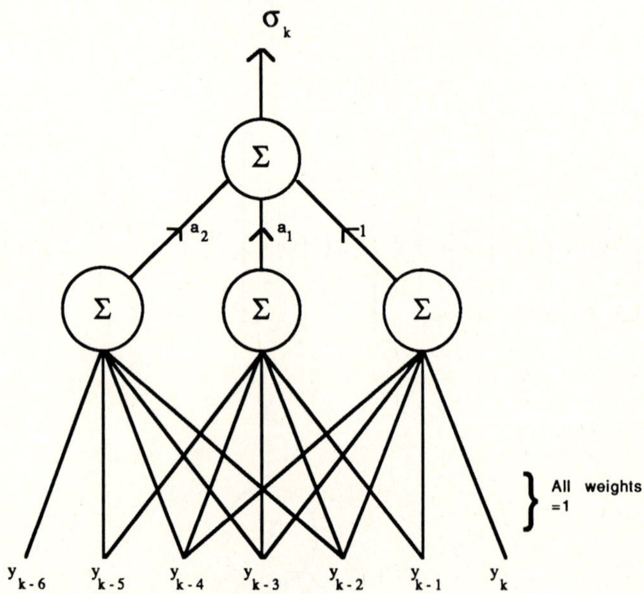

Figure 3c Alternative form of network

We note four features of the net:

(i) From eqn (44) if we redraw the example net of Fig.3(a) as in Fig.3(b) and we see how it is incorporating the constraints

$$e_i \;=\; y_i + a_1\, y_{i-1} + a_2\, y_{i-2} \tag{45}$$

and forming the output as the sum of the m estimation errors e_i as a result in

$$\sigma_k \;=\; e_k + e_{k-1} + e_{k-2} + e_{k-3} + e_{k-4} \tag{46}$$

(ii) A feature of the weight values is that they are a function of the constant and the two variables in $[1\ a_1\ a_2]^T$ and that L+1-2p of the weights from w_p to w_{L-p} have the same value of

$$w_i = \sum_{j=o}^{p} a_j \qquad ; \qquad a_o = 1\ ,\ p \le i \le L\text{-}p \tag{47}$$

(iii) For a data set of say D points, the first network window is $(y_1, y_2, .. y_7)$, the second window, shifted along m=5 points is $(y_6, y_7, .. y_{12})$ and so on, thus

$$J \;=\; (e_3 + e_4 + e_5 + e_6 + e_7)^2 + (e_8 + e_9 + e_{10} + e_{11} + e_{12})^2 + .. \tag{48}$$

$$+ (e_{D-4} + e_{D-3} + e_{D-2} + e_{D-1} + e_D)^2$$

and if the e_i are uncorrelated then

$$J \rightarrow \;=\; e_3{}^2 + e_4{}^2 + .. + e_D{}^2 \tag{49}$$

(iv)
$$Y_k \;=\; y_k + y_{k-1} + y_{k-2} + y_{k-3} + y_{k-4} \tag{50}$$

the connectionist predictor is

$$\sigma_k \;=\; Y_k + a_1\, Y_{k-1} + a_2\, Y_{k-2} \tag{51}$$

and the connectionist model can be reduced to the alternative form shown in Fig. 3(c).

4. Results

A few preliminary results are now given. These are based on the two speech waveforms shown in Fig.4, (a) for the fricative sound SH and Fig.4 (b) for the voiced sound XX.

4.1 Weights

Results for the weights **a** for the two single-layer connectionist models, which minimise J, for the two sounds are given in Table 1. These were evaluated by an lp analysis of the data in the form of eqn (21) for D=255, p=10 and values of m=1,2,10 corresponding to L=9,10,19. In

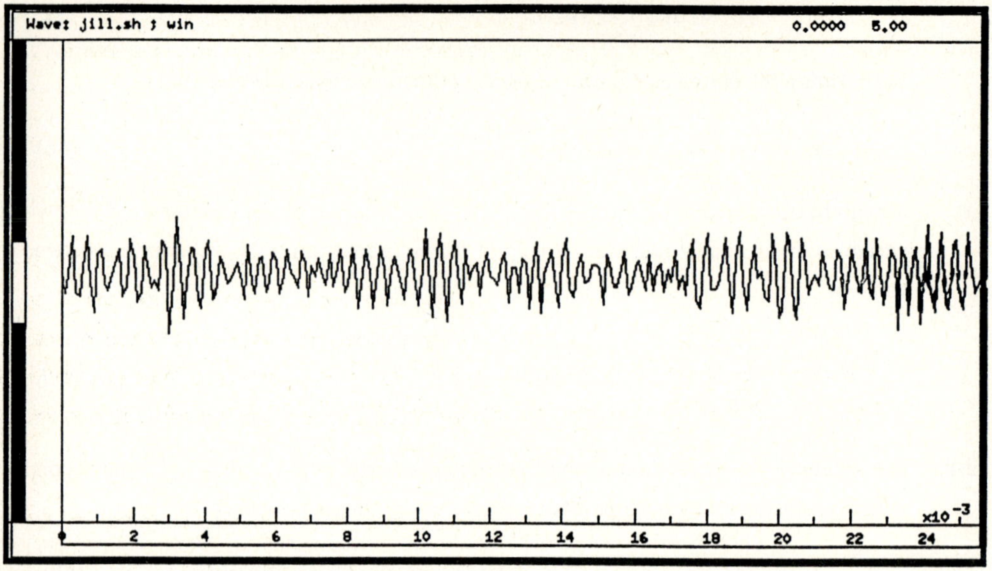

(a)

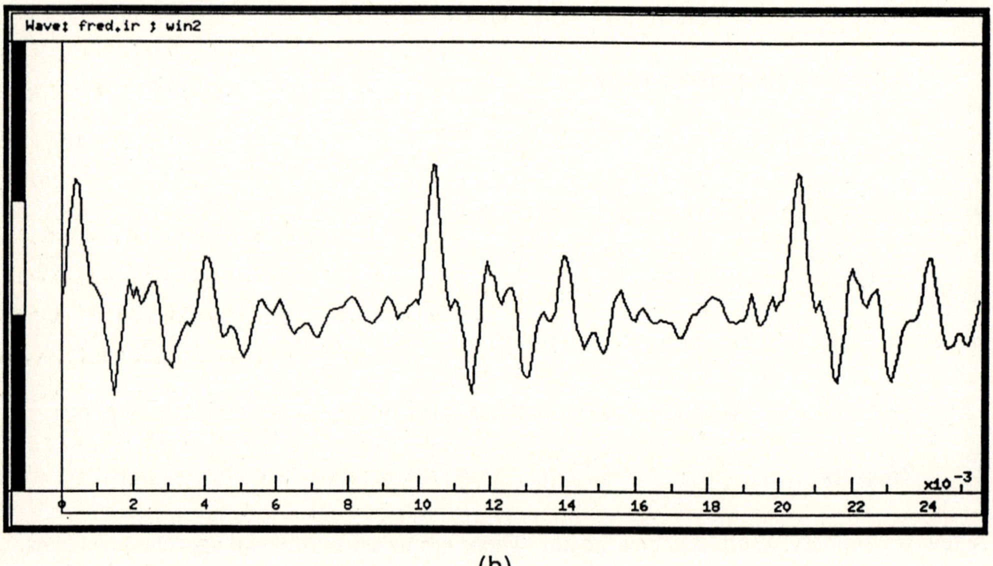

(b)

Fig.4 Speech data (a) SH (b) XX

each case the complete $\{Y_i\}$ data set was Hamming windowed and the speech data was differenced.

	m	1	2	10
SH	a[0]	1.0000e+00	1.0000e+00	1.0000e+00
	a[1]	1.9182e+00	1.0612e+00	9.5530e-01
	a[2]	3.1613e+00	2.2368e+00	1.2481e+00
	a[3]	3.6465e+00	1.7159e+00	6.5549e-01
	a[4]	3.3922e+00	1.8578e+00	- 1.4257e-02
	a[5]	2.4098e+00	7.7389e-01	- 6.2322e-01
	a[6]	1.4004e+00	6.3805e-01	- 5.4530e-01
	a[7]	6.1027e-01	4.7522e-02	- 1.6082e-01
	a[8]	2.6004e-01	1.7009e-01	1.5763e-01
	a[9]	8.8384e-02	8.7972e-03	2.0119e-01
	a[10]	8.1398e-02	7.3252e-02	3.4179e-01
XX	a[0]	1.0000e+00	1.0000e+00	1.0000e+00
	a[1]	- 5.7751e-01	- 1.3096e-01	- 1.4638e+00
	a[2]	- 2.7614e-02	9.9194e-01	4.7755e-01
	a[3]	1.3903e-01	- 6.1721e-01	1.2726e-01
	a[4]	5.8045e-01	1.0194e+00	7.3267e-01
	a[5]	- 4.8825e-01	- 1.1269e+00	- 1.0681e+00
	a[6]	1.2586e-01	7.7592e-01	1.2313e-01
	a[7]	1.7913e-01	- 2.1720e-01	4.2442e-01
	a[8]	7.2381e-02	1.1211e-01	3.6772e-02
	a[9]	- 1.7274e-01	- 5.1237e-02	- 1.4219e-01
	a[10]	4.9896e-01	2.6461e-01	7.2076e-02

Table 1 Weight vectors **a** for the two waveforms

It can be seen that the weight vectors for each sound, which would be constant if the e_i were uncorrelated, are not particularly constant. Also we would expect them to be more constant in the case of the fricative SH, than the voiced sound XX, since in the former case the excitation is less correlated.

However it is well known that the coefficients **a** are sensitive to the excitation even in the m=1, lp case and a strict constancy cannot be expected as a result. Also a rather longer dataset would be needed for the lack of correlation of e_i to make itself felt.

4.2 Cost functions

A more practical test of the value of the class is how well it classifies different sounds. This is investigated here in a preliminary way by computing the output cost functions and the results are given in Table 2. Here, using the values of **a** shown in Table 1 above the values of the normalised output cost function J for the SH networks with input SH and then input XX are given for m=1,2,10 and then similarly for the XX networks. In each case the Y_k form of network was used, the complete $\{Y_k\}$ data set was Hamming windowed, the speech data was differenced and J'=J/(energy of $\{Y_k\}$ data).

m	1	2	10
SH net input SH	2.9233e-02	1.6996e-02	3.3537e-03
SH net input XX	3.1062e+01	1.7694e+01	7.1154e+00
XX net input XX	1.6661e-01	3.3856e-02	1.1707e-02
XX net input SH	1.0611e+00	6.2910e-01	2.7708e-01

Table 2 Normalised output cost functions J'

We see that for this limited set of data the nets are performing a useful classification of the two sounds. Also that where a net has its 'own' sound as input J' is broadly constant as would be expected from eqn (33). It would be precisely constant if the estimation errors were uncorrelated.

These results are perhaps the most practical attributes of the class, suggesting that a form of connectionist vector quantisation (CVQ) structure as shown in Fig.5 is possible, where a set of connectionist models of the type studied are trained to span an appropriate region of the **a** space, analogous to conventional VQ structures [8]. The codebook entry for the current speech data is then specified by the network 0_{Ci}, with the lowest output cost function. Results for this will be published later.

5. Single layer connectionist model for autoregressive moving average (ARMA) processes.

Another common form of time series is the ARMA process [9]. In this case the current sample y_i is estimated as $\hat{y}_i$ a linear combination of previous y_i and of another sequence u_i as

$$\hat{y}_i = -\sum_{j=1}^{p} a_j y_{i-j} - \sum_{j=o}^{n} b_j u_{i-j} \tag{52}$$

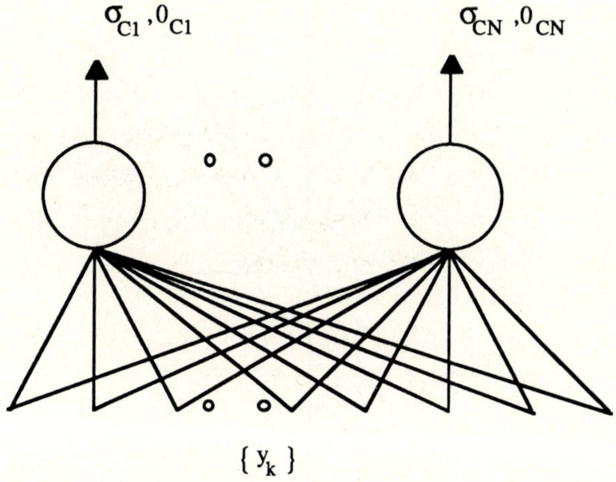

Figure 5 Connectionist vector quantisation (CVQ) structure

This can be used for example to model a linear system with an input sequence $\{u_i\}$ and an output sequence $\{y_i\}$ and without loss of generality we can take n=p. Introducing an estimation error $e_i = y_i - \hat{y}_i$ the ARMA filter is

$$e_i = \sum_{j=o}^{p} a_j \, y_{i-p} + \sum_{j=o}^{n} b_j \, u_{i-j} \qquad ; \quad a_o = 1 \tag{53}$$

The connectionist result for this case is found to be a simple extension of the result for the autoregressive case of the previous sections. *

We now consider the single layer net of Fig.6(a) with L+1 inputs for $\{u_i\}$ and for $\{y_i\}$. For the linear case, with $\sigma_T = 0$, the minimisation is

$$E = \min_{w_1..w_L \; v_o..v_L} \sum_{N} \sigma_k^{\,2} \tag{54}$$

subject to the constraint of eqn (53) which we can write

$$e_i = y_k + \mathbf{zw} + \mathbf{qv} \tag{55}$$

* I am grateful to Dr Joseph Mariani of LIMSI,Orsay Cedex, France who suggested investigating this extension.

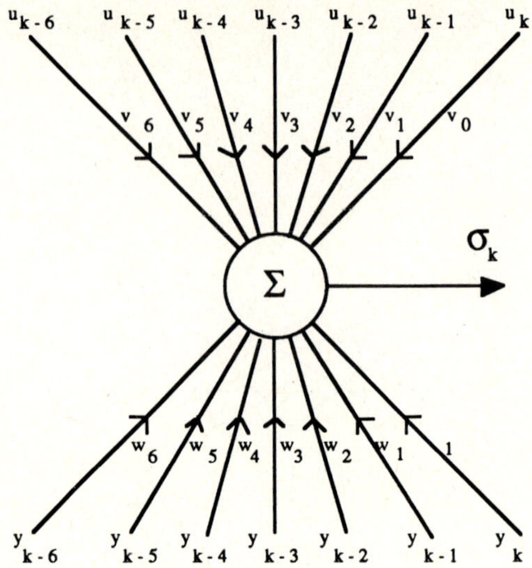

Figure 6(a) ARMA model, L=6

Taking as generating solutions

$$\mathbf{w} = \mathbf{I}_L + \alpha\mathbf{a} \tag{56}$$
$$\mathbf{v} = \beta\mathbf{b}$$

we find that for

$$\mathbf{w} = \mathbf{I}_{L,p} + \mathbf{S}_m\mathbf{a} \tag{57}$$
$$\mathbf{v} = \mathbf{S}_{m+1}\,\mathbf{b}$$
$$\sigma_k = \mathbf{I}_{T,m}\,\mathbf{e}_m \tag{58}$$

Then on introducing the variable

$$U_k = \sum_{j=o}^{m} u_{k-j} \tag{59}$$

The connectionist ARMA filter is

$$\sigma_k = \sum_{j=o}^{p} a_j\, Y_{k-j} + \sum_{j=o}^{p} b_j\, U_{k-j} \qquad ; \quad a_o = 1 \tag{60}$$

Proceeding as before

$$\sigma = \mathbf{Y} + \mathbf{Xa} + \mathbf{Qb} \tag{61}$$

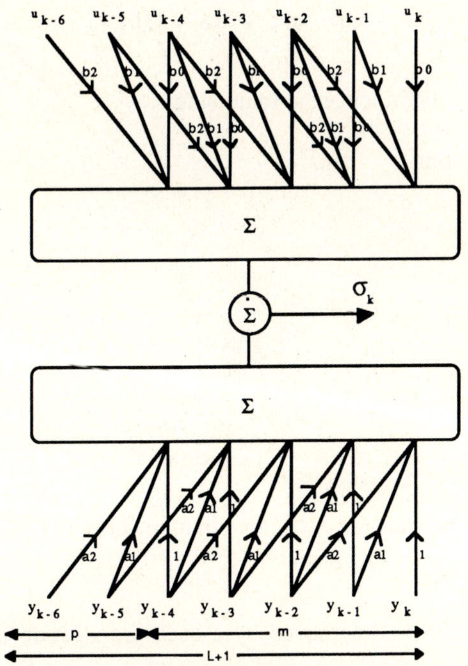

Figure 6(b) Single layer ARMA model with expanded weight values

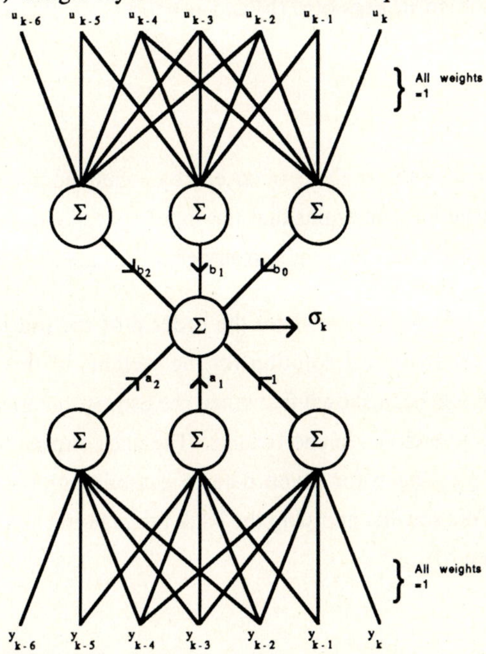

Figure 6(c) Alternative form of ARMA network

$$\sigma^T\sigma \quad = \quad (\mathbf{Y} + \mathbf{Xa} + \mathbf{Qb})^T \; (\mathbf{Y} + \mathbf{Xa} + \mathbf{Qb})$$

On applying the orthogonality principle the solution for

$$E = \min_{w_1..w_L \; v_0..v_L} \sigma^T\sigma \tag{62}$$

is found to be

$$\begin{bmatrix} \mathbf{X}^T\mathbf{X} & \mathbf{X}^T\mathbf{Q} \\ \mathbf{Q}^T\mathbf{X} & \mathbf{Q}^T\mathbf{Q} \end{bmatrix} \begin{bmatrix} \mathbf{a} \\ \mathbf{b} \end{bmatrix} = - \begin{bmatrix} \mathbf{X}^T\mathbf{Y} \\ \mathbf{Q}^T\mathbf{Y} \end{bmatrix} \tag{63}$$

$$E = \sigma^T\mathbf{Y} \tag{64}$$

Again under the same conditions on $g(\sigma)$, the solution for the non-linear problem E_N is the same as for the linear problem E.

The solution is the same as that achieved by a back-propagation algorithm and the same conditions exist for **a** and **b** if the e_i are uncorrelated. Examples of the network structures for an ARMA process are shown in Figs 6(a),(b) and (c) corresponding to the AR structures of Figs 3(a),(b) and (c).

6. Conclusions

The paper has concentrated on the analysis of speech by connectionist models with the speech data as input and including the constraint that the input speech can be modelled by a linear predictive process. (It applies more generally to autogressive time series data).

It has focussed on a class of networks where the order p of the linear predictive process is specified and produced an analytical solution for the weights of this class to minimise the network cost function. It has been shown that when the estimation errors are uncorrelated the solution establishes the conventional lp coefficients. The class chosen forces the analysis to be pth order, the effect of varying p for given data to establish global minima has not been explored in this paper. (We see that applying the back propagation algorithm to the weights **w** establishes the minimum cost).

The solution for the network weights of the class have been shown to apply to both a linear network and within restrictions, a non-linear network. These restrictions are satisfied by many of the non-linear functions used in current neural networks. It was shown that the same solution is achieved by the back propagation algorithm.

The few preliminary results given, show that the nature of speech, with its correlated excitation, mitigates against the weight values of the class corresponding exactly to the conventional lp coefficients, as predicted by the theory. However as in the case of conventional lp analysis, good classification of sounds has been indicated by preliminary results and this in turn has suggested a form of connectionist vector quantisation (CVQ) structure. The weight values of the class exhibit an interesting uniformity, which speculatively might have a physiological analogue.

A solution has also been given for the case of a network whose input is an ARMA process.

7. References

[1] Atal, B., Hanauer, S.L.: Speech analysis & synthesis by linear prediction. In J. Acoust. Soc. Amer., 50, 637-655, (1971).

[2] Rumelhart, D.E., McClelland, J.L.: Parallel distributed processing: Explorations in the Microstructure of cognition, Cambridge, Mass-London: Bradford/MIT Press, (1986).

[3] Waibel, A., Hanazawa, T., Hinton, G., Shikano, K., Lang, K.: Phoneme recognition using time-delay neural networks, ATR Interpreting Telephony Research Laboratories, Tech. Rep. TR-1-006, (1987).

[4] Robinson, A.J., Fallside, F.: A Dynamic connectionist model for phoneme recognition, Proc. nEuro'88, Paris, (1988).

[5] Elman, J L & Zipser, D: Learning the hidden structure of speech, ICS Report 8701, University of California, San Diego, (1987).

[6] Fallside, F.: On the analysis of linear predictive data such as speech by a class of single layer connectionist models. 2nd Symposium on Advanced Man-Machine Interface. Hawaï, nov.1988 and Tech. Rep. CUED/F-INFENG/TR27, (1988).

[7] Parsons, T.: Voice & speech processing, New York-San Francisco-Toronto-London: McGraw-Hill, (1986).

[8] Buzzo, A., Gray, A.H., Gray, R.M., Markel, J.D.: Speech coding based on vector quantisation, IEEE Trans., Vol.ASSP-28, 5, 562-574, (1980).

[9] Hannan, E.J.: Multiple time-series, New York-London: Wiley, New York, (1977).

High Level Speech Processing by Competitive Neural Networks From Psychology to Simulation

Thierry Michaux , Pedro L. Galindo and Susana Gonzalez

Computer Science Faculty
Universidad Politecnica de Madrid
&
LAFORIA
Université Pierre et Marie Curie
Paris VI
4 place Jussieu.Tour 46-00; 2e.
F-75252 PARIS Cedex 05

Abstract

The aim of this paper is to show that on the basis of the new paradigms defined by Hinton (1986) and Rumelhart (1986), it is possible to define a new approach of High Speech Processing that fits perfectly with the current theories in psychology and biology.

0. Introduction

Too many works actually consider neural networks as mere fashionable engineering tools and forget the scientific implications of these models. Any scientific domain needs to fulfill certain criteria (experiments, theories, simulation) and " a certain kind of integrity" [Feynmann, 1987] which makes the difference between "cargo-cult-sciences" and science .

Crick [1989] pointed out recently that there is a gap between engineering neural networks and biological neural networks. Engineering is often based on science, but the aims are different ("A successful piece of engineering is a machine that does something useful. Understanding the brain, on the other hand, is a scientific problem"). Churchland and Sejnowski [1988] introduced another notion between biological realistic models which are genuinely and strongly predictive of some aspect of nervous system dynamics or anatomy, and biological simplifying models, which though not so predictive, demonstrate that the nervous system could be governed by specific principles.

One of the consequences of the great success and possibilities of the artificial neural networks has been their application to classical problems with traditional concepts. This is especially true in speech processing where neural networks are used to replace Markov models or more traditional engineering tools.

NATO ASI Series, Vol. F 68
Neurocomputing
Edited by F. Fogelman Soulié and J. Hérault

This paper tries to demonstrate that by using simplified neural networks models for High Level Speech Processing (morphological structure), it is possible to give a good account of what could be a realistic model of speech perception.

If we want to study speech perception we have the possibility to adopt two points of view: the engineering or the scientific approach.

The engineering approach considers the problem independently of the context. All the solutions to speech perception can be carried out by pure signal processing. During the last decade, this approach has had a certain success. However, it is quite limited in comparison with other artificial intelligence disciplines. Research along that line was essentially a problem of pattern matching and the target was simple: isolated words speech recognition. Continuous speech recognition seems, with this approach, quite problematic. Problems become exponential and the target seems imposible to reach in comparison with the difficulties.

The second possibility is to view speech as an adaptive system that evolves and stabilizes through philogenetic and ontogenetic processes. Thus, if we want to simulate this process, we need to have a good understanding of the underlying biological and psychological phenomena. This is our scientific paradigm.

In the last 20 years, knowledge of neural perception, brain processing and ontogenetic evolution has considerably increased . A wide litterature exists on the subject and it seems possible to define a new approach of speech recognition based on this scientific knowledge.

This paper presents a model of acquisition, storage, and processing of spanish morphology using a competitive learning model that takes into account various scientific results.

In the first step, the aternative to lexicon arbitrary definition will be justified.The second step will recall the last results of experimental psychology in speech perception.The third step will present a theoretical model of storage and process of spanish lexicon using competitive learning. The fourth step will show the results of the simulation using a competitive learning algorithm derived from the ART1 model of Grossberg [Carpenter and Grossberg, 1987], [Grossberg, 1987]. Finally, it will be shown that the critics developed by [Pinker, 1987] and [Lachter, 1987] against the works of [Rumelhart, 1986, a] are not founded .

Lexicon can be considered as an adaptive non arbitrary system.

1. Speech and Language as an adaptive system

One of the dogmatic principles upon which linguistics is based, is arbitraryness of the sign.

This paradigm is explicitly expressed in Saussure´s "Cours de Linguistique Générale " and implicitly recognized in the anglosaxon linguistic school by the differenciation between superficial structure (the sound) and deep structure (the sense). It means that the concatenation of sound refered to a meaning is totally arbitrary. It is also admitted that the concatenation of sounds to form words is arbitrary too.

One of the consequences in the engineering approach has been to define arbitrary subwords structures that have no reality in speech recognition. It is this paradigm of arbitraryness which ruins the scientific approach and prevents it from a good understanding of speech perception.

We will propose here an alternative.We will try to demonstrate by a real scientific approach (experiments, systematic study, theory and simulation) that the lexicon is not arbitrary. If that is true, we should find a clue of this structure in the process of perception and storage of the lexicon in our brain.

2. Experimental psychology data: lexicon storage and learning as an adaptive parallel process.

2.1 The different schools.

The first attempt to understand how language is stored and processed in the brain is quite recent. Nowadays there are two main streams of research: the process explanation and the representational theory.

The process explanation assumes that all words are represented separately in the lexicon. Representation of a word causes activation of other morphologically related words. This theory follows the linguistic principle of lexicon arbitraryness. We can apply to it the same criticism as to language arbitraryness. As these experiments do not bring new information, we will not consider them here.

On the other hand, the representational theory supposes that effects of morphological structures are reflections of the nature of the representation in memory. One of the main streams of that school is the morphemic decomposition model proposed in [Taft and Forster,1975, 1976] and elaborated by Taft [Taft, 1979a, 1979b, 1981, 1985].

It is based on the following principles:

- Words are multiply represented and accessed sequentially
- A master file or lexicon contains a complete specification of words but this master file is accessed through a morphological peripherical file.

- the morphological peripherical file is achieved by morphemic decomposition in prefixes [Taft and Forster, 1975 1976], suffixes [Taft, 1979b] and the stem.
- Words are accessed by the stem.

More recent studies by Lukatela confirm the decomposition of words into morphological subunits but refute the existence of a master file with full representation of the words.

One of the problems of this approach is the sequential access to the stem file. It is not compatible with our actual knowledge of brain processing. On the other hand, it does explain how and why different elements exist.

2.2 The point of recognition as point of discrimination.

A more realistic approach would be to define the access to the main file in a parallel way using the first letters that the words share. Hence the one adopted and defined by Marslen-Wilson and Tyler for speech perception.
Let us consider the following example. We have five words which we want to store in the memory: cabo
caballo
caballero
caballerismo

The points of recognition are symbolized by "/".

stage of learning	words	subunits
1	cab/o, cab/all/o	cab, o, all
2	caball/o, caball/er/o	cab, o, all, er
3	caballer/o caballer/ism/o	cab, o, all, er, ism, o

Whatever could be the order of the words we could arrive at this final storage decomposition.

The process which Marsler-Wilson defined is the way perception is carried out. He established where the point of recognition in speech recognition was.

What we suggest is to consider the point of recognition as a point of discrimination and organization in subunits. Thus it is posible to conceive the learning and storing process as an adaptive competitive system [MacWinney, 1987].

2.3 An evolutive function: attention

We will complete this overview by outlining that the attention of a child a few days old is not the same as that of a two years old child. It depends on the maturity of the brain and of the data processed.

To sum up, we can state, on the basis of experimental psychology that a realistic model of speech recognition and storage of a lexicon should involve:

- A parallel process to retrieve and store the information
- A competitive system to decompose words in (morphological?) subunits.

The next step of a scientific study should be to first try to divide the lexicon into morphological subunits.

If we prove that the lexicon can be decomposed in such a way, then, all the structure of the master file is adaptive (non arbitrary). So, the structure should evolve in function of the data and of the stage of the competitive process and the attention level should play an important role during learning.

These points will be considered in the following paragraphs.

3. A formal competitive approach of the spanish lexicon

To see if spanish lexicon is non-arbitrary (adaptive) we tried to divide it all into morphological subunits.

We took the inverse dictionnary of **** and stripped it of the last elements that were most frequent.

As we stated before, this is equivalent to finding the recognition point. In the same way we processed the words before the last ones and the previous ones each time it was possible. In such a way we divided 85 percent of the spanish lexicon. The remaining words are composed of non asserted spanish words or words whose decomposition resulted ambiguous (for example trabajo in trab-aj-o or tra-baj-o). This morphological decomposition was done manually and directly on a copy of the lexicon. Two years were necessary to achieve this task. A compilation and analysis of all the results is still under completion.

We have now the experimental studies on which to base a theory of speech perception, recognition and storage. We have a formal study of the spanish lexicon process using competitive learning which proves that it is a non arbitrary adaptive system. The next step is the simulation on computer of this complex competitive parallel and adaptive system, which is what we now present .

4. Simulation on computer of learning and storage of spanish morphological structures

4.1. The previous models

There exist already two models of acquisition of morphological structures by adaptive systems.

The first one has been developed by Rumelhart [Rumelhart, 1986a]. It consists in the learning of the structure of regular and irregular past tenses. The model is a two layer perceptron, the learning rule is the Widrow-Hoff delta rule. The input is the infinitive form of the verb, the output the regular or irregular form of the verb in the past tense. Words were coded using Wickelphones and Wickelfeatures. Rumelhart intended to show that the system behaved in a way similar to a child. We would prefer to rephrase the results saying that the discrimination realized by the system showed that the irregular past tense system is not arbitrary. This model has been extensively criticized in a special issue of "Cognition" (1988).

The second one was NETtalk [Sejnowsky, 1987]. It uses the more recent back-propagation model. The learning rule is the general delta rule. The input of the system is a written text that runs through a window of seven units, the output is the phoneme corresponding to the pronunciation of the central letter. Phonemes are coded using phonetic articulatory features. The system is trained to pronounce one text correctly and generalizes to other texts.

It is another proof of the non-arbitrary relation between phonemes and morphemes.

The problem of these two systems is the numerical codification of knowledge in the weights. Interpretation of the results is quite difficult and rather subjective.

4.2. Competitive learning model for speech perception

There exist today different simulation models of competitive learning: [Rumelhart, 1986], [Fukushima, 1988], [Grossberg, 1988],etc. We have chosen the Grossberg ART 1 for the following reasons:

- It is the model which seems to have the highest pretention in speech processing [Stone & Grossberg, 1987].
- The author has not still been involved in the fight of connectionist/traditional approach and could not be considered as a part in this conflict.

The problem with Grossberg's model is its use of a different vocabulary than the one traditionnally accepted.To summarize, we will use:

Notation	Grossberg	ours
I_i	input	input
X_i	short term memory of F_1	activation at F_1
$\lvert X_i \rvert$	activity at F_1	number of active nodes at F_1
T_j	input F_2	signal from F_1 to F_2
Y_j	short term memory of F_2	activation at F_2
V_i	input F_1	signal from F_2 to F_1
X'	new STM of F_1	new activation at F_1
$\lvert X'_i \rvert$	new activity at F_1	number of new active nodes at F_1
W_{ij}	long term memory	weights of connections from F_1 to F_2
W'_{ji}	long term memory	weights of connections from F_2 to F_1

Note: i refers to index in F_1, j to index in F_2. ρ is the attentional parameter

Initially F_2 is inactive, and nodes in F_2 are ready for learning.

Input signal

$$I_i = \begin{cases} 1 & \text{if } i \in I \\ 0 & \text{if } i \notin I \end{cases}$$

Activation at F1

For simplicity: $X_i = I_i$

Signals from nodes in F_1 to nodes in F_2

$$T_j = \Sigma_i X_i W_{ij}$$

Activation at F_2

(Simplified version of the model)

$$Y_j = \begin{cases} 1 & \text{if } T_j = \max \{T_k \,/\, \text{node k is not reset for learning}\} \\ 0 & \text{otherwise} \end{cases}$$

Winner node is J if $Y_J = 1$.

Signals from nodes in F_2 to nodes in F_1

$$V_i = \Sigma_j Y_j W'_{ji} = Y_J W'_{Ji}$$

New activation at F_1

At this moment, both, signal input I, and top-down signal V, excite F_1.

$$X_i' = I_i * V_i$$

Reset rule (Winner node = J)

if $\frac{|X'|}{X|} < \rho$ reset node J for learning of pattern I, making a new iteration.

if $\frac{|X'|}{|X|} \geq \rho$ make learning on weigths related to J.

Fast Learning on J.

We have the following learning rule for weights related to winner node J :

Bottom up (W_{iJ} from F_1 to F_2)

$$W_{iJ} = \begin{cases} \frac{1}{|X'|} & \text{if } i \in X' \\ 0 & \text{otherwise} \end{cases}$$

Top down (W'_{Ji} from F_2 to F_1)

$$W'_{Ji} = \begin{cases} 1 & \text{if } i \in X' \\ 0 & \text{otherwise} \end{cases}$$

To tune the algorithm, we used the example proposed in [Grossberg, 1987] and got the same results. We need to outline here that what Grossberg defines as unitization is the full representation of the object represented and not the division in subunits.

The results are dependent on two factors: the level of attention, ρ, and the order of presentation of the patterns.

If we present the set of inputs several times, in a random order, the network stabilizes. Results obtained after different simulations are the same. This lets us conclude that those patterns were invariances, and not errors. Their completion is proportional to the level of ρ defined and independent of the number of iterations needed to stabilize the system. We can interpret those data as invariant basic units.

The next step was to see what could be the results with words.

One of the main criticisms made to the previous systems by [Pinker and Prince, 1987], [Lachter and Bever, 1987] consisted in saying that all the results were fixed. The trick was to use a special codification. The correlation that the system was "discovering" was, in reality, inside the codification.

To avoid this criticism we decided an arbitrary codification. If a morphological adaptive system does exist, whatever could be the codification, the structure has to appear through competitive learning.

We used 26 letters of the alphabet (ch and ll were coded as two letters, not as one letter). Each letter was coded on 26 bits such as:
a: 10000000000000000000000000
b: 01000000000000000000000000
...
z: 00000000000000000000000001

We used a training set of five verbs conjugated in different tenses (present, past and future) organized according to three different criteria:
- alignment on the left, alphabetical order.
- alignment on the right, inverse alphabetical order.
- alignment on the stress.

It is with this last organization that we got the best results. Simulation of the basic Grossberg ART1 model and the same algorithm with several presentations of training set follows:

Simulations

The basic algorithms as presented in [Grossberg, 1988] cannot pretend to divide the lexicon in subunits. The unitization in such a system can only be conceived as a representation of the lexicon with the words as units. This resut can be obtain with a maximal level of attention where $\rho = 9$ or 10. If we put $\rho < 9$ we get a mixture of heterogeneous subunits in which we find some similarity to those defined previously in the formal analysis.One possible interpretation is to think that we are in presence of bugs! The other could be to interpret these units as the invariants of the distributed representation. It exists a third one which consists in considering that we deal with a dynamical competitive system and that we get then a local image of the transition period between two instants of stabilization

Scientific studies show that the level of attention of a child increases during the critical learning period. This is why in consideration of this experimental fact, we tried to make evolve the attentional parameter ρ of the Grossberg's model using a sigmoid function.

Different modifications of ρ have been made. The best function for which we get the best results is:

$\rho\ (t) = 1/[1 + \exp\ (-\ t)]$ $\qquad\qquad$ $\rho(t+ dt) = 1/[\ 1 + \exp\ (-dt) * (1 - \rho\ (t))\ /\ \rho(t)]$

For a good comprehension of what is occuring, our explanation will be limited to the set of eight spanish verbs, conjugated in present, past and future for first, second and third person of singular and plural. Similar results have been obtained with larger vocabularies and our present experiments with french and english languages coded phonologically are very encouraging. The contrast of performances between a simulation of Art1 for a value of ρ=0.5 with the model proposed when ρ just reachs 0.5 is quite important. With Art1 we have an heterogenous mixture. With the model proposed, verbs are divided in morphological subunits.

ART1 (ρ=0.5)	model proposed (ρ=0.5)		
a o	o	em	reis
m s	i	aba	temia
temia	a	tap	vivi
viv	e	iamos	viv
a a	dur	eis	teme
vivi	re	mos	amos
a a	a a	ara	cenar
ir	ia	ira	vivir
lati	a a	iais	durar
e n	ra	temer	cena
re	m s	ias	aban
aba	is	are	latir
is	vi	abamos	picar
latir	e n	ire	tapar
ra	lati	emos	abas
cen	pic	ais	tapa
pic	cen	ian	picais
dur	lat	abais	duraba
late			tapaban
tem			
reis			

But that is not the most astonishing. If we let the system stabilize with a value of $\rho = 0.9$ we get the following results.

We will consider two examples with $\rho = 0.9$. The inputs are the verbs **picabais** and **durare**.

INPUT = P I C A B A I S

1	A	1° The stress vowel, class of the verb.
2	A A	2° Correlation of the stressed vowel with the next vowel
3	A B A	3° Determination of the tense: imperfect.
4	P I C	4° Determination of the stem.
5	A B A I S	5° Composition of tense + person (2° of plural).
6	P I C A B A	6° Composition of stem + tense (imperfect).
RES 7	P I C A B A I S	7° Word recognized = stem + tense + person

INPUT = D U R A R E

1	E	1° The stress vowel.
2	R E	2° Correlation of the strss vowel with the previous one.
		tense = future, person = 1° of the singular
3	A R E	3° Composition class of the verb + tense + person.
4	D U R	4° Determination of the stem.
RES 5	D U R A R E	5° Word recognized = stem + stem + tense + person.

The system has made a decomposition of the verbs in morphological subunits and has learnt their conjugation. We need to repeat here that the system has no linguistic information at all. It does not know what is a letter, a vowel, a consonant, a verb, a tense or a person. The codification is arbitrary too. The information we get cannot be then the one we coded. The system only has determined a certain number of classes that it considers successfully before stating what the input is. The most astonishing is that the system, without any kind of linguistic information, considering the different possibilities, makes a morphological analysis and composes the stem, the tense and the person like in a conjugation.

The question to answer now is: why do we get such results.

5 Conclusion: Lexicon as an adaptive self-organized distributed system

In the first part of this article, we have proposed an alternarive to arbitraryness of the lexicon. In the second paragraph we have shown how experimental psychology could help us to find a solution. The formal approach of competitive learning presented in part 3 was a good clue of what could be the result but had to be proved by a simulation where there was no exterior information. The simulation developed and presented in part 5 shows that the lexicon alined on the stress (point of recognition in spanish) processed by a competitve learning model self-organizes choosing the morphological unit as subunits of the word. The lexicon cannot be considered as an arbitrary system. **It is an adaptive self-organized system.** The basic subunits that the self organization produces are Vowels, Vowels Consonant, CVC that are all used in higher level afterward. **The system is distributed.** The basic V, CV, VC, CVC **subunits are all pertinent units that determine the upper level**: the conjugation of the verbs. In the same way the division between V, VC, and CV could be a good representation of the lower level between constant frequencies CF and transitions (Modulated frequencies: MF). This is quite close to the results obtained by [Suga, 1989] with cortical maps representation. Should this result be confirmed by further studies, it would reinforce the hypothesis of [Rumelhart, 1986] and [Bates, 1987] that there does not exist for **language processing** different modules with different kinds of processing [Fodor, 1987] but one **global system with a unique process which determines the different hierarchical steps**. All those steps are accessed in parallel during perception.

References.

1. Churchland, P. S. & Sejnowski, T. J.: "Perspectives on cognitive neuroscience". Science, 242, 741-745, (1988).
2. Crick, F.: " The recent excitement about neural networks" Nature 337, 129-132, (1989).
3. Carpenter, G. A. & Grossberg, S.: " A massively parallel architecture for self-organizing neural pattern recognition machine". Computer Vision, Graphics and Image Processing, 37,54-115, (1987).
4. Feynmann, D.: "Cargo Cult Science". 338-346 in "Surely, you're joking, Mr Feynmann". Counterpoint. London.
5. Grossberg , S.: " Competitive learning: from interactive activation to adaptive resonance" Cognitive Science, 11, 23-63, (1987).
6. Hinton, G. E., McClelland, J. L. & Rumelhart, D. E.: " Distributed Representation" In Rumelhart & McClelland (1986).
7. Lachter, J. & Bever, T. J.: "The relation between linguistic structure and theories of language learning: a constructive critic of some connectionist learning models". Tecnich Report N44. Cognitive Science. Department of Psychology. Rochester University. Rochester, NY.
8. McClelland, J. L. & Rumelhart, D. E.: Parallel distributed processing: exploration in the microstructure of cognition. V2: Psychological and biological models". Cambridge , Mass. MIT Press. (1986).
9. Pinker, S. & Prince, A.: On language and connectionism: analisis of a parallel distributed processing model of language acquisition .Occasional paper=33. Center for Cognitive Science. MIT. Cambridge. (1987).
10. Rumelhart, D. E. & McClelland, J. L.: "On learning the past tenses of english verbs". 216-272 in McClelland, J. L. & Rumelhart, D. E. (1986a).
11. Rumelhart, D. E. & McClelland, J. L.: Parallel distributed processing: exploration in the microstructure of cognition. V1: Foundations Cambridge , Mass. MIT Press. (1986, b).
12. Sejnowsky, T.J. & Rosenberg, C. R.: "Parallel networks that learn to pronounce english text"Complex Systems, 1, 145-168, (1987).
13. Slobin, D.I.: The cross linguistic study of Language acquisition. Hillsdale, N.J.Lawrence Erlbaum. (1986).
14. Waibel, A., Hanazawa, T., Hinton, G., Shikano, K., & Lang, K.: "Phoneme recognition using time delay neural networks". ATR Tech Report TR-1-0006 ATR Interpreting Telephony Research Laboratories. Osaka. Japon. (1987).
15. Waibel, A.,Sawai, H. & Shikano, K.: " Modularity and scaling in large phonemic neural networks". ATR Tech Report TR-1-0034 ATR Interpreting Telephony Research Laboratories. Osaka. Japon.(1988).

CONNECTED WORD RECOGNITION USING NEURAL NETWORKS

Umit Dağıtan, Neşe Yalabık

Computer Engineering Department

Middle East Technical University

Ankara

Turkey

Abstract

A connected word recognition system which makes use of two neural network models, namely, Kohonen's Network and a Multilayer Perceptron is implemented. The digitized speech signal is represented by a sequence of Linear Predictive Coding (LPC) coefficients and segmented into syllables. The Kohonen's Network is used to perform vector quantization to compress LPC data for the input of the Multilayer Perceptron (MP). MP is used to perform recognition in syllable basis with the Back-Propagation algorithm used for training. The words are constructed by using the sequence of recognized syllables. The system was trained and tested with ten Turkish words with sixteen syllables, with an overall recognition rate of 90 percent.

1. Introduction

The use of neural networks (NN) in speech recognition is a recent area of research. Usually the recognition is performed in phoneme level using various NN models [1,2]. However, in case of isolated or connected word recognition with limited vocabularies, it might be performed in the word or syllable level [3] using a Multilayer Perceptron (MP), although the word-level recognition with a MP may not be very practical.

This study aims to examine the performance of a MP as a syllable recognizer for a speaker independent connected word recognition system with a small vocabulary. Another model, namely, Kohonen's Network in its one-dimensional form is used for data compression with computational concerns for the input and overall size of MP. Syllable segmentation and word reconstruction are also implemented as pre and post recognition stages.

Figure 1 shows the overall block diagram of the system, whose details will be given in the following sections.

NATO ASI Series, Vol. F 68
Neurocomputing
Edited by F. Fogelman Soulié and J. Hérault

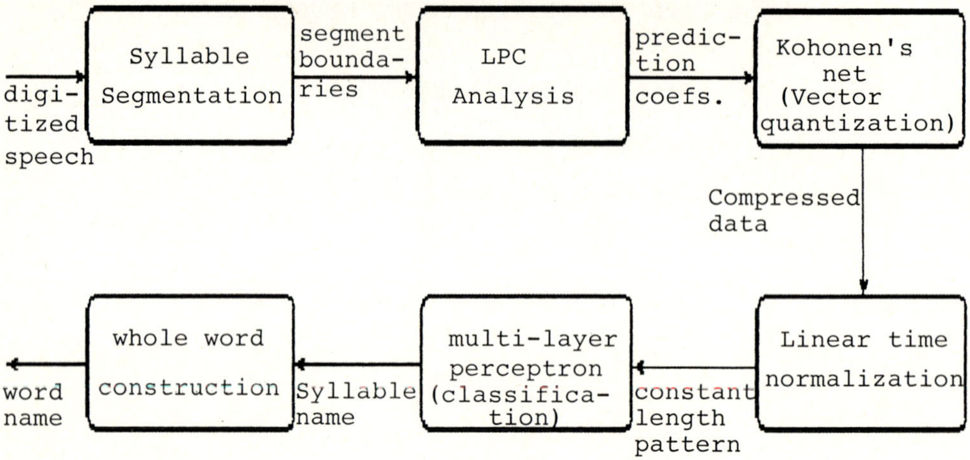

Figure 1. System Block Diagram

2. Syllable Segmentation

Before it is converted into a form suitable for MP, the digitized speech signal is segmented into syllables. This is basically performed by examining the signal energy, finding local minima and making use of Zero Crossing Rate. The algorithm used for segmentation is similar to Mermelstein's Convex-Hull algorithm [4] which recursively subdivides the speech segment into potential syllables using convex-hull of the energy function. It works in a split-merge fashion to combine over-segmented parts by taking into account of the length of the subdivided parts.

3. LPC Analysis and Kohonen's Vector Quantizer

The segmented speech is modeled by an 8-coefficient LPC vector for each of overlapped frames of 24 msecs, with a varying number of frames/syllable. Since the implementation is performed on a microcomputer, the computational requirements for the size of the perceptron creates a need for the compression of LPC data. For that purpose, Kohonen's 1-d "Feature Map" is used as a vector quantizer [1] resulting with a scalar code per LPC vector. In 1-d form (Figure 2) model is a single layer network that is trained in an unsupervised fashion and will map to an integer of a range that corresponds to the number of outputs, which is chosen to be 512 here. The adaptation algorithm here starts with a neighborhood of 128, which is reduced slowly for determining the connection weights.

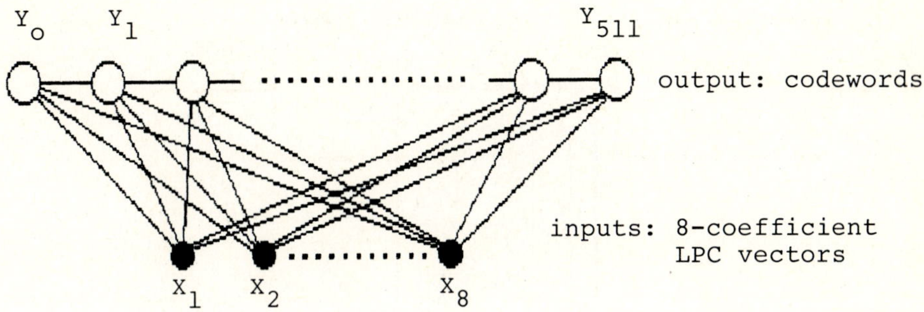

Figure 2. Kohonen's 1-d Feature Map as used in the study.

4. Linear Time Normalization and Multilayer Perceptron

The outputs of Kohonen's network are accumulated in time by a buffer until all frames in the syllable are quantized (Figure 3). The resultant sequence is of varying length. To obtain a fixed length feature set for the MP, the sequence is linearly time normalized to longest possible length, which was 14 here.

A 3-layer perceptron is implemented to obtain better discriminatory power compared to 1 or 2-level networks (Fig.3). The network has 16 outputs corresponding to 16 syllables that appear in ten Turkish digits. The number of nodes at each level is determined experimentally to give the best performance.

The perceptron was trained by well-known back propagation algorithm whose details can be found elsewhere [5]. The details of the training and the recognition results will be given in section 5.

Word reconstruction is performed by examining the recognition scores for succesive syllables and hopefully recovering from misclassified ones by using these scores. This approach will help in increasing overall word recognition rate.

5. Experimental Results and Conclusions

Among 450 words connected in groups of at most 10, 95 % are correctly segmented. The MP resulted with a 93 % correctly trained samples, with 80 syllables in training set. With 5 male and 5 female speakers, 80 % are correctly recognized among 80 test syllables. Together with the word reconstruction step,an overall correct word recognition ratio of 90 % is obtained.

The results seem quite promising although further analysis in the topology of MP for better and faster training might be performed.

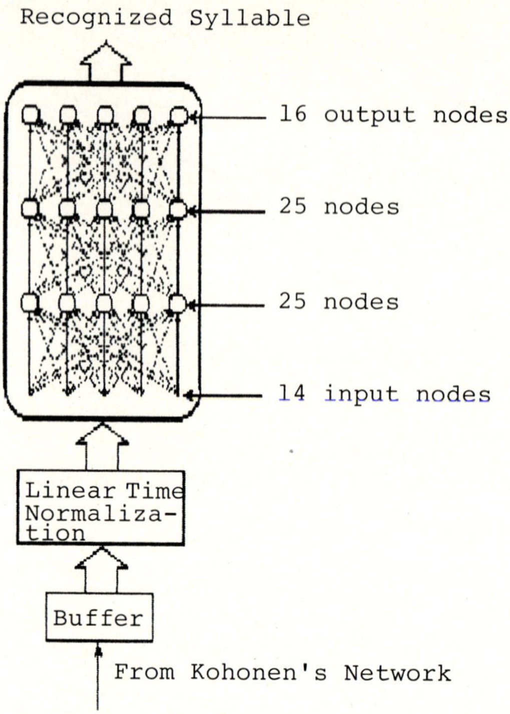

Figure 3. Multilayer Perceptron

References

[1] T.Kohonen, K.Masisara, T.Sarimaki "Phonotopic Maps-Insightful Representation of Phonological Features for Speech Representation" Proc.IEEE 7th Inter. Conf. on Pattern Recognition, Montreal, Canada, 1984 pp 182-185.

[2] Y.Bengio, R.Cardin, R.de Mori, E.Merlo "Programmable Execution of Multilayered Networks for Automatic Speech Recognition" Comm. ACM, Vol.32, No.2 February 1989, pp 195-199

[3] D.J.Burr "Experiments on Neural Net Recognition of Spoken and Written Text" IEEE Truns. on ASSP, Vol.ASSP-36, No.7, July 1988, pp 1162-1168.

[4] P.Mermelstein "Automatic Segmentation of Speech into Syllabic Units" Acoust-Soc.Am.Vol.58, No.4 October 1975, pp 880-883.

[5] D.E.Rumelhart, G.E.Hinton, R.J.Williams "Learning Internal Representations by Error Propogation" in D.E. Rumelhart, J.L. McClelland (Eds) "Parallel Distributed Processing". Vol 1., MIT Press, 1986, pp 318-362.

4 IMAGE

Handwritten Digit Recognition: Applications of Neural Net Chips and Automatic Learning

Y. Le Cun, L. D. Jackel, B. Boser, J. S. Denker, H. P. Graf, I. Guyon, D. Henderson, R. E. Howard, and W. Hubbard

AT&T Bell Laboratories, Holmdel, N. J. 07733

Abstract

We describe two neural-net approaches to digit recognition. One method uses a neural-network chip to perform line thinning and local feature extraction. This preprocessing stage was designed by hand and did not involve any learning. However, automatic learning was used in the final classification step. The chip can process about 100 characters/sec, but the interface to the host computer limits the throughput to about 1 character/sec.

The other method uses constrained automatic learning on pixel images with no preprocessing other than segmentation and size-normalization. It appears that good generalization performance cannot be obtained unless some *a priori* knowledge about the task is built into the system. This paper demonstrates how such knowledge can be integrated into a back-propagation network by providing hints and constraints on the architecture. Most of the computational burden of this method can be borne by a digital signal processor, resulting in a throughput of about 10 characters/sec.

Both methods have 1% error rate and about a 12-13% reject rate when trained on 7300 digits taken from U.S. Zipcodes and tested on 2000 such digits. These results appear to be at the state-of-the-art in handwritten digit recognition.

1 Introduction

The massively parallel architecture of connectionist systems is an obvious candidate for performing image recognition, but few results on real-world applications have been published so far. This paper describes two methods for achieving handwritten digit recognition. The task of handwritten digit recognition was chosen because it has considerable practical interest, because it is relatively well defined, and because it has sufficient complexity to constitute a meaningful test of connectionist methods.

NATO ASI Series, Vol. F 68
Neurocomputing
Edited by F. Fogelman Soulié and J. Hérault

Simple classification techniques directly applied to pixel images do not provide high recognition rates because systems based on these techniques contain little prior knowledge about the task topology. Knowledge can be built into the system by changing the representation of an input pattern from a pixel image to a predefined feature description. The first of our methods implements this idea by performing feature extraction with a neural-network chip. The feature representation can then be used by a relatively simple classifier, consisting of a two-layer network trained with Back-Propagation.

Finding the proper feature representation for a particular problem is a very complex task. To circumvent this, our second method incorporates sufficient knowledge of the task topology into the classifier so that it automatically learns the features and generates an appropriate change of representation. This is done by using an adaptive network that has constraints on its architecture that capture the two-dimensional topology of the data. The network is trained on pixel images directly, using the Back-Propagation algorithm, thus demonstrating the ability of BP networks to deal with large amounts of low level information.

Section 2 describes the data base and shows some examples. Section 3 discusses the first method based on a neural-network chip that performs line-thinning and feature extraction using local template matching. Section 4 discusses the second method, which is implemented on a digital signal processor, and makes extensive use of constrained automatic learning. Some concluding remarks are made in Section 5.

2 The Data Base

A recurring problem in evaluating character recognition systems is the lack of a reliable measure of the difficulty of the task. In particular, for digit recognition the performance of the system is highly test-set dependent. A system may successfully recognize 99% of test data consisting of well-formed digits but score only 80% when confronted with the poorly-formed digits that are both routinely produced and easily recognized by people. We chose to perform our experiments on a rather difficult data set: isolated handwritten digits that were taken from postal Zipcodes. The Zipcode images were collected by the U.S. Postal Service from envelopes that passed through the Buffalo, NY post office. A postal Service contractor converted the original Zipcode images to binary images, and segmented the digits. The resulting database consists of 9298 binary images of isolated digits, 7291 of which are used as the training set, and the remaining 2007 as the test set. Most of the images are fairly clean; however, a significant fraction are very blotchy or incomplete. The latter defect is quite common among '5's in which the top horizontal stroke is often missing. It should be stressed that such mistakes in the segmentation are inevitable: high level, contextual information is needed to perform a perfectly reliable segmentation on connected character sequences, and no such information is available at the early preprocessing stage without any feedback from the recognition stages.

In our laboratory we performed some additional preprocessing to normalize the shape and the skew (tilt) of the digits [2, 10]. We scaled the bit maps to fit into either a 32 by 32 or 16 by 16 pixel window. Typical scaled and "de-skewed" examples taken from this data set are shown in Figure 1. As can be seen, many of the digits are of poor quality.

Figure 1. Examples of normalized data.

3 Digit Recognition Using a Neural-Net Template Matching Chip

For this method [4], extensive preprocessing was done beyond the simple scaling and de-skewing described above. The objective here was to change the representation of the digit from a bit map to a feature map with the expectation that the classes will be more tightly clustered in a well-constructed feature map than in a scaled bit map. The features were designed by hand on the basis of neurobiological models, and stored on a general-purpose neural-net chip, with the dual objectives of speeding a compute-intensive feature extraction process and demonstrating the utility of the chip. The Back-Propagation algorithm (see for example [12]) was used to train a network that has feature maps as inputs and digit classes as outputs.

3.1 The Chip

The chip used for computing the feature map has been described extensively elsewhere [5]; here we will only outline its function. The chip stores 49 templates, each with 49 components. Binary input vectors, up to 49 bits long are loaded on the chip and are compared in parallel to each of the 49 stored templates. The comparison of the input vector with the stored templates is done by taking an analog dot product of the input with each template. The components of the templates can have relative values of 1 (excitation), 0 (don't care), or -2 (inhibition), and are set by the state of the 2 static RAM cells assigned to each template component. (The value -2 arises from differences in the conductance of the P and N channel load transistors.) The dot product for each template plus a programmable bias is then passed through a comparator circuit. When the dot product plus the bias is greater than zero, the comparator reports a "1" (match); otherwise it reports a "0" (no match).

All signals and storage elements on the chip are accessed through an external 8-bit bus. This includes the 2916 RAM cells used for storing templates, as well as the 49 input bits and the 49 output bits. It is the external bus and its interface board to the host computer that limits the chip throughput. The chip itself calculates the 49 dot products simultaneously in less than 1 microsecond, but the experimental interface board can only pass the input and output for this data in 20 microseconds.

In our application the chip is basically used as an engine to perform parallel, thresholded convolutions. The templates represent the convolution kernels and the input vector is a local neighborhood of the processed image. The size of the neighborhood is either 5 by 5 pixels or 7 by 7 pixels and sequentially scanned through the image. Two sets of convolutions are done: the first is used to "skeletonize" the scaled digit image, and the second is used to extract key features in the skeletonized image and thus form feature maps. Both these steps are described below.

For the low accuracy dot products required in template matching, analog electronic circuits on our chip have advantages over digital circuits: the analog circuits can be faster and more compact. This is because the summation in the dot product is computed "for free" just by adding the component currents in a summing wire.

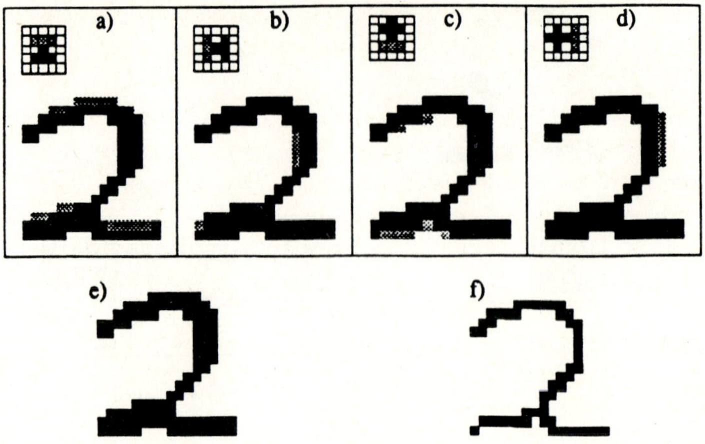

Figure 2. The skeletonization process. e) shows a scaled binarized image. f) shows the result after skeletonization using one pass with 20 templates. a) - d) show typical templates used for thinning in the upper left of each box. Black is excitation, gray is inhibition, and white is don't care. The pixels deleted by each template are shown in gray on the large image in each box

3.2 Skeletonization

The width of written line strokes for characters varies with character size, writing instruments, and writing style. To compensate for this variation, our 32 by 32 normalized image is processed by a "skeletonization" or line-thinning step. Although features can be extracted reliably for any particular width of lines, the width does not carry much information and a smaller number of features suffices to analyze the skeletonized images. The objective for a skeletonizer is to eat away pixels of the image until only a backbone of the character remains. Thus broad strokes are reduced to skinny lines. This process is traditionally done by scanning a 3 by 3 window across the image, and then using table look up to determine whether or not the middle pixel in the window ought to be deleted [9]. The table is designed so that pixels that are crucial to maintaining connectivity are not deleted. With larger windows, such as 5 by 5, table look up becomes impractical. But larger windows offer the possibility of more clever skeletonization which can be less noise sensitive and can preserve straight edges. In our experiment we used such 5 by 5 windows to illustrate the potential of neural-net hardware.

Skeletonization with our chip proceeds in the following way. A 5x5 pixel window is raster scanned across the image. The 25 bits representing the pixels in each window are compared to twenty 25-bit templates stored on the chip. Each template tests for a particular condition that allows the deletion of the middle pixel in the window. If the match of the image data to any of the templates exceeds a preset threshold, the center pixel is deleted. Examples of some of the templates used for skeletonization are shown in Figure 2. These templates were chosen in a systematic, but ad hoc, manner.

It should be noted that although the skeletonization is performed in a raster scan fashion, it can be performed entirely in parallel with a sufficient amount of special

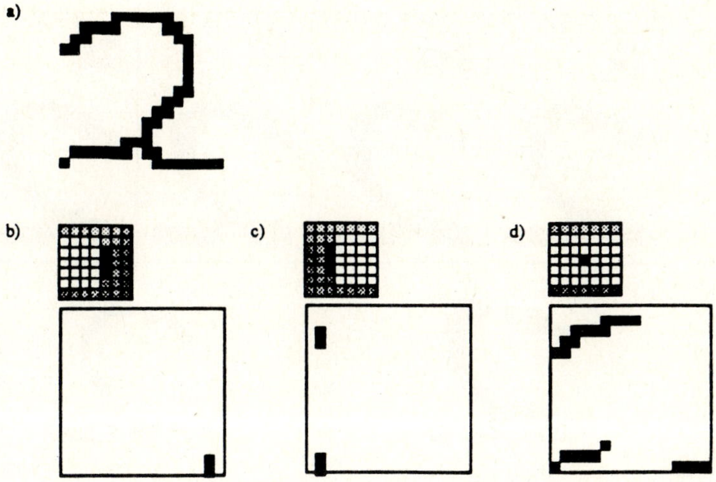

Figure 3. The feature extraction process. a) shows a skeletonized image. b), c) and d) show examples of feature templates, and the resultant feature maps for the image shown in a). In the templates, black is excitation and gray is inhibition. b) and c) check for line endstops, d) checks for horizontal lines.

purpose hardware.

3.3 Feature Extraction

In the feature extraction process, the skeletonized image is raster scanned with a 7 by 7 pixel window. The templates for feature extraction, which are loaded on the chip after skeletonization is complete, were inspired by results from experimental neurobiology [6], but their precise shapes were fine tuned by hand, in part to conform to the constraints imposed by the chip. The templates check for the presence of oriented lines, oriented line end-stops, and arcs. Examples of some of the 49 templates are shown in Figure 3.

Whenever a feature template match exceeds the preset threshold, a 1 is set in the map for that corresponding feature. Thus, there is a feature map for every template. Some of the templates search for the same feature, but on a different size scale. The maps for such features are logically ORed together after the scan is completed.

The feature extraction process generates forty-nine 32 by 32 maps from the 32 by 32 normalized image. Some of these maps are combined by logical operations to produce eighteen 32 by 32 feature maps. To reduce the amount of data, each feature map is coarse-blocked into a 3 by 5 array by simply ORing neighboring bits in each feature map. The eighteen 3 by 5 feature maps make up a 270-bit vector which is used for digit classification. The coarse blocking also has the effect of building a fair amount of translation and rotation invariance into the processing.

3.4 Classification and Results of Chip-Based system

The Back-Propagation algorithm was used to train the final classification network. The network had 270 input units, corresponding to the coarse-blocked feature maps, 40 hidden units fully connected to the input layer, and 10 output units, one for each digit class with full interconnects to the hidden units. Thus, there were about 11,000 weights for the classification network. The raw generalization performance on the 2007 test examples was around 94% and was obtained after about 15 learning passes through the training set.

In a realistic application, the user is less interested in the raw error rate than in the number of rejections necessary to reach a given level of accuracy. In our case, we measured the percentage of test patterns that must be rejected in order to get 1% error rate on the *remaining* test patterns.

Our rejection criterion was based on three conditions: the activity level of the most-active output unit should be larger than a given threshold t_1, the activity level of the second most-active unit should be smaller than a given threshold t_2, and finally, the difference between the activity levels of these two units should be larger than a given threshold t_d.

It should be emphasized that the rejection thresholds were obtained using performance measures on the *test set.* Thus we measure performance by setting output unit activation criteria which must be attained in order to accept a classification. For activations below this level we reject the digit as unclassifiable. We find that to obtain a misclassification rate no higher than 1% we must reject 13% of the digits. We expect that a patient human could achieve the same error rate by rejecting about 5% of the digits.

3.5 Time Budget

As stated earlier, the chip has enough computing power to evaluate all the templates at one window location in one microsecond. Thus, a few milliseconds should be required for the skeletonization and feature extraction across the whole 32 by 32 image. Actual processing times were about two orders of magnitude slower. Although the chip-host interface costs an order of magnitude in throughput, currently the bottleneck in the process is the speed at which the host computer formats the pixel-window data to be sent to the chip. This bottleneck and the I/O problem could be eliminated if the chip were incorporated into an special-purpose image-processing system.

3.6 Degrees of Freedom in the Network

We can interpret the combination of skeletonization, feature extraction, and classification as one huge feed-forward network. In that case about 2 million connections must be evaluated to perform the three skeletonization passes and an additional 2 million are required for the feature extraction. Thus, 99.5% of the connection evaluations involve a "hand-crafted" change of representation from bit maps to feature maps; the final classification requires only 0.5% of the connections. We note, however, that relatively few bits are required to specify the weights for the skeletonization and feature extraction. There are 25 skeletonization kernels of 25 coefficients each. Each coefficient has one of three values ($\approx$ 1.6 bits). Most of the kernels are rotations or reflections of other kernels. Furthermore most of the kernels have symmetry axes. We estimate that once these geometric constraints are imposed, about 150 bits are required to specify the skeletonization kernels, and by similar arguments about 400 bits are required to specify the feature extraction kernels. Thus, the network of 4 million connections can be parameterized by just several hundred bits. These arguments suggest that by imposing sufficient constraints on the weights in a multilayered network, high recognition accuracy might be achieved by *learned* convolution kernels. Such a network is discussed in the following sections.

4 Digit Recognition Using Constrained Automatic Learning

The experiments described above suggest that a large network is probably needed to perform accurate digit recognition. If we were to design a large unconstrained network, it is very unlikely that it could be trained on a data base even as large as ours with any hope of achieving good generalizing ability (i.e. good scores on the test data). Previous work performed on simple digit images [8] showed that the architecture of the network strongly influences the network's generalization ability. Good generalization can only be obtained by designing a network architecture that contains a certain amount of *a priori* knowledge about the problem. The basic design principle is to reduce the number of free parameters that can be modified by the learning algorithm as much as possible without overly reducing the computational power of the network. Application of this principle increases the probability of correct generalization because it results in a specialized network architecture that has a reduced entropy [3, 11, 13, 8]. On the other hand, some effort must be devoted to the design of the architecture.

Classical work in visual pattern recognition has demonstrated the advantage of extracting local features and combining them to form higher-order features. Such knowledge can be easily built into the network by forcing the hidden units to combine only local sources of information. We know that the digit recognition task is a 2-dimensional geometric problem, so we ought to incorporate this knowledge in the network design. One way we can do this is by forcing the early layers in the network to perform 2-dimensional convolutions over the image. Following this approach, we designed the network shown in Figure 4.

4.1 Architecture

The input to the network is a 16 by 16 gray-scale image that is formed by normalizing the raw image. The image is gray-scale rather than binary since a variable number of pixels in the raw image can fall into a given pixel in the normalized image.

All of the connections in the network are adaptive, although heavily constrained, and are trained using Back-Propagation. This is in contrast with the chip-based method where the first few layers of connections were hand-chosen constants. The architecture is a direct extension of the one proposed in [8]. In addition to the input and output layer, the network has three hidden layers respectively named H1, H2 and H3. Connections entering H1 and H2 are local and are heavily constrained.

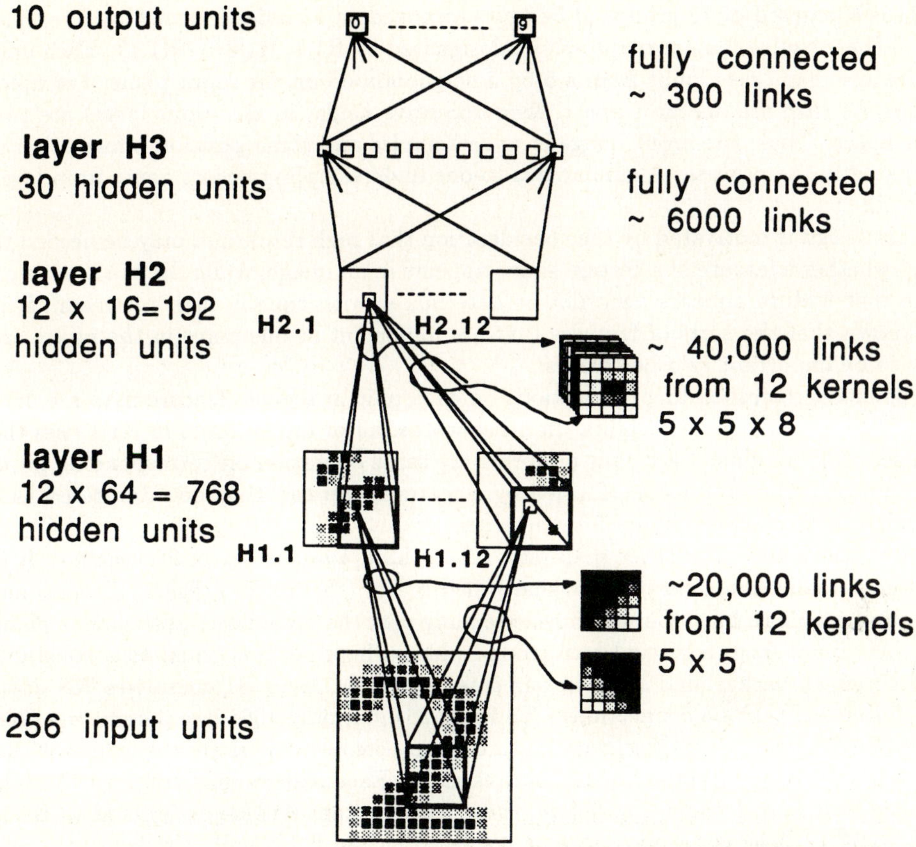

Figure 4. Network Architecture.

H1 is composed of 12 groups of 64 units arranged as 12 independent 8 by 8 feature maps. These twelve feature maps will be designated by H1.1, H1.2 ⋯ H1.12. Each unit in a feature map takes input from a 5 by 5 neighborhood on the input plane. For units in layer H1 that are one unit apart, their receptive fields (in the input layer) are two pixels apart. Thus, the input image is *undersampled* and some position information is eliminated in the process. A similar two-to-one undersampling occurs going from layer H1 to H2.

This design is motivated by the consideration that high resolution may be needed to detect whether a feature of a certain shape appears in an image, while the exact position where that feature appears need not be determined with equally high precision. It is also known that the sorts of features that are important at one place in the image are likely to be important in other places.

Therefore, corresponding connections on each unit in a given feature map are constrained to have the same weights. In other words, all of the 64 units in H1.1 uses the same set of 25 weights. Each unit performs the same operation on corresponding parts of the image. The function performed by a feature map can thus be interpreted as a generalized convolution[1] with a 5 by 5 kernel.

Of course, units in another map (say H1.4) share *another* set of 25 weights. It is worth mentioning that units *do not* share their biases (thresholds). Each unit thus has 25 input lines plus a bias. Connections extending past the boundaries of the input plane take their input from a virtual background plane whose state is equal to a constant, pre-determined background level, in our case -1. Thus, layer H1 comprises 768 units (8 by 8 times 12), 19968 connections (768 times 26), but only 1068 free parameters (768 biases plus 25 times 12 feature kernels) since many connections share the same weight.

Layer H2 is also composed of 12 features maps. Each feature map contains 16 units arranged in a 4 by 4 plane. As before, these feature maps will be designated as H2.1, H2.2 ⋯ H2.12. The connection scheme between H1 and H2 is quite similar to the one between the input and H1, but slightly more complicated because H1 has multiple 2-D maps. Each unit in H2 combines local information coming from 8 of the 12 different feature maps in H1. Its receptive field is composed of eight 5 by 5 neighborhoods centered around units that are at identical positions within each of the eight maps. Thus, a unit in H2 has 200 inputs, 200 weights, and a bias. Of course, all units in a given map are constrained to have identical weight vectors. The eight maps in H1 on which a map in H2 takes its inputs are chosen according to the following scheme. There are four maps in the first hidden layer (namely H1.9 to H1.12) that are connected to all maps in the next layer and are expected to compute coarsely-tuned features.

Connections between the remaining eight maps and H2 are as shown in the first eight rows of Table 1. The idea behind this scheme is to introduce a notion of functional contiguity between the eight maps. Because of this architecture, H2 units in consecutive maps receive similar error signals, and are expected to perform similar operations. As in the case of H1, connections falling off the boundaries of H2 maps take their input from a virtual plane whose state is constant equal to 0. To summarize, layer H2 contains 192 units (12 times 4 by 4) and there is total of 38592 connections between layers H1 and H2 (192 units time 201 input lines). All these connections are controlled by only 2592

[1]Because of the non-linear saturating function of the units, and because of the undersampling, the total effect cannot be expressed as a convolution in the strict sense, although the spirit is the same.

	1	2	3	4	5	6	7	8	9	10	11	12
H1.1	X	X	X							X	X	X
H1.2	X	X	X							X	X	X
H1.3	X	X	X	X	X	X						
H1.4	X	X	X	X	X	X						
H1.5				X	X	X	X	X	X			
H1.6				X	X	X	X	X	X			
H1.7							X	X	X	X	X	X
H1.8							X	X	X	X	X	X
H1.9	X	X	X	X	X	X	X	X	X	X	X	X
H1.10	X	X	X	X	X	X	X	X	X	X	X	X
H1.11	X	X	X	X	X	X	X	X	X	X	X	X
H1.12	X	X	X	X	X	X	X	X	X	X	X	X

Table 1. Connections between H1 and H2.

free parameters (12 feature maps times 200 weights plus 192 biases).

Layer H3 has 30 units, and is fully connected to H2. The number of connections between H2 and H3 is thus 5790 (30 times 192 plus 30 biases). The output layer has 10 units and is also fully connected to H3, adding another 310 weights. In summary, the network has 1256 units, 64660 connections and 9760 independent parameters.

4.2 Experimental Setup

All simulations were performed using the BP simulator SN [1] running on a SUN-4/260. Before training, the weights were initialized with random values using a uniform distribution between $-2.4/F_i$ and $2.4/F_i$ where F_i is the number of inputs (fan-in) of the unit to which the connection belongs. Each unit in the network computes a dot product between its input vector and its weight vector. This weighted sum, denoted a_i for unit i, is then passed through a sigmoid squashing function to produce the state of unit i, denoted by x_i:

$$x_i = f(a_i)$$

The squashing function we use is a scaled hyperbolic tangent:

$$f(a) = A\tanh(Sa)$$

where A is the amplitude of the function and S determines its slope at the origin. This is an odd function, with horizontal asymptotes $+A$ and $-A$.

Symmetric functions are believed to yield faster convergence, although the learning can be extremely slow if all the weights are too close to 0. The cause of this problem is that the origin of weight space is a stable point for the learning dynamics, and, although it is a saddle point, it is attractive in almost all directions. For our simulations, we use $A = 1.716$ and $S = 2/3$. With this choice of parameters, $f(1) = 1$ and $f(-1) = -1$. The rationale behind this choice is that the overall gain of the squashing transformation is around 1 in normal operating conditions, and the interpretation of the state of the network is simplified. Moreover, the absolute value of the second derivative of f is maximum at $+1$ and -1, which, as we will see later, improves the convergence at the end of the learning session.

The output cost function is the usual mean squared error:

$$MSE = \frac{1}{OP}\sum_p\sum_o\frac{1}{2}(d_{op} - x_{op})^2$$

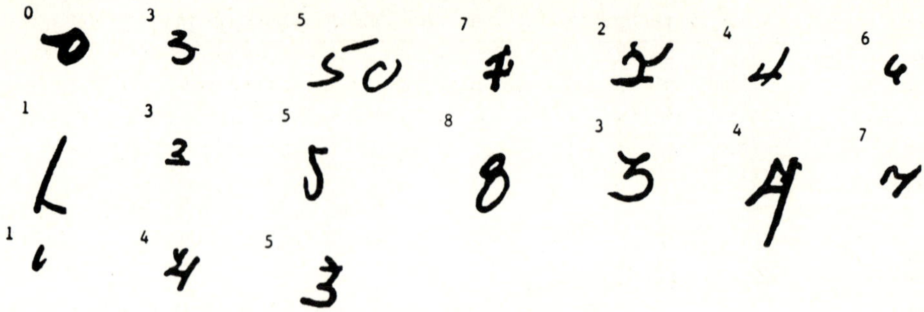

Figure 5. Misclassified Images

where P is the number of patterns, O is the number of output units, d_{op} is the desired state for output unit o when pattern p is presented on the input. x_{op} is the state of output unit o when pattern p is presented. The target values for the output units are -1 and $+1$: well within the range of the sigmoid function. Additionally, since the second derivative of the sigmoid is maximum near the target values, the curvature of the objective function in the vicinity of the solution is maximized and the convergence speed during the final phase of the learning process is improved.

During each learning experiment, the patterns were presented in a constant order, and the training set was repeated 30 times. The weights were updated according to the so-called stochastic gradient or "on-line" procedure (updating after each presentation of a single pattern) as opposed to the "true" gradient procedure (averaging over the whole training set before updating the weights). Experiments show that the stochastic gradient converges significantly faster than the true gradient on highly redundant data sets such as ours. We used a variation of the Back-Propagation algorithm that computes a diagonal approximation to the Hessian matrix to optimally set the learning rate. This "pseudo-Newton" procedure is not believed to bring a considerable increase in learning speed, but it produces a reliable result without requiring extensive adjustments of the parameters [7].

4.3 Results

Training was stopped after 23 passes through the training set. The MSE was then 2.5×10^{-3} on the training set and 1.8×10^{-2} on the test set. The percentage of misclassified patterns was 0.14% on the training set (10 mistakes) and 5.0% on the test set (102 mistakes). The percentage of rejections was then 12.1% for 1% error on what is left.

Figure 5 shows *all 17* of the images in the test set that were misclassified by the network. In most cases there is a reasonable explanation, or at least apology, for the mistake. The main problem, accounting for six of the cases, is erroneous segmentation. Segmentation is a very difficult problem, especially when the characters overlap extensively. Improving the segmentation would greatly improve the overall performance of the system, but would require considerable effort. In four cases, the image is ambiguous even to humans. This contribution to the error rate obviously cannot be eliminated by any method. In three cases, the raw image is unambiguous, but the 16 by 16 image (at the input of the network) is ambiguous because of its low resolution. In two cases, the characters have an unusual style which is not represented in the training set; a modest increase in training set size should reduce the number of such failures. We have no good explanation for the two remaining cases.

Figure 6 shows some specific weight values connecting the input to layer H1, and then H1 to H2. The leftmost column in the figure represents the 12 kernels used by the feature maps in layer H1. The bottom 4 rows contain the maps in H1 that are seen by all maps in H2 (see Table 1). Each one of these 5 by 5 kernels is used by all units in a given map in H1. The three remaining columns are representative examples of the connection weights from H1 to H2. The first column represents the 200 incoming weights to any unit in H2.1, the second column represents weights of H2.5 and the third column represents the weights of H2.8. These columns are divided into a series of eight 5 by 5 kernels that come from the H1 feature map corresponding to the vertical position of the kernel in the figure. For example, units in H2.1 take inputs from H1.1, H1.2, H1.3, H1.4, H1.9, H1.10, H1.11 and H1.12.

Within each kernel, a white square represents a positive connection and a black square represents a negative connection; the area of the square is proportional to the magnitude of the connection strength. The biases are not shown.

Certain of the kernels in figure 6 can be interpreted as feature detectors remarkably similar to those found to exist in biological vision systems [6] and/or designed into previous artificial character recognizers. We emphasize that the weight patterns in figure 6 were learned, not designed in. Most of the kernels are non-ideal and coarsely tuned, more like biological feature detectors than (possibly overly) precise and ideal kernels designed by hand.

Specifically, H1.11 (first column, eleventh line) clearly calculates a derivative in the vertical direction, and responds maximally to horizontal edges. Similarly, H1.6 responds maximally to lines running from Northwest to Southeast. Several kernels, for instance H1.9 and H1.12, are roughly off-center/on-surround type feature detectors. Kernel H1.8 discriminates between horizontal and vertical lines.

Similar geometrical structures can be seen in the H2 kernels. For example, H2.1 clearly detects Southwest-Northeast edges, mainly by combining outputs from H1.9 and H1.10. Kernel H2.5 detects vertical bars, and kernel H2.8 detects horizontal lines, by having strong weights coming from H1.11. Most kernels, however, are difficult to interpret, especially in the later layers.

4.4 DSP Implementation

During the classification process, almost all the computation time is spent performing multiply/accumulate operations. A digital signal processor (DSP) is thus a natural choice for implementing the neural network because of its efficiency in performing multiply-accumulate operations. We used an off-the-shelf board that contains 256 kBytes of local memory and an AT&T DSP-32C general purpose DSP with a peak performance of 12.5 million multiply-add operations on 32 bit floating point numbers (25MFLOPS). The DSP operates as a coprocessor; the host is a personal computer

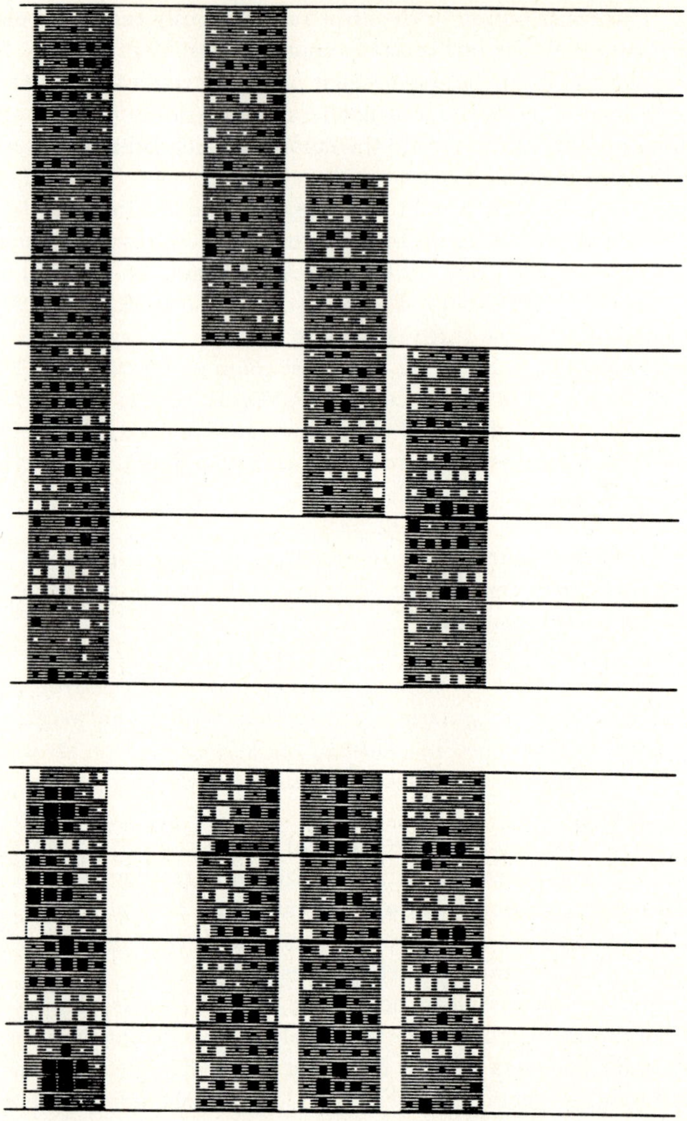

Figure 6. Example of connection weights from input layer to H1 and from H1 to H2. Connections from input layer to H1 are represented on the leftmost columns. Connections from H1 to H2.1, H2.5 and H2.8 are represented on the three rightmost columns

(PC), which also contains a video acquisition board connected to a camera.

The personal computer first digitizes an image and binarizes it using an adaptive thresholding technique. The thresholded image is then scanned and each connected component (or segment) is isolated. Components that are too small or too large are discarded; remaining components are sent to the DSP for normalization and recognition. The PC gives a variable sized-pixel map representation of a single digit to the DSP which in turn performs the normalization and classification steps.

The overall throughput of the digit recognizer including image acquisition is 10 to 12 classifications per second and is limited mainly by the normalization step. On normalized digits, the DSP performs more than 30 classifications per second.

5 CONCLUSION

In past years, much was learned about neural networks by studying small test problems. To make further progress, more can be learned by attacking large, real-world tasks, especially if the tasks have been attempted in the past with other methods. In particular, real applications contain the surprises and secrets of the natural world. Just as in other types of research and engineering, there are aspects of the system that would not appear in a idealized model, and must be discovered through experiments on real systems. We believe that our experiments on digit recognition, described in this paper, uncover aspects of real data that cannot be inferred from small problems.

We have successfully applied neural-network methods to a large, real-world task. Our results appear to be at the state of the art in digit recognition. We demonstrated that a general-purpose neural-net chip can be incorporated as an accelerator in a large network.

We also showed that a network can be trained on a low-level representation of data that has minimal preprocessing (as opposed to elaborate feature extraction). The network had many connections but relatively few free parameters. The network architecture and the constraints on the weights were designed to incorporate geometric knowledge about the task into the system. Because of the redundant nature of the data and because of the constraints imposed on the network, the learning time was relatively short considering the size of the training set. Scaling properties were far better than one would expect just from extrapolating results of Back-Propagation on smaller, artificial problems.

The final network of connections and weights obtained by Back-Propagation learning was readily implementable on commercial digital signal processing hardware. Throughput rates, from camera to classified image, of more than ten digits per second were obtained.

Acknowledgments

We thank the US Postal Service and its contractors for providing us with the database. The Neural Network simulator SN is the result of a collaboration between Léon-Yves Bottou and the first author.

References

[1] L.-Y. Bottou and Y. le Cun. Sn: A simulator for connectionist models. In *Proceedings of NeuroNimes 88*, Nimes, France, 1988.

[2] R. G. Casey. Moment normalization of handprinted characters. *IBM Journal of Research and Development*, 548, 1970.

[3] J. Denker, D. Schwartz, B. Wittner, S. A. Solla, R. Howard, L. Jackel, and J. Hopfield. Large automatic learning, rule extraction and generalization. *Complex Systems*, 1:877–922, 1987.

[4] J. S. Denker, W. R. Gardner, H. P. Graf, D. Henderson, R. E. Howard, W. Hubbard, L. D. Jackel, H. S. Baird, and I. Guyon. Neural network recognizer for hand-written zip code digits. In D. Touretzky, editor, *Advances in Neural Information Processing Systems*, pages 323–331. Morgan Kaufmann, 1989.

[5] H.-P. Graf, W. Hubbard, L. D. Jackel, and P. G. de Vegvar. A cmos associative memory chip. In *Proc. IEEE First International Conference on Neural Networks*, pages III–461. IEEE, 1987. San Diego, CA.

[6] D. H. Hubel and T. N. Wiesel. Receptive fields, binocular interaction and functional architecture in the cat's visual cortex. *Journal of Physiology*, 160:106–154, 1962.

[7] Y. le Cun. *Modèles Connexionnistes de l'Apprentissage.* PhD thesis, Université Pierre et Marie Curie, Paris, France, 1987.

[8] Y. le Cun. Generalization and network design strategies. In R. Pfeifer, Z. Schreter, F. Fogelman, and L. Steels, editors, *Connectionism in Perspective*, Zurich, Switzerland, 1989. Elsevier.

[9] N. J. Naccache and R. Shingal. Spta: A proposed algorithm for thinning binary patterns. *IEEE Trans. Systems, Man, and Cybernetics*, SMC-14:409, 1984.

[10] W. C. Naylor. Some studies in the interactive design of character recognition systems. *IEEE Transaction on Computers*, page 1075, 1971.

[11] S. Patarnello and P. Carnevali. Learning networks of neurons with boolean logic. *Europhysics Letters*, 4(4):503–508, 1987.

[12] D. E. Rumelhart, G. E. Hinton, and R. J. Williams. Learning internal representations by error propagation. In *Parallel distributed processing: Explorations in the microstructure of cognition*, volume I., Bradford Books, Cambridge, MA, 1986.

[13] N. Tishby, E. Levin, and S. A. Solla. Consistent inference of probabilities in layered networks: Predictions and generalization. In *Proceedings of the International Joint Conference on Neural Networks*, Washington DC, 1989.

A method to de-alias the scatterometer wind field: a real world application

F. Badran*,**, S. Thiria*,**, M.Crépon***,

(*) Laboratoire de Recherche en Informatique
bât 490
Université de Paris Sud
91405 ORSAY Cedex - FRANCE

(**) Conservatoire National des Arts et Métiers
292 rue Saint Martin
75 003 PARIS - FRANCE

(***)Laboratoire d'Océanographie
LODYC
Université de Paris 6
4 place Jussieu
75 006 PARIS - FRANCE

1. Introduction

By the 1990's several scatterometers are going to fly on board satellites dedicated to earth and ocean observation. The Europeen ERS.1 AMI (Advanced Microwave Imager) is planned to be launched in 1991 and the US N.SCAT (Navy SCATterometer) is supposed to be launched in 1992. These scatterometers will provide wind vectors on a grid mesh of 50*50 km with a time and space coverage which will be dramatically improved with respect to conventionnal means of observations (see figure 1). For the first time oceanographers can expect to obtain an adequate description of the forcing of ocean circulation which depends on the wind-stress vector for the surface layers and on the wind-stress curl for the large scale and deep motions. These scatterometers will measure the wind with three antennas oriented in different directions. As the radar backscatter σ_o varies harmonically with the horizontal angle χ between the wind and the antenna, with maxima backscatter in the upwind and downwind directions and minima at the crosswind angle, it is possible to compute the wind direction [1]. In the absence of noise the determination of the direction of the wind would be unique. As the backscatter signal is noisy ambiguities can arise in its determination. The functional relationship between σ_o and the azimuth angle χ is nearly $\sigma_o = \cos(2\chi)$, which results in two major ambiguities which are approximately 180° apart, and two others which are at 90°. Several techniques have been proposed to remove these ambiguities[2]. In the present paper we propose an alternative approach based on concepts developed in the frame of neural networks. The method we use can be related to image processing and two dimensional filtering. Its conceptual framework is to determine two optimal filters to dealias the wind direction. First, the weights of the so-called filters which are represented by neural networks are computed automatically from some

NATO ASI Series, Vol. F 68
Neurocomputing
Edited by F. Fogelman Soulié and J. Hérault

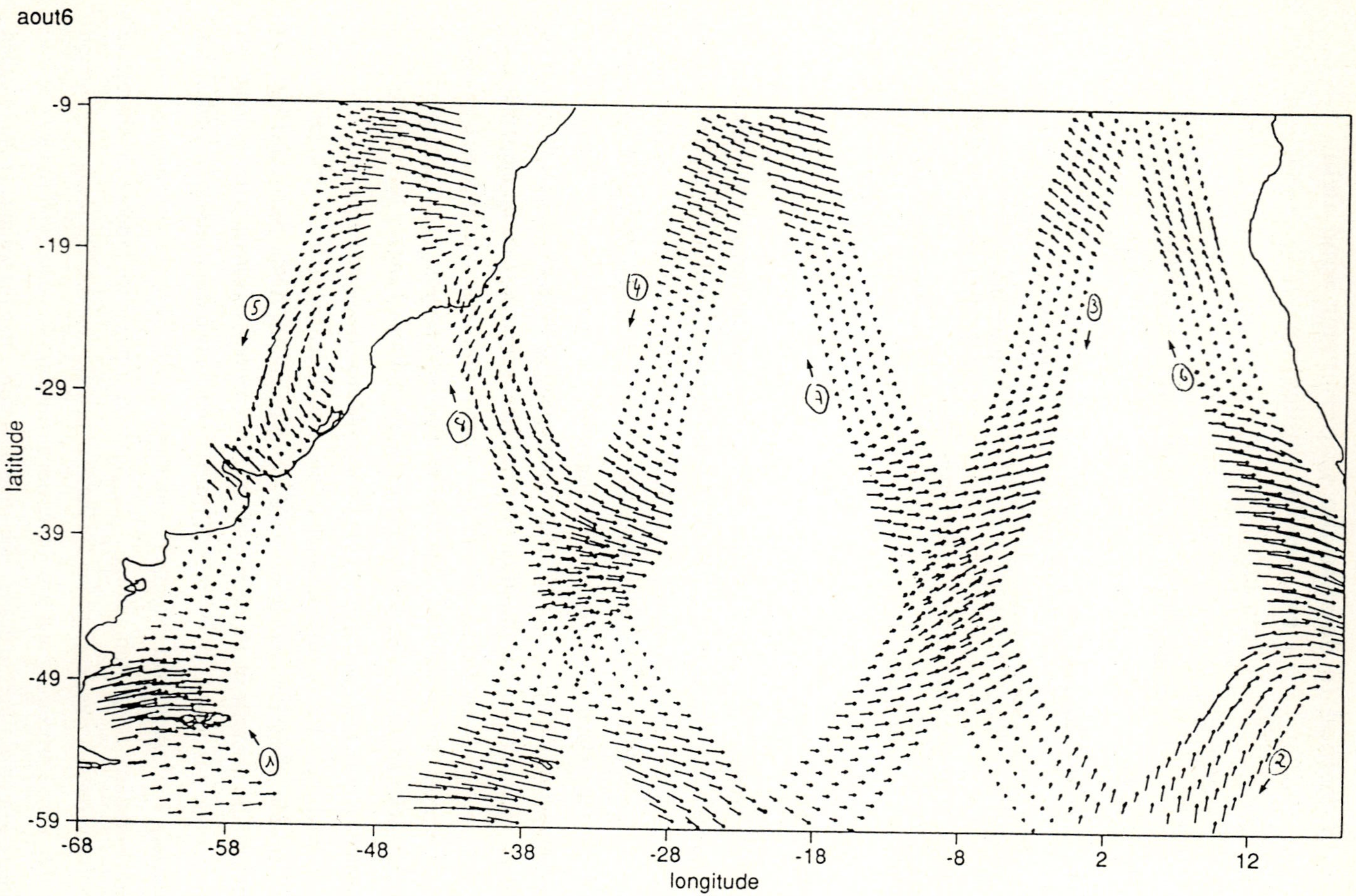

Figure 1. Scatterometers provide wind vectors on a grid mesh of 50*50 km

specific situations where the wind is perfectly known. We use for that, during the learning phase, the Back Propagation algorithm.Then the neural networks are applied on wind fields which have never been seen before, using a dynamic process in order to remove ambiguities.

2. The method

Two **optimal " machines"** are built with the aim of de-aliasing the wind direction, wherein each "machine" is dedicated to removing one of the ambiguities. One machine is made of 3 filters i.e. 3 multilayered networks depending on the position of the point to be de-aliased in relation to the boundary of the swath. Each filter takes into account the 25 wind measurements uniformly spread over a square of 200*200 km (see figure 2)

Type 1	Type 2	Type 3
VVVVV	VVVVV	VVVVV
VVVVV	VVVVV	VVVVV
VVPVV	VPVVV	PVVVV
VVVVV	VVVVV	VVVVV
VVVVV	VVVVV	VVVVV

Figure 2. presentation of the 3 classes of neighbourhoods for a 5x5 window .P is the point to be examined, V are those to deal with.

Back-propagation [3] is used during **the learning phase** to compute the weights of the filters. Each filter has the same **architecture** composed of 3 layers (see figure 3): One input layer with 50 automata (25 are forced with the sine of the corresponding wind vectors and 25 with the cosine of the same vectors); one hidden layer with 25 automata; and the output layer with 2 automata (each corresponding to a possible answer (i.e. the wind direction is correct or the wind direction is not correct). Full connection is used between layers.

3. The experiments

Because the actual data are not available, we test the method on simulated data provided by meteorological models. Noise has been added to the data according to the rate of ambiguities provided by scatterometers. First, Gaussian noise with constant standart deviation of 10° has been superimposed on the direction of each vector of the grid. Second, in order to test each filter independently, 20% of the wind direction has been inverted to simulate the first ambiguity of the learning set and to test sets of the first "machine".

Similarly 7% of the wind direction has been rotated by $\pm 90°$ to simulate the second ambiguity for the second "machine". In each case, the learning set was made up of 2000 windows from the 18th August wind map and the generalization was performed on three wind maps never used. The two "machines" have given a consistently good performances (see table 1, table 2).

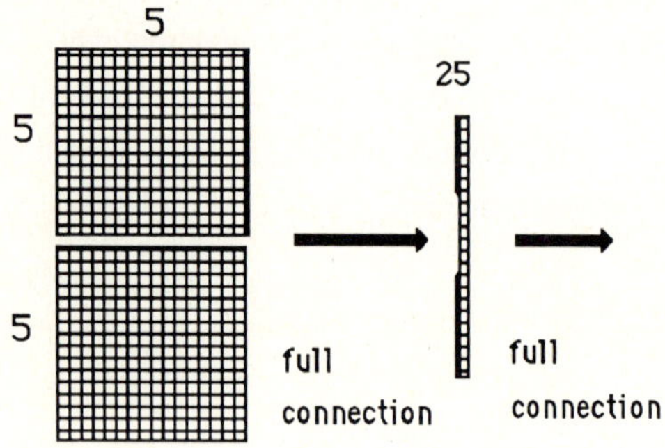

Figure 3. architecture of the network

neighbourhood type	August18th	August16th	August6th	September1th
type 2	98%	97,5%	98%	98%
type 1	99.47%	98.5 %	99,12%	98,3%
type 0	98.93 %	98.2 %	99%	98,14%

Table 1. generalization rate for the first removal ambiguity (180°)

neighbourhood type	August18th	August16th	August6th	September1th
type 2	99.95%	99.95%	99.95%	99.95%
type 1	97.86%	97.7 %	97.6%	97.23%
type 0	99.5 %	99.37 %	99.6%	98,96%

Table 2. generalization rate for the second removal ambiguity (±90°)

For a wind map the generalization rate is the ratio of the number of windows correctly classified to the total number of windows. Because this recognition is just local, these rates represent a lower bound of the global process - i.e the generalization rate of the "machine".

4. The relaxation process

The filters are used as in image analysis processessing. First the "180°-machine" proceeds and corrects most of the 180°-errors , point by point. Then the " 90°-machine" focuses on the other ambiguity (± 90°) and finds most of the errors. Some are badly corrected because in this case we have just rotated the vector by + 90°, taking no notice of the real error (± 90°). Finally the first machine is used again in order to improve the corrections (see figure 4).

5.Conclusion

The time required to de-alias the whole wind-map is very fast. This fact and the good performances obtained shows that from now on "neural networks" are actualy usable for real applications.

6. References

1. Cavanie, A., Lecompte, P.: Study of a method to De-Alias Winds from ERS-1 data, final report of ESA contract n°6874/87/GP-I (sc), (1987).
2. Roquet, H., Ratier, A.: Toward direct variational assimilation of scatterometer backscatter measurements into numericalweather prediction model, proceeding of IGARSS 88 symposium, Edinburgh, Scotland, 13-16 Septembre 1988. Ref ESA SP-284 (IEEE 88CH2497-6), (1988).
3. Rumelhart, D.E., McClelland, J.L.: Parallel distributed processing: explorations in the microstructures of cognition. MIT Press, (1986).

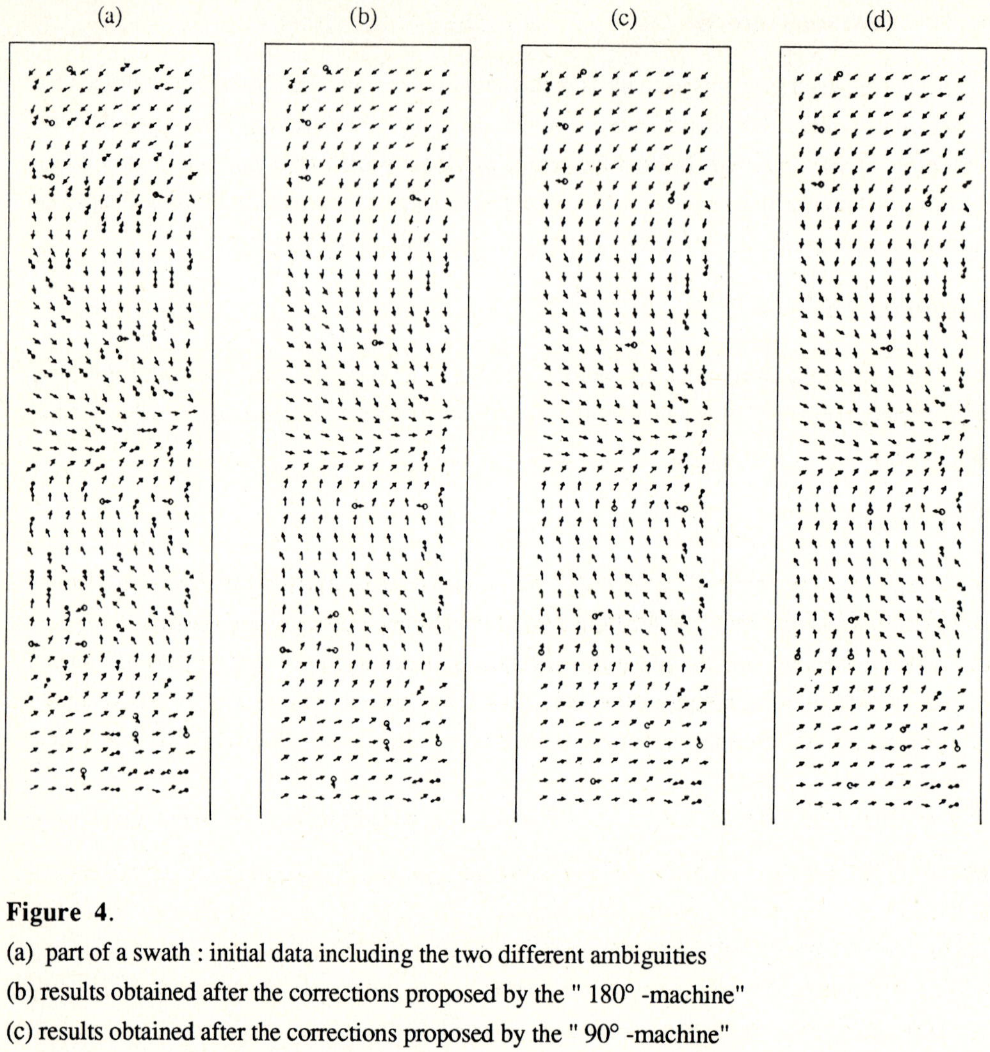

Figure 4.

(a) part of a swath : initial data including the two different ambiguities

(b) results obtained after the corrections proposed by the " 180° -machine"

(c) results obtained after the corrections proposed by the " 90° -machine"

(d) results obtained after the corrections proposed by the second passage of the" 180° -machine" note that the two columns on the right have not been corrected

Detection of microcalcifications in mammographic images

Catherine Bourrely*, Serge Muller**

* Laboratoire de Recherche en Informatique
Bât. 490
Université Paris-Sud, Centre d'Orsay
91405 Orsay, FRANCE

** General Electric CGR
Département Etudes Avancées
Dir. Etudes et Produits Nouveaux
283 rue de la Minière- Z.I. Nord
78530 Buc, FRANCE

Abstract

This paper presents an application of multi-layered networks to medical images analysis. Different architectures of networks are tested for a detection task on mammograms. Their training with the Gradient Back Propagation algorithm is realized on small images extracted from digitized mammograms and labeled according to the presence of microcalcifications amongst the breast parenchyma background structures. The classification performances we obtain demonstrate that an appropriate network architecture for this task should involve local connections, probably combined with shared weights, and also suggest that some adequate pre-processing might lead to more efficient results.

1. Introduction

Microcalcifications are one of the main radiological signs which detection is of great interest in mammograms analysis [4,10]. Since their tiny dimensions (from 10 to 3000 μm) and homology with the surrounding parenchyma heterogeneities make them hardly detectable on a radiological film — even by an experienced observer — it seems appropriate to take advantage of connectionist models abilities in Pattern Recognition [7,3,11] and use a neural network to achieve this detection task on digitized mammographic images.

We intend to train a network to discriminate between two classes of selected patterns: microcalcifications and heterogeneous background structures. A network showing good capabilities for that classification task should perform quite well on an entire mammogram, by labeling the scanning windows containing the microcalcification patterns it previously learned.

The data base we used for training is described in section 2. In section 3 we present various network architectures trained on that base with the Gradient Back Propagation algorithm [5], and display the most interesting results obtained so far.

NATO ASI Series, Vol. F 68
Neurocomputing
Edited by F. Fogelman Soulié and J. Hérault

2. The data

The data base is a set of small images selected in original mammograms of about 2048 x 2048 pixels, digitized on 4096 gray levels [8]. The selected windows have to include either a microcalcification or a part of the breast parenchyma, and must take into account the variable size of microcalcifications, as well as the heterogeneity in shape and density of both structures, so as to be representative of any pattern that may be encountered in an entire mammogram. We thus select 334 windows of 20 x 20 pixels, 163 of them containing a microcalcification and the other 171 showing the background. These labeled data are randomly arranged, and logarithmically processed [9] in order to provide a second data base. The pixels intensities are translated in the [-1,+1] interval in order to fit the sigmoidal transition function used in the G.B.P. algorithm [2]. The raw and log. bases are both divided into two parts: the first 200 examples provide the training set, and the remaining patterns are kept apart to test for generalization.

3. The method and results

Given the data structure, the general architecture of the networks is designed as follows:
- an input layer of 20 x 20 cells, fitted to the 20 x 20 matrices of real numbers
- at least one hidden layer
- an output layer of 2 cells, coding for the class-membership of the input image.

The connections between the layers may be total or local, including shared weights [1,6,11]. Depending on the activity of the two output cells, we define 3 possible class-memberships:
- microcalcification: -1 and +1
- background: +1 and -1
- unknown: any other output

We allow a maximum variation of 0.2 around these desired values. The evolution of the network performances during the training phase is measured by the learning and generalization rates.

After training, we evaluate the network reliability through the following rates:
- <u>correctly-classified patterns:</u>

TP (true-positive rate): microcalcifications classified as microcalcification / total number of microcalcifications

TN (true-negative rate): backgrounds classified as background / total number of backgrounds
- <u>misclassified patterns:</u>

FN (false-negative rate): microcalcifications classified as background / total number of microcalcifications

FP (false-positive rate): backgrounds classified as microcalcification / total number of backgrounds

- non-classified patterns:

NCM: non-classified microcalcifications rate

NCB: non-classified backgrounds rate

The following figures show the classification results we obtained for the 3 types of connection structure we tested, either on raw or log. bases:

network number	type of connection	base
1	total	raw
2	local	raw
3	local	log
4	shared weights	raw

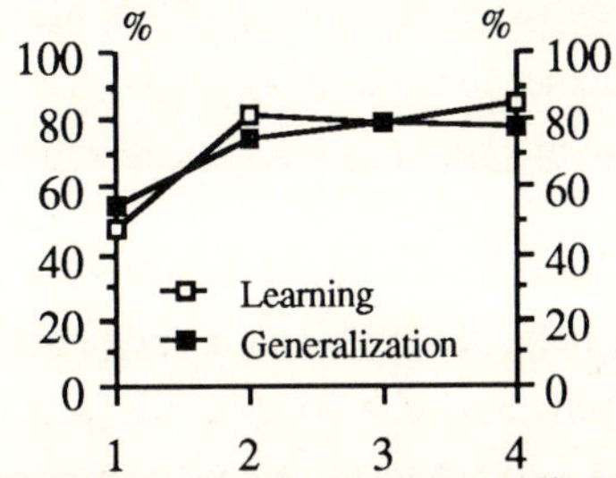

FIGURE 1. learning and generalization rates for networks 1 to 4.

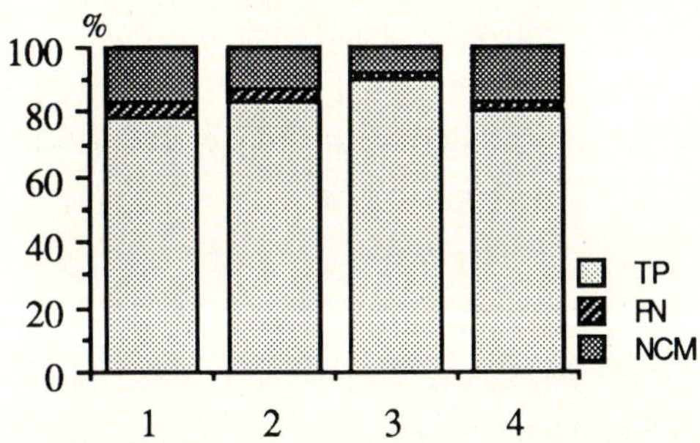

FIGURE 2. classification of microcalcification patterns for networks 1 to 4.

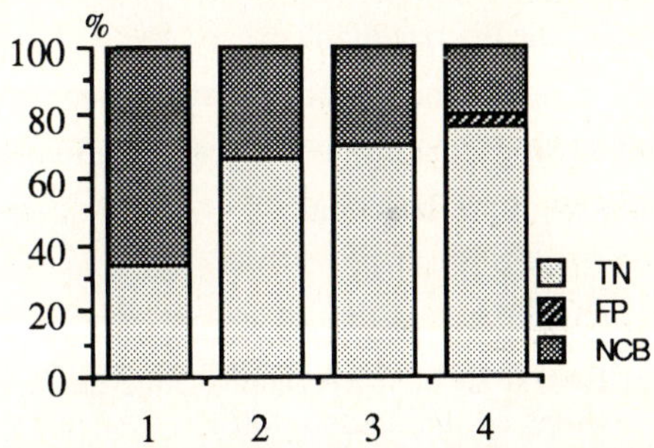

FIGURE 3. classification of background patterns for networks 1 to 4.

4. Discussion

Figure 1 displays for each network (1 to 4) the learning and generalization rates obtained after the training phase was performed. It mainly shows that, in all cases, the learning was successful since the generalization performances always lie very close to the learning ones.

Figures 2 and 3 display more information about generalization performances for classification of microcalcification (fig.2) and background (fig.3) patterns: the rate of correctly-classified microcalcifications (TP) is always larger than 80%, which shows that all networks achieved a good internal representation of this pattern through the learning phase. On the other hand, the recognition of the background pattern seems much more difficult to learn, since the TN rate only reaches from 37% to 75%. Network 4 reaches the highest correct-classification rates (TP and TN) for both patterns at the same time, and the lowest non-classified patterns rate (NCM and NCB). Nevertheless, network 3 allows the best discrimination between the two patterns, since its FN and FP rates are the lowest.

5. Conclusion

Given that our purpose is to build the best microcalcification detection system, we should take advantage of the following observations:

1. the *logarithmic preprocessing* yields better discrimination performances, since it allows a lower confusion between microcalcification and background patterns (and thus a minimal microcalcification oversight);
2. the use of *shared weights* appears to reduce the gap between the two patterns classification performances.

In that extent, we expect an improvement of the system performances by combining a shared weights structure with a simple adequate preprocessing of the data: background patterns should be far better recognized, and for both patterns the non-classified share should totally disappear, with the lowest possible increase in false-negative (and false-positive) rate.

So far, the FN rate didn't exceed 5%; a slight increase in this value wouldn't automatically lead to a failure of the detection system, since one must define a critical FN threshold according to the significance of the microcalcifications frequency in an entire mammogram for the given purpose of the detection.

References

[1] Bottou L. Y.: "Reconnaissance de la parole par réseaux multi-couches", Proc. Neuro-Nîmes 88, EC2 eds (1988).
[2] Bottou L. Y., Le Cun Y.: "SN, un simulateur pour réseaux connexionnistes", Proc. Neuro-Nîmes 88, EC2 eds (1988).
[3] Gorman R. P., Sejnowski T. J.: Analysis of hidden units in a layered network trained to classify sonar targets, Neural networks, vol. 1, n° 1, 75-89, (1988).
[4] Lamarque J. L.: Le Sein, radiodiagnostic clinique, Medsi (1981).
[5] Le Cun Y.: Modèles Connexionnistes de l'Apprentissage, Thesis, Paris (1987).
[6] Le Cun Y.: "Character recognition", unpublished manuscript.
[7] Lehky S. R., Sejnowski T. J.: Extracting curvatures of 3-D objects using a neural network, Soc. for Neuroscience Abstracts, 13, (1987), 1451.
[8] Obellianne C.: Mise au point d'un système connexionniste pour la détection de microcalcifications dans des images mammographiques numérisées. Internal report EHEI (January, 1989).
[9] Rosenfeld A., Kak A. C.: Digital Picture Processing, Academic Press, Vol. 1 (1982).
[10] Tabár L., Dean P. B.: Teaching Atlas of Mammography , Georg Thieme Verlag (1985).
[11] Waibel A., Hanazawa T., Hinton G., Shikano K.: "Phoneme recognition using time-delay neural networks", Tech. Report TR-I-0006, Adv. Telecom. Res. Inst., Japan (1987).

What is a feature, that it may define a character, and a character, that it may be defined by a feature ?

Ethem ALPAYDIN
Laboratoire de microinformatique
Ecole Polytechnique Fédérale de Lausanne
37 Ave. de Cour 1007 Lausanne
Switzerland

We can only do what is possible and proceed from there toward what is desirable.
David Marr

1. Introduction

Whereas artificial neural networks (ANN) provide a powerful scheme for evaluation of multiple simultaneous constraints and inferences, it is not that evident how a given problem, i.e. a conceptual structure, can be mapped on a low-level structure within plausible resource requirements. This is also true in optical character recognition.

Recognition is the mapping of a low-level vector to a high-level concept, for example, mapping bitmaps to characters. If there exists only one low-level reference vector for each concept as in single font recognition, the mapping can be done using nearest neighbor search. The precursor of this work similarly can recognize one font family only [3]. Having a preprocessor that performs size normalization and skeletonization, it is independent of the size of the character image and thickness of strokes. Thanks to a flexible interface, it can rapidly learn a new font family. Experience gained from that system directed the design of a more general one, while keeping intact most of the basic useful characteristics.

2. In defense of the approach

When more than one vector exist to be mapped to the same concept, as in multi-font or handwritten character recognition, they should be closer to each other than any other vector. Formally, the following condition should hold (x, y, and z are low-level vectors, I and J are concepts, MAP(x,I) denotes that x is to be mapped to class I and DISTANCE(x,y) returns the distance between vectors x and y in a measure that makes sense according to their interpretation):

(For all x, for all y, MAP(x,I) and MAP(y,I) and
there does not exist z, MAP(z,J) and (J#I) and
(DISTANCE(x,z) $\leq$ DISTANCE(x,y)) or (DISTANCE(y,z) $\leq$ DISTANCE(x,y))). (1)

NATO ASI Series, Vol. F 68
Neurocomputing
Edited by F. Fogelman Soulié and J. Hérault

In character recognition, size normalization and alignment operations can be applied to make images more similar when viewed from the point of view of individual pixel values and their positions. If (1) does not hold, two possibilities exist, each being a variant :

i) The concept *I* can be divided into two classes, i.e., two units which both correspond to the same concept. For example, having two output units for 'A' for members of two different fonts. This is in fact, Kohonen's Learning Vector Quantization [8].

ii) The second possibility is to change the parameter space, thus changing the distance measure to find one that will satisfy (1). This implies a feature extraction mechanism, thus a multi-layer network. This is the approach taken in the rest of this paper, as (i) can always be equally depicted as another hidden layer.

The idea is that "the 'same' objects --members of the same class-- have more similar features than objects that are not the same" [9]. These features e.g. lines, corners, and meta-features, i.e., features of the features, inter-relations between them; e.g. to-the-left-of, bigger-than, can be used as distance measures in comparison. Besides, "the use of a good set of features is an excellent type of preprocessing ... the great reduction in dimensionality of the stimulus allows the system to discard irrelevant information and eliminate noise, while making later stages simpler and more reliable since they have to cope with less complex inputs" [4]. The two 'b's in fig. 1 when compared as bitmaps are quite different, but same if compared as:

(circle,line,right(circle,line),longer(line,circle),touches(circle,line)).

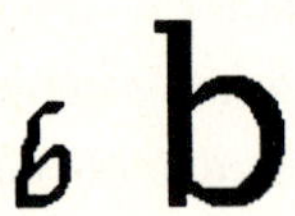

Fig. 1. Two b or not two b.

Such a scheme maps nicely on an ANN where features map to units and meta-features to connections or hidden units depending on the order of the relation. The network carries out a relaxation by simultaneously checking multiple hypotheses using the empirical evidence passed by the input units versus the positive/negative inferences between these various hypotheses. The states of the units evolve in time where highest consistency is achieved between evidence and rules at which point the activations of the output units imply corresponding confidence levels in the possible identities.

The feature idea in the context of character recognition inherently contains the following assumption. The image of a printed character carries contributions from two sources: its universal form, and anything else added in this particular instantiation. The Platonic universal form idea implies that "underneath all 'A's there is just one grand, ultimate abstraction that can be captured in a finitely parametrizable computational structure" [7]. This structure then can be described using features and meta-features as parameters, and all existing 'A's e.g. of fonts, handwritten versions, can be taken as particular examples of the common form "A-ness." During recognition, if program detects these features and meta-features, it will detect the underlying "A-ness" only, ignoring everything that is particular to font or writer, and therefore be able to recognize all 'A's. The rest of the paper lies on the assumption that this is possible.

The difficulty lies in the determination of correct features and meta-features. Algorithms to discover features and the correct order of the relations in between them; learning rules, act by modifying the connection weights once the structure of the network i.e., number of hidden layers, hidden units etc. are specified. The learning algorithm of the Boltzmann machine has the capability of self-structuring in that, from a network with complete connectivity, hidden units when necessary appear and act as required [1]. Incremental learning or self-growing algorithms where the network starts only with the input and output units and add hidden units, i.e. feature detectors, as necessary, are also proposed. The Grow-and-learn algorithm is one-shot using Hebbian rule [2]. Its iterative version has recently been proposed (Mézard, this volume). Both suffer from exponential growth. A second pass after learning to unite certain functions and eliminate insignificant units and links seems necessary.

3. The network model for handwritten numeral recognition

The input to the system is a skeletonized 16*16 bitmap. The first feature detectors are 3*3 masks that are applied to all positions in the bitmap. These masks check for corners, junctions, and short line segments with various orientations. There are altogether 13 of these. The second layer is fed with the features thus detected and try to combine values of neighboring feature detectors as more sophisticated features, e.g. longer lines. These 4*4 features check for 25 partially overlapping zones each returning only one feature which include lines with various orientations, line ends, arcs, corners, and junctions. Feeding to 10 output units, there is an adaptive layer where definition of 10 arabic numerals in terms of these 4*4 features are learned in one-shot by a variant of the Hebbian rule.

The system is implemented on a transputer network to exploit the property of synchronous operation of the processing units. The basic computational characteristic of a neuron i.e. little computation, more I/O, does not map well to the idea of a transputer, i.e. more computation, less I/O. Forking individual processes for individual neurons is not a good idea as they will quickly fill up and slow down the processor due to frequent context switching. Thus, instead of parallelizing each step, we have decided to parallelize the complete task as a pipeline. Each transputer handles one of the phases which are inputting image, 3*3 feature detection, 4*4 feature detection, and recognition, and data are transferred in between as large packets to minimize the time lost for synchronization.

4. Conclusions and future directions

Experience gained from the two systems shown that character recognition cannot be handled just by detecting a bunch of features and some straightforward geometrical relations in between them. What we thought in an ad hoc fashion as features are not sufficient. There are two options. If one insists on a pure parallel bottom-up approach, he should find more detailed features and meta-features to satisfy condition (1). This implies a more sophisticated representation and most possibly such features would be sensible to particular conditions with quite low probabilities of occurrences. They cannot be determined in advance as they depend largely on particular examplars to be learned. In other words, in lower levels there are basic features that are shared by a great number --a distributed representation. Higher up, features get more complicated and less general, more dependent on the examplars --a local representation.

The second option which extends the first, is to sacrifice from a pure parallel feed-forward approach. Sequentiality in decision may be introduced, thus results of previous partial results affect further operations, decreasing search space in time. Division of operation in time, as computational resources can be reused over time implies a need for less and better utilization. The network correspondant of such an idea is a recurrent network, i.e. with internal feedback. A multi-layer network in the form of a processing cone as in the previous option exists but processing is not one-shot. Instead, there is a top-down activation spread for guidance, for hypothesis generation and a bottom-up spread for verification of such hypotheses. The complete network then, relaxes into a state by validating one hypothesis that is most consistent with the external evidence supplied from input units, and the internal rules denoted by connections [5], [6].

Acknowledgements. The author wants to thank P. Buzzi for careful programming. The work is supported by Fonds National Suisse de la Recherche Scientifique.

References

[1] Ackley, D., G. Hinton, and T. Sejnowski (1985). "A learning algorithm for Boltzmann machines," *Cognitive Science*, **9**, 147-169.

[2] Alpaydin, E. (1988). "Grow-and-learn network," *EPFL-LAMI, Internal note*, September 1988.

[3] Alpaydin, E. and P. Marchal (in press). "Snark, a neural optical reader," to appear in *Proc. of Connectionism in Perspective*, Zurich, Switzerland October 1988.

[4] Anderson, J., J. Silverstein, S. Ritz, and R. Jones (1977). "Distinctive features, categorical perception, and probability learning: some applications of a neural model," *Psychological Review*, **84**, 413-451.

[5] Fukushima, K. (1988). "Neocognitron: a hierarchical network capable of visual pattern recognition," *Neural Networks*, **1**, 119-130.

[6] Grossberg, S. (1988). "Nonlinear neural networks: principles, mechanisms, and architectures," *Neural Networks*, **1**, 17-62.

[7] Hofstadter, D. (1985). *Metamagical themas*, New York: Basic books.

[8] Kohonen, T. (1984). *Self-organization and associtative memory*, Berlin: Springer.

[9] Marr, D. (1982). *Vision*, San Francisco: Freeman.

A STUDY OF IMAGE COMPRESSION WITH BACKPROPAGATION

M. Mougeot* **, R. Azencott, B. Angeniol*.**

* Thomson-CSF
1 rue des mathurins
F. 92223 Bagneux

** Laboratoire Mathématiques appliquées
U.A. 743 du C.N.R.S.
Universite Paris Sud
F. 91405 Orsay

Abstract:

Backpropagation is one possible algorithm used to achieve image compression with a multi-layer neural net [1] . Associated with a quadratic cost function in a linear case, it is nothing but an indirect way to compress images with the Karhunen-Loève method [2] . So, in this case, this algorithm brings no improvement. However, the knowledge of the optimal solution helps us to study in detail, how the backpropagation algorithm solves the compression problem. We show that the convergence of the learning process can be accelerated by setting some constraints on the weights. The error function is then minimized for an unique value around which it is strictly convex.

In order to improve the visual appearance of restored images, we use the same algorithm associated to other cost functions (p-Hölder norms). Unlike the quadratic case, the theoretical optimal solution for the p-Hölder norms ($p \neq 2$) is not known, and backpropagation is shown to provide a relevant tool to compute the optimal solution.

1. Description of the neural net:

The neural net has three layers of respectively n,p and n cells ($p<n$). The first matrix of weights (A) performs the image compression, the second one (B) the image restoration on the output layer. Let X represents the image

$$X = (x_{ij}) \qquad 1 \le i \le n \quad 1 \le j \le N$$

Figure 1.

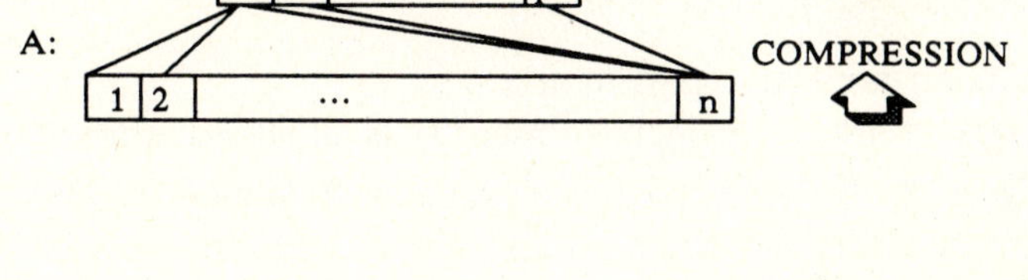

NATO ASI Series, Vol. F 68
Neurocomputing
Edited by F. Fogelman Soulié and J. Hérault

2. Analysis of the optimal weights:

The quadratic error function used is : $E_2^2 = \sum_{j=1}^{N} \sum_{i=1}^{n} (x_{ij} - y_{ij})^2$

where (y_{ij}) represents the computed output for example j.

After convergence, figure 2 shows that the weights are not well organized and do not extract salient features as the ones obtained through Karhunen–Loève do. Backpropagation does not decorrelate the data in the middle layer. The middle cells values, which are a compressed representation of the input vector, have all the same importance. Therefore , we can not hope to use an adaptive code, to improve the compression, as for the Karhunen–Loève method. These results are representative for lots of images.

Figure 2.

Representation of the optimal weights for 5 middle cells : the karhunen–Loève method

Matrix A:

Representation of the optimal weights computed with backpropagation. (7 grey levels)

Matrix A:

3. A significant decrease in convergence time:

The convergence of the learning process can be accelerated by setting some constraints on the weights. After the linear learning phase, at the optimal solution, the two matrices of weights A and B verifie : $BA = UU^*$

U is a (n,p) matrix formed by the first p normalized eigenvectors of XX^* associated with the eigenvalues $\lambda 1 \geq \lambda 2 \geq \ldots \geq \lambda p$

So, to solve the compression problem with backpropagation in auto–association mode, we just have to code U and U^* in the neural net weight matrices [2] :

$$B = U T^{-1} \qquad A = T U^*$$

where T is an arbitrary (p,p) matrix.

T (T different from the identity matrix) is obtained when backpropagation minimizes the quadratic cost function. T gives a weights solution always different from identity.

We prove that the hessien matrix has p^2 zero eigenvalues, at the optimal solution. We decide to constrain p^2 weights during the gradient descent, so that $A = [Ip \mid A']$

Let note $U^* = [V \mid W]$ where V is a (p,p) matrix. We suppose that V is invertible. (This was always verified with the pictures we tested)
The optimal solution obtained with backpropagation is then unique:

$$B=UV \text{ and } A=V^{-1}U^*$$

The surface near the optimal solution is then convex [3]. This constrained back-propagation finds very quickly the optimal solution (figure 3). The convergence is then largely accelerated.

Figure 3. Image compression using an auto-association network : Convergence comparison of
0 standard and
• constrained backpropagation :

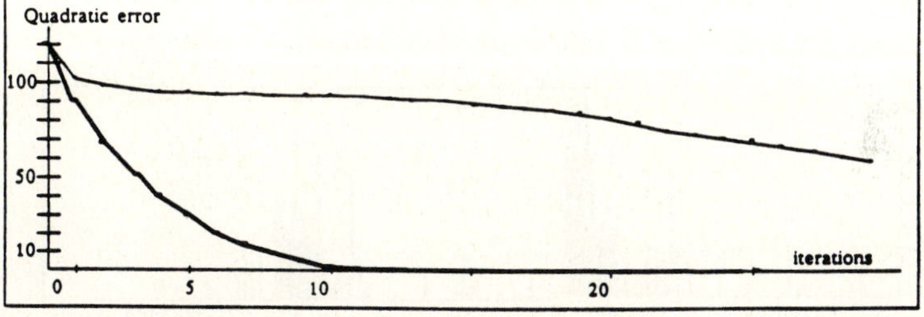

4. Using other error functions to improve restoration:

We want to improve the restoration quality for a compressed and subsequently restored image, without decreasing the compression rate. Classically, a mean square criterion E_2 is used to objectively measure the difference between the original and reconstructed images. Backpropagation tends to minimize this quadratic deviation. Unfortunately, the mean square error spreads degradations all over the image.

We find other error functions that are able to "hide" the local errors generated by compression, in places, where they cannot be seen easily. For that purpose, we use p–Hölder norms (norm Lp) instead of the quadratic error function, to compress images with backpropagation (3).

$$E_p^{\,p} = \sum_{j=1}^{N}\sum_{i=1}^{n} | x_{ij} - y_{ij} |^p \qquad p>=1$$

The computation of the gradient with a p–Hölder norm is not any harder than the computation with a quadratic error.The gradient is computed locally, as for the quadratic error (p=2). We are working here with a transition function equal to identity (linear case).

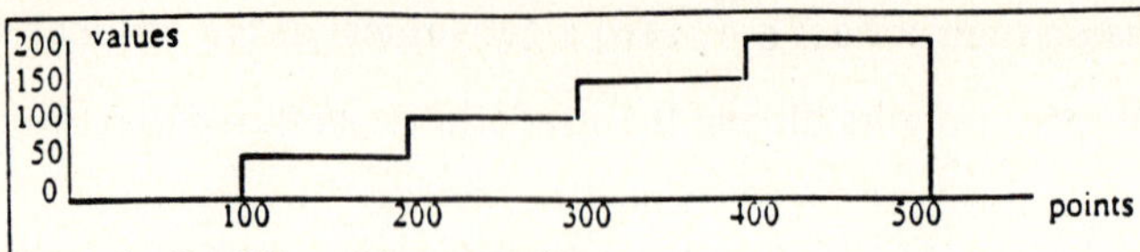

Figure 4. Signal S1, used for compression.

In order to decide which p–Hölder norm is more appropriate, we compute, for a given compression rate, the optimal encoding of a signal S1 (figure 4) for different values of p, with backpropagation. We can then compare the quality of the different reconstructed images produced (figure 5 and 6).

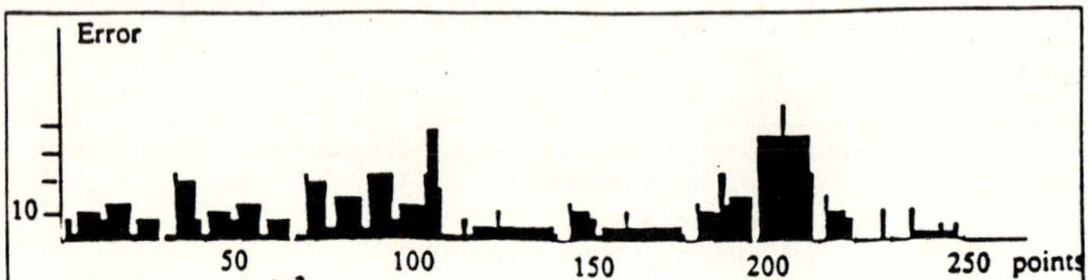

Figure 5. p=2
Absolute difference between the original and restored signals S1.

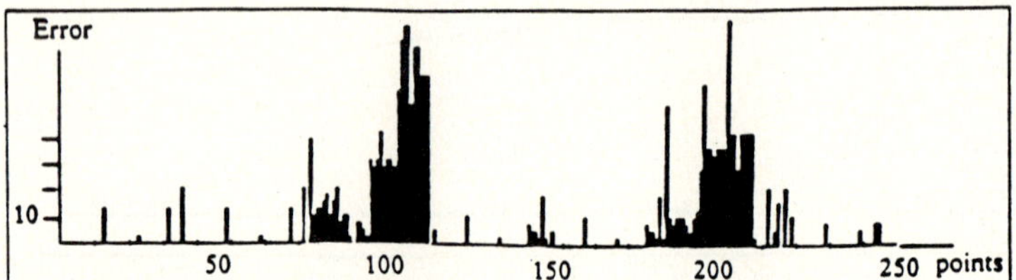

Figure 6. p=1
Absolute differences between the original and restored signals S1.

Figures 5,6 only sketch the first 250 points of the signals. We just want to point out the differences between uniform regions and regions containing steps. We find that the results are quite improved by the case of the L1 norm:
the degradations are much around the steps, (figures 5 and 6), but in uniform areas, we observe almost perfect restoration, and a few peaks. Least square minimization tends to lead to smooth errors. On the other hand, the L1 norm criterion favours spiky and sparse solutions. In the case of the Lp norm, $1<=p<=2$, values close to 1 produce more spiky solutions than those closer to 2.
The differences illustrated in the previous pictures are confirmed if we compute the quadratic energies of the difference between the restored and original signals.

[1] G. Cottrell, P. Munro, D. Zipser. Image compression by backpropagation: An example of extensional programming. In N.E. Sharkey (Ed). Advances in Cognitive science (Vol. 3). Norwood, NJ : Ablex.

[2] H. Bourlard, Y. Kamp. Autoassociation by multilayer perceptrons and singular values decomposition. Manuscript 217. Philips research laboratory. Brussels. November 87.

[3] P. Baldi, K. Hornik. Neural Network and Principal Component Analysis. Learning from examples without local minima. 1988. preprint.

Distortion Invariant Image Recognition by Madaline and Back-Propagation Learning Multi-Networks

V. Cruz, G. Cristobal, T.Michaux, S. Barquin

Laboratorio de I.A.Facultad de Informática,
Campus de Montegancedo s/n. Boadilla del Monte
28660 Madrid. SPAIN.

Abstract

In this paper, a new model which permits visual patterns to be invariant to affine transforms (translations, rotations and dimensions) is presented.

After the training process, this system is able to extract the generalized invariant image from an arbitrary picture and recover the input image without distortions.

I. Introduction

Automatic image recognition has been considered an area of special interest for over thirty years. The extraction of invariant patterns in varying positions, orientations and dimensions, would lead to the development of more robust and flexible systems.

We can find a first aproximation to solve this problem in the MADALINE neural network proposed by B. Widrow et al. [1,2]. A MADALINE neural network is a multilayer fully connected net with many hidden layers. The main property of these nets is that, when an input pattern is presented, the output pattern is invariant to certain distortions. The learning rule is based on the LMS algorithm for recovering the input pattern from the MADALINE network output. The LMS is appropriate for patterns with low dimensionality, but its computational requirements rise exponentially when increasing the size of the input pattern.

One other interesting method has been proposed by D. Zipser et al. [3] as an extensional programming model for solving the image compression problem. This technique is based on the back-propagation algorithm developed by Rumelhart et al. [4]. A multilayer neural network fully connected with a hidden layer is used. The supervised network learning procedure requires labeled training data representing the function to be learnt. The training algorithm operates by adjusting the weights between the elements of the network in such a way as to

NATO ASI Series, Vol. F 68
Neurocomputing
Edited by F. Fogelman Soulié and J. Hérault

reduce the overall error in the output. Zipser et al. [3] use the internal representation of the input pattern (from the hidden units) to solve the image compression problem. They show the representation of images in an efficient format by neuronlike computing elements, recovering the input image from the intermediate representation using a decodification function and a neural net trained by back-propagation. The problem is that the intermediate image is not invariant to input picture distortions.

The system proposed here is a multilayer neural network that uses combined features from both neural nets explained above (the invariant extraction of the MADALINE nets and the recovering capabilities of the Zipser model). This system is able to recover an undistorted image from a distorted input.

First, MADALINE neural networks are used in a preprocessing step. These networks are extensions of those proposed by Widrow et al. [1,2]. On the other hand, a fully connected neural network with a hidden layer is used to recover the original picture from the invariant image obtained as output of the MADALINE nets. We use networks of simple neuronlike processing units connected by links of random weights. The units communicate by passing real-valued activations across the links. The network is arranged in layers, with the outer layers corresponding to input and output, and activation only passing one way through the network. The back-propagation algorithm is used as the supervision learning scheme for the network.

II. System Architecture

An input image to the system is defined as a discretized NxN light intensity function f(x,y), where x and y correspond to the spatial coordinates within the image, and f(x,y) is the gray level range from 0 to 2^k-1. In this study, the image size selected was 256x256 pixels quantized into 256 gray levels. Let us consider a frame as a window of MxM pixels taken from an image of NxN pixels with $M<N$. Frames used in this paper have 16x16 pixels.

The system proposed (Fig. 2) is divided into three subsystems:

- Preprocessing subsystem. This contains two steps :

Step 1.- The invariants of the frames from the original image are obtained using a MADALINE neural network.
Step 2.- The generalized invariant image is obtained using a MADALINE net.

- Processing subsystem. A multilayer neural network trained by the back-propagation algorithm is used. The relationship between the generalized invariant and the invariants of the picture without distortions is established.

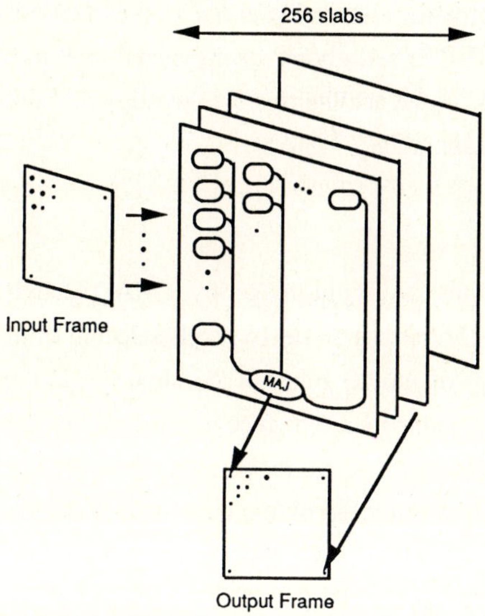

Figure 1- MADALINE neural nets invariant to distortions used in the preprocessing of the input picture

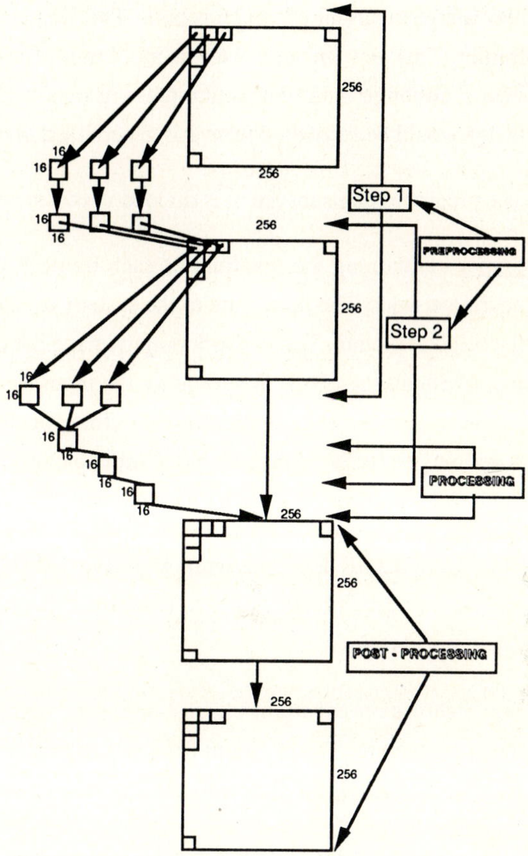

Figure 2 - Schematic diagram of the system

- Post-processing subsystem. This step gives a reordination to obtain the input picture without distortions.

A. Preprocessing Subsystem

The computational requirements in order to process an invariant image of 256x256 pixels leads to a large effort in a conventional serial computer. In this case 65536 slabs of 65536 ADALINE cells would be needed, requiring a storage space for the weight matrices of 10^{13} MB. of memory.

To avoid it, we divided the preprocessing subsystem in two steps. First, all the 16x16 frames from the original image are presented as input of a MADALINE network, obtaining their invariants step by step. Second, for each invariant frame a characteristic value is obtained and a new image invariant of 16x16 is built. This image contains information about all the invariant frames. This new image is used as input to a MADALINE net, giving a generalized invariant image, although the input picture presents distortions. In the next subsystem the original input image would be recovered from this generalized invariant image.

The preprocessing subsystem is divided in two steps:

Step 1.- Obtaining the invariant of each frame from the real input image, by a MADALINE neural network. The input data to the system are the 256 frames of 16x16 pixels selected from the original picture. The network output image consists of another frame of the same size as the input with all the pixels invariant to the input frame distortions. The recovery process of the frames requires less computational effort for 16x16 frames. Moreover, for generalizing purposes, the recovery process of the input picture only would need to find the relation between the weight matrices in the preprocessing step.

The MADALINE neural network will have 256 slabs of 256 ADALINE cells. 256 matrices of weights are used for the upper left-hand corner of each slab $W_1, W_2, W_3, \ldots W_{256}$ with values randomly chosen.

Fig. 3 shows the invariant images obtained from an image and two different shifts images of the same picture. The invariant frames that build the invariant image are the same in the three pictures. However, the situations are different for the three images according to the input image translation.

Step 2.- Obtaining the generalized invariant . The output image of Step 1 has its frames invariant, but the picture obtained still has distortions. It is necessary to obtain an invariant image from this picture of invariant frames. A MADALINE neural network with only one slab per frame is used for this purpose. In this way, from an input frame of 16x16 pixels a single output value would be obtained. With these values we build up a 16x16 input image for a MADALINE net. The MADALINE net of Step 1 is used to obtain an output image of 16x16 pixels : the generalized invariant image.

The first step in the preprocessing system, would be appropriate as a first computational process in the study of the stereoscopic vision and motion detection. This computational visual model yield an invariant extraction in incremental levels of processing, according to the biological hierarchical models proposed in the literature [5].

B. Processing Subsystem

The output of the preprocessing subsystem will be the input of the processing subsystem. From this input image of 16x16 pixels, the processing subsystem computes the characteristic image values of the invariant frames without distortions.

A multilayer neural net with a hidden layer is used. The network architecture with 256 input cells, 256 hidden cells and 256 output cells is trained using the back-propagation algorithm. This training procedure relates the generalized invariant image, and the invariant image of the real input picture without distortions.

The learning process is supervised. First, a real image without distortions is set as input to the system. The preprocessed picture is computed. The processing step gives the image that contains the characteristic values of the invariant frames. This image was obtained in the first part of the second step in the preprocessing subsystem. If an undistorted image is introduced to the system, the input image to the process subsystem is the same. Therefore, the output of the processing subsystem is the same.

The achievement of this subsystem is to build a neural net that relates the generalized invariant of a given input image with the characteristic values of the invariant frames of this image without distortions. It is proved experimentally that a neural net like this can be obtain the real image from a coded image and generalize for other pictures [3]. Here the coded image is the generalized invariant image and the output is the image of the characteristic values of the invariant frames.

C. Post-processing Subsystem

The output of the last step gives us the clues to obtain an undistorted image from a distorted picture. That image of 16x16 pixels has the characteristic values of the invariant frames of the input picture to the system only if that input image has no distortions. If the input image has distortions its invariant frames are the same, but are distributed in different order as can be seen in Fig. 3. If the output image of Step 2 in the preprocessing subsystem is compared with the input image to this subsystem, it is possible to reorder the invariant images frames in order to obtain the invariant image frames of the input picture without distortions.

A 256x256 image is built for the invariant frames of the input picture to the system without distortions. This image is used (frame to frame) as input to a multilayer neural net trained by the back-propagation algorithm. This neural net has 256 input cells, 126 hidden cells and 256 output cells. The weight matrices are randomly chosen.The goal of this multilayer net is to find the relation between and image and its invariants, that is, the inverse application of a MADALINE network. Because of the MADALINE network used in the preprocessing step works always with the same weight matrices (once initialized randomly) , the multilayer neural net used in this subsystem can generalize for every input image.

III. Simulation Results

Figure 4 shows the whole process for a given picture presented three times with different distortions. First the invariant images frames are computed, obtaining three pictures of 256x256 pixels. The generalized invariant images are obtained in the second preprocessing step. These generalized images are the same for the three pictures. The output of the processing step is just the characteristic values of the invariant frames in the first picture (the picture without distortions). The reordering of the invariant frames gives the same result for the three test pictures. The output image is quite similar to the input image without distortions in the three cases.

Several test image have been computed, and the evaluation of the results shows that the global invariant features have a similar shape in the standard image case (Lena, cameraman, etc.). The learning procedure and the generalization for solving images with close global invariants require less computational effort in comparison with the general case of images without perceptual similarity. In this way, this kind of architecture would be appropriate for military (target recognition invariant to distortions), medical and robotics applications. Further research is being pursued in order to extend the kind of distortions (blur, motion, etc.), for restoration purposes. Also this kind of model would be appropriate for stereoscopic vision research and motion detection.

IV. References

[1] Widrow, B. et al.: Layered Neural Nets for Pattern Recognition, IEEE Trans. on ASSP, 36, 7, 1109-1118 (1988)

[2] Widrow, B., Winter, R.: Neural Nets for Adaptive Filtering and Adaptive Pattern Recognition", IEEE Computer, 21, 3, 25-39 (1988)

[3] Cottrell, G. et al.: Image Compression by Back-Propagation. An Example of Extensional Programming, Tech. Rep. 8702, U.C. San Diego, Institute for Cognitive Science (1987)

[4] Rumelhart, D.E., McClelland, J.L. (eds.): Parallel Distributed Processing, MIT Press, Cambridge, Mass. (1986)

[5] Marr, D.:Representing Visual Information. In: Hanson, A., Riseman, E.M. (eds.) Computer Vision System. Academic Press, New York, 61-80 (1978)

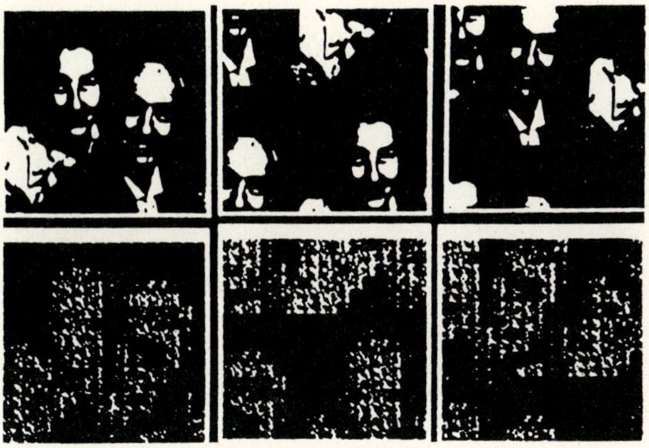

Figure 3 Invariant images (below left) from the original image (above left) and the corresponding invariants (bellow middle and right) from two different shift images (above middle and right)

Figure 4 General process corresponding to a given picture (top-left) and two different shift images (middle and bottom left). The output of the system is presented at right

AN ALGORITHM FOR OPTICAL FLOW

E.De Micheli, G.Radonich [+], S.Uras & V.Torre
Dipartimento di Fisica
Via Dodecaneso, 33
16146 Genova
Italy

1 - INTRODUCTION

The analysis of time-varying image sequences is a classical problem of machine vision (Aggarwal & Nandhakumar, 1988; Ullman, 1979), but is likely to be very useful in robotics, passive navigation and several other fields. Two major approaches have been proposed for the analysis of image sequences: one based on differential techniques aims at computing a dense optical flow, and the other recovers the displacement of selected tokens on the images, by tracking tokens from one image to the next one.

In this paper we present a general approach to the problem, which is based on the computation of optical flow obtained by a procedure similar to that proposed by Girosi, Verri & Torre (1989), which also utilizes procedures of tracking tokens from one image to another. By exploiting mathematical properties of the 2D motion field (Verri, Girosi & Torre, 1989) several 3D motion parameters, such as *time-to-collision* and angular velocity, can be recovered with a precision which is dependent on the image texture. The computed optical flow can also be used to track, in the sequence edge segments, from one image to the next thus greatly improving the information which can be extracted from an image sequence. The optical flow is also useful in obtaining good segmentation of the changing image in areas where different motions occur and in order to recover a coarse depth map. This paper, which is a continuation of previous work (Verri et al 1989; Girosi et al 1989), aims at presenting different experimental results, which appear to prove that the proposed approach for the analysis of time varying images is practical and useful. The major application that has been considered is in the vision system of a robot moving in indoor scenes.

[+] Istituto per la Ricerca Scientifica e Tecnologica, 38050 Povo, Trento, Italy

NATO ASI Series, Vol. F 68
Neurocomputing
Edited by F. Fogelman Soulié and J. Hérault

2 - THE COMPUTATION OF OPTICAL FLOW

When an opaque object is moving in front of an artificial or a biological eye, it defines a 3D velocity field $\vec{V} = (V_x, V_y, V_z)$ in the space where in an appropriate system of reference $\vec{V} = \vec{V}(\vec{R})$ and $\vec{R} = (R_x, R_y, R_z)$ possibly solid to the image plane of the eye. Because of the imaging device, the 3D velocity field $\vec{V}$ is transformed into a 2 motion field $\vec{v} = (v_x, v_y)$ on the image plane (Verri et al. 1989). The available information, however, is not for the 2D motion field $\vec{v}$, but for the scalar field $E(x,y,t)$ of the image brightness at location (x,y) on the image plane at time t. By optical flow we mean any 2D vector field derived from $E(x,y,t)$ which is close to the 2D motion field $\vec{v} = (v_x, v_y)$. It is therefore evident that many different optical flows exist and have different properties and behaviour.

2.1 - OPTICAL FLOW AND 2D MOTION FIELD

It has recently been shown (Girosi, et al.1989) that optical flow $\vec{u} = (u_x, u_y)$ computed as:

$$\vec{u} = -H^{-1} \frac{\partial}{\partial t} \text{grad } E \tag{2.1}$$

where the 2x2 matrix H is the Hessian of $E(x,y,t)$ or

$$H = \begin{pmatrix} \dfrac{\partial^2 E}{\partial x^2} & \dfrac{\partial^2 E}{\partial x \partial y} \\ \dfrac{\partial^2 E}{\partial x \partial y} & \dfrac{\partial^2 E}{\partial y^2} \end{pmatrix} \tag{2.2}$$

$\text{grad } E = \left(\dfrac{\partial^2 E}{\partial x \partial t}, \dfrac{\partial^2 E}{\partial y \partial t} \right)$, is related to the 2D velocity field $\vec{v}$, by the equation:

$$\vec{u} = \vec{v} + H^{-1} \left(J\, \vec{v}^{\,T} \cdot \text{grad } E - \text{grad } \frac{dE}{dt} \right) \tag{2.3}$$

where $J\, \vec{v}^{\,T}$ is the Jacobian of $\vec{v}$

$$J\, \vec{v}^{\,T} = \begin{pmatrix} \dfrac{\partial v_x}{\partial x} & \dfrac{\partial v_x}{\partial y} \\ \dfrac{\partial v_y}{\partial x} & \dfrac{\partial v_y}{\partial y} \end{pmatrix} \tag{2.4}$$

where $\dfrac{dE}{dt} = \vec{v} \cdot \text{grad } E + \dfrac{\partial E}{\partial t}$ is the total derivative of the image brightness $E(x,y,t)$. Equation (2.3), which is simply an identity, indicates that:

a) whenever $\frac{dE}{dt}$ and $J\,\vec{v}^{\,T}$ are bounded, then the optical flow $\vec{u}$ will approach to the true 2D motion field $\vec{v}$ when the entries of the matrix H^{-1} are small. Since $\frac{dE}{dt}$ and $J\,\vec{v}^{\,T}$ are likely to be bounded with the exception of those points near object boundaries or motion discontinuities, we can determine whether the computed optical flow $\vec{u}$ is close to $\vec{v}$ by simply evaluating H^{-1}. It is evident that the entries of H^{-1} will be small whenever the two eingenvalues λ_1 and λ_2 of the symmetric matrix H are large.

An inspection of equation (2.1), from which the optical flow is derived, shows that:

b) Numerical stability of the computation of optical flow is guaranteed whenever the inversion of the matrix H is numerically stable. This last condition is fulfilled when det H is large and the conditioning number C_H of H is close to 1 (Lanczos, 1961). Since the matrix H is symmetric, we have that $C_H = |\frac{\lambda_{max}}{\lambda_{min}}|$ where λ_{max} and λ_{min} are the two real eingenvalues of H with largest and smallest absolute value.

By a simple inspection of conditions a) and b) we see that det H large and $C_H \sim 1$ imply both numerical stability in the computation of $\vec{u}$ and similarity between optical flow $\vec{u}$ and 2D motion field $\vec{v}$. Consequently, when det H is large and $C_H \sim 1$ an optical flow is obtained, which is numerically stable and almost correct.

Fig. 1. Four frames of a box translating towards the camera in front of a fixed background. Each image was composed by 256x256 pixels and was acquired with a PULNIX TM46 camera and digitized by an Imaging Technology FG100 board.

2.2 LINEAR FILTERING

Fig. 1 illustrates 4 frames in which a box is translating towards the camera in front of a fixed background. Fig. 2A reproduces the optical flow on a 60x60 grid obtained from the image sequence of Fig. 1 by using equation (3.1). Many vectors with an inconsistent direction or magnitude are present, and the simplest way to remove these erroneous vectors is to smooth the flow of Fig. 2A, by linear filtering.

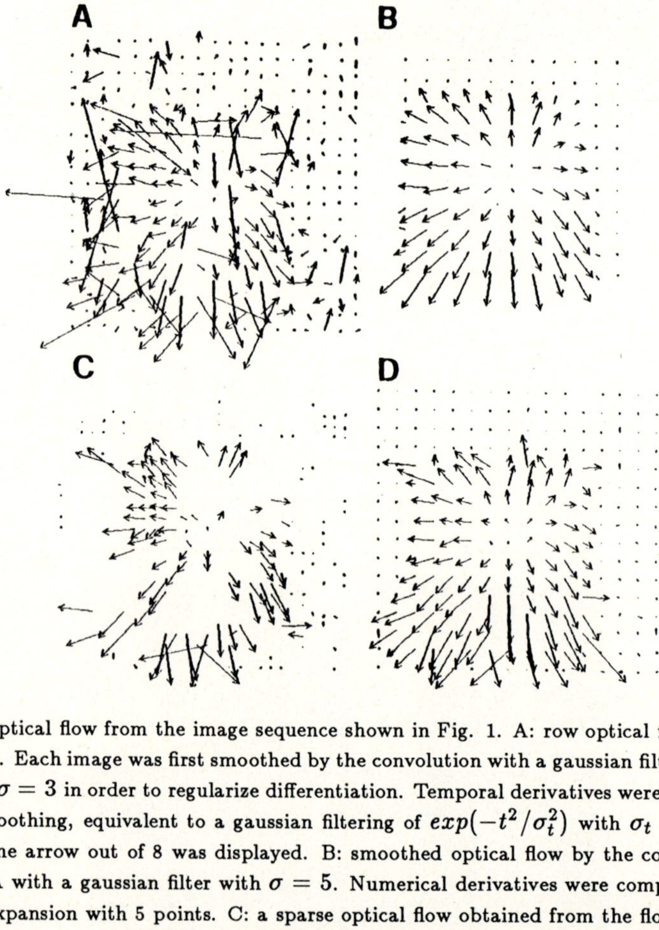

Fig. 2. Optical flow from the image sequence shown in Fig. 1. A: row optical flow obtained by solving eq.(3.1). Each image was first smoothed by the convolution with a gaussian filter $exp(-(x^2+y^2)/\sigma^2)$ with $\sigma = 3$ in order to regularize differentiation. Temporal derivatives were computed using a temporal smoothing, equivalent to a gaussian filtering of $exp(-t^2/\sigma_t^2)$ with $\sigma_t = 1$. For better visualization one arrow out of 8 was displayed. B: smoothed optical flow by the convolution of the flow of Fig. 2A with a gaussian filter with $\sigma = 5$. Numerical derivatives were computed by using a Taylor series expansion with 5 points. C: a sparse optical flow obtained from the flow of Fig. 2A by choosing those vectors with det H > 0.3 and $C_H < 5$. D: filling-in and interpolation of the sparse optical flow of Fig. 2C. The filling-in procedure recursively expands the mean value of the sparse optical flow, computed in the 3×3 neighborhood of the running point, into the empty regions until the difference between $\frac{\partial E}{\partial t}$ computed in two close points becomes greater than 20%. The left empty regions are then filled linearly interpolating the values of the region boundary.

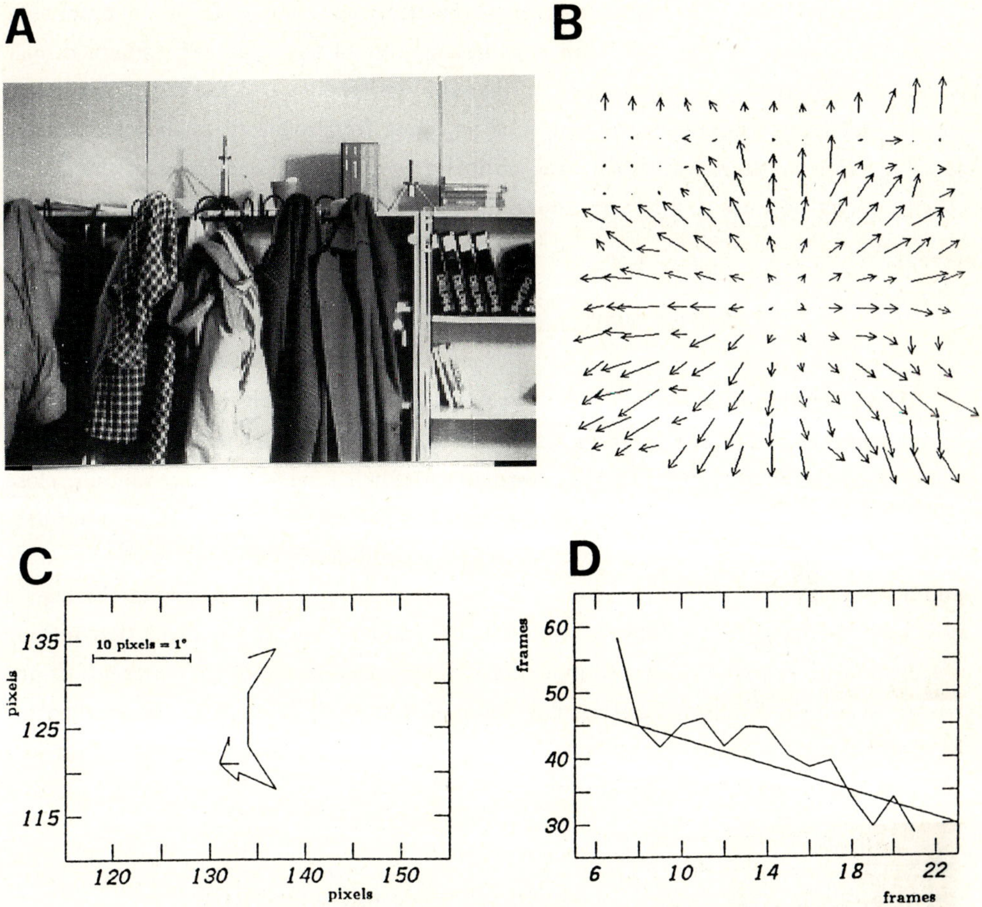

Fig. 3. Recovery of optical flow of a pure translation. A: an image of an office in IRST. The image sequence was composed by 27 frames. The displacement of the camera between each acquired frame was about 5 cm, and it was obtained sliding the camera on the rail of an optical bench. B: the smoothed optical flow relative to a frame of the sequence of Fig. 3A. The optical flow was computed as described in Fig. 2. C: the localization of the focus of expansion of the optical flow obtained from the image sequence of Fig. 3A. The focus of expansion (i.e. the singular point) of the flow was located as the intersection on the image plane of the two curves $u_x = 0$ and $u_y = 0$. The focal length of the camera was 8 mm and the width of a pixel was 0.014 mm so an angular displacement of 1 degree corresponds to a displacement on the image plane of about 10 pixels. D: comparison with the true *time-to-collision* (straight line) and the computed *time-to-collision* (polygonal line). The *time-to-collision* at each frame was computed as described in the text.

The optical flow of Fig. 2B has been obtained by convolving the two components of the optical flow of Fig. 2A with a gaussian filter of the type $e^{\frac{x^2}{\sigma^2}}$ where $\sigma = 3$ pixels. The filtered optical flow (see Fig. 2B) appears smooth and has a singular point, which is a focus of expansion, as would be expected from a pure translation (Verri et al 1989). It is clear, however, that the optical flow near the boundaries of the box is clearly wrong because it shows an apparent motion of the fixed background.

2.3 NON LINEAR FILTERING

The erroneous apparent motion introduced by the linear filtering can be removed by appropriate non-linear filtering. It is possible to select only those vectors, which are likely to be correct, because they were obtained when det H is large and C_H close to 1. By using this procedure the sparse optical flow, shown in Fig. 2C, is obtained. A dense optical flow can easily be obtained by a combination of a filling-in procedure and a linear interpolation. By using the procedure explained in details in the legend of Fig. 2, the dense optical flow of Fig. 2D is obtained. It is now evident that motion discontinuities are well preserved and no clearly erroneous vectors are present. If one wishes to use the computed optical flow for a further analysis, such as the localization of singular points, a final smoothing step may be useful in order to clearly evidentiate the location of the focus of expansion.

3 - THE RECOVERY OF MOTION PARAMETERS

The obvious test of any procedure for motion analysis is the comparison between 3D motion parameters directly measured with those recovered from the analysis of the image sequence. Here we discuss the recovery of 3D motion parameters in two special, but pratically relevant cases: pure translation and pure rotation.

It has been shown elsewhere (Verri et al 1989) that in the case of pure translation the 2D motion field has, at most, one singular point, which is a focus and does not change its location on the image plane with time. Moreover if P_T is the singular point the *time-to-collision* between the image plane and the point projected into P_T is simply $1/\lambda$, where λ is the eingenvalue of P_T, or more precisely the eingenvalue of the matrix

$$M = J\,\vec{v}|_{P_T} \tag{3.1}$$

In the case of a pure axial rotation, the angular velocity ω is simply

$$\omega^2 = \det M = \det J\ \vec{v}|_{P_R} \tag{3.2}$$

where P_R is the immobile point of the pure rotation (Verri et al 1989).

In this section we present experimental results showing that whenever there is enough texture in the image (or more precisely when a significant portion of points in the image has a large value for det H and a conditioning number C_H close to 1) the computed optical flow is adequate for a reliable recovery of *time-to-collision* and angular velocity. When very few features are present in the image the computed optical flow does not provide a good estimate of 3D motion parameters, but it is still able to efficiently drive the tracking of edge segments.

3.1 TIME TO COLLISION

Fig. 3A illustrates an image taken in an office while the camera was translating on a rail of an optical bench. During the camera translation 27 images were taken, the camera being displaced by 5 cm each time. From this sequence of 27 images a sequence of 15 optical flows was obtained, one of which is shown in Fig. 3B. The optical flows were obtained following the procedure explained in section 2 (see legend of Fig. 2 for further details). In each computed optical flow the singular point P_T was located and its eingenvalues computed. In Fig. 3C the location of P_T in pixel coordinates for each optical flow is reproduced. P_T moves around the average location (133, 124) by at most 10 pixels, corresponding to a fluctuation in the direction of translation of about one degree. Fig. 3D reproduces a comparison with the true *time-to-collision* (straight line) with the computed *time-to-collision* (points connected by straight segments). The comparison between the computed and directly measured 3D motion parameters is satisfactory. Better results are obtained for more textured scenes, but the method is not satisfactory for scenes with little texture.

3.2 ANGULAR VELOCITY

Fig. 4A reproduces an image of some objects placed on a platform, which was rotated by 5 degrees between each image acquisition. The computed optical flow, shown in Fig. 4B, shows a singular point, which appears as a center as expected from

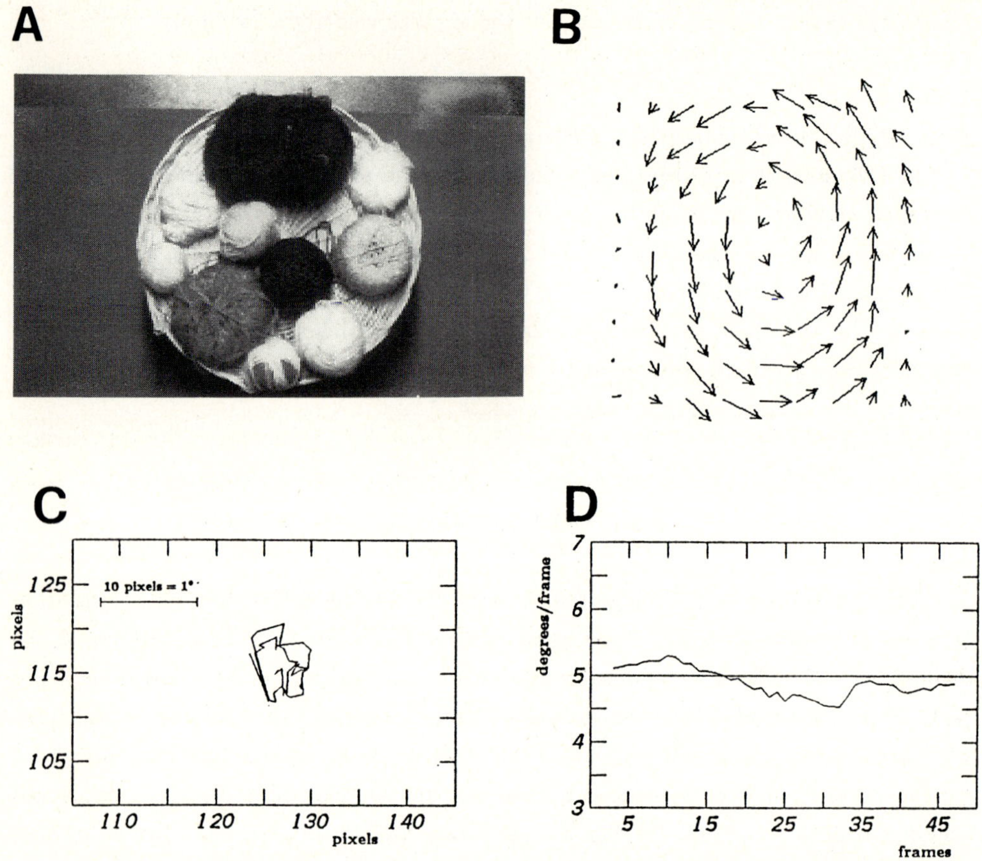

Fig. 4. Recovery of optical flow of a pure rotation. A: an image of a sequence composed by 50 frames. The camera viewed from above pointing towards a rotating platform, on which different objects were mounted. The platform was rotated by 5 degrees between each frame. B: the smoothed optical flow relative to the image of the sequence. The optical flow was computed as described in Fig. 2. C: the localization of the immobile point of the optical flow obtained from the image sequence of Fig. 4A. The immobile point (i.e. the singular point) of the flow was located as the intersection on the image plane of the two curves $u_x = 0$ and $u_y = 0$. D: comparison with the true angular velocity (straight line) and the computed angular velocity (polygonal line). The angular velocity at each frame was computed using the technique described in the text.

an axial rotation (Verri et al 1989). The trajectories appear elliptical because of the distortion introduced by the different horizontal and vertical width of the pixel, which was not corrected. Fig. 4C and 4D reproduce the location of the singular point and the computed angular velocity for each flow of the sequence. It can be seen that even in this case the computed angular velocity is in reasonable agreement with the true angular velocity.

3.3 THE RECOVERY OF MOTION PARAMETERS FROM A SPARSE OPTICAL FLOW

It is useful to check whether a dense optical flow is really necessary for the recovery of the *time-to-collision* and angular velocity or whether a sparse optical flow could also be useful. Fig. 5A illustrates an image reproducing a photograph of a greek sculpture, so as to have a simple textured plane. In Fig. 5B we reproduce the unfilled or sparse optical flow, obtained by considering only those vectors, where det H was large and the conditioning number C_H close to 1. By using the sparse optical flows of Fig. 5B it is possible to locate the singular point $P_T = (\bar{x}, \bar{y})$ and to analyse the nature of the singular point by estimating the 6 parameters $\bar{x}, \bar{y}, a, b, c$ and d, such that

$$\begin{aligned} u_x &= a(x - \bar{x}) + b(y - \bar{y}) \\ u_y &= c(x - \bar{x}) + d(y - \bar{y}) \end{aligned} \tag{3.3}$$

represents the mean square approximation of the flow in Fig. 5B.

In the case of a pure translation expect b and c can be expected to be negligible and the values of a and d to be very similar. The values of b and c turned out to be of the order of 10^{-4} $frames^{-1}$ and a and d 10^{-4} $frames^{-1}$. The *time-to-collision* can be taken as $\frac{1}{a}$.

This procedure of recovering motion from a sparse optical flow proved to be quite precise, and also robust, as shown by the comparison between the computed and true *time-to-collision* (see Fig. 5D). In the case of Fig. 5 the agreement is rather good and in addition the location of the focus of expansion (see Fig. 5C) was not affected by large fluctuations and proved to be correct.

An extensive experimentation on sequences of images of different objects has shown that an accuracy of about 98 % can be obtained in the special case of a highly textured plane parallel to the image plane. This configuration, which is optimal from a theoretical point of view (the 2D motion field becomes linear), also proved experimentally

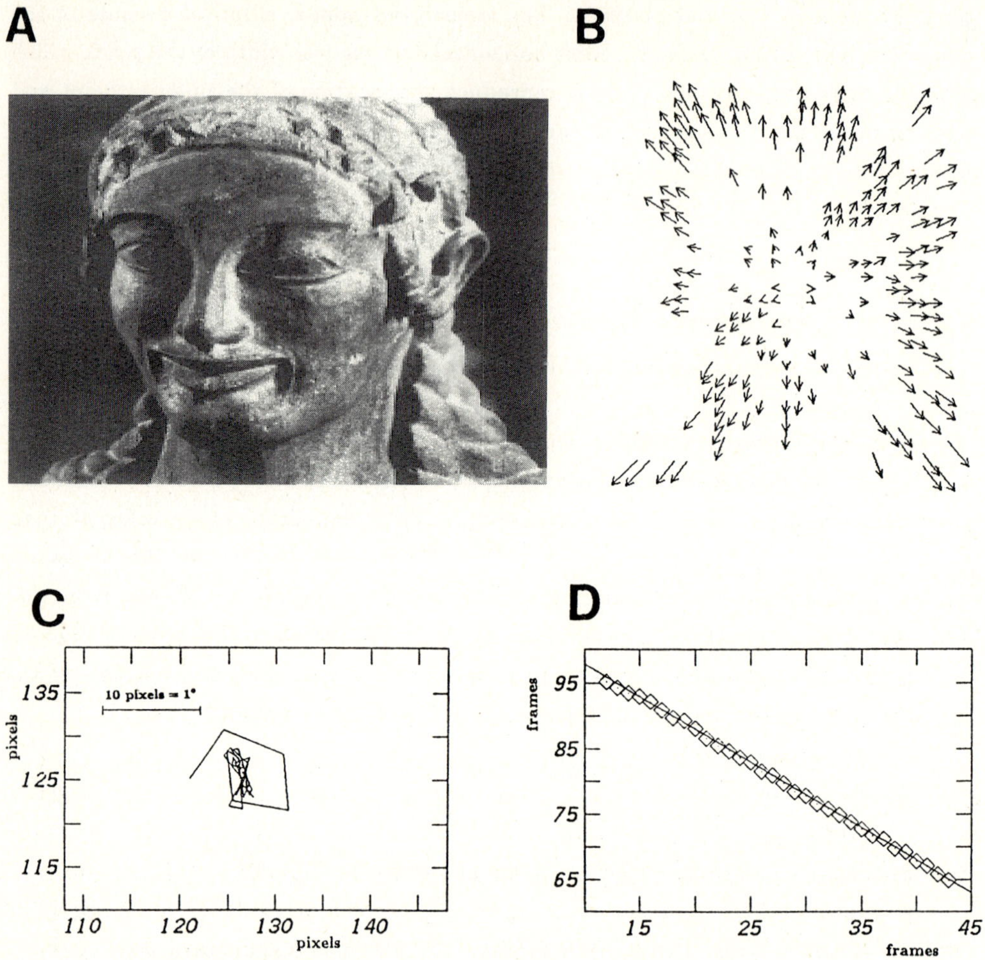

Fig. 5. Recovery of *time-to-collision* from a sparse optical flow. A: an image of a photograph of a greek Apollon. The image sequence was composed by 50 frames. The displacement of the camera between each frame was about 2 cm. B: the sparse optical flow obtained as described in the legend of Fig. 2C. C: the location of the focus of expansion. D: comparison between the true (straight line) and computed *time-to-collision* (polygonal line). Localization $(\bar{x}, \bar{y})$ and *time-to-collision* $\frac{1}{a}$ were obtained by a mean square approximation of equations (4.3) with the sparse optical flow of Fig. 5B.

to be the most favourable. For scenes with either little texture, or depart from a planar structure or for scenes which do both, the agreement between computed and directly measured 3D motion parameters deteriorates and may become poor.

DISCUSSION

The aim of this paper is to evaluate whether or not the computation of optical flow by differential techniques can be a useful tool for recovering 3D motion parameters, motion discontinuities and depth from image sequences. The major application considered here, is the vision system of a mobile vehicle moving in indoor scenes and eventually in an outdoor environment. The great majority of image sequences, analysed here, were obtained by sliding the viewing camera on a rail of an optical bench and therefore were not affected by disturbances and shocks likely to occur on a camera mounted on a mobile robot.

It is now useful to summarize the main conclusions:

1- The recovery of *time-to-collision* and angular velocity is usually successful in the presence of textured images, and when the viewed scene can be approximated by a planar surface parallel to the image plane (see Fig. 5). When the scene has a more complex structure the accuracy of the estimation of the *time-to-collision* decreases (see Fig. 3). When the scene is not textured the estimation of the *time-to-collision* becomes poor.

2- Even when the optical flow is inadequate to reliably estimate the *time-to-collision*, it is still adequate enough to help the matching of edge segments in two successive frames. Therefore it is usually possible to use the computed optical flow to track edge segments and so to obtain a more complete 3D reconstruction of the scene and the motion.

To conclude, the proposed technique for the analysis of image sequence is suitable for the vision system of a mobile robot and so many industrial applications. Many improvements are under study, such as the use of Kalman filtering and the integration of motion information with other sensory modalities.

REFERENCES

1. Aggarwal, J.K. & Nandhakumar, N. : On the Computation of Motion from Sequences of Images - A Review. Proceedings of the IEEE, Vol. 76, No. 8, pp.917-935.
2. Ullmann, S. : The Interpretation of Visual Motion. MIT Press, Cambridge and London 1979.
3. Girosi, F., Verri, A., & Torre, V. : Constraints in the Computation of Optical Flow. Proceedings of the IEEE Workshop on Visual Motion, Irvine CA 1989.
4. Lanczos, C. : Linear Differential Operators. D. Van Nostrand Company, London 1961.
5. Verri, A., Girosi, F. & Torre, V. : Mathematical Properties of the $2D$ Motion Fields: from Singular Points to Motion Parameters. Proceedings of the IEEE Workshop on Visual Motion, Irvine CA 1989.

5 NEURO-BIOLOGY

MULTICELLULAR PROCESSING UNITS FOR NEURAL NETWORKS : MODEL OF COLUMNS IN THE CEREBRAL CORTEX

Yves BURNOD
Lab. Neurobiologie Cellulaire
Institut Pasteur
25 rue Dr.Roux, Paris, FRANCE

ABSTRACT

We develop a theory which models the adaptive capacities of the neuronal circuits in the cerebral cortex. This theory shares common features with connectionist models but with closer links with the physical reality of the cerebral cortex, particularly with what is known of its hierarchical organizational levels.
Basic processing units are not considered at the single cell level but at the level of cortical "columns", which are stereotyped neuronal circuits repeated throughout the cortical tissue. We derive from experimental results a set of rules governing the activation of columns by layered inputs (feedback, feedforward, reciprocal), and show that the resulting process is a searching mechanism. Local learning rules generalize operant conditioning properties and construct functional networks which combine cortical actions (sensory matches, movements) in order to reach a goal, whatever the initial conditions. These rules generalize learning in multi-layered networks which process different types of information and may perform different types of adaptive actions in the external world; this simplified model of the cortical column may help to fill the gap between, on one hand, parallel distributed processing and, on the other hand, more classical algorithms (goal-oriented programs).
Furthermore, we propose a model of the network linking columns and thus cortical areas. This network, which is auto-constructed by cells having a limited amount of genetic information, has very important combinatorial properties: the symmetries of the cortical network form an organizing topographic substrate which favor progressive learning of elaborate functions such as language.

Properties of real neural networks are determined by a whole set of "cellular programs" such as oriented growth of neurites or synthesis of specific ionic channels. Cells first construct a neural network with configurations at higher spatial levels such as neural structures, layers of neurons, cell types, and local circuits. The basic organization of several neural tissues (including the cerebral cortex) is a cellular "texture" which forms a repetitive multicellular circuit perpendicular to the surface of the tissue (1,2). Different neuronal textures produce different types of information processing, such as temporal patterning of motor programs or spatial filtering of sensory information, and they give complementary learning capacities.

Though we are still far from an exhaustive knowledge of the cortical structure, it has been known for some time that this tissue has a typical morphological and functional unit, the "cortical column" (3,4,5), schematized in Figure 1A : it is formed by small group of pyramidal neurons and interneurons closely related (called a mini-column, 30 microns); a functional sensory-motor unit is formed by a redundant set of such circuits (called a "maxi-column", 500 microns width).

We attempt to model the basic features of this multicellular organization (6), by a processing unit with activation and learning rules which are based upon the architectural and functional properties of the cortical column. These rules can be interpreted in terms of Artificial Intelligence, and units can be assembled in multi-layer connectionist networks for pattern and speech recognition (see ref. 7 , this volume).

NATO ASI Series, Vol. F 68
Neurocomputing
Edited by F. Fogelman Soulié and J. Hérault

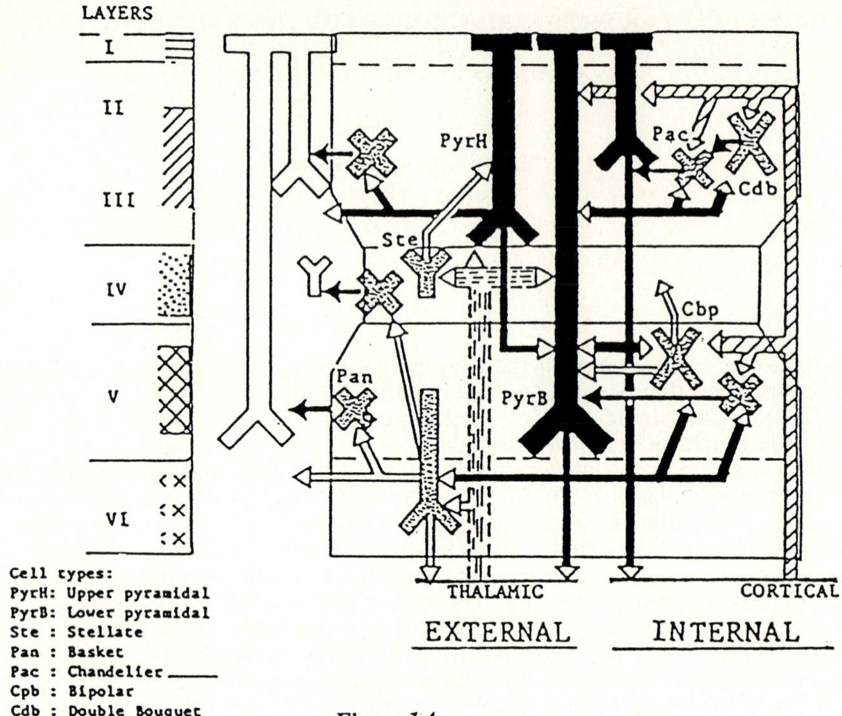

Figure 1A
Connectivity of a cortical column

I. In/out connectivity and activation rules

The basic processing unit has two output divisions and two different types of inputs (Figure 1A). They are in direct correspondence with the 6 layers which form the thickness of the cortex, since they can be grouped in 2 divisions of pyramidal neurons, separated by the "granular" layer IV, with two specialized outputs (1,8):

1. External outputs: Pyramidal neurons of the lower infragranular layers (V and VI) project outside the cortex toward other neural structures; they also participate in the "feed-back" connections from associative toward receptive areas (9).
2. Internal output: Pyramidal neurons of the "upper" supragranular layers (II and III) project mainly toward other cortical regions; since they contact the supragranular pyramidal cells of other columns, they form a recursive network between columns. Their transmitter is the glutamate which has an excitatory effect (3,8).

The basic unit combines two major types of inputs organized in layers:

1. External input: Inputs from thalamus are limited mostly to layer IV intermediate between the two output divisions. They bring to the cortex information about the outside world.
2. Internal input: Cortical inputs are axons of pyramidal cells which arrive from directly adjacent columns or from more distant columns in other areas.

Figure 1B
Repetitive neuronal circuits on the cortical surface

On a top view of the cortical surface, such units can be modeled as a crystal structure, as illustrated in Figure 1B, with several types of neurons (circles) organized in repetitive circuits: within each unit, a central neuron schematizes lower pyramidal neurons (external output) with external inputs centered around this position. A crown of eight neurons (in black) represents the upper pyramidal neurons in direct relation with four cortico-cortical inputs (symbolized by hatched squares) which can have different origins. Inhibitory interneurons (open circle) or excitatory ones (open circles with central dots) are branched in parallel on the main in-out connections.

The activation rules are shaped by combining several neuronal features of the cortical column, which can be grouped in an input-output table (See Fig. 3 in ref. 7, this volume).

In first approximation, the non-linear behaviour of a column is thus modeled with three levels of activation, as shown in Figure 1C: (1) inhibited level "E0" , unmodulated; (2) low level "E1" representing low frequencies of action potentials (1 to 10/sec) which can be observed even in the absence of behaviour; (3) high level "E2" representing higher frequencies (10 to 100/sec), more phasic, which are observed in response to specific stimuli in receptive sensory areas (3,4), or before voluntary movements in motor areas (10).

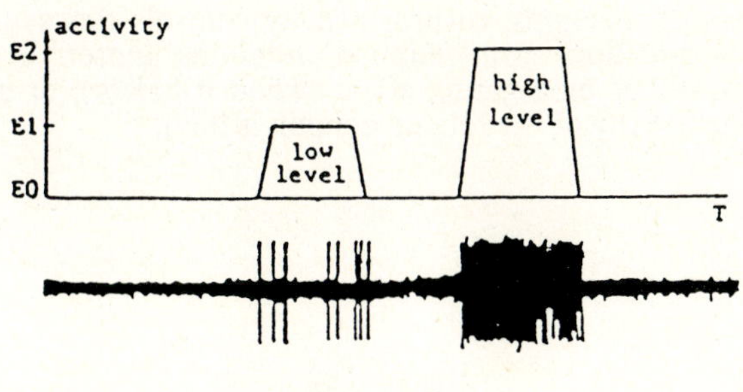

Figure 1C
Levels of activity

These three levels are not arbitrary: differences between E1 and E2 correspond: (1) to the non-linear response of a column when several types of inputs (internal and external) are synchronized (recruitment of excitatory transversal circuits); (2) to conditions required for learning. This simplification of cortical activity enables to describe the internal logic of activation rules and learning rules.

1) The operation upon external inputs on layer IV can be modeled by a filtering process which amplify stimuli which are oriented in the sensory map, with a lateral inhibition (3,4). The amplitude of the response is modulated as a function of cortical areas: strong (E2) in visual and somatosensory cortex, low (E1) in associative and frontal areas (3,4).

2) Internal inputs, when moderate (E1), have a gating effect on other inputs (11,12). Synchronization of both inputs produces a strong non-linear amplification (E2) . This "gating" effect can explain the large increase of cell activity in associative areas when a stimulus matches behavioral "expectancies", probably induced by activities of cortical inputs (10, 13). The "internal" output can be more sensitive than the external one (for example due to the intermediate position of layer IV) and transmit gating signals in the cortical network, without significant output in the extrinsic network (by lower layers).

3) Relations between columns become inhibitory when their differences of activity increase. Connections between pyramidal cells of neighboring modules are excitatory, but there is a parallel inhibitory pathway via Basket interneurons: they can produce a strong lateral inhibition in response to focal stimuli (3), or in response to a direct cortical stimulation which provokes limited muscular contractions (12). With reciprocal connections, the more a column inhibits, the less it is inhibited. In consequence, the strength of inhibition between two columns augments with the difference of their activities.

4) Feedforward/feedback connections.

Corticocortical connections between two distant zones are reciprocal, but the laminar pattern may be different, as illustrated in Figure 3B. For example, the cortical connections from "primary" sensory maps toward "secondary" associative maps ("feed-forward" connections) arise from supragranular layers and project to layer IV (and not to layers II and III); but the reciprocal connections from secondary areas to primary maps ("feed-back" connections) arise from both infra and supra-granular layers and project mostly to the supragranular layers II and III (9).

On the feedforward connections, cortical inputs in layer IV have similar roles as thalamic inputs (external) and are mostly excitatory for columns on register: these inputs represent a sensory information previously processed by more primary areas.

On the feedback connections, cortical activity controls this sensory information flow in the reverse direction, with laminar relations closer to those between neighbouring columns: either by a gating effect (when it is low), or an inhibitory one (when it is high and the activity of the related column is low).

II. Learning properties of a cortical column

Learning rules in a cortical column can be assumed from the component neuronal properties, and give interesting properties to the processing unit which models the column (see ref. 7, this volume, Fig. 4)

It has been proposed that learning at the cellular level depends upon the correlation between a presynaptic activity due to sensory stimuli and a postsynaptic depolarization due to another cortical activation (14). Such a mechanism could explain changes of sensory map during critical developmental periods for ocular dominance columns (4), or in adults where representation of fingers (15) can extend when fingers are used repetitively with sustained attention.

At the cellular level, critical patterns of activation correspond to a temporal sequence closer to operant conditioning than to pavlovian conditioning (16). An efficient pattern, due to voltage properties of glutamate receptors (NMDA), is first a strong depolarization of a neuron (E2), and then a strong reactivation by an input (E2): these receptors and thus glutamate inputs become more efficient when the cell is depolarized, resulting in calcium accumulation and potentiation.

Different types of neurons within a column (5,17) can give great finesse to the learning process, as illustrated in Figure 2. If one assumes that cellular memorization is a general phenomenon, every cell type in a column can register information according to its own logic that depend upon: (1) excitatory (Glutamate) or inhibitory action (GABA); (2) position in the circuit with respect to the specific inputs and outputs; (3) orientation of dendrites and axons coupling either the upper and lower layers of a column, or two neighboring columns.

Local registrations (for example by dendritic spines) can also occur, and result in a precise quantitative adjustment of the transmission between columns and between layers.

Intercolumnar connections (and connections between layers) are both excitatory and inhibitory: excitation by upper pyramidal neurons, is paralleled by inhibition of "Basket" cells (1,5,17). These two types of cells can change their transmission coefficients for two contrasting form of activation (Fig. 2A, left): (1) an excitatory pattern when cortical inputs are strongly activated (E2) just after high activity (E2) in pyramidal neurons (changes of pyramidal neurons), or (2) input excitation following inhibition (E0) of the column (changes of inhibitory neurons which are highly active).

These activation patterns can change the relations between two adjacent columns with two possible consequences: the columns can merge into one single functional module with an homogeneous activity, or they can be subdivided in two independent modules. Such effects modify the functional maps on the cortical surface.

Long-range relations between columns are also characterized by a balance between an excitatory and an inhibitory influence. The influence of a cortical input will depend upon the relative probability of occurrence of the two main potentiating conditions (Figure 2A, on the vertical axis): "activation" or "inhibition" patterns may occur "always", "sometimes", or "never". Each activity pattern preferentially modifies a type of neuron and thus favors an information pathway in the cortical column (Figure 2A, middle and right part, on respectively transversal and lateral axis of the cortex):

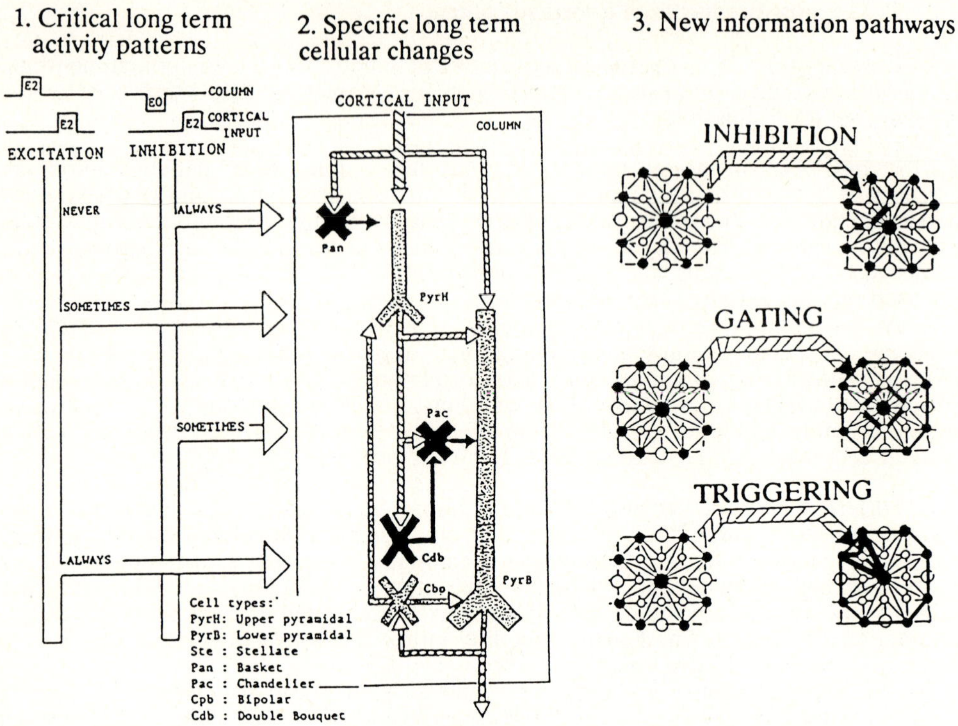

Figure 2
Learning properties of a cortical column

1) INHIBITION: if a column is always inhibited before strong cortical inputs, such input will "learn" an inhibitory effect, by a reinforced influence of Basket cells.

2) GATING: a weak transversal coupling between upper divisions of columns may be learned when a column is SOMETIMES highly active before strong cortical inputs. This pattern reinforces transmission in upper pyramidal cells; transversal inhibitory interneurons such as "Chandelier cells" (1,5,17) limit the coupling between the upper and lower layers of the column, since the inhibition pattern may also sometimes occur. With this learning, the cortical inputs cannot produce a strong external output, but can "gate" the efficiency of the other inputs, thus producing a preparation or an anticipation that "orients" cortical activity toward possible actions: the production of a behavioral sequence will depend upon environmental conditions (thalamic inputs).

3) TRIGGERING: A strong increase in the coupling between cortical inputs and lower layer of the receptor column can occur when the "activation" pattern ALWAYS occurs. In this case, an active coupling between the upper and lower layers, can be produced by two types of interneurons: excitatory "Bipolar" cells, and "Double bouquet" cells which can inhibit the inhibitory interneurons that were previously uncoupling the upper and lower columnar divisions (1,5,17). After this learning, a moderate cortical input can trigger an external output, even if all other inputs are inactive: an action can be "spontaneously" performed (internal drive), independently of environmental conditions.

III . Interpretation of the cortical processing

Taken together, these activation and learning rules define a simple realistic model of a cortical column (reference 7, this volume): as shown in Figure 3A, it combines "external stimuli" (layer IV inputs, dotted lines) and "internal expectations" or hypotheses (cortical inputs, hatched lines) in order to generate answers or actions (lower layer outputs, in black).

1. When external inputs match internal ones in some units, these units effect precise "actions" or give precise "answers" while inhibiting other units emitting only hypotheses (E1).

2. When a single input is active (E1), it corresponds to an hypothesis which can then be transmitted to other units: answers are triggered by units where this propagating "call" is in register with external stimuli. The propagation of the internal expectation continues until the external effects of cortical actions can re-activate the calling units, via an external feedback loop; the resulting strong activity inhibits the propagation and the call stops.

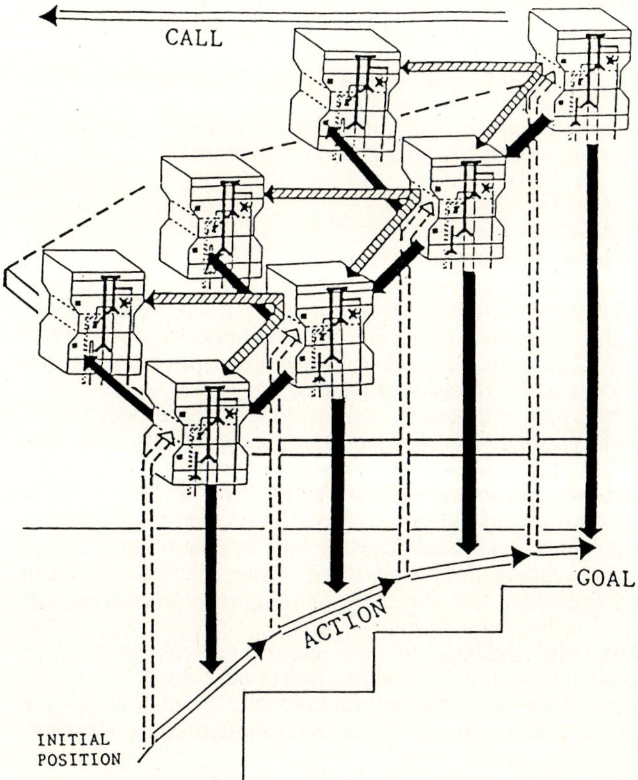

Figure 3A
Cortical call tree after learning

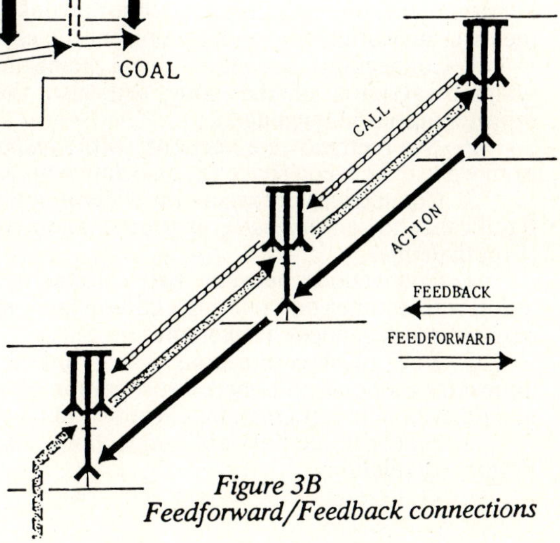

Figure 3B
Feedforward/Feedback connections

A contrasted activity (E2-E0) which result in "answers" or "actions" represents, in this sense, an equilibrium position, a kind of "goal"; a partial cortical activation (E1-E1) is interpreted as an hypothesis, or a question: the processing mechanism produces an exploration, a internal search for specific answers which are confirmed by external stimuli.

The learning rules assemble new functional networks which combine four types of "cortical actions" that are likely to accomplish "cortical goals": (1) random actions that search a solution by the trial and error method; (2) inhibition of inefficient actions; (3) "orientation" of the call toward actions which were sometimes efficient, but the final choice will depend upon environmental conditions; (4) generation of fixed combinations and sequences of actions which were always efficient independently of external conditions. These different strategies result in a precise behavioral adaptation to the regular features of the environment.

The equivalence between "goal" and "action" is a very powerful property of the cortical system to construct programs of actions with subgoals. Learning rules generate ramified hierarchical "call trees" around goals and partial goals, as illustrated in Figure 3A. A partial activation spreads in this tree (from right to left in Figure 3A) until it is in register with other stimuli. In response to these "initial conditions", the call tree then produces an appropriate combination and sequence of actions which bring in cascade the whole system close to the goal (from left to right in Figure 3A). These call trees can organize motor programs and placement in space, whatever the initial positions; they can also perform parallel and dynamic processing of diverse sensory information, whatever their initial forms on the receptive maps (recognition algorithms).

IV . Combinatorial properties of the cortical network

The network between cortical areas is complex: we propose a simplified model which focus on the main information flows and underline the combinatorial properties of this network. Figure 3A schematizes this model for one hemisphere, with the connections linking the main cortical regions (black rectangles).

Connections between cortical areas are usually symmetrical with respect to the sulci and gyri of the cortical surface (18,19,20): for example between left and right hemisphere; between somatosensory areas and motor areas, and between parietal and frontal areas, with respect to the central sulcus. These symmetries are functionally important because they induce isomorphic links between the different representations of the external world. Our model represent the cortical network with at least 6 symmetries:

1. Connections between the 2 hemispheres favor not only relations between symmetrical parts of the body, but also the symbolic "coding" of sensori-motor representations in language.

2. Symmetrical connections with respect to the central sulcus induce an isomorphism between space (in associative areas) and time (in frontal areas).

3. Connections between the lateral and medial face of the hemispheres give significance to sensory patterns (visual, auditor) in relation with fundamental programs (hypothalamic).

4. Connections between two cortical pathways, one relating manipulation and vision with another one relating audition and phonation, form a substrate to link cortical images and sequences of phonemes.

5 .Reciprocal connections which link temporal and parietal regions allow an important cooperation between recognition of forms (What ? in the temporal pathway) and determination of positions (Where ? in the parietal pathway) .

6. Feedback-feedforward connections show reciprocal patterns for top-down and bottom-up relations.

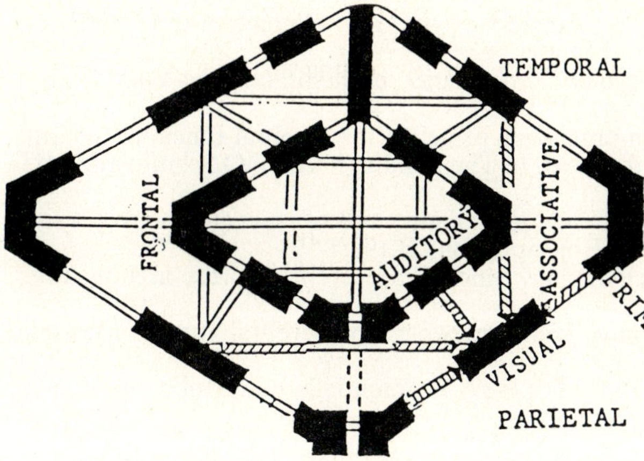

Figure 4A
Model of the network linking cortical areas.

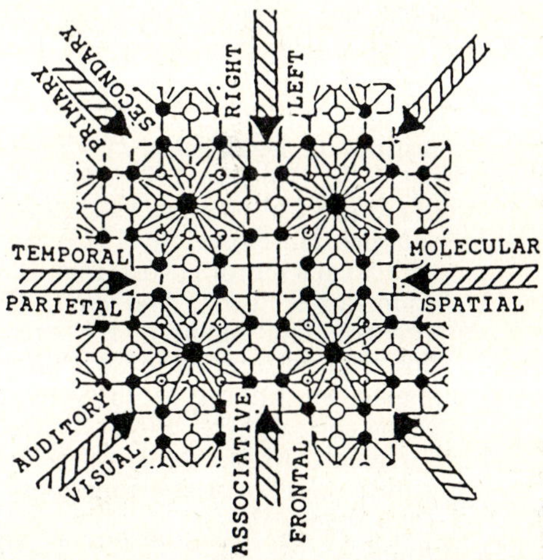

Figure 4B
Standard connections of columns

In our simplified but realistic model, cortical regions can be viewed as the end product of successive growth and subdivisions of the cortical sheet; the main important aspect of cortical connectivity is that the specialized cortical regions are formed by six steps of subdivision which are balanced by six sets of systematic and symmetrical connections. Every cortical "module" (set of adjacent mini-columns) is linked with six other modules in six other areas, with the same connectivity pattern which only depends upon the basic symmetries of the cortical sheet. The symmetries of the network between cortical areas (Figure 4A) and the standard connections of every local subset of columns (Figure 4B) are thus in complete correspondence.

This global architecture is close to an hypercube (6) with six dimensions. This is due to the very simple mode of construction of the cortical network (successive subdivisions balanced by systematic connections) . Hypercube geometry is an optimal trade-off between the number of connections of each processing module and the number of intermediate relays in the pathway between any two modules of the cortical surface. In our model, every cortical zone has six standard cortico-cortical relations and the maximal number of relays between two cortical modules is also six.

1. Cajal, S. (1911). Histologie du Système Nerveux de l'Homme et des Vertébrés. Maloine, Paris.
2. Shepherd, G.M. (1979). The synaptic organization of the brain. New-York, Oxford University Press.
3. Mountcastle, V.B. (1978). An organizing principle for cerebral function: the unit module and the distributed system. In The mindful brain, F.O.Schmitt ed., MIT Press, Cambridge,Mass.
4. Hubel, D.H., Wiesel T. (1977). Functional architecture of macaque monkey visual cortex. Ferrier Lecture Proc. Roy. Soc. Lond.B,198:1-59.
5. Szentagothai, J. (1975). The "module concept" in cerebral cortex architecture. Brain Res., 95:475-496.
6. Burnod, Y. (1988) "An adaptive neural network: the cerebral cortex". Masson, Paris.
7. Guyot, F., Alexandre, F., Haton, J.P. (1989) A potentially powerful connectionist unit: the cortical column. This volume.
8. Jones, E.G. (1981). Anatomy of cerebral cortex: columnar input-output organization. In The organization of the cerebral cortex, F.Schmitt et al. eds., Cambridge, Mass., MIT Press.
9. Van Essen, D.C., Maunsell, J.H.R. (1983). Hierarchical organization and functional streams in the visual cortex. Trends in neurosciences. 6.9
10. Evarts, E.V., Tanji, J. (1974). Gating of motor cortex reflexes by prior instruction. Brain Res., 71:479-494.
11. Vogt, B.A., Gorman, L.F. (1982). Responses of Cortical Neurons to Stimulation of Corpus Callosum in Vitro. J.Neurophysiol,48:6
12. Asanuma, H., Rosen, I. (1973). Spread of mono and poly synaptic connections within cat's motor cortex. Exp. Brain Res., 16:507.
13. Mountcastle, V.B., Andersen, R.A., Motter,B.C. (1981). The influence of attentive fixation upon the excitability of the light-sensitive neurons of the posterior parietal cortex. J. Neurosci., 1:1218-1235.
14. Fregnac, M., Imbert, M. (1984) Development of neuronal selectivity in primary visual cortex of cat . Physiological Reviews 64(1).
15. Merzenich, M.M., Jenkins, W.M., Middlebrooks J.C. (1984) In "Dynamic aspects of neocortical functions" G.M.Edelman, W.E.Gall, W.M.Cowan eds, John Wiley NY.
16. Burnod, Y., Maton, B. Calvet, J. (1982). Activity of neurons in area 4 and in area 5 of monkey during operant conditioning of a flexion movement. In Conditioning, C.D.Woody ed.,Plenum.
17. Peters, A., Jones, E.G. (1984). Classification of cortical neurons . In "Cerebral cortex Vol(1): cellular components of the cerebral cortex " A.Peters and E.G.Jones eds. Plenum Press.
18. Nauta, W.J.H., Karten, H.J. (1970). A general profile of the vertebrate brain, with sidelights on the ancestry of cerebral cortex. In The Neurosciences, Second Study Program, F.O.Schmitt, ed., New York, Rockefeller, pp.7-25.
19. Pandya, D.N. and Kuypers, H.G.J.M. (1969). Cortico-cortical connections in the rhesus monkey. Brain Research, 13:13.
20. Jones, E.G., Coulter, J.D. Hendry, S.H.C. (1978). Intracortical connectivity of architectonic fields in the somatic sensory, motor and parietal cortex of monkeys. J. comp. Neurol.,181:292.

A POTENTIALLY POWERFUL CONNECTIONIST UNIT: THE CORTICAL COLUMN

F. Guyot, F. Alexandre, J.P. Haton
CRIN/INRIA
BP 239, 54506 Vandoeuvre-les-Nancy
France

Y. Burnod
Institut Pasteur
25, rue du docteur Roux
75015 Paris

ABSTRACT

We propose a novel approach to neuron-like models that consists in simulating cortical columns, i.e. associations of elementary neurons having a specific, functionnal activity. This model is built according to a theory which is consistent with neurobiological data. It provides autonomous units, each computing its output as a function of its inputs, modulated by such internal features as learning coefficients.

Implementing this model is achieved through a network of columns that simulates the inherently parallel functionning of the nervous system. Since each column behaves autonomously, the network is functionnaly specified by just describing the connectivity pattern of each area.

We describe in details this model and present the experimental conditions in which it has been and is now tested. Results already obtained show the efficiency of the model in terms of recognition rate as well as its ability to deal with higher level problems. We shall also discuss main general points such as topology, connectivity, temporal processing, etc.

NATO ASI Series, Vol. F 68
Neurocomputing
Edited by F. Fogelman Soulié and J. Hérault

1. INTRODUCTION

In order to deal with cognitive functions of higher level than pattern matching, we propose a new connectionist unit which integrates more sophisticated behaviour than neuron-like unit. This unit is based on significant neurobiological observations and was adapted to computer implementation through psychological considerations. So the unit stands at the crossroad of Artificial Intelligence, Neurosciences and Cognitive Psychology.

Automatic Speech Recognition is among the most difficult problems studied in Artificial Intelligence. It is consequently a good touchstone for an automaton with such properties and behaviour. We have therefore chosen this field as a test bed in order to validate our model.

After a recall of the model we have built, of its principles and of the properties which have so arisen, we present the classical realizations implemented until now. We then expose open questions about our simulations for speech processing but also common to many speech processing techniques (time dependance, representation, selective attention, topology, ...) and propose the solutions we have retained for implementation.

2. THE MODEL

The principles.

Our goal was to design a more powerful connectionist unit than the classically used formal neuron. The initial point of the studies stands in a neurobiological modelization of the cortical column [1], on which we add, as computer scientists, some general basic principles which are proposed as a solution to efficient reasoning in a neural network. The first model used for visual (and auditory) recognition is based upon the following principles:

1. We assume as the major principle that the connectivity between automata has to remain local; the network is **not** fully interconnected. The consequence of this principle is that information has to spread over in the network step by step thanks to an appropriate mechanism.

2. Most of the human-like data processing (perception, recognition, analysis) use three kinds of information: external stimuli, external actions (answer) and internal concepts. In our automaton, we want to keep this distinction with more specified inter-automata messages.

3. The last principle to be retained corresponds to the way analysis will be done; we believe that information flow coming from external world is tremendously important (see for example visual information) and that pertinent cues are few. That is the reason why we chose to have a kind of top-down analysis, starting from

general inital goal (such as "recognition of the digit 4") and recursively triggering those subgoals that are efficient for reaching the initial concept. As a consequence, learning has to create appropriate links between a goal and its subgoal.

As these principles provide us with general constraints on the software implementation of such units, we have to design the main features of the automaton through these constraints.

Architecture:
We distinguish at first two kinds of inputs for an automaton, coming from the external world (stimuli) or from the internal world (concept or subgoal), and also two kinds of outputs going to the external world (actions) or to the internal world (concept or subgoal). We mainly outline here the biological reality of such a division [2,3].

Connectivity:
The way automata are linked together takes into account the above distinction between inputs and outputs. We define three kinds of automata: sensory automata which receive direct information from the external world, associative automata with no links with the external world, and motor ones which are able to trigger external actions. We gather each type of unit in a map (sensory map, associative map, motor map), so that the connectivity should become clear, as indicated in Figure 1.

Maps \ Links	External input from:	Internal input from:	External output to:	Internal output to:
Sensory	– initial encoding	– itself – associative	– feed–back on initial encoding	– itself – associative
Associative		– sensory – itself – motor		– sensory – itself – motor
Motor	– answer during learning	– itself – associative	– answer during recognition	– itself – associative

Figure 1. Connectivity types following Maps types.

This table illustrates the inter-map network; more precisely, we have to define the symetrical (input, output) internal links at the level of the automaton. If a path exists between two units, it is sufficient to make these two units interact, following principle 1. We can thus imagine many different networks, from minimal length pathways constraints (fully interconnected nets) to the minimal connection number constraints (mono-dimensional nets).

We choose to connect a unit with its neighbours on the same map and with its symetrical image in a related map, which seems to us the maximal simplification we can make on biological data [4]. Concerning the map network, further works on larger networks (more than 8 maps) will show the advantages to use an hypercubic structure.

The general connectivity between units of different maps is depicted in Figure 2:

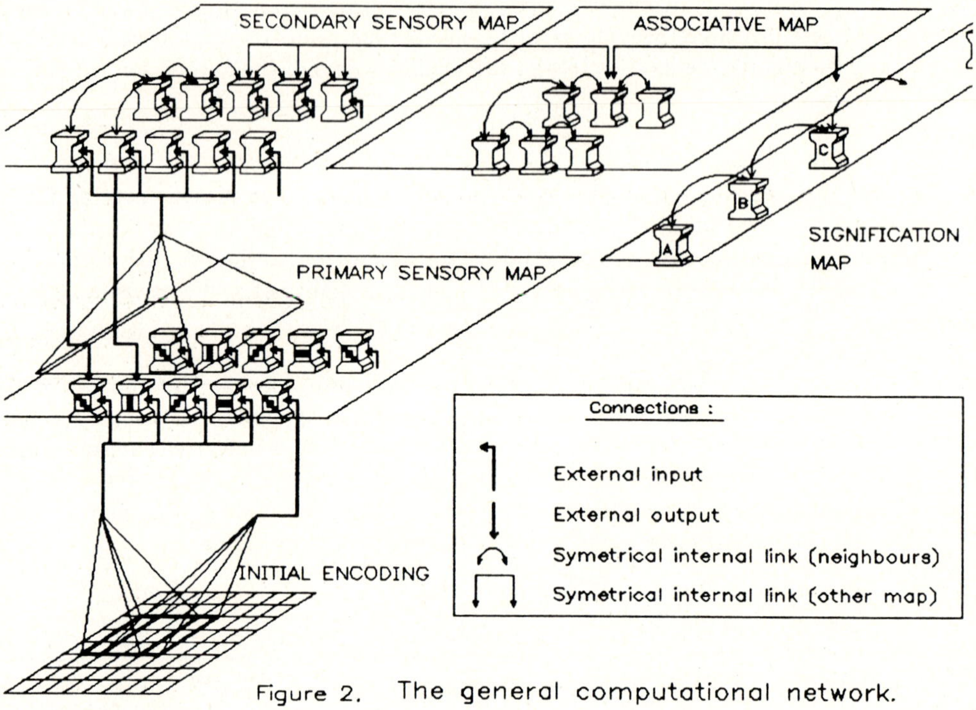

Figure 2. The general computational network.

Levels of activity:

Because of principle 1 (local connectivity), a specially adapted state of activation is needed to perform a step by step data propagation. We call this level of activation E1. According to its definition, such a state represents a precise type of processing, which corresponds neither to full activity nor to inhibition. We can consider it as a sensibilisation state [5] occuring when the network holds some hypothesis upon the external world; in this case, no actions are triggered. We must lay emphasis on the importance of such a signal for a major psychological characteristic of human processing, i.e. selective attention. To be complete with the description of the levels of activation, we also define (i) a state E0 standing for a non activated automaton; no distinction is made between an inhibited automaton and a non activated one; (ii) a state E2 corresponding to the attainement of a concept and therefore to the triggering of an action.

From a logical point of view, these three levels define a trivalued logic where E0, E1 and E2 respectively means no, perhaps and yes.

Activation rules:

Having described the concrete basis of the C-automaton, we have to add rules (activation rules and learning rules) to describe inferences in the systeme. An in-out table (truth table) is given below in Figure 3, where the two kinds of outputs (external action or internal concept) are set as a function of the two inputs. These rules must suit the three main principles: memorization has to relate a concept with its subgoals, actions and stimuli, thanks to a step by step pathway in the map:

Inputs		column prior state	Ouputs		Comments:	Depends upon:
internal	external		internal	external		
E0	E0	E0 E1	E0	E0		
			E2	E2	Sensory	
E0	E1	E0 E1	E1	E0	Associative	Map
			E0	E0	Motor	
			E0	E0	Inhibition	
E1	E0	E0 E1	E1	E0	Gating	Learning
			E2	E2	Triggering	
E1	E1	E0 E1	E2	E2	Amplification	
E2	E0 E1	E0 E1	E0	E0	Inhibition	
			E1	E0		
E2	E0 E1	E2	E2	E2	Reactivation	

Figure 3. Input/Ouput table of the C–automaton

The interpretation of this table follows:

- line 2: a distinction is made between the three kinds of maps, either directly receiving stimuli (sensory map), or directly triggering actions (motor map), or combining relations between a sensory map and a motor one (associative map).
- line 3: the learning dependent case represents the effect of an hypothesis hold by a concept onto a potential subconcept which is, of course, modulated by learning.
- line 4: the gathering of a stimulus and a conceptual hypothesis produces an action (an answer).
- line 5: inhibition of an attained goal upon concurrential units usefully limits the number of active automata.
- line 6: the fully coactivation of two modules will produce learning.

Learning rules:

In a typical learning session, stimuli are proposed to the network thanks to sensory map and motor map, then activities E1 (active search) spread within the different maps until meeting.

By measuring the probability of coactivation of two linked attained concepts, the learning process is able to distinguish three kinds of relations between two units (following Figure 4), and during a recognition session to infere three kinds of activity (inhibition, gating, triggering: see Figure 3).

Repetition Factors		Outputs for the learning dependant case		
P2	P0	Internal	External	
–	–	E0 E1	E0	Random
0	1	E0	E0	Inhibition
>0	<1	E1	E0	Gating
1	0	E2	E2	Triggering

Figure 4. Memorization rules of the C–automaton.

3. REALIZATION

The first network we made was elaborated in order to realize a classical matching problem [6] of visual recognition of characters masked with random noise. The network includes a Primary Sensory Map, a Secondary Sensory Map, an Associative Map, all standing for cortex-like areas, and a Significative Map which proposes the solutions (see Figure 2). This non-cortical area makes problems arise on which we will discuss later.

After the encouraging results [7] obtained for this simulation, we then used the same network in a different way: instead of a 8x8 grid where characters were digitized as an initial encoding, we introduced spectrogram images, to solve another classical problem of spoken digit recognition [6]. Results for this simulation have first been reported [7] as speech recognition, because speech tokens were on the input layer. Nevertheless, we want to point out that this is only a visual recognition of spectrograms and **not real** speech recognition. This visual approach of speech recognition is at the root of many problems encountered in this simulation. This point made us decide a completely new approach in order to build a more biologically plausible network for efficient speech processing.

The point here is to fit more closely to the human way to process speech and to extract data from Biology as well as from Cognitive Sciences.

4. DISCUSSION

Initial encoding and biological structures.

It is well known that the auditory cortex has been less studied than the visual one. Nevertheless, structural data can be found on this part of the cortex, and, moreover, many properties of the peripheral organization (from external to internal ear) are available. We present now the characteristics we chose to represent the speech processing chain:

- In the cochlea, a spectral analysis is carried out: fibers are representative of a characteristic frequency and code the intensity of a sound up to a saturation threshold [8]. These fibers also react stronger to the novelty brought by the signal (e.g. burst amplification).
- The thalamic nucleus MGM enhances intensity contrast and distributes the auditive information on the cortical maps [9]. This nucleus can also selectively amplify parts of the signal, responding to cortical feedback actions.
- The main important property of the auditive cortex (which is common to the whole cortex) is its two-dimensional structure. The thalamic nucleus has to allocate the auditive cues on two main axes. It is known [9] that the frequency axis is often represented on the auditive maps which are related through associative areas to temporal areas for semantic relations and parietal areas for muscular representation of speech production.

To summarize, a preprocessing for computer simulations is achieved through:

- a spectrum analysis (FFT, LPC, ARMA...),
- a novelty and contrast enhancement,
- a one frequency axis representation.

Temporal signal and temporal processing:

In the visual recognition of spectrograms two main problems have arisen:

-First, the detection of the beginning of the utterance eliminates pertinent cues like silence before burst.

-the second point arises from a non-constant rate of production that makes the temporal axis less precise than the frequency one.

That is the reason why the mental representation shows weak probalistic coefficients at the end of the word.

A first solution consists of a pre-processing which compresses the spectrogram on the temporal axis; but, once again, the efficient work is done by the pre-processing instead of the network itself.A more elegant solution is to take time into account at the processing unit level [10]. This will be done if the input layer is no longer the entire static spectrogram but rather successive frames which change with time and make progressively the system evolve toward a temporal representation of the word [11].

Integration of time allows the network to provide different interesting behaviours:

- Selective attention can selectively enhance pertinent indices in the data flow; this selectivity can be context dependent.
- Anticipation: the network is able, after learning, to foresee different possible events.
- Too strong anticipations can lead to errors and ask for complementary behaviour: a backtrack to previous information badly interpreted. For example, in vision, while reading, misunderstanding (lexical, syntaxic, or semantic) necessitates to go back to the previous character (or word, or sentence).

Moreover, this approach for integration of time has benefic consequences:

- Most of the information is represented by a continuous temporal pathway through the network; hence the local connectivity principle is extremelly well adapted for dealing with such data [12];
- This principle goes against the fully-parallel processing. We assume that this mixed sequential-parallel processing is a powerful way to deal with more cognitive functions than matching; many human cognitive behaviours use this mixed strategy (reading, walking, decision-making...).

Distributed data and distributed output:

Another class of problems relates to architectural aspect; as mentionned above, the network follows a cortex-like organization except for the output map called "Significative Map" and standing for the motor areas giving a meaning by a behaviour (like speech or hand writing) in a distributed way and not by "grand-mother units". Human being does not have LEDS on his forehead to recognize phonemes, but parallely and sequentially use a set of muscles to give an answer.

To solve this particular point, we can point out the internal direct link in the human brain between audition and speech production, improved by an external feed-back loop. As a consequence, phonemes using the same muscles for the prodution, have simular representation for audition.

Using a "Motor Map" (simulating a set of muscles) as an output map, is an elegant way to take into account coarticulation phenomenons which are nothing but **temporal muscular constraints**.

Moreover, this kind of distributed output representation gets ride of the grand-mother units problem.

5. CONCLUSION

We are now investigating the integration in the unit of these three discussion items as three new principles:

- a biologically plausible initial encoding,
- a temporal processing providing ad-hoc behaviours,
- a distributed output for solution extraction.

6. REFERENCES

[1] Y. Burnod, "An adaptive neural network: The cerebral cortex", Masson, Paris, 1988.

[2] D.H. Ballard, " Cortical connections and parallel processing: Structure and function", The behavioral and brain sciences 9,67-120, 1986.

[3] Y. Burnod, This volume.

[4] C.D. Gilbert,T.N. Wiesel, "Laminar specialization and intra-cortical connections in cat primary visual cortex", In the organization of the cerebral cortex, F.Schmitt et al eds., Cambridge, Mass., MIT Press, 1981.

[5] P. Anizan, "Modèle à régulations hiérarchisées", 3èmes Journées Neurosciences, Univ. Aix-Marseille I-II, 1986.

[6] F. Fogelman Soulie, P. Gallinari, Y. Le Cun, S. Thiria. "Network learning", Machine learning, vol 3, Y. Kodratoff, R. Michalski Eds.

[7] F. Guyot, F. Alexandre, J.P. Haton, Y. Burnod, "The Cortical Column, a New Processing Unit for Cortex-Like Networks", Proc. CEC Workshop "From the Pixels to the Features", Elsevier, 1989.

[8] B. Delgutte, "Codage de la Parole Dans le Nerf Auditif", Thèse, Université Paris VI, 1984.

[9] E. I. Knudsen, S. du Lac, S. D. Esterly, "Computational Maps in the Brain", Neurosciences, 10, p. 41-65, 1987.

[10] J. Leboeuf, "Un Systeme Connexionniste Appliqué au Traitement Automatique de la Parole", Thèse, Université de Paris-Sud, 1988.

[11] F. Guyot, F. Alexandre, J.P. Haton, "Toward a Continuous model of the cortical column: application to speech recognition", Proc. ICASSP-89, Glasgow, 1989.

[12] T. Kohonen, "Self Organization and Associative Memory", Springer, 1984.

Complex information processing in real neurones

Jørn Hounsgaard, Jens Midtgaard

Institue of Neurophysiology - Blegdamsvej 3C
2200 Copenhagen N. - DENMARK

Introduction

Although networks of real and modelled neurones have much in common they are studied for very different reasons and in very different ways. Brains are historical entities handed over by the process of natural selection and shaped by their individual lives. They are given and we are well aware of their overall abilities to direct body function and movement and to provide sensation, mental activity and social interaction. Apart from how brains are put together during development the key question in neurobiology is - not what they do - but how they do it!

Attempting to understand how the brain works is a good reason for studying signal processing in nerve cells. Neurones are the most obvious functional building blocks in the brain. They constitute ontogenetic and metabolic entities and are also conveniently viewed as units of signal processing. Typically and in general terms a nerve cell receives chemical signals from presynaptic terminals of other nerve cells at its dendrites. The postsynaptic responses are translated into impulse patterns in the axon and finally transmitted chemically to the nerve cells contacted by the axon terminals.

In terms of information processing the interesting part is the mapping of presynaptic impulse activity into postsynaptic impulse activity. Usually a nerve cell has 10^3-10^5 presynaptic axons to direct the activity of just one postsynaptic axon. Since most presynaptic information is discarded in the process, postsynaptic translation may be viewed as the prime origin of complexity at the single cell level (Kuhn, 1988; Landauer 1988a, b) - the remaining signalling in nerve cells mainly being involved with information transport. In the following we sketch the translational properties of nerve cells, with examples from our own work, and discuss their possible contribution to the function of networks of real and modelled neurones.

NATO ASI Series, Vol. F 68
Neurocomputing
Edited by F. Fogelman Soulié and J. Hérault

Two kinds of current generators, three ways of regulation

Independent of the postsynaptic translational mechanism the output patterns that a nerve cell can produce are ultimately limited by the biophysical properties of the axonal membrane. Within these bounds impulse activity is determined by the generator potential at the origin of the axon. This potential is modulated by distributed current generators in the membrane of the cell body and dendrites, mainly in the form of ion channels. The analysis of synaptic translation in neurones is therefore primarily an account of ion channels, their interactions and regulation. Ion channels are aqueous pores formed by membrane spanning proteins. Those with which we are concerned here oscillate between open and closed states. In the open state specific species of ions, determined by the selectivity of the channel, can permeate and generate current according to the pore conductance and the difference between the membrane potential and the Nernst potential for the permeant ions. The variable of functional importance for the generator potential has proved to be the kind and number of open channels.

There are three separate ways of regulating the open state probability of ion channels. Transmitter regulation is confined to channels in the membrane facing synaptic terminals. The open state probability of this class of channels increase dramatically when they associate with the specific transmitter liberated by their opposing terminal. Voltage regulated channels are thought to be located in the non-synaptic membrane. These channels oscillate between open and several non-conducting states, the state probabilities changing with the postsynaptic membrane potential. The voltage sensitivity of state probabilities and the kinetics of state shifts vary widely among the different subclasses of voltage sensitive channels. Finally state probabilities and transmitter affinity of some of the synaptic and non-synaptic channels are also affected by specific members of a heterogeneous group of substances in the cell interior known as second messengers. The concentration and distribution of second messengers, of which Ca^{++}, cyclic nucleotides and phosphoinositides are good examples, is affected by certain neurotransmitters and postsynaptic activity. Detailed reviews of ion channels and their regulation have appeared elsewhere (Hille, 1984; Miller 1988; Levitan 1988).

The translational process in principle

We are now equipped to deal more directly with the translational process. The activity of each presynaptic axon control the open state probability of the transmitter gated channels in the subsynaptic membrane of its own terminals. For the present purpose this process can be considered independent of the activity in other presynaptic axons and of the postsynaptic membrane potential. In a sense the spatial distribution of open synaptic channels in the postsynaptic membrane is a faithful map of the pattern of presynaptic activity. The changes in postsynaptic potential induced by the changing patterns of open synaptic channels do however alter the state probabilities of voltage sensitive channels in the non-synaptic membrane. Since these current generators react to a voltage change independent of its source, their states are determined by the overall pattern of open synaptic channels and by their own mutual voltage and time dependent interactions.

The translational process relate to the history of synaptic inputs and resulting interacting state-shifts in voltage sensitive channels. Since the kinetics of state shifts cover time ranges from less than a millisecond to more than a minute the detailed pattern of synaptic input in this time window condition the nonsynaptic component of the response to a presynaptic action potential. Likewise a presynaptic action potential will influence subsequent synaptic translation on a similar time scale (Hounsgaard and Midtgaard, 1989).

The translational process in real neurones

As we have detailed elsewhere (Midtgaard and Hounsgaard, 1989) the non-linearly interacting nonsynaptic current generators, intercalated between the primary synaptic responses and the axonal impulse activity, assign a high probability to a small subset of the physically possible output patterns in the axon (intrinsic output selection). At the same time the non-synaptic interactions allow input in a broad time window to excert intricate heterosynaptic modulation of the intrincically preferred outputs (conditional synaptic interaction). The overall effect is enhanced computational power at the single cell level.

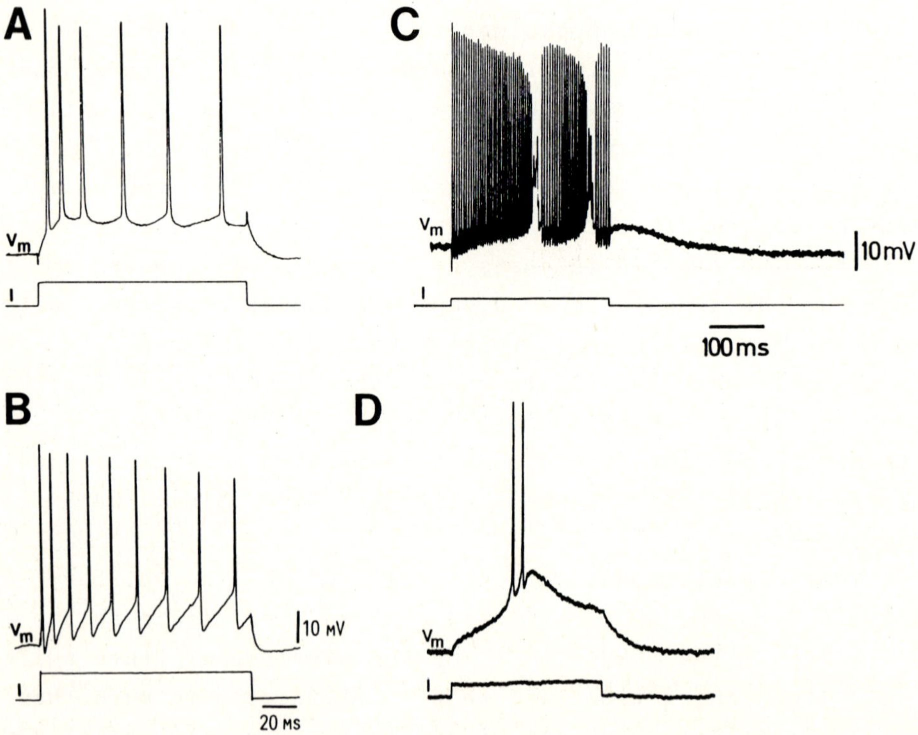

Figure 1.
Response pattern in four different cell types to a depolarizing current pulse delivered through the recording electrode. A, hippocampal pyramidal cell. B, hippocampal interneurone. C, cerebellar Purkinje cell. D, thalamic neurone. (The record in D kindly provided by H. Jahnsen & R. Llinás).

Even casual examination of the brain reveal that far from being universal computers each region subserve very specific, non-interchangeable functions. As shown in figure 1 the response pattern to the same stimulus is dramatically different in different cell types. We believe that this difference which is due to the different collection of voltage sensitive channels carried by different cell types is essential for dedicated and differentiated function of networks with a limited number of neurones available. It is sufficiently obvious that the translational process - output selection and conditional synaptic interaction - is highly cell specific. Even in the same local network neurones that share most of their synaptic input may end up with entirely different output due to different translational properties. An example is the stellate and Purkinje cells in the cerebellum sharing their parallel fiber input, but stellate cells operating in a time window of a few hundred milliseconds and Purkinje cells over minutes (Midtgaard, 1988).

Modifiable translation

What we have seen so far is that the intrinsic properties of real neurones, as compared with McCollough-Pitt neurones and their like, let many more inputs interact in many more ways. For some nerve cells, however, the functionally required outputs and the relevance of presynaptic input patterns may vary so much at different times that optimal function cannot be satisfied by fixed translational properties. The same motoneurone may engage in postural control that require regulated levels of tonic firing and in movements that require precisely timed phasic activity. An elegantly simple voltage dependent shift between intrinsic states that favour output patterns of either the tonic or the phasic type was recently described in thalamic neurones (Jahnsen and Llinás, 1984). In many nerve cells, however, including motoneurones, a more elaborate synaptic regulation of the translational properties is provided by a special class of neurotransmitters - neuromodulators - that regulate the functional properties of voltage gated ion channels via second messengers (Levitan, 88).

We have initiated a study of how neurotransmitters of this class regulate the intrinsic response properties in motoneurones. So far we have shown that serotonin induce a bistable state that allow tonic firing to be initiated by a brief burst of excitatory synaptic potentials and terminated by a brief burst of inhibitory synaptic potentials (Hounsgaard and Kiehn, 1989; Hounsgaard et al., 1988). We have also shown that intrinsic bursting pacemaker properties are induced by activating muscarinic acetylcholine receptors or NMDA receptors (Mintz, 1987). It is tempting to suggest that the bistable mode of activity induced by serotonin optimally favour the output patterns needed for postural control, while the phasic mode induced by NMDA and acetylcholine favour the patterned activity that could be useful in locomotion. Synaptically regulated translational properties - mediated by second messengers - obviously reduce the need for precise presynaptic regulation of synaptically controlled current generators and may thus help to minimize the number of neurones required for a given network operation.

Proposals for networks of real neurones

We have attempted to point out how real neurones differ from the modelled neurones so far used in computational networks. It is our claim that the translational process in real neurones, based on spatially and temporally diverse non-linear molecular interactions, is a basic source of time scale and processing density in brain function (Midtgaard and Hounsgaard 1989). The translational properties preassign a high probability to a small subset of the physically possible output patterns in a cell-specific manner. In effect this reduce the role of the synaptically controlled current generators to that of triggering and shaping the output patterns rather than creating them de novo. At the same time the molecular network in nerve cells expand input interactions and increase the number of computational steps between the input and the output. In the quest for useful output, modulation of translational properties by second messengers may allow neurones to meet changing demands in a dedicated fashion.

Despite the lucid analysis of certain invertebrate ganglia (Selverston and Moulins 1985) it is fair to say that the specific contribution of complex translational properties in nerve cells to network operations is virtually unknown. However preliminar, it seems useful to align the results from real neurones and networks with their modelled counterparts.

Most artifical neural networks deliver discrete output from metastable states defined by synaptic strengths. In contrast the output (and input) in real networks is contineous in time. Furthermore, since the translational properties of neurones in real networks change dynamically during processing, it may be more fruitful to picture the output as the activity that arise in the pursuit of flighty attractors. (It is assumed that attractors in real networks are defined not only by a connectivity matrix but also by the 'matrix of translational properties'). We predict that erratic behaviour in real networks is protected against 1) by the output constraints at the single cell level favouring useful outputs, 2) by the modular organisation of local networks, 3) by the existence of global synaptic systems (e.g. n. coeruleus, substantia nigra, the raphé nuclei etc. in vertebrates) with a concerted regulatory potential on single cell translational properties and local attractors based on non-local information.

In modelled networks learning is usually implemented by rules for changing connectivity. While obvious analogies exist in real networks (TINS 1988) it is to be expected that changes in translational properties also play a role in the long term adaptive behaviour of brains. Irrespective of learning rules it seems essential to identify mechanisms that condition network modification locally and coordinate modifications globally. Recent evidence indicate that both purposes are served by interacting second messenger systems operated on by single cell activity and local and global synaptic systems. (Stevens 1989, Bear and Singer 1986).

The behaviour of heterogeneous networks of neurones with complex translational properties as they occur in brains is not well understood. Experiments and models in concert may none the less give some clues (Kleinfeld and Sompolinsky 1988, Getting 1989).

References

1. Bear, M.F. and Singer, W.: Modulation of visual cortical plasticity by acetylcholine and noradrenaline. Nature 320, 172-176 (1986)

2. Getting, P.A.: Emerging principles governing the operation of neural networks. Ann. Rev. Neurosci. 12, 185-204 (1989)

3. Hille, B.: Ionic Channels of Excitable Membranes. Sinauer Associates Inc. Publishers, Sunderland, Massachusetts (1984)

4. Hounsgaard, J. and Midtgaard, J.: Synaptic control of excitability in turtle cerebellar Purkinje cells. J. Physiol. 409, 157-170 (1989)

5. Hounsgaard, J. and Kiehn, O.: Serotonin induced bistability of turtle motoneurones caused by a nifedipine sensitive calcium plateau. J. Physiol. In press. (1989)

6. Hounsgaard, J., Hultborn, H., Jespersen, B. and Kiehn, O.: Bistability of α-motoneurones in the decerebrate cat and in the acute spinal cat after intravenous 5-hydroxytryptophan. J. Physiol. 405, 345-367 (1988)

7. Jahnsen, H.: Responses of neurons in isolated preparations of the mammalian central nervous system. Progress in Neurobiology 27, 351-372 (1986)

8. Kleinfeld, D. and Sompolinsky, H.: Associative neural network model for the generation of temporal patterns. Biophys. J. 54, 1039-1051 (1988)

9. Kuhn, H.: Origin of life and physics: diversified microstructure - Inducement to form information-carrying and knowledge-accumulating systems. IBM J. Res. Develop. 32, 37-46 (1988)

10. Landauer, R.: Dissipation and noise immunity in computation and communication. Nature 335, 779-784 (1988a)

11. Landauer, R.: A simple measure of complexity. Nature 336, 306-307 (1988b)

12. Levitan, I.B.: Modulation of ion channels in neurons and other cells. Ann. Rev. Neurosci. 11, 119-136 (1988)

13. Midtgaard, J.: Electroresponsiveness of interneurons in the turtle cerebellar cortex in vitro. Euro. J. Neurosci., Suppl. ENA Meeting (1988)

14. Midtgaard, J. and Hounsgaard, J.: Nerve cells as source of time scale and processing density in brain function. Int. J. Neur. Syst. 1, in press (1989)

15. Mintz, I.: Analyse <u>in vitro</u> des propriétés membranaires actives des motoneurones de tortue et de leur contribution aux oscillation induites par l'acide N-méthyl-D-aspartique

et les agonistes muscariniques. Thése de Doctorat de l'Université Paris 6 (thesis) (1987)

16. Selverston, A.I. and Moulins, M.: Oscillatory neural networks. Ann. Rev. Physiol. 47, 29-48 (1985)

17. Stevens, C.F.: Strengthening the synapses. Nature 338, 460-461 (1989)

18. TINS. Learning and memory. 11, No. 4. P.26 (1988)

Formal Approach and Neural Network Simulation of the Co-ordination between Posture and Movement

Michel Dufossé[1]

Institut Méditerranéen de Technologie
Marseille, France

1. Living bodies as autonomous systems

Motor control in living bodies must be considered in relation to a given number of finalities. It may consist of global finalities that are essential for an autonomous system, such as prey catching or escaping a predator, and more elementary finalities which are derived from displacement, target detection, maintenance of internal energizing state... etc. The living creature always tries to maintain and preserve its internal cohesion. Each motor act and information sampling bring an interaction between the system and the external medium.

A systemic study of autonomy was worked out, according to which a given number of couplings exist between the living system and its environment (21) One may cite the resting point on the ground, the visual anchorage on a target, the vestibular informations... etc. The resting points for example are not inputs or outputs of the system at this level of analysis but simply interaction points; the interaction being related to the principle of equality between action and reaction.

Proposition 1: *Sensorimotor control is aimed at the maintenance of the autonomy of the system constituted by a living body or by an autonomous robot. It results from various couplings between the system and its environment. These couplings are bidirectional. Sensorimotor control is performed via a structured set of actions exerted on the various couplings.*

2. Frame of reference for a goal directed movement

A movement corresponds to a modification of the couplings between the autonomous system and its environment. Schematically, one might separate voluntary movements resulting from an action of the system and induced movements resulting from a perturbation of the environment.

---

[1] Laboratoire de Neurosciences Fonctionnelles, CNRS, Marseille and (present address) Institut Méditerranéen de Technologie, Avenue Grand Pré, 13009 Marseille, France

NATO ASI Series, Vol. F 68
Neurocomputing
Edited by F. Fogelman Soulié and J. Hérault

This distinction is not always clear. Many voluntary movements are initiated by a modification of the environment, detected by the system. Learning the relation between an event and its context must be considered as an interference between the perturbing sphere and the sollicited living system (22).

Outside the biological system, the position and the movement of a point must be referred to a frame of reference. Roughly speaking, a frame of reference is a set of points at fixed distances, such as the visual background of a target (Fig. 1).

Proposition 2: *The choice of an appropriate frame of reference for a target position is an essential prerequisite of movement initiation in a living body or of a multijoint robot moving in a complex environment. This choice depends upon the action's goal and constitutes one objective of sensorimotor control.*

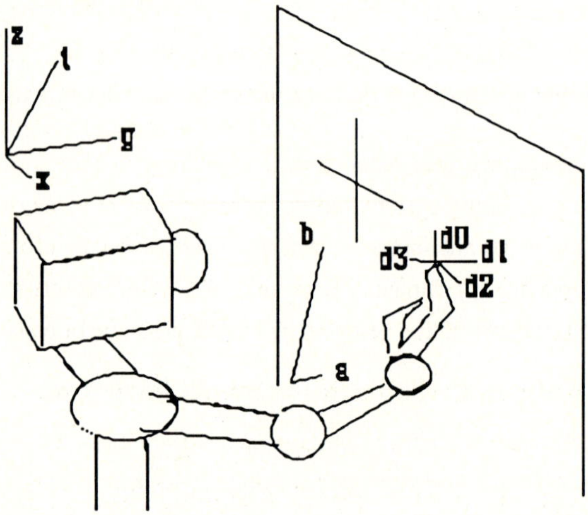

FIGURE 1. A movement (d0,d1,d2,d3...) directed towards a sensory cue depends upon one or more reference frames (18) such as the body support (x,y,z,t,..) and the goal's context (a,b,..). In a living system or compliant robot, learning the relation between those frames is one of the basic aims of movement control.

3. Posture as a reference frame.

The muscle provides the body with a compliant interface to the environment. Together with the spinal reflexes, it constitutes a servoregulation of stiffness (11). This spring-like property of muscles allows for ballistic movements which must be controlled in a feedforward manner. The disadvantage of such an interface is the perturbations on the position in remote segments resulting from the forces on which the movement is based, causing loss of both stability and equilibrium. Effects of these perturbations are reduced by anticipatory postural adjustments.

Both movement and posture controls involve sensorimotor actions on one or more couplings. The distinction between these two components can be made according to their respective goals. Movement's goal is a change of state (hand manipulation for example), posture's goal is the maintenance of a given state (holding the object with the controlateral hand, fixation of trunk and shoulder during manipulation... etc) notwithstanding external or internal perturbations.

The various segments under postural control, including resting points with external objects, can be considered as a body reference frame for movement. Thus, in order to maintain this frame, the nervous system adaptively corrects any modification of body segments resulting from postural perturbations, whatever the cause, being a self-motion or an environmental action (7).

Similarly, movement control in a compliant, multi-jointed, autonomous robot must include two components: the action that is aimed towards a focal goal and the compensation for internal perturbations provoked by this action on remote segments through viscoelastic joints. These two aspects have been defined as teleokinetic and ereismatic (9).

Proposition 3: *At least, two reference frames must coexist, one being related to the autonomous system, the other being related to the action's goal. Postural control is aimed at the maintenance of a preselected body reference frame with regards to the goal reference frame.*

4. Distinct roles of nervous structures in reference frame control

The organization of a movement by the central nervous system involves not only the planning of muscular control, but also the anticipation of the putative consequences of the action, such as the sensory inflow relating to the execution of the motor action or the mechanical effects of this action on other body segments or equilibrium (15). Both cases can be related to a modification of the relationship between body and goal reference frames.

Two concepts of "control augmentation" and "stabilization augmentation", devoted respectively to the cerebellum and basal ganglia, have been introduced (13). The cerebellum together with the precerebellar nuclei and the inferior olive is involved in motor co-ordination or control augmentation (10,12). The motor part of the basal ganglia, whose output is linked to the supplementary motor area of the cerebral cortex, seems to solve the problem of postural stability (stability of the relation between body and goal reference frames). Experimental results in parkinsonian patients during bimanual tasks provide some support for this hypothesis (16).

In the present simulation, both structures are related to two kinds of control. The cerebellum would control the relation between the goal itself and its frame of reference, the basal ganglia the selection and stabilization of the body frame as regards to the goal reference frame.

5. Neural network simulation

As opposed to current neural net methods, the basic element of the simulation is not a formal neurone but the basic unit of each nervous structure involved (20) (Fig. 2). The simulation, performed in parallel computer language (Occam), takes into account the following basic units: the cerebral columnar automata (4,5), the cerebellar microzone considered as a perceptron device (1,12,17), the elementary striato-pallido-nigral circuit of the basal ganglia and the elementary spinal circuit of stiffness servomechanism (11). Internal and external loops which include adaptive neural structures are then considered as part of an autopoïetic system whose structure evolves by adaptation to external perturbations.

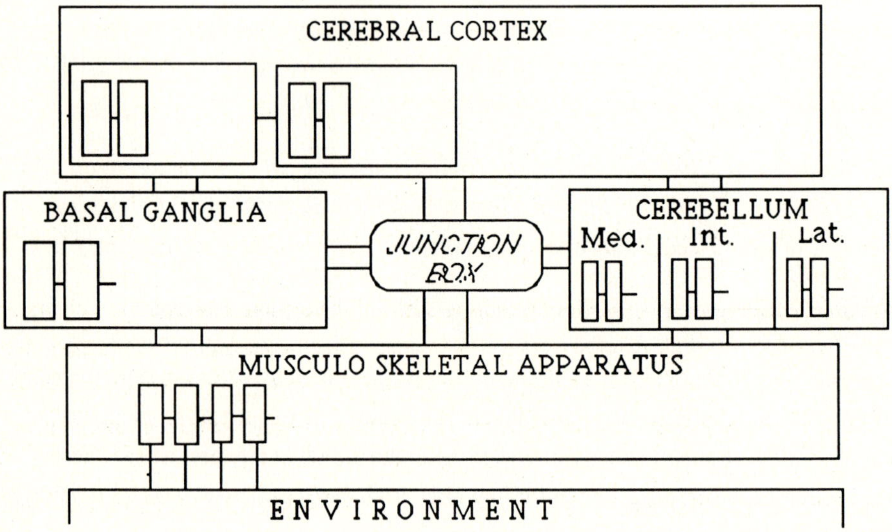

FIGURE 2. Parallel simulation includes four major block systems, each being divided in areas. Inside each area, the basic element is indicated by a small rectangle. The junction box defines the connections between areas according to physiological data (2,14).

During the learning phase, movement and posture control can be distinguished by their respective spatial and temporal frequencies, higher for movement, lower for posture (8). Thus, a fuzzy logic simulation is well suited, involving two kinds of signals: position and change of position, each of which being characterized as zero (adequate), positive or negative, small, medium or large (23).

Preliminary simulations indicate that the nervous system is not an input-output device performing matrix-like operations between sensory and motor vectors, as previously described (19). Although the use of tensor theory has been criticized in such case (3), it is well suited to metric operations such as distance computation in non orthogonal frames of reference. This formalism can be redefined in a more general sense for sensorimotor co-ordination, covariant coordinates being related to postural adjustment (reference frame), contravariant ones being related to movement itself (6).

References

1. Albus, J.: A theory of cerebellar function. Math. Biosci. 10,25-61 (1971).
2. Allen, G.I., Tsukahara, N.: Cerebrocerebellar communication systems. Physiol. Rev. 54, 957-1006 (1974).
3. Arbib, M.A., Amari, S.I.: Sensori-motor transformations in the brain (with a critique of the tensor theory of cerebellum). J. Theor. Biol. 112, 123-155 (1985).
4. Burnod, Y.: An adaptive neural network, the cerebral cortex. Masson (1988).
5. Daegelen, P., Burnod, Y., Guoignon, E.: Reconnaissance de structures secondaires d'ARN's: Utilisation de réseaux d'automates neuronaux. RBMI, Juin (1985).
6. Dufossé, M.: Tensorial scheme of the co-ordination between posture and movement. (submitted).
7. Dufossé, M., Hugon, M., Masion, J.,Paulignan, Y.: Two modes of adaptive changes to perturbations of forearm posture. In: Posture and gait: development, adaptation and modulation. Excerpta Medica,B. Amblard, A. Berthoz, F. Clarac, eds., 217-225 (1988).
8. Guiard, Y.: Asymetric division of labor in human skilled bimanual action: the kinematic chain as a model. J. Motor Behav. 19, 4, 486-517 (1987).
9. Hess, W.R.: Teleokinetisches and ereismatisches kräftesystem in der biomotorik. Helv. Physiol. Pharmacol. Acta 1, C62-C63, (1943).
10. Holmes, G.: The cerebellum of man. Brain 1, 62, 1-30
11. Houk, J.C., Rymer, W.Z.: Neural control of muscle length and tension. In: Handbook of physiology, V.B. Brooks ed., Section I, Vol 2, 257-323 (1981).
12. Ito, M.: The cerebellum and neural control. Raven Press (1984).
13. Ito, M.: Neural systems controlling movement. TINS, 515-518 (1986).
14. Kawato, M., Furukawa, K., Suzuki, R.: A hierarchical neural-network model for control and learning of voluntary movement. Biol. Cybern. 57,169-185 (1987).
15. Massion, J., Dufossé, M: Co-ordination between posture and movement: Why and How ? NIPS 3,88-93 (1988).

16. Massion, J., Viallet, F., Massarino, R., Khalil, R.: La région de l'aire motrice supplémentaire est impliquée dans la coordination entre posture et mouvement. C.R.Acad.Sci. Paris 308, 417-423 (1989).

17. Marr, D: A theory of cerebellar cortex. J. Physiol. 202,437-470 (1969).

18. Paillard, J., Beaubaton, D.: De la coordination visuomotrice à l'organisation de la saisie manuelle. In: Du contrôle moteur à l'organisation du geste (H. Hecaen , M. Jeannerod, eds). Masson (1978).

19. Pellionisz, A., Llinas, R.: Tensorial approach to the geometry of brain function: cerebellar coordination via a metric tensor. Neurosci. 5,1125-1136 (1980).

20. Shepherd, G.M.: The synaptic organization of the brain. Oxford Univ. Press (1979).

21. Varela, F.: Principles of biological autonomy. Elsevier (1979).

22. Winograd, T.: Des machines savantes mais incultes. Science et Vie, July (1985).

23. Yamakawa, T.: A simple fuzzy computer hardware system employing min and max operations. A challenge to 6th generation computer. IFSA congress, Tokyo, 827-830, July 20-25 (1987).

Cheapmonkey : Comparing an ANN and the Primate Brain on a Simple Perceptual Task: Orientation Discrimination

Guy A. Orban, Mark Devos and Rufin Vogels

Laboratorium voor Neuro- en Psychofysiologie, KU Leuven Medical School, Campus Gasthuisberg, Herestraat ,B-3000 Leuven, Belgium

Introduction

For a number of years our laboratory has been involved in the study of the neuronal mechanisms underlying simple discriminations such as speed or orientation discriminations made by humans (Orban et al. 1984a,b) and model species such as cats (Vandenbussche et al. 1986b) and monkeys (Vandenbussche et al. 1986a; Vogels et al. 1988). The reason for studying these simple perceptual tasks is to reduce the complexity of the study by having an extremely complex brain performing a relatively simple operation, which we hope to understand with the presently available neuroscience techniques. As such these studies are an alternative to neuroscience studies of the behaviour of invertebrates (Kandel 1976). One approach has been to record from different structures along the visual pathways while monkeys perform the discrimination. We (Vogels et al. 1989, Vogels and Orban 1989, Orban and Vogels 1989) have recently finished such a study of monkey striate neurons recorded while the monkey was performing an orientation discrimination task. We have used the orientation tuning curves obtained in that study as characteristics of input units of a multilayer perceptron trained with backpropagation and performing an orientation discrimination task similar to that of the monkeys.

The aims of this study were fourfold. Artificial neural networks (ANNs) are supposed to be powerful computational devices of which the operation is not always well understood. In order to test how powerful these device are it is useful to compare them to a genuine brain. Since we have both the input (striate tuning curves) and output (just noticeable differences) characteristics of the monkey behaviour we can compare the monkey performance with that of different network configurations using input units similar to the monkey striate neurons. In order to understand the functioning of ANNs we can use the same strategy as used for the primate brain and test them in simple perceptual tasks. Indeed as will be shown we can study how input unit characteristics and connection strengths determine the overall network performance. The study

NATO ASI Series, Vol. F 68
Neurocomputing
Edited by F. Fogelman Soulié and J. Hérault

can contribute to the better understanding of computations in ANNs but also in the primate brain. The orientation tuning characteristics of hidden units of the multilayer perceptron may provide some clue to which properties single neurons beyond striate cortex involved in orientation discrimination should have, facilitating their search in the monkey visual cortical areas. A similar strategy was followed by Lehky and Sejnowski (1988). Finally this study may reveal which parameters of the orientation tuning of cortical cells determine the behavioural performance of primates.

Methods

Action potentials of striate neurons were recorded with a microelectrode and eye movements with a scleral search coil while the monkey was performing an orientation discrimination task. When the monkey was fixating an LED, two grating stimuli (diameter 8 deg., contrast 80 %, mean luminance 10 cd/m^2) were presented in succession (inter-stimulus interval 300 msec, stimulus duration 350 msec) over the receptive field of the cortical neuron under study. The task of the monkey was to maintain fixation when the two gratings had the same orientation and to saccade to the grating when the two gratings differed in orientation. Correct responses were rewarded by juice drops. Tested in this way, monkeys, after considerable training, are able to discriminate (at the 75% correct level) orientation differences as small as 1.5 deg. Orientation tuning curves were collected by changing the orientation of the first grating in 10 ,15 or 30 deg. steps, depending on the sharpness of tuning of the neuron under study. For each orientation tested both the average response and the variance were measured (Fig. 1). As shown in this figure the sharpness of orientation tuning of striate neurons, captured by the tuning width at half height, varies considerably: the cell in Figure 1A had a tuning width of 11 deg. compared to 80 deg. for the cell of Figure 1C.

These orientation tuning curves plotting mean response and variance as a function of orientation, were modeled by gaussian curves with the parameters maximum response or maximum variance, optimal orientation and standard deviation representing the sharpness of tuning. For the mean response curve of the cell in Figure 1A the sigma was 4.1 compared to 29 for the cell of Figure 1C. These gaussian-shaped curves were used as characteristics of the input units of the multilayer perceptron (Fig. 2). The units of the perceptron had a classical sigmoid activation function. The number of input and hidden units was variable but the number of output units was fixed at two. The network was trained with a variant of backpropagation called Self Adapting backpropagation (Devos and Orban 1988) which is less sensitive to the initial choice of the learning parameters. During each learning step all orientations were presented to the input layer. The orientations were presented symmetrically with respect to the reference orientation, i.e. the orientation from which others had to be distinguished.

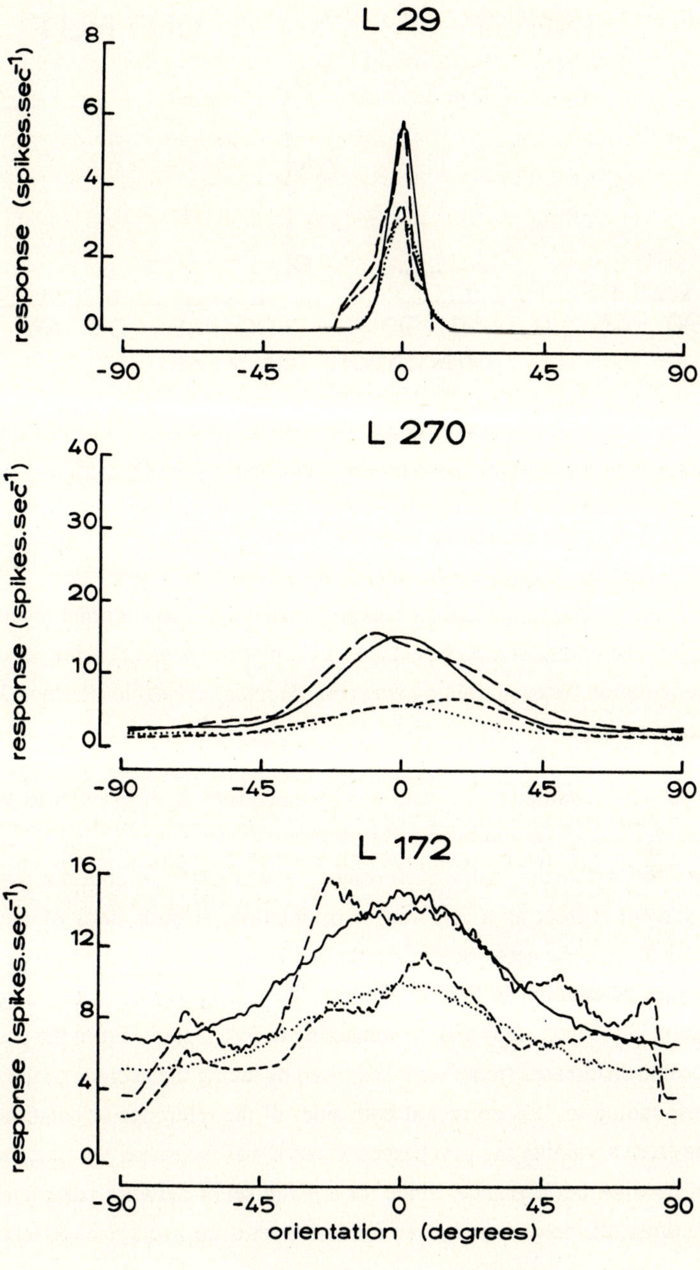

Figure 1 Modeling of orientation tuning of monkey striate neurons by a gaussian distribution. The mean response and the variance are plotted as a function of stimulus orientation for the monkey data (large stippled line, mean, short stippled line, variance) and the gaussian models (full line, mean, dotted line, variance). Zero represents the optimal orientation of the model gaussian distribution. The tuning width at half height was 11 deg. for L29, 52 deg. for L270 and 80 deg. for L172; the standard deviation (sigma) of the model curves was 4.1, 19 and 29 for these three cells respectively

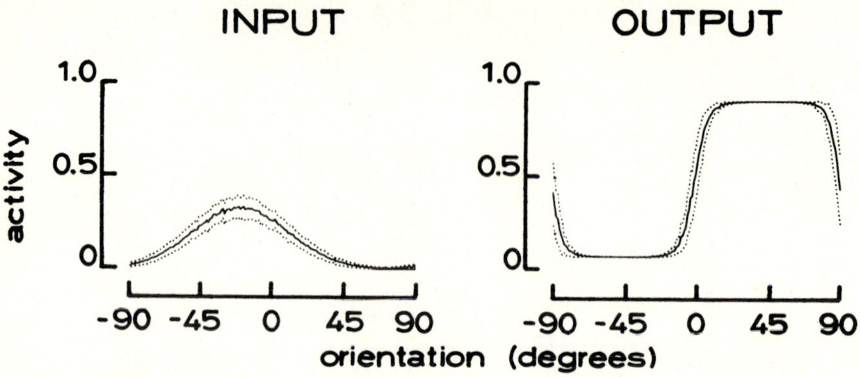

Figure 2 Activity profile of network input and output neurons : full lines represent the mean activity and stippled lines the mean plus or minus the standard deviation

Orientations within 5 deg. of the reference orientation were presented in 0.5 deg. steps. those between 5 and 10 deg. in 1 deg. steps, and those beyond in 5 deg. steps. Errors were accumulated over one training step and then backpropagated to the lower order layers. Training was terminated when the orientation performance curve, plotting percent correct discrimination as a function of orientation for each training step (Fig. 3) remained stable (Pearson X^2 test) for five successive training steps.

For each set of network parameters, training was repeated five times in order to evaluate the variability in convergence speed and in connection strengths between units in different layers. Once the network had reached a stable performance it was tested to obtain a psychometric curve, plotting percent correct as a function of orientation, at both sides of the reference orientation (Fig. 3). To test the network all orientations were again presented, those within 2.5 deg. of the reference orientation in 0.25 deg. steps, those between 2.5 and 5 deg. from the reference orientation in 0.5 deg. steps and the remaining in 5 deg. steps. From the psychometric curves, just noticeable differences (jnds) were estimated by taking the average of the orientation differences corresponding to 75% correct at both sides of the reference orientation. For each network resulting from a training the psychometric curve was measured ten times to establish the variability of network performance. Since for a given set of network parameters training was repeated five times, the network jnd given for such a set is the average of 50 tests.

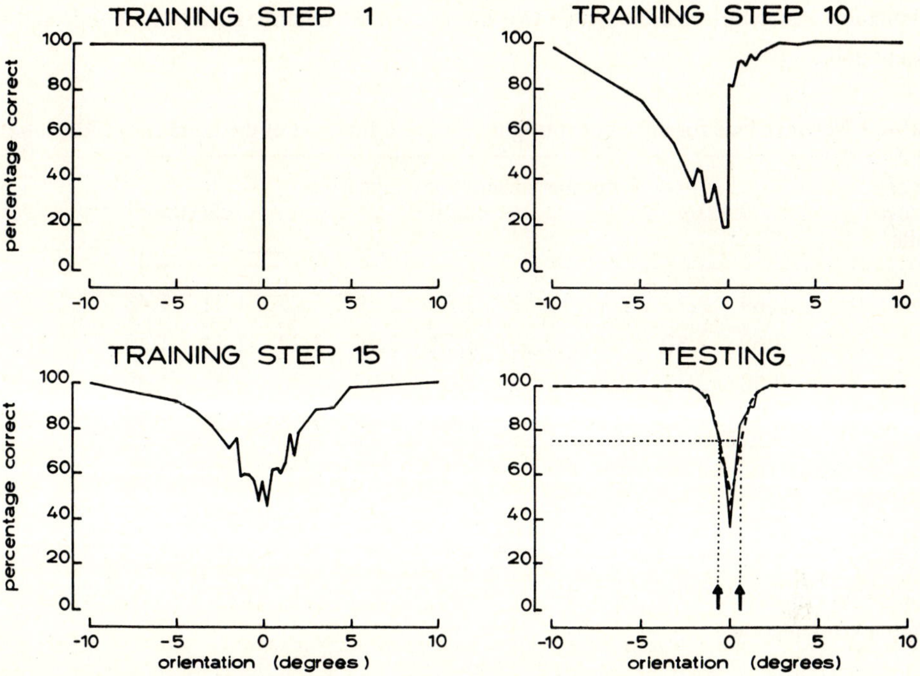

Figure 3 Training and testing of a network. The network performance (percent correct) is plotted as a function of stimulus orientation (zero represents the reference orientation). The total training of this network took 18 steps. In the testing of the network, the performance at either side of the reference orientation was averaged. In the example the jnds for the two sides were -0.55 deg and +0.45 deg yielding an average value of 0.5 deg. The network jnds reported in this study are the medians of 50 of these test values

Results

Monkeys are able to discriminate orientations at all reference orientations after some training. The network was initially trained and tested at a single reference orientation. This is a linearly separable problem which can be solved by a two-layer network without need for hidden units. Indeed after training a three-layer network for orientation discrimination at a single reference orientation we measured the activity of the hidden units as a function of orientation. This revealed that the activity profile of the hidden units was not different from that of the output units (Fig. 2B). This indicated that for a single reference orientation no further processing was required beyond the second layer. This was confirmed by studying the performance of the network, i.e. its jnd in orientation as a function of the number of hidden units for a large number of network parameters. In all cases the performance of a three-layer network was no better than a two-layer network (Table 1). The remainder of the study at a single reference orientation was therefore done with a two-layer network containing only input units and two output units.

Table 1 Network jnds for different configurations as a function of the number of hidden units

nb of hidden units	<4,0>			<4,20>			<20,0>		
0	2.69	2.72	2.85	2.48	2.57	2.79	1.29	1.41	1.48
2	2.69	2.80	3.00	2.53	2.57	2.94	1.22	1.44	1.53
4	2.60	2.73	2.96	2.39	2.88	3.02	1.24	1.37	1.49
8	2.70	2.85	2.91	2.57	2.67	2.76	1.28	1.34	1.40

(Column groups: < number of input units, phase >)

The table indicates the first, second (median) and third quartiles of the network jnds for different network configurations defined by the number of input units and the phase, i.e. the angle between the preferred orientation of the unit closest to the reference orientation and the reference orientation.

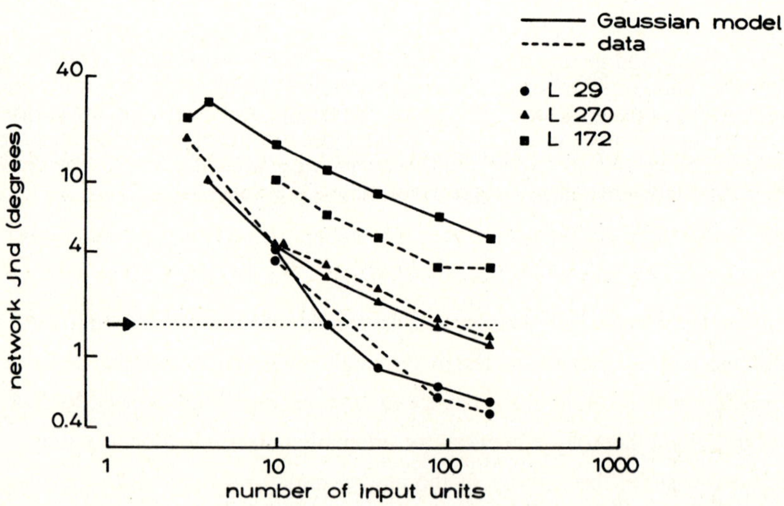

Figure 4 The jnd network plotted as a function of the number of input units, for the neurons of which the tuning characteristics were shown in Fig. 1: stippled lines, the monkey data and full lines, the gaussian model curves. The arrows indicate the average jnd of monkeys

The orientation tuning curves of monkey striate neurons were modeled with gaussian curves. Although the fit between the data and the model was generally satisfactory, one has to evaluate how much this approximation influences the network performance. We therefore compared the performance of networks with same parameters except that the real tuning curves were replaced by their model gaussian curves. As shown in Figure 4 this had little influence on the network performance. In about two thirds of the cases there was hardly any difference between the network performance with data and model tuning curves as in Figure 4B. In the remaining cases the network with the model curves performed better than that with the data curves as in Figure 4A or the reverse as in Figure 4C. It is worth mentioning that the difference in performance only depended on the difference in maximum steepness of the two curves . In Figure 4A the model curve (Fig. 1A) had steeper slopes then the data curve and the reverse was true for the cell of the Figure 4C network (Fig. 1C). We conclude that on average the modelling of the data by gaussian curves does not influence the conclusions derived from the study of these networks.

Since the number of output units was fixed only the number of input units and their tuning characteristics can determine the network performance. As shown in Figure 4, the jnd of the network decreases with an increasing number of input units. This relationship seems to follow a power law of the number of input units. The tuning characteristics however also contribute to the performance of the network. The network of Figure 4A used cells of Figure 1A as input units. These units had a small sigma (4.1) and no spontaneous activity. The networks of Figures 4B and 4C used the cells of Figures 1B and 1C respectively as input units. These units had a broader tuning indicated by a larger sigma and spontaneous activity. Their performance was poorer than that of the network in Figure 4A. The Figure 4A network needed only about 20 input units to match the monkey performance, while the Figure 4B network needed about 50 and the Figure 4C network failed to match the monkey's performance even with 200 input units. Figure 4 also indicates however that wider tuning of input units has advantages and not just disadvantages. Indeed the network in Figure 4B needed only four input units to be trainable, while the network in Figure 4A, using narrower input units, needed at least 10 input units to converge.

In order to understand which input units contributed most to the performance of the network we have investigated the strength of the connections between the input units and the output units. These are shown in Figure 5A. Depending on the number of input units, the input unit with the strongest connection to the output unit was located two or three sigma from the reference orientation. Since at two or three sigma the response of a tuned unit is weak this thus does not indicate which input unit contributed the most input to the output units. These contributions are

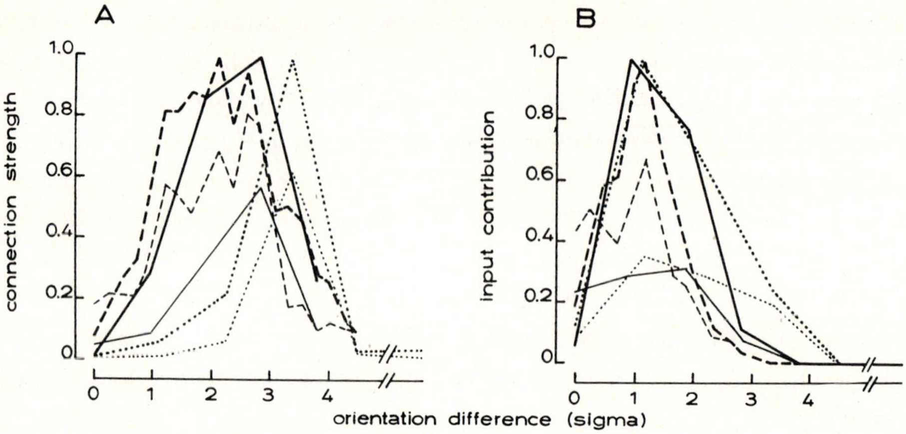

Figure 5 Which input units are used in this discrimination ? The curvature strength and the input contribution (see text for definition) of the different input neurons are plotted as a function of the difference between their optimal orientation and the reference orientation expressed in standard deviations.

obtained by multiplying the connection strength by the mean activity of the input unit for the reference orientation. These values are plotted as a function of the preferred orientation of the input units in Figure 5B. For all network parameters the unit of which the preferred orientation differed one sigma from the reference orientation contributed the most to the output unit.

Discussion and Conclusions

We modeled orientation tuning curves of monkey striate neurons recorded in awake discriminating monkeys with gaussian curves and used these as characteristics of input units of a multilayer perceptron trained with a variant of backpropagation.

The conclusion of our study depend either little or not at all on the substitution of the original tuning curves by model curves.

Multilayer perceptrons using backpropagations are powerful computational devices since only a few tens of input units are required to match the performance of the primate brain. For the discrimination at a single reference orientation no hidden units are required since it is a linear problem.

The multilayer perceptrons are so powerful because they use the input units which have the steepest slope at the reference orientation. Indeed gaussian curves have the steepest slope at one sigma from the optimal orientation, and units with their preferred orientation at one sigma from the reference orientation contribute the most to the output units.

When compared to other models for human orientation discrimination (Paradiso 1988),the small number of input units required by multilayer perceptrons is striking. This indicates that if the primate brain could use the striate units with steepest slope it would have to combine the input from few cells to perform this simple orientation discrimination task.

Our study provides a possible functional significance for the wide range in orientation tuning observed in monkey striate cortex. While narrowly tuned cells are useful to achieve fine discrimination efficiently, i.e. with fewer input units, more broadly tuned cells are useful to learn thc discrimination more efficiently, i.e. with fewer input units.

The present study provides no insight into the stages involved in orientation discrimination beyond the striate cortex since for the simple problem of discrimination at a single reference orientation hidden units were not required. We are presently studying harder problems involving several reference orientations.

Aknowledgements. The research reported was supported by a grant of the National Artificial Intelligence Program (RF/AI/01) of the Belgian Ministry of Science. RV holds a research fellowship from the Belgian National Research Council (NFWO).

References

1. Devos, M.R., Orban, G.A.: Self-adapting back-propagation. Neuro-Nîmes, EC2 ed., 104-112 (1988)
2. Kandel, E.R.: Cellular Basis of Behavior. San Francisco: Freeman (1976)
3. Lehky, S.R., Sejnowski, T.J.: Network model of shape-form shading: neural function arises from both receptive and projective fields. Nature, 333, 452-454 (1988)
4. Orban, G.A., De Wolf, J., Maes, H. Factors influencing velocity coding in the human visual system. Vision Res., 24, 33-39 (1984)
5. Orban, G.A., Vandenubssche, E., Vogels, R. Human orientation discrimination tested with long stimuli. Vision Res., 24, 121-128.
6. Orban, G.A., Vogels, R.: Orientation tuning characteristics of V1 neurons measured in the discriminating monkey. Soc. Neurosci. Abstr., in press (1989)
7. Paradiso, M.A.: A theory for use of visual orientation information which exploits the columnar structure of striate cortex. Biol. Cybern., 58, 35-49 (1988)
8. Rumelhart, D.E., Hinton, G.E., Williams, R.J.: Learning internal representations by error propagation. In D.E. Rumelhart & J.L. McClelland (eds.), Parallel Distributed Processing: Explorations in the Microstructure of Cognition. Vol. 1: Foundations. MIT Press, 318-362 (1986)

9. Vandenbussche, E., Orban, G.A., Maes, H.: Velocity discrimination in the monkey. Soc. Neurosci. Abstr., 12, 1183 (1986a)

10. Vandenbussche, E., Orban, G.A., Maes, H.: Velocity discrimination in cat. Vision Res., 26, 1835-1849 (1986b)

11. Vogels, R., Orban, G.A., Eeckhout H., Spileers, W.: Visual orientation discrimination in the primate. Arch. internat. Physiol. Biochim., 96, P31 (1988)

12. Vogels, R., Orban, G.A.: Orientation discrimination thresholds of single striate cells in the discriminating monkey. Soc. Neurosci. Abstr., in press (1989)

13. Vogels, R., Spileers, W., Orban, G.A.: The response variability of striate cortical neurons in the behaving monkey. Exp. Brain Res., in press (1989)

REFERENCES

Ackley, D.H., Hinton, G.E. and Sejnowski, T.J.: A learning algorithm for Boltzmann machines. Cognitive Science, vol. 9, 147-169 (1985)

Adda-Decker,M.: Evaluation d'unités de décision pour la reconnaissance de la parole continue, Thèse 3ème cycle, Orsay (December 1988).917-935.

Aggarwal, J.K., Nandhakumar, N.: On the computation of motion from sequences of images-A review. Proceeding of the IEEE, Vol.76, n° 8.

Albus, J.: A theory of cerebellar function. Math. Biosci. 10, 25-61 (1971).

Allen, G.I., Tsukahara, N.: Cerebrocerebellar communication systems. Physiol. Rev. 54, 957-1006 (1974).

Almeida, L.: A Learning Rule for Asynchronous Perceptrons with Feedback in a Combinatorial Environment. In Proceedings of the 1987 IEEE First Annual International Conference on Neural Networks, S. Diego, CA (1987).

Alpaydin, E. : Grow-and-learn network. EPFL-LAMI, Internal note (September 1988).

Alpaydin, E., Marchal, P.: Snark, a neural optical reader. In "Connectionism in Perspective", R. Pfeifer, Z. Schreter, F. Fogelman Soulié, L. Steels eds, North Holland, 309-315 (1989).

Alspector, J., Allen, R. B., Hu, V. and Satyanarayana, S.: Stochastic learning networks and their electronic implementation. In: Neural Information Processing Systems, Natural and Synthetic, D.Z.Anderson, ed., American Institute of Physics (1988)

Anderson, J., Silverstein, J., Ritz, S., Jones, R.: Distinctive features, categorical perception, and probability learning: some applications of a neural model. In Psychological Review, 84, 413-451 (1977).

Angéniol, B., Le Texier, J.Y., Mateu, J.B.: SLOGAN: an object-oriented language for neural network specification.In: Neural networks, from models to applications, L.Personnaz and G.Dreyfus, eds., IDSET, 641-652 (1989).

Anizan, P.: Modèle à régulation hiérarchisées. 3èmes Journées Neurosciences, Univ. Aix-Marseille I-II (1986).

Ans, B., Gilhodes, J.-C., Hérault, J.: Simulation de réseaux neuronaux (SIRENE). II - Hypothèse de décodage du message de mouvement porté par les afférences fusoriales Ia et II par un mécanisme de plasticité synaptique. C. R. Acad. Sc., Paris, 297, série III, 419-22 (1983).

Arbib, M.A., Amari, S.I.: Sensori-motor transformations in the brain (with a critique of the tensor theory of cerebellum). J. Theor. Biol. 112, 123-155 (1985)

Asanuma, H., Rosen, I.: Spread of mono and polysynaptic connections within cat's motor cortex. Exp. Brain Res., 16.507 (1973).

Anizan,P.: Modéle a régulations hiérarchisées, 3ème journées Neurosciences, Univ. Aix-Marseille I-II (1986).

Atal, B., Hanauer, S.L.: Speech analysis & synthesis by linear prediction. In J. Acoust. Soc. Amer., 50, 637-655 (1971).

Azencott, R.: Markov fields and low-level vision tasks. Proc. Int. Cong. Appl. Math., ICIAM, Paris (1987).

Azencott, R.: Gibbs fields, simulated annealing and low-level vision tasks. Proc. Cong. on Pattern Recognition, AFCET-INRIA, Antibes (1987).

Azencott, R.: General Boltzmann machines with multiple interactions. IEEE PAMI, to appear.

Azencott, R.: Parameter estimation for synchronous Markov fields. to appear (1990) p.236.

Bahl, L.R., Brown, P.F., de Suza, P.V., Mercer, R.L.: Maximum mutual information estimation of hidden model parameters. In Proc. IEEE ICASSP 86, pages 49-52 (1986).

Bahl, L.R., Jelinek, F.: Decoding for Channels with Insertions, Deletions, and Substitutions with Applications to Speech Recognition, IEEE Trans. on IT, vol. 21, no. 4, 404-411 (1975).

Baiardi, F., Mussardo, R., Serra, R., Valastro, G.: Feedforward layered networks on message passing parallel computers. In Parallel architectures and neural networks, E. Caianiello ed. World Scientific, Singapore (1989).

Baldi, P., Hornik, K.: Neutral Network and principal component analysis. Learning from examples without local minima. preprint (1988).

Ballard, D.H.: Cortical connections and parallel processing: Structure and function. The behavioral and brain sciences 9, 67-120 (1986).

Baum, E., Haussler, D.: What Size Net Gives Valid Generalization ?, Neural Computation, Vol. 1. n° 1. 151-160 (1989).

Baum, E., Wilczek,F.: Supervised learning of probability distribution by neural networks. In Neural Information processing systems, D Anderson, editor, Am. Inst. of Physics. 52-61 (1988).

Bear, M.F., Singer,W.: Modulation of visual cortical plasticity by acetylcholine and noradrenaline. Nature 320. 172-176 (1986).

Becker, S., Le Cun, Y.: Improving the convergence of back-propagation learning with second order methods. In "Proceedings, 1988 Connectionist models Summer School", Morgan Kaufman, 29-37 (1988).

Bengio, Y., De Mori, R.: Speaker normalization and automatic speech recognition using spectral lines and neural networks. In Proceedings of the Canadian Conference on Artificial Intelligence (CSCSI-88), Edmonton, Al. (May 1988).

Bengio, Y., Cardin, R.,De Mori, R., Merlo, E.: Programmable execution of multilayered networks for automatic speech recognition, Comm. ACM, Vol. 32, N° 2, 196-199 (1989) .

Benveniste, A., Métivier, M., Priouret, R.: Algorithmes stochastiques. Masson, Paris (1988).

Béroule, D.: Un modèle de mémoire adaptative, dynamique et associative pour le traitement automatique de la parole, Thèse 3ème cycle, Orsay. (1985).

Béroule, D.: Guided propagation inside a Topographic Memory, IEEE First International Conference on Neural Networks, San Diego. (1987).

Béroule, D.: The Never-Ending Learning, Neural Computers, R. Eckmiller, C.v.d. Malsburg (Eds), Springer Verlag (1988a).

Béroule, D.: SunADAM: a software simulation of the Adaptive, Dynamic and Associative Memory Model for the SunWorkstation, IPO report, Eindhoven. (1988b).

Béroule, D.: The adaptive, dynamic and associative memory model : a possible future tool for vocal Human-Computer Communication, The structure of multi-modal Dialogue, M.M. Taylor, F. Néel, D.G. Bouwhuis (Eds.), Amsterdam: North-Holland. (1989a).

Béroule, D.: Traitement connexionniste du Langage, in Histoire, Epistémologie et Langage, tome 11 fascicule 1: Sciences du langage et recherches cognitives, F. Rastier Ed. (1989b).

Béroule, D.: Management of time distorsions through rough coincidence detection, Proceeding of the &st European Conference on Speech Communication and Technology , Paris. (1989c).

Béroule, D., Schwartz, J.L.: Essai de formalisation de faits et hypothèses de physiologie concernant le traitement de l'information pour la reconnaissance automatique de la parole. Proceedings of the 15th JEP, Aix-en-Provence. (1986).

Beynon, T., Dodd, N.: The implementation of multi-layer perceptorns on transputer networks. Proc. 7th Occam user group, Grenoble, (1987).

Bienenstock, E., Fogelman Soulié, F., Weisbuch, G.: Disordered systems and Biological organization. NATO ASI Series, F20, Springer Verlag, (1986).

Blanchet, P., Coupet,P.,Dore,L., Lajaunie,T.: Approche d'un apprentissage syntaxique par un modèle connexionniste, D.E.A. report, LIMSI, Orsay. (1986).

Blayo, F., Hurat, P.: A systolic architecture dedicated to neural networks. In: Neural networks, from models to applications , L. Personnaz and G. Dreyfus, eds., IDSET, 701-709, (1989).

Bloch, V., Laroche, S.: Facts and hypotheses related to the search of the engram, Neurobiology of learning and memory, Guilford, New-York. (1984).

Bottou, L.Y.: Reconnaissance de la parole par réseaux multi-couches. In Proc. Neuro-Nîmes 88, EC2 eds (1988).

Bottou, L.Y., Le Cun, Y.: SN, un simulateur pour réseaux connexionnistes. In Proc. Neuro-Nîmes 88, EC2 eds (1988).

Bottou, L.Y., Le Cun, Y.: SN: Un simulateur pour réseaux connexionnistes. "Neuro-Nîmes 88", EC2 Ed., 371-382, (1988).

Bottou, L., Fogelman Soulié, F., Liénard, J.S., Blanchet, P.: Speaker independent isolated digit recognition: multi layer perceptrons vs dynamic time warping. Neural Networks, to appear.

Bourlard, H., Kamp, Y.: Auto-Association by Multilayer Perceptron and Singular Value Decomposition, manuscript M217, Philips Research Laboratory, Brussels, Belgium, November (1987).

Bourlard, H., Wellekens, C.J.: Multilayer perceptrons and automatic speech recognition. In IEEE 1st ICNN, San Diego, M. Caudill, C. Butler eds, IEEE catalog n° 87TH0191-7, vol. IV, 407-416, (1987).

Bourlard, H., Wellekens, C.J.: Speech Pattern Discrimination and Multilayer Perceptrons, Computer, Speech and Language, vol. 3, 1-19, (1989).

Bourlard, H., Wellekens, C.J.: Links between Markov Models and Multilayer Perceptrons, Advances in Neural Information Processing Systems 1, Morgan Kaufmann, 502-510, (1989).

Bout, D.E., Miller, T.K.: A traveling salesman objective function that works. Proc. 2nd IEEE ICNN, San Diego, vol. II, 299-304, (1988).

Bowler, K.C., Bruce, A.D., Kenway, R.D., Pawley, G.S., Wallace, D.J., McKendrick, A.: Scientific computation on the Edinburgh DAPS. Tech. report, Univ. of Edinburgh, (dec. 1987).

Bowler, K.C., Kenway, R.D., Pawley, G.S., Roweth, D.: An introduction to Occam 2 programming. Chartwell-Bratt, Bromley, (1987).

Bridle, J.S.: Probabilistic Scoring for Back-Propagation Networks, with Relationships to Statistical Pattern Recognition, Neural Network for Computing, Snowbird, UT, (1989).

Brodatz, P.: Textures- A photographic album for artists and designers. Dover, New York, (1966).

Brown, P.: The Acoustic-Modeling Problem in Automatic Speech Recognition, Ph.D. thesis, Comp. Sc. Dep., Carnegie-Mellon University, (1987).

Burnod, Y.: An adaptive neural network, the cerebral cortex. Masson (1988).

Burnod, Y.: Cerebral Cortex and Behavioral Adaptation: a possible mechanism, Masson. (1988).

Burnod, Y., Daegelen, P.: Hypercube structure of the network between cortical areas. In Y. Burnod: An adaptive neural network, the cerebral cortex. Masson, (1988).

Burnod, Y., Maton, B., Calvet, J.: Activity of neurons in area 4 and in area 5 of monkey during operant conditioning of a flexion movement. In Conditioning , C.D. Woody ed. Plenum.(1982).

Burr, D.J.: Experiments on Neural Net Recognition of Spoken and Written Text. IEEE Trans. on ASSP, Vol. ASSP-36, n°. 7, 1162-1168, (1988).

Buzzo, A., Gray, A.H., Gray, R.M., Markel, J.D.: Speech coding based on vector quantisation, IEEE Trans., Vol.ASSP-28, 5, 562-574, (1980).

Cajal,S., Ramon,Y.: Histologie du système nerveux de l'homme et des vertebres. Maloine, Paris. (1911).

Carnevalli P. & al.: Image processing by simulated annealing. IBM J. of Res. & Devlpt., Vol. 29, N° 6, 569-579, (Nov. 1985).

Carnevali, P., Patarnello, S. : Europhys. Lett. 4, 1199, (1987).

Carpenter, G.A., Grossberg, S.: The ART of Adaptive Pattern Recognition by a Self-Organizing Neural Network. Computer, (March 1988).

Carpenter, G. A., Grossberg, S.: A massively parallel architecture for self-organizing neural pattern recognition machine. Computer Vision, Graphics and Image Processing, 37, 54-115, (1987).

Carpenter, G.A., Grossberg, S.: The ART of Adaptive Pattern Recognition by a Self-Organizing Neural Network. Computer, (March 1988).

Casey, R.G.: Moment normalization of handprinted characters. IBM Journal of Research and Development, 548, (1970).

Cavanie, A., Lecompte, P.: Study of a method to De-Alias Winds from ERS-1 data, final report of ESA contract n°6874/87/GP-I (sc)(1987).

Chalmond, B.: Image restoration using an estimated Markov model. IEEE PAMI, (1988).

Changeux, J.P., Courrege, P., Danchin, A.: A Theory of the Epigenesis of Neuronal Networks by Selective Stabilisation of Synapses, Proc. Nat. Acad. Sci. USA, Vol 70, N° 10, 2974-2978. (1973).

Chavel P. & al.: Utilisation du speckle comme générateur rapide de tableaux aléatoires binaires: optimisation des paramètres. Annales des Télécommunications, (March 1988).

Chollet, G., Choukri, K., Montacié, C.: A test workstation for the evaluation of speech recognition algorithms, applications, and data bases. In proc. 7th FASE Symposium (Speech '88), Edinburgh 145-151, (August 1988).

Chou, P.Y., Fasman, G.D.: Empirical prediction of protein conformation. ANN. Rev. Biochem., 47, 251-276, (1978).

Choukri, K.: Several approaches to Speaker Adaptation in Automatic Speech Recognition Systems. PhD Thesis, ENST, Paris, France, (1987).

Choukri, K., Chollet, G.: Unsupervised and Dynamic learning of Spectral transformations using canonical correlation analysis for adaptation of ASR to new speakers. In Computer and Speech Language, Vol 1, N 2, Academic Press Inc., 95-107, 1986.

Churchland, P. S., Sejnowski, T. J.: Perspectives on cognitive neuroscience. Science, 242, 741-745, (1988).

Clarke, L.J.: The Tiny User Guide. ECS project, Edinburgh University Computing Service.

Clarke, L.J.: Rian User Guide. ECS project, Edinburgh University Computing Service.

Collingridge, G.L., Bliss, T.V.P.: NMDA receptors: their role in long-term potentiation. Trends Neuroscience. 10, 288-293, (1987)

Comon, P.: Statistical approach to the Jutten-Hérault algorithm for separating independent signals. In this volume.

Comon, P.: Separation of Stochastic Processes whose Linear Mixture is Observed. ONRNSF - IEEE Workshop on Higher-Order Spectral Analysis, Vail, Colorado, (june 28-30 1989).

Compiani, M. Montanari, D., Serra, R., Valastro, G.: Classifier systems and neural networks. In Parallel architectures and neural networks, E. Caianiello ed. World Scientific, Singapore, 105, (1989).

Compiani, M. Montanari, D., Serra, R., Simonini, P., Valastro, G.: Dynamical systems in Artificial intelligence: the case of classifier systems. In "Connectionism in perspective", R. Pfeifer, Z. Schreter, F. Fogelman Soulié, L. Steels eds, North Holland, 331-340, (1989).

Compiani, M. Montanari, D., Serra, R., Simonini, P.: Asymptotic behaviour of classifier systems. In Proc. 3rd Int. Conf. on Genetic algorithms and their applications, Los Altos, Morgan Kaufman, (1989).

Conrad, M.: The lure of molecular computing. IEEE Spectrum. vol. 23, 55-60, (1986).

Cosi, P., Bengio, Y., De Mori, R.: On the generalization capabilities of multilayer networks in the extraction of speech properties. In Proceedings of the 11th International Joint Conference on Artificial Intelligence, Detroit Mi., (Aug. 1989).

Cottrell, G., Munro, P.W., Zipser, D.: Image compression by back propagation: a demonstration of extensional programming. In " Advances in Cognitive Science", N.E. Sharkey Ed., vol2, Norwood NJ Ablex. to appear.

Cottrell, G.: Image Compression by Back-propagation. An example of Extensional Programming. Tech. Rep. 8702, U.C. San Diego, Institute for Cognitive Science, (1987).

Cover, T.: Geometrical and statistical properties of systems of linear inequalities with applications in pattern recognition. IEEE Trans. Elect. Comp. 14, 326-334, (1965).

Cox, D.R., Millar, H.D.: The theory of stochastic processes. Methuen, (1965).

Crick, F.: The recent excitement about neural networks. Nature 337, 129-132, (1989).

Daegelen, P., Burnod, Y., Guoignon, E.: Reconnaissance de structures secondaires d'ARN's: Utilisation de réseaux d'automates neuronaux. RBMI, (Juin 1985).

Davis, M.: An active process in cochlear mechanisms, Hearing Research, N° 91, (1984).

Delgutte, D.: Codage de la parole dans le nerf auditif, Thèse d'état, Paris VI. (1984).

Denker, J., Schwartz, D., Wittner, B., Solla, S., Hopfield, J.J. Howard, R., Jackel, L.: Automatic Learning, Rule Extraction and Generalization. In Complex Systems vol 1, 877-922, (1987).

Dencer, J., Gardner, W.R., Graf, H.P., Henderson, D., Howard, R.E., Hubbard,W., Jankel,L.D., Baird, H.S., Guyon, I.: Neural network recognizer for hand-written zip code digits. In D; Touretzky, editor, Advances in Neural Information Processing Systems, Morgan Kaufmann, 323-331, (1989).

Devijver, P.A., Kittler, J.: Pattern Recognition: A Statistical Approach, Prentice Hall International, (1982).

Devos F. & al. : Optical generation of random number arrays for on-chip massively parallel Monte Carlo cellular processors. Optics Letters, Vol. 12, N° 3, (March 1987).

Devos, M.R. and Orban, G.A.: Self-adapting back-propagation. Neuro-Nîmes, EC2 ed., 104-112 (1988)

Diederich, S., Opper, M.: Learning of correlated patterns in spin-glass networks by local learning rules. Phys. Rev. Lett., vol. 58, no. 9, 949-952, (1987)

Dodd, N.: Texture discrimination using multi-layer perceptrons. Pattern Recognition Letters, in press.

Doddington, G.R., Schalk, T.B.: Speech recognition: turning theory to practice. In IEEE Spectrum, 26-32, 1981.

Duda R., Hart, P.: Pattern Recognition and Scene Analysis. John Wiley & Sons, (1973).

Dufossé, M.: Tensorial scheme of the co-ordination between posture and movement. (submitted).

Dufossé, M., Hugon, M., Masion, J., Paulignan, Y.: Two modes of adaptive changes to perturbations of forearm posture. In: Posture and gait: development, adaptation and modulation. Excerpta Medica,B. Amblard, A. Berthoz, F. Clarac, eds., 217-225 (1988).

Duranton, M., Gobert, J. and Mauduit, N.: A digital VLSI module for neural networks. In: Neural networks, from models to applications. L.Personnaz and G.Dreyfus, eds., IDSET, 720-724, (1989)

Durbin, R., Rumelhart, D.E.: Product units: a computationally powerful and biologically plausible extension to back propagation networks. Neural Computation. 1, 133-142, (1989).

Eckmiller, R., von der Malsburg, C.: Neural computers. Springer Verlag, (1988).

Eisele, I.: Delta-type doping profiles in silicon. Appl. Surface Science, vol. 36, 39-51, (1989).

Elman, J.L.: Finding Structure in Time, CRL Tech, Report 8801,University of California, San Diego, (1988).

Elman, J.L., Zipser,D.: Learning the hidden structure of speech, ICS Report 8701, University of California, San Diego, (1987).

Evarts, E.V., Tanji, J.: Gating of motor cortex reflexes by prior instruction. Brain Res.71-479, (1974).

Fahlman, S.E.: Faster learning variations on back-propagation: an empirical study. In "Proceedings, 1988 Connectionist models Summer School", Morgan Kaufman, 38-51, (1988).

Feynmann, D.: Cargo Cult Science.In "Surely, you're joking, Mr Feynmann". Counterpoint. London.338-346

Féty, L.: Méthodes de traitement d'antenne adaptées aux radiocommunications.Thèse de l'ENST, Paris, (1988).

Fogelman Soulié, F., Goles, E., Weisbuch, G.: Transient length in sequential iteration of threshold functions. Disc. Appl. math. 6; 95-98, (1983).

Fogelman Soulié, F., Robert, Y. Tchuente, M.: Automata networks in computer science. Manch. Univ. Press, (1987).

Fogelman Soulié, F., Gallinari, P., Le Cun, Y., Thiria, S.: Evaluation of network architectures on test learning tasks. In IEEE 1st ICNN, San Diego, M. Caudill, C. Butler eds, IEEE catalog n° 87TH0191-7, vol. II, 653-660, (1987).

Fogelman Soulié, F., Gallinari, P., Le Cun, Y., Thiria, S.: Network Learning. In Machine Learning, vol. 3, Y. Kodratoff, R. Michalski eds, Morgan Kaufman, to appear.

Fogelman Soulié, F., Goles, E., Martinez, S., Mejia, C.: Energy functions in neural networks with continuous local functions. Complex Systems, to appear.

Foo, Y.P.S, Takefuji, Y.: Integer linear programming neural networks for job-shop scheduling. Proc 2nd IEEE ICNN, vol. II, 341-348, (1988).

Forrest, B.M. : J. Phys. A21, 245 (1988).

Forrest, B.M.: Restoration of binary images using networks of analogue neurons. In Parallel Architectures and Computer vision, I. Page ed., Oxford Univ. press, 19-31, (1988).

Forrest, B., Roweth, D., Stroud, N., Wallace, D., Wilson, G.: Neural network models. Edinburgh preprint n°87/419; (1987).

Fox, G.C., Furmanski, W.: The physical structure of concurrent problems and concurrent computers. In Scientific applications of multiprocessors, R.J. Elliott, C.A.R. Hoare eds, Prentice Hall Int. Series in Computer Science, 55-88, (1989).

Fregnac, M., Imbert, M.: Developement of neuronal selectivity in primary visual cortex of cat. Physiological Reviews 64. (1984).

Friedman, J.H., Baskett, F., Shustek, L.J.: An algorithm for finding nearest neighbors. IEEE Trans. Comp. vol. C-24, 1000-1006, (october 1975).

Fukunaga, K., Narendra, P.M.: A branch and bound algorithm for computing k-nearest neighbors. IEEE Trans. Comp. vol. C-24, 750-753, (july 1975).

Fukushima, K.: Neocognitron: a hierarchical network capable of visual pattern recognition. In Neural Networks, 1, 119-130, (1988).

Gallant, S.I.: Optimal Linear Discriminants. Eighth International Conference On Pattern Recognition, Vol. 2, 849, Paris, France, (1986).

Gallinari, P., Thiria, S., Fogelman-Soulié, F.: Multilayer Perceptrons and Data Analysis. Second annual International Conference on Neural Networks, San Diego, vol. I, 391-401, (1988).

Gallinari, P., Thiria, S., Fogelman Soulié, F.: Multilayer Perceptrons and Data Analysis. IEEE 2nd ICNN, San Diego, vol. I, 391-401, (1988).

Garda, P. et al.: A massively parallel image processor for stochastic relaxation using optical random number generation. Optical Computing 88, Toulon , 08-30/09-02, (1989).

Gardner, E., Stroud, N., Wallace, D.: Training with Noise, and the Storage of Correlated Patterns in a Neural Network Model, Edinburgh Preprint 87/394, University of Edinburgh, (1987).

Gardner, E. : Europhys. Lett. 4, 481 (1987)

Gardner, E. Derrida,B.: Optimal Storage Properties of Neural Network Models. In J. Phys. A: Math. Gen., 21, 271-284, (1988).

Garnier, J., Osguthorpe, D.J., Robson, B.: Analysis of thje accuracy and implications of simple methods for predicting the secondary structure of globular proteins. J. Mol. Biol., 120, 97-120, (1978).

Gascuel, O., Golmard, J.L.: A simple method for predicting the secondary structure of globular proteins: implications and accuracy. Centre de Recherche en Informatique de Montpellier, Technical report, (1988).

Gauvain, J.L.: Reconnaissancede mots enchainés et détection de mots dans la parole continue, Thèse 3ème cycle, Orsay. (1982).

Geman S., Geman, D.: Stochastic relaxation, Gibbs distributions and the Bayesian restoration of images. IEEE Trans. PAMI, Vol. PAMI-6, n°6, 721-741, (1984).

Geman, S., Graffigne, C.: Gibbs fields and image segmentation. Proc. Int. Congress MAth. (1987).

Getting, P.A.: Emerging principles governing the operation of neural networks. Ann. Rev. Neurosci. 12, 185-204 (1989).

Gilbert, C.D., Wiesel, T.N.: Laminar specialization and intra-cortical connections in cat primary visual cortex. In the organization of the cerebral cortex, F. Schmitt et al eds., Cambridge, Mass., MIT Press. (1981).

Gillick, L.: Probability scores for backpropagation networks. Personal communication. (1987).

Girosi, F., Verri, A., Torre, T.: Constraints in the computation of optical flow. Proceedings of the IEEE Workshop on visual motion, Irvine CA. (1989).

Goles, E.: Fixed point behaviour of threshold functions. SIAM J. Disc. and Alg. Meth., 4, 529-531, (1982).

Goles, E.: Dynamics on positive automata networks. Theor. Comp. Sci., 41, 19-32, (1985).

Goles, E.: Antisymmetric neural networks. Disc. appli. math. 13, 97-100, (1986).

Goles, E., Fogelman Soulié, F., Pellegrin, D.: Decreasing energy functions as a tool for studying threshold functions. Disc. Appl. math., 12, 261-277, (1985).

Goles, E., Martinez, S.: Dynamics on generalized neural networks. Kluber Pub. to appear.(1990).

Goles, E., Martinez, S.: Properties on positive functions and the dynamics of associated automata networks. Disc. Appl. math. vol. 18, 39-46, (1987).

Goles, E., Martinez, S.: Lyapunov functionals for automata networks defined by cyclically monotone functions. Res. Rep. Univ. Chile, (1987).

Goles, E., Martinez, S.: Exponential transient classes of symmetric neural networks for synchronous and sequential updating. Res. Rep. Univ. Chile, (1989).

Goles, E., Olivos, J. : The convergence of symmetric threshold automata. Inf. and Control. vol. 51, 2; 98-100, (1981).

Goles, E., Olivos, J. : Comportement périodique des fonctions à seuil binaires et applications. Disc. Appl. maths; 3, 93-105, (1981).

Goles, E., Vichniac, G.: Lyapunov functions for parallel neural networks. In Neural Networks for computing, Snowbird 1986, J. Denker ed., Am. Inst. Phys. 151, 165-181, (1986).

Gori, M., Bengio, Y., De Mori, R.: BPS : A learning algorithm for capturing the dynamic nature of speech. In Proceedings ICNN-89, Washington, D. C., (1989).

Gorman, R.P., Sejnowski,T.J.: Analysis of hidden units in a layered network trained to classify sonar targets. In Neural networks, vol. 1, n° 1, 75-89, (1988).

Gorman, R.P., Sejnowski, T.J.: Analysis of hidden units in a Layered network trained to classify sonar targets. Neural Networks, vol.1, n°1, 75-89, (1988).

Goser, K.: Basic VLSI circuits for neural networks. NATO advanced research workshop on neuro computing: Algorithms, Architectures and applications, Les Arcs (1989). In this book.

Goser, K. Fölster, C., Rückert, U.: Intelligent memories in VLSI. Inf. Sci. vol. 34, 61-62, (1984).

Graf, H.P. de Vegvar, P.: A CMOS implementation of a neural network model. Proc. Stanford Conf. on Advanced Research in VLSI, P.Losleben (ed.), MIT Press, (1987).

Graf, H.P., Hubbard, W., Jackel L.D., de Vegvar P.G.: A CMOS associative memory chip. In Proc. IEEE 1st ICNN, San Diego, Vol. 3,461. (1987).

Grossberg, S.: Nonlinear neural networks: principles, mechanisms, and architectures. In Neural Networks, 1, 17-62, (1988).

Grossberg , S.: Competitive learning: from interactive activation to adaptive resonance. Cognitive Science, 11, 23-63, (1987).

Guiard, Y.: Asymetric division of labor in human skilled bimanual action: the kinematic chain as a model. J. Motor Behav. 19, 4, 486-517 (1987).

Guyon, I., Personnaz L., Dreyfus, G.: Of points and Loops, Neural Computers, R. Eckmiller, C.v.d. Malsburg (Eds), Springer Verlag. (1988)

Guyot, F., Alexandre, F., Haton, J.P.: A potentially powerful connectionist unit: the cortical column. This volume.

Guyot, F., Alexandre, F., Haton, J.P.: Toward a continuous model of the cortical column: application to speech recognition, Proc. ICASSP-89, Glasgow. (1989).

Guyot, F., Alexandre, F., Haton, J.P., Burnod, Y.: The cortical column, a new processing unit for cortex-like networks. Proc. CEC Workshop: From the pixels to the features, J.C. Simon ed., Elsevier.(1989).

Hannan, E.J.: Multiple time-series, Wiley, New York, (1977).

Hanson, S.J., Burr, D.J.: Knowledge representation in connectionist networks. Tech. Report, Bell Comm. Research, Morristown, NJ, (1987).

Heite, C., Goser, K., Schumacher, K.: Fuzzy logic cells in CMOS. ESSCIRC'89. Vienna. To appear.

Hebb, D.: The organization of Behaviour, Wiley, New-York. (1949).

Hérault, J.: Brain and neuro computing. IEEE EUSIPCO'80. Grenoble, (1980).

Hérault, J., Juttcn, C., Ans, B.:Détection de grandeurs primitives dans un message composite par une architecture de calcul neuromimétique en apprentissage non supervisé. Xème GRETSI, 1017-22, Nice, (1985).

Hess, W.R.: Teleokinetisches and ereismatisches kräftesystem in der biomotorik. Helv. Physiol. Pharmacol. Acta 1, C62-C63, (1943).

Hille, B.: Ionic channels of excitable membranes. Sinauer associates inc. Publishers, Sunderland, Massachusetts. (1984).

Hilleringmann, U., Goser, K.,: CMOS-Schaltungen in laser-kristallisierten siliziumschisten. GME-Fachtagung Mikroelektronik. Baden-Baden'89. (1989).

Hinton, G.E.: Connectionist learning procedures. Technical report. Carnegie Mellon Univ. CM4-CS-87-115 (1987).

Hinton, G.E., Sejnowski, T.J., Ackley, D.H.: Boltzmann Machines: constraint satisfaction networks that learn. Tech. report, Carnegie Mellon Univ. CM4-CS-84-119 (1984).

Hinton, G.E., Sejnowski, T.J.: Learning and relearning in Boltzmann machines. In Parallel Distributed Processing : Exploration in the Microstructure of Cognition, D.E. Rumelhart, J.L. McClelland eds, MIT Press, vol. 1, 282-317, (1986).

Hinton, G. E., McClelland, J. L. & Rumelhart, D. E.: Distributed Representation. In Parallel Distributed processing, D.E. Rumelhart, J.L. McClelland eds, MIT Press, (1986).

Hofstadter, D.: Metamagical themas, New York: Basic books, (1985).

Holland, J.H.: Escaping brittleness. In Machine Learning, R.S. Michalski et al. eds., vol. 2, Los Altos, Morgan Kaufman, 592-623, (1986).

Holland, J.H., Holyoak, K.J., Nisbett, R.E., Thagard, P.R.: Induction. Cambridge, MA, MIT Press, (1986).

Holley, L.H., Karplus, M.: Protein structure prediction with a neural network. PNAS, USA, 86, 152-156, (1989).

Holler, M., Tam, S., Castro, H.and Benson, R.: An electrically trainable artificial neural network with 10240 "floating gate" synapses. Proceedings of International Joint Conference on Neural Networks, Washington D.C., (June 1989)

Holmes, G.: The cerebellum of man. Brain 1, 62, 1-30

Hopfield, J.J.: Neural networks and physical systems with emergent collective computational abilities. Proc. Natl. Acad. Sci. USA, vol.79, 2554-2558, (April 1982).

Hopfield, J.J.: Neurons with graded response have collective computational properties like those of two-state neurons. In Proceedings of the National Academy of Sciences of the USA, Vol. 81, 3088-3092, (May 1984).

Hopfield, J.J.: On the effectiveness of neural network hardware. Proceedings of the workshop "Hardware implementation of neuron nets and synapses", San Diego (USA), P.Mueller ed, 120-124, (January 1988)

Hopfield, J.J., Feinstein, D., Palmer, R.: Unlearning has a Stabilizing Effect in Collective Memories, Nature, vol. 304, 158-159, (1983).

Hopfield, J.J., Tank, D.W.: Neural Computation of Decisions in Optimization Problems. Biol. Cyb., vol. 52, 141-152, (1985).

Houk, J.C., Rymer, W.Z.: Neural control of muscle length and tension. In: Handbook of physiology, V.B. Brooks ed., Section I, Vol 2, 257-323 (1981).

Houk, J. C., Rymer, W. Z., Crago, P. E.: Nature of the dynamic response and its relation to the high sensitivity of muscle spindles to small changes in length. In "Muscle Receptors and Movement" H. Taylor and A. Prochazka, Eds., MacMillan (London), 33-43, (1981).

Hounsgaard, J.,Hultborn, H., Jespersen, B., Kiehn, O.: Bistability of L-motoneurones in the decerebrate cat and in the acute spinal cat after intravenous 5-hydroxytryptophan. J. Physiol. 405. 345-367 (1988).

Hounsgaard, J., Midtgaard, J.: Synaptic control of excitability in turtle cerebellar Purkinje cells. J. Physiol. 409, 157-170 (1989).

Hounsgaard, J.,Kiehn, O.: Serotonin induced bistability of turtle motoneurones caused by a nifedipine sensitive calcium plateau. J. Physiol. In press. (1989).

Huang, W.M., Lippmann, R.P.: Neural net and traditional classifiers. In D Anderson, editor, Neural Processing systems, pages 387-396, Am. Inst. of Physics, (1988).

Hubel, D.H., Wiesel, T.N.: Receptive fields, binocular interaction and functional architecture in the cat's visual cortex. Journal of Physiology, 160,106-154 (1962).

Hubel, D.H., Wiesel, T.N.: Functional architecture of macaque monkey visual cortex. Ferrier lecture Proc. Roy. Soc. Lond. B. 198.1-59 (1977).

Ito, M.: The cerebellum and neural control. Raven Press (1984).

Ito, M.: Neural systems controlling movement. TINS, 515-518 (1986).

Jahnsen, H.: Responses of neurons in isolated preparations of the mammalian central nervous system. Progress in Neurobiology 27. 357-372 (1986).

Jelinek, F.: The development of an experimental discrete dictation recognizer. In IEEE Proceedings, 1616-1624, (November 1984).

Jones, E.G.,: Anatomy of cerebral cortex: columnar input-output organization. In The organization of the cerebral cortex, F. Schmitt ed. Cambridge, Mass., MIT Press. (1981).

Jones, E.G., Coulter, J.D., Hendry, S.H.C.: Intracortical connectivity of architectonic fields in the somatic sensory, motor and pariental cortex of monkeys. J. comp. Neurol., 181, 292 (1978).

Jordan, M.L.: Serial Order: A Parallel Distributed Processing Approach, UCSD, Tech. Report 8604, (1986).

Jordan, M.L.: Supervised learning and systems with excess degrees of freedom. COINS Tech. Rep. 88-27, (1988).

Jutten, C.: Calcul Neuromimétique et Traitement du Signal. Analyse en Composantes Indépendantes. Thèse d'état ès Sciences Physiques, INP-USM Grenoble, (1987).

Jutten, C., Hérault, J., Ans, B.: Détection de Grandeurs Primitives dans un Message Composite. Colloqium GRETSI, Nice, France, (1985).

Jutten, C., Hérault, J.: Independent Component Analysis versus Principal Component Analysis. Conference EUSIPCO, Grenoble, France, (sept 1988).

Jutten, C., Hérault, J.: Analog Implementation of a Permanent Unsupervised Learning Algorithm. NATO Workshop on Neuro-Computing, feb 27-march 3, 1989, Les Arcs, France, this volume.

Jutten, C., Hérault, J.: Une solution neuromimétique au problème de séparation de sources.Traitement du Signal. To appear.

Kabsch, W., Sander, C.: Dictionnary of protein secondary structure: pattern recognition of hydrogen-bonded and geometrical features. Biopolymers, 22, 2577-2637, (1983a).

Kabsch, W., Sander, C.: How good are predictions of protein secondary structure? FEBS Letters, 155, 179-182, (1983b).

Kamgar-Parsi, B., Kanal, L.N.: An improved branch and bound algorithm for computing k-nearest neighbors. Pattern recognition lett. 3, 7-12, (1985).

Kandel, E.R.: Cellular Basis of Behavior. San Francisco: Freeman (1976)

Kawato, M., Furukawa, K., Suzuki, R.: A hierarchical neural-network model for control and learning of voluntary movement. Biol. Cybern. 57,169-185 (1987).

Kim, B.S., Park, S.B.: A fast k nearest neighbor finding algorithm based on the oredered partition. IEEE Trans. PAMI, vol. PAMI-8, n°6, 761-766, (nov. 1986).

Kirkpatrrick, S., Gelatt, C.D., Vecchi, M.P.: Optimisation by simulated annealing. Science, 220, 671-680, (1983).

Klar, H., Ramacher, U.: Microelectronics for artificial neural nets. VDI-Verlag, (1989).

Kleene, S.C.: Representation of events in nerve nets and finite automata. In Automata Studies, C.E. Shannon, J. McCarthy eds, Princeton Univ. Press, (1956).

Kleinfeld, D. Sompolinsky, H.: Associative neural network model for the generation of temporal patterns. Biophys. J. 54. 1039-1051 (1988).

Knudsen, S., Du Lac, S., Esterly, S.D.: Compulational maps in the brain. Neurosciences.10, 41-65 (1987).

Kohonen, T.: Self-Organization and Associative Memory. Springer-Verlag, Berlin, (1988).

Kohonen, T., Masisara, T.K., Sarimaki ,T.: Phonotopic maps-insightful representation of phonological features for speech representation. proc. IEEE,7th Inter. Conf. on Pattern recognition Montréal. 182-185 (1989).

Koikkalainen, P., Oja, E.: Specification and implementation environment for neural networks using communicating sequential processes. Proc. IEEE ICNN-88, San Diego, 533-540, (1988).

Koutsougeras, C., Papachristou, C.A.: Training of a neural Network for Pattern Classification Based on an Entropy Measure. In IEEE International Conference on Neural Networks, vol I, 247, San Diego, (July 1988).

Krauth, W., Mézard, M. : Learning algorithms with optimal stability in neural networks. J. Phys. A, 20, L 745, (1987).

Krauth, W., Nadal, J.P., Mézard, M. : Basins of attraction in a perceptron-like neural network. Complex Systems 2, 387 (1988).

Krauth, W., Nadal, J.P., Mézard, M.: The roles of stability and symmetry in the dynamics of neural networks. J. Phys. A, 21, 2995-3011, (1988).

Kreuzer, I., Goser, K.: A modified model of Boltzmann machines for WSI-realization. EUSIPCO'88 Grenoble. (1988).

Kubo, M., Masuda, I., Miyata, K., Ogiue, K.: Perspective on BiCMOS VLSI's. In IEEE JSSC, Vol 23, n° 1, (February 1988).

Kuhn, H.: Origin of life and physics: diversified microstructure- Inducement to form information-carrying and knowledge-accumulating systems. IBM J. Res. Develop.32. 37-46 (1988).

Lachter, J., Bever, T. J.: The relation between linguistic structure and theories of language learning: a constructive critic of some connectionist learning models. Tec. Report N44. Cognitive Science. Department of Psychology. Rochester University. Rochester, NY.

Lamarque, J.L.: Le Sein, radiodiagnostic clinique. Medsi (1981).

Lanczos, C.: Linear differential operators. D. Van Nostrand Company, London (1961).

Landauer, R.: Dissipation and noise immunity in computation and communication. Nature 335. (1988a).

Landauer, R.: A simple measure of complexity. Nature 336. 306-307 (1988b).

Leboeuf, J., Béroule,D.: Processing of noisy patterns with a connexionist system using a topographic representation of speech, European Conference on speech technology, Edinburg. (1987).

Leboeuf, J.: Un système connectionniste appliqué au Traitement Automatique de la Parole, Thèse Doctorat, Orsay. (1988).

Le Cun, Y.: Character recognition, unpublished manuscript.

Le Cun, Y.: Une procédure d'apprentissage pour réseau à seuil asymétrique, Cognitiva 85, Paris. Cesta ed. 599-604 (1985).

Le Cun, Y.: Modèles connexionnistes de l'apprentissage, Thèse, Paris, (1987).

Le Cun ,Y.: Constrained Networks For Handwritten Numeral Recognition. Snowbird Conference on "Neural Networks for Computing", Snowbird, (April 1989).

Le Cun, Y.: Generalization and network design strategies. In "Connectionism in perspective", R. Pfeifer, Z. Schreter, F. Fogelman Soulié, L. Steels eds, North Holland, 143-156, (1989).

Le Cun, Y., Fogelman Soulié, F.: "Modèles connexionnistes de l'apprentissage", Intellectica vol. 1, n°2/3, 114-143, (1987).

Lee, M.K.O.: Neural networks for knowledge based systems. Res. note RN/89/36, Univ. Coll. London, (1989)

Lehky, S.R., Sejnowski, T.J.: Network model of shape-form shading : neural function arises from both receptive and projective fields. Nature, 333, 452-454 (1988)

Lehky S. R., Sejnowski, T.J.: Extracting curvatures of 3-D objects using a neural network. In Soc. for Neuroscience Abstracts, 13, 1451, (1987).

Levin, J., Robson, B., Garnier, J.: An algorithm for secondary structure determination in proteins based on sequence similarity. FEBS Letters, 205, 303-308,(1986).

Levitan, I.B.: Modulation of ion channels in neurons and other cells. Ann. Res. Neurosci. 11. 119-136 (1988).

Liénard, J.S.: Analyse, Synthèse et Reconnaissance Automatique de la Parole Continue, Thèse d'état Paris VI. (1972).

Lim, V.I.: Algorithms for prediction of alpha-helical and beta-structural regions in globular proteins. J. Mol. Biol., 88, 873-894, (1974).

Lippman, R.: Computing with neural nets, in IEEE ASSP, Vol. 4, n° 2, 4-22, (1987).

Lippmann, R.P., Gold, B.: Neural Classifiers Useful for Speech Recognition, 1st Int. Conf. on Neural Networks, vol. IV, 417, San Diego, CA, (1987).

Little, W.A.: The existence of persistent states. Math. Bios., 19, (1974).

Ljung, L., Soderstrom, T.: Theory and Practice of Recursive Identification, MIT Press, (1983).

Loncelle, J.: Détection de contours par rétro-propagation du gradient. "Neuro-Nîmes 88", EC2 Ed., 373-394, (1988).

Mannel, F.: Are artificial neural networks finally ready for market? Electronics, 61, 85-88, (Aug. 1988).

Mariani, J.J.: ESOPE: un système de compréhension de la parole continue, Thèse d'état, Orsay. (1982).

Marino, G., Morasso, P., Zaccaria, R.: Motor knowledge representation. Proc. IJCAI, los Angeles, 1110-1112, (1985).

Marino, G., Morasso, P., Zaccaria, R.: NEM: a language for the representation of motor knowledge. In Human movement understanding, P. Morasso, V.Tagliasco, eds, North Holland, Amsterdam, 125-156, (1986).

Marslen-Wilson, W.D.: Speech Understanding as a psychological process, Spoken Language Generation and Understanding , D. Reidel. (1980).

Marr, D.: Representing visual information. In Computer Vision System, A. Hanson, E.M. Riseman Eds., Academic Press, New York, 61-80, (1978).

Marr, D.: Vision, San Francisco: Freeman, (1982)..

Marr, D: A theory of cerebellar cortex. J. Physiol. 202,437-470 (1969).

Massion, J., Dufossé, M: Co-ordination between posture and movement: Why and How ? NIPS 3,88-93 (1988).

Massion, J., Viallet, F., Massarino, R., Khalil, R.: La région de l'aire motrice supplémentaire est impliquée dans la coordination entre posture et mouvement. C.R.Acad.Sci. Paris 308, 417-423 (1989).

Maxwell, T., Giles, C.G., Lee, Y.C.: Generalization in neural networks, the contiguity problem. In Proc. IEEE 1st ICNN, vol.2, 41-45, (1987).

McAllester, D.A.: An outlook of truth maintenance. Rep. AIM-551; AI Lab, MIT, (1980).

McClelland, J. L., Rumelhart, D. E.: Parallel distributed processing: exploration in the microstructure of cognition. V2: Psychological and biological models". Cambridge , Mass. MIT Press. (1986).

McCulloch, W., Pitts, W.: A logical calculus of the ideas immanent in nervous activity. Bull. Math. Biophys. 5, (1943).

Mead, C.A.: Analog VLSI and Neural Systems. Addison-Wesley, (1988).

Mehring, M., Sixl, H.: Molecular electronics: storage and transport. WOPPLOT'86, Springer Verlag. (1987).

Mermelstein, P.: Automatic segmentation of speech into syllabic units, Acoust-Soc. Am. Vol. 58, N° 4 880-883 (1975).

Merzenich, M.M., Jenkins, W.M., Middlebrooks, J.C.: In Dynamic aspects of neocortical functions. G.M. Edelman, W.E. Gall, W.M. Cowan eds., John Wiley NY. (1984).

Metropolis N. & al. : Equations of State calculations by fast computing machines. J. Chem. Phys., 21, 1087, (1953).

Mézard, M., Nadal, J.P. : Learning in feed-forward layered networks: the tiling algorithm. J. Phys. A, 22, 2191-2203, preprint LPS-ENS. (1989).

Mézard M.: Learning algorithms in layered networks, this book. (1989).

Midtgaard, J.: Electroresponsiveness of interneurons in the turtle cerebellar cortex in vitro. Euro. J. Neurosci., Suppl. ENA Meeting (1988).

Midtgaard, J., Hounsgaard, J.: Nerve cells as source of time scale and processing dentisity in brain function. Int. J. Neur. Syst. 1, in press (1989).

Minsky, M. , Papert, S.: Perceptrons. MIT Press, Cambridge MA, (1969).

Mintz, I.: Analyse in vitro des propriétés membranaires actives des motoneurones de tortue et de leur contribution aux oscillations induites par l'acide N-méthyl-D-aspartique et les agonistes muscariniques. Thèse de Doctorat de l'Université Paris 6, (1987).

Mitchison, G.J., Durbin, R.M.: Bounds on the learning capacity of some multi-layer networks. Biol. Cyber., 60, 345-356, (1989).

Moopenn, A., Langenbacher, H., Thakoor, A. P. and Khanna, S.K.: A programmable binary synaptic matrix chip for electronic neural networks. In: Neural Information Processing Systems, Natural and Synthetic, D.Z.Anderson, ed., American Institute of Physics, (1988)

Morasso, P., Mussa Ivaldi, F.A.: The role of physical constraints in natural and artificial manipulation. Proc. IEEE Conf. Robotics and Automation. San Francisco, 1901-1905, (1986).

Morasso, P., Mussa Ivaldi, F.A., Zaccaria, R.: Redundant robotic manipulators. I: Regularizing by mechanical impedance. NATO ARW Kinematic and Dynamic Issues in Sensor Based Control. (1987).

Morasso, P., Vercelli, G., Zaccaria, R.: Rappresentazione del movimento in Robotica: modello, ricostruzione, data base cognitivo in un caso antropomorfo. 4th SIRI Nat. Conf. Milano, (1988).

Morgan, N., Bourlard, H.: Generalization and Parameter Estimation in Feedforward Nets: Some Experiments, Neural Networks for Computing, Snowbird, UT, also in ICSI Technical Report TR-089-017, (1989).

de Mori, R., Lam, L., Gilloux, M.: Learning and plan refinement in a knowledge-based system for automatic speech recognition. IEEE Transactions on Pattern Analysis and Machine Intelligence, vol. PAMI-9, N°.2, 289-305, (1987).

Morton,J.: A functional model of memory, Psychological Review. (1969).

Mountcastle, V.B.: An organizing principle for cerebral function: the unit module and the distributed system. In the mindful brain, F.O. Schmitt ed., MIT Press. (1978).

Mountcastle, V.B., Andersen, R.A. Motter, B.C.: The influence of attentive fixation upon the excitability of the ligh-sensitive neurons of the posterior parietal cortex. J. Neurosci. 1.1218-1235 (1981).

Mourad, K., Portinaro, N.: Progetto e Ottimizzazione di un Sommatore Analogico per Reti Neurali in Tecnologia CMOS. Internal Report, Politecnico di Torino, (April 1989).

Muhlenbein, H., Gorges-Schleuter, M., Kramer, O.: Evolution algorithms in combinatorial optimisation. Parallel Computing, 7, 65-85, (1985).

Murray D.W. & al. : A parallel approach to the picture restoration algorithm of Geman and Geman. Image Vision Computing, Vol. 4, N° 6, 133-142, (August 1986).

Murray, A.F., Smith, A.V.W.: Asynchronous VLSI Neural Networks Using Pulse-Stream Arithmetic. In IEEE JSSC, Vol 23, n° 3, (June 1988).

Murray, A. F., Smith, V. W., Butler, Z. F.: Bit-serial neural networks. In: Neural Information Processing Systems, Natural and Synthetic, D.Z.Anderson, ed., American Institute of Physics, (1988)

Murray, D.W., Kashko, A., Buxton, B.: A parallel approach to the picture restoration algorithm of Geman and Geman. IVC, 3, 133-142, (1985).

Murveit, H., Brodersen, R.W.: An Integrated-Circuit-Based Speech Recognition System, IEEE Trans. ASSP, vol. 34, n° 6, 1465-1472, (1986).

Murveit, H.,Weintraub, M.: 1000-Word Speaker-Independent Continuous -Speech Recognition Using Hidden Markov Models, Proc. Int. Conf. on ASSP-88, 115-118, New York, (1988).

Mussa Ivaldi, F.A., Morasso, P., Zaccaria, R.: Kinematic networks-A distributed model for representing and regularizing motor redundancy. Biol. Cyb. in press.

Naccache, N.J., Shingal, R.: Spta: A proposed algorithm for thinning binary patterns. IEEE Trans. Systems, Man, and Cybernatics, SMC-14:409, (1984).

Nadal, J.P. : Study of a growth algorithm for a feedforward network. In Intl Journal of Neural Networks, 1, 55-59, (1989).

Nadas, A., Nahamoo, D., Picheny, M.A.: On a Model-Robust Training Method for Speech Recognition, IEEE Trans. on ASSP, vol. 35, n° 9, 1432-1436, (1988).

Nature's 11th international conference "How the brain works", Cambridge (USA), September 1988. Nature vol.335, 489-491, (October 1988).

Nauta, W.J.H., Karten, H.J.: A general profile of the vertebrate brain, with sidelights on the ancestry of cerebral cortex. In the Neurosciences, F.O. Schmitt ed., N.Y., Rockfeller, 7.25 (1970).

Naylor, W.C.: Some studies in the interactive design of character recognition systems. IEEE Transaction on Computers, 1075 (1971).

Norman, M.G., Mclachlan, S.: submitted to Conf. on Eng. Appl. of transputers, Liverpool, (1989).

Norman, M.G., Fisher, R.B.: Surface tracking within three dimensional datasets, using a generalised message passing harness. In Developments using Occam, J. Kerridge ed., IOS Amsterdam, 77-82, (1988)

Norman, M.G., Wilson, S.: The TITCH User Guide. ECS project, Edinburgh University Computing Service.

Norman, M.G.: A genetic approach to topology optimisation for multiprocessor architecture. submitted to Parallel Computing.

Obellianne, C.: Mise au point d'un système connexionniste pour la détection de microcalcifications dans des images mammographiques numérisées. Internal report EHEI (January, 1989).

Omohundro, S.M.: Efficient algorithms with neural network behavior. Complex Systems, 1, 273-347, (1989).

Oppenheim, A., Schafer, R.: Digital Signal Processing. Englewood Cliffs, NJ: Prentice Hall, (1975).

Orban, G.A., De Wolf, J. and Maes, H. Factors influencing velocity coding in the human visual system. Vision Res., 24, 33-39 (1984)

Orban, G.A., Vandenubssche, E. and Vogels, R. : Human orientation discrimination tested with long stimuli. Vision Res., 24, 121-128.(1984).

Orban, G.A., Vogels, R.: Orientation tuning characteristics of V1 neurons measured in the discriminating monkey. Soc. Neurosci. Abstr., in press (1989)

Ouali, J., Saucier, G., Trilhe, J.: A flexible wafer scale network. ICCD Conference, Rye Brook, (USA), (September 1989)

Paillard, J., Beaubaton, D.: De la coordination visuomotrice à l'organisation de la saisie manuelle. In: Du contrôle moteur à l'organisation du geste (H. Hecaen , M. Jeannerod, eds). Masson (1978).

Palm, G.: Neural assemblies, an alternative approach to Artificial intelligence. Springer verlag, (1982).

Pandya, D.N., Kuypers,H.G.J.M.: Cortico-cortical connections in the rhesus monkey. Brain Research. (1969).

Paradiso,M.A.: A theory for use of visual orientation which exploits the columnar structure of striate cortex. Biol. Cybern. 58. 35-49 (1988).

Parker, D. B., Learning-Logic. Invention report, S81-64, File 1, Office of Technology Licensing, Standford University, (October 1982).

Parsons, T.: Voice & speech processing, New York-San Francisco-Toronto-London: McGraw-Hill, (1986).

Patarnello, S., Carnevali, P.: Learning networks of neurons with boolean logic. Europhysics Letters, 4(4): 503-508.(1987).

Pellionisz, A., Llinas, R.: Tensorial approach to the geometry of brain function: cerebellar coordination via a metric tensor. Neurosci. 5,1125-1136 (1980).

Peretto, P.: Collective properties of neural networks. preprint, (1984).

Personnaz, L., Guyon, I., Dreyfus, G.: Information Storage and Retrieval in Spin-Glass Like Neural Networks. In J. Physique Lett., 46, L-359 - L-365, (1985).

Personnaz, L., Guyon, I., Dreyfus, G.: Collective computational properties of neural networks: new learning mechanisms. Phys. Rev. A, vol. 34, 4217-4228, (1986)

Personnaz, L., Guyon, I., Dreyfus, G.: Designing a neural network satisfying a given set of constraints. In: Neural networks for computing, J.S.Denker ed., American Institute of Physics, (1986)

Personnaz, L., Johannet, A., Dreyfus, G., Weinfeld, M.: Towards a neural network chip: a performance assessment and a simple example. In: Neural networks, from models to applications, L.Personnaz and G.Dreyfus, eds., IDSET, 682-691 (1989)

Peters, A., Jones, E.G.: Classification of cortical neurons. In Cerebral cortex Vol. 1: cellular components of the derebral cortex. A. Peters and E.G. Jones eds. Plenum Press. (1984).

Peterson, G.E., Barley, H.L.: Control methods used in a study of vowels. J. Acoust. Soc. Amer., 24(2):175-184, March 1952.

Peterson, W.W., Weldon, E.J.: Error correcting codes, MIT Press, (1972)

Pineda, F.: Generalization of Backpropagation to Recurrent and Higher Order Networks. In Neural Information Processing Systems, D. Anderson (ed.), American Institute of Physics, (1988).

Pinker, S., Prince, A.: On language and connectionism: analysis of a parallel distributed processing model of language acquisition. Occasional paper n°33. Center for Cognitive Science. MIT. Cambridge. (1987).

Plout, D.C., Hinton, G.E.: Learning sets of filters using back propagation. In Computer Speech and Language, vol. 2,.35-61, (1987).

Pœppel G. and Krey U. : Europhys.Lett. 4, 481, (1987).

Poggio, T., Reichardt, W.: On the representation of multi-input systems: computational properties of polynomial algorithms. Biol. Cyber. 37, 167-186, (1980).

Poritz,A.B. : Hidden Markov Models: A Guided Tour, Proc. Int. Conf. on ASSP-88, 7-13, New York, (1988).

Prager, R.W., Harrison, T.D., Fallside, F.: Boltzmann Machines for Speech Recognition, Computer, Speech and Language, vol. 1, 3-27, (1986).

Pratt, W.K.: Digital image processing. John Wiley & Sons, (1978).

Prior, D., Radcliffe, N.J., Norman, M.G., Clarke, L.J.: Concurrency: practice and experience. To appear.

Quian, N., Sejnowski, T.J.: Predicting the secondary structure of globular proteins using neural network models. J. Mol. Biol., 202, 865-884, (1988).

Rabiner, L.R., Juang, B.H.: An introduction to Hidden markov models. IEEE ASSP Magazine, 3:1; 4-16, (1986).

Radcliffe, N.J.: Early clustering around optima. Tech. rep. Univ. of Edinburgh, in preparation.

Rayner,K., Pollatsek,A.: Eye movement control during reading: Evidence for direct control, Quartely Journal of experimental psychology, (1981).

Richards, G.D.: Implementation of back-propagation on a transputer array. In proc. 8th Tech. meeting of the Occam user group, J. Kerridge ed., IOS Amsterdam, 173-179, (1988).

Richards, G.D.: Documentation from Rhwydaith. ECS project, Edinburgh University Computing Service.

Riolo, R.: CFS-C: A package of domain independent subroutines for implementing classifier systems in arbitrary, user-defined environments. Int. rep. Univ. of Michigan, (1986).

Robert, F., Wang, S.: Implementation of a neural network on a hypercube FPS-T20. IFIP Working Group 10.3, Conference on Parallel Processing, Pisa, Italy (April 1988).

Robertson, G.G., Riolo, R.: A tale of two classifier systems. Machine Learning, 3, 139-160, (1988).

Robinson, A.J., Fallside, F.: A Dynamic connectionist model for phoneme recognition, In Neural Networks: from models to applications. L. Personnaz, G. Dreyfus eds, IDSET, 541-550 (1989).

Robinson, A.J., Fallside, F. : The Utility Driven Dynamic Error Propagation Network, Tech. Report, CUED/F-INFENG/TR.1, Cambridge Univ., UK, (1987).

Roll, J.P., Contribution de la proprioception musculaire à la perception et au contrôle du mouvement chez l'homme. Thèse d'état, Univ. d'Aix-Marseille I, (1981).

Roques,M.: Apprentissage et reconnaissance de séquence de classe lexicales, DEA report, LIMSI. (1989).

Roquet, H., Ratier, A.: Toward direct variational assimilation of scatterometer backscatter measurements into numerical weather prediction model. Proceeding of IGARSS 88 symposium, Edinburgh, Scotland. Ref ESA SP-284 (IEEE 88CH2497-6), (13-16 Septembre 1988).

Rosenblatt, F.: Principles of Neurodynamics. Spartan, New York, (1962)

Rosenblatt, F.:The perceptron: A probabilistic model for information storage and organization in the Brain, Psychological Review. (1959).

Rosenfeld, A., Kak, A.C.: Digital Picture Processing, Academic Press, Vol. 1 (1982).

Rückert, U., Kreuzer, I., Goser, K.: VLSI architectures for associative networks. IEEE ISCAS, Helsinki, june 6-8, (1988).

Rückert, U., Goser, K.: VLSI design of associative networks. In: VLSI for artificial intelligence, J.G. Delgado-Frias and W.Moore eds., Kluwer Academic, (1989).

Rückert, U., Kreuzer, I., Tryba, V., Goser, K.: Fault tolerance of associative memories based on neural networks. IEEE COMPEURO'89, Hamburg, to be published.

Rujan P., Marchand, M.: Learning by activating neurons: a new approach to learning in neural networks. KFA Jülich preprint, (1988).

Rumelhart, D.E., McClelland, J.L.: Parallel Distributed Processing: explorations in the microstructures of cognition. Bradford Books, Cambridge MA, MIT Press, (1986).

Rumelhart, D. E., McClelland, J. L.: On learning the past tenses of english verbs. In Parallel Distributed processing, D.E. Rumelhart, J.L. McClelland eds, MIT Press, 216-272, (1986)

Rumelhart, D.E., Hinton, G.E., McClelland, J.L.: A general framework for parallel distributed processing. In Parallel Distributed processing, D.E. Rumelhart, J.L. McClelland eds, MIT Press, vol.1, 45-76, (1986).

Rumelhart, D.E., Hinton, G.E., Williams, R.J.: Learning internal representations by error propagation. In Parallel Distributed Processing, D.E. Rumelhart, J.L. McClelland, eds., MIT Press, vol. 1, 318-362, (1986).

Sage, J.P., Thompson, K., Withers, R.S.: An artificial network integrated circuit based on MNOS/CCD principles. In: Neural networks for computing, J.S.Denker ed., American Institute of Physics, (1986)

Schwartz, J.L.: L'organisation de l'information nerveuse à la sortie du système auditif périphérique, LIMSI report 83-1 Orsay. (1983).

Schwartz, D. B., Howard, R. E., Denker, J. S., Epworth, R. W., Graf, H. P., Hubbard, W., Jackel, L. D., Straughn, B. and Tennant, D. M.: Dynamics of microfabricated electronic neural networks. Appl. Phys. Lett., vol. 50, 1110-1112, (1987)

Schwartz, D. B., Howard, R. E.: Analog VLSI for adaptive learning, Neural Networks for Computing, Snowbird, 1988 (unpublished).

Segui,J.: The syllable: A basic perceptual unit?, Attention and performance: Control of language process, Hillsdale. (1983).

Shepherd, G.M.: The synaptic organization of the brain. N.Y. Oxford University Press. (1979).

Sejnowski, T.J., Rosenberg, C.M.: NetTalk: A parallel network that learns to read aloud. Tech. report JHU/EECS-86/01, Johns Hopkins U. EE1CS (1986).

Sejnowski, T.J., Rosenberg, C.M.: Parallel networks that learn to pronounce english text. Complex Systems, vol.1, n°1, 145-168, (1987).

Selverston, A.I., Moulins, M.: Oscillatory neural networks. Ann. Rev. Physiol. 47.29-48 (1985).

Serra, R.: Dynamical systems and expert systems. In "Connectionism in perspective", R. Pfeifer, Z. Schreter, F. Fogelman Soulié, L. Steels eds, North Holland, 265-275, (1989).

Shepherd, G.M.: The synaptic organization of the brain. Oxford Univ. Press (1979).

Shingai, R.: Maximum period of 2-dimensional neural networks. Inf. and Control, 41, 324-341, (1979).

Shriver, B. ed: Artificial neural systems. IEEE Computer, vol. 21, 8-117, (1988).

Sivilotti, M., Emerling, M. R., and Mead,C.: A novel associative memory implemented using collective computation. In: Proc. Chapel Hill Conf. on VLSI, 329-342, Computer Science Press (1985)

Simmen, M., Wilson, G.V.: A comparison of two parallel implementations of the Durbin and Willshaw algorithm for solving the travelling salesman problem. Submitted to Concurrency: practice and experience.

Slobin, D.I.: The cross linguistic study of Language acquisition. Hillsdale, N.J.Lawrence Erlbaum. (1986).

Smieja, F.J.: The significance of underlying correlations in the training of a layered net. INNS Conf. Boston and Tech. report, Univ. of Edinburgh, (1988).

Smieja, F.J.: MLP solutions, generalization and hidden unit representations. In Proc. DANIP workshop, Bonn, (1989).

Smieja, F.J., Richards, G.D.: Hard learning the easy way- backpropagation with deformation. Complex Systems. To appear.

Solla, S., Levin, E., Fleisher, M.: Accelerated learning in layered neural networks. Complex systems. (1989).

Sorenson, H.W.(ed): Kalman filtering: theory and application. IEEE Press, New York, (1985).

Steels, L.: Connectionist problem solving- An AI perspective. In "Connectionism in perspective", R. Pfeifer, Z. Schreter, F. Fogelman Soulié, L. Steels eds, North Holland, 215-228, (1989).

Stevens, C.F.: Strengthening the synapses. Nature 338, 460-461 (1989).

Szentagothai, J.: The "module concept" in cerebral cortex architecture. Brain Res. 95.475.496 (1975).

Tabár L., Dean, P.B.: Teaching Atlas of Mammography , Georg Thieme Verlag, (1985).

Taylor & Taylor, Psychology of Reading, Academic Press, New-York London.

Tchuente, M.: Sequential simulation of parallel iterations and applications. Theor. Comp. Sci., 48, 135-144, (1986).

Tishby, N., Levin, E., Solla, S.A.: Consistent inference of probabilities in layered networks: Predictions and generalization. In Proceedings of the International Joint Conference on Neural Networks, Washington DC.(1989).

Torinmi, A., Yoshimi, M., Iwase, M., Akiyama, K., Tamigushi, K.: A study of photon emission from m-channel MOSFET's. IEEE Trans. on Electron Dev. ED-34, 1501-1507, (1987).

Trouvé, A.: Parallelization of simulated annealing. C.R. Ac. Sci. (1988).

Tsividis, Y.P. and Anastassiou, D.: Switched capacitor neural network. Electronic Lett. vol. 23, 958-959, (1987).

Ullmann, S.: The interpretation of visual motion. MIT Press, Cambridge and London.(1979).

Valiant, L.G.: Optimally universal parallel computers. In Scientific applications of multiprocessors, R.J. Elliott, C.A.R. Hoare eds, Prentice Hall Int. Series in Computer Science, 17-20, (1989).

Vandenbussche, E., Orban, G.A., Maes, H.: Velocity discrimination in the monkey. Soc. Neurosci. Abstr., 12, 1183 (1986a)

Vandenbussche, E., Orban, G.A., Maes, H.: Velocity discrimination in cat. Vision Res., 26, 1835-1849 (1986b).

Van Essen, D.C., Maunsell, J.H.R.: Hierarchical organization and functional streams in the visual cortex. Trends in neurosciences. 6.9. (1983).

Varela, F.: Principles of biological autonomy. Elsevier (1979).

Verleysen, M., Sirletti, B., Vandemeulenbroecke, A.M., Jespers, P.: Neural networks for high-storage content-adressable memory: VLSI circuit and learning algorithm. IEEE Journal of solid-state circuits, vol. 24, no. 3, 562-569, (1989)

Verri, A., Girosi, F., Torre,V.: Mathematical properties of the 2D motion fields: from singular points to motion parameters. Proceedings of the IEEE Workshop on Visual motion, Irvine CA.(1989).

Verzeano,M.: The activity of Neuronal Networks in Memory Consolidation, Sleep and Memory, Drucker-Colin J. Mc Gaugh Eds., New-York Academic Press. (1877).

Viterbi, A.J.: Principles of digital communication and coding. Mc Graw-Hill, (1979).

Vogels, R., Orban, G.A., Eeckhout H., Spileers, W.: Visual orientation discrimination in the primate. Arch. internat. Physiol. Biochim., 96, P31 (1988)

Vogels, R., Orban, G.A.: Orientation discrimination thresholds of single striate cells in the discriminating monkey. Soc. Neurosci. Abstr., in press (1989)

Vogels, R., Spileers, W. and Orban, G.A.: The response variability of striate cortical neurons in the behaving monkey. Exp. Brain Res., in press (1989).

Vogt, B.A., Gorman, L.F.: Responses of cortical neurons to stimulation of corpus callosum in vitro. J. Neurophysiol, 48:6 (1982).

Waibel, A., Hanazawa, T., Hinton, G., Shikano, K., Lang, K.: Phoneme recognition using time-delay neural networks, ATR Interpreting Telephony Research Laboratories, Tech. Rep. TR-1-006, (1987).

Waibel, A., Hanazawa, T., Hinton, G.E., Shikano, K., Lang, K.: Phoneme Recognition: Neural Networks vs. Hidden Markov Models, Proc. Int. Conf. on ASSP-88, 107- 110, New York, (1988).

Waibel, A., Hanazawa, T., Hinton, G.E., Shikano, K., Lang, K.: Phoneme Recognition Using Time-Delay Neural Networks. In IEEE Transactions on Acoustics, Speech and Signal Processing, Vol. 37, N° 3, 328, (March 1989).

Waibel, A., Hanazawa, T., Hinton, G.E., Shikano, K., Lang, K.: Phoneme Recognition: Neural Networks vs. Hidden Markov Models, Proc. Int. Conf. on ASSP-88, 107- 110, New York, (1988).

Waibel, A., Sawai, H. & Shikano, K.: Modularity and scaling in large phonemic neural networks. ATR Tech Report TR-1-0034 ATR Interpreting Telephony Research Laboratories. Osaka. Japon.(1988).

Watrous, R.L.: Learning algorithms for connectionist networks: applied gradient methods of non linear optimization. In IEEE 1st ICNN, San Diego, M. Caudill, C. Butler eds, IEEE catalog n° 87TH0191-7, vol. II, 619-627, (1987).

Watrous, R.L., Shastri, L.: Learning phonetic features using connectionist networks. In Proceedings of the 10th International Joint Conference on Artificial Intelligence, 851-854, (1987).

Watrous, R.L., Shastri, L.: Learning Phonetic Features Using Connectionist Networks: an Experiment in Speech Recognition, 1st Int. Conf. on Neural Networks}, vol. IV, 381-388, San Diego, CA (1987).

Weaver, C.S.: Some Properties of Threshold Logic Unit Pattern Recognition Networks. In IEEE Transactions on Computers, Vol. c-24, N°. 3, 290, (March 1975).

Weinfeld, M.: A fully digital integrated CMOS Hopfield network including the learning algorithm. In: VLSI for artificial intelligence, J.G. Delgado-Frias and W.Moore eds., Kluwer Academic, (1989)

Wexler, J., Wilson, G.V.: Edinburgh Supercomputer Project Directory, (1988).

Widrow, B.: Layered Neural Nets for Pattern Recognition. IEEE Trans. on ASSP, 36, 7, 1109-1118, (1988).

Widrow, B., Winter, R. : Neural Nets for Adaptive Filtering and Adaptive Pattern Recognition. IEEE Computer, 21, 3, 25-39, (1988).

Wilson, G.V., Pawley, G.S.: On the stability of the travelling salesman problem of Hopfield and Tank. Biol. Cyber. 58, 63-70, (1988).

Winograd, T.: Des machines savantes mais incultes. Science et Vie, July (1985).

Yair, E., Gersho, A.: The Boltzmann perceptron network: a soft classifier. Tech. report CIPR TR 88-11, Center for information processing research, Dep. of E&CE, UCSB.(1988).

Yamakawa T.: A simple fuzzy computer hardware system employing min and max operations. A challenge to 6th generation computer. IFSA congress, Tokyo, 827-830, July 20-25 (1987).

Younes, L.: Parameter estimation for Gibbs fields. Ann. Inst. H. Poincaré (1988) and thesis, Univ. Paris Sud, (1988).

Yunck, T.P.: A technique to identify nearest neighbors. IEEE Trans. Syst. Man Cyber., vol. SMC-6, 678-683, (oct. 1976).

Zadeh, L.A.: Fuzzy logic. IEEE Computer, 21, 83-92, (1988).

Zambrano, J., Besson, R.: Studies on the use of telephone networks for deaf communications. In X Congress of deaf world federation. Helsinki, (1987).

LIST OF CONTRIBUTORS

Name	Address	Page
F. Alexandre	CRIN - BP 239 54 506 VANDOEUVRE-LES-NANCY FRANCE	369
L. Almeida	INESC - Rua Alves Redol 4-2° 1096 LISBOA Codex - PORTUGAL	27
E. Alpaydin	Microprocessor Laboratory (LAMI) Swiss Federal Institute of Technology of Lausanne - Cour 37 1007 LAUSANNE - SWITZERLAND	329
B. Angéniol	THOMSON CSF-DSE 1, rue des Mathurins - BP 10 92223 BAGNEUX Cedex - FRANCE	333
R. Azencott	Laboratoire de Mathématiques Bât. 425 - Université de Paris Sud 91405 ORSAY Cedex - FRANCE	51, 333
F. Badran	Laboratoire de Recherche en Informatique Bât. 490 Université Paris Sud 91405 ORSAY-FRANCE	319
F. Baiardi	Dipartimento di Informatica Università de Pisa Corso Italia 40 56100 PISA-ITALIA	161
S. Barquin	Laboratorio de Inteligencia Artificial Universidad Politecnica de Madrid Campus Monte Gancedo 28 660 BOADILLA DEL MONTE MADRID - ESPANA	337
Y. Bengio	Departmento of Computer Science Mc Gill University MONTREAL H3A-2K6-CANADA	207
D. Béroule	LIMSI-CNRS - BP 30 91 406 ORSAY Cedex - FRANCE	241
P. Blanchet	LIMSI-CNRS - BP 30 91 406 ORSAY Cedex - FRANCE	237
B. Boser	AT & T Bell Labs Crawfords Corner Road HOLMDEL-NJ 07733-USA	303

H. Bourlard	Philips Research Laboratory Avenue van Becelaere 2 Box 8 1170 BRUXELLES - BELGIUM	217
C. Bourrely	Laboratoire de Recherche en Informatique Bât. 490 Université Paris Sud 91 405 ORSAY - FRANCE	325
J. Bridle	Royal Signal and Radar Establishment St Andrews Road MALVERN- Worcestershire WR 14 3PS - UK	227
Y. Burnod	Laboratoire de Neurobiologie Cellulaire Département de Biotechnologie Institut Pasteur - 25, rue du Dr Roux 75015 PARIS - FRANCE	359
R. Cardin	Department of Computer Science Mc Gill University MONTREAL H3A-2K6- CANADA	207
P. Chavel	I.O.T.A. C.N.R.S L.A. 14, BP 43 91406 ORSAY-FRANCE	167
G. Chollet	C.N.R.S. URA 820 ENST, Dept SIGNAL 46 Rue Barrault 75013 PARIS -FRANCE	261
K. Choukri	Cap Sesa Innovation 118 rue de Tocqueville 75 017 PARIS - FRANCE	261
J.F. Collins	Biocomputing Research Unit and Molecular Biology University of EDINBURGH - UK	181
D. Collobert	CNET Département TIC 22301-LANNION Cedex - FRANCE	173
P. Comon	THOMSON SINTRA BP 53 06801 CAGNES SUR MER Cedex - FRANCE	81
M. Compiani	ENITADA- Via Aldo Moro 38 BOLOGNA 40127- ITALY	103
P. Cosi	Centro di Studio per la Ricerche di Fonetica CNR Via G. Oberdan 10 35122 PADOVA-ITALY	207

M. Crépon	Laboratoire d'Océanographie LODYC Université de Paris 6 4 Place de Jussieu 75006 PARIS -FRANCE	319
G. Cristobal	Laboratorio de Inteligencia Artificial Universidad Politecnica de Madrid Campus Monte Gancedo 28 660 BOADILLA DEL MONTE MADRID - ESPANA	337
V. Cruz	Laboratorio de Inteligencia Artificial Universidad Politecnica de Madrid Campus Monte Gancedo 28 660 BOADILLA DEL MONTE MADRID - ESPANA	337
U. Dagitan	Department of Computer Engineering Middle East Technical University 06531 ANKARA-TURKEY	297
D. Del Corso	Dipartimento di Elettronica Politecnico di Torino Corso Duca degli Abruzzi 24 10129 TORINO - ITALY	157
J.S. Denker	AT & T Bell Labs Crawfords Corner Road HOLMDEL-NJ 07733-USA	303
B. Derot	Thomson CSF-DSE 1 Rue des Mathurins BP 10 92223 BAGNEUX-FRANCE	89
F. Devos	Institut d'Electronique Fondamentale Bât 220 91 405 ORSAY - FRANCE	167
G. Dreyfus	ESPCI - 10, rue Vauquelin 75231 PARIS Cedex 05 - FRANCE	41
M. Dufossé	IMT - Avenue Grand Pré 13 009 MARSEILLE - FRANCE	389
R. Durbin	Department of Psychology Stanford University - STANFORD CA 94 305 - 2130 - USA	15
F. Fallside	Department of Engineering University of Cambridge Trumpington Street CAMBRIDGE CB2 1PZ - UK	265

J.P. Haton	CRIN - BP 239 54 506 VANDOEUVRE-LES-NANCY - FRANCE	369
S.J. Hayward	Biocomputing Research Unit and Molecular Biology University of EDINBURGH - UK	181
D. Henderson	AT&T Bell Labs Crawfords Corner Road HOLMDEL-NJ 07733 - USA	303
J. Hérault	Institut National Polytechnique de Grenoble L.T.I.R.F. 46,avenue Félix Viallet 38031 GRENOBLE Cedex - FRANCE	145
J. Hounsgaard	Neurofysiologisk Institut Blegdamsvej 3C DK-2200 KOBENHAVN - DENMARK	379
R.E. Howard	AT&T Bell Labs Crawfords Corner Road HOLMDEL-NJ 07733 - USA	303
W. Hubbard	AT&T Bell Labs Crawfords Corner Road HOLMDEL-NJ 07733 - USA	303
L.D. Jackel	AT&T Bell Labs Crawfords Corner Road HOLMDEL-NJ 07733 - USA	303
P. Jespers	Université Catholique de Louvain Laboratoire de Microélectronique Bâtiment Maxwell Fai place du Levant 3 B-1348 LOUVAIN LA NEUVE - BELGIUM	141
C. Jutten	Institut National Polytechnique de Grenoble L.T.I.R.F. 46,avenue Félix Viallet 38031 GRENOBLE Cedex - FRANCE	145
S. Knerr	ESPCI - 10, rue Vauquelin 75231 PARIS Cedex 05 - FRANCE	41
G. de La Croix Vaubois	Thomson CSF-DSE 1 rue des Mathurins BP 10 92 223 BAGNEUX - FRANCE	89
P. Lalanne	I.O.T.A. C.N.R.S L.A. 14, BP 43 91406 ORSAY-FRANCE	167

J. Lampinen	Lappeenranta University of Technology Box 20 SF LAPPEENRANTA - FINLAND	65
Y. Le Cun	AT&T Bell Labs Crawfords Corner Road HOLMDEL-NJ 07733 - USA	303
M. Lee	University College London Computer Science - Gower street LONDON WC1E 6BT - UK	117
K. Madani	Institut d'Electronique Fondamentale Bât 220 91 405 ORSAY - FRANCE	167
C. Mejia	Laboratoire de Recherche en Informatique Bât. 490 Université Paris Sud 91 405 ORSAY - FRANCE	3
E. Merlo	Department of Computer Science Mc Gill University MONTREAL H3A-2K6 - CANADA	207
M. Mézard	Ecole Normale Supérieure Groupe de Physique Statistique 24 rue Lhomond 75231PARIS Cedex 05 - FRANCE	75
T. Michaux	Laboratorio de Inteligencia Artificial Universidad Politecnica de Madrid Campus Monte Gancedo 28660 BOADILLA DEL MONTE MADRID - ESPANA	285, 337
E. De Micheli	Dipartimento di Fisica Via Dodecaneso, 33 16146 GENOVA ITALY	345
J. Midtgaard	Neurofysiologisk Institut Blegdamsvej 3C DK-2200 KOBENHAVN - DENMARK	379
D. Montacié	C.N.R.S. URA 820 ENST, Dept SIGNAL 46 Rue Barrault 75013 PARIS -FRANCE	261
D. Montanari	Enidata - Via Aldo Moro 38 BOLOGNA 40127 - ITALY	103

E. Pasero	Dipartimento Ing. Elettronica-II Universita Roma "Tor Vergata" Via O. Raimondo 1 00173 ROMA - ITALY	153
P. Peretto	DAF/LIH - CEN - BP 85X 38041 GRENOBLE Cedex - FRANCE	195
L. Personnaz	ESPCI - 10, rue Vauquelin 75231-PARIS Cedex 05 - FRANCE	41
N.J. Radcliffe	Physics Department University of Edinburgh JCMB The King's Buildings Mayfield Road EDINBURGH EH9 3JZ - UK	181
G. Radonich	Instituto per Ricerca Scientifica e Technologica 38050 POVO, TRENTO, ITALY	345
M. Reyneri	Dipartimento di Elettronica Politecnico di Torino Corso Duca degli Abruzzi 24 10129 TORINO - ITALY	153, 157
G.D. Richards	Physics Department University of Edinburgh JCMB The King's Buildings Mayfield Road EDINBURGH EH9 3JZ - UK	181
D. Rumelhart	Department of Psychology Stanford University STANFORD CA 94 305 - 2130 - USA	15
S. Salaun	CNET Département TIC 22301-LANNION Cedex - FRANCE	173
R. Serra	Enidata - Via Aldo Moro 38 BOLOGNA 40127 - ITALY	103
P. Simonini	Enidata - Via Aldo Moro 38 BOLOGNA 40127 - ITALY	103
F.J. Smieja	Physics Department University of Edinburgh JCMB The King's Buildings Mayfield Road EDINBURGH EH9 3JZ - UK	181
J. Taboury	I.O.T.A. C.N.R.S L.A. 14, BP 43 91406 ORSAY-FRANCE	167

S. Thiria	Laboratoire de Recherche en Informatique Bât. 490 Université Paris Sud 91 405 ORSAY - FRANCE	319
V. Torre	Dipartimento di Fisica Via Dodecaneso, 33 16 146 GENOVA - ITALY	345
S. Uras	Dipartimento di Fisica Via Dodecaneso, 33 16146 GENOVA ITALY	345
G. Valastro	Enidata Via Aldo Moro 38 BOLOGNA 40127 - ITALY	161
F. Vallet	Thomson-CSF Laboratoire Central de Recherche Domaine de Corbeville BP 10 91 401 ORSAY - FRANCE	37
G. Vercelli	Universita di Genova Faculta di Ingegneria Dipartimento di Informatica, Sistemistica e Telematica Via Opera Pia 11 A 16 145 GENOVA - ITALIA	109
M. Verleysen	Université Catholique de Louvain Laboratoire de Microélectronique Bâtiment Maxwell Fai place du Levant 3 B-1348 LOUVAIN LA NEUVE - BELGIUM	141
C. Vinouze	CNET Département TIC 22301-LANNION Cedex - FRANCE	173
R. Vogels	Labo voor Neuro an Psychfysiologie K.U. Leuven - Campus Gasthuisberg O en W Herestraat 59 3000 LEUVEN - BELGIUM	395
D. Wallace	Physics Department University of Edinburgh JCMB The King's Buildings Mayfield Road EDINBURGH EH9 3JZ - UK	181
M. Weinfeld	LIX Ecole Polytechnique 91128 PALAISEAU Cedex - FRANCE	123

C. Wellekens	Philips Research Laboratory Avenue van Becelaere 2 Box 8 1170 BRUXELLES - BELGIUM	217
N. Yalabik	Department of Computer Engineering Middle East Technical University 06 531 ANKARA - TURKEY	297
R. Zaccaria	Universita di Genova Faculta di Ingegneria Dipartimento di Informatica, Sistemistica e Telematica Via Opera Pia 11 A 16 145 GENOVA - ITALIA	109
R. Van Zurk	DAF/LIH - CEN - BP 85X 38041 GRENOBLE Cedex - FRANCE	195

INDEX

A

B

C

O

P

NATO ASI Series F

Including Special Programmes on Sensory Systems for Robotic Control (ROB) and on Advanced Educational Technology (AET)

Vol. 1: Issues in Acoustic Signal – Image Processing and Recognition. Edited by C. H. Chen. VIII, 333 pages. 1983.

Vol. 2: Image Sequence Processing and Dynamic Scene Analysis. Edited by T. S. Huang. IX, 749 pages. 1983.

Vol. 3: Electronic Systems Effectiveness and Life Cycle Costing. Edited by J. K. Skwirzynski. XVII, 732 pages. 1983.

Vol. 4: Pictorial Data Analysis. Edited by R. M. Haralick. VIII, 468 pages. 1983.

Vol. 5: International Calibration Study of Traffic Conflict Techniques. Edited by E. Asmussen. VII, 229 pages. 1984.

Vol. 6: Information Technology and the Computer Network. Edited by K. G. Beauchamp. VIII, 271 pages. 1984.

Vol. 7: High-Speed Computation. Edited by J. S. Kowalik. IX, 441 pages. 1984.

Vol. 8: Program Transformation and Programming Environments. Report on a Workshop directed by F. L. Bauer and H. Remus. Edited by P. Pepper. XIV, 378 pages. 1984.

Vol. 9: Computer Aided Analysis and Optimization of Mechanical System Dynamics. Edited by E. J. Haug. XXII, 700 pages. 1984.

Vol. 10: Simulation and Model-Based Methodologies: An Integrative View. Edited by T. I. Ören, B. P. Zeigler, M. S. Elzas. XIII, 651 pages. 1984.

Vol. 11: Robotics and Artificial Intelligence. Edited by M. Brady, L. A. Gerhardt, H. F. Davidson. XVII, 693 pages. 1984.

Vol. 12: Combinatorial Algorithms on Words. Edited by A. Apostolico, Z. Galil. VIII, 361 pages. 1985.

Vol. 13: Logics and Models of Concurrent Systems. Edited by K. R. Apt. VIII, 498 pages. 1985.

Vol. 14: Control Flow and Data Flow: Concepts of Distributed Programming. Edited by M. Broy. VIII, 525 pages. 1985.

Vol. 15: Computational Mathematical Programming. Edited by K. Schittkowski. VIII, 451 pages. 1985.

Vol. 16: New Systems and Architectures for Automatic Speech Recognition and Synthesis. Edited by R. De Mori, C.Y. Suen. XIII, 630 pages. 1985.

Vol. 17: Fundamental Algorithms for Computer Graphics. Edited by R.A. Earnshaw. XVI, 1042 pages. 1985.

Vol. 18: Computer Architectures for Spatially Distributed Data. Edited by H. Freeman and G.G. Pieroni. VIII, 391 pages. 1985.

Vol. 19: Pictorial Information Systems in Medicine. Edited by K. H. Höhne. XII, 525 pages. 1986.

Vol. 20: Disordered Systems and Biological Organization. Edited by E. Bienenstock, F. Fogelman Soulié, G. Weisbuch. XXI, 405 pages.1986.

Vol. 21: Intelligent Decision Support in Process Environments. Edited by E. Hollnagel, G. Mancini, D.D. Woods. XV, 524 pages. 1986.

NATO ASI Series F

Vol. 22: Software System Design Methods. The Challenge of Advanced Computing Technology. Edited by J.K. Skwirzynski. XIII, 747 pages. 1986.

Vol. 23: Designing Computer-Based Learning Materials. Edited by H. Weinstock and A. Bork. IX, 285 pages. 1986.

Vol. 24: Database Machines. Modern Trends and Applications. Edited by A.K. Sood and A.H. Qureshi. VIII, 570 pages. 1986.

Vol. 25: Pyramidal Systems for Computer Vision. Edited by V. Cantoni and S. Levialdi. VIII, 392 pages. 1986. *(ROB)*

Vol. 26: Modelling and Analysis in Arms Control. Edited by R. Avenhaus, R.K. Huber and J.D. Kettelle. VIII, 488 pages. 1986.

Vol. 27: Computer Aided Optimal Design: Structural and Mechanical Systems. Edited by C.A. Mota Soares. XIII, 1029 pages. 1987.

Vol. 28: Distributed Operating Systems. Theory und Practice. Edited by Y. Paker, J.-P. Banatre and M. Bozyiğit. X, 379 pages. 1987.

Vol. 29: Languages for Sensor-Based Control in Robotics. Edited by U. Rembold and K. Hörmann. IX, 625 pages. 1987. *(ROB)*

Vol. 30: Pattern Recognition Theory and Applications. Edited by P.A. Devijver and J. Kittler. XI, 543 pages. 1987.

Vol. 31: Decision Support Systems: Theory and Application. Edited by C.W. Holsapple and A.B. Whinston. X, 500 pages. 1987.

Vol. 32: Information Systems: Failure Analysis. Edited by J.A. Wise and A. Debons. XV, 338 pages. 1987.

Vol. 33: Machine Intelligence and Knowledge Engineering for Robotic Applications. Edited by A.K.C. Wong and A. Pugh. XIV, 486 pages. 1987. *(ROB)*

Vol. 34: Modelling, Robustness and Sensitivity Reduction in Control Systems. Edited by R.F. Curtain. IX, 492 pages. 1987.

Vol. 35: Expert Judgment and Expert Systems. Edited by J.L. Mumpower, L.D. Phillips, O. Renn and V.R.R. Uppuluri. VIII, 361 pages. 1987.

Vol. 36: Logic of Programming and Calculi of Discrete Design. Edited by M. Broy. VII, 415 pages. 1987.

Vol. 37: Dynamics of Infinite Dimensional Systems. Edited by S.-N. Chow and J.K. Hale. IX, 514 pages. 1987.

Vol. 38: Flow Control of Congested Networks. Edited by A.R. Odoni, L. Bianco and G. Szegö. XII, 355 pages. 1987.

Vol. 39: Mathematics and Computer Science in Medical Imaging. Edited by M.A. Viergever and A. Todd-Pokropek. VIII, 546 pages. 1988.

Vol. 40: Theoretical Foundations of Computer Graphics and CAD. Edited by R.A. Earnshaw. XX, 1246 pages. 1988.

Vol. 41: Neural Computers. Edited by R. Eckmiller and Ch. v. d. Malsburg. XIII, 566 pages. 1988.

NATO ASI Series F

Vol. 42: Real-Time Object Measurement and Classification. Edited by A. K. Jain. VIII, 407 pages. 1988. *(ROB)*

Vol. 43: Sensors and Sensory Systems for Advanced Robots. Edited by P. Dario. XI, 597 pages. 1988. *(ROB)*

Vol. 44: Signal Processing and Pattern Recognition in Nondestructive Evaluation of Materials. Edited by C.H. Chen. VIII, 344 pages. 1988. *(ROB)*

Vol. 45: Syntactic and Structural Pattern Recognition. Edited by G. Ferraté, T. Pavlidis, A. Sanfeliu and H. Bunke. XVI, 467 pages. 1988. *(ROB)*

Vol. 46: Recent Advances in Speech Understanding and Dialog Systems. Edited by H. Niemann, M. Lang and G. Sagerer. X, 521 pages. 1988.

Vol. 47: Advanced Computing Concepts and Techniques in Control Engineering. Edited by M.J. Denham and A.J. Laub. XI, 518 pages. 1988.

Vol. 48: Mathematical Models for Decision Support. Edited by G. Mitra. IX, 762 pages. 1988.

Vol. 49: Computer Integrated Manufacturing. Edited by I.B. Turksen. VIII, 568 pages. 1988.

Vol. 50: CAD Based Programming for Sensory Robots. Edited by B. Ravani. IX, 565 pages. 1988. *(ROB)*

Vol. 51: Algorithms and Model Formulations in Mathematical Programming. Edited by S.W. Wallace. IX, 190 pages. 1989.

Vol. 52: Sensor Devices and Systems for Robotics. Edited by A. Casals. IX, 362 pages. 1989. *(ROB)*

Vol. 53: Advanced Information Technologies for Industrial Material Flow Systems. Edited by S.Y. Nof and C.L. Moodie. IX, 710 pages. 1989.

Vol. 54: A Reappraisal of the Efficiency of Financial Markets. Edited by R.M.C. Guimarães, B.G. Kingsman and S.J. Taylor. X, 804 pages. 1989.

Vol. 55: Constructive Methods in Computing Science. Edited by M. Broy. VII, 478 pages. 1989.

Vol. 56: Multiple Criteria Decision Making and Risk Analysis Using Microcomputers. Edited by B. Karpak and S. Zionts. VII, 399 pages. 1989.

Vol. 57: Kinematics and Dynamic Issues in Sensor Based Control. Edited by G.E. Taylor. XI, 456 pages. 1990. *(ROB)*

Vol. 58: Highly Redundant Sensing in Robotic Systems. Edited by J.T. Tou and J.G. Balchen. X, 322 pages. 1990. *(ROB)*

Vol. 59: Superconducting Electronics. Edited by H. Weinstock and M. Nisenoff. X, 441 pages. 1989.

Vol. 60: 3D Imaging in Medicine. Algorithms, Systems, Applications. Edited by K.H. Höhne, H. Fuchs and S.M. Pizer. IX, 460 pages. 1990.

Vol. 61: Knowledge, Data and Computer-Assisted Decisions. Edited by M. Schader and W. Gaul. VIII, 421 pages. 1990.

Vol. 62: Supercomputing. Edited by J.S. Kowalik. X, 425 pages. 1990.

Vol. 63: Traditional and Non-Traditional Robotic Sensors. Edited by T.C. Henderson. VIII, 468 pages. 1990. *(ROB)*

Vol. 64: Sensory Robotics for the Handling of Limp Materials. Edited by P.M. Taylor. IX, 343 pages. 1990. *(ROB)*

Vol. 65: Mapping and Spatial Modelling for Navigation. Edited by L.F. Pau. VIII, 357 pages. 1990. *(ROB)*

NATO ASI Series F

Vol. 66: Sensor-Based Robots: Algorithms and Architectures. Edited by C. S. G. Lee. 1990. *(ROB)*

Vol. 67: Designing Hypermedia for Learning. Edited by D. H. Jonassen and H. Mandl. XXV, 457 pages. 1990. *(AET)*

Vol. 68: Neurocomputing. Algorithms, Architectures and Applications. Edited by F. Fogelman Soulié and J. Hérault. XI, 455 pages. 1990.